LEADERSHIP

LEADERSHIP

Six Studies in World Strategy

————◆————

HENRY KISSINGER

PENGUIN PRESS

NEW YORK

2022

PENGUIN PRESS
An imprint of Penguin Random House LLC
penguinrandomhouse.com

Image credits appear on page 417.

ISBN 9780593489444 (hardcover)
ISBN 9780593489451 (ebook)

Printed in the United States of America
1   3   5   7   9   10   8   6   4   2

To Nancy,
The inspiration of my life

Contents

Acknowledgements

This book is what it is largely because of Stuart Proffitt, publishing director at Penguin Press UK and editor extraordinaire. Thoughtful publishers raise issues that are elusive and thereby inspire their authors to their best reflections. Stuart has performed this task with aplomb, persistence and wisdom. Few have understood – or challenged – my thinking with comparable subtlety and range of knowledge. Throughout dozens of Zoom calls over more than two years, Stuart has been an indispensable partner in the conception and execution of this book.

Another remarkable collaborator complemented Stuart's impact with exceptional editorial skill. Neal Kozodoy reviewed every chapter. A genius in slicing Gordian knots of clotted prose and a profound amateur historian, he broadened the perspective and elevated the prose.

As with previous books, I have benefited from dedicated associates who explored the vast source materials. Matthew Taylor King gave sage counsel on both substance and style. Leaving an imprint on every chapter, he helped shepherd the book from its midway point with extraordinary commitment and perception.

Eleanor Runde, who combines enthusiasm, efficiency, and remarkable intellect, undertook valuable research in the first phase of the book and later returned on a part-time basis to make a penetrating contribution to the Sadat chapter. Vance Serchuk was helpful and incisive in the development and analysis of the Nixon chapter. Ida Rothschild provided effective line edits and thoughtful organizational comments.

Meredith Potter, Ben Daus, and Aaron MacLean submitted research on statecraft at an early stage. Joseph Kiernan and John Nelson at the beginning undertook useful background research. Austin Coffey was valuable in collating the key chapters for publication.

The principal chapters were submitted for review to distinguished authors on the subject whose work I admire. Daniel Collings, who also undertook research on Margaret Thatcher, reviewed the completed Thatcher text together with Charles Powell (Lord Powell of Bayswater) and Charles Moore. Professor Julian Jackson perceptively read the de Gaulle chapter, and Professor Christopher Clark the Adenauer chapter. Martin Indyk, diplomat and scholar, offered discerning comments for the Sadat chapter. I am indebted to each of them for their help.

The veteran diplomat Charles Hill, collaborator and friend for half a century, contributed trenchant memos and an especially useful treatment of Richard Nixon. Over his remarkable career, Charlie made a seminal contribution by service to the State Department and to Yale University and to the elevation of our society.

A number of friends permitted me to impose on their goodwill for incisive judgment on specific issues. They included Ray Dalio, Samantha Power, Joel Klein, Roger Hertog, Eli Jacobs, and Bob Blackwill.

In recent years, Eric Schmidt has broadened my vistas by introducing me to the world of high-tech and artificial intelligence. Together with Dan Huttenlocher, we collaborated on *The Age of AI*, which influenced the strategic discussions in these pages.

In the preparation of this volume – our seventh such collaboration – Theresa Cimino Amantea once again demonstrated her indispensability. As the book took shape, Theresa not only deciphered my handwriting and retyped chapters over many rounds of revisions with her trademark diligence and eagle-eyed acuity. She also liaised with Penguin Press, the Wylie Agency, and my outside readers and editors.

Assisting with the typing during a critical period was the tireless Jody Iobst Williams, another trusted associate of many decades. Jessee LePorin and Courtney Glick capably managed my schedule throughout the process. Chris Nelson, Dennis O'Shea, and Maarten Oosterbaan of my personal staff provided invaluable assistance during long stretches of pandemic-imposed seclusion and on many administrative matters.

Ann Godoff, president and editor of Penguin Press, reprised her traditional role managing important matters for the American release with characteristic professionalism. On the UK side, Richard Duguid, Alice Skinner, and David Watson all performed ably under time pressure, particularly in copy-editing and collating the manuscript.

Andrew Wylie, my literary agent over many years, and his UK deputy

James Pullen represented me around the world with indefatigable commitment and ability.

This book is dedicated to Nancy, my wife of just under a half-century. She has fulfilled my life and given it meaning. As with my other books, Nancy read and uplifted every chapter.

Needless to say, the shortcomings in this book are my own.

Introduction

THE AXES OF LEADERSHIP

Any society, whatever its political system, is perpetually in transit between a past that forms its memory and a vision of the future that inspires its evolution. Along this route, leadership is indispensable: decisions must be made, trust earned, promises kept, a way forward proposed. Within human institutions – states, religions, armies, companies, schools – leadership is needed to help people reach from where they are to where they have never been and, sometimes, can scarcely imagine going. Without leadership, institutions drift, and nations court growing irrelevance and, ultimately, disaster.

Leaders think and act at the intersection of two axes: the first, between the past and the future; the second, between the abiding values and aspirations of those they lead. Their first challenge is analysis, which begins with a realistic assessment of their society based on its history, mores, and capacities. Then they must balance what they know, which is necessarily drawn from the past, with what they intuit about the future, which is inherently conjectural and uncertain. It is this intuitive grasp of direction that enables leaders to set objectives and lay down a strategy.

For strategies to inspire the society, leaders must serve as educators – communicating objectives, assuaging doubts and rallying support. While the state possesses by definition the monopoly of force, reliance on coercion is a symptom of inadequate leadership; good leaders elicit in their people a wish to walk alongside them. They must also inspire an immediate entourage to translate their thinking so that it bears upon the practical issues of the day. Such a dynamic surrounding team is the visible complement of the leader's inner vitality; it provides support for the leader's journey and ameliorates the dilemmas of decision. Leaders can be magnified – or diminished – by the qualities of those around them.

The vital attributes of a leader in these tasks, and the bridge between the past and the future, are courage and character – courage to choose a direction among complex and difficult options, which requires the willingness to transcend the routine; and strength of character to sustain a course of action whose benefits and whose dangers can be only incompletely glimpsed at the moment of choice. Courage summons virtue in the moment of decision; character reinforces fidelity to values over an extended period.

Leadership is most essential during periods of transition, when values and institutions are losing their relevance, and the outlines of a worthy future are in controversy. In such times, leaders are called upon to think creatively and diagnostically: what are the sources of the society's well-being? Of its decay? Which inheritances from the past should be preserved, and which adapted or discarded? Which objectives deserve commitment, and which prospects must be rejected no matter how tempting? And, at the extreme, is one's society sufficiently vital and confident to tolerate sacrifice as a waystation to a more fulfilling future?

THE NATURE OF LEADERSHIP DECISIONS

Leaders are inevitably hemmed in by constraints. They operate in scarcity, for every society faces limits to its capabilities and reach, dictated by demography and economy. They also operate in time, for every era and every culture reflects its own prevailing values, habits and attitudes that together define its desired outcomes. And leaders operate in competition, for they must contend with other players – whether allies, potential partners or adversaries – who are not static but adaptive, with their own distinct capacities and aspirations. Moreover, events often move too quickly to allow for precise calculation; leaders have to make judgments based on intuitions and hypotheses that cannot be proven at the time of decision. Management of risk is as critical to the leader as analytical skill.

'Strategy' describes the conclusion a leader reaches under these conditions of scarcity, temporality, competition and fluidity. In finding the way ahead, strategic leadership may be likened to traversing a tightrope: just as an acrobat will fall if either too timid or too audacious, a leader is obliged to navigate within a narrow margin, suspended between the relative certainties of the past and the ambiguities of the future. The penalty for excessive ambition – what the Greeks called hubris – is exhaustion, while the price for resting on one's laurels is progressive insignificance and eventual decay. Step by step, leaders must fit means to ends and purpose to circumstance if they are to reach their destinations.

The leader-as-strategist faces an inherent paradox: in circumstances that call for action, the scope for decision-making is often greatest when relevant information is at its scantiest. By the time more data become available, the margin of maneuver tends to have narrowed. Amid the early phases of a rival power's strategic arms buildup, for example, or in the sudden appearance of a novel respiratory virus, the temptation is to regard the emerging phenomenon as either transitory or manageable by established standards. By the time the threat can no longer be denied or minimized, the scope for action will have constricted or the cost of confronting the problem may have grown exorbitant. Misuse time, and limits will begin to impose themselves. Even the best of the remaining choices will be complex to execute, with reduced rewards for success and graver risks in failure.

This is when the leader's instinct and judgment are essential. Winston Churchill understood it well when he wrote in *The Gathering Storm* (1948): 'Statesmen are not called upon only to settle easy questions. These often settle themselves. It is where the balance quivers, and the proportions are veiled in mist, that the opportunity for world-saving decisions presents itself.'[1]

In May 1953, an American exchange student asked Churchill how one might prepare to meet the challenges of leadership. 'Study history. Study history,' was Churchill's emphatic reply. 'In history lie all the secrets of statecraft.'[2] Churchill was himself a prodigious student and writer of history who well understood the continuum within which he was working.

But knowledge of history, while essential, is not sufficient. Some issues remain forever 'veiled in mist', forbidding even to the erudite and experienced. History teaches by analogy, through the ability to recognize comparable situations. Its 'lessons', however, are in essence approximations which leaders are tested to recognize and are responsible for adapting to the circumstances of their own time. The early twentieth-century philosopher of history Oswald Spengler captured this task when he described the 'born' leader as 'above all a valuer – a valuer of men, situations, and things ... [with the ability] to do the correct thing without "knowing" it'.[3]

Strategic leaders need also the qualities of the artist who senses how to sculpt the future using the materials available in the present. As Charles de Gaulle observed in his meditation on leadership, *The Edge of the Sword* (1932), the artist 'does not renounce the use of his intelligence' – which is, after all, the source of 'lessons, methods, and knowledge'. Instead, the artist adds to these foundations 'a certain instinctive faculty which we call inspiration', which alone can provide the 'direct contact with nature from which the vital spark must leap'.[4]

Because of the complexity of reality, truth in history differs from truth in science. The scientist seeks verifiable results; the historically informed strategic leader strives to distill actionable insight from inherent ambiguity. Scientific experiments support or cast doubt on previous results, presenting scientists with the opportunity to modify their variables and repeat their trials. Strategists are usually permitted only one test; their decisions are typically irrevocable. The scientist thus learns truth experimentally or mathematically; the strategist reasons at least partly by analogy with the past – first establishing which events are comparable and which prior conclusions remain relevant. Even then, the strategist must choose analogies carefully, for no one can, in any real sense, experience the past; one can only imagine it as if 'by the moonlight of memory', in the phrase of the Dutch historian Johan Huizinga.[5]

Meaningful political choices rarely involve a single variable; wise decisions require a composite of political, economic, geographical, technological and psychological insights, all informed by an instinct for history. Writing at the end of the twentieth century, Isaiah Berlin described the impossibility of applying scientific thinking beyond its remit and, consequently, the enduring challenge of the strategist's craft. He held that the leader, like the novelist or landscape painter, must absorb life in all its dazzling complexity:

> what makes men foolish or wise, understanding or blind, as opposed to knowledgeable or learned or well informed, is the perception of [the] unique flavors of each situation as it is, in its specific differences – of that in it wherein it differs from all other situations, that is, those aspects of it which make it insusceptible to scientific treatment.[6]

SIX LEADERS IN THEIR CONTEXT

It is the combination of character and circumstance which creates history, and the six leaders profiled in these pages – Konrad Adenauer, Charles de Gaulle, Richard Nixon, Anwar Sadat, Lee Kuan Yew and Margaret Thatcher – were all shaped by the circumstances of their dramatic historical period. They all then also became architects of the postwar evolution of their societies and the international order. I had the good fortune to encounter all six at the height of their influence and to work intimately with Richard Nixon. Inheriting a world whose certainties had been dissolved by war, they redefined national purposes, opened up new vistas and contributed a new structure to a world in transition.

Each of the six leaders, in his or her way, passed through the fiery furnace of the 'Second Thirty Years' War' – that is, the series of destructive conflicts stretching from the beginning of the First World War in August 1914 to the end of the Second World War in September 1945. Like the first Thirty Years' War, the second began in Europe but bled into the larger world. The first transformed Europe from a region where legitimacy was derived from religious faith and dynastic inheritance to an order based on the sovereign equality of secular states and bent on spreading its precepts around the globe. Three centuries later, the Second Thirty Years' War challenged the entire international system to overcome disillusionment in Europe and poverty in much of the rest of the world with new principles of order.

Europe had entered the twentieth century at the peak of its global influence, imbued with the conviction that its progress over the previous centuries was certain – if not destined – to be unending. The continent's populations and economies were growing at an unprecedented rate. Industrialization and increasingly free trade had midwifed historic prosperity. Democratic institutions existed in nearly every European country: dominant in Britain and France, they were underdeveloped but gaining in relevance in Imperial Germany and Austria, and incipient in pre-revolutionary Russia. The educated classes of early twentieth-century Europe shared with Lodovico Settembrini, the liberal humanist in Thomas Mann's novel *The Magic Mountain*, the faith that 'things were taking a course favorable to civilization'.[7]

This utopian view reached its apotheosis in the English journalist Norman Angell's bestselling 1910 treatise *The Great Illusion*, which held that growing economic interdependence among the European powers had rendered war prohibitively expensive. Angell proclaimed 'man's irresistible drift away from conflict and towards cooperation'.[8] This and many other comparable predictions would be exploded in short order – perhaps most notably Angell's claim that it was 'no longer possible for any government to order the extermination of a whole population, of the women and children, in the old Biblical style'.[9]

The First World War exhausted treasuries, terminated dynasties and shattered lives. It was a catastrophe from which Europe has never fully recovered. By the signing of the armistice agreement on November 11, 1918, nearly 10 million soldiers and 7 million civilians had been killed.[10] Of every seven soldiers who had been mobilized, one never returned.[11] Two generations of the youth of Europe had been depleted – young men killed, young women left widowed or alone, countless children orphaned.

While France and Britain emerged victorious, both were exhausted and politically fragile. Defeated Germany, shorn of its colonies and gravely indebted, oscillated between resentment of the victors and internal conflict among its competing political parties. The Austro-Hungarian and Ottoman empires both collapsed, while Russia experienced one of the most radical revolutions in history and now stood outside any international system.

During the interwar years, democracies faltered, totalitarianism marched, and privation stalked the continent. The martial enthusiasms of 1914 having long since subsided, Europe greeted the outbreak of the Second World War in September 1939 with premonition tinged with resignation. And, this time, the world at large shared in Europe's suffering. From New York, the Anglo-American poet W. H. Auden would write:

> Waves of anger and fear
> Circulate over the bright
> And darkened lands of the earth,
> Obsessing our private lives;
> The unmentionable odor of death
> Offends the September night.[12]

Auden's words proved prescient. The human toll exacted by the Second World War ran to no fewer than 60 million lives, primarily concentrated in the Soviet Union, China, Germany and Poland.[13] By August 1945, from Cologne and Coventry to Nanjing and Nagasaki, cities had been reduced to rubble through shelling, aerial bombing, fire and civil conflict. The shattered economies, widespread famine and exhausted populations left in the war's wake were daunted by the costly tasks of national reconstitution. Germany's national standing, almost its very legitimacy, had been obliterated by Adolf Hitler. In France, the Third Republic had collapsed under the impact of the Nazi assault of 1940 and was, by 1944, only just beginning its recovery from that moral void. Of the major European powers, Great Britain alone had preserved its prewar political institutions, but it was effectively bankrupt and would soon have to deal with the progressive loss of its empire and persistent economic distress.

On each of the six leaders profiled in this book, these upheavals left an indelible mark. The political career of Konrad Adenauer (born 1876), who served as mayor of Cologne from 1917 to 1933, would include the interwar conflict with France over the Rhineland as well as the rise of Hitler; during the Second World War, he was twice imprisoned by the Nazis. Beginning in 1949, Adenauer shepherded Germany past the lowest point of its history by abandoning its decades-long quest for domination of Europe, anchoring Germany in the Atlantic Alliance, and rebuilding it on a moral foundation which reflected his own Christian values and democratic convictions.

Charles de Gaulle (born 1890) spent two and a half years during the First World War as a prisoner of war in Wilhelmine Germany; in the Second, he initially commanded a tank regiment. Then, after the collapse of France, he rebuilt the political structure of France twice – the first time in 1944 to restore France's essence, and the second time in 1958 to revitalize its soul and prevent civil war. De Gaulle guided France's historical transition from a defeated, divided and overstretched empire to a stable, prosperous nation-state under a sound constitution. From that basis, he restored France to a significant and sustainable role in international relations.

Richard Nixon (born 1913) took from his experience in the Second World War the lesson that his country had to play an enhanced role in the emerging world order. Despite being the only US president to resign from office, between 1969 and 1974 he modified the superpower tensions of the high Cold War and led the United States out of the conflict in Vietnam. In the process, he put American foreign policy on a constructive global footing by opening relations with China, beginning a peace process that would transform the Middle East and emphasizing a concept of world order based on equilibrium.

Two of the leaders discussed in these pages experienced the Second World War as colonial subjects. Anwar Sadat (born 1918), as an Egyptian army officer, was imprisoned for two years for attempting in 1942 to collaborate with German Field Marshal Erwin Rommel in expelling the British from Egypt and then for three years, much of it in solitary confinement, after the assassination of the pro-British former Finance Minister Amin Osman. Long animated by revolutionary and pan-Arab convictions, Sadat was projected, in 1970, by the sudden death of Gamal Abdel Nasser into the presidency of an Egypt that had been shocked and demoralized by defeat in the 1967 war with Israel. Through an astute combination of military strategy and diplomacy, he then endeavored to restore Egypt's lost territories and self-confidence while securing long-elusive peace with Israel with a transcendent philosophy.

Lee Kuan Yew (born 1923) narrowly escaped execution by the occupying Japanese in 1942. Lee shaped the evolution of an impoverished, multiethnic port city at the edge of the Pacific, surrounded by hostile neighbors. Under his tutelage, Singapore emerged as a secure, well-administered and prosperous city-state with a shared national identity providing unity amid cultural diversity.

Margaret Thatcher (born 1925) huddled with her family around the radio listening to Prime Minister Winston Churchill's wartime broadcasts during the Battle of Britain. In 1979, Thatcher inherited in Britain a former imperial power permeated by an air of weary resignation over the loss of its global reach and the decline of its international significance. She renewed her country through economic reform and a foreign policy that balanced boldness with prudence.

From the Second Thirty Years' War, all six leaders drew their own conclusions as to what had led the world astray, alongside a vivid appreciation of the indispensability of bold – and aspirational – political leadership. The historian Andrew Roberts reminds us that, although the most common understanding of 'leadership' connotes inherent goodness, leadership 'is in fact completely morally neutral, as capable of leading mankind to the abyss as to the sunlit uplands. It is a protean force of terrifying power' that we must strive to orient toward moral ends.[14]

EPITOMES OF LEADERSHIP: THE STATESMAN AND THE PROPHET

Most leaders are not visionary but managerial. In every society and at every level of responsibility, day-to-day stewards are needed to guide the institutions entrusted to their care. But during periods of crisis – whether of war, rapid technological change, jarring economic dislocation or ideological upheaval – management of the status quo may be the riskiest course of all. In fortunate societies, such times call forth transformational leaders. Their distinction can be categorized into two ideal types: the statesman and the prophet.[15]

Farsighted statesmen understand that they have a pair of essential tasks. The first is to preserve their society by manipulating circumstances rather than being overwhelmed by them. Such leaders will embrace change and progress, while ensuring that their society retains its basic sense of itself through the evolutions they encourage within it. The second is to temper vision with wariness, entertaining a sense of limits. Such leaders assume responsibility not only for the best but also for the worst outcomes. They tend to be conscious of the many great hopes that have failed, the countless good intentions that could not be realized, the stubborn persistence in human affairs of selfishness and power-hunger and violence. In that definition of leadership, statesmen are inclined to erect hedges against the possibility that even the most well-made plans might prove abortive, or that the most eloquent formulation might hide ulterior motives. They tend to be suspicious of those who personalize policy, for history teaches the fragility of structures dependent largely on single personalities. Ambitious but not revolutionary, they work within what they perceive as the grain of history, moving their societies forward while viewing their political institutions and fundamental values as an inheritance to be transmitted to future generations (albeit with modifications that sustain their essence). Wise leaders in the statesman mode will recognize when novel circumstances require existing institutions and values to be transcended. But they understand that, for their societies to thrive, they will have to ensure that change does not go beyond what it can sustain. Such statesmen include the seventeenth-century leaders who fashioned the Westphalian state system* as well as nineteenth-century European leaders such as Palmerston, Gladstone, Disraeli and Bismarck. In the twentieth century, Theodore and Franklin Roosevelt, Mustafa Kemal Ataturk and Jawaharlal Nehru were all leaders in the statesman mode.

The second type of leader – that of the visionary, or prophet – treats prevailing institutions less from the perspective of the possible than from a vision of the imperative. Prophetic leaders invoke their transcendent visions as proof of their righteousness. Craving an empty canvas on which to lay down their designs, they take as a principal task the erasure of the past – its treasures along with its snares. The virtue of prophets is that they redefine what appears possible; they are the 'unreasonable men' to whom George Bernard Shaw credited 'all progress'.† Believing in ultimate solutions, prophetic leaders tend to distrust gradualism as an unnecessary concession to time and circumstance; their goal is to transcend, rather than manage, the status quo. Akhenaten, Joan of Arc, Robespierre, Lenin and Gandhi are among the prophetic leaders of history.

The dividing line between the two modes may appear absolute; but it is hardly impermeable. Leaders can pass from one mode to the other – or borrow from one while largely inhabiting the ways of the other. Churchill in his 'wilderness years' and de Gaulle as leader of the Free French belonged, for these phases of their lives, in the prophetic category, as did Sadat after 1973. In practice, each of the six leaders profiled in this book managed a synthesis of the two tendencies, though with a tilt toward the statesmanlike.

For the ancients, an optimal blend of the two styles was exemplified in the leadership of Themistocles, the Athenian leader who saved the Greek city-states from being absorbed by the Persian empire. Thucydides described Themistocles as being 'at once the best *judge* in those

---

* Established in the seventeenth century after the Thirty Years' War, the Westphalian system grouped the survivor states of that conflict on the basis of national interest and sovereignty to replace the religious or dynastic foundation of the preceding medieval period.

† 'The reasonable man adapts himself to the world: the unreasonable one persists in trying to adapt the world to himself. Therefore all progress depends on the unreasonable man' (George Bernard Shaw, *Man and Superman*).

sudden crises which admit of little or no deliberation, and the best *prophet* of the future, even to its most distant possibilities'.[16]

The encounter between the two modes is often inconclusive and frustrating, resulting from their distinctive measures of success: the test of statesmen is the durability of political structures under stress, while prophets gauge their achievements against absolute standards. If the statesman assesses possible courses of action on the basis of their utility rather than their 'truth', the prophet regards this approach as sacrilege, a triumph of expediency over universal principle. To the statesman, negotiation is a mechanism of stability; to the prophet, it can be a means of converting or demoralizing opponents. And if, to the statesman, preservation of the international order transcends any dispute within it, prophets are guided by their objective and willing to overturn the existing order.

Both modes of leadership have been transformational, especially in periods of crisis, though the prophetic style, representative of moments of exaltation, will usually involve greater dislocation and suffering. Each approach also has its nemesis. The statesman's is that equilibrium, though it may be the condition of stability and of long-term progress, does not supply its own momentum. For the prophet, the risk is that an ecstatic mood may submerge humanity in the vastness of a vision and reduce the individual to an object.

THE INDIVIDUAL IN HISTORY

Whatever their personal characteristics or modes of action, leaders inevitably confront an unrelenting challenge: preventing the demands of the present from overwhelming the future. Ordinary leaders seek to manage the immediate; great ones attempt to raise their society to their visions. How to meet this challenge has been debated as long as humanity has considered the relationship between the willed and the inevitable. In the Western world since the nineteenth century, the solution was increasingly ascribed to history as if events overwhelmed men' and women by a vast process of which they were tools, not creators. In the twentieth century, numerous scholars, such as the eminent French historian Fernand Braudel, have insisted on viewing individuals and the events they shape as mere 'surface disturbances' and 'crests of foam' in a wider sea of vast and ineluctable tides.[17] Leading thinkers – social historians, political philosophers and international relations theorists alike – have imbued inchoate forces with the strength of destiny. Before 'movements', 'structures' and 'distributions of power', one is told, humanity is denied all choice – and, by extension, cannot but abdicate all responsibility. These are, of course, valid concepts of historical analysis, and any leader must be conscious of their force. But they are always applied through human agency and filtered through human perception. Ironically, there has been no more efficient tool for the malign consolidation of power by individuals than theories of the inevitable laws of history.

The issue this presents is whether these forces are endemic or subject to social and political action. Physics has learned that reality is altered by the process of observation. History similarly teaches that men and women shape their environment by their interpretation of it.

Do individuals matter in history? A contemporary of Caesar or Mohammed, Luther or Gandhi, Churchill or FDR would hardly think of posing such a question. These pages deal with leaders who, in the unending contest between the willed and the inevitable, understood that what seems inevitable becomes so by human agency. They mattered because they transcended the circumstances they inherited and thereby carried their societies to the frontiers of the possible.

LEADERSHIP

Konrad Adenauer:
The Strategy of Humility

THE NECESSITY OF RENEWAL

In January 1943, at the Casablanca Conference, the Allies proclaimed that they would accept nothing less than the 'unconditional surrender' of the Axis powers. US President Franklin Delano Roosevelt, who was the driving force behind the announcement, sought to deprive any successor government to Hitler of the ability to claim that it had been deluded into surrender by unfulfilled promises. Germany's complete military defeat, together with its total loss of moral and international legitimacy, led inexorably to the progressive disintegration of the German civil structure.

I observed this process as part of the 84th Infantry Division of the US army as it moved from the German border near the industrial Ruhr territory to the Elbe River near Magdeburg – just 100 miles away from the then-raging Battle of Berlin. As the division was crossing the German border, I was transferred to a unit responsible for security and prevention of the guerrilla activity that Hitler had ordered.

For a person like me, whose family had fled the small Bavarian city of Fürth six years earlier to escape racial persecution, no greater contrast with the Germany of my youth could have been imagined. Then, Hitler had just annexed Austria and was in the process of dismembering Czechoslovakia. The dominant attitude of the German people verged on the overbearing.

Now, white sheets hung from many windows to signify the surrender of the population. The Germans, who a few years earlier had celebrated the prospect of dominating Europe from the English Channel to the Volga River, were cowed and bewildered. Thousands of displaced persons – deported from Eastern Europe as forced labor during the war – crowded the streets in quest of food and shelter and the possibility of returning home.

It was a desperate period in German history. Food shortages were severe. Many starved, and infant mortality was twice that of the rest of Western Europe.[1] The established exchange of goods and services collapsed; black markets took its place. Mail service ranged from impaired to nonexistent. Rail service was sporadic and transport by road made extremely difficult by the ravages of war and the shortage of gasoline.

In the spring of 1945, the task of occupying forces was to institute some kind of civil order until trained military government personnel could replace combat troops. This occurred around the time of the Potsdam conference in July and August (of Churchill/Attlee, Truman and Stalin). At that summit, the Allies divided Germany into four occupation zones: for the United States, a southern portion containing Bavaria; for Britain, the industrial northern Rhineland and Ruhr Valley; for France, the southern Rhineland and territory along the Alsatian border; and for the Soviets, a zone running from the Elbe River to the Oder–Neisse Line, which formed the new Polish frontier, reducing prewar German territory by nearly a quarter. The three Western zones were each placed under the jurisdiction of a senior official of the occupying powers with the title of high commissioner.

German civil governance, once demonstrably efficient and unchallengeable, had come to an end. Ultimate authority was now exercised by occupation forces down to the county (*Kreis*) level. These forces maintained order, but it took the better part of eighteen months for communications to be restored to predictable levels. During the winter of 1945–6, fuel shortages obliged even Konrad Adenauer, who was to become chancellor four years later, to sleep in a heavy overcoat.[2]

Occupied Germany carried not only the burden of its immediate past but also of the complexity of its history. In the seventy-four years since unification, Germany had been governed successively as a monarchy, a republic and a totalitarian state. By the end of the war, the only memory of stable governance harked back to unified Germany's beginning, under the chancellorship of Otto von Bismarck (1871–90). From then until the outbreak of the First World War in 1914, the German empire was hounded by what Bismarck would call the 'nightmare' of hostile external coalitions provoked into existence by Germany's military potential and intransigent rhetoric. Because unified Germany was stronger than any of the many states surrounding it and more populous than any save Russia, its growing and potentially dominant power turned into the permanent security challenge of Europe.

After the First World War, the newly established Weimar Republic was impoverished by inflation and economic crises and considered itself abused by the punitive provisions included in the postwar Treaty of Versailles. Under Hitler after 1933, Germany sought to impose its totalitarianism on all of Europe. In short, throughout the first half of the twentieth century, united Germany had been by turns either too strong or too weak for the peace of Europe. By 1945, it had been reduced to its least secure position in Europe and the world since unification.

The task of restoring dignity and legitimacy to this crushed society fell to Konrad Adenauer, who had served as lord mayor (*Oberbürgermeister*) of Cologne for sixteen years before being dismissed by Hitler. Adenauer was by his background fortuitously cast for a role that required at once the humility to administer the consequences of unconditional surrender and the strength of character to regain an international standing for his country among the democracies. Born in 1876 – only five years after German unification under Bismarck – Adenauer was for the rest of his life associated with his native city of Cologne, with its towering Gothic cathedral overlooking the Rhine and its history as an important locus in the Hanseatic constellation of mercantile city-states.

As an adult, Adenauer had experienced the unified German state's three post-Bismarck configurations: its truculence under the Kaiser, domestic upheavals under the Weimar Republic, and adventurism under Hitler, culminating in self-destruction and disintegration. In striving to remake a place for his country in a legitimate postwar order, he faced a legacy of global resentment and, at home, the disorientation of a public battered by the long sequence of revolution, world war, genocide, defeat, partition, economic collapse and loss of moral integrity. He chose a course both humble and daring: to confess German iniquities; accept the penalties of defeat and impotence, including the partition of his country; allow the dismantling of its industrial base as war reparations; and seek through submission to build a new European structure within which Germany could become a trusted partner. Germany, he hoped, would become a normal country, though always, he knew, with an abnormal memory.

FROM EARLY LIFE TO INTERNAL EXILE

Adenauer's father, Johann, once a non-commissioned officer in the Prussian army, was for three decades a clerical civil servant in Cologne. Lacking education beyond mandatory primary school, Johann was determined to provide his children with educational and career opportunities. Adenauer's mother shared this objective; the daughter of a bank clerk, she supplemented Johann's income through needlework. Together, they assiduously prepared young Konrad for school and strove to transmit their Catholic values to him.[3] Cognizance of sin and social responsibility ran as an undercurrent throughout Adenauer's childhood. As a student at the University of Bonn, he achieved a reputation for commitment through his habit of plunging his feet into a bucket of ice water to overcome the fatigue of late-night studies.[4] Adenauer's degree in law and family background of service induced him to join the Cologne civil service in 1904. He was given the title of *Beigeordneter*, or assistant mayor, with particular responsibility for taxation. In 1909, he was promoted to senior deputy mayor and in 1917 became lord mayor of Cologne.*

Mayors of Cologne were typically former civil servants who strove to elevate their conduct above the violent and intensely partisan politics of the era. Adenauer's reputation grew to the extent that, in 1926, there were even discussions in Berlin as to whether he might be drafted as chancellor of a national unity government. The effort fell apart because of the difficulty of finding a nonpartisan alliance, Adenauer's condition for accepting the position.

Adenauer's first conspicuous national conduct occurred in connection with Hitler's designation as chancellor on January 30, 1933. To fortify his position, Hitler called a general election and proposed to the German parliament the so-called Enabling Act, suspending the rule of law and the independence of civil institutions. Adenauer, in the month after Hitler's designation as chancellor, undertook three public

---

* In 1917, Kaiser Wilhelm II changed the title of Cologne's mayor to lord mayor (*Oberbürgermeister*). See Dr Matthias Oppermann, 'Biography of Konrad Adenauer', Konrad Adenauer Foundation (Konrad-Adenauer-Stiftung) online archives, https://www.kas.de/en/konrad-adenauer.

demonstrations of opposition. In the Prussian Upper House, to which he belonged ex officio as lord mayor of Cologne, he voted against the Enabling Act. He refused an invitation to welcome Hitler at Cologne airport during the election campaign. And in the week before the election he ordered the removal of Nazi flags from bridges and other public monuments. Adenauer was dismissed from office the week after Hitler's foreordained electoral victory.

After his dismissal, Adenauer appealed for sanctuary to an old school friend who had become the abbot of a Benedictine monastery. It was granted, and in April Adenauer took up residence in Maria Laach Abbey, 50 miles south of Cologne on the Laacher See. There, his main occupation was to immerse himself in two papal encyclicals – promulgated by Popes Leo XIII and Pius XI – which applied Catholic teaching to social and political developments, especially the evolving condition of the modern working class.[5] In these encyclicals, Adenauer encountered doctrines that meshed with his political convictions: emphasizing Christian rather than political identity, condemning communism and socialism, ameliorating class struggle through humility and Christian charity, and ensuring free competition instead of cartel practices.[6]

Adenauer's time at Maria Laach was not to last. While attending a Christmas Mass – which had drawn people from the surrounding area to see and support him – Nazi officials pressured the abbot to evict his admired guest. Adenauer left the following January.

The next decade of his life brought difficulty and instability. There were moments of grave danger, especially after the unsuccessful plot on Hitler's life in July 1944 organized by representatives of the Prussian upper class and including remnants of pre-Nazi political and military life. Hitler's vengeance sought to destroy all these elements. For a while, Adenauer escaped their fate by traveling peripatetically, never staying in one place for more than twenty-four hours.[7] Danger never altered his rejection of Hitler for trampling on the rule of law, which Adenauer considered to be the *sine qua non* of the modern state.[8] Although a known dissenter, Adenauer had been unwilling to join with anti-regime conspirators, whether civilian or military, largely because he was skeptical of their possibilities of success.[9] On the whole, as one scholar describes it, 'he and his family did their best to live as quietly and inconspicuously as possible'.[10]

Despite his departure from politics, the Nazis eventually imprisoned

him. In fall 1944, he spent two months in a prison cell from the window
of which he witnessed executions, including that of a sixteen-year-old
boy; above him he heard the screams of other inmates as they were
tortured.

In the end, his son Max, who was serving in the German army, managed to secure his release. As American tanks entered the Rhineland in
February 1945, Adenauer began to think about whether he might find a
role in his militarily defeated, morally devastated, economically reeling
and politically collapsed country.[11]

THE ROAD TO LEADERSHIP

Hitler's savage reaction to the July coup in the frenzied final year of the
Second World War had decimated the ranks of those who might try to
succeed him. Some senior Social Democratic Party politicians had
survived the concentration camps – including Adenauer's later rival
Kurt Schumacher – and possessed the political stature for the position
of chancellor. But they lacked followings large enough to win the public
support needed to implement the country's unconditional surrender and
its accompanying penalties – preconditions for gaining the confidence
of the Western Allies.

In May 1945, the American forces that first occupied Cologne
reinstated Adenauer as mayor, but with the transfer of the city to British
authority as a result of the Potsdam agreement, tensions arose, and the
British dismissed him within a few months. Though he was temporarily
excluded from political activity by the occupying power, Adenauer
quietly concentrated on building a political base in preparation for the
re-emergence of German self-government.

In December 1945, Adenauer attended a meeting to form a new party
influenced by both Catholic and Protestant Christianity. Former members of the Catholic Center Party, with which Adenauer had been
associated as mayor of Cologne, as well as of the conservative German
National People's Party and the liberal German Democratic Party, were
in attendance. Many had opposed Hitler, and some had been imprisoned
for their resistance. The group lacked a clear political direction and doctrine; indeed, the tone of discussions at this initial meeting was more
socialist than classically liberal. In part because of Adenauer's objections,

the question of first principles was put aside, and the group simply settled on its name: the Christian Democratic Union.[12]

The following month, Adenauer helped to imbue the CDU with its
political philosophy as the party of democracy, social conservatism and
European integration, rejecting Germany's recent past as well as totalitarianism in any form. At a January 1946 congress of the CDU's
important members in the British occupation zone in Herford, Westphalia, Adenauer elaborated on these principles and consolidated his
leadership of the nascent party.

Adenauer's first public speech after the end of the war on March 26,
1946, was a preview of his subsequent political leadership. Criticizing
Germany's conduct under Hitler, Adenauer asked an audience of thousands in the severely damaged main hall of the University of Cologne
how it was possible that the Nazis had come to power. They had then
committed 'great crimes', he said, and the Germans could find their way
toward a better future only by coming to terms with their past.[13] Such
an effort would be necessary for their country's revival. From this perspective, Germany's attitude after the Second World War needed to be
the opposite of its reaction to the First. Instead of indulging in self-
pitying nationalism once again, Germany should seek its future within
a unifying Europe. Adenauer was proclaiming a strategy of humility.

Tall and seemingly imperturbable, Adenauer tended to speak tersely,
though mitigated by the lilting tones of the Rhineland, more conciliatory than Prussian speech, in which, according to Mark Twain, sentences
march across conversations like military formations. (The Rhineland had
had an autonomous history until it was acquired by Prussia in 1814–15.)
At the same time, he exuded vitality and self-assurance. His style was the
antithesis of the blaring charismatic quality of the Hitler era and aspired
to the serene authority of the pre-First World War generation, which had
operated while governed by restraint and shared values.

All of these qualities, together with the standing he had acquired by
a decade of ostentatious aloofness from Hitler, made Adenauer the
most obvious candidate to lead the new democratic party. But he was
not above practical maneuvers to achieve his end. The first CDU meeting was set up with one chair positioned at the head of the table.
Adenauer strode up to it and announced, 'I was born on 5 January
1876, so I am probably the oldest person here. If nobody objects, I will
regard myself as president by seniority.' That elicited both laughter

and acquiescence; from that point on, he would steward the party for over fifteen years.[14]

The CDU program, which Adenauer played a key role in developing, urged Germans to reject their past and to embrace a spirit of renewal based on Christian ideals and democratic principles:

> Away with the slogans of a vanished time, away with the fatigue of life and state! The same hardship forces all of us to get to work. It would be a betrayal of one's own family and of the German people to sink now into nihilism or indifference. The CDU appeals to all those forces newly willing to build on unflinching confidence in the good qualities of the German people and the indomitable determination to make the Christian idea and the high ideal of true democracy the basis of renewal.[15]

Throughout, Adenauer was always conscious of – perhaps obsessed by – the possibility of tragedy. Germany, in his view, was not strong enough morally or materially to stand alone, and any attempt to do so would end in disaster. Located in the center of the continent, the new Germany needed to abandon many of its previous policies and attitudes – particularly the opportunistic manipulation of its geographic position and the Prussian inclination for good relations with Russia. (Prussia, the taproot of German militarism, would be formally abolished as a state within Germany by the Allies in 1947.) Adenauer's Germany would instead anchor its democracy domestically in its Catholic regions and ecumenical Christian values and internationally in federation with the West – especially in security ties with the United States.[16]

Untouched by wartime air attacks, the bucolic university town of Bonn had been selected as the temporary capital of the FRG pending reunification, when Berlin would once again serve as the capital. It was also Adenauer's personal preference, situated close to his home village of Rhoendorf and away from the turmoil of politics. Adenauer was able to affect the choice of Bonn in September 1948 – before becoming chancellor – because of his influence as leader of the CDU and president of the Parliamentary Council, a group of German political figures that had been tasked by the Allies with planning the political evolution and drawing up a new constitution, or Basic Law. He later quipped that he had convinced the council to endorse Bonn only because Rhoendorf was too small (population under 2,000) to serve as a capital.[17] He had also, less humorously, rejected the much more cosmopolitan Munich because of Bavaria's reputation for impetuous sentimentality and, as he deprecatingly remarked, because the capital should not lie cheek by jowl with potato fields. Adenauer also disdained major cities such as Frankfurt, site of a short-lived parliament in 1848, where democracy's prospects might be distorted by public demonstrations and riots.

THE RESTORATION OF CIVIL ORDER AND THE INAUGURATION OF THE CHANCELLOR

In 1946, German reconstruction slowly began. Elections were called for progressively higher levels of administration, restoring structures and shifting political responsibility steadily to the Germans themselves. In January 1947, the US and Britain established a common economic policy for their zones. France joined the following year, making it the 'Trizone'. The economist Ludwig Erhard was appointed as director of the Economic Council and oversaw the smooth transition to the new currency, the Deutschmark. He coupled it with eliminating both price controls and rationing. Erhard's bold economic policy inspired a recovery that eventually enabled political reconstruction based on a constitution approved by the Allied Powers.[18]

On May 23, 1949 – four years after unconditional surrender – the new German constitution (the Basic Law) took effect, and the Federal Republic was formally established, comprising the three Western zones. The German Democratic Republic, replacing the Soviet occupation zone, would be formally constituted several months later.

The partition of Germany now mirrored the dividing lines in Europe. The process culminated in an election for a parliament, the Bundestag, in August. On September 15, the Bundestag voted for a chancellor who, by the constitution, required an absolute majority and who could only be removed by an absolute majority vote for a named successor – a stabilizing measure. Although Adenauer was elected by a margin of only one vote (presumably his own) in this parliament of a rump state, he managed to win four consecutive elections, serving for fourteen years.

Germany's sovereignty, however, remained severely constrained. The Allies, who exercised paramount authority over occupied West Germany through their respective high commissioners, officially averred that the German people would 'enjoy self-government to the maximum possible degree'. But they identified a set of issues – ranging from foreign affairs to the 'use of funds, food, and other supplies' – over which the three high commissioners and other occupation authorities would have final say.[19] The Occupation Statute, from which the quotations above are drawn and which was enacted two weeks prior to the Federal Republic's establishment in May, stood above the Basic Law. A related document, the Ruhr Statute, established Allied control over the eponymous industrial center and laid out criteria for the dismantling of German industry for reparations.[20] Another industrial base – the Saar Valley – was however given a special autonomous status at a comparatively early stage.

The tension between maintaining Allied authority and restoring German self-government was especially evident on September 21, 1949, when the three high commissioners gathered in Bonn to welcome Adenauer as the new chancellor of the Federal Republic and the first legitimate successor to Hitler. Adenauer had affirmed before the ceremony that he would not challenge the partition of Germany and the impairment of its sovereignty by the various statutes imposed by the Allies as a price for unconditional surrender. But he used the occasion of inauguration to demonstrate that he would do so with dignity and self-respect. Beyond the border of the red carpet where the high commissioners had assembled, a place had been set aside for him. As the ceremony began, and in utter violation of protocol, Adenauer abandoned his place and moved to the carpet *alongside* the high commissioners – indicating that the new Federal Republic would insist on equal status in the future, even as it accepted the consequences of Germany's past transgressions.

In a brief acceptance speech, Adenauer emphasized that, as chancellor, he accepted the Occupation Statute and other limitations on sovereignty. Germany's subordination to its provisions, he pointed out, had been combined in the statute with its partition; in recognition of his acceptance of these sacrifices, he therefore urged the high commissioners to apply the provisions of the various statutes in a 'liberal and generous manner' and to make use of the clauses allowing for changes and developments that might enable the German people to achieve 'full freedom' in due course.

The core of his acceptance speech was not the appeal to the victors for generosity but Adenauer's unprecedented vision of the new Europe to which he was committing the new Germany. Disavowing any return to the nationalism or motivations of prewar Europe, Adenauer outlined the case for building 'a positive and viable European federation' designed to overcome

> the narrow nationalistic conception of states as it prevailed in the 19th and early 20th centuries ... If we now turn back to the sources of our European civilization, born of Christianity, then we cannot fail to succeed in restoring the unity of European life in all fields of endeavor. This is the sole effective assurance for maintaining peace.[21]

Adenauer's speech implied a profound transformation of his country. Within the context of unconditional surrender, it was also a shrewd appeal to equality with the victors, the only such claim available to Germany.

The speech also opened more fundamental vistas. The new chancellor was simultaneously accepting the indefinite (possibly permanent) division of his country and proclaiming a foreign policy in partnership with the foreign powers that were now occupying it. While acknowledging Germany's submission, he was announcing national objectives of federation with his country's historic adversaries in Europe and of alliance with the United States.

Adenauer put forward these visionary ideas without rhetorical flourish. The duties of nations, as he viewed them, were their own justification; oratorical embellishment could only distract from that basic understanding. Adenauer's unobtrusive style also suggested the role he foresaw for the new Germany in helping to shape a new Europe through consensus.

Not for more than a century had a European leader confronted the challenge of returning his country to the international order. France had been totally defeated at the end of the Napoleonic wars and its capital occupied by foreign forces, but French national unity was unimpaired, and the postwar Congress of Vienna accepted Talleyrand as a senior representative of France with equal rights as a historic state. Konrad Adenauer shouldered his comparable task under much more forbidding circumstances. His neighbors did *not* accept his country as an equal. For them, Germany was still very much 'on probation'.

For a demoralized, defeated society, the passage to the restoration of democratic sovereignty presents one of the most difficult challenges to statesmanship. The victors are reluctant to grant to an erstwhile enemy the legal authority, much less the capacity, to recover its strength. The prostrate loser assesses progress by the degree and speed at which it is able to regain control over its future. Adenauer had the inner resources to transcend these tensions. His strategy of humility was composed of four elements: accepting the consequences of defeat; regaining the confidence of the victors; building a democratic society; and creating a European federation that would transcend the historic divisions of Europe.

THE PATH TO A NEW NATIONAL IDENTITY

Adenauer considered strengthening ties with the West and especially the United States as the key to the restoration of Germany's place in the world. In his memoirs, Dean Acheson would enthusiastically describe his first meeting as US secretary of state with Adenauer in 1949:

> I was struck by the imagination and wisdom of his approach. His great concern was to integrate Germany completely into Western Europe. Indeed, he gave this end priority over the reunification of unhappily divided Germany, and could see why her neighbors might look upon it as almost a precondition to reunification . . . He wanted Germans to be citizens of Europe, to cooperate, with France especially, in developing common interests and outlook and in burying the rivalries of the past few centuries . . . They must lead in the rebirth of Europe.[22]

The United States was instrumental in supporting these goals with an economic revival plan. On June 5, 1947, General George C. Marshall, Acheson's predecessor as secretary of state and formerly army chief of staff, had articulated it at Harvard University:

> Our policy is directed not against any country or doctrine but against hunger, poverty, desperation, and chaos. Its purpose should be the revival of a working economy in the world so as to permit the emergence of political and social conditions in which free institutions can exist.[23]

Adenauer took the Marshall speech and subsequent formal plan as reason to acquiesce to the 1949 Ruhr Agreement, one of the other means by which the Allies retained control over German industry. He interpreted the Marshall Plan as a brake on exactions from Germany, but more crucially as a first step toward the federalization of Europe:

> If [the Ruhr Statute] is used as an instrument to hold down the German economy, the Marshall Plan is nonsense . . . If, however, the Ruhr Statute is used as an instrument in the German and the European interest, if it means the beginning of a new economic order in Western Europe, then it can become a promising starting point for European cooperation.[24]

It was ironic that the German Social Democratic Party (SPD), under the leadership of Kurt Schumacher, now emerged as Adenauer's principal domestic opponent. The SPD had a history of deep commitment to democracy, dating back to the creation of the German state; but during the imperial period it had been isolated from the leadership groups since, as a Marxist party, it had not been considered reliably nationalist. Its current leader, Schumacher, in ill health as a result of over a decade of imprisonment under Hitler, convinced himself that his party would never win a postwar election unless it established itself as *national* in its purpose. He therefore opposed Adenauer's strategy of restoration by submission: 'As a people we have to make German policy, which means a policy which is not determined by a foreign will, but which is the product of the will of our people.'[25] A kind of populism became Schumacher's insistent demand. However understandable in terms of SPD history, it was incompatible with unconditional surrender or with Europe's experience of Germany under Hitler.

Adenauer shared the SPD's democratic principles, but there was also a strategic rationale for his embrace of democracy. He was determined to turn submission into a virtue, and he saw that a temporary inequality of conditions was the precondition to equality of status. During parliamentary debates in November 1949, he emphasized this by shouting (which was highly unusual for him): 'Who do you think lost the war?'[26] Submission was the only way forward: 'The Allies have told me that the dismantling of factories would be stopped only if I satisfy the Allied desire for security,' he explained before wryly asking: 'Does the Socialist party want dismantling to go on to the bitter end?'[27]

Another basic Adenauer objective was reconciliation with France. Adenauer had met Robert Schuman, then France's foreign minister, for the first time in 1948. At that time French policy was aimed at disabling German industrial production and placing the Saar region under French control. Adenauer redefined the issue; the ultimate challenge was not strategic or financial but political and ethical. In July 1949, before becoming chancellor, he pursued this theme in a letter to Schuman:

> In my view, any economic advantage gained by [another] country as a result of being allocated dismantled factories is dwarfed by the great damage being done to the morale of the German people ... I implore you, since you have such a special appreciation of the issue of reconciliation between France and Germany and of the principle of European cooperation, to find ways and means to terminate these completely incomprehensible measures.[28]

At home, Adenauer stressed that cooperation with the Allies' various punitive measures was the only wise course. On November 3, 1949, he gave an interview to the German weekly *Die Zeit*:

> If we simply show a negative response towards the statute of the Ruhr and the Ruhr Authority, France will interpret this as a sign of German nationalism, as an act of defiance rejecting all surveillance. Such an attitude would appear to be passive resistance against security itself. And that above all must be avoided.[29]

Adenauer's approach proved effective. Later that month, the Allies invited him to negotiate a new relationship with the Occupation Authority reducing the number of factories marked for dismantlement and establishing a path for Germany's accession to the Council of Europe, which had been founded that year. On November 24, he presented the new agreement to a Bundestag in which nationalism was still rampant. Schumacher was so carried away that he called Adenauer the 'chancellor of the Allies'. Suspended from parliament for this slur, Schumacher was soon reinstated and immediately renewed his attack.[30] In reply, Adenauer stressed that humility was the road to equality:

> I believe that in everything we do, we must be clear that we, as a result of total collapse, are without power. One must be clear that in the negotiations, which we Germans must conduct with the Allies in order to come progressively into ever-greater possession of power, the psychological moment plays a very large role. One cannot demand and expect trust from the outset. We cannot and must not assume that with the others there has occurred suddenly a complete change in mood toward Germany, but that instead trust can only be recovered slowly, bit by bit.[31]

Adenauer's approach was more warmly received by Germany's neighbors than by his domestic critics. In March 1950, the Council of Europe invited the Federal Republic to join it, albeit only as an associate member. In a memorandum to his cabinet, Adenauer urged accession despite the discriminatory status: 'It is as yet the only way. I must warn against saddling Germany with the odium of having brought the European negotiations to nothing.'[32]

Three months later, Robert Schuman, eager to tie Germany to France, put forward a plan to supersede and replace the Ruhr Authority. Published on May 9, 1950, the Schuman Plan would lead to the creation of a European Coal and Steel Community (ECSC), superficially a common market for these commodities, but whose essential goal was political. With such an agreement, Schuman declared, 'war between France and Germany becomes not merely unthinkable, but materially impossible'.[33]

At a press conference, Adenauer endorsed the plan in similar terms, saying it had 'created the genuine foundation for the elimination of all future conflict between France and Germany'.[34] In a meeting with Jean Monnet, commissioner-general of the French National Planning Commission and later first president (1952–5) of the ECSC High Authority, Adenauer reinforced Schuman's point: 'The various governments involved should not be so much concerned with their technical responsibilities as with their moral responsibility in the face of the great hopes that this proposal has aroused.'[35] In a letter to Schuman on May 23, 1950, Adenauer again emphasized the non-material objectives: 'In fact, we will succeed only if we do not let our work be guided solely by technical and economic considerations, but put it on an ethical basis.'[36]

The Schuman Plan accelerated German entry into a unifying Europe. As Adenauer put it in a February 1951 speech in Bonn:

> The Schuman Plan serves [the] goal of building a unified Europe. For that reason, from the very beginning we have taken up the idea that animates the Schuman Plan with approval. We have stayed true to this idea even though sometimes things have been extremely difficult for us.[37]

The ECSC charter was initialed on March 19, 1951. The following January, the Bundestag ratified it by a vote of 378 to 143.[38] The Bundesrat (the upper house representing the ten states of the Federal Republic) demonstrated lingering German national sentiment by calling on

Adenauer to 'ensure that the Allied High Commission abolished all the restraints on iron and steel production in Germany and that West Berlin was expressly included in the territory covered by the ECSC'.[39] In the event, West Berlin was specifically included in ECSC territory, and German steel and coal production increased under the auspices of the new Community. What is more, as Schuman had proposed, the ECSC officially replaced the unpopular (at least in Germany) Ruhr Authority.

In only two years after becoming chancellor, Adenauer had achieved Germany's participation in European integration – and he had done so by a policy which strove to overcome Germany's past. His motivation was undoubtedly partly tactical and national as well as ethical. But tactics had been merged with strategy, and his strategy was being transformed into history.

THE SOVIET CHALLENGE AND REARMAMENT

The Soviet Union considered the rebuilding of the West German economy and the progressive establishment of German political institutions as a direct challenge. The communist threat began to eclipse the Western democracies' fear of a resurgent Germany when, in June 1948, the Soviet Union blockaded the access routes to Berlin from the surrounding Soviet occupation zone. This was a challenge to the four-power arrangement for the governance of Berlin, which had been established at the Potsdam Summit in 1945. In the end, the US airlift to West Berlin overcame Soviet blackmail. America made clear that it would not permit the collapse of Berlin and would resort to military escalation to open the access routes if necessary. In May 1949, Stalin called off the blockade. On October 7, 1949, the Soviet Union turned its occupation zone into a sovereign (though satellite) state, sealing the partition of Germany.

In this process of escalating commitment, the United States and its allies established what grew into a pillar of American policy: the North Atlantic Treaty Organization. In what amounted to a unilateral American guarantee of its territory, the Federal Republic was put under the protection of NATO in 1949, although it still remained unarmed and was not technically a member of the organization. But one year later, in

1950, the North Korean invasion of South Korea persuaded the Allies that they were facing an overriding communist challenge. President Truman, responding to European pleas, appointed General Dwight D. Eisenhower as supreme allied commander of NATO. The general insisted that the defense of Europe required thirty divisions (approximately 450,000 soldiers),[40] a number that could not be reached without German participation.

America's allies were understandably ambivalent at the prospect that the very country under whose aggression they had suffered a few years earlier should now contribute a significant military component to Western defense. At first, Western Europe's leaders insisted that the troops assigned to the defense of Germany should be supplied by other countries. But upon reflection – and under American pressure – most European leaders accepted that the defense of Germany could not be assured without a German military contribution.

In his memoirs, Adenauer would reflect on how the Korean War had put an end to the remnants of the policy of weakening Germany:

> It was in the interest of the United States that Germany should become strong once more. Therefore, the many examples of discrimination, such as the Ruhr Statute, the Occupation Statute, and the provisions regarding the rearming of Germany, could only be of a transitory nature.[41]

Adenauer considered German rearmament to be necessary for the sake of Europe as well as for the recovery of Germany's political identity. Having first discouraged public debate on the subject so as not to interfere with progress toward German membership in European institutions, he soon reversed himself. Allied confidence might be shaken, he argued, if West Germany could not be trusted, or did not trust itself, with its own defense.[42]

German rearmament was formally proposed by Britain and the United States in August 1950 and quickly endorsed by Germany. France reacted half-heartedly with the 'Pleven Plan', which in October 1950 proposed a European army of mixed nationalities including German units. A draft treaty was drawn up, providing for the creation of a European Defense Community (EDC) that would include an integrated German contingent. A bitter controversy followed after Adenauer briefed key deputies of the German parliament on the contents of the draft treaty.[43] Schumacher went so far as to call the treaty 'a triumph for the Allied–clerical coalition against the German people'.[44]

In March 1952, to head off a European defense community and German rearmament, Stalin formally offered German unification under five conditions: (a) all occupying forces, including Soviet, would be withdrawn within one year; (b) united Germany would have a neutral status and not enter into any alliances; (c) united Germany would accept the 1945 frontiers – that is, the Oder–Neisse Line that constituted the disputed postwar border with Poland; (d) the German economy would not be limited by conditions imposed by outsiders – in other words, abolishing the Ruhr Statute limiting the German economy; and (e) united Germany would have the right to develop its own armed forces. These proposals were addressed to the Western Allies, emphasizing Germany's secondary position.

Was Stalin's offer genuine, or was he attempting to embarrass Adenauer by maneuvering him into the position of appearing to prefer a divided Germany within Europe over a united, national, neutral Germany? In effect, Stalin was asking Adenauer to abandon all the progress he had made toward European integration in return for unification.

Contemporary evidence suggests that Stalin made this offer only after receiving repeated assurances from his foreign minister that it would be refused. Nonetheless it put Adenauer in a difficult position. For the first time since unconditional surrender, the issue of the country's unification had been formally placed before the Allied powers and the German people. In Germany, Schumacher argued that the opportunity to negotiate must not be missed and that the German Bundestag should refuse to ratify the European Defense Community until the Stalin note had been explored. 'Anybody who approves the EDC in these [present] circumstances,' he argued, 'can no longer call himself German.'[45]

Adenauer stood fast. He understood that a negotiation was likely to deadlock and move the unification of Germany onto an ideological terrain on which it stood alone, to be feared by all sides. Should it act unilaterally, the negotiation would turn into the battleground on which Europeans fought out their internecine rivalries.

To avoid such choices, Adenauer evaded taking a public position on the Stalin offer by postponing discussion of it until the concept of free elections had been accepted by all the occupying countries and built into the constitution of a unifying Germany. In the meantime, he advocated the ratification of the EDC Treaty in the name of a common Allied defense.

This approach set off what the British Foreign Secretary Anthony Eden called a 'battle of the notes'. Adenauer was supported by Eisenhower, then a candidate for the presidency of the United States and, until May 30, 1952, still supreme allied commander of NATO. More concerned by the prospect of a neutral Germany than by Soviet pressure, Britain and France acceded to Adenauer's gambit. The consensus was expressed in Allied notes sent to the Kremlin on March 25 and May 13, which demanded free elections in both West and East Germany as a prelude to unification. The Soviet response on May 24 asserted that the Allied notes had stalled any possibility of German reunification 'for an indefinite period'.[46]

With renewed urgency to demonstrate the potential of the European project, now that it had come at the apparent expense of German unification, on May 26, 1952, Adenauer signed the contractual agreements on the European Defense Community.* But many in France remained unwilling to reconcile themselves to sharing an army with a nation with which their country had fought wars in every generation since the sixteenth century, which had devastated part of their country in the First World War and occupied all of it in the Second. Two years after the agreement, on August 30, 1954, the French National Assembly refused to ratify the EDC – while also discarding the Pleven Plan.

Calling this a 'black day for Europe',[47] Adenauer expressed his concerns to the representatives of Luxembourg and Belgium:

> I am firmly convinced, 100 percent convinced, that the national army to which [French Prime Minister Pierre] Mendès-France is forcing us will be a great danger for Germany and Europe. When I am no longer on hand, I don't know what will become of Germany, unless we still manage to create Europe in time.[48]

Because of these premonitions, Adenauer abandoned the EDC project and personally conducted secret negotiations with the Allies on the outlines of a German national army.

American leadership proved pivotal. Elected president in November

---

* The following day the treaty was signed in Paris.

1952, Eisenhower had decided that the unification of Europe and its joint defense, including the Federal Republic of Germany, was, in the words of one historian, a

> kind of skeleton key, unlocking the solution to a number of problems at once, and most important, providing a type of 'dual containment'. The Soviet Union could be kept out, and Germany kept in Europe, with neither able to dominate the Continent.[49]

Together with British Foreign Secretary Eden, Eisenhower forged a modification of the EDC Treaty that allowed the development of a German army. Less than a decade after unconditional surrender, NATO would consist of federated national forces including those of Germany.

A trip by Adenauer to Washington in 1953 marked a high point of these efforts. On April 8, he visited the Tomb of the Unknown Soldier. The German flag – the black, red and gold tricolor of the Federal Republic, not the black, sword-bearing eagle of Prussia or the swastika of the Thousand Year Reich – was raised above Arlington National Cemetery. As the chancellor strode toward the tomb, a twenty-one-gun salute sounded in a scene with which Adenauer would end the 1945–53 volume of his memoirs:

> An American band played the German national anthem. I saw how tears were running down the face of one of my companions, and I, too, was deeply moved. It had been a long and hard road from the total catastrophe of the year 1945 to this moment of the year 1953, when the German national anthem was heard in the national cemetery of the United States.[50]

Adenauer rebuilt the German armed forces throughout his remaining years in office without resurrecting Germany's historical intermittent militarism. By early 1964, the Bundeswehr had reached an overall strength of 415,000 officers and enlisted men. One historian describes it as 'the tip of the spear' of the NATO alliance and 'linchpin' of the defense of Western Europe against a conventional Soviet attack.[51] More than this, the army was the backstop of the FRG's re-entry into international diplomacy – a tangible sign that the new Germany was both trusted by the Atlantic Alliance and a responsible contributor to the common defense.

Adenauer would draw on the political capital accumulated during the formation of NATO to achieve his underlying quest to bring the occupation of Germany to an end. To attain full membership in NATO and proceed with the dismantling of the Occupation Statute, Adenauer agreed in 1954 to postpone the resolution of the Saar territory – which Paris sought to maintain as a neutral protectorate under French occupation – until 1957. It took complicated parliamentary maneuvers to induce the Bundestag to ratify both treaties in February 1955.[52]

When the treaties took effect on May 5, 1955, the Federal Republic became a sovereign state once more. Whereas, six years earlier, Adenauer's election had been ratified by the Allied high commissioners, now they accepted their own dissolution. Adenauer stood on the steps of his office complex – the Palais Schaumburg – as the German flag was raised over government buildings throughout Bonn. Adenauer's first great task – ensuring the peaceful, swift and amicable end of the Occupation Statute – had been accomplished.[53]

Two days later, to symbolize his country's commitment to full partnership in Europe and the Atlantic Alliance, Adenauer led a delegation to Paris, where Germany assumed equal status within NATO. In six fateful years, Adenauer had brought his country from postwar partition, restrictions under the Occupation Statute and reparations to participation in the European Community and full membership in NATO. The strategy of humility had achieved its goal of equality in a new structure for Europe that Adenauer's inauguration had signified.

THE INEXTRICABLE PAST: REPARATIONS TO THE JEWISH PEOPLE

The ethical basis for foreign policy on which Adenauer had relied in Germany's dealings with the Western Allies was especially complex in relation to the Jewish people. Nazi crimes against Jews had been uniquely sweeping, savage and single-minded. Some six million, more than one-third of the world Jewish population, were murdered in a methodically planned and executed policy of wholesale extermination.

Toward the end of the war, the Western Allies assigned Nazi crimes to automatic-arrest categories, to be implemented by Allied intelligence personnel and based in part on an accused perpetrator's rank in the Nazi Party. By the beginning of the occupation, such criminal categorization applied to tens of thousands of individuals. As the government was progressively turned over to the Federal Republic, so was the denazification process, which thereby became a German domestic political issue. Adenauer considered reparations to the Jewish people a moral duty as well as unqualifiedly in the German national self-interest; his commitment to the denazification process was more opaque, since he was also head of the CDU and in that capacity keenly aware that a rigorous effort would affect a significant proportion of voters.

Adenauer therefore restricted the denazification process to a politically manageable number and argued less for retribution than for domestic reconciliation and compensation for the Holocaust's surviving victims. In practice, this meant focusing war crime investigations primarily on high-ranking former Nazis or on officials whose specific crimes could be proved in a court of law. This of course allowed for a wide span of ambiguity, illustrated by the fact that Hans Globke – a drafter of the Nuremberg race laws – became Adenauer's chief of staff. At the same time, Adenauer never wavered from affirming the moral obligations imposed on Germany by the Nazi past. Therefore, as a symbol of repentance and as a bridge toward justice and reconciliation with the Jewish people, he committed the Federal Republic to discussions on reparations with Jewish leaders and also with Israel, which he acknowledged as representative of the Jewish people as a whole.

In March 1951, the Israeli government sent a request to the four occupying powers and the two German governments for reparations to survivors and heirs in the amount of $1.5 billion. Neither the Soviet Union nor the German Democratic Republic ever replied directly. Adenauer replied, however, on behalf of the Federal Republic, addressing the Bundestag on September 27, 1951:

> In the name of the German people . . . unspeakable crimes were committed which require moral and material reparation [*Wiedergutmachung*]. These crimes concern damage to individuals as well as to Jewish property whose owners are no longer alive . . . The first steps have been taken on this level. A great deal remains to be done. The government of the Federal Republic will support the rapid conclusion of a law regarding restitution and its just implementation. A portion of identifiable Jewish property is to be returned. Further restitution will follow.[54]

It was now Germany's duty, Adenauer continued, to resolve this issue so as 'to ease the way to an inner purification'.[55]

The reparations law passed the Bundestag on May 18, 1953. The fourteen members of the Communist Party rejected it, appealing to German nationalism. The Social Democratic Party supported reparations unanimously. For the government, the outcome was more ambiguous: 106 members of parliament from the CDU-led coalition voted yes; 86, primarily from the CDU's conservative Bavarian wing, abstained.[56]

Despite these parliamentary reservations, Adenauer had achieved his goal. The historian Jeffrey Herf has summarized the benefits reaching Israel from Germany:

> The West German deliveries to Israel of ships, machine tools, trains, autos, medical equipment, and more amounted to between 10 and 15 percent of annual Israeli imports. According to reports of the Federal Republic, restitution payments to individual survivors of Nazi political, racial, and religious persecution, most of whom were Jewish survivors, amounted to 40.4 billion [German] marks by 1971, 77 billion marks by 1986, about 96 billion marks by 1995, and would total about 124 billion marks in all.[57]

Nevertheless, Israel's citizens were deeply divided over the prospect of accepting 'blood money' as some kind of expiation for genocidal slaughter. Debates in the Knesset, the Israeli parliament, were fiercely contested and accompanied by street demonstrations. Throughout, Adenauer maintained personal contact with Nahum Goldmann, the founder of the World Jewish Congress.

The Federal Republic would establish full diplomatic relations with Israel in 1965, two years after Adenauer's departure from office. The following year, Adenauer visited Israel, by then the home of some 150,000 survivors of the Holocaust, as a private citizen. When he arrived he said, 'this is one of the most solemn and beautiful moments of my life . . . never did I think, when I became Chancellor, that I would one day be invited to visit Israel.'[58]

Despite this opening, the visit was the occasion for an eruption of tension – perhaps unsurprising – between the ninety-year-old Adenauer and the Israeli prime minister, Levi Eshkol. 'We have not forgotten and we shall never forget,' Eshkol said to Adenauer at a dinner he was giving in the German statesman's honor, 'the terrible Holocaust in which we lost 6,000,000 of our people. German–Israeli relations cannot be normal relations.'[59] He added that Germany's reparations to Israel were 'only symbolic' and could not 'erase the tragedy which occurred'. Ever composed, Adenauer replied: 'I know how difficult it is for the Jewish people to forget the past but should you fail to recognize our good will, nothing good can come of it.'[60]

The most memorable images of Adenauer's time in Israel came from a (for all involved) wrenching visit to Yad Vashem, Israel's Holocaust memorial and museum, located on the western slope of Mount Herzl in Jerusalem.[61] Maintaining a dignified silence, Adenauer was led into the Remembrance Chamber – a cavernous, dimly lit hall with a roof resembling a tent canopy – where he was invited to kindle a flame and lay a wreath at a memorial to the unknown victims of the death camps. Unexpectedly presented with a badge bearing the Hebrew word for 'remember', he replied, 'even without this badge, I never could have forgotten.'[62]

TWO CRISES: SUEZ AND BERLIN

For Adenauer, the end of the occupation and the introduction of Germany into the European and international order marked the culmination of a historic effort. But history does not grant respites. A year after the restoration of German sovereignty in 1955, the Middle East conflict challenged the premises underlying the NATO Alliance.

In late October 1956, Adenauer was shaken by the US decision to sponsor a UN General Assembly resolution condemning the Franco-British military operation to reverse the Egyptian nationalization of the Suez Canal. Adenauer had assumed that the Alliance by definition would protect the core interests of each member. Now the US formal opposition to Britain and France at the UN separated America from its key allies while they were engaged in military action in what they conceived as their national interest. Might in some future circumstance others – and especially Germany – suffer a similar fate?

Adenauer chose the occasion of a routine visit to Paris in November 1956 for a discussion of Euratom (the European Atomic Energy Community) to express this view – albeit in a very restricted group including French Prime Minister Guy Mollet and Foreign Minister Christian Pineau. Adenauer's train arrived in Paris on November 6, one day after Premier Bulganin of the Soviet Union, chief patron of and arms supplier to the Nasser regime, had threatened missile attacks on Britain and France if they continued their military operations along the Suez Canal.

The French government greeted Adenauer with unusual warmth. A company of the Garde Civile gave the salute. The two national anthems were played.[63] A member of Adenauer's entourage described the scene:

> The Chancellor took the salute like a statue, motionless. I was thinking of the scene at the National Cemetery in Arlington near Washington [in 1953]. Even the most hard-boiled must have been touched by the significance of the moment and its symbolism. In the most serious hour France had experienced since the end of the war, the two governments were standing shoulder to shoulder.[64]

Adenauer learned of America's refusal to arrest a run on the pound sterling, a major blow to its British ally, during the Paris trip. He was dismayed but not to the point of questioning the significance of NATO. On the contrary, he thought it imperative for Europe to maintain its ties to America. The NATO alliance, he argued, was the most important component of the security of every European country. He warned his hosts against public controversy with the United States, and especially against any kind of retaliation, even verbal. Rather, America's European allies should enhance their cooperation *within* Europe:

> France and England will never be powers comparable to the United States and the Soviet Union. Not Germany, either. There remains to them only one way of playing a decisive role in the world: that is to unite to make Europe ... We have no time to waste: Europe will be your revenge.[65]

It was during the Suez crisis that Adenauer began to consider the need to use European integration – and particularly the Franco-German relationship – as a hedge against American vacillation.

France, in the decade after de Gaulle's return to the presidency in 1958, followed this precept, though (as we shall see in the next chapter) de Gaulle required no German encouragement to move in the direction of European autonomy.* The Franco-German relationship did become more intense during the de Gaulle presidency after Adenauer's overnight

* See Chapter 2, pages 105–7 and 112–13.

visit to de Gaulle's home in Colombey-les-Deux-Églises in September 1958 – an invitation never extended to any other foreign leader.*

Two years after Suez, Adenauer's doubts about American reliability resurfaced when, in November 1958, Soviet leader Nikita Khrushchev challenged the status of Berlin. While the Four Power Occupation Authority formally continued to function, West Berlin had since 1957 been governed de facto by the laws of the Federal Republic; its legal structure was based on free elections contested by the FRG's major parties in the Allied-occupied portions of the city.† In the eastern part of Berlin, the German Democratic Republic governed by Soviet imposition. A vestige of four-power control enabled officials of West and East to circulate throughout the city.

Khrushchev's ultimatum to the Western Allies, demanding a new status for Berlin within six months, directly challenged the foundations of Adenauer's foreign policy and of the Atlantic Alliance. Any significant change to Berlin's status under Soviet threat would signal eventual communist dominance in the city and imperil his vision of building the Federal Republic under an Allied, especially American, nuclear umbrella. Yet though Khrushchev threatened force, he did not have the confidence to execute it within the time frame of his ultimatum.

Eisenhower skillfully deferred a confrontation by drawing Khrushchev into a prolonged, largely procedural exchange over the issues his ultimatum implied, culminating in an invitation for the Soviet leader to make a personal tour of the US in September 1959. British Prime Minister Harold Macmillan pursued a similar strategy with a visit to Moscow in February 1959. Among the principal allies, only de Gaulle stood aloof from this strategy, insisting on withdrawal of the Soviet ultimatum before entering negotiations.

Khrushchev, at a loss over how to implement his threats – or at least unwilling to face the military consequences – withdrew his deadline in May 1959. During his US visit, he and Eisenhower agreed to a joint communiqué containing the phrase 'all outstanding international questions [such as Berlin] should be settled not by the application of force

---

* See Chapter 2, page 104.

† In Adenauer's period, Willy Brandt, the mayor of the Western sector of Berlin from 1956 to 1966, would become a national figure in West Germany. Brandt was elected chancellor in 1969, when East Berlin would, for all practical purposes, become part of the GDR.

but by peaceful means through negotiations,' which engendered a brief warming in US–Soviet relations.[66]

Despite this agreement, Khrushchev remained persistent in striving to isolate and demoralize Adenauer's Germany. In May 1960, Khrushchev's efforts produced a summit about Berlin to be held in Paris among the leaders of the four occupying powers – without the Federal Republic, thus implying the possibility that the outcome might be imposed on Germany.

The summit assembled on schedule when fate, or accident, intervened. An American U-2 spy plane was shot down over Russia on May 1, 1960, and Khrushchev used the incident to demand an American apology before proceeding with any substantive discussions. When Eisenhower refused, Khrushchev aborted the summit without, however, reinstating his threat. The issues of Berlin – and American reliability – were left for Adenauer to discuss with Eisenhower's successor, John F. Kennedy.

THREE CONVERSATIONS WITH ADENAUER

By an ironic twist of fate, more than twenty years after fleeing with my family from Nazi Germany, I had the opportunity to participate in shaping long-term American policy toward the country – now part of the NATO Alliance – as a consultant to the Kennedy White House.

First as an academic in the late 1950s pursuing studies in European history, and then as a White House consultant in the early 1960s, I began meeting with officials of foreign governments. My admiration of Adenauer's leadership notwithstanding, I remained concerned during this period about the impact of Germany's turbulent political culture on the decisions imposed on it by the Cold War. As I wrote in a memo for President Kennedy in April 1961:

> A country which has lost two world wars, undergone three revolutions, committed the crimes of the Nazi era, and seen its material wealth wiped out twice in a generation, is bound to suffer from deep psychological scars. There is an atmosphere of hysteria, a tendency toward unbalanced actions. A German friend, a creative writer, said to me that Germany

alone of the major countries of Europe suffered no visible psychic shock
after the war. It sublimated its problems in the frenzied effort to rebuild
economically. But it remains a candidate for a nervous breakdown.[67]

This passage captures the unstable atmosphere in which Adenauer was
acting and the psychological challenges to his policies.

I met Adenauer the first time in 1957 during an academic trip to
Germany and would continue our meetings until his death a decade
later. The last few of our ten or so meetings were conducted after his
retirement in 1963, when I became a sympathetic listener to his occasionally melancholy reflections on his life and the future of his people in
a country that – in spite of the end of occupation – appeared fated to
host the British, French and American armies indefinitely, now as a
deterrent to Soviet aggression.

The chancellor's office was located in the Palais Schaumburg, once
the residence of a nineteenth-century Rhenish aristocrat. Elaborate by
those standards, it was too small to accommodate the machinery of a
modern bureaucratic-technological state. In the chancellor's office, easy
chairs and sofas dominated, with a minimum of visible technical para-
phernalia; it had the character more of a living room than of a center of
power. Except for a very few key advisors, the operational personnel
were situated elsewhere in Bonn, a city in truth too modest to serve as
the capital of a major country.

Adenauer's authority derived in part from his personality, which
combined dignity with strength. His face, left partly rigid by injuries
sustained in an automobile accident during his early forties, and his
demeanor, simultaneously courtly and aloof, conveyed an unmistakable
message: one was entering a world guided by principle and immune to
slogans or pressure. He spoke calmly, only occasionally using his hands
for emphasis. Always well prepared on contemporary issues, he never
discussed his personal life in my presence. Nor did he inquire into
my own, though – given the perennial effectiveness of the German
bureaucracy – surely he knew my family history and understood the
paths onto which fate had placed each of us.

Adenauer had a sharp eye for character, and his observations were
occasionally phrased sardonically. In a discussion on the qualities of
strong leadership, he cautioned me 'never to confuse energy with
strength'. On another occasion, he was ushering me into his office just

as another visitor, who had recently won media attention by attacking him, was leaving. My surprise must have been evident at the cordial manner of their parting. Adenauer began the conversation with: 'My dear Mr Professor, in politics it is important to retaliate in cold blood.'

October 1957

The first conversation opened with the West's relations with the Soviet Union. Adenauer insisted that the conflict was both fundamental and permanent and warned of concessions to the Soviets or the East Germans. Berlin's currently divided status, while difficult, was tenable, he said, adding that any Soviet-backed proposal to 'modify' or 'improve' it was designed to weaken Western unity and Berlin's autonomy – just as Stalin's crafty unification offer of five years earlier had been.

Nor was the Soviet Union the only threat facing the world order as Adenauer saw it. Was I aware, Adenauer asked, that in the judgment of serious observers a split between China and Russia was imminent? In the face of such evolving challenges, he continued, the West should take special care not to weaken itself by inter-Allied disputes. Since an overt Sino-Soviet split was not a widespread expectation at that time, I refrained from commenting. Adenauer chose to treat silence as agreement. In his introductory conversation with President Kennedy in 1961, he would repeat his cautionary message, adding 'and Professor Kissinger agrees with me'.[68]

The overriding purpose of Adenauer's first conversation with me was to explore the reliability of the American nuclear guarantee. Nuclear weapons at that time were little more than a decade old, and no comparable experience in history could serve as a precedent for one country risking its devastation on behalf of another. In the early phase of the alliance, NATO, by its own admission, did not have sufficient forces for a conventional defense. Therefore, the central question became: would the United States assume the nuclear risks?

When I argued that, in the emerging world order, America would make no distinction between Allied interests and its own, Adenauer pointed out courteously yet firmly that during the Suez crisis only a year earlier, America had failed to treat the interests of even its major allies (Britain and France) in that spirit.

Once broached, Adenauer's concern over US reliability on the nuclear issue grew ever more explicit, leading him to devise ingenious hypothetical scenarios that might test American presidential determination. Could, for instance, a US leader run the risks of nuclear devastation in the last months of his presidency? Or in the three-month interval between election and inauguration? Or after a hydrogen bomb had exploded over a major American city? At this stage of the US–Germany relationship, Adenauer's questions, however blunt, were designed primarily to evoke reassurance. I repeated the standard American answer of an unqualified reiteration of the US commitment. But Adenauer's concern about nuclear strategy escalated in scope and intensity in all our later conversations.

May 1961 – Flexible Response

My next conversation with Adenauer occurred on May 18, 1961, in an altered political framework. John F. Kennedy, the new American president, was a leader for whom Adenauer's previous experience had not prepared him. Eloquent, youthful and dynamic, with distinguished service in the Pacific during the Second World War, Kennedy represented a generational break with his predecessors, all of whom had been born before the First World War. Imbued with the confidence of the 'Greatest Generation', Kennedy set about to channel that generation's energy and faith in the country into a design for achieving America's global goals.* Although he had spent time in Europe during his father's service as ambassador to Britain (1937–40) and had toured Germany on several occasions as a student and as a senator, Kennedy was just beginning to grapple with how to reassure a defeated Germany engaged simultaneously in the reconstruction of Europe and the defense of its political structure from Soviet threats.

Kennedy was obliged to make policy in the face of a growing stockpile of Soviet nuclear weapons. The Soviets had tested a nuclear weapon for the first time in 1949. By Eisenhower's inauguration in 1953, they

---

* The Kennedy administration included an unprecedented number of academics – among them Arthur Schlesinger, Jr, John Kenneth Galbraith and Carl Kaysen – with direct access to the president. More familiar with the informal atmosphere of the academy than with the intricate clearance systems by means of which diplomacy protects itself (and the country), they sometimes engaged in public reflections that were interpreted abroad as presidential preferences. This complicated dialogues with foreign leaders.

had built some 200 nuclear weapons; when Kennedy became president in 1961, they possessed about 1,500 warheads and were beginning to develop intercontinental delivery systems – thereby creating premature concerns about a so-called missile gap. The apprehensions would turn out to be exaggerated because, in the early 1960s, the United States was still in a position to prevail with a preemptive first strike.

Adenauer, for his part, continued to regard the Atlantic Alliance as the key to Germany's strategic and political future. But the Alliance was having internal disputes on both overall political goals and a common military strategy. As Adenauer had expressed to me in our previous conversation, the disagreements over nuclear strategy were about whether the Alliance would always be able to depend on an almost reflexive American self-identification with Alliance objectives when allies were threatened with aggression.

Kennedy and his advisors, most notably Defense Secretary Robert McNamara, sought to mitigate the impact of such a conundrum with a doctrine of flexible response, by which they envisioned creating various thresholds in combat to enable adversaries to consider responses other than massive retaliation. But the weapons were so colossally destructive that the technical design of these hypothetical scenarios proved more persuasive than the diplomacy put forward on their behalf.

The German defense minister, Franz Josef Strauss, became a vocal opponent of American nuclear strategy. A quintessential Bavarian, voluble and passionate, with a girth testifying to his enjoyment of his region's libations, Strauss raised the applicability of 'flexible response' to a Berlin crisis in a conversation with me on May 11, during this same visit to Bonn. [69] How much territory would be lost, he asked, before the 'threshold' response was reached? What would be the duration of a 'pause'? Who would make the decisions at each envisioned stage, especially on the leap from conventional to nuclear warfare? He doubted whether America would be either able or willing to carry out so complex and ambiguous a policy. Other German participants at the meeting supported Strauss, especially the chief of staff of the newly created armed forces.

Adenauer demonstrated the impact of Strauss's thinking by bluntly opening our conversation, once again in his office in the Palais Schaumburg, with the sentence, [70] 'You Americans have sinned a great deal against NATO.' Adenauer had been put off by a US proposal that the

NATO allies work out a system for controlling the independent nuclear forces of Britain and France and relating them to an integrated strategy via a Multilateral Force. How, Adenauer asked, could countries without nuclear weapons of their own be expected to make sensible proposals? The NATO secretary-general's staff was too thin and too unfamiliar with nuclear affairs to undertake such an assignment. If nuclear coordination was truly sought, he argued, the authority of the secretary-general needed to be strengthened and his staff increased.

The White House proposal to which Adenauer was referring had been drafted with the expectation that he and his entourage would conclude from their unfamiliarity with nuclear strategy that responsibility for it should remain with America. But Adenauer had drawn the unexpected conclusion that Europe's capability for autonomous nuclear forces should be enhanced.

This is why Adenauer next turned to the subject of de Gaulle. De Gaulle had warned him that America, despite its promises, had abandoned France at the United Nations over Algeria just as it had previously done in 1956 over Suez. According to Adenauer, de Gaulle had argued that the diplomacy conducted by the Allies with respect to Berlin had lacked decisiveness and direction. Instead of temporizing, America should boldly take the lead and flatly reject Soviet demands. De Gaulle had briefed him on a conversation between Eisenhower and Khrushchev which, as Adenauer interpreted it, might tempt the Soviets to keep pressing forward, especially given the soft posture of British Prime Minister Macmillan. Firmness was all the more necessary because Adenauer was also convinced that the Soviets would never risk self-destruction over Berlin.

I answered by recapitulating what I had said in our first conversation: that, from what I knew about American thinking, the freedom of Berlin and of Europe as a whole was regarded as inseparable from our own. That led Adenauer to the subject of France's independent nuclear force. Did it strengthen the Alliance? Was it necessary? I expressed my skepticism that the Kremlin would interpret a distinct French nuclear force as a substitute for the American nuclear commitment. At this, Adenauer called for Foreign Minister Heinrich von Brentano to join us and asked me to repeat my observations to him. How could a professional military man such as de Gaulle come to so unrealistic an ambition? Adenauer promised to explore this with him at their next meeting.

The following month, Adenauer's concerns over the future of German–American relations were intensified when Khrushchev reaffirmed the Berlin ultimatum. In response, Kennedy mobilized National Guard units and appointed General Lucius Clay as 'Personal Representative with the rank of Ambassador', in effect making him the key American official in Berlin. Khrushchev further escalated the crisis on August 13 by building a wall across the city, brutally dividing it. The Four Power status of Berlin had been obliterated.

Side by side with military readiness measures, the Kennedy administration elaborated a number of political proposals to put access to Berlin under the jurisdiction of an international authority in place of the Four Powers; it was to be composed of an equal number of NATO and Warsaw Pact commissioners (eight for each) – plus three from neutral European countries. In this scheme, final determination on which peace and war depended would be removed from the Atlantic Alliance and placed into the hands of countries that had declared themselves neutral mainly to remove themselves from day-to-day issues. The proposal was never formally explored, as Adenauer refused to entertain the prospect of trading American supervision of the access routes for that of three European neutrals.

Another set of ideas for resolving the Berlin impasse involved ways for Germany to accept the Oder–Neisse Line, which had reduced pre-war German territory by nearly a quarter at the end of the Second World War. Adenauer rejected this, too, though he would actually have been prepared to accept it under the appropriate framework – such as a settlement on German unification. In his judgment, altering access procedures to Berlin – which he believed were already functioning adequately – did not qualify for so large a concession. Above all, the constant quest for separate negotiating formulae isolated Germany. Adenauer's strategy relied on the containment policy devised by George Kennan and implemented by US Secretaries of State Dean Acheson and John Foster Dulles. It assumed that the Soviet bloc would eventually weaken if confined to its own resources and obliged to confront its internal dilemmas. That, in Adenauer's view, would be the moment to negotiate unification.

February 1962 – Kennedy and Adenauer

There was a melancholy element in the encounters between Kennedy and Adenauer. Both pursued important goals, but their policies derived from opposite starting points and were sought by different methods – endurance by Adenauer, diplomatic flexibility by Kennedy. Adenauer had assumed office at the nadir of German history; America, when Kennedy became president, was at the acme of its power and self-confidence. Adenauer saw his task as rebuilding democratic values on the basis of Christian morality amid the chaos of unconditional surrender; Kennedy's sweeping purposes reflected unchallenged belief in America's providential mission based on its historic democratic values and dominant power. For Adenauer, the reconstruction of Europe involved a reaffirmation of traditional values and verities; for Kennedy, it was the affirmation of faith in scientific, political and moral progress in the modern world. For Adenauer to succeed, it was necessary to stabilize the soul of Germany; for an American president, and especially for Kennedy, the goal was to mobilize an existing idealism. What started as a historic partnership gradually became strained in execution as American idealism overestimated the diplomatic flexibility available to Germany.

On the way to constructing an Atlantic Community, American and German objectives had run parallel. The structures formed during the period of creativity in the late 1940s and early 1950s were based on a substantially common vision in the political field and a de facto American monopoly in the nuclear arena. But once the journey was completed, and especially under the pressures of Khrushchev's repeated Berlin ultimatums, history demanded its due; national interests and even national styles, reflecting centuries of different internal evolution, reasserted themselves. As a result, by 1962, Washington was receiving reports that Adenauer was challenging the credibility of American nuclear commitments and the policy on Berlin.

McGeorge Bundy, Kennedy's national security advisor, asked me in February 1962 as an established acquaintance of Adenauer to meet with him to help restore trust on nuclear matters. I responded that, in Adenauer's mind, political issues were both paramount and permanent while nuclear issues were symbols of political and ethical reliability. To overcome Adenauer's reservations, it was agreed that he should receive a special briefing from me on American security policy and nuclear capabilities. This was developed by Secretary of Defense McNamara and approved by Secretary of State Dean Rusk, and it included details about US nuclear force structures and planning not previously shared with leaders of Allied countries (except for the UK). Because of the briefing's nuclear component, Adenauer was accompanied only by an interpreter.* (Since I did not know the technical terms for nuclear strategy in German, I conducted my part of the conversation in English.)

As I began my presentation on February 16,[71] elaborating upon the firmness of the American commitment, Adenauer interrupted: 'They have already told me this in Washington. Since it did not convince me there, why would it convince me here?' I replied that I was mainly an academic, not an official; might the chancellor defer judgment until he heard my entire presentation? Unshaken, Adenauer responded: 'How much of your time are you spending on your Washington consultation?' When I replied by saying about a quarter, Adenauer replied: 'Let us assume then you will tell me three-quarters of the truth.'

This volley might well have discomfited Walter Dowling, the American ambassador in Bonn, who had accompanied me to the meeting. But, as a professional, he did not bat an eye. As I developed the nuclear presentation, which demonstrated the enormous disparity that existed at that time between American and Soviet strategic nuclear forces, Adenauer's attitude was transformed. As I was now answering questions he had previously addressed without satisfaction to other American visitors, the briefing emphasized that American second-strike forces were larger and far more effective than Soviet first-strike forces, and that an American first strike would be overwhelming.

The final paragraph of Ambassador Dowling's report summed up the conversation's effect on the chancellor:

> On two occasions when Kissinger and I sought to leave, [Adenauer] asked
> us to stay in order to give him another opportunity to express his grat-
> itude for what had been said and his strong concurrence with it. He said
> he was relieved to see what strength existed to defend freedom and that
> [the] main task was to see to it that there would be no human failings.

* The briefing took place in the chancellor's office in Bonn. Though born in Germany, I generally spoke English in official conversations but did not ask for a translation if my opposite number spoke German.

Upon leaving, Kissinger said that when we spoke of our power and our
dedication to [the] Atlantic Community, these were not simply idle
phrases. The Chancellor replied, 'Thank God for this!' On this note, the
meeting broke up.[72]

The 'human failings' to which Adenauer referred clearly included his
concern over developing an appropriate strategy and America's possible
unwillingness to apply its overwhelming power.

A few decades later, I would receive a letter from Germany that illustrated the value Adenauer placed on honoring his commitments. Bearing
a sender's name I did not recognize, it informed me that the writer had
served as the interpreter during that long-ago conversation. Following
White House instructions, I had asked Adenauer not to distribute the
nuclear information I shared with him, and he had given his word of
honor to respect the request. The writer now confided that he had, in
fact, made a record of the entire briefing – as was his duty as interpreter –
and given it to the chancellor the next day. Adenauer, however, had
directed him to destroy the nuclear portion since he could not guarantee
that his promise to me would continue to be kept once he left office.

History had thrown Adenauer and Kennedy into a kind of mutual
dependence, but it could not make up for the generational gap and the
resulting differences. Kennedy saw his objective as first reducing and
then ultimately eliminating the possibility of nuclear war; in that effort,
he meant to engage Soviet participation in a long journey that required
tactical flexibility, including on the part of the German chancellor. From
Adenauer's perspective, however, the American president's tactics
threatened to dissipate the stability and solidity he had wrought from
the disintegration of Hitler's Germany. Kennedy had the more global
approach, Adenauer the fortitude to face the moral and physical collapse of his country, living with its partition and building a new
European order based on Atlantic partnership.

GERMAN UNIFICATION:
THE TORMENTING WAIT

The German people had never been governed within borders that corresponded to those of the postwar period.[73] Absent an East–West agreement, or a collapse of the existing balance of power, their establishment seemed to augur the indefinite partition of Germany between the communist East and the democratic West. True, the goal of a unified Germany was tacitly affirmed by the existence of a Four-Power Control Council for the whole of Occupied Germany and was explicitly embraced by the three Western powers; but inevitably internal German politics would seek unity between West and East more explicitly than would the occupying powers. Unification became a perennial political issue in West Germany and was used as a strategic instrument by the Soviet Union – starting with Stalin's offer of 1952 and culminating in Khrushchev's ultimatums on Berlin.

Adenauer's policy was based on treating the partition of the country as provisional; he believed that unification would come eventually through the dismantling of the Soviet satellite orbit, the Federal Republic's superior economic growth, the strength and cohesion of the Atlantic Alliance and internal tensions arising within the Warsaw Pact. This assumed a collapse of the East German satellite – much, in fact, as happened in 1989. Until such a collapse, the FRG's top priorities would continue to be the Atlantic Alliance, close relations with America, and integration into Europe. The difficulty of the strategy that replaced submission to the Allies with endurance was that Moscow was unlikely to remain passive in the interval and would doubtless attempt to forestall such an outcome by diplomatic and even military pressures, as happened in the various Berlin crises. The resulting controversies gradually weakened Adenauer's domestic position.

When the East German Soviet satellite had declared itself sovereign in October 1949, Adenauer had responded with the so-called Brentano Doctrine (named after his foreign minister from 1955 to 1961), according to which the Federal Republic would suspend diplomatic relations with any country that recognized the GDR. But with time, and in the face of internal German pressures for contact at least with Eastern Europe and East Germany, this policy proved increasingly difficult to maintain.

Reeling from electoral defeats, and impacted by Khrushchev's maneu-vers, the SPD began to change course, mobilizing support by emphasizing its stance in favor of negotiations with Eastern Europe and especially with East Germany. Herbert Wehner, its most forceful leader (though ineligible for the top post because of his wartime arrest and internment in Sweden as a Soviet agent), led an internal process that in 1959 culmin-ated in the party's acceptance of German membership in NATO. As the SPD increasingly put itself forward as an instrument of unification, it revived its immediate postwar policy of seeking greater flexibility in negotiating with the Eastern countries and the Soviet Union, albeit now within a NATO framework – the so-called *Ostpolitik*.[74]

Adenauer and the CDU argued that progress toward eventual unifi-cation was undermined by turning the status of Berlin, the historic capital of Germany, into a negotiation in which the communists held all the geographic and military assets. The affirmation of the final goal, in Adenauer's view, could paradoxically render the provisional partition bearable – in contrast to the early days of the Federal Republic, when Adenauer strove to set the issue aside.

The debates between the CDU and the SPD began to overlap with divisions within the CDU over Adenauer's succession. A combination of his age – he was eighty-six by 1962 – and disputes with the US over Soviet strategy gradually weakened his domestic position. Adenauer's refusal to oppose de Gaulle's veto of British accession to the EEC* was criticized by a substantial minority in the CDU. When, in the 1961 elec-tion, the CDU lost its majority in the Bundestag, a coalition government became necessary. The Liberal Democrats – a moderately conservative, free-trade party and the sole available coalition partner – agreed, on the condition that Adenauer leave office before the end of the coalition's term in 1965.

In the fall of 1962, this issue of Adenauer's retirement came to a head. Defense Minister Franz Josef Strauss charged the magazine *Der Spiegel* with violations of national security when it published leaked government documents that he was exploring the idea of securing tact-ical nuclear weapons for the FRG's defense.[75] In response, Strauss accused *Der Spiegel* of sedition and recommended that the Hamburg

* See Chapter 2, pages 111–12.

police raid the magazine's office. In addition, the journalist responsible for the story was arrested in Spain, where he had been vacationing.

All five Liberal Democrat cabinet ministers resigned in protest on November 19, and Strauss too was subsequently forced to resign. Adenauer himself had been aware of Strauss's plan – distracted by the Cuban missile crisis, in his telling – and, though he surmounted the immediate wave of resignations, his time was now clearly limited.

As Adenauer prepared to leave office, he was especially concerned to put his foreign-policy achievements on firm ground for the future. One of the pillars of his foreign policy had been the containment of Soviet power – a strategy that had been supported by every American president since Truman. Premised on the conviction that Soviet ideology and strategic assertiveness could be overcome through building situations of Allied strength, especially in Central Europe, the concept turned out to be prescient. Containment's shortcoming, however, was that it included no prescription for the conveying of Western strength to the adversary, nor the diplomacy that would implement it, unless there was a direct attack or other pressures. As a result, in internal domestic politics, Adenauer's fortitude and endurance had to yield ground to *Ostpolitik*.

The other main pillar was Adenauer's conviction that the future of Germany and of a united Europe depended on moral faith and commitment to democratic principles. He explained this in a 1956 speech about Europe's future:

> 'The greatest thoughts spring from the heart' is a famous saying. And we, too, must let the great thought of a united Europe spring from our hearts if it is to materialize. Not as though the unity of Europe were a matter of the emotions, of sentiment, but rather in the sense that a firm heart, dedicated to a great task, can give us the strength to carry out in the face of all difficulties what our reason has recognized as right. If we find this strength, then we shall do justice to all the necessities I have mentioned. We shall then complete the great work of unification which each of our nations needs, which Europe needs, and which the whole world needs.[76]

During his period in office, Adenauer achieved his goal of implanting democracy in Germany and the shaping of a European structure within which Germany could be a major part. By a merging of Adenauer's strategy and Kennedy's tactics, the ultimate goal – German unification – was reached with the collapse of the Soviet empire more than two decades after they had both left the stage.

FINAL CONVERSATIONS

Adenauer resigned as chancellor in April 1963 after fourteen years of service.

Dean Acheson once observed that many leaders after leaving office act as if they had concluded a great love affair. They find it difficult to separate themselves from the issues that had occupied their days; reflections on alternative courses of action fill many of their hours and conversations.

It was different with Adenauer, and especially so I thought during my last visit on January 24, 1967, three months before he passed away. Age had not enfeebled him. He was especially concerned about long-term trends of Germany rather than the issues of the moment. He raised a theme always present in his thinking but heretofore obscured from me: the evolution of what the Germans thought of themselves. The Germans were a deeply troubled and conflicted people, Adenauer said, not only because of their Nazi past but also, in a deeper sense, because of an absence of a sense of proportion or of historical continuity. The evolution of history would present the Germans with surprising developments to which they might react in an unanticipated manner. Maintaining the inner stability of Germany could turn into a perpetual problem.

To my question as to whether the recently formed grand coalition between the two leading parties – the CDU and the SPD – had overcome the inherent absence of national consensus, Adenauer replied that both major parties were very weak. He wondered aloud: 'Are any leaders still able to conduct a genuine long-range policy? Is true leadership still possible today?' The SPD, he said, had only one strong leader, Herbert Wehner, who was ineligible for the chancellorship because of his communist past. Moreover, the SPD was divided between political tacticians on their right and a pacifist left wing. Over time, this could cause the party to edge toward the East German Communists (the SED), the East German Soviet satellite or even the Soviet Union on a nationalist basis.

As for the CDU, Adenauer's own party, its weakness resided in its opportunism. The then chancellor, Kurt Georg Kiesinger, who in 1966 had replaced Adenauer's immediate successor, Ludwig Erhard, was an able orator but not so much strong as handsome and overly concerned with appearances. Still, he was better than Erhard, who in Adenauer's view had been too 'stupid' for the office of chancellor, his postwar economic wizardry notwithstanding. When I interjected that 'too non-political' might be the more appropriate adjective, Adenauer replied: 'For a political leader, the adjective "non-political" is the definition of stupidity.'

Adenauer was emphatic about America's role in the Vietnam War. It was beyond him why the United States had extended itself so far from the arena of its main interests and why it now found it so difficult to extricate itself. In response to my comment that in defending our partners in Asia we were concerned about protecting our credibility as an ally in the main theater, he said that he wanted to think about this aspect: 'Could you come back tomorrow for my reaction?'

The next day, he seated us so that we were face to face and said in a solemn way: *'Schau mir in die Augen* [Look me in the eyes].' And then, returning to my assurances of the day before, he said:

> Do you think that I still believe you will protect us unconditionally? . . . Your actions over recent years here make it clear that, for your country, détente with the Soviet Union will also be a top priority in crisis situations. I do not believe that any American president will risk nuclear war on behalf of Berlin in every circumstance. But the alliance remains important. What is protecting us is that the Soviet leaders themselves cannot be sure of this element of doubt.

Thus, in a poignant summary, Adenauer had returned to the subject of our first conversation of ten years earlier: the inherent ambiguity of a nuclear threat. But he was also articulating another key principle he had come to in his years of service: the decisive importance of the Atlantic Alliance.

What had started as a plea for reassurance in a crisis had turned into a long-term strategic perception. Adenauer reaffirmed, in his last words to me, his commitment to the Atlantic partnership – even while expressing reservations about the complexity of implementing it. Accepting the strategy that would contain the Soviet Union for almost half a century, he realized that this very ambiguity created the deterrence on which America's allies could count for their evolution within a European political structure and in partnership with America.

THE ADENAUER TRADITION

Great leadership is more than an evocation of transitory exultation; it requires the capacity to inspire and to sustain vision over time. Adenauer's successors found that the principles of his formative vision were essential for the future of Germany. This was true even of Willy Brandt, who in 1969 became the first SPD chancellor of the Federal Republic.

Brandt had spent the Hitler years in exile, first in Norway and then in neutral Sweden. As mayor of West Berlin during the Berlin Crises of 1958–62, he had displayed strong leadership and rhetorical powers that fortified his people and helped sustain their morale.

Once in office as chancellor, Brandt conducted himself in a manner distinct from the traditionalism of Adenauer. Most importantly, he promoted *Ostpolitik*, which involved opening to the communist world while maintaining Germany's relationships with its Allies. Both President Richard Nixon and I, as his national security advisor, were at first uneasy about the potential evolution of *Ostpolitik* into a new variety of German nationalism masked as neutralism with which the Federal Republic might seek to maneuver between East and West.

While some of Brandt's foreign policy moved away from that of Adenauer, he was committed enough to the Atlantic Alliance that he consulted closely with Washington in any negotiations with Moscow. In his first week in office, Brandt sent his friend and foreign policy advisor Egon Bahr to Washington. To our surprise, Bahr affirmed the Federal Republic's commitment to NATO and to continuing the Adenauer-era efforts to unify Europe. The new chancellor, Bahr told us, would coordinate *Ostpolitik* with his allies and especially with the White House. In response, Nixon overcame our premonitions and acted on Bahr's assurances through a consultation process set up through my office.

Brandt kept Bahr's word. Developing an imaginative policy toward Eastern Europe, especially Poland, he opened negotiations with the Soviet Union on the overall relationship and also on guaranteed access to Berlin. These negotiations were completed in 1972 and facilitated by us through the policy of linkage.* Together with the Western allies, Brandt concluded an agreement on access to Berlin, which continued without challenge until unification.

At the same time as Brandt retained Adenauer's commitment to consultation within NATO, so did he develop *Ostpolitik* with neighboring peoples to the east. Brandt traveled to Warsaw in 1970 and visited the memorial for the 1943 Warsaw Ghetto Uprising, where Polish Jews had fought the Nazi attempt to deport them to death camps only to be brutally put down. Brandt did penance before the memorial, placing a wreath and then falling to his knees.

This silent gesture, which represented a moral underpinning for Germany's postwar reconciliation with the world, spoke for itself. Brandt, to be sure, considered the FRG's relationship with Poland of great strategic value, but he also described it as of substantial 'moral-historical significance'. It was the continuation of Adenauer's commitment to both repentance and dignity – indeed, dignity through repentance.[77]

Whatever further ambitions might have been entertained by the advocates of *Ostpolitik* were overtaken by Brandt's resignation from office in 1974. His successor was Helmut Schmidt (1974–82), a socialist primarily by the accident of his birth in the city-state of Hamburg, where the Social Democrats were the governing party and where he would serve as a city senator in the 1960s. In his formative years, the youthful Schmidt experienced more chaos than stability. He served in the Luftwaffe as an anti-aircraft artillery officer on the Eastern Front in 1941[78] but was too young to be politically active during the Nazi period.

Schmidt centered German foreign policy substantially on Adenauer's principles. Like his great predecessor, he was convinced of the crucial role of morality. 'Politics without a conscience tends towards criminality,' he said on one occasion, adding, 'As I see it, politics is pragmatic action for the sake of moral ends.'[79] In 1977, Schmidt recounted to me how a few weeks earlier a German commando unit undertook a daring raid to rescue German hostages who had been hijacked by terrorists to Mogadishu, Somalia, leaving him in anguish during the hours before word arrived of the raid's success. If he could feel so deeply about the survival

* See Chapter 3, pages 141–5.

of eighty-six hostages and their rescuers, he mused, how would he ever be able to implement NATO nuclear-weapons strategy?

And yet, when in the early 1980s the time came to decide on the deployment of American medium-range missiles in Germany, Schmidt carried out what he considered to be his duty, in opposition to the majority of his own party – even though this courageous act was the proximate cause of his fall from office.

Schmidt was also a driving force behind a second aspect of Adenauer's policy: the unification of Europe. Like Adenauer, he gave special priority to France. He and his French counterpart President Valéry Giscard d'Estaing renewed the Adenauer–de Gaulle cooperation, reinforced once again by personal friendship. The pair supplied the impetus behind the European Security Conference of 1975, which accelerated the process of delegitimizing the Soviet domination of Eastern Europe. They, with strong support from President Gerald Ford, advocated for meetings of democratic heads of government – then the G5, now the G7 – to express a joint approach to world order.[80]

The fulfillment of Adenauer's vision of a unified Germany within a unifying Europe came about during the chancellorship of Schmidt's successor, Helmut Kohl, when Soviet rule in Eastern Europe collapsed from its overexertions and internal contradictions. A thoughtful student of German history who spoke in the dialect of his Rhenish birthplace, Kohl was less intellectual than Schmidt and less philosophical than Adenauer. He governed through his mastery of the attitudes of his people. Like Adenauer, he was determined to avoid repeating Germany's vacillations among the various temptations presented by its central geographic location and the complexity of its history. Kohl resisted mass demonstrations, on a scale not previously seen in Germany, against the deployment of medium-range American missiles in Europe to counterbalance comparable Soviet deployment. His fortitude was rewarded by a US–Soviet negotiation which, by 1988, led to the INF arms-control agreement requiring the mutual withdrawal of this class of nuclear weapons on both sides – the first, and so far sole, agreement designed to eliminate a category of nuclear weapons.

The disintegration of the East German communist regime began as its population fled in increasing numbers to neighboring countries. In August 1989, the political balance shifted irretrievably when 9,000 East Germans who had fled to Hungary were permitted to leave that country for West Germany. By October, thousands of East Germans were sheltering in the West German embassy in Prague. The final disintegration of the East German satellite government was confirmed when it felt obliged to allow the refugees onto trains which, with the assistance of officials from the Federal Republic, traversed East German territory before reaching West German refuge.[81]

The fall of the Berlin Wall in November 1989 made German reunification an immediate domestic issue again. Important elements in West Germany, including its president, the distinguished Richard von Weizsäcker, argued that the West should declare itself satisfied – at least initially – with the introduction of democratic elections in the former Soviet occupation zone. Kohl thought otherwise. In the Adenauer tradition, he argued that, if two separate German states should continue to exist, even if both were democratic, they would never be unified without developing the legitimacy for their separate existence, in effect inviting a series of escalating crises.

Kohl solved the problem in a decisive and courageous act of leadership. When the East German regime announced free elections, Kohl conducted himself as if the GDR no longer existed and simply scheduled campaign visits to East Germany as if the election were in West Germany. The East German counterpart of the CDU achieved an overwhelming electoral victory, opening the way to the formal unification of Germany – together with continued German membership in NATO – on October 3, 1990.

Kohl still had to persuade France and Britain – both of which had understandable reservations stemming from two world wars. British Prime Minister Margaret Thatcher was especially reluctant.* The process would not be completed until, in May 1990, the Soviets agreed to withdraw their troops from East Germany[82] and that a united Germany could remain in NATO. In this, Soviet domestic difficulties played a role. But it would not have occurred without the policies that Adenauer's successors and the Allies had followed in pursuit of his vision, described by him after unconditional surrender as a way to give his people and his divided country the courage to start again.

An unforeseen consequence of the collapse of the Berlin Wall was

---

* As described in Chapter 6, pages 380–82.

that in December 1989 an obscure researcher in physics at the East
German Humboldt University, a pastor's daughter who had never
engaged in politics, decided to join a new party in East Germany called
the 'Democratic Awakening'. Angela Merkel was then thirty-five years
of age and without any political experience whatsoever, but with a
strong moral core. By late 1990, her party had merged with the CDU.
In November 2005, she was elected chancellor of Germany. She stayed
in office for sixteen years, steadying her country through manifold
crises, raising its purposes in a world of high technology and emerging
as one of the principal leaders in the post-Cold War international order,
fulfilling Adenauer's dream of the future role of his country. She retired
in December 2021, the only chancellor of the FRG to do so in the
absence of a political crisis.

In 2017, on the fiftieth anniversary of Adenauer's death, Angela
Merkel paid tribute to his historic contribution:

> Today we honor a great statesman who, with foresight and skill, gave our
> country perspective and stability after the failure of the Weimar Republic
> and the horrors of National Socialism. We bow to Konrad Adenauer with
> great gratitude. We also take his merit as an obligation for our tasks in a
> confusing, difficult world. In view of what Konrad Adenauer and his con-
> temporaries have achieved, we should have the courage to continue this
> work.[83]

For his part, Konrad Adenauer did not linger over posterity's judgment. When asked how he wanted to be remembered, he replied simply:
'He has done his duty.'[84]

2

Charles de Gaulle: The Strategy of Will

CLOSE ENCOUNTERS

Within a month of his inauguration as president on January 20, 1969, Richard Nixon undertook what was described as a working visit to the capitals of Europe to emphasize the importance he attached to Atlantic relations. Nixon was warmly received by his European counterparts in Brussels, London and Bonn, all of whom he had met previously and who were eager to affirm America's leading role in Atlantic relations.

The atmosphere in Paris was subtly different. A half-dozen years earlier, not long after Nixon's defeat in the November 1962 California gubernatorial election, Charles de Gaulle had received him for lunch at the presidential residence, the Élysée Palace. The French president's praise for the foreign-policy acumen Nixon had displayed while serving as Dwight Eisenhower's vice president (1953–61) meant a great deal to the American, then at the low point of his political career. Now, de Gaulle personally welcomed Nixon and his entourage at the airport, having raised the occasion to the level of a state visit.

This was the first time I encountered de Gaulle. He used the occasion for a succinct yet warm welcoming statement for Nixon, emphasizing France's distinct and historic identity:

> For two hundred years, during which so much has happened, nothing could shake the feeling of friendship our country has for yours. On another note, you have come to see us so that we might specify our thoughts and intentions on the subject of world affairs and so you could clarify your own views and initiatives. How could we not grant the greatest interest and highest importance to these exchanges?[1]

The welcome was based entirely on the French national interest and de Gaulle's personal regard for Nixon. It avoided mention of NATO, the Common Market and European multilateralism – all of which had been the standard rhetoric of other leaders in Europe's capitals.

A reception followed at the Élysée. In the course of it, a de Gaulle aide drew me away from the crowd and into the presence of the austere figure towering above the assemblage. De Gaulle did not radiate warmth and gave no indication of previous contact[2] or current welcome. His first words to me were a challenge: 'Why don't you leave Vietnam?' – an odd question considering that he had preceded his own decision to leave Algeria only seven years earlier with nearly three years of intensified military efforts. When I responded, 'Because a sudden withdrawal would damage American international credibility,' he replied with a curt 'For example, where?' ('Par exemple, où?') I fared no better with my next response: 'For example, in the Middle East.' This seemed to throw de Gaulle into a moment of reflection, which he broke with: 'How very odd. Until this moment, I thought it was your enemies [that is, the Soviets] who had the credibility problem in the Middle East.'

The following day, de Gaulle arranged a substantive meeting with Nixon in the elegant Grand Trianon chateau on the grounds of the Versailles palace called into being by Louis XIV. When the discussion turned to Europe, de Gaulle used the occasion to elaborate his welcoming statement for some thirty-five minutes in an exposition of extraordinary passion, elegance and eloquence.

Historically, he said, Europe had been the arena of diverse nationalities and convictions. There was no such thing as a political Europe. Each part of Europe had created its own identity, undergone its own suffering, developed its own authority and mission. The countries of Europe were in the process of recovering from the Second World War and seeking to defend themselves on the basis of a strategy that defined their character. The situation since the war had produced necessities and dangers that required close cooperation among the states of Europe – and between Europe and the United States. France was prepared to cooperate in common tasks and would prove a loyal ally. It would not, however, give up its capacity to defend itself or surrender the determination of its future to multilateral institutions.

These were principles in the name of which de Gaulle had contested the Atlantic policies of the prior two US presidents, Lyndon B. Johnson and John F. Kennedy. Nixon, who admired de Gaulle and was not willing to engage in a comparable debate in the early days of his presidency, invited me to comment as a professor of history.

Somewhat stunned by the unexpected request, I said: 'That was a profound and moving presentation. But how does President de Gaulle propose to keep Germany from dominating the Europe he has described?' He was silent for a moment and then replied: '*Par la guerre.*' ('By war.')

Another substantive conversation developed at the lunch shortly afterward. Acknowledging that he was aware of my scholarly efforts, de Gaulle asked about statesmanship in the second half of the nineteenth century: which figure had impressed me most? When I mentioned the German chancellor Otto von Bismarck (1871–90), he inquired into which of Bismarck's qualities I most admired. 'For his moderation, which unfortunately failed him in the settlement after the Franco-Prussian war of 1871,' I said. De Gaulle ended the conversation by evoking the aftermath of that settlement: 'It was better that way, for it gave us the opportunity to reconquer Alsace.'

Only six years earlier, de Gaulle had signed a Treaty of Friendship with Chancellor Konrad Adenauer of Germany, with whom he enjoyed warmer personal relations than with any other world leader. But, for de Gaulle, friendship did not do away with the lessons of history or the requirements of strategy. It is also quite possible that his combative remarks were designed to see how his interlocutor would react.

Two months after the meeting with Nixon, de Gaulle resigned. He was under no domestic or international pressure to do so. He chose the moment of his own final departure because of its suitability for a historic transition.

Who, then, was this towering figure, so eloquent in his reflections on world order, so confident that he could casually invoke war with Germany over canapés, so assured of his legacy that he could resign when he judged the moment suitable? De Gaulle knew full well that he had sustained his legendary stature by cloaking himself in mystery. Who was the colossus behind the veil?

THE BEGINNING OF THE JOURNEY

On March 21, 1940, in reaction to the defeat of French forces seeking
to repel the German assault on Norway, Paul Reynaud was appointed
to replace Édouard Daladier as prime minister. Five years earlier,
Reynaud had taken an interest in the views of then-Lieutenant
Colonel Charles de Gaulle, who would become an advisor to the senior
politician.

In mid-May 1940, the still little-known forty-nine-year-old professional soldier would be promoted from colonel to acting brigadier
general in recognition of his extraordinary leadership of an armored
regiment in the struggle to turn back the German invasion of Belgium.
Two weeks later, Reynaud, acting simultaneously as minister of defence,
selected de Gaulle as his undersecretary of defence.

De Gaulle established his office in the Defence Ministry on June 5,
the very day Luftwaffe airstrikes reached the outskirts of Paris. Within
a week, the French government retreated from the capital. On June 17,
the newly appointed undersecretary, learning of Reynaud's resignation
and the plan to seek an armistice with Adolf Hitler, abruptly flew to
London from Bordeaux. De Gaulle's plane passed over the harbors of
Rochefort and La Rochelle, where the Germans had set scores of ships
afire, as well as the Breton hamlet of Paimpont, where his mother Jeanne
lay dying. As he left, he ordered that passports be rushed to his wife
and three children so that they could follow him to London.[3] The next
day, he delivered an address on the BBC announcing the formation of
a resistance movement in opposition to the policies of the French
government:

> The destiny of the world is at stake. I, General de Gaulle, now in London,
> call on all French officers and men who are at present on British soil, or
> may be in the future, with or without their arms, and I invite all engineers
> and skilled workmen from the armaments factories who are at present on
> British soil, or may be in the future, to get in touch with me. Whatever
> happens, the flame of French resistance must not and shall not die.[4]

Here, to say the least, was an extraordinary declaration by someone
as yet entirely unknown to the overwhelming majority of the French
people. A junior minister, France's lowest-ranking general, was brazenly

soliciting opposition to the government of France that he himself had joined less than two weeks earlier and of which he was nominally still a member. The broadcast's succinct phrases, unlike the elevated rhetoric customary in other historic statements such as the American Declaration of Independence (1776), was exactly what it sounded like: an invitation to French nationals on British soil to revolt against their government, extended on behalf of an undefined enterprise.

A few days before, the British government had been focused on dissuading France's leaders from entering into a separate peace with Hitler. To prevent it, Prime Minister Winston Churchill had gone so far as to propose a merging of French and British sovereignty to forestall the most feared outcome: a complete collapse followed by the absorption of France into the German sphere.[5] De Gaulle favored the gesture – even if he was wary of some of the particulars – because he thought it would encourage the government to endure for longer without capitulating.

The initiative was devised by Charles Corbin and Jean Monnet, who was later to play a significant role in the concept of a European union.[6] The plan for the de facto union advanced rapidly on June 16. De Gaulle, then in England to negotiate with the British, read it on the telephone to Reynaud, who asked if Churchill had formally approved. De Gaulle put Churchill on the line, who repeated the offer. Reynaud replied that he would submit it to his cabinet in an hour's time. As one historian writes:

> Churchill, Attlee, Sinclair and the chiefs of staff were all set to be transported by the cruiser *Galatea* that night to Concarneau, off the coast of Brittany, to discuss with Reynaud and his colleagues the prolonging of the battle – and the future of this new nation. They . . . got as far as Waterloo [Station], where they took their seats in a special train primed to depart at 9:30 p.m. for Southampton.
>
> But . . . the train never left the station. Churchill received a hand-delivered note from a private secretary that the trip was off because of a 'ministerial crisis' in Bordeaux [to which the French government had fled].[7]

Reynaud had been ousted. Marshal Philippe Pétain, at eighty-seven years old, had been made premier.

While the final outcome of the armistice negotiations remained uncertain, the British kept de Gaulle officially at arm's length. His proclaimed rallying of what soon became known as 'Free French' officers and men was accorded no formal standing, and a proposed follow-up BBC broadcast was canceled.[8] But then the die was cast quickly: France signed a ceasefire with Germany on June 22 that placed the entire Atlantic coast and half of the country under German occupation. This was precisely what de Gaulle had been determined to prevent. His overarching aim from then on was to restore French sovereignty by means of a liberation in which the Free French would play a significant part, and then to turn the process of liberation into the rebirth of French society made necessary by the moral and military collapse of 1940.

On June 23, now with the permission of the British cabinet, de Gaulle again spoke on the BBC. Defiantly, he addressed himself to Marshal Pétain of Vichy France – so named for the resort in central France where the retreating government would establish itself, and which for the next two years became the ruling authority, in collaboration with Germany, over the rump of unoccupied France.

Pétain, who in the early 1920s had served as de Gaulle's mentor, was venerated for having repelled the German assault at Verdun during the First World War. Now, ignoring the gap in their military ranks, the most junior French general addressed the most senior (and heretofore most highly esteemed) with withering condescension. Asserting that the ceasefire had reduced France to bondage, de Gaulle issued a stinging rebuke: 'To accept such an act of debasement we did not need you, M. le Maréchal. We did not need the victor of Verdun. Anyone else would have done.'[9]

The insult at once completed de Gaulle's break with official France and accelerated his efforts to establish himself as the head of the emerging Free French movement. By then several notable French refugees, mainly from the academic world, were already residing as exiles in London, but they lacked either the stature or the necessary conviction to claim leadership of a wartime movement. For its part, British intelligence had been entertaining the idea of persuading two eminent French political figures of the Third Republic in as-yet unoccupied France – Édouard Daladier, the former prime minister, and Georges Mandel, the last interior minister – to form a dissident government in exile. But that plan was dropped when the two men, having escaped to Algeria, were prevented by French colonial officials loyal to Vichy from pursuing contact with the British and were then expelled to metropolitan France.

It was Churchill's conviction of the need for a symbolic expression of French resistance that resolved any uncertainties. 'You are alone,' he said to de Gaulle. 'Well, I will recognize you alone.' On June 28, a mere eleven days after his arrival, the government of the United Kingdom recognized Charles de Gaulle 'as leader of the Free French wherever they might be'.[10] It was a characteristically courageous decision by Churchill, who could not have known de Gaulle's views in any depth and did not foresee the rows he would stoke within the Allied camp.

Soon afterward, Britain formalized the relationship with de Gaulle, accepting the general's own unique conception of French national dignity. He insisted, for instance, that while Britain would supply the Free French with resources and funds, these should come as loans to be repaid, not as gifts. Again, although Free French forces (which did not yet exist in any formal sense) would be under overall British or Allied high command, they would operate as autonomous units under Free French officers. Such a charter represented a considerable achievement for 'a penniless Brigadier exiled in a land whose language he did not know'.[11]

THE SOURCES AND AIMS OF DE GAULLE'S CONDUCT

Before 1940, de Gaulle had been known as an outstanding soldier and progressive strategic analyst, but nothing suggested that one day he would emerge as a mythic leader. On August 15, 1914, he had been among the first French soldiers to be wounded in the First World War when he took a bullet to the knee in the fierce fighting at Dinant, a Belgian town along the Meuse. After a brief convalescence, he returned to the front. In January 1915, he was awarded the Croix de Guerre in recognition of his leadership of daring reconnaissance missions in which he and his soldiers would crawl to the edge of no man's land to listen for conversations in the German trenches. On March 2, 1916, after sustaining a bayonet wound in the thigh, de Gaulle was taken prisoner. Despite five attempts to escape, he would remain imprisoned in Germany until the armistice of November 11, 1918.

De Gaulle had learned German in school, and while in prison he consumed German newspapers with the appetite of an eager student and the curiosity of a journeyman military analyst. He wrote extensively about the German war effort, read novels, engaged in spirited discussions of military strategy with his fellow prisoners and even delivered a series of lectures on civil–military relations throughout French history. Much as he pined to return to the front, internment was his graduate school. It was also a crucible of solitude. In his prison notebook, the twenty-six-year-old de Gaulle wrote: 'Dominating oneself ought to become a sort of habit, a moral reflex acquired by a constant gymnastic of the will especially in the tiniest things: dress, conversation, the way one thinks.'[12]

A sensitive reader and author of poetry as a schoolboy, de Gaulle by early adulthood seemed to be withdrawing into the solitude that the seventeenth-century French playwright Pierre Corneille suggested was the price of statesmanship: 'To whom can I confide / The secrets of my soul and the cares of my life?'[13] The virtue of self-mastery sketched in his journal was to become a central feature of his character. Hereafter, stoicism would be his public face, tenderness reserved mainly for his family – especially his wife, Yvonne, and their disabled daughter, Anne.

Upon his return to peacetime army service, de Gaulle recognized that the distinction he could no longer fulfill on the battlefield might be achieved by intellectual efforts. In 1924, he published *The Enemy's House Divided*, a penetrating analysis of the causes underlying the collapse of the German war effort in 1918. The book, based on his reading of German newspapers, brought de Gaulle to the attention of Marshal Pétain, who made de Gaulle an aide, a kind of research assistant for a book-in-progress – later abandoned – on the history of the French army. He showed his respect for the younger man's abilities by recommending him to deliver a series of lectures at the French War College – and by personally attending the first one.

The capacity for gratitude not being among de Gaulle's most highly developed traits, neither Pétain's gesture nor the gap in rank between them prevented the younger man from confronting his mentor over what he considered inadequate credit for his literary contributions. As his relations with Pétain declined, he returned to command and to writing.

In his most influential book, *Toward a Professional Army*,[14] de Gaulle challenged the defensive policies of the French military, urging instead a strategic posture based on offensive armored warfare. At that time, France was constructing the presumably impregnable Maginot Line along its eastern frontier with Germany, which in 1940 would prove spectacularly useless against an armored German invasion via Belgium. His recommendations, ignored by the French army, would instead be adopted in Germany in the mid-1930s and vindicated by the German victory over France only a few years later.

De Gaulle grasped early in the war that America would eventually be drawn in, thereby tipping the balance of forces against the Axis powers. Woe to the side that would array America against it. 'In the free world, immense powers have not yet made their contributions,' de Gaulle proclaimed in July 1940, adding:

> One day, these powers will crush the enemy. On that day France must be on the side of victory. If she is, she will become what she was before, a great and independent nation. That, and that alone, is my goal.[15]

But, in a repeating pattern, de Gaulle was alone among his French military contemporaries in getting this analysis correct.

Under normal circumstances, with his battlefield experience, promotion to brigadier general and intellectual brilliance, de Gaulle might have aspired to a top command in the army and, after another decade or so of service, perhaps to a position in the French cabinet. That he would, instead, emerge as the symbol of France itself was scarcely conceivable.

Yet leaders who alter history rarely appear as the endpoint of a linear path. We might expect that the arrival on the scene of a low-ranking brigadier general declaring the establishment of a resistance movement amid the chaos of France's capitulation to Hitlerite Germany would have ended by meriting perhaps a footnote acknowledging his role as an auxiliary actor in a future that would be determined by the ultimate victors. Yet, arriving in London with effectively nothing but his uniform and his voice, de Gaulle catapulted himself out of obscurity and into the ranks of world statesmen. In an essay I wrote over fifty years ago, I described him as an illusionist.[16] First as a leader of the Free French during the war, later as founder and president of the Fifth Republic, he conjured up visions that transcended objective reality, in the process persuading his audiences to treat them as fact. For de Gaulle, politics was not the art of the possible but the art of the willed.

Wartime London teemed with Poles, Czechs, Danes, Dutch and nationals from a half-dozen other countries who had fled their occupied homelands. All considered themselves part of the British war effort. None made any claim to an autonomous strategy. Only de Gaulle did so from the start. Although he accepted British management of military operations because his forces were yet too small to do otherwise, his ultimate war aim was different from that of his allies.

Britain and, after 1941, the United States fought for the defeat of Germany and Japan. De Gaulle fought for these aims too, but primarily as a waystation to his ultimate goal: the renewal of the soul of France.

DE GAULLE IN THE HISTORY
OF FRANCE

It is unlikely that even Churchill, at the beginning of their relationship, grasped the magnitude of de Gaulle's vision. According to it, France, over nearly two centuries, had dissipated its *grandeur*, the mystical quality that signifies material success combined with moral and cultural preeminence. Now, at his country's nadir, de Gaulle presented himself as the emissary of destiny, whose task it was to reclaim France's national greatness. That he had not received and could not proffer any portents of this mission was not relevant; his legitimacy derived from an innate sense of personal authority buttressed by unshakeable faith in France and its history.

As de Gaulle saw it, France had accumulated the elements of its lofty stature over a long historical process beginning in medieval Europe, when feudal principalities settled their disagreements through adjustments to the balance of power. By this means, the core of France developed as a centrally governed polity as early as the sixth century under the Frankish King Clovis.

By the early seventeenth century, with the Habsburg monarchy in Austria expanding over Central Europe and as far west as Spain, France needed an enhanced central authority and a complex strategy to defend itself from encirclement. The task fell to Armand-Jean du Plessis, Cardinal Richelieu, who served as chief minister to Louis XIII from 1624 to 1642 and was the principal architect of France's later becoming the preeminent European power under Louis XIV. Rejecting the prevailing strategies based on dynastic loyalty or confessional affiliation, Richelieu instead oriented France's internal and external policies in accord with 'reasons of state' (*raisons d'état*): that is, the flexible pursuit of the national interest based entirely on a realistic judgment of circumstances.

This, for de Gaulle, marked the first truly grand strategic approach to European affairs since the fall of Rome. France would now seek to exploit the multiplicity of states in Central Europe by encouraging their rivalries and exploiting their divisions in a manner that would ensure its own status as always stronger than any possible combination of them. Ignoring France's and their personal Catholicism, Richelieu and his successor Jules Mazarin supported the Protestant states in the Thirty Years' War, which devastated Central Europe, leaving France the arbiter of its rivalries.

In this manner, France emerged as the most influential country of the Continent, with Britain playing a balancing role against it. By the early eighteenth century, the so-called European Order of the *ancien régime* consisted of two partially overlapping coalitions, at times at war with each other, at times making settlements, but never driving conflicts to the extreme of threatening the survival of the system. The primary elements of this order were the equilibrium in Central Europe manipulated by France and the overall balance of power managed by Britain throwing its navy and financial resources against the strongest European power of the day, usually against France.

De Gaulle lauded the basic strategy of Richelieu and his successors in a speech in 1939:

> France has always found natural allies when she wished it. To fight against Charles V, then against the House of Austria, and finally against the growing Prussia, Richelieu, Mazarin, Louis XIV, and Louis XV used each of those allies in turn.[17]

Under Napoleon at the beginning of the nineteenth century, instead of advancing its interests by alliances and limited warfare, France proceeded to overthrow the prevailing order by *conquering* rather than simply defeating its rivals, all the while invoking the French Revolution's new principle of popular legitimacy. But, in the end, even the might of Napoleon and his 'nation in arms' was overcome by his fatal miscalculation: invading Russia. De Gaulle considered Napoleon a once-in-a-millennium genius but also blamed him for squandering

French power and prestige: 'He left France smaller than he found her.'[18] Napoleon's brilliance and his capacity for catastrophic errors of judgment, de Gaulle believed, could not easily be separated; France's sweeping Napoleonic victories laid the groundwork for its eventual disasters. This is why de Gaulle dated France's decline as a world power to the era of Napoleon even though France remained at the center of events after Napoleon quit the stage.

As rising powers such as Germany surpassed France in economic performance, France continued to demonstrate cultural eminence. In the 1820s, French scholars decoded hieroglyphics of the Rosetta Stone, unlocking ancient languages. In 1869, French engineers connected the Red Sea to the Mediterranean through the Suez Canal. In the last quarter of the nineteenth century – when Renoir, Rodin, Monet and Cézanne took the visual arts to sublime new heights – France was the artistic leader of Europe and still a significant economic and commercial power. As Baron Georges Haussmann drove great boulevards through its medieval past and imposed modernity, Paris was the heart of Western civilization, 'the capital of the nineteenth century'.[19] Overseas, fielding armies equipped with the latest weapons, the French Third Republic established a vast colonial empire under the banner of the *mission civilisatrice*.*

These imperial and cultural triumphs obscured the decay of France's inner strength. At the conclusion of the Napoleonic Wars in 1815, France counted 30 million inhabitants, outstripping any European state except backward Russia. By the dawn of the twentieth century, the figure had increased only to 38.9 million,[20] while the United Kingdom's population grew from 16 million to 41.1 million[21] and Germany's from 21 million to 67 million.[22] In industrial production, France by 1914 lagged behind the United States, Germany, Britain and Russia – especially in the key industries of coal and steel.[23]

A renewed and now anxious quest for alliances followed to mitigate the growing imbalance with Germany. An alliance with Russia in 1894

---

* The French 75 mm field gun, debuted in 1897, was a groundbreaking artillery piece combining long range with extreme accuracy. French service weapons, such as the 1866 Chassepot rifle, were excellent bolt-action rifles which could be adapted to metallic cartridges. (Chris Bishop, 'Canon de 75 modèle 1897', in *The Illustrated Encyclopedia of Weapons of World War II* (London: Amber Books, 2014); Roger Ford, *The World's Great Rifles* (London: Brown Books, 1998).)

and the 1904 Entente Cordiale with Britain were the most significant. With the major powers solidified into two alliance groups, diplomacy became rigid and allowed an otherwise unremarkable Balkan crisis between Serbia and Austria in the summer of 1914 to precipitate a world war, in which casualties for all participants were way out of proportion to historical experience.

But they were greatest for France, which suffered two million dead – 4 percent of its population – and the devastation of its northern regions.[24] Russia, heretofore France's principal ally, was convulsed by revolution in 1917 and was then pushed hundreds of miles to the east by the various peace settlements. As a result of Austria's defeat combined with Woodrow Wilson's doctrine of national self-determination and democratic ideology, a plethora of states weak in structure and inadequate in resources now faced Germany in Eastern and Central Europe. Any future resurgence of German military capacity would have to be defeated by a French offensive into the German Rhineland.

Although victorious in 1918, France knew better than any of its allies how close to defeat it had come. And it had lost its psychological and political resilience. Drained of its youth, fearful of its defeated antagonist, feeling abandoned by its allies and assailed by premonitions of impotence, France experienced the 1920s and 1930s as an almost uninterrupted succession of frustrations.

Nothing could have better expressed France's feeling of insecurity after 1918 than its decision to begin building the Maginot Line at a moment when its army was the largest in Europe and Germany's was limited by the peace treaty to 100,000 men. What made the decision all the more poignant was that the Treaty of Versailles had specifically prohibited Germany from stationing military forces in the Rhineland – the territory that had to be crossed before an attack on France could be launched. In the aftermath of its victory, France had come to feel so unsure of itself that it did not think it could counter a flagrant breach of the peace treaty by its disarmed enemy with its own offensive.

As a lieutenant colonel in 1934, de Gaulle had subjected French military doctrine to a seminal critique in *Toward a Professional Army*. Mobility, he wrote, was the key to strategy, with air power and tanks as principal implementing forces.[25] But the army in which he served had designed a strategy of static defense, which would prove disastrously inadequate.

In a passage from that 1934 book, de Gaulle expressed his melancholy conclusion:

> Once upon a time there was an old country all hemmed in by habits and
> circumspection. At one time the richest, the mightiest people among those
> in the center of the world stage, after great misfortunes it came, as it were,
> to withdraw within itself. While other people were growing around it, it
> remained immobile.[26]

This was the attitude which de Gaulle, at all stages of his career, was
determined to reverse.

DE GAULLE AND THE SECOND
WORLD WAR

De Gaulle's position in London in the summer of 1940 apparently provided no scope at all for the restoration of *grandeur*. The European
heartland had been subjugated by Hitler. The Soviet Union, the last
remaining Continental power, had signed a nonaggression pact with
Germany the year before.[27] France, now governed by Pétain under partial German occupation, veered between neutrality and collaboration.

De Gaulle had neither been appointed to lead Free France by any
constituted French authority nor had his leadership been confirmed by
elections. His claim to command derived from its proclamation. 'The
legitimacy of a governing power,' he would later write, 'derives from its
conviction, and the conviction it inspires, that it embodies national
unity and continuity when the country is in danger.'[28] Alluding to
another moment of national peril, he chose as the banner of his movement the two-barred Cross of Lorraine – the symbol of the martyred
Joan of Arc, who with her mystical visions had rallied the French five
centuries earlier to retake their land from foreign occupiers. De Gaulle's
claim – with no obvious evidence to support it – was that he was
'invested' with the 'supreme authority' of an eternal, invincible France
that transcended whatever temporal tragedies might have taken place
within its physical borders.[29]

In the months and years that followed, de Gaulle would conduct
himself with a self-assurance and refusal to compromise that allowed
him to extract concessions from the (frequently vexed) leaders of the

Alliance – Churchill, Franklin D. Roosevelt and even Stalin – all of whom he obliged to reckon with France's self-proclaimed indispensability to a reconstituted Europe.

Beginning with his appeal of June 18, 1940, de Gaulle conducted himself as if the Free French embodied not an aspiration but a reality. He launched his enterprise with a group of advisors assembled from the distinguished French personalities self-exiled to London and a military force recruited largely from the decimated French ranks that had been evacuated from Dunkirk. By the end of 1940, when an Empire Defense Council of civilian supporters was formed, there were only 7,000 effective Free French fighters.

How to realize his vision with such meager forces? De Gaulle understood that he had few military options. He therefore decided to focus on creating a geographical base for legitimacy by rallying to his side the dispersed fighting forces of the French empire. To this end, he traveled across its scattered colonies to detach them from Vichy as a first step to the liberation of the motherland. Throughout, his main enemy was not Germany but Vichy; his main objective, not to win the war (though he would help) but to create the conditions for France's territorial, institutional and moral renewal in the peace that would follow.

It would be two months before de Gaulle's territorial efforts bore fruit. In the meantime, a draining decision loomed for the Allies: what to do about the French fleet anchored at Mers-el-Kébir naval base outside the Algerian city of Oran? Were it to fall into German hands, it would risk tipping the naval balance against Britain – or even aiding a potential Nazi invasion of the British Isles. Churchill decided this was a risk he would not run. On July 3, after demanding that the fleet sail to British ports, he ordered the bombardment of the Algerian naval base. The attack killed nearly 1,300 French sailors and sank three vessels, including the battleship *Bretagne*. De Gaulle, although anguished, reacted calmly and defended the episode on the BBC: 'No Frenchman worthy of the name can for a moment doubt that a British defeat would seal forever his country's bondage.'[30] After the war, he said that had he been in Churchill's place, he would have done the same thing.[31]

Good news for the Free French finally arrived on August 26, when Governor-General Félix Éboué of Chad, France's first high-level colonial administrator of African descent, pledged the colony's support for de Gaulle. In a radio broadcast the following day, de Gaulle lauded the development: 'France is France. There is in her a secret spring which has always surprised the world, and which has not finished surprising it. France, crushed, humiliated, abandoned, is beginning to climb back from the abyss.'[32]

The climb would not be easy, as French West Africa remained firmly in Vichy's grip. In September, a Franco-British flotilla steamed toward Dakar harbor with the aim of rallying Senegal and neighboring colonies to the Free French side. It ended in fiasco. For a few days, de Gaulle was devastated.[33] A rapturous welcome in Douala, Cameroon, on October 7 lifted his spirits, and soon Brazzaville in French Congo was made the new capital of Free France. A small Free French military operation succeeded in taking Gabon on November 10, putting all of French Equatorial Africa in de Gaulle's column.

Whatever the financial and military limitations of his movement, de Gaulle had struck a chord. Armistice Day, November 11, featured popular demonstrations in Paris in favor of the Free French, including students who subversively carried pairs of fishing rods ('*deux gaules*').

Strategically located along historic trans-Saharan trade routes, Chad would prove a vital staging ground for Free French military operations, especially into Italy's Libyan colony. In early 1941, Free French Colonel Philippe Leclerc de Hauteclocque led a column of 400 men across 1,000 miles of forbidding terrain to carry out a daring raid on Kufra, a southern Libyan oasis town where a full Italian garrison was stationed. On March 1, after a ten-day siege, the Italians surrendered. In what soon became known as the 'Oath of Kufra', Leclerc had his men swear that they would not rest until the day when 'our colors, our beautiful colors, will wave from the cathedral of Strasbourg'.[34]

The battle of Kufra was the first major Free French military victory in the war, a major lift of morale and a vindication of de Gaulle's precept: 'In our position, whoever stands still falls behind.'[35] Two years later, after the Allied landing in North Africa, Leclerc would lead a Free French column, consisting of 4,000 Africans and 600 French, from Chad across Libya to Tunisia, on de Gaulle's orders, where they joined the British in a pitched battle against German Field Marshal Rommel's Afrika Korps.

But, before Leclerc could march through Libya a second time, the Free French had to prove their mettle in other theaters. Their operations were designed to liberate with Allied help Vichy-controlled territories in order to demonstrate to the world that the Free French were spirited, capable and determined to restore France's position as a leading power in the world. In these procedures, de Gaulle would insist that Free France would cooperate as a partner, not a supplicant.

The June 1941 invasion of Syria and Lebanon, territories that had been established as French mandates under the League of Nations following the First World War, repeated the African pattern. While Britain was seeking to forestall Germany from establishing airbases in the Levant, de Gaulle joined the effort with his limited forces in order to vindicate France's historic position in the region – which involved, in no small part, a fierce rivalry with Britain.

Since the Vichy authorities in Syria refused to deal with the Free French, the British commander negotiated with Henri Dentz, the Vichy high commissioner. An agreement in July 1941, dubbed the Armistice of Saint Jean d'Acre, effectively granted Britain suzerainty of the entire Levant. That French territory could be the subject of a British negotiation with Vichy was, however, anathema to de Gaulle. The treaty's provisions for repatriating French troops to Vichy compounded his displeasure. He had hoped to augment his small army with deserters from the Vichy forces in Syria, and above all he was concerned lest a precedent be set for the eventual disposition of France itself. More specifically, he feared that after ultimate victory France's governance would be placed under Allied control and that a new French government would be legitimized by the Allies rather than by France's own actions.

On July 21, Oliver Lyttelton, Britain's minister resident for the Middle East, received de Gaulle in his Cairo office. De Gaulle icily threatened to withdraw his men from the joint force – and the Free French from subordination to British command.[36] 'In the permeable, intrigue-ridden, venal medium which the Levant laid open to England's plans,' de Gaulle would write of this episode in his memoirs, 'the game . . . was easy and tempting. Only the prospect of a rupture with us and the necessity of conciliating the feelings of France could impose on London a certain moderation.'[37] Lyttleton summarily produced an interpretation of the armistice that would placate de Gaulle: 'Great Britain has no interest in Syria or the Lebanon except to win the war. We have no desire to encroach in any way upon the position of France.'[38] In his memoirs, de Gaulle would also acknowledge the sobering truth – that 'the moral and material damage which separation from Great Britain would entail for us was bound, obviously, to make us hesitate'.[39]

When de Gaulle met Churchill on September 12, the conversation was at first punctuated by anger and bouts of silence. One of the prime minister's aides wondered if they 'had strangled each other', and although the two leaders emerged smoking cigars they nonetheless could not even agree on joint minutes.[40]

Having challenged Churchill, the leader who had made his eminence possible, de Gaulle did not hesitate to take on an even more formidable figure, President Roosevelt, over essentially the same issues: the fate of French territories reconquered by Allied arms. Here he encountered a less tolerant perspective. Roosevelt was focused single-mindedly on winning the war, and disputes over status within the coalition irritated him, especially when put forward by a figure whose claim was in no way buttressed by comparable power. He had only disdain for what he saw as de Gaulle's Joan of Arc complex.[41]

De Gaulle's controversies with America began over St Pierre and Miquelon, two tiny islands off the coast of Newfoundland: vestigial remnants of France's North American empire that had been spared by the Treaty of Paris of 1763. Following the attack on Pearl Harbor, Roosevelt had contacted the Vichy official responsible for France's Western Hemisphere possessions, requesting the islands' formal neutralization – which would preclude their radio station from broadcasting to passing German submarines. Though Vichy granted that request, de Gaulle found it unacceptable that any foreign country, even if benevolent, should interfere in French internal matters without his agreement. He therefore ordered the commander of his tiny navy, Admiral Émile Muselier, to occupy the islands in the name of the Free French.

What made this initiative all the more brash was that the landing took place on December 23, just as Churchill was arriving in Washington to confer with Roosevelt for their first wartime meeting as allies. Writing to Muselier on Christmas Eve, de Gaulle instructed him not to be deflected by US protestations:

> We threw a paving stone into a frog pond. Stay quietly in Saint-Pierre, organize the government and the radio station. Any representative of any foreign government who addresses you regarding the islands should be requested by you to address the [Free French] National Committee.[42]

Muselier's forces seized the islands without resistance and, on December 26, organized a plebiscite to confirm their allegiance to the Free French.

Any possibility of a surprise attack in the Western Hemisphere, even a minuscule one such as this, was bound to upset Washington, especially two weeks after Pearl Harbor. Secretary of State Cordell Hull was so outraged that in a protest communiqué he referred to the 'so-called Free French', a phrase widely criticized in the media and Congress.[43] De Gaulle retaliated by, from then on, calling Hull the 'so-called Secretary of State'. By February 1942, Sumner Welles, Hull's deputy, had restored cooperation between the Free French and Washington.[44]

In this way, de Gaulle's apparently absurd stroke became a symbol of France's political recovery. Indeed, his impulse, consistent and in many ways heroic, to defend France's historical identity in the face of great disparities of power became the prerequisite to restoring French greatness. He was well aware of how exasperating this was for his allies: 'They think perhaps that I am not someone easy to work with,' he mused. 'But if I were, I would today be in Pétain's General Staff.'[45]

De Gaulle's challenging behavior was rooted in the concept of *grandeur* he sought to reenact. Derived, as we have seen, from French conduct in quest of preeminence on the Continent – a preeminence always on the verge of being achieved, ever thwarted by Britain's balance-of-power policies – it infused de Gaulle's interpretation of his responsibility as leader of the Free French. Inevitably it included an effort to forestall any temptations on the part of the British to settle historic disputes pre-emptively during the course of the war.

Occasionally exasperated, Churchill once quipped: 'Yes, de Gaulle does think he is Joan of Arc, but my bloody bishops won't let me burn him.' Yet in the end, de Gaulle and Churchill managed an ambivalent kind of cooperation throughout the war. Churchill made de Gaulle's efforts financially possible and protected him from Roosevelt's hostility – as in May 1943, when the president half-seriously suggested exiling de Gaulle to Madagascar.*

In the fall of 1943, de Gaulle seemed to realize that he was approaching the limits of British tolerance. He asked the Soviet ambassador Ivan Maisky whether he might be received on Russian territory if

---

* This French possession had been invaded by the British in May 1942 without giving prior notice to de Gaulle.

disagreements with Churchill grew too intense. Without rejecting the approach altogether, the Soviet ambassador urged de Gaulle to consider it carefully before submitting a formal proposal. It is unlikely that de Gaulle was suggesting that the Free French should be moved onto Russian soil; much more likely, he was exploring options for the future and demonstrating to Stalin that Russia was an essential part of his long-term calculations.

De Gaulle understood that, before long, his vision would need to be realized in France itself. He carefully prepared himself for that battle. After the founding of the Free French National Committee (*Comité national français* or CNF) in September 1941, he created legal structures that could be moved to the mother country when the time arrived. In the absence of a legislature and courts, and following a longstanding French tradition, the CNF used a gazette (*Journal officiel*) to promulgate 'laws' and decrees.* De Gaulle also remained in close contact with the substantial émigré community in London, presenting himself as the embodiment of the true France. His legitimacy was never challenged, and he attracted a distinguished group of admirers. Finally, he cultivated a following inside metropolitan France while courting diverse factions of the Resistance, including the communists.

All of these elements were held together by his personality: commanding, aloof, passionate, visionary, ineffably patriotic. Thus on June 18, 1942, at a rally at the Royal Albert Hall in London to mark the second anniversary of the founding of the Free French, de Gaulle declared:

> Once our task is finished, our role complete, following on from all those who have served France since the dawn of her history, preceding all those who will serve her for the eternity of her future, we will say to France, simply, like [the poet Charles] Péguy: 'Mother, look upon your sons who have fought for you.'[46]

The Free French would need all of this unquestioning, near-mystical devotion to overcome their next challenge.

---

* The *Journal officiel* has been in place since the late Second Empire (1869) and throughout the Third Republic; Vichy also had its own version. A digital version is in place today.

NORTH AFRICAN CONTEST

On November 8, 1942, in 'Operation Torch', American and British forces landed in French Morocco and the vast territory of Algeria. The latter's three coastal regions were administered not as colonies but as departments of France – part of its domestic territory.* Algeria held strategic importance for the Allies, not least because the territory was the base of a substantial army that might be recruited to augment Allied forces in the eventual invasion of Europe. But for the Free French it above all brought to the fore the question of the governance of France itself. Whichever of the contending forces inside Algeria prevailed could have a decisive claim to be the legitimate government of the French homeland when the war was over.

The 'Anglo-Saxon' powers, as de Gaulle was wont to call them, were little interested in handing such a powerful capacity to the troublesome leader of the Free French. They never informed him of their planning; he learned of the invasion only after the event. More significantly, the Allies brought with them to Algeria a possible rival to de Gaulle's leadership.

A veteran of the First World War, General Henri Giraud had commanded French troops in the Netherlands during the 1940 campaign. Taken prisoner, he was imprisoned at the hilltop Königstein Fortress near Dresden, from which the then-sixty-three-year-old escaped in April 1942 by rappelling down a 150-foot cliff. This daring escape reinforced Giraud's already heroic reputation,[47] established in a previous escape from a German prison camp in the First World War. Returning to Vichy France, he labored in vain to persuade Pétain that Germany would lose the war and that France should defect to the Allied camp. Though Pétain rejected Giraud's arguments, he refused to extradite him to Germany. On November 5, 1942, Giraud was spirited out of France to Gibraltar in a British submarine under nominal American command. On November 9, following the Operation Torch landings, he flew to Algiers, where both Roosevelt and Churchill sought to anoint him as the dominant figure.

---

* The three coastal regions of Oran, Alger and Constantine were governed as departments of France from 1848 to 1957. A fourth, Bône, was added from 1955 to 1957. Beyond the coast, the desert regions of Algeria were never considered part of 'metropolitan France'.

In this critical contest for political legitimacy, a third contender was also in Algiers, having arrived in his case shortly before the Allied landings. This was Admiral François Darlan, commander of the Vichy navy, who had come ostensibly to visit his ailing son.

Was this the first step in a disengagement by Pétain from the Germans? Or a means to organize the defense of Algeria against a possible Anglo-American invasion? In such an ambiguous situation, the roles of collaborator and patriot could merge. On November 10, Eisenhower, as supreme commander of the Allied forces, decided to exploit Darlan's presence to negotiate an armistice with Vichy forces and appointed him high commissioner of France in Africa in exchange for his cooperation with the Allies' campaign in North Africa.

Darlan's claim to authority lasted only forty-one days. He was assassinated on Christmas Eve by a killer whose motive has never been discovered. All the contending parties had an interest in Darlan's removal, none in disclosing a role in it.

This left Giraud as de Gaulle's principal rival. In effect, he represented Vichy France's aspiration for redemption.

Before the dispute between the two generals could go very far, Roosevelt, Churchill and their staffs met in Casablanca in January 1943 to plan the Anglo-American war strategy and to settle the dispute between, as Roosevelt saw it, two French prima donnas. Roosevelt presented his view of the matter to de Gaulle in their first encounter on January 22. He advocated de Gaulle's nightmare of an Anglo-Saxon trusteeship over reconquered France:

> The President again alluded to the lack of power on the part of the French people at this time to assert their sovereignty. The President pointed out that it was, therefore, necessary to resort to the legal analogy of 'trusteeship' and that it was his view that the Allied Nations fighting in French territory at the moment were fighting for the liberation of France and that they should hold the political situation in 'trusteeship' for the French people.[48]

Roosevelt's challenge forced the implicit to become explicit. De Gaulle used Archbishop Francis Spellman of New York to stress his determination to accept only a French solution. Spellman was visiting American troops in Morocco and had been enlisted by Roosevelt to convince the general to accept a subordinate role in a Giraud-dominated structure. Far from submitting, de Gaulle replied with a threat: it would be imprudent for Anglo-Americans to subvert the French national will lest the French body politic turn toward a third party for salvation – by clear implication, the Soviet Union.[49] It was a variation on the maneuver he had carried out a little earlier in his visit to the Soviet ambassador in London.[50]

Roosevelt, supported by Churchill, retreated to proposing a duumvirate of the two generals. De Gaulle refused, again on the grounds that it was he who represented the genuine France, a position in which he had persisted for all three days he attended the Casablanca conference.

Had Giraud possessed the slightest political talent, he might have achieved a propitious outcome for himself. His limitations in this area were well described by Harold Macmillan, then British resident minister in Algiers and later prime minister:

> I would suppose never in the whole history of politics has any man frittered away so large a capital in so short a space of time . . . He sat down to play cards with every ace, every king, and almost every queen in the pack . . . but succeeded by some extraordinary sleight of hand in cheating himself out of his own stake.[51]

Giraud's undoing was accelerated by the political skill of his rival. When the issue became how best to keep the 'Anglo-Saxon' leaders from imposing a solution on an internal French issue, de Gaulle suddenly displayed unexpected flexibility. In April 1943, although still treating Giraud with disdain – 'All France is with me . . . Giraud should look out! . . . Even if he eventually goes to France victorious but without me, they will fire upon him'[52] – he invited Giraud to a meeting (which finally materialized on May 31). There he accepted the *principle* of joint leadership that he had rejected a few months earlier and proposed a committee consisting of two chairmen: himself as head of the political department, and Giraud as head of the military. Over it would be a French Committee of National Liberation (CFLN) composed of three individuals appointed by de Gaulle, three by the Algerian authorities and three by Giraud.

It was a daring gambit by de Gaulle, based on the conviction that his superior governance skills would convince the members of the CFLN appointed by Algerian authorities to back him in the long run.[53] And indeed, within the CFLN's overall framework – de Gaulle's structural proposal having been accepted – he outmaneuvered the older, far less subtle general. Ultimately, Giraud's military command became subordinate to the nominal 'civilian' control of the Committee, presenting the Allies with the fait accompli of a unified French authority. In the process, a new defense committee was created, with de Gaulle at the helm, to oversee military operations, effectively pushing Giraud into staff status.[54]

De Gaulle himself would later describe Giraud's political collapse thus:

> It was therefore inevitable that Giraud should find himself gradually isolated and rejected, until the day when, walled within limitations he did not accept and, moreover, deprived of the external supports which were the source of his dizzying ambitions, he determined to resign.[55]

Subtly and ruthlessly, with infinite self-belief and patience, de Gaulle deprived Giraud of any pathway to authority and transformed the CFLN itself into the foundation of the eventual republican government of France.

Under de Gaulle's leadership, the CFLN in Algiers proceeded to outline the institutions that would govern France's internal and foreign affairs after liberation – forestalling an Anglo-Saxon trusteeship. A June 1944 CFLN ordinance established special courts to conduct jury trials – unusual in the French civil-law tradition – of Nazi collaborators after liberation. Only citizens with 'proof of national sentiments', or an unvarnished war record approved by the local liberation committee, would be eligible to serve as jurors.[56] From the beginning, de Gaulle's proto-state took the form of a strong executive aided by advisory councils with limited power, all of which reported to de Gaulle, thus making him the obvious leader of a future government.

In his dealings with Roosevelt and Churchill, de Gaulle acted as if he were already a head of government and never lost sight of the mission whose major task would come after victory. By the time the British and American Allies landed in metropolitan France in June 1944, the penurious, unrecognized junior general of June 1940 had become the unchallenged leader of the Allies' French contingent and of the potential government.

ACHIEVING POLITICAL POWER

The test would come when the Western Allies carried out the liberation of France, which they had promised Stalin at the Teheran summit in late 1943. In the prelude to the June 1944 landings on the French coast of Normandy, de Gaulle concentrated on avoiding civil war between his forces and the political forces inside France representing the Resistance. This was all the more important because his American and British partners, though they reluctantly accepted his control of the existing French army, were not yet prepared to treat him as their equal in the future governance of France. Both Roosevelt and, to a lesser extent, Churchill strove to reserve the ultimate decision on this matter until the conclusion of the war. Roosevelt shared his prediction of France's political evolution with Secretary of War Henry L. Stimson: 'De Gaulle will crumble . . . Other parties will spring up as the liberation goes on and de Gaulle will become a very little figure.'[57]

Despite de Gaulle's triumphs in rallying the French overseas empire to his side, and in overcoming Giraud's challenge to his leadership, Free French control over metropolitan France was anything but fore-ordained. The Vichy authorities had enjoyed considerable popular support at the beginning of the German occupation. Internal Resistance groups had not begun to organize themselves into larger units until the Allies landed in North Africa. Among the Resistance forces, the communists were the best organized; the socialist presence was also significant. In the end, the various internal groups never coalesced under a single command.

De Gaulle's nightmare was that Allied forces entering France might form a transitional government and fulfill Roosevelt's prediction. It was therefore essential that he appear in France at the earliest opportunity before such a government could be established and in Paris as a national figure transcending the divisions of the Third Republic.

On June 6, 1944, American and British forces landed in Normandy, soon establishing beachheads 100 kilometers long and 25 kilometers deep. Six weeks would pass before sufficient Allied forces could assemble before breaking through determined German resistance.

De Gaulle would not wait that long to begin establishing his authority. From the day of the landing, he insisted on visiting recaptured territory. Churchill reluctantly agreed to a visit to the British sector, instructing the British commander General Montgomery that he welcome de Gaulle not at the airfield on French soil but at British headquarters.

This slight turned out to be useful to de Gaulle's purpose, which was to establish his personal political presence. On June 14, after a brief visit to British headquarters, he set out for Bayeux, the largest town (pop. 15,000) in British-captured territory. There, de Gaulle refused a glass of champagne from the Vichy sub-prefect still in place, greeted the local Vichy dignitaries aloofly and proceeded to the center square for his main purpose, which was to deliver his first speech on the soil of metropolitan France. In the shadow of Bayeux's magnificent medieval cathedral, he addressed the assemblage as if they had been members of the French Resistance through the entire war ('You have never stopped [fighting] since the beginning of the war') and as if he had the legitimacy to give them orders:

> We will continue to wage war with our forces of land, sea, and air as we do today in Italy, where our soldiers have covered themselves with glory, as they will do tomorrow in metropolitan France. Our Empire, fully gathered around us, provides tremendous help . . . I promise you that we will continue the war until the sovereignty of every inch of French territory is restored. No one will stop us from doing it.
>
> We will fight alongside the Allies as an Ally. And the victory we will win will be the victory of freedom and the victory of France.[58]

There was no mention of the British troops who had actually liberated Bayeux or of the American forces that had suffered many of the casualties in the landing. De Gaulle was seeking to transform, in the minds of his listeners, what was essentially an Anglo-American expedition into a singular French victory. In visiting Bayeux, he sought not so much to claim the nation's territory as to summon its spirit. Not for the last time, he strove to persuade his listeners to accept as gospel an account bearing little relation to reality.

De Gaulle concluded his visit with a supremely political gesture. Taking his leave of Montgomery, he remarked almost casually that some of his party were staying behind. Montgomery reported the episode, adding: 'I have no idea what is their function.' But de Gaulle did: they were to establish his authority by means of a new civil government.[59]

In the following two months, de Gaulle sought to reinforce his position among the Allies and visited Rome to meet French troops from Algeria that had joined the Allied Italian campaign. Afterward he paid his first visit to Washington to improve relations with his American ally. Barely four weeks were left to prepare for the culmination of three years of turmoil and hope and ambition – to be accepted as the incarnation of French political legitimacy on French soil.

Paris was the only place where this could be achieved, and only in retrospect does his triumph there appear inevitable. He had no military force of his own. The Free French forces that, courtesy of General Omar Bradley, had taken the lead in the final approach to Paris were under Allied command. The Resistance was by then strong enough to fight the German occupying forces on its own. Nevertheless, de Gaulle came not to celebrate their victory over the Germans but to proclaim his mission.

After his arrival by car in Paris on August 26, 1944, he stopped at Gare Montparnasse, where the Resistance had accepted the surrender of the German occupation forces in the city, to thank General Leclerc of the Free French division. From there, he moved to the office at the Defense Ministry where he had served as undersecretary for exactly five days before exiling himself to London. He found that not a piece of furniture, not even a curtain, had been moved since his departure. De Gaulle treated the intervening four years as an ellipsis in French history. He would write in his memoirs: 'Nothing was missing except the State. It was my duty to restore it.'[60]

To symbolize the continuity of French history, de Gaulle's next stop was the Hôtel de Ville (seat of the Paris city government), because both the Second and Third Republics had been proclaimed there.[61] Many expected him to proclaim a Fourth Republic, ending the Third, which had lost the war. But that would have been the opposite of his design. When Georges Bidault, the titular head of the Resistance, inquired whether de Gaulle would proclaim a Republic during his Paris visit, he replied curtly: 'The Republic has never ceased to exist ... Why should I proclaim it?'[62] His intention was to create a new political reality for the French people before proclaiming its nature.

De Gaulle was greeted at the Hôtel de Ville with emotional speeches by Bidault and Georges Marrane, vice president of the Parisian Liberation Committee and a high-ranking member of the Communist Party. He responded with a moving statement about the meaning of the day:

> How can one hide the emotion that grips all of us, who are here, *chez nous*, in Paris which has risen up to defend itself and which has done so by itself. No! We will not hide this sacred and profound emotion. There are moments which go beyond each of our poor lives. Paris! Paris outraged! Paris broken! Paris martyred! – but Paris liberated! Liberated by itself, liberated by its people with the help of the armies of France, with the help and assistance of the whole of France, of that France which fights, of the only France, of the true France, of eternal France.[63]

The extraordinary metaphysical elevation of de Gaulle's oratory expressed his faith in the singularity of his country. The Allied armies at the gates of Paris, which had graciously stepped aside to permit the Free French to enter before them, were not mentioned. Nor were Britain and the United States, though they had been fighting the war with enormous losses and sacrifices. The liberation of Paris was treated as a purely French achievement. By proclaiming it to be so, he was persuading his listeners that it was so: the creation of political reality by sheer force of will.

This seeming lack of gratitude to the liberators and obsessional emphasis on the alleged French role reflected another purpose. De Gaulle was only too aware that much of the French population had adjusted to the occupation. Emphasizing that period would have disclosed too many ambivalences, while stressing the role of the American and British forces would have impeded his ultimate purpose of restoring France's faith in itself.

A parade down the Champs-Élysées, unprecedented in scale and perhaps never equaled in French history for its fervor, sealed de Gaulle's legitimacy. It provided the first opportunity for Parisians to see the physical embodiment of what had previously been but a voice on the BBC. The crowds, enthusiastic and emotional, observed an unusually tall officer walking on the long route from the Arc de Triomphe to the Place de la Concorde. With his delegate for Paris on his right and Bidault on his left, de Gaulle strode a half-step ahead, obviously moved though rarely smiling, occasionally shaking a few hands. At the Place de la Concorde, the crowd was so thick that he had to be driven the rest of the way to Notre Dame. At both places, sniper fire rang out. As during later assassination attempts – and as previously in war – de Gaulle made no move to protect himself and forbore commenting. The unflinching physical courage he displayed in those days helped to cement his leadership of France.

The Resistance was quickly folded into the new provisional government. In private conversation the week following the liberation of Paris, de Gaulle abruptly cut off one former resister who prefaced a comment with, 'The Resistance . . .' by responding, 'We have moved beyond the Resistance. The Resistance is finished. The Resistance must now be integrated into the Nation.'[64]

Two years earlier, in a speech at London's Royal Albert Hall in 1942, when he was still establishing himself, de Gaulle had cited the eighteenth-century aphorist Nicolas Chamfort: 'The reasonable have survived. The passionate have lived' (that is, fulfilled themselves). He then declared that the Free French would prevail because they carried within them the two French qualities of reason and passion. In his own case, reason was responsible for the callousness with which he ignored some of those who had fought on his side. Passion prevailed in the parade down the Champs-Élysées and the mass at Notre Dame.

By September 9, de Gaulle had formed a new cabinet under his authority as president of the provisional government. Longtime Free French associates, experienced Third Republic politicians unblemished by Vichy service, communists, Christian democrats, former Resistance leaders and technocrats were all persuaded to join this government of national unity. The stern manner in which de Gaulle opened the first cabinet meeting – 'The government of the Republic, modified in its composition, continues' – reflected his conviction that, without the state, there would be only chaos.[65] Convinced that France's divisions had caused its decline, de Gaulle was determined that his country begin the postwar period with a unity worthy of its historic *grandeur*.

A VISIT TO MOSCOW

The events of August 26 had, in effect, marked the coronation of a republican monarch. Rejecting any form of Allied occupation authority in France, de Gaulle's provisional government established order with remarkable swiftness. He balanced popular and judicial reprisals against Vichy leaders and Nazi sympathizers with a liberal use of the power of pardon. Though earlier having striven to build up the political components of the Resistance, now he insisted on a strong presidential system that would transcend the divisive partisanship of the late Third Republic.

With his authority in France established, de Gaulle left for Moscow on November 24, only three months after the liberation of Paris. 'Let us hope there is no revolution,' he deadpanned only half-jocularly upon departure.[66] German forces still occupied parts of Alsace and Lorraine. War still raged on French soil; the tasks of reconstruction were daunting. A new German invasion – the Ardennes Offensive – was imminent though unperceived by Allied generals.

De Gaulle saw France's reentry into international diplomacy as a vital step toward the consolidation of his domestic authority, as well as for the moral regeneration of the nation. France's defeat in 1940 had left it sidelined in international diplomacy. It had been excluded from the Teheran conference in 1943, when Churchill, Roosevelt and Stalin had settled on the strategy of the war. It would be similarly absent from the Yalta and Potsdam conferences in 1945, which established the structure of postwar Europe. De Gaulle could not restore France's influence if he behaved as a supplicant seeking admission to international conferences; he had to demonstrate to Britain and the US that France was an autonomous actor with independent choices for whose goodwill it was important to contend. If France were to rejoin the first tier of international diplomacy, it would have to create its own opportunities – beginning with his daring mission to Moscow to parley with Stalin.

Before this visit, Churchill and American diplomats such as Averell Harriman and Wendell Willkie had flown the northern route to Murmansk when seeking conferences with Stalin. But de Gaulle had no planes suitable for that route and no fighters with the range to act as escort. He chose instead to travel a circuitous route by French plane via Cairo and Teheran to Baku on the Caspian Sea, followed by a five-day journey in a special train, provided by Stalin, across a landscape devastated by the battle of Stalingrad and the fighting around Moscow. The discomfort of the journey was a price worth paying. It enabled de Gaulle to discuss with the Soviet autocrat the postwar peace settlement before the next Anglo-American meeting with him, and to do so as the representative of a power in its own right. He thus became the first Allied leader to discuss the postwar settlement with Stalin.

When he reached the Kremlin, the main subject of conversation was the postwar structure of Europe. Stalin left no doubt that his objective was the domination of Eastern Europe. He proposed that France recognize the Lublin government, which he had established in Soviet-occupied Poland as an eventual successor to the internationally recognized Polish government in support of whose territorial integrity Britain had declared war on Germany in 1939. De Gaulle evaded the request by saying he needed to learn more about the Lublin government, implying that its endorsement by the Soviet Union alone was insufficient for recognition by France but also that, for an appropriate return, it was a goal not impossible for Stalin to achieve.

In his turn, de Gaulle put forward his own proposal for Central Europe, which amounted to a reversal of 200 years of European history. As he saw it, the German territories west of the Rhine should be ceded to France – including the Saar region (a major coal-producing area) and parts of the Ruhr industrial region. In the reconstituted Germany, Bavaria would become the largest state and Prussia would be dissolved, its major portion assigned to the restructured province of Hanover.

De Gaulle made no mention of consulting his allies, and Stalin undoubtedly understood that the Americans and the British would never agree to such an upheaval in the map of Europe. So he replied that he needed to discuss the proposal with the British – for whose sensibilities he had not previously demonstrated any special concern. But by omitting any reference to the United States, Stalin also implied that a separate European deal excluding the US might be available.

In the end, the two leaders settled for a mutual-assistance pact aimed at deterring postwar German aggression but, in a startling additional clause, pledged joint action if either side, after taking 'all necessary measures to eliminate any new threat from Germany', were to be invaded. Such a mutual assistance treaty, reminiscent of the Franco-Russian alliance preceding the First World War, was deprived of immediate practical effectiveness by the geographical distance separating the two powers and by the fact that the French government had only been established three months earlier.

In the process, de Gaulle had an early exposure to the Soviet negotiating style that would become stereotypical years later in the Cold War. Soviet Foreign Minister Vyacheslav Molotov, who was supervising the preparation of the final documents for Stalin, rejected the first French draft, promising to produce an alternative quickly. Two days later, at what had been planned as the final dinner of the visit, the draft had still not made an appearance. De Gaulle did not buckle. After sitting through the meal and a series of seemingly endless toasts, he arose from his seat shortly after midnight (early, for a Stalin banquet) and requested an early-morning departure for his train.

To return home empty-handed from such a daunting journey would have been humiliating, but the challenge worked. At 2 a.m. a Soviet counter-draft appeared and, with modification, proved acceptable to de Gaulle. It was signed at 4 a.m. in the presence of Stalin, who joked that the French had outwitted him. Given Stalin's reputation for slyness and brutality, self-deprecating remarks of this nature had succeeded in gratifying many an earlier interlocutor, including Hitler's foreign minister, Joachim von Ribbentrop.*

De Gaulle's return from Moscow on December 17, 1944 was celebrated in Paris as France's reentry into Europe after an absence of four years and as a personal diplomatic triumph.[67] The agreement also strengthened de Gaulle's position domestically vis-à-vis the French communists. Within days, however, warfare returned to the fore with the start of the German offensive into the Ardennes forest and Alsace.

DE GAULLE AND THE PROVISIONAL GOVERNMENT

Throughout his leadership of the Free French, de Gaulle's statements and actions had evoked a common theme: to reconstruct a legitimate and powerful French state, which alone could restore order after the liberation and deal with the Allies as an equal in the endgame against

---

* American negotiators would subsequently be exposed to similar tactics, given an especially sinister twist by Stalin's reputation for vindictiveness. During the Cold War, testing the psychological endurance of one's adversary by procrastination became almost standard in Soviet East–West diplomacy. And so was the rush to agreement in the final phase (a good example being the Nixon–Brezhnev summit in Moscow in May 1972) – almost as if design and self-discipline, assiduously cultivated over months of negotiation, were suddenly overwhelmed by the fear that the patiently pursued fruits might be snatched away through a fatal misjudgment of the adversary's staying power.

Germany. 'The state, which is answerable for France,' de Gaulle wrote in his presidential memoir, 'is in charge at one and the same time of yesterday's heritage, today's interests, and tomorrow's hopes.'[68] In conceiving of the state as a generational compact, de Gaulle was echoing Edmund Burke, who defined society as 'a partnership . . . between those who are living, those who are dead, and those who are to be born.'[69]

This idea of state served to salvage France's self-respect by portraying Vichy as an erroneous interregnum between a glorious past and a bright future – and Free France as the true continuity of the state. Had de Gaulle not been as determined a fighter for French identity during the war years – or had he not asserted his leadership of an internationally based French alternative to Vichy – the myth of continuity would have been implausible. As we have seen, only a comparatively small share of the French public actively supported the Free French; yet the spell cast by de Gaulle was sufficiently powerful that it effectively banished this fact from French memory. Forgetfulness, paradoxically, is sometimes the glue for societies that would not otherwise cohere.

Downplaying Vichy's importance also gave de Gaulle in October 1944 the flexibility to dissolve the Patriotic Militia, a group of former Resistance fighters engaged in vigilantism against alleged Nazi collaborators. In its place he imposed the more uniform system of justice he had previously prepared in Algiers. The state either possessed a monopoly of legitimate violence within its territory or it did not; summary executions had no place in de Gaulle's France.

Military developments moved apace. By the end of 1944, the French ranks had swollen to 560,000 troops. On November 23, the French First Army commanded by General Jean de Lattre retook the medieval city of Strasbourg, thereby fulfilling Leclerc's oath at Kufra. But an offensive launched by Germany in December 1944 into Alsace – twinned with the earlier Ardennes offensive – threatened now to surround the city. This development raised the perennial question of whether war strategy should be shaped by military or by political considerations. As long as the military battlefield was on French soil, de Gaulle gave priority to the political.

The American field commander, General Bradley, wanted to establish a defensive line along the Vosges Mountains from which to rally for a counteroffensive – a strategy that implied the evacuation of Strasbourg. De Gaulle's reaction was unambiguous. French forces, he insisted, would not withdraw from a city that had changed hands between Germany and France four times in the previous century. Setting up a conflict between his national and Allied obligations, de Gaulle instructed de Lattre to refuse Eisenhower's orders. At the same time, he appealed to Roosevelt, Churchill and Eisenhower himself to reconsider, announcing a personal visit to Allied headquarters to argue his case.

Arriving at headquarters in Versailles on January 3, 1945, he found Churchill already there, seeking to prevent an open conflict among the Allies in the midst of a German offensive. In this instance, fortune was kind both to their cause and to de Gaulle's place in history. The military situation had improved, Eisenhower had already changed his mind, and French forces were permitted to remain in Strasbourg. Eisenhower's acquiescent response preempted what might have been, for de Gaulle, the spectacle of a French refusal to obey the supreme commander while a battle was raging. Yet, while de Gaulle prevailed, his victory came at an increased cost in the American willingness to accommodate him in the future.

The final phase of the war in April 1945 provoked another assertion of French autonomy: de Gaulle ordered his forces to occupy the south-west German industrial city of Stuttgart, even though it had been assigned to the future American zone of occupation and for operational purposes to the American army. Following his usual tactics, de Gaulle did not alter his command when the discrepancy was pointed out to him; nor, as usual, did his initiative invite dialogue.

Harry Truman, who had succeeded Roosevelt as president on April 12, was unimpressed by de Gaulle's explanation of his defiance – that, in effect, France should supplant Britain as America's major European ally. Britain, de Gaulle argued, had become too exhausted by war to play that role. Truman, insisting on the agreed delineation of occupation zones, threatened a complete reconsideration of existing undertakings. De Gaulle had no alternative but to relent, though he felt no compulsion to do so gracefully.

Meanwhile, privation ruled the home front. 'We lacked food to satisfy the barest needs of existence,' de Gaulle would write of the period after liberation in his war memoirs.[70] Individuals were restricted to 1,200 calories a day. The black market provided some relief for those with means, but almost everywhere scarcity prevailed:

Since there was no wool, no cotton and scarcely any leather, many citizens were wearing threadbare clothes and walking on wooden shoes.
There was no heat in the cities, for the small amount of coal being mined
was reserved for the armies, railroads, power plants, basic industries, and
hospitals . . . At home, at work, in offices and in schools, everyone shivered
with cold . . . It would take years before we returned to prewar living
standards.[71]

The French were living in a state of spiritual as well as material penury.
Communism presented itself as the expression of solidarity with the down-
trodden and a vessel of prestige by dint of its outsized representation in the
ranks of the Resistance – as well as Stalin's victories on the Eastern Front.
De Gaulle therefore identified the government's 'immediate task' as the
realization of, in his words, 'reforms by which he could regroup alle-
giances, obtain worker support, and assure economic recovery' – all
salutary ends in themselves, and all having the secondary effect of preventing the Communist Party from seizing control of France.[72]

Reforms that in more placid times might have been achieved in decades were unveiled in weeks. The provisional government established a
family allowance to support the raising of children and revive the French
birthrate. French women were able to exercise the right to vote for the
first time, fulfilling de Gaulle's longstanding conviction that a modern
society required universal suffrage. Social security expanded dramatically: 'Thus vanished the fear, as old as the human race, that sickness,
accident, old age, or unemployment would fall with crushing weight
upon the workers,' wrote de Gaulle.[73] Wartime planning did not subside
so much as rebrand itself as *dirigiste* economic policy. Air France,
Renault, coal, gas and electricity – all were nationalized. The High Commission of Atomic Energy and National School of Administration, two
pillars of postwar France, were both founded in the second half of 1945.

De Gaulle demonstrated that revolutionary changes did not require
a revolution. He stood between communists and free-market liberals,
renters and property owners, recalling the equipoise the Athenian law-
giver Solon displayed toward the rich and poor of his society: 'Before
them both I held my shield of might, / And let not either touch the
other's right.'[74]

Mighty as de Gaulle's shield was, however, it threatened to buckle
under domestic political stress. Postwar France's political institutions

remained embryonic; de Gaulle could rely on no structure to support what he would later call his 'certain idea of France'. To contain the violent schisms that had long divided France between Catholics and secularists, monarchists and republicans, socialists and conservatives, a legitimate central authority was crucial.

De Gaulle did not advocate a dictatorship: the central authority could be tested by periodic expressions of the popular will. Rather, he envisioned a strong executive under a republican system with a bicameral legislature and an independent judiciary:

> in order that the state should be, as it must be, the instrument of French unity, of the higher interests of the country, of continuity in national policy, I considered it necessary for the government to derive legitimacy not from the parliament, in other words the parties, but, over and above them, from a leader directly mandated by the nation as a whole and empowered to choose, to decide, and to act.[75]

On October 21, 1945, French voters elected the Constituent Assembly, a provisional legislature tasked with drawing up a new constitution. Three weeks later, it affirmed de Gaulle as head of government by a nearly unanimous vote, which, as he wryly noted in his memoirs, was more a recognition of past services than an understanding of his vision for the future.

As soon as the government began to operate, the historic dilemmas of the Third Republic reemerged. They started with the very formation of the government on November 21, which, according to the constitution, needed to be approved by parliament. As the largest party in the Constituent Assembly, the Communists demanded the three most important cabinet portfolios: Foreign Policy, Defense and Interior. Although de Gaulle refused to entertain this demand, he did feel obliged to grant the Communists significant domestic ministries, such as Economy and Labor.

Within weeks, de Gaulle realized that he was losing the struggle to shape the new constitution. A conventional political leader might have accepted such a disappointment as the price of holding power, but de Gaulle was not prepared to trade his conviction for what others judged practical. All along his tortuous wartime course, he had demonstrated that the improbable could be transformed into the realistic; if he could not achieve the moral renewal of his society, he would give up what most political leaders would consider fulfillment and what he had struggled and suffered to achieve.

On November 19, he asked the Canadian ambassador whether Canada would provide domicile should he resign. In a January 1, 1946 speech to the Assembly in advocacy of his defense budget, he suggested that it might be the last time he would speak 'in this hemicycle'.[76] Five days later, he left on vacation, returning on January 14 to tell Interior Minister Jules Moch in confidence:

> I do not feel I am made for this kind of fight. I do not want to be attacked, criticized, contested every day by men whose only claim is to have had themselves elected in some small corner of France.[77]

On January 20, a Sunday, not quite eighteen months after his triumphant return to liberated Paris, de Gaulle convened a special meeting of the cabinet. There, he read a brief statement outlining his disdain for 'the exclusive regime of parties' and his 'irrevocable' decision to resign, giving no indication of future plans.[78] After shaking hands with his colleagues, he got into his car and drove off. His stunned associates were left with a task none could have imagined when entering the room: choosing a successor to an already mythic personality. They elected Félix Gouin of the Socialist Party, who would serve for five months.

Historians have puzzled over the timing of de Gaulle's resignation. Clearly he was at odds with the procedures of the Third Republic, in place until the Constituent Assembly would complete its work on a constitution, which itself was trending in a direction he disfavored. But attacking the institutions he led as head of government could have appeared to demonstrate either political impotence or, possibly, an invitation to a Bonapartist coup. Yet, paradoxically, if he intended to realize the vision to which he had unfailingly kept faith through all adversity and doubt – namely, assuming power so as to infuse republican government with broad legitimacy – he needed to resign before the Assembly's work had been completed and not in protest at an existing constitution.

What this master of timing may have miscalculated was the interval required for the political leadership to recognize his indispensability and mend its ways.

THE DESERT

De Gaulle's abrupt resignation, like his flight to London five-and-a-half years earlier, affirmed his readiness to break with official France when his convictions could no longer support its direction. In doing so, he elected to 'withdraw from events before they withdrew from me'.[79] But whereas the relocation to London elevated him to the center of world historical events and the epic task of sustaining France in exile, he now found himself shrouded in provincial solitude, an exile in his own country.

The gesture was in keeping with de Gaulle's carefully cultivated image as a man of destiny, standing apart from politics-as-usual, uninterested in power for power's sake. The de Gaulle family settled in 'la Boisserie', a country house dating to the early nineteenth century, which lay in the village of Colombey-les-Deux-Églises, some 140 miles east of Paris. German Chancellor Konrad Adenauer would later describe it as 'a very simple house that has only a few well-furnished rooms on the ground floor but otherwise ... is very primitive'.[80] Winters were gray and harsh, for there was no central heating. 'This is not a gay place,' said de Gaulle to a visitor. 'One does not come here to laugh.'[81]

In the war memoirs he composed during his self-exile, he described how he found peace in his austere existence:

> This section of Champagne is imbued with calm – wide, mournful horizons; melancholy woods and meadows; the frieze of resigned old mountains; tranquil, unpretentious villages where nothing has changed its spirit or its place for thousands of years. All this can be seen from my village ... From a rise in the garden, I look down on the wild depths where the forest envelops the tilled land like the sea beating on a promontory. I watch the night cover the landscape. Then, looking up at the stars, I steep myself in the insignificance of earthly things.[82]

During this period, de Gaulle made only one public intervention of long-term significance: a speech on June 16, 1946 in Bayeux propounding his vision for France's political institutions. Two years and two days earlier, when the Allied beachhead was still tenuous a week after the invasion, de Gaulle first visited the Norman town. Six months after his resignation, he recalled the importance of his installing a prefect there:

'It was here on the soil of the ancestors that the State reappeared.'[83] Yet the work of reconciling France's institutions with its historic mission was incomplete; the constitution for what would become the Fourth Republic was being drafted at the time, and de Gaulle remained convinced that whatever emerged from the Constituent Assembly would be a dead end.

De Gaulle laid out his diagnosis of France's malaise with characteristic frankness: 'During a period no longer than two generations, France was invaded seven times and went through thirteen regimes.' Such 'numerous disturbances in our public life' had intensified France's 'ancient Gallic propensity for divisions and quarrels', finally resulting in 'the disaffection of the citizens toward institutions'.[84] A strong presidency was needed, 'situated above the parties', which would represent 'the values of continuity', as de Gaulle himself had done as leader of the Free French.[85]

Following Montesquieu, de Gaulle also argued for a strict separation of powers. It was very important that the president not be at the mercy of the legislative power, for this would result in 'a confusion of powers in which the Government would soon be nothing more than an assemblage of delegations'; in which the national interest would find no advocate; and in which any cabinet minister would be reduced to a mere 'party representative'.[86] A bicameral legislature would provide constituents with an upper house entitled to review and amend legislation passed by the lower house but also to propose bills to the National Assembly. In this manner, the French constitution would harness 'the fertile grandeurs of a free nation grouped under the aegis of a strong State'.[87]

This second Bayeux speech was also notable for an exposition of de Gaulle's thinking on democracy, a subject about which he rarely spoke. Unlike his American counterparts, de Gaulle identified democracy more commonly with its institutional framework than an enumeration of individual liberties. This is why, in the seminal Bayeux speech, he advocated democracy in the form of a biting analysis of the defects and ultimate futility of dictatorship:

> It is the fate of dictatorship to exaggerate what it undertakes. As the citizens become impatient with its constraints and nostalgic for their lost freedom, the dictatorship must, whatever the cost, be able to compensate

with broader and broader accomplishments. The nation becomes a machine on which the master imposes a regime of unchecked acceleration. In the end something has to give way. The grandiose edifice collapses in blood and misfortune. The nation is left broken and worse off . . .[88]

In sum, republican government served as the best bulwark between chaos and tyranny. De Gaulle's appeal at Bayeux did little to hinder the final draft of the constitution of the Fourth Republic, which retained parliamentary supremacy and the weak executive of its predecessor. It was ratified via referendum in October 1946.

Despite de Gaulle's expectation that the country would quickly recall him, no summons came. He struggled against bouts of gloom with demonstrative stoicism, at times reaching apocalyptic moods. In 1947, he attempted to launch a national political movement that stood separately from the established parties; it evoked a brief exuberance before sputtering out.

Meanwhile, overall domestic conditions stabilized and improved. Although France indulged in a merry-go-round of prime ministers, wellsprings of vitality reemerged. The economy, with the aid of the US-led European Recovery Program (or Marshall Plan), began to recover, and, by the early 1950s, France's well-educated workforce, technical expertise and integration into a US-sponsored system of open trade combined to achieve historic prosperity.

The Fourth Republic collapsed in 1958 not so much from domestic challenges as from its inability to establish priorities regarding its colonial possessions. It spent too many of the political gains of the economic recovery on three colonial crises: the effort to hold on to Indochina, the Suez intervention and, above all, the Algerian crisis.

FAILURE IN INDOCHINA AND
FRUSTRATION IN THE MIDDLE EAST

Indochina was the first in a series of postwar trials testing the Fourth Republic's claim to France's former spheres of geopolitical influence. Conquered piecemeal by France from 1862 to 1907, the colony had been under dual Japanese occupation and Vichy administration since the fall of France in June 1940. In March 1945, fearing an Allied invasion and suspecting that the French colonists might mount an uprising, the Japanese overthrew their erstwhile collaborators and established direct rule.

By the time of the Japanese surrender in August, two powerful forces were preparing to exploit the vacuum: Ho Chi Minh's communist Vietminh insurgency, which had opposed both the French and the Japanese during the war; and an Allied military campaign to retake the colony – involving Chinese, British and Indian troops, as well as a French expeditionary corps under General Leclerc's command.

By early 1946, French forces appeared to have largely reasserted control over Indochina. But France's strenuous efforts achieved only a brief interregnum of tranquility. On the night of December 19, 1946, the Vietminh set off dramatic explosions in Hanoi, signaling the beginning of another long and bloody war.

By 1954, colonial rule in Vietnam had become untenable. Laos and Cambodia had gained their independence from France the year before. The Eisenhower administration, emerging from the Korean War, was unwilling to back France militarily in Vietnam. General Henri Navarre's strategy of luring Vietminh General Võ Nguyên Giáp into an open battle by concentrating forces in the cauldron-like valley of Dien Bien Phu had resulted in a debacle. Over the course of eight weeks, Chinese-supplied North Vietnamese forces had trapped the French and in early May brought about their surrender.

In the aftermath of this catastrophe, Pierre Mendès-France, the only Fourth Republic premier for whom de Gaulle would later express respect, moved swiftly to conclude negotiations in Geneva over the future of Vietnam. According to the resulting agreement, France would abandon the colony, which would be divided along the 17th parallel between the communist north and the anti-communist south.

De Gaulle, not in office during that drama, never forgot the lesson. Meeting with President Kennedy in May 1961, he warned the young American president against involvement in the region. As recorded in an official memorandum,

> President de Gaulle recalled the war France waged in Indochina. He stated his feeling that a new war could not lead anywhere even if waged by the U.S. If the U.S. feels that its security or honor compelled it to intervene, the French will not oppose such an intervention but will not

participate in it, except of course if it were to lead to a worldwide war, in which case France would always be at the side of the U.S.[89]

The second postwar shock to France resulted from a joint Franco-British military operation to restore the West's position in the Middle East by invading the Suez Canal region in 1956 in league with Israel, which was pursuing its own separate national objectives.

In 1954, Gamal Abdel Nasser had taken over Egypt, deposing General Muhammad Naguib, who two years earlier had replaced the monarchy. Nasser created a nationalist regime that increasingly moved toward Soviet economic support and armed itself with Soviet weapons. In July 1956, he nationalized the Suez Canal, which had been under French and British ownership. Britain was thus faced with the end of its preeminence in the region, and France with the prospect that an emboldened Nasser might redouble his support for insurgent nationalists in its own North African possessions, especially Algeria.

In October 1956, in a secretly agreed coordination, British and French forces moved to seize the canal days after Israeli forces had invaded the Sinai Peninsula. The Eisenhower administration, viewing the Cold War as an ideological contest for the allegiance of the developing world, was transfixed by fear that the Soviet Union would use the occasion to coopt the Middle East. This is why, on October 30, twenty-four hours after Israel's initial attack, the United States submitted a resolution in the Security Council ordering Israeli armed forces 'immediately to withdraw ... behind the established armistice lines'. When this resolution was vetoed by Britain and France, Eisenhower took the issue to the General Assembly. On November 2, the General Assembly demanded an end to the hostilities by an overwhelming vote of sixty-four to five. At an overnight session on November 3–4, it passed an even stronger resolution and began to discuss a United Nations peacekeeping force for the canal. On November 6, a run on the pound sterling took on alarming proportions. Contrary to previous practice, America stood at the sidelines and refused to step in and calm the market.[90] These measures convinced Britain and France to call off the operation.

Washington's disavowal of the Anglo-French action at Suez exposed the limits of NATO as an intergovernmental military alliance – and of America's commitments to its allies. London and Paris drew antithetical lessons from their misadventure. Britain, shocked by the decline of its historic role and chastened by its schism with Washington, strove to restore the special relationship with America. It would return to modifying elements of historic policies in exchange for enhancing its influence over US decision-making. France, by contrast, with far less prospect of achieving this kind of influence over American choices, festered in frustration – creating a rift in perception within the Atlantic Alliance that would achieve its full expression after de Gaulle's return.

Before that could happen, however, the chronic instabilities of the Fourth Republic merged with France's colonial crisis in North Africa.

ALGERIA AND THE RETURN OF DE GAULLE

Conquered by France in 1830, Algeria held a special status amongst the French territories overseas. In the decades after annexation, waves of French and Southern European colonists settled along its coastline. By the 1950s, there were approximately one million of them, mostly French and known as the *pieds-noirs*.

The North African littoral, as we have seen, played a critical role in Allied military strategy during the Second World War; Algeria in particular advanced de Gaulle's personal strategy for attaining power. Unlike Tunisia, Morocco or France's sub-Saharan colonies, the Algerian littoral had been constitutionally treated as an integral component of metropolitan France, with a status comparable to Corsica. It was regarded so much as part of the French homeland that, as late as 1954, Prime Minister Mendès-France planned to move French weapons factories there, out of range of the Soviets.

The notion of Algeria as a kind of sanctuary would not survive the year. That November, the territory was struck by a wave of guerrilla attacks organized by the National Liberation Front (FLN), which called for an independent state, 'sovereign, democratic, and social, within the framework of the principles of Islam'.[91] In response to the challenge, Mendès-France declared: 'Never will any French government yield on the principle that Algeria is France.'[92] Although the French governor, Jacques Soustelle, among others, believed that economic development initiatives could stem the budding insurgency, convictions intensified over the following months.

The CIA had first predicted an 'Algerian settlement' within a year.[93] After a few months, its analysts reversed their view and argued that France's humiliation at Dien Bien Phu and its unwillingness 'to face the realities' – never defined – were helping to fuel the conflict in Algeria. Even left-leaning French governments found themselves locked in a cycle of military escalation. François Mitterrand, the future Socialist Party standard-bearer and French president who was then serving as Mendes-France's interior minister, spoke for many on the left when he reiterated the prime minister's assertion: 'Algeria is France.' But now he added, 'the only negotiation is war'.[94]

What had been originally acquired as a beachhead for the projection of French power was turning into a cancer eating at the country from within. *Pieds-noirs*, enraged by the inability of the French government in Paris to protect them, formed vigilante groups defiant of elected authority. The French army grew resentful of the political class, whose indecisiveness it blamed for the stalemate. As government after government tumbled – six collapsed between the FLN's attacks in November 1954 and de Gaulle's return in June 1958 – French public opinion became increasingly exasperated by this seemingly irresolvable crisis. With key elements of French society revolting against state authority, what started as an insurrection by Arab nationalists against French colonialism risked metastasizing into a French civil war.

Algeria was the last act in the saga of French imperial retreat and the first act in de Gaulle's return to save France a second time. De Gaulle had been observing the growing paralysis from Colombey. First, he expected that his indispensability would be quickly recognized. But no party leader undertook the responsibility to encourage, much less support, a revision of the constitution compatible with de Gaulle's public list of the preconditions for his return.

By May 1958, the domestic situation had reached the critical phase that de Gaulle had stipulated. A group of generals including General Jacques Massu, the paratroop commander, in a coup-like appeal to French President René Coty, demanded that de Gaulle be appointed the head of a government of national safety. Simultaneously, the National Assembly was searching for a strong premier. It settled on Pierre Pflimlin, a member of the Christian Democratic Party, who proved at first hesitant and then unable to form a stable majority. Algeria continued to boil.

De Gaulle maneuvered masterfully among the contending factions, refusing to take sides. He did not declare himself ready for office until all the parties had become deadlocked due to their incompatible goals. The Assembly increasingly feared a military coup and looked to de Gaulle to avert it; the army was drawn to the idea of de Gaulle's return because the former soldier was championing a strong state, which it interpreted as resolve to crush the Algerian insurgents. To reinforce the fear of a parachute descent in Paris, officers of the Algerian corps bloodlessly seized Corsica, prompting Pflimlin's resignation.

Each of de Gaulle's supporters misunderstood him to some extent. He used the army's pressure as a tool but did not aim to seize power from the barrel of a gun. His purpose was in fact not a new Bonapartism but a constitutional state strong enough to dispatch the army to the barracks. By the same token, de Gaulle sought to be recalled to office in a constitutional manner and to abolish, not to serve, the existing political system.

De Gaulle put forward no specific demand; instead, he maintained an artful ambiguity, made himself available for exploration by each faction and without restricting his flexibility appeared to each as the best last solution to its worst fears. Maneuvering each of the contending forces into the position of supplicant, he was always negotiating from a position of strength.

As de Gaulle well understood, the political constellation in the spring of 1958 had by now brought about what was likely to be his last opportunity to fulfill what he believed to be the task assigned to France by history. But he had the wisdom to play it like a game of Chinese Wei-Ch'i or Go, which starts on a blank board, each party possessing 180 pieces, and where success is achieved through patience and a superior grasp of the evolving tactical situation.

To have shared his ultimate program would have risked alienating all factions or driving them into precipitous action. Instead, he persuaded each group that advancing his candidacy was the best way to thwart its rivals. In the end, on May 29, 1958, President Coty invited de Gaulle to become the last prime minister of the Fourth Republic, extending the invitation through the Secretary of the Presidency.

Throughout this period, de Gaulle conducted only one press conference, on May 19 – near the end of the crisis – in which he described himself as a 'man who belongs to nobody and who belongs to everybody' and said he would return to power only by means of an exceptional act by the National Assembly that would recall him to office for the purpose of introducing a new constitution.[95] He had a word for all concerns. To the army, he said that its normal role was to be a servant of the state, on the condition that there was a state. To those worried about the threat he might pose to democracy, he pointed out that he had restored democratic institutions in France in 1944. 'Why should I, at age 67, begin a career as a dictator?'[96] He ended the press conference by saying: 'I have said what I have to say. Now I am going to return to my village and hold myself at the disposition of the country.'[97]

On June 1, the multiple consultations came to an end, and de Gaulle appeared before the National Assembly for the first time since his resignation in January 1946. He read without emotion the edict that would dissolve the chamber and give him full power for six months for the drafting of a new constitution, which would then be submitted to a referendum. The debate lasted only six hours. The final vote was 329 to 224 for the investiture of de Gaulle as prime minister, a temporary springboard to his constitutional presidency.

Twice in a lifetime de Gaulle had assumed the leadership of France: the first time in 1940 to rescue it from the consequences of national catastrophe; the second in 1958 as the only means of avoiding civil war. The first time, the once-unknown brigadier general brought four years of solitary vision to their culmination with the liberation of Paris. The second time, already a legendary figure, he was recalled from internal exile to save the constitutional government from itself and to lead the French people to a post-imperial, but nonetheless dynamic and independent, role in the world. In this great task de Gaulle envisioned four phases: restoring France's constitutional structure so as to create a government with authority; finishing France's colonial adventures in a way that removed them as a canker in the body politic; designing a French military and political strategy which made clear the international indispensability of France in both defense and diplomacy; and, finally, defending that strategic concept against allies, especially a reluctant America.

THE FIFTH REPUBLIC

De Gaulle ascribed the process by which the Fourth Republic was overthrown to three factors. In order to 'save the country while preserving the Republic', it was essential, first, to 'change a discredited political system'; second, to restore the army 'to the path of obedience without delay'; and, third, to place himself in a leading role as the only person who could bring about the requisite changes.[98]

Entering office, de Gaulle needed to transform his deliberate tactical ambiguity into a strategic design for overcoming the revolutionary turmoil he had inherited. Leftist domestic critics envisioned France's radical dissociation from Algeria as a simple and unambiguous task; in reality, the processes of French administration and settlement that had lasted for more than a century, as well as the war that had been ongoing since 1954, could not be switched off with the abruptness of changing a television channel. The army's commitment to keeping Algeria French had brought de Gaulle into office; now he acted on the conviction that returning the military to its role as an instrument of national policy was not achievable by a single dramatic decision. It would require a process that, by gradually reducing the military role in civilian order, would preclude the possibility of military dominance.

Governing by decree, de Gaulle had been given six months to develop a new constitution. In accordance with principles laid down in his Bayeux speech of 1946, the new constitution replaced the parliamentary supremacy of the Third and Fourth Republics, and its attendant tendency toward factionalism, with a largely presidential system. In the Fifth Republic, control of defense and foreign policy would be reserved to the president, who was elected for a seven-year term by indirect suffrage via electors (modified to direct election in 1962). To oversee the functioning of the government, the president would appoint a prime minister representing a majority in the popularly elected National Assembly. But, to prevent a deadlock between the executive and legislative branches, the president also had the right to dissolve the Assembly and call parliamentary elections.

On matters of overriding national importance, the president could make recourse to popular referenda – a method de Gaulle, if not his successors, employed with relish. In October 1962, he spearheaded the referendum campaign allowing for direct election of the president. While extricating France from Algeria, he deployed two referenda as demonstration that a majority of the country endorsed his program.

It is likely that at the beginning of the presidency de Gaulle did not have a precise sense of his ultimate destination in Algeria, although he was determined to end a war that was preventing France from fulfilling its international and domestic missions. Returning to office, he undertook several simultaneous strategies, each compatible with these two desiderata which had won him his position, all without committing to a specific outcome.

De Gaulle's artful ambiguity was on full display during his visit to Algeria in June 1958, shortly after becoming head of government. Addressing a rapturous crowd of *pieds-noirs*, who took him to be their savior, de Gaulle said: 'Je vous ai compris' ('I have understood you'). The phrase encouraged the faith of those whose commitment to French Algeria had helped to put him in office, while doing nothing to limit his options. His choice of words may also have saved his life: a would-be assassin was on the scene in a nearby building as de Gaulle spoke, but set down his rifle when he heard the leader's words.[99]

As a first move, de Gaulle ordered General Maurice Challe, the commanding general, to launch an all-out offensive to clear rebels from the countryside. The purpose was to crystallize his two options: either integrating Algeria into France via military victory or, if that failed, discrediting the army's case against a political settlement.

At the same time, de Gaulle accompanied armed force with sweeping domestic reform. His Constantine Plan, named for the eastern Algerian city in which it was announced in October 1958, marked an ambitious humanitarian and economic development effort to industrialize and modernize Algeria. He was thus outflanking left-wing and Algérie française voices simultaneously.[100]

In implementing his strategic direction, de Gaulle turned to the referendum procedure, this time brilliantly linking the ratification of the new constitution to a new arrangement for France's colonial possessions. Both the metropole and the colonies were invited to vote by universal suffrage on the new constitutional framework. By putting forward the concept of a 'French Community', de Gaulle was able to supersede a thorny constitutional debate between two leaders of French colonial Africa: Léopold Sédar Senghor (later president of Senegal), who favored a federal solution in which Africans would become full citizens of France and the colonies would be merged into two regional groupings, and Félix Houphouët-Boigny (former French health minister and later president of the Ivory Coast), who preferred a looser confederation.

For each colony, there was a choice: approve the constitution and join the French Community or be granted immediate independence. All but Guinea under Sekou Touré chose to remain in the French Community – a vague institution sharing security functions. But the winds of political independence were blowing across Africa, and the Community arrangement buckled within two years. In 1960, the 'Year of Africa', fourteen Francophone states gained their independence, thereby largely avoiding wars of national liberation. The two exceptions were Cameroon, where a bloody contest between nationalist insurgents and the French military raged for nine years, and Algeria, which retained an intermediate status compatible with either a military or a diplomatic outcome.

To secure African support for the Community, de Gaulle undertook a five-day cross-continental campaign in August 1958, during which he spoke in unusually rapturous tones of the new mission for France. In Madagascar's capital, gesturing to the ancient palace nearby, he declared: 'Tomorrow you will be a State once again, as you were when the palace of your kings was inhabited!'[101] His *Memoirs of Hope* record his reception in the French Congolese capital of Brazzaville: whether in the 'beflagged streets of the city center' or 'in the seething suburbs of Bas-Congo and Potopoto', the crowds were 'delirious with enthusiasm' for the referendum.[102]

In a May 1969 memorandum to President Richard Nixon, I described the significance of de Gaulle's extraordinary constitutional referendum:

> There was [in it] more than sympathy for African nationalists or a shrewd leaning with the anti-colonial tide. De Gaulle's African policy mirrored his concept of grandeur as well as gratitude. His memoirs show clearly an obsession with France's civilizing mission, and he qualified the colonies' independence with political, economic, and personal ties that left French influence and culture still dominant. In turn, the French-speaking Africans came to rely on his special brand of patronage. The result was that in Africa, if anywhere, de Gaulle made France a great power.[103]

THE END OF THE ALGERIAN CONFLICT

Having completed the constitutional framework, de Gaulle steered his Algerian policy to its conclusion. One who saw France's predicament clearly was Mao Zedong, who predicted to FLN leader Ferhat Abbas that France would not be able to sustain a military commitment to the conflict at its current scale: 'You will see that they face many difficulties. France needs to support an 800,000-strong military and spend three billion francs a day. If that continues for a long time, they will collapse.'[104]

De Gaulle left no record of the precise moment he arrived at the same conclusion. Nor was that unusual for him. Withal his dramatic way of proclaiming ultimate goals, he generally presented them in a manner as to obscure the nature of the journey.

A couple of instances illustrate this aspect of his conduct, one of them related to me by Paul Stehlin, then-chief of the French Air Force. At a meeting discussing French national strategy, de Gaulle had asked the participants for their views on his NATO policy. Shortly afterward, Stehlin, who had remained silent, was invited to de Gaulle's office. 'Was your silence an expression of disagreement?' Stehlin then indicated his reasons for disagreement, to which de Gaulle cryptically replied: 'And how do you know that I am not traveling to the same destination but on my own route?'[105]

A second example of de Gaulle's aloof style of decision-making emerged in December 1958, during the drafting of his program for domestic fiscal reform. The proposed plan, the handiwork of a senior civil servant and economist named Jacques Rueff, proved highly controversial. While considering it, de Gaulle summoned Roger Goetze, a financial aide, to his office and observed that, in assessing the prospects of even the best-thought-out proposal, a policymaker would be wise to reserve a one-third element of doubt. 'You are the expert,' de Gaulle said. 'You will tell me tomorrow morning if you consider whether the plan has a two-thirds chance of success. If yes, I will adopt it.'[106] The next morning, Goetze affirmed his confidence in the Rueff plan, and de Gaulle accepted it. Proclaimed by edict and put before the French public in a radio address, it provided the economic basis for the de Gaulle presidency, which officially began on January 8, 1959.

On September 16, 1959, de Gaulle abruptly crystallized the Algerian choices before France in a televised address. He put forward three options without definitively committing himself to any. As his biographer Julian Jackson writes:

The first was independence or 'secession' (*scission*), as de Gaulle dubbed it . . . A second option was what he described by the neologism of 'francisation', which was his way of describing what advocates of *Algérie française* called 'integration' . . . The third option was 'the government of Algeria by the Algerians, supported by the aid of France and in close union with her', with a federal system internally in Algeria where the different communities would cohabit peacefully.[107]

De Gaulle favored the third option, which he called 'association', but privately he mused that it might be too late to avoid the first, Algeria's total break from France.[108] The first and third options involved a substantial element of self-determination for the country's Muslim-majority population, while the second envisioned the gradual merging of French and Algerians into a single people.

Four months later, in January 1960, with the military situation still not substantially improved, *pied-noir* activists uneasy with de Gaulle's options began constructing barricades in Algiers. When the news was first reported, I was in Paris, having spent an early part of the day with a group of French military officers who had invited me to discuss my book *Nuclear Weapons and Foreign Policy*. Understandably, the impact of the barricades overrode concern over nuclear strategy. Several of my interlocutors (mostly at the rank of colonel or brigadier general) blamed their president for the troops' sympathy for the *pied-noir* rebels, arguing that whenever de Gaulle appeared on the scene he divided France, and hence he needed to be removed.

The same day, I had lunch with Raymond Aron, the great French political philosopher. In a Left Bank café, he exclaimed his dismay over the barricades: 'I am becoming ashamed to be French; we are acting like Spaniards, in a state of permanent revolution.' At these words, a diner at a nearby table rose, came over to ours, identified himself as a reserve officer and demanded an apology in the name of the French army.

By January 29, many in France – and all of my acquaintances there – expected a military coup, perhaps even a parachutist descent on Paris. De Gaulle went on television that evening wearing his wartime uniform. After a stark description of the situation in Algiers, he addressed the French army, ordering it to tear down the barricades unconditionally: 'I must be obeyed by all French soldiers. No soldier must, at any moment, and even passively, associate himself with the rebellion. In the end, public order must be reestablished.'[109] The next day, the barricades went down. It was an extraordinary demonstration of charismatic leadership.

In April 1961, an abortive coup staged by the army marked the last upheaval of the Algerian settlers against what de Gaulle understood as his historic task: disengagement. Again, he took to television to denounce the rogue action in Algeria:

> Now the State is flouted, the Nation defied, our power degraded, our international prestige lowered, our role and our place in Africa jeopardized. And by whom? Alas! Alas! By men whose duty, honor, and *raison d'être* was to serve and obey.[110]

The putsch failed, but opposing sentiments did not disappear. On August 22, 1962, de Gaulle and his wife Yvonne remarkably escaped death by machine-gun-wielding Secret Armed Organization (OAS) assassins in the Paris suburb of Petit-Clamart. (As with the sniper fire during the mass at Notre-Dame Cathedral on August 26, 1944, de Gaulle refused to duck.) Others were not so lucky: some 2,000 French citizens were killed by the OAS in bombings and targeted assassinations in two years.*

In August 1961 – three years into his presidency – de Gaulle began the process of preparing the French people for the eventual outcome. He started withdrawing troops from Algeria with the justification that they were needed for the defense of Europe. To the French colonists, subordinating the security of what was legally a province of France to European defense represented a blow to their self-image and a revolutionary change in France's priorities. The French public may have become exhausted from colonial wars, but the colonists themselves, and most of all the army, had borne the brunt of the sacrifice and felt deeply deceived.

The endgame came in the form of the Evian Accords, negotiated in secret between de Gaulle's ministers and representatives of the FLN in early 1962. This ninety-three-page document created an independent state while safeguarding French strategic equities on its territory, including access to military facilities and preferential treatment for its energy companies. Of the three options de Gaulle earlier considered, this was 'secession lite'. De Gaulle announced an April referendum on the pact in metropolitan France. It won over 90 percent – overwhelming support

---

* As dramatized in Frederick Forsyth's 1971 novel *The Day of the Jackal*.

that was bolstered by public disaffection with terrorist attacks by OAS remnants seeking to derail the accord. A subsequent vote in Algeria itself on July 1 endorsed the Evian Accords with 99.72 percent backing. Two days later, France recognized the new state. Yet the promised mineral rights did not materialize, and France would conduct its final nuclear test in the Algerian desert four years later, in 1966.

De Gaulle had turned Algérie française from a self-evident fact in the mid-1950s into an extremist slogan uttered primarily by the *pieds-noirs* five years later. But by that time, the wide-ranging integrationist forces that in 1958 had helped propel de Gaulle into the presidency had been reduced to a fringe terrorist movement. 800,000 French colonists were expelled from Algeria by the new regime – which combined aspects of Islamism, socialism and Arab nationalism – or left to their own devices shortly after the signing of the peace accords. Fearing violence, 150,000 of the remaining 200,000 elected to migrate by 1970.[111] As for the Algerian Muslims who had remained loyal to France – the *harkis* – withdrawal left them defenseless against reprisals by the FLN, which considered them traitors. Around 40,000 were able to flee to France, but tens of thousands remained in Algeria and were massacred.[112]

De Gaulle viewed his action as a patriotic service in the cause of restoring French national self-respect and the French voice in international affairs. Algerian disengagement made available more resources for French economic development and military modernization. Once embarked on the process, he exhibited the same implacability that had propelled him forward ever since arriving in London in 1940.

De Gaulle never responded to several suggestions that he express compassion for the French settlers fleeing what they regarded as their homeland; nor is there any record of his ever having discussed the impact of his Algerian policy on himself. Though he *did* on occasion express emotions in public – the speeches in Bayeux and Paris in June and August 1944, for example – de Gaulle made it a practice never to permit personal feelings to override his sense of duty or the requirements of the historical process, as he saw it. In his judgment, Algeria had become a drain on France, isolating it among allies and handing to the Soviet Union and other radical forces an irresistible opportunity for intervention. Amputating Algeria saved the vitality of the Fifth Republic; it was the price France had to pay for the ability to conduct its own independent foreign policy and to fulfill de Gaulle's vision of its role in the emerging world order. He was hardly engaging in hyperbole when, as his Algeria policy was unfurling in 1959, he privately characterized it as 'perhaps ... the greatest service I will have rendered to France'.[113] De Gaulle had defied history in order to channel it in a different direction.

GERMANY AS A KEY TO FRENCH POLICY: DE GAULLE AND ADENAUER

On September 14, 1958, three months after becoming prime minister, de Gaulle took a major step in advancing the policy of reconciliation with Germany that had been started by his Fourth Republic predecessors. Ever since the Thirty Years' War, each country had regarded the other as its hereditary enemy. In the twentieth century alone, France and Germany had fought each other in two world wars.

Implementing that tradition, de Gaulle, on his 1944 visit to Moscow, had advocated that a defeated Germany be broken up into its component states and that the Rhineland become part of France's economic domain. He submitted a similar plan to his European allies in 1945.

But in 1958, returning from exile, de Gaulle reversed the policy of centuries by initiating a Franco-German partnership. To free energies for broader tasks and to create a bloc that might lead to European autonomy, de Gaulle invited German Chancellor Konrad Adenauer for an overnight stay at la Boisserie in Colombey-les-Deux-Églises. No other leader, foreign or domestic, was ever to receive a comparable invitation; when French ambassador to the United Kingdom Jean Chauvel suggested a parallel visit for Prime Minister Harold Macmillan, de Gaulle informed him boldly that Colombey was too small for an appropriate meeting.[114]

The courtesies extended to Adenauer – such as personally conducting him through the house – were emblematic of the importance de Gaulle attached to the new relationship. Another gesture extended to Adenauer, no less unique, was to hold their discussions without the presence of aides, and largely in German. Indeed, the etiquette of the whole meeting was skillfully orchestrated to appeal to the psychology of the guest and to allow two old men, both born in the nineteenth century, to feel at ease with each other in practicing traditional courtesies.

Concrete agreements between them were neither proposed nor concluded. Instead, a mere thirteen years after the conclusion of the Second World War, de Gaulle sought to bring about a complete reversal of their past relations. He did not propose a mutual obliteration of memories, many of which would necessarily remain. But, in place of centuries of hostility, he offered French support for the rehabilitation of Germany and its quest for a European identity. Further, he suggested that a close relationship be established to promote the balance of power and the unity of Europe. In return, he asked for German acceptance of existing European frontiers (including that of Poland), an end to the German quest to dominate Europe. As he would put it later in his memoirs:

> France for her part had nothing to ask of Germany with respect to unity, security, or rank, whereas she could help to rehabilitate her erstwhile aggressor. She would do so – with what magnanimity! – in the name of the entente to be established between the two peoples, and of the balance of power, the unity, and the peace of Europe. But to justify her support, she would insist that certain conditions be fulfilled on the German side. These were: acceptance of existing frontiers, an attitude of goodwill in relations with the East, complete renunciation of atomic armaments, and unremitting patience with regard to [German] reunification.[115]

What de Gaulle demanded as a quid pro quo for this revolutionary reconfiguration of French foreign policy was an abandonment of the traditional foreign policy of the national Germany that de Gaulle had encountered in his youth. Adenauer went along with the main trends of the North Atlantic Treaty Organization as opening the road for Germany into a European system. For Adenauer it was a step into the future.

DE GAULLE AND THE ATLANTIC ALLIANCE

A comparable transformation of established policy trends with even greater impact on world order occurred with the creation of the Atlantic Alliance. At the end of the Second World War, America emerged from its historic isolation into an unprecedented global role. Its 6 percent of the world's population was economically preeminent; it possessed half of the world's global industrial capacity together with a monopoly on atomic weapons.

Until then, America's behavior internationally outside the Western Hemisphere had been confined to rallying only against strategic threats and withdrawing into isolation when the lessening of danger made it seem safe to do so. Now, between 1945 and 1950, in two great initiatives – NATO and the Marshall Plan – America abandoned its previous mode of conduct and assumed a permanent role in world affairs. Alongside the East River in midtown Manhattan, the new, modernist United Nations headquarters symbolized that America had become part of an international order.

The new initiatives remained based on premises about the nature of international relations that were as unique, indeed as idiosyncratic, as American history itself: that cooperation among nations was natural, that universal peace was the inherent outcome of international relations, and that a principled division of labor would provide adequate motivation and resources for the conduct of the Atlantic Alliance.

De Gaulle's historical experience produced diametrically different conclusions. He led a country made cautious by too many enthusiasms shattered, skeptical by too many dreams proved fragile, and conditioned by a sense not of national power or cohesion but of latent vulnerability. Nor did he believe that peace was the natural condition among states: 'The world is full of opposing forces ... The competition of efforts is the condition of life ... International life, like life in general, is a battle.'[116]

Washington, confident of America's dominance, focused on immediate, practical tasks; it urged an alliance structure that, in the name of integration, would encourage joint Allied action and impede autonomous initiatives. De Gaulle, governing a country racked by generations of international and civil conflict, insisted that the *manner* of cooperation was as important as the goal. France, if it were to recover its identity, had to be perceived as acting out of choice, not compulsion, and it therefore needed to preserve its freedom of action.

Imbued by these convictions, de Gaulle rejected any view of NATO that would place French forces under international command or a view of Europe that would dissolve French identity in supranational institutions. He warned against a kind of supranationalism that was taking hold (as if 'self-renunciation were henceforth the sole possibility and even the only ambition') which was at odds with France's national character and purposes.[117]

Paradoxically, de Gaulle considered this view to be compatible with a united Europe – 'so that gradually there may be established on both sides of the Rhine, of the Alps, and perhaps of the Channel the most powerful, prosperous, and influential complex in the world'.[118] Even as he always affirmed the practical importance of the American alliance, he doubted that it applied to all challenges relevant to France. Specifically – like Adenauer – he questioned whether America could, or would want to, retain its all-out commitment to Europe indefinitely – especially in the area of nuclear weapons.

De Gaulle's assertive style resulted from a combination of personal confidence and historical experience, tempered by an awareness of the nightmare in which the unexpected had formed the most central French experience. By contrast, American leaders, though personally modest in their conduct, based their own views on confidence in their mastery of the future.

During a visit to Paris in 1959, President Eisenhower addressed the issue of French reservations head-on: 'Why do you doubt that America would identify its fate with Europe?'[119] It was an odd question in light of Washington's imperious conduct toward both Britain and France during the Suez crisis a few years earlier. Avoiding the temptation to bring up Suez, de Gaulle reminded Eisenhower that in the First World War, America came to the rescue only after France had endured three years of mortal peril, and that America had entered the Second World War only after France had already been occupied. In the Nuclear Age, both interventions would have come too late.[120]

The sheer geographical vulnerability of France also preoccupied de Gaulle. He opposed various schemes for negotiating the disengagement of American forces from Central Europe, of which the most notable was the one put forward in the Reith Lectures in 1957 by George Kennan. De Gaulle rejected any symmetrical withdrawal from the dividing lines in Europe because that would leave American forces too far away and the Soviet army too near: 'if disarmament did not cover a zone which is as near to the Urals as it is to the Atlantic, how would France be protected?'[121]

De Gaulle's assessment of the Soviet challenge was made explicit when, in 1958, Soviet Premier Nikita Khrushchev repeated an ultimatum threatening Allied access to Berlin. De Gaulle was adamant in refusing to negotiate under threat. With characteristic eloquence, he attributed the latest challenge to the volatility of the Soviet domestic system:

> There is in this uproar of imprecations and demands organized by the Soviets something so arbitrary and so artificial that one is led to attribute it either to the premeditated unleashing of frantic ambitions or to the desire of drawing attention away from great difficulties. This second hypothesis seems all the more plausible to me since, despite the coercions, isolation, and acts of force in which the Communist system encloses the countries which are under its yoke ... actually its gaps, its shortages, its internal failures, and above all its character of inhuman oppression, are felt more and more by the elites and the masses, whom it is more and more difficult to deceive and subjugate.[122]

On the basis of this assessment, de Gaulle was prepared to cooperate whenever, in his view, French and American interests genuinely converged. Thus, during the 1962 Cuban Missile Crisis, American officials were astonished by de Gaulle's all-out support for their forceful reaction to the Soviet deployment of ballistic missiles in the island nation; indeed, his was the most unconditional backing extended to them by any Allied leader. When Dean Acheson, the former secretary of state acting as special emissary of President Kennedy, confirmed an imminent move to blockade Cuba and offered him a White House briefing, de Gaulle declined on the grounds that when a great ally acts in an hour of need, that urgency is sufficient justification in itself.

THE NUCLEAR DIRECTORATE

Upon assuming office, de Gaulle accelerated the existing French military nuclear program. Within months, he inaugurated his Atlantic policy with a proposal to reorganize NATO on the issue of nuclear strategy. The United States had grave reservations about independent European nuclear forces in principle; in Washington's view, such forces needed to be integrated into NATO plans and joint commands;[123] they were treated as diversions from the conventional forces preferred by America. De Gaulle considered abstention from developing a major military capacity as a form of psychological abdication. On September 17, 1958, he sent a proposal to Eisenhower and Macmillan for a tripartite arrangement among France and NATO's two nuclear powers at the time: Britain and the United States. To prevent each country from being drawn into a nuclear war against its will, de Gaulle proposed giving each a veto over the use of nuclear weapons except in response to a direct attack.[124] By the same token, the tripartite directorate would also devise common strategy for specific global regions outside of Europe.[125]

Did de Gaulle envisage the directorate as a stopgap until a French nuclear arsenal could be developed and strong enough for an autonomous strategy? Or was he aiming at a new and unprecedented relationship with Washington and London that would provide France with a special leadership role on the Continent based on nuclear weapons? The answer will never be known because, incredibly, the proposal for a directorate never received a response.[126]

Eisenhower and Macmillan had dealt with de Gaulle in Algiers when he was still a contestant for leadership – and hence in no position to implement his views unilaterally. They therefore thought they could afford to ignore him. Their tactics made sense, however, only on the assumption that de Gaulle was being grandiloquently frivolous and had no practical alternative. These assumptions turned out to be mistaken.

To de Gaulle, the issue went to the heart of France's role in the world. His determination to retain control over decisions affecting his nation's destiny was the central feature of his strategy.

De Gaulle reacted to the American and British silence by demonstrating that, in fact, he did have options. In March 1959, he withdrew the French Mediterranean fleet from the integrated NATO command; in June of that year, he ordered the removal of American nuclear weapons from French soil; in February 1960, France conducted its first nuclear test in the Algerian desert; and in 1966 he pulled France out of the NATO command structure altogether.[127] He must have judged that Britain and the US would have no choice but to support him in case of Soviet attack while he retained freedom of decision.

In a televised speech on April 19, 1963, de Gaulle explained his rationale for moving swiftly to establish an independent nuclear deterrent:

to dissuade us, the voices of immobility and demagogy are as always simultaneously raised. 'It is useless,' say some. 'It is too costly,' say others ... But this time we shall not allow routine and illusion to invite invasion of our country. Moreover, in the midst of the strained and dangerous world in which we live, our chief duty is to be strong and to be ourselves.[128]

On August 24, 1968, France conducted its first thermonuclear (hydrogen bomb) test. It was now technologically a full-fledged nuclear power.

FLEXIBLE RESPONSE AND NUCLEAR STRATEGY

In 1961, newly inaugurated President John F. Kennedy ordered a review of American defense policy. He was especially concerned with modifying the then-prevalent doctrine of massive retaliation (first advanced by Eisenhower's secretary of state John Foster Dulles), which proclaimed that the United States would resist aggression by means of overwhelming nuclear retaliation at places of its own choosing.

So long as the United States possessed a vastly superior nuclear arsenal, the doctrine held considerable plausibility, though even then questions were raised about the eventual American readiness actually to employ such weapons in every contingency.[129] With the expansion of Soviet nuclear capability, the credibility of massive retaliation diminished; allies concluded from their own hesitancy to use nuclear weapons that America would be similarly inhibited.

At the same time, Britain, whose nuclear weapons were to be delivered largely by airplanes, feared that growing Soviet anti-aircraft defenses might jeopardize the British ability to retaliate. It therefore sought to acquire an American weapon then in the process of development: an air-launched standoff missile named Skybolt. At first, Kennedy overrode the resistance of his secretary of defense, Robert McNamara, who was opposed to autonomous nuclear capabilities in principle.

Kennedy was soon to change his mind. The simultaneous operation of different autonomous forces seemed to him and, above all, to McNamara too dangerous, and he pressed allied countries to phase out their nuclear forces altogether. In July 1962, McNamara made a statement opposing independent nuclear forces: 'limited nuclear capabilities, operating independently, are dangerous, expensive, prone to obsolescence, and lacking in credibility as a deterrent.'[130]

Concerns over the utility of a British independent nuclear force had never previously been brought to the surface; the special relationship with America seemed to preclude autonomous nuclear actions by Britain. But in November 1962, McNamara canceled the US-UK Skybolt program – ostensibly on technical grounds. In Britain, the cancellation of Skybolt was treated with outrage as eradicating its status as a nuclear power and as undermining Britain's special status among America's alliances.

At a meeting in Nassau in December 1962, President Kennedy and Prime Minister Macmillan fashioned a compromise: the United States would offer assistance to Britain to build Polaris submarines, whose missiles would be able to overcome Soviet air defenses. The submarines would be put under NATO command but, in cases involving the 'supreme national interest,' Britain could employ them autonomously. A similar arrangement was offered to France.

Macmillan agreed, relying on the 'supreme national interest' escape clause to give Britain latitude because an autonomous use of nuclear weapons would occur, by definition, only when a supreme national challenge was involved.

De Gaulle's reaction was quite the opposite. He treated the Nassau agreement as a direct challenge, all the more as it had been communicated to him publicly without any prior effort to consult him. At a press conference on January 14, 1963, he repudiated the American offer as publicly as he had received it, observing acidly: 'Of course, I am only speaking of this proposal and agreement because they have been published and because their content is known.'[131]

In the process, de Gaulle also rejected Kennedy's view that Atlantic relations should be based on a twin-pillar concept and that the European pillar should be organized along supranational lines: 'such a system would undoubtedly find itself powerless to sweep along and lead the peoples and, to begin with, our own people, in the domains where their souls and their flesh are in question.'[132]

Finally, at the same press conference, and despite Macmillan's assiduous wooing of him over the previous two years, de Gaulle vetoed British membership in the European Economic Community, thus undercutting Macmillan's own grand strategy and the American notion of a twin-pillar partnership.

WHAT IS AN ALLIANCE?

Alliances have historically been formed to establish congruence between a nation's capability and its intentions in five ways: 1) to assemble forces adequate to defeat or deter a possible aggressor; 2) to convey this capability; 3) to proclaim obligations beyond the calculus of a power relationship – were these unambiguous, no such formal expression would have been required; 4) to define a specific *casus belli*; and 5) to remove, as a means of diplomacy in a crisis, any doubt about the intentions of the parties.

All of these traditional objectives were altered by the emergence of nuclear weapons. For countries relying on America's nuclear guarantees, no deployment of forces beyond those already fielded was meaningful; everything depended on the credibility of American assurances. The effort to strengthen NATO by building the allies' conventional forces, therefore, never fulfilled its objective. The allies did not consider that conventional weapons added significantly to the common strength and never reached their conventional-weapons commitments partly for fear that, in so doing, they could render American nuclear might dispensable. When they did participate in American military action – for example, in Afghanistan and Iraq – it was not so much in pursuit of their strategic interests in those countries as a device to continue sheltering under the American nuclear umbrella.

De Gaulle operated in the interstices of these ambivalences. In order to justify an independent French nuclear deterrent, he invoked the inherent uncertainty of nuclear guarantees. But he would have persisted in the course of nuclear autonomy regardless of the phrasing of American assurances. For de Gaulle, leadership was the elaboration of national purpose from a careful analysis of the meshing of existing power relationships with historical evolution. For France to rely on 'foreign arms' for its own security, he wrote in his *War Memoirs*, 'would poison its soul and its life for many generations'.[133] He sought in the 1960s to rebuild a powerful military complete with an independent nuclear deterrent, which would enable his country to fulfill its duty to shape the future.[134] An auxiliary role would never be appropriate for France. And this was a moral, not a technical, issue:

> As for the immediate future, in the name of what were some of [France's] sons to be led out to a fight no longer its own? What was the good of supplying with auxiliaries the forces of another power? No! For the effort to be worthwhile, it was essential to bring back into the war not merely some Frenchmen, but France.[135]

In de Gaulle's view, international obligations were inherently contingent, for two reasons: the circumstances in which they might evolve were, by definition, unpredictable; and the obligations themselves would be modified by changes in the geopolitical environment or the perception of leaders. As a result, de Gaulle was, on the one hand, among the most solid supporters of the Atlantic Alliance when there was an actual Soviet challenge to the international order, as during the Cuban Missile Crisis in 1962 or the Soviet ultimatum over the status of Berlin. But, on the other hand, he never abandoned his insistence on his country's freedom to judge the consequences of occasions as they arose.

The American concept of NATO preserved the peace of the world for over a half-century. US presidents treated alliances as a form of legal contract to be implemented on the basis of a quasi-legal analysis of the Alliance's terms. The contract's essence lay in the uniformity of the promised response to a challenge seen as undifferentiated with respect to the Alliance as a whole. For de Gaulle, the essence of alliances resided in the soul and the convictions of his country.

President Nixon put an end to the theoretical controversies over control of nuclear weapons, and tensions between France and the US substantially subsided. Thereafter, the autonomous French nuclear forces developed without harassment from the United States and with occasional assistance when compatible with US law. While the French Fifth Republic has launched a number of conventional military operations – especially in Africa and the Middle East – it has never threatened to use its nuclear weapons independently, and US and French nuclear policies have ranged from compatible to coordinated. Continuing on the path set by de Gaulle, France has preserved its national objectives by choosing autonomy.

THE END OF THE PRESIDENCY

By the end of the 1960s, de Gaulle had revived France, rebuilt its institutions, removed the blight of the Algerian war and become a central participant in a new European order. He had placed France in a position to prevent international policies with which it felt uncomfortable, while fostering a set of arrangements to whose management France had become indispensable. Richelieu had originated this style of statecraft in the seventeenth century; in the twentieth, de Gaulle had revived it.

After ten years in the presidency, de Gaulle had achieved the historical tasks available to him and was left with the management of day-to-day events. But such mundane matters were not what had motivated his legendary journey. Observers began to detect the settling-in of boredom, almost melancholy. In 1968, then-Chancellor of Germany Kurt Georg Kiesinger told me of a conversation in which de Gaulle hinted at a resignation: 'For centuries, we and the Germans have traversed the world, usually competitively, looking for a hidden treasure, only to find that there is no hidden treasure, and only friendship is left to us.' Speculation began about another withdrawal from public life and a possible succession.

But history would not permit de Gaulle's odyssey simply to peter out. In May 1968, a student revolt that grew into a general protest – one expression of a Europe-wide movement – consumed much of Paris. Students occupied the Sorbonne, where they festooned windows and columns with Maoist posters.[136] They erected barricades in the Latin Quarter and engaged in street battles with police. Everywhere graffiti proclaimed the protesters' anarchic sensibilities: 'It is forbidden to forbid.'[137] Emboldened by the students, and sensing government dithering, the trade unions launched a nationwide strike.

The end of the de Gaulle presidency seemed imminent. Pierre Mendès-France and François Mitterrand – two vestiges of previous regimes – began exploratory talks for succession, with the latter slated as president and the former as prime minister. Prime Minister Georges Pompidou initiated negotiations with the protesters, though to what end – whether to arrange a transition or to replace de Gaulle – has never been clear. In Washington, Secretary of State Dean Rusk informed President Johnson that de Gaulle's days were numbered.

But de Gaulle had not designed the state as the central element of France's revival to permit his authority to be dissolved in Third Republic-style maneuvers. On May 29, a Wednesday, he suddenly left Paris with his wife and flew to Baden-Baden to meet with General Jacques Massu, commander of the French Cold War garrison in West Germany.

Massu had been commander of French paratroopers in Algeria and had every reason to feel betrayed by de Gaulle. Moreover, de Gaulle had actually dismissed him from his command for stating publicly that he would not automatically carry out the orders of the head of state. But in Algeria he had also been exposed to the national myth with which de Gaulle had infused his actions and which proved sufficiently powerful to restore Massu's allegiance. When de Gaulle hinted at resignation, Massu replied that it was his duty not to abandon the arena and to prevail. The president had no right to flee when the battlefront was inside France. A time to resign might come, but it was not now; duty demanded that he carry on the struggle – an enterprise in which he had Massu's full support.*

With this reassurance in hand, de Gaulle flew back to Paris and reinstated governmental authority – largely without the use of force. As during his rise to the leadership of France a decade earlier, he chose to challenge the political structure by an appeal to the French public – this time by calling for a new national election rather than by assuming emergency powers – and even though Massu's support had provided him with a last recourse to the army (which he never needed to invoke).

The following day, de Gaulle addressed a massive demonstration at the Place de la Concorde, involving at least 400,000 people who had gathered on behalf of public order. Leaders of the Free French, the Third and Fourth Republics and the Resistance all rallied behind de Gaulle and, by extension, the constitutional order of the Fifth Republic. Paris had not seen such an expression of unity since the march in August

---

* A mystery remains about the Baden-Baden trip. De Gaulle had ordered that the German government be notified of his presence. And reliable witnesses have testified that baggage for the family was on the airplane. In the event that he failed to persuade Massu, did de Gaulle plan to stay for an interval while he allowed the Pompidou negotiation to proceed? It is inconceivable that de Gaulle would have gone into permanent exile in Germany. It is more likely that without Massu he would have awaited the outcome of Pompidou's negotiation and returned afterwards to deal with chaos or internal exile (if Pompidou brought it off). See 'Secrecy Marked de Gaulle's Visit', *New York Times*, June 2, 1968; Henry Tanner, 'Two Tense Days in Elysée Palace', *New York Times*, June 2, 1968.

1944 that de Gaulle had led down the Champs-Élysées on the day after the city's liberation.

Pompidou, reading the signals on the day after the rally, promptly offered his resignation. Then, a day later, he attempted to withdraw it – only to be told by an aide of de Gaulle's that Maurice Couve de Murville had just been appointed in his place an hour earlier. In the subsequent election, the supporters of de Gaulle achieved an over-whelming majority – the first absolute majority for one political grouping in the entire history of the French Republics.[138]

The sole challenge remaining for de Gaulle was the management of his exit. To assert that the office had become too taxing was incompat-ible with the posture that had transported him from low-ranking brigadier general to the realm of myth. But retirement after political defeat was similarly incompatible with that myth.

De Gaulle chose as his vehicle a technical issue. A national refer-endum had been called regarding two provincial-reform measures that had for some time lingered on the legislative calendar. Though neither was of constitutional significance, de Gaulle announced a preference in the wording of each measure that was difficult to rec-oncile with the other. The referendum was scheduled for April 27, 1969, a Sunday. Before leaving for his regular weekend retreat in Colombey-les-Deux-Églises, de Gaulle ordered that his possessions and papers be packed.

De Gaulle announced from Colombey that he was resigning the presidency the day after losing the referendum, offering no explanation. He would never return to the Elysée Palace or make any public state-ment. When asked later why he had chosen these particular issues as the occasion for retiring from office, de Gaulle replied: 'Because of their triviality.'

My last encounter with de Gaulle had occurred four weeks earlier in connection with the funeral of President Eisenhower in March 1969. De Gaulle announced his intention to be present, and Nixon asked me to meet him at the airport on the president's behalf. He arrived around 8 p.m., which would have made it 2 a.m. Paris time. He seemed very tired. I informed him of a few technical arrangements Nixon had made to facilitate his travels, especially in arranging communications for him. I spoke in English, and he replied in English, which he employed on only the rarest occasions: 'Please thank the president for how he welcomed me and for all the courtesies he has extended.' There was no further conversation.

The next day, de Gaulle spent an hour with Nixon and then attended a reception at the White House for foreign leaders and Washington dignitaries attending the funeral. Some sixty heads of state and prime ministers were present, along with members of Congress and other American leaders. Quite a few of the Washington contingent were liberals, not in principle very enthusiastic about de Gaulle.

When the reception was already well under way, de Gaulle arrived in the uniform of a French brigadier general. His presence transformed the character of the event. A scene of scattered groups engaged in random interchanges drew into a circle around de Gaulle, prompting my remark to an aide that I hoped de Gaulle would not move to a window lest the whole room tip over. He seemed to respond to comments and questions politely but with a minimum of commitment; he had come to pay the respects of France to Eisenhower, not for the purpose of chit-chat. After at most fifteen minutes, he went over to Nixon to express his sympathy and left the reception for the airport.

A month later, he retired. Twenty months afterward, he died.

THE NATURE OF DE GAULLE'S STATESMANSHIP

De Gaulle is often remembered by Americans today – if he is remembered at all – as a caricature: the egotistical French leader with delusions of grandeur, perpetually aggrieved over slights real and imagined. As often as not, he was a thorn in the side of his peers. Churchill occasionally raged about him. Roosevelt schemed to marginalize him. In the 1960s, the Kennedy and Johnson administrations constantly feuded with him, believing his policy was one of opposition to American goals.

The criticisms were not without foundation. De Gaulle could be haughty, cold, abrasive and petty. As a leader, he radiated mystique, not warmth. As a person, he inspired admiration, even awe, but rarely affection.

Yet in his statesmanship, de Gaulle remains exalted. No twentieth-century leader demonstrated greater gifts of intuition. On every major strategic question facing France and Europe over no fewer than three decades, and against an overwhelming consensus, de Gaulle judged correctly. His extraordinary prescience was matched by the courage to act on his intuition, even when the consequences appeared to be political suicide. His career validated the Roman maxim that fortune favors the brave.

As early as the mid-1930s, while the rest of the French military was wedded to a strategy of static defense, de Gaulle grasped that the next war would be decided by motorized offensive forces. In June 1940, when almost the entire French political class concluded that resistance to the Germans was futile, de Gaulle made the opposite judgment: that sooner or later the United States and the Soviet Union would be drawn into the war, that their combined strength would eventually overwhelm Hitler's Germany, and that the future therefore lay on the side of the Allies. But, he insisted, France could play a role in the future of Europe only if it restored its political soul.

After the liberation of France, he again broke with his countrymen – recognizing that the emerging political system was a recipe for dysfunction. He therefore refused to continue at the head of the provisional government, abruptly resigning from the paramount position that he had so carefully carved out for himself during his wartime service. He withdrew to his home in Colombey-les-Deux-Églises, in the expectation that he would be summoned back if the political paralysis he predicted came to be.

That moment of opportunity took twelve years to arrive. Amid a looming civil war, de Gaulle engineered a transformation of the French state which restored the stability that had been missing throughout his lifetime. Simultaneously, for all his nostalgia about France's historic glories, he ruthlessly amputated Algeria from the body politic, having concluded that its retention would be fatal.

De Gaulle's statesmanship is singular. Relentless in its commitment to the French national interest, transcendent in its legacy, his career produced few formal lessons in policy making, no detailed guidance to be followed in specific circumstances. But the legacy of leadership needs to be inspirational, not solely doctrinal. De Gaulle led and inspired his followers by example, not by prescription. More than a half-century after his death, French foreign policy can still adequately be described as 'Gaullist'. And his life is a case study in how great leaders can master circumstance and forge history.

DE GAULLE AND CHURCHILL
COMPARED

The opening chapter of this book contains reflections on categorizing great leaders as either prophets or statesmen. The prophet is defined by his vision; the statesman by his analytical ability and diplomatic skill. The prophet is in quest of the absolute, and for him compromise can be a source of humiliation. For the statesman, compromise can be a stage on a road made up of comparable adjustments and accumulations of nuance but guided by the vision of the destination.

De Gaulle defined his goals in the visionary mode of the prophet, but his execution was in the mode of the statesman, steely and calculating. His style of negotiation was to act unilaterally to create a fait accompli and to conduct negotiations primarily over modifications of his purposes, not their alterations. He adopted this style even toward Winston Churchill, on whom he was totally dependent in 1940 for financial and diplomatic support and to whom he owed his position and his continuation in office.

It was one measure of Churchill's greatness to have recognized de Gaulle's ability immediately upon the latter's arrival in England without resources, arms, constituency or even language, and to have accepted him as leader of the Free French, then existing as a political force primarily in the imagination of this one Frenchman. He soon learned that that vision embraced a memory of centuries of militant rivalry between their two nations, and that de Gaulle considered British dominance in theaters adjacent to Europe, such as the Middle East or Africa, as regrettable, even offensive.

Nevertheless, and despite their occasionally serious conflicts, Churchill stood by de Gaulle on the key issues. Without his support, de Gaulle could not have survived the opposition of Roosevelt – which continued up to the gates of Paris.

Churchill supported the formation of the Free French as a vestige of his seminal and romantic experience of the French–British alliance in the First World War, which had culminated in Britain's offer to formally merge the two states as France stood at the edge of disaster in the Second. Churchill maintained and strengthened this commitment as de Gaulle evolved from a convenience to greatness.

Both of these giants of leadership possessed unusual analytical gifts and a special sense for the nuances of historical evolution. Yet they have left different legacies and drew from different wellsprings. Churchill grew out of participation in British politics; like de Gaulle, he understood his times and prospects better – and ran greater risks – than almost all his contemporaries. Because his vision outpaced his nation's understanding, he had to wait for highest office until the challenges faced by his contemporaries would confirm his foresight. When his hour at last arrived, he was able to lead his people through their direst period by his character, which attracted both respect and affection, but also because he saw the effort they were impelled to make as part of a continuum with British history, which he was able to evoke with unique mastery. He became the symbol of their endurance and triumph.

While Churchill viewed his leadership as enabling the British people to flourish and to culminate in their history, de Gaulle conducted himself as a singular event destined to lift his people toward an eminence that had been importantly dissipated. Defiantly out of joint with the times in which he lived, de Gaulle strove for consensus by proclaiming the moral and practical importance of a vanished grandeur; he appealed not so much to a historic continuum as to what had been, centuries earlier, and might again be. By this narrative, he helped France recover from its downfall and then led it to a new vision of itself. As André Malraux described him, he was 'a man of the day before yesterday and the day after tomorrow'.[139]

In the seventeenth century, Richelieu had devised the policy of a great state, but did so on behalf of a king whom he needed to persuade of the correct course. De Gaulle had to define the vision while he was in the process of implementing it, and it was the French people whom he had to convince at distinct stages. His statements do not therefore have the character of maxims; they are designed less to direct than to inspire. And he always referred to himself in the third person, as if his views were not his own but were to be perceived as expressions of destiny.

Though both Churchill and de Gaulle saved their societies and peoples, there was a fundamental difference in their styles of leadership. Churchill reflected the quintessence of British leadership, which is based on a high but not exceptional level of collective performance out of which, with good fortune, an exceptional personality can appear at a moment of great necessity. Churchill's leadership was an extraordinary emanation of a tradition, fitting to its circumstances; his personal style was ebullient and leavened by delightful humour. De Gaulle's leadership was not an elaboration of a historic process but a unique expression of a personality and of a special set of principles. His humor was sardonic, designed to stress the distinctness, as well as the distinctiveness, of its subject matter.* Where Churchill saw his leadership as the culmination of a historical process and a personal fulfillment, de Gaulle treated his encounter with history as a duty, one to be born as a burden separated from any personal satisfaction.

In 1932, the forty-two-year-old de Gaulle, then serving as a major in the French army far removed from a foreseeable personal eminence, sketched a concept of greatness as not for the faint of heart:

> Aloofness, character, and the personification of greatness, these qualities . . . surround with prestige those who are prepared to carry a burden which is too heavy for lesser mortals. The price they have to pay for leadership is unceasing self-discipline, the constant taking of risks, and a perpetual inner struggle. The degree of suffering involved varies according to the temperament of the individual; but it is bound to be no less tormenting than the hair shirt of the penitent. This helps to explain those cases of withdrawal which, otherwise, are so hard to understand. It constantly happens that men with an unbroken record of success and public applause suddenly lay the burden down . . . Contentment and tranquility and the simple joys which go by the name of happiness are denied to those who fill positions of power. The choice must be made, and it is a hard one: whence that vague sense of melancholy which hangs about the skirts of majesty . . . One day somebody said to Napoleon, as they were looking at an old and noble monument: 'How sad it is!' 'Yes,' came the reply, 'as sad as greatness.'[140]

BEHIND THE MYSTERY

Charles de Gaulle attracted admirers, who were useful to him, but a relationship with him implied neither reciprocity nor permanence.

* A comparable distinction can be seen in the country residences of Churchill and de Gaulle. Chartwell was a retreat where relaxed and sociable life could buttress intellectual fulfillment, and pleasant surroundings encouraged conversation with trusted friends. Colombey-les-Deux-Églises was an austere retreat for solitude and reflection.

He walks through history as a solitary figure – aloof, profound, courageous, disciplined, inspiring, infuriating, totally committed to his values and principles and vision and refusing to diminish them by personal emotion. While a prisoner of war in Germany in the First World War, he wrote in his diary: 'One must become a man of character. The best way to succeed in action is to know how to dominate oneself perpetually.'[141]

And yet. Reflecting on the passage of the seasons at Colombey, in the mid-1950s, de Gaulle ended his war memoir with a poem in which, for the only time in his writing, he used the personal pronoun: 'As age triumphs, nature comes closer to me. Each year, in the four seasons which are so many lessons, I find consolation in her wisdom.' Spring makes all bright, 'even the snow flurries', and turns everything young, 'even the wizened trees'. Summer proclaims the glories of nature's bounty. Nature retires in autumn, still beautiful in her 'robe of purple and gold'. And even in winter, when all is 'barren and frozen ... a secret labor is being accomplished', preparing the ground for new growth, perhaps even resurrection:

> Old Earth, worn by ages, racked by rain and storm, exhausted yet ever ready to produce what life must have to go on!
>
> Old France, weighed down with history, prostrated by wars and revolutions, endlessly vacillating from greatness to decline, but revived, century after century, by the genius of renewal!
>
> Old man, exhausted by ordeal, detached from human deeds, feeling the approach of the eternal cold, but always watching in the shadows for the gleam of hope![142]

De Gaulle's seemingly impenetrable armor masked a deep reservoir of emotion, even gentleness, which we can see most clearly in his relationship with his disabled daughter Anne.

Anne had Down syndrome, but Charles and Yvonne de Gaulle elected to raise her in their home, defying the contemporary practice of sending disabled children away to grow up in a psychiatric hospital. A photograph from 1933 captures the tenderness of their relationship: De Gaulle and Anne are seated on a beach, he aged forty-two, dressed in a dark three-piece suit and tie with a top hat lying at his side – in uniform even in civilian clothes – and she in white beach clothes. They appear to be playing patty-cake.

Anne died of pneumonia in 1948 at the age of twenty. 'Without Anne, maybe I never would have done what I did. She gave me the heart and the inspiration,' de Gaulle later divulged to his biographer Jean Lacouture.[143] After her death, he carried a framed picture of her in his breast pocket for the rest of his life.

De Gaulle died of an aneurysm less than two years after resigning the presidency, on November 9, 1970, at la Boisserie. He was, most appropriately, playing a game of solitaire. He was buried beside Anne in the parish churchyard of Colombey-les-Deux-Églises.

3

RICHARD NIXON: THE STRATEGY OF EQUILIBRIUM

THE WORLD TO WHICH NIXON CAME

Richard Nixon was one of the most controversial presidents in American history and the only president obliged to resign from office. He also had a seminal impact on the foreign policy of his period and its aftermath, as a president who reshaped a failing world order at the height of the Cold War. After five and a half years in office, Nixon had ended American involvement in Vietnam; established the United States as the dominant external power in the Middle East; and imposed a triangular dynamic on the previously bipolar Cold War through the opening to China, ultimately putting the Soviet Union at a decisive strategic disadvantage. From December 1968, when he asked me to serve as his national security advisor, to the end of his presidency in August 1974, I was a close collaborator to his leadership and decision-making. We stayed in regular contact for the remaining twenty years of his life.

At the age of ninety-nine, I return to Nixon not to rehearse the controversies of a half-century ago (which I have addressed in three volumes of memoirs), but to analyze the thinking and character of a leader who assumed office amid unprecedented cultural and political turmoil and who transformed the foreign policy of his country by embracing a geopolitical concept of the national interest.

By January 20, 1969, when Nixon took the presidential oath of office, the Cold War had reached full maturity. Commitments that the United States had assumed abroad during its postwar period of seemingly limitless power were beginning to prove beyond its material and emotional capacity to sustain. Domestic conflict over Vietnam was nearing an apex of intensity, spurring calls in some quarters for American military withdrawal and political retreat. Both the US and the Soviet Union were deploying missiles distinguished by enhanced payloads, improved accuracy and intercontinental range. The Soviet Union was nearing parity with the US in the number of long-range strategic nuclear weapons and, according to some analysts, might even be attaining strategic superiority, raising concerns about sudden doomsday attacks and an extended period of political blackmail.

In the months before Nixon's election in November 1968, the challenges his presidency would face began to take shape in three major strategic theaters: Europe, the Middle East and East Asia.

In August 1968, the Soviet Union, together with its Eastern European satellites, occupied Czechoslovakia, whose sin had been to liberalize its system within the Soviet orbit. In Germany, the Soviet threat to West Berlin – initiated by Premier Nikita Khrushchev's 1958 ultimatum to the Western occupying powers to remove their forces within six months – persisted, periodically recurring in the form of a threat by Moscow to blockade the beleaguered city. Europe and Japan, both of which had recovered from the devastation of war under the security umbrella of the US, began to compete economically with the US and to nurse their own sometimes differing perceptions of the evolving world order.

At the same time, the People's Republic of China (PRC) had become the fifth country to possess the world's most devastating weapons – after the United States, the Soviet Union, the United Kingdom and France – following a successful nuclear test in October 1964. Beijing swung between engaging with and withdrawing from the international system, training and financing Maoist guerrillas around the world, yet also, by spring 1967, withdrawing its ambassadors from nearly every country in the world amidst the upheaval of the Cultural Revolution.[1]

In the Middle East, Nixon faced a region in the throes of conflict. The Sykes–Picot Agreement of 1916, whereby Britain and France had agreed to subsume the territories of the faltering Ottoman empire under their respective spheres of influence, had led to the formation of largely Arab and Muslim polities that seemed, on the surface, members of a state system comparable to the one created by the Peace of Westphalia. But only on the surface: unlike the European territories still under the essentially Westphalian system, mid-twentieth-century Middle Eastern states did not reflect common national identities or histories.

Despite France and Britain's historical preeminence in the Middle East, each grew progressively less capable of projecting its power there after the bloodletting of the two World Wars. Local upheavals, initially sparked by anti-colonial movements, were being swept into larger conflicts within the Arab world – and between Arab countries and the state of Israel. The latter, having been recognized by most Western countries within two years of its independence in 1948, was now seeking recognition from neighbors that regarded it as inherently illegitimate and as occupying territory rightfully theirs.

During the decade preceding Nixon's inauguration, the Soviet Union began to exploit this gathering Middle East maelstrom and to exacerbate it by establishing ties with the authoritarian military regimes that had replaced the largely feudal governing structure left by the Ottoman empire. Newly equipped with Soviet weapons, Arab armies extended the Cold War into a Middle East previously dominated by the West, sharpening the region's disputes and intensifying the risk that they might unleash a global cataclysm.

Overshadowing all of these concerns as Nixon assumed office was the bloody stalemate in Vietnam. The preceding Johnson administration had dispatched more than 500,000 American troops to a region as remote from America culturally and psychologically as it was geographically. Over 50,000 more were still on the way there at the time of Nixon's inauguration. The task of extricating the United States from an inconclusive war – and of doing so under the most turbulent domestic circumstances since the American Civil War – fell to Nixon. The five years before his election had also witnessed domestic political controversy of an intensity without antecedent in postbellum American history: the assassinations of President John F. Kennedy, his brother (and then-Democratic presidential frontrunner) Robert and the pathbreaking civil rights leader Martin Luther King, Jr. Violent protests over Vietnam, and demonstrations against the assassination of King, racked the streets of US cities and shut down Washington for days on end.

American history is replete with raucous domestic controversies, but the situation confronting Nixon was unprecedented in that, for the first time, an emerging national elite had convinced itself that defeat in war was at once strategically inevitable and ethically desirable. Such a conviction implied the breakdown of the centuries-long consensus that the national interest represented a legitimate, even moral, end.

In some respects, this set of beliefs marked the reemergence of an earlier isolationist impulse, according to which America's 'entanglement' in foreign troubles was not only unnecessary for the nation's well-being but corrosive to its character. But now, rather than arguing that the nation's values were too elevated to countenance involvement in faraway conflicts, this new strand of isolationism held that America itself had become too corrupted to serve as a moral guidepost overseas. Proponents of this position, having secured a foothold – and eventually a near-dominant influence – in institutions of higher learning, viewed the Vietnam tragedy neither within a framework of geopolitics nor as an ideological struggle, but as the herald of a national catharsis that would spur a long overdue turn inward.

AN UNFORESEEN INVITATION

While teaching at Harvard University, I had also acted as a part-time foreign-policy advisor to New York Governor Nelson Rockefeller, Nixon's principal rival for the Republican nomination in both 1960 and 1968. In consequence, I did not expect any invitation to serve on the staff of the newly elected president. Yet such a call came, and I was offered the post of national security advisor, the second-highest-ranking presidential appointment not subject to Senate confirmation (behind the White House chief of staff). Nixon's decision to bestow such a responsibility on a Harvard professor with a record of opposing him illustrated both the president-elect's generosity of spirit and his willingness to break with conventional political thinking.

Shortly after his electoral victory in November 1968, Nixon invited me to our first substantive meeting at his New York transition headquarters in the Pierre Hotel. (I had encountered him only once before, fleetingly, at a Christmas party hosted by the formidable Clare Boothe Luce.) The meeting provided an occasion to review the current international situation via a thoughtful, relaxed promenade through major foreign-policy challenges, in the course of which Nixon shared his views and invited my comments. He offered no hint that the meeting was related to staffing his administration, let alone intended to assess my suitability for a particular position.

As I was leaving, Nixon introduced me to a lanky Californian whom he identified as his chief of staff, H. R. Haldeman; without explanation, Nixon then ordered Haldeman to establish a direct telephone link to my office at Harvard. Haldeman wrote down the president-elect's order on a yellow pad but proceeded to do nothing about it – thus providing, along with my introduction to the multifaceted personality of the incoming president, an advance lesson in the nature of bureaucratic conduct in a Nixon White House: some presidential statements were symbolic, suggesting a direction but not a call for an immediate action.

Intrigued but somewhat uncertain, I returned to Harvard to await developments. A few days later, John Mitchell, a law partner in the same firm as Nixon and on the verge of being nominated as attorney general, telephoned me with a query: 'Are you going to take the job or not?' When I replied, 'What job?', he muttered something that sounded like 'another screw-up' before inviting me to meet with the president-elect again the following day.

This time, the position of national security advisor was offered explicitly. Awkwardly, I requested some time for reflection and consultation with associates familiar with my previous political positions. Other presidents or chief executives I have known, hearing such a vacillating reply, would have relieved me of the need for reflection by ending the discussion then and there. Instead, Nixon told me to take a week and – touchingly – suggested that I consult Lon Fuller, his former contract-law professor at Duke, who was then teaching at Harvard Law School and was familiar with Nixon's way of thinking and conduct.

The next day, I consulted with Nelson Rockefeller, who had just returned from a trip to his ranch in Venezuela. Rockefeller's reaction not only put an end to any ambivalence but also demonstrated that there was still underlying unity in the country. He chided me for postponing my decision and urged me to accept Nixon's offer immediately; when the president invites you to important service, he observed, delay is not an appropriate response. 'Keep in mind,' Rockefeller added, 'that Nixon is taking a much bigger chance on you than you are on him.' I telephoned Nixon that afternoon to say that I would be honored to serve in his administration.

Nixon and I would eventually develop a relationship which, in its operational character, might have been described as a 'partnership' – although true partnership rarely exists when the power is so unequally distributed between the two sides. The president can dismiss his security advisor without procedure or warning and has the authority to impose his preferences without formal notice or discussion. And, whatever contribution the security advisor might make, the president bears the ultimate responsibility for the decisions.

These realities notwithstanding, Nixon never treated me as a subordinate when it came to issues of national security and foreign policy; rather, he dealt with me as a kind of academic colleague. The same regard did not extend to domestic policy or electoral politics. I was never invited to meetings on these subjects (except during the 'Pentagon Papers' episode, when classified Defense Department documents had been leaked).

Our relationship assumed this collegial form from the beginning. Throughout, Nixon avoided derogatory references about my previous association with Nelson Rockefeller. Even when he was under great pressure, his conduct toward me was invariably courteous. This consistent graciousness was all the more remarkable because, side by side with the decisive and thoughtful Nixon described in these pages, there was another Nixon – insecure about his image, uncertain of his authority and plagued by a nagging self-doubt. This other Nixon was accompanied by a version of Adam Smith's 'impartial spectator': that is, a second 'you', standing outside yourself, observing and judging your actions. Nixon seemed to me to have been haunted by such critical self-awareness all his life.

This part of Nixon involved a restless pursuit of approbation – a prize frequently withheld by the very groups that mattered most to him. Even within his established relationships, an element of reserve was palpable, while encounters outside his inner circle – particularly those involving persons of stature – were likely to be treated as demanding a kind of performance. Nixon's purpose was not always to communicate information; rather, his language was often meant to convey an impression of some end that had not necessarily been revealed to the other party.

Given these complexities, Nixon would, on occasion, make statements that did not reflect the full scope of his designs. This conduct should not be confused with indecision. He was clear about his goals and pursued them with determination and subtlety. At the same time, however, he often sought to preserve his options by selecting the most advantageous time and forum in which to debate them.

The combination of these qualities produced the special characteristics of the Nixon administration. Extremely knowledgeable, especially about foreign policy issues, and highly effective in presenting his analyses, Nixon nevertheless recoiled from face-to-face confrontations. Loath to transmit direct orders to disagreeing cabinet members, he would choose Haldeman or Mitchell for that task – or me, on issues of foreign policy.

Serving as an assistant to Nixon required an awareness of this modus operandi: Not every comment made or order issued by the president was intended to be interpreted or carried out literally. The instruction to Haldeman to install a direct phone line to my office at the end of our first meeting is one example: he wanted to convey to his staff that he was going to seek to add me to his team, but he was not yet ready to offer me the position in circumstances in which I might refuse it in the hearing of others.

Another more consequential example: in August 1969, an American airliner en route from Rome to Israel was hijacked by Palestinian terrorists and flown to Damascus. When I communicated the news to Nixon, who was enjoying a Saturday-evening dinner with old friends in Florida, he replied, 'Bomb the airport of Damascus.' Rather than serving as an official directive, this statement was intended to impress both his advisors and his dining companions with his determination to put an end to hijackings.

As Nixon well knew, however, initiating any such military action requires more than a simple order from the president. There needs to be a follow-up directive containing operational instructions to the implementing departments. In anticipation of such a follow-up decision, Secretary of Defense Melvin Laird, Chairman of the Joint Chiefs of Staff General Earle Wheeler and I spent much of the evening ensuring that preliminary steps for such a strike were taken – specifically, moving a Sixth Fleet aircraft carrier toward Cyprus to position it to carry out the order. Although a president's staff is pledged to execute his orders, it is also obliged to give him the full opportunity to reflect on the implications of his actions.

In this case, Nixon settled the issue the following morning. As part of his morning briefing, I updated him on the Damascus airport hostage situation, conveying that the Sixth Fleet's ships were now near Cyprus. 'Did anything else happen?' he asked. When I replied that nothing had, he responded with a single word – 'Good' – delivered without moving a facial muscle. Nothing further was said or done about the airstrike.[2]

Thus Nixon's immediate entourage learned that sweeping statements were not necessarily intended to result in explicit actions. Often, they conveyed a mood or were used to assess an interlocutor's views. To postpone irreversible actions until the president could make a considered decision, Haldeman set up a staff system seeing to it that Nixon's Oval Office meetings took place in the presence of a presidential assistant. The senior advisors, in turn, were obliged to pass on directives through the White House chief of staff. Trouble could arise when those with no regular contact with the president found themselves in his company as he debated his options on an issue with himself. Illustrative here is former Eisenhower aide – and friend of Nixon – Bryce Harlow's pithy explanation for the Watergate debacle: 'Some damn fool got into the Oval Office and did what he was told.'

Unsurprisingly, Nixon's own assessment of his qualities was less oblique than the foregoing account might suggest. Shortly after my July 1971 secret visit to China – and Nixon's announcement that he himself would make the journey the following year – Nixon sent me recommendations for briefing the press. Referring to himself in the third person, he wrote:

> One effective line you could use in your talks with the press is how RN is uniquely prepared for this meeting and how ironically in many ways he has similar characteristics and background to [Chinese Premier Zhou Enlai]. I am just listing a few of the items that might be emphasized.
> (1) Strong convictions.
> (2) Came up through adversity.
> (3) At his best in a crisis. Cool. Unflappable.
> (4) A tough bold strong leader. Willing to take chances where necessary.
> (5) A man who takes the long view, never being concerned about tomorrow's headlines but about how the policy will look years from now.
> (6) A man with a philosophical turn of mind.
> (7) A man who works without notes – in meetings with 73 heads of state and heads of government RN has had hours of conversation without any notes . . .

(8) A man who knows Asia and has made a particular point of traveling in Asia and studying Asia.

(9) A man who in terms of his personal style is very strong and very tough where necessary – steely – but who is subtle and appears almost gentle. The tougher his position usually, the lower his voice.[3]

That the note is evidence of both significant insecurity and determined self-promotion requires no elaboration. Yet Nixon's self-assessment was essentially accurate: he did have a wealth of foreign-policy experience; he was at his most effective in a crisis; he was bold but given to careful, occasionally excruciating deliberation and analysis; he had an enormous appetite for information; he took the long view, engaged in careful reflections about the nation's challenges and was often at his best in high-pressure, set-piece meetings with other world leaders – at least those involving presentation rather than negotiation. That he was preoccupied with the appearance of being in charge – to the point that he sometimes embellished the record – does not contradict the achievements of his administration.

Given the national stakes involved and the time pressure under which decisions often need to be made, no senior White House relationship can be entirely free of friction. In my own case, Nixon's insecurities occasionally led to presidential resentment when the media emphasized my contribution to national policy to the derogation of his own. The French philosopher Raymond Aron – my lifelong friend and intellectual mentor – once commented that the press's prominent coverage of my role served as an alibi for its hostility to Nixon. The resulting tensions were explicitly addressed only rarely – and, even then, never by Nixon himself, but by associates such as Haldeman or Domestic Affairs Advisor John Ehrlichman.

Nonetheless, I never experienced the kind of language which, I later learned, Nixon occasionally inflicted on others. When the transcripts of Nixon's Oval Office conversations became public, I called George Shultz (who had served as budget director and secretary of the treasury) to ask whether I had become so inured to profanity that I did not remember Nixon's use of it. Shultz's recollections were comparable to mine; in our dealings with him, Nixon's language was courteous and fastidious.

Nixon's handicaps – his anxiety, the insecurities that prompted his need to extract maximum respect, his reluctance to confront face-to-face disagreements – ultimately damaged his presidency. But the achievements of Nixon's career require recognition as a stupendous effort to transcend inhibitions that would have defeated a lesser leader.

NATIONAL SECURITY DECISION-MAKING IN THE NIXON WHITE HOUSE

Every White House establishes a framework for decision-making to facilitate the choices only the commander-in-chief is in a position to make. As soon as he was appointed chief of staff, Haldeman created a White House organization that enabled Nixon to balance his convictions and his inhibitions, obscuring his weaknesses while achieving a considerable measure of coherence.

Access to the president, as a general matter, was in the presence of one of two White House presidential assistants: Ehrlichman for domestic policy, me for national security issues. Our offices were responsible for preparing the president for each upcoming meeting, sketching both issues that might be raised and potential responses to offer. Nixon would study these recommendations carefully before meetings but never had notes in front of him during the actual conversation.

When Nixon and I were both in Washington, I was generally his first appointment of the day. I accompanied him on his foreign trips and attended every official meeting. When either of us was traveling domestically, we typically communicated by phone at least once a day. The first subject on our agenda was generally the Presidential Daily Brief, prepared by the Central Intelligence Agency. Absent a crisis, Nixon spent relatively little time on day-to-day issues and much more on the historical background or dynamics of a particular region or situation. He was always focused on what constituted potential turning points or key impending decisions. During these discussions, which frequently extended over many hours, the strategic thinking of the Nixon administration was shaped.

Having served as Eisenhower's vice president, Nixon sought to replicate his predecessor's national security procedures while adapting them to his requirements. To that end, he asked General Andrew Goodpaster, who for a period had coordinated Eisenhower's National Security

Council, to work with me in setting up a comparable structure.[4] Under Eisenhower, NSC staff had essentially prepared for meetings by collecting departmental views. During the subsequent Kennedy and Johnson periods, the Goodpaster staff was transformed by McGeorge Bundy and Walt Rostow to about fifty professionals, including academics, who participated in substantive preparations for the NSC meetings. In the Nixon administration, it retained a similar size; in the contemporary period, it has grown to as many as 400.[5]

When, early during the presidential transition, Goodpaster and I called on Eisenhower, then a patient with terminal heart illness at Walter Reed Hospital, I still harbored the notion (inherited from my Harvard days) that the former president's mind was as vague as the grammar he occasionally deployed in his press conferences. I quickly learned otherwise. He was familiar with national security issues in substance as well as their administrative ramifications. Eisenhower's facial features were vivid and expressive, exuding self-assurance produced by decades of command. His manner of speaking was forceful, direct and eloquent.

After welcoming Goodpaster, Eisenhower wasted no time in making his initial point. I might learn that he had not favored my appointment as security advisor, he said, because he did not consider academics adequately prepared for high-level decision-making. Nevertheless, he would give me whatever help he could. His assessment was that President Johnson's approach, in which the State Department had chaired the interdepartmental aspect of the national security process, had not worked because the Defense Department had resisted State leadership, and in any case State personnel were better suited to dialogue than strategic decision-making.

Eisenhower then outlined his recommendations, the essence of which was to place the national security operation under the White House security advisor. The security advisor or his designee would chair various regional and technical subcommittees. A committee at the deputy-secretary level should then vet the groups' deliberations for the National Security Council.

Goodpaster drafted these recommendations, and Nixon adopted them. The structure has remained essentially intact ever since. Within any given administration, however, intangibles of personality will inevitably affect the actual distribution of power.

During NSC meetings in which the designated cabinet officials (secretaries of state, defense and treasury as well as CIA director) were
present, Nixon was skillful at formulations that implied a desired goal
without committing to a particular implementation. Exploration of
options became his way of eliciting information about potential courses
of action without involving a confrontation over a decision; this
approach enabled the president to separate long-range policy from day-
to-day processes. It also permitted him to grasp the range of options as
if he were dealing with an abstract intellectual problem, independent of
personal preferences or departmental prerogatives. Wherever feasible,
Nixon's actual decision would be conveyed subsequently, when – I can
think of no exception – he would not have to confront any disagreement face to face.

Adopting Eisenhower's NSC plan facilitated Nixon's longtime determination to control foreign policy from the White House. A Decision
Memorandum issued in his name would announce his plan of action. In
particularly controversial situations – as, for example, in the 1970
incursion into Cambodia in pursuit of North Vietnamese divisions
stationed there – Haldeman or Attorney General John Mitchell personally reinforced the final decision to the relevant cabinet secretary,
indicating that it was beyond further discussion.

Nixon's inhibitions did not constrain his decisiveness. In moments of
crisis, he drove the process, if indirectly, via my staff. And at several key
points – such as during the 1972 response to North Vietnam's 'Easter
Offensive' against the South, or the October 1973 strategic airlift of
weapons and supplies to Israel during the Yom Kippur War – he intervened by issuing a direct order.

By January 1969, when Nixon took office, the nature of the American debate over Vietnam had undergone an upheaval. The early domestic
disputes about Southeast Asia had remained traditional: they concerned
disagreements over the means for achieving agreed-upon ends. Universities debated Vietnam at 'teach-ins', which took the good faith of the
opposing sides for granted. By the Johnson presidency, judgments of the
American conduct in Vietnam turned on precisely that issue of good
faith. Opponents declared the war immoral and contrary to traditional
American values. Their response was a challenge to both established
policies and the moral legitimacy of successive administrations – to the
point where some antiwar activists sought to undermine the very

operation of government through huge public demonstrations, sometimes for days on end. Another tactic was the massive leaking of
classified governmental information, justified by a definition of open
government incompatible with any element of secrecy.

'Secrecy', Nixon acknowledged in his memoirs, 'unquestionably
exacts a high price in the form of a less free and creative interchange of
ideas within the government.' But, he added, in some quantity it is
always necessary in affairs of state: 'I can say unequivocally that without secrecy there would have been no opening to China, no SALT
agreement with the Soviet Union, and no peace agreement ending the
Vietnam war.'[6]

In this connection, Eisenhower taught me an essential lesson about
serving in Washington. In mid-March 1969, when the former president
was clearly weakening, Nixon invited me to join in briefing his predecessor on a recent NSC meeting regarding the Middle East, which
had discussed the growing Soviet military presence in the region and the
balance in our response between diplomatic and other measures. As
he was in the process of coming to a decision, Nixon asked me to outline for Eisenhower the options discussed by the NSC.

The next morning, the content of the NSC meeting appeared in the
media. General Robert Schulz, Eisenhower's military aide, called very
early that morning to connect me with the former president. Unleashing
a torrent of expletives not commonly associated with his benign public
persona, Eisenhower castigated me for the constraint on Nixon's options
brought about by the leakage of NSC deliberations. When I asked
whether he thought my office had done the leaking, he went through
another catalog of invectives to underline that my assignment was to
protect the secrecy of classified information throughout the entire
national security system. I had not carried out that assignment if I con-
strued it as only applying to the security of my own office.

My reply – that we had been in office for only two months and had
done our utmost to control the leaking during that time – found no
greater favor. 'Young man' – I was then forty-six – 'let me give you one
fundamental piece of advice,' Eisenhower said in an almost fatherly
tone. 'Never tell anyone that you are unable to carry out a task entrusted
to you.' Those were the last words I heard from Eisenhower. He died
two weeks later.

NIXON'S WORLDVIEW

Nixon's assessments of the past and intuitions about the future were derived both from his substantial international experience as a political figure and his years of reflection while out of office. International travel in his position as vice president – and presumed future presidential candidate – had brought him into contact with world leaders who sought to understand American thinking and to gauge his own future prospects. In these circles he was treated as a serious figure – an attitude not always in evidence among domestic adversaries or journalists.

Nixon's convictions about foreign policy did not fit neatly into existing political categories. In his congressional career, he had been conspicuously engaged in the debate over the trial of the former State Department official and alleged Soviet agent Alger Hiss, whom much of the political establishment regarded as the victim of a 'witch hunt' – until (and even after) he was convicted of perjury and imprisoned. Thus, by the time Nixon was inaugurated, both conservatives and liberals had a well-formed conception of him. Conservatives saw him as a staunch anti-communist and hardline cold warrior, expecting him to display a confrontational style of diplomacy. Liberals worried he might initiate a period of American muscle-flexing abroad and domestic controversy at home.

Nixon's foreign-policy views were far more nuanced than his critics' perception of them. Molded by his experiences of public service in the navy during the Second World War, in Congress and as vice president, he was unshakably convinced of the basic legitimacy of the American way of life, particularly the opportunities for social mobility, as his own life personified. In keeping with the foreign-policy verities of the day, he believed in America's special responsibility to defend the cause of freedom internationally, and especially the freedom of America's democratic allies. In seeking to end the conflict in Vietnam, which he had inherited, he was driven by the specter of the impact of an American retreat on the nation's credibility as an ally but also as a power and presence in the world at large.

Nixon's view of America's international duties was put forward during an address on July 6, 1971, as he explained the US obligation in Vietnam in essentially nonpartisan terms, blaming neither his Democratic predecessors nor the antiwar left. He acknowledged and specified the then-prevalent criticisms of US policy:

the United States can't be trusted with power; the United States should recede from the world scene and take care of its own problems and leave world leadership to somebody else, because we engage in immorality in the conduct of our foreign policy.[7]

Accepting that the US had made initial missteps in Vietnam, as it had in other wars, he then asked the central question: 'What other nation in the world would you like to have in the position of preeminent power?' America was:

> a nation that did not seek the preeminent world position. It came to us because of what had happened in World War II. But here is a nation that has helped its former enemies, that is generous now to those that might be its opponents . . . that the world is very fortunate . . . to have in a position of world leadership.[8]

While Nixon reiterated his postwar vision of US global leadership, he challenged prevailing American foreign-policy assumptions. Then, as now, an important school of thought maintained that stability and peace were the normal state of international affairs, while conflict was the consequence of either misunderstanding or malevolence. Once hostile powers were decisively overcome or defeated, the underlying harmony or trust would reemerge. In this quintessentially American conception, conflict was not inherent but artificial.

Nixon's perception was more dynamic. He viewed peace as a state of fragile and fluid equilibrium among the great powers, a precarious balance that in turn constituted a vital component of international stability. In an interview for *Time* in January 1972, he stressed a balance of power as a prerequisite for peace:

> It is when one nation becomes infinitely more powerful in relation to its potential competitor that the danger of war arises. So I believe in a world in which the United States is powerful. I think it will be a safer world and a better world if we have a strong, healthy United States, Europe, Soviet Union, China, Japan, each balancing the other, not playing one against the other, an even balance.[9]

Any of the great British statesmen of the nineteenth century would have made a comparable statement about the balancing of power in Europe.

Although Europe* and Japan never did materialize as powers of comparable capacity during Nixon's period in office, 'triangulation' between China and the Soviet Union became a principle of US policy from Nixon's tenure until the end of the Cold War and beyond; indeed, it contributed importantly to the conflict's successful outcome.

Nixon placed his strategy into a specific American context. At the dawn of the twentieth century, Theodore Roosevelt (1901–9) had expressed the view that one day America would inherit Britain's role of upholding the global equilibrium – which was itself based on the experience of maintaining a balance of power on the European continent.[10] But subsequent presidents eschewed this kind of analysis. Instead, the vision championed by Woodrow Wilson (1913–21) became dominant – namely, that international stability must be sought by means of collective security, defined by the joint enforcement of international law: in Wilson's words, 'not a balance of power, but a community of power; not organized rivalries, but an organized common peace'.[11]

Nixon sought to restore the balance-of-power thinking of Theodore Roosevelt to American foreign policy. Like Roosevelt, he considered the national interest to be the defining objective in the pursuit of national strategy and foreign policy. Recognizing that national interests are often in tension with each other and not always reconcilable in so-called 'win-win' outcomes, he saw the statesman's task as identifying and managing those differences; this could be accomplished either by mitigating them or, when necessary and as a last resort, by overcoming them with force. In such extreme cases, he was prone to apply a maxim he frequently put to his associates: 'You pay the same price for conducting policy halfheartedly or hesitantly as for doing it the correct way and with conviction.'

In Nixon's foreign-policy vision, the United States should be the principal shaper of a fluid system of shifting balances. This role had no definable terminal point, but if America resigned from it, he believed, there would be global chaos. America's permanent responsibility was to participate in an international dialogue and to take leadership of that dialogue where appropriate. In his first inaugural address, Nixon therefore proclaimed a 'new era of negotiations'.

---

* Though Europe *cumulatively* was powerful, it was not a powerful *unity*.

DIPLOMACY AND LINKAGE

Nixon's foreign policy emphasized a twofold approach toward advers-aries: one was to build American strength and alliances, especially the Atlantic Alliance; the other was to maintain a constant dialogue with adversaries, like the Soviet Union and China, via the 'era of negotiations'. By linking geopolitical and ideological designs, Nixon sought to over-come two obstacles that had made it difficult for Americans to meet their international challenges.

In *Diplomacy* (1994), I would label these concepts the psychiatric versus the theological approach. The former holds that negotiations are ends in themselves, so that, once state adversaries meet face to face, their dispute may be dealt with as a manageable and potentially resolv-able misunderstanding, almost similar to personal quarrels. The theological approach conceives of adversaries as infidels or apostates and treats the very fact of negotiations with them as a kind of sin.[12]

By contrast, Nixon conceived negotiations as an aspect of overall strategy, part of a seamless web of relevant factors – among them the diplomatic, economic, military, psychological and ideological. Despite being a veteran anti-communist, Nixon did not regard ideological dif-ferences with communist states as barriers to diplomatic engagement. Rather, he viewed diplomacy as a preferred method for thwarting hos-tile designs and transforming adversarial relations into either engagement or the isolation of the adversary. Thus, the opening to China was based on the conviction that Mao Zedong's communist rigidities could be off-set by exploiting the Soviet threat to China's security. Likewise, during the October 1973 Arab–Israeli war, his conviction that Moscow's Middle East clients would be unable to achieve their regional objectives by force created a strategic and psychological opening to weaken Soviet influence and put America in the position to broker peace.

Nixon was never tempted by the conceit that establishing personal rapport with foreign leaders could transcend conflicting national inter-ests. 'We all must recognize that the United States and the Soviet Union have very profound and fundamental differences,' Nixon said during a 1970 speech to the UN General Assembly, explaining that to think otherwise 'would slight the seriousness of our disagreements. Genuine progress in our relations calls for specifics, not merely atmospherics. A true détente is built by a series of actions, not by a superficial shift in the apparent mood.'[13] Negotiating with ideological adversaries from a position of strength would lead to an order favorable to American interests and security aspirations.

Following these principles, Nixon early in his first term obtained congressional approval for national missile defense – an initiative that many regarded as a hawkish provocation of Moscow. Yet in the following decades, missile defense has proven an indispensable component of strategy. Similarly, when Soviet-backed and -equipped Syrian forces invaded Jordan in 1970, Nixon invoked a regional alert; and when Soviet Premier Leonid Brezhnev threatened intervention at the end of the Yom Kippur War in October 1973, he raised a global alert. Although he was adamant about containing the Soviet Union, his ultimate goal was to build a structure of peace. Explaining his perspective during the 1970 UN General Assembly, Nixon said, 'Power is a fact of international life. Our mutual obligation is to discipline that power, to seek together with other nations to ensure that it is used to maintain peace, not to threaten the peace.'[14]

Still, how was 'peace' to be defined and achieved? George Kennan, the visionary architect of the post-Second World War containment policy – along with Secretaries of State Dean Acheson and John Foster Dulles – had seemed content to wait out the Soviet Union by building up American strength, confident that history would eventually bring about a Soviet transformation or collapse. But two decades marked by tense thermonuclear stalemate, compounded by the trauma of Vietnam, had left the US in need of a more active strategy. Nixon's policy was designed to move Moscow and Beijing to accept the legitimacy of the international system and behave according to principles compatible with America's security interests and values by exploiting their differences via diplomacy.

Nixon described himself as a skilled negotiator. This was accurate with respect to big-picture discussions designed to draw an interlocutor into a strategic dialogue. But his reluctance to deal with direct confrontation disinclined him to engage in the reciprocal balancing and adjustment of nuances by which diplomacy operates.

In any event, negotiating detailed diplomatic settlements is a craft from which presidents would be well advised to refrain. Given the vast self-confidence needed to achieve their eminence, presidents as negotiators are likely to prove either too accommodating or too confrontational (or both) – the former when they rely on their ability to manipulate by personal charm, the latter when, drawing on the pressures that enabled their domestic rise, they equate diplomacy with confrontation.

A diplomatic deadlock between top leaders complicates any adjustment *within* the internal governance of both sides – another reason why detailed issues should be dealt with at lower levels, where technical expertise is more concentrated and accommodation less personally threatening. If only a few issues remain for the final phase, leaders will be liberated to crown a substantive outcome with symbolic adjustment and a celebratory flourish.

Nixon's strengths as a statesman resided at the two ends of geo-political strategy: analytical rigor in design and great boldness in execution. He was at his best in dialogues over long-range objectives and in efforts to draw his counterpart onto the edges of a strategic undertaking. While restless during face-to-face negotiations over the minutiae of strategic-arms limitations with Brezhnev at the Moscow summit of 1972, Nixon was eager to discuss principles of US–Chinese geopolitics with Zhou Enlai (and effective in doing so) during the Beijing summit that same year, laying the groundwork for a parallel US–China strategy to thwart the Soviet drive for global hegemony.

Nixon combined his attitude to negotiations with a strategy that was uncongenial to the foreign-policy establishment: linkage. On February 4, 1969, he sent a letter to Secretary of State William Rogers and Defense Secretary Melvin Laird emphasizing the new administration's approach.[15] Its essence was a dramatic move away from the previous administrations' tendency to compartmentalize seemingly disparate issues:

> I recognize that the previous administration took the view that when we perceive a mutual interest on an issue with the USSR, we should pursue agreement and attempt to insulate it as much as possible from the ups and downs of conflicts elsewhere. This may well be sound on numerous bi-lateral and practical matters such as cultural or scientific exchanges. But, on the crucial issues of our day, I believe we must seek to advance on a front at least broad enough to make clear that we see some relationship between political and military issues.[16]

The memorandum elicited unease, to put it mildly, among advocates of the prevailing view, which was to negotiate on issues as they emerged to prevent them from contaminating realms of potential cooperation.

Such an approach mirrored the government's departmental structure in which disparate departments and offices lobby for their preferred 'line of effort'. Nixon recognized that such segmentation ran the risk at that period of enabling the Soviet Union to prescribe the agenda and use negotiations as a cover to advance its imperial aims.

In the end, Nixon's approach powerfully altered the Soviet calculus. Three weeks after the announcement on July 15, 1971 of Nixon's intention to visit to China, he was invited to a summit in Moscow. In May 1972 – only three weeks after he had ordered the bombing of North Vietnam and the mining of Haiphong harbor, and three months after the summit in Beijing – a week-long US–Soviet summit in Moscow would demonstrate the Soviet Union's eagerness to stabilize relations with America. The Strategic Arms Limitation Treaty (SALT I), the Anti-Ballistic Missile (ABM) treaty and the Incidents at Sea Agreement were signed by Nixon and Brezhnev during that summit as steps toward the goal Nixon put forward in his first inaugural address: strengthening the 'structure of peace'. The 1974 Threshold Test Ban Treaty continued the process, as did the 1975 Helsinki Accords, which were agreed during the succeeding Gerald Ford administration.

These agreements highlighted another term – détente – that came to be associated with Nixon's foreign policy and evoked controversy. Derived from the French infinitive *détendre* ('to loosen'), and therefore shrouded in inscrutable implications, it implied a relaxation of tensions among the superpowers. The primary objection to it was the contention that American diplomacy should focus on undermining and eventually destroying the Soviet system and those of other adversaries. Contrarily, Nixon and I argued that declaring overthrow of the entire system as the defining objective would overshadow every controversy with the risk of an ultimate confrontation in an age of weapons of mass destruction and revolutionary technology in other fields. Instead, we favored a strong military position coupled with a diplomacy that achieved the defense of American strategic interests via multiple options.

Another purpose of détente was to give the Soviets a stake in key aspects of the US–Soviet relationship. Relations were to be fostered when Soviet conduct was responsible and reduced or modified in periods of stress. The approaches of strength and of diplomacy were kept on the table simultaneously and executed as part of the same strategy. As we shall see, the United States responded strongly to high-risk challenges, posing a maximum incentive for restraint by the other side – as in the Jordan crisis of 1970, the South Asia conflict of 1971 and the Middle East war of 1973. At the same time, it always kept open a vision of coexistence with adversaries.

A TRIP TO EUROPE

Nixon's first foreign trip as president took place a month after his inauguration, from February 23 to March 2, 1969. The proclaimed purpose was to 'restore a new spirit of cooperation' after differences over Vietnam and Middle East policy had strained America's relationship with its European allies.

But the trip's elevated purpose ran up against the complexities of Europe's growing quest for a new identity. While the continent had substantially recovered economically from the ravages of the Second World War, it was still only beginning the process of creating common institutions and remained far from its avowed goal of devising a common geopolitical strategy. For four centuries, Europeans' military prowess and contributions to political philosophy had shaped the world. Now, however, the nations of Europe, above all, feared Soviet pressures backed by military force. As a result, although the allies considered American military support via NATO indispensable, they were also moving to gain greater autonomy in shaping their political and, especially, economic future.

Nixon's first venture into foreign policy had been as a Congressman on the 1947 Herter Committee – a forerunner of the 1948 Marshall Plan. The committee's fall 1947 trip to Europe helped shape Nixon's lasting commitment to an organic link between America and the continent. At that time, Europe was eager for a deeper American connection. A quarter-century later, when Nixon became president, European leaders were still preoccupied with the continent's internal evolution, while only nominally committed to enhancing their political partnership with the US.

To complicate matters, within a year of Nixon's visit, every major European government would be replaced for domestic reasons. Two

months later, Charles de Gaulle – who had twice vetoed British membership in the European Community, the predecessor of the EU – retired
and was succeeded by Georges Pompidou. Likewise, Chancellor Kurt
Georg Kiesinger, our host in Germany, who basically followed the Adenauer course, would be replaced before the year was out by Willy
Brandt, who would adopt a more flexible policy toward the Soviet
Union under the aegis of *Ostpolitik*.* Prime Minister Harold Wilson,
our British host, would lose an election to the Conservative leader Edward
Heath, who would seek to put distance between London and Washington by giving greater priority to securing membership in a united
Europe than to fostering the UK's established ties with America. Nixon
therefore found himself on a journey to convey America's long-term
reassurances to a group of leaders focused on their domestic political
horizons.

Nor were these the only ironies attending his eight-day visit. Even as
his hosts encouraged him to initiate talks on nuclear arms control with
the Soviet Union and on ending the Vietnam War, they grew uneasy
when he accepted their recommendations on a broad basis. 'In due
course, and with proper preparation, the United States will enter into
negotiations with the Soviet Union on a wide range of issues,' Nixon
stated during remarks at NATO headquarters in Brussels, acknowledging that such talks 'will affect our European allies' though they would
be conducted by the United States on its own. With that in mind, he
stressed the importance of maintaining cooperation and unity: 'We will
do so on the basis of full consultation and cooperation with our allies,
because we recognize that the chances for successful negotiations
depend on our unity.'[17]

The address generated ambivalence. European allies welcomed support against the Soviet threat yet remained uneasy about what US–Soviet
negotiations might actually entail. Nixon's purported intention of
injecting diplomatic fluidity into a frozen international situation produced a mixture of approval and anxiety, while his call for 'genuine
consultation with the allies before the fact' raised questions about the
alliance's cohesiveness that have continued into our present moment.

The US relationship with Europe under Nixon evolved at a cooperative, consultative level, and Nixon's personal commitment to NATO

* See Chapter 1, pages 44–5.

was pervasive. Still deeper structural issues were explored but not resolved: what degree of cooperation was needed outside the Treaty area, for example in the Middle East or Asia? How much unity did the Alliance need amidst a fragmenting world and an exploding technology? How much diversity could it stand?

Part of the ambivalence can be ascribed to the Vietnam War, which European leaders generally perceived as a diversion from their own central security interests. Differential assessments of global risk between America and Europe created further challenges, such as the German *Ostpolitik*, which advocated a forward political approach to the Soviet Union.

A significant transformation of Atlantic relations occurred during the third year of the Nixon presidency in the economic field. The 1944 Bretton Woods agreement had established fixed exchange rates between foreign currencies and the dollar and allowed governments to exchange dollars for gold at $35 per ounce. It had worked well for two decades but by the late 1960s was coming under increasing strain.[18] As Western Europe and Japan recovered from the Second World War, they accumulated dollar reserves – $40 billion by 1971, compared with US gold reserves worth $10 billion. Lacking confidence in the US ability to sustain gold convertibility, foreign governments, led by France, demanded that ever more dollars be exchanged for gold.[19]

Nixon reacted with characteristic decisiveness. Over three days at Camp David in August 1971, he conferred with his economic advisors. Federal Reserve Chairman Arthur Burns sought to preserve the Bretton Woods system, while Treasury Secretary John Connally and Office of Management and Budget Director George Shultz favored an end to the dollar–gold link, with Shultz going so far as to propose a new system of floating exchange rates.[20] Siding with Connally and Shultz, Nixon judged that dollar–gold convertibility could not be preserved and that any attempt to maintain it would invite speculative attacks on the dollar. He announced a temporary suspension of dollar convertibility to gold on Sunday, August 15.*

Both this decision and the unilateral manner in which it was made unsettled some allies. France was strongly opposed to the suspension of

---

* That Sunday, I was traveling to Paris for negotiations with the North Vietnamese, described in Chapter 3, pages 155–60.

the link. French Finance Minister Valéry Giscard d'Estaing (later to become president) worried that, without the tether of the link, American economic inflation might spread throughout the global financial system.[21] On its part, West Germany was concerned that the sudden and unilateral change heralded a resurgence of economic nationalism.[22] To assuage these anxieties and develop the outlines of a new long-term monetary arrangement, Undersecretary of the Treasury Paul Volcker met with European counterparts.

These efforts culminated in the Smithsonian Agreement of December 1971, which devalued the dollar and established new exchange rates. But fixed exchange rates proved difficult to sustain without the gold standard, and the agreement fell apart by February 1973, leading the major economies to adopt floating exchange rates.[23] Despite initial fears, the system still endures. Nixon's dramatic decisions at Camp David shifted the global monetary order to a more flexible – but ultimately more sustainable – equilibrium.

In 1973, Nixon responded to the continuing debates over the monetary system as well as the European uneasiness about nuclear weapons and the Vietnam War by proposing the 'Year of Europe'. This involved a declaration of long-term partnership between Europe and the United States following the then-approaching conclusion of the Vietnam War.

In a speech delivered in New York in April 1973, I proposed, on behalf of Nixon, that the US and its European partners reach by the end of the year a statement of common purposes in both political and strategic fields – modeled on the Atlantic Charter signed by Franklin Roosevelt and Winston Churchill on August 14, 1941. The purpose was to bring the common security efforts up to date with technological development and to define common political purposes in light of the evolution of the crisis in different parts of the world. The proposal proved premature. Our allies were receptive to a restatement of strategic goals that involved their immediate security, but resisted global definitions of transatlantic political unity.

Nixon supported the NATO structure, vigorously defended the freedom of Berlin and achieved an enhanced status for that city, which put an end to more than a decade of crisis and threats to Berlin access. He also maintained a continuous political dialogue with NATO and the principal leaders of Europe. After his presidency, US initiatives outside the NATO area – as in counter-insurgency operations in Afghanistan or Iraq, for example – received European support, but more in order to maintain the American commitment to European defense against Russia than to express a common global purpose. Nixon's ultimate goal of an organic relationship with Europe on global issues has therefore remained on the agenda to this day.

THE VIETNAM WAR AND ITS CONCLUSION

By the time Nixon took office, the US had been involved in Vietnam for nearly two decades; as he was being inaugurated in January 1969, 30,000 American servicemen had already died in battle, and multiple antiwar protests, some of them violent, had taken place all over the country. At my first meeting with Nixon after the election at the Pierre Hotel, he emphasized that he was determined to end the war in Vietnam during his first term. He vowed to the families of fallen servicemen an outcome compatible with America's honor. He would seek to achieve it by a diplomacy of linkage with the Soviet Union. Conceivably his idea of an opening to China would also play a role. But he would not sell out. The security of free peoples, as well as international peace and progress, depended on restoring and eventually renewing American leadership. Military and political efforts had to remain concurrent.

The US had joined the defense of South Vietnam against communist insurgents by sending military advisors as early as the presidency of Harry Truman. Eisenhower increased American aid and augmented the number of military advisors attached to the US embassy in Saigon from 35 to nearly 700 by 1956.[24] Toward the end of his presidency, Eisenhower concluded that new supply routes being opened by North Vietnamese encroachment into Laos and Cambodia, two weak and neutral countries bordering South Vietnam, were progressively threatening the safety of Saigon and needed to be resisted.

This supply system, later dubbed the Ho Chi Minh Trail, stretched through rugged jungles along South Vietnam's 600-mile-long western border, rendering it difficult to discover, target or intercept. It had become the linchpin of the North Vietnamese strategy to undermine and ultimately overthrow the South Vietnamese government.

During the presidential transition of 1960, Eisenhower advised his successor, John F. Kennedy, to deploy American combat forces in the region and, if necessary, resist incursions into the neutral border countries. Kennedy did not immediately act on Eisenhower's advice, seeking instead a political solution via negotiation with Hanoi. The outcome was the 1962 International Agreement on the Neutrality of Laos. But when Hanoi later violated Laotian neutrality through increased infiltration, Kennedy responded by assigning 15,000 American troops to train and advise South Vietnamese combat units. Believing South Vietnam's autocratic ruler, Ngo Dinh Diem, lacked broad support and the political will to win, the Kennedy administration encouraged the country's military to replace him. That coup, which led to Diem's assassination on November 2, 1963, hollowed out the South Vietnamese government amidst a civil war in which, by definition, the besieged government is the principal prize. The North Vietnamese used this opportunity to introduce regular combat units to reinforce their guerrilla forces.

After Kennedy's assassination on November 22, 1963, Lyndon B. Johnson escalated US military efforts in Vietnam on the advice of the national security team he had inherited from Kennedy (the sole dissenter being George Ball, the undersecretary of state).* Johnson would soon realize, however, that the political ambiguities in the region were compounded by the complexity of devising a military strategy.

The sheer scale of the US deployment to so distant a location created an imperative for America to end the war quickly. But Hanoi's strategy was to protract the conflict so as to exhaust the Americans psychologically. In a contest between a mechanized army and jungle-based guerrilla forces, the latter enjoy the advantage, in that they win as long as they do

---

* In so doing, Johnson went with the prevalent school of thought that held that the communist challenges in Asia were of the same character as those in Europe during the 1940s and 1950s and therefore could be resisted by drawing secure lines behind which the threatened populace could rally in pursuit of its freedom. Unhappily, there was a critical difference between the two cases: European societies were essentially cohesive and thus able, once security was provided, to rebuild their historic identities. Indochina, by contrast, was ethnically divided and rent by civil war. Aggression was thus taking place not only across geographical dividing lines but also within civil society. In 1965, Mao's deputy Lin Biao issued a manifesto calling on the world's rural populations to rise up and defeat the cities. Both the Kennedy and Johnson administrations interpreted the communist challenge as a global crusade in which Indochina represented the first stage.

not lose. By January 1969, North Vietnam had consolidated the western third of Laos and portions of Cambodia out of reach of American power as bases through which it sent most of its supplies to South Vietnam – imperiling the southernmost portion of South Vietnam, including Saigon. It was thus in a logistical position to test American domestic endurance by applying a strategy which North Vietnamese Premier Pham Van Dong had told *New York Times* correspondent Harrison Salisbury was based on the belief that the North Vietnamese were more profoundly committed to Vietnam than the Americans – in essence, that more Vietnamese would be prepared to die for Vietnam than would Americans.[25]

Deadlock on the battlefield and growing casualties created a civic fracturing on the American home front. It began on college campuses during the Johnson administration as a debate over objectives and feasibilities. By the time Nixon took his oath of office, it had exploded into a confrontation over the relationship between American values and American methods: was the war just? If it was unjust, would it not be better to abandon the entire enterprise? While the latter position was initially considered radical, it soon became the conventional wisdom among broad swaths of the American elite.

American exceptionalism was turned on its head; the righteous idealism that had inspired and sustained the country's post-Second World War assumption of international responsibilities was now, in light of Vietnam, invoked in wholesale repudiation of America's global role. The crisis of faith ignited by Vietnam extended well beyond the war to the very character and essence of American purposes.

As college teach-ins dissolved into mass demonstrations, a point was reached where, in the election year of 1968, President Johnson was precluded from making public appearances except on military bases. Nonetheless, unilateral withdrawal from the war remained unpopular with the general public, and both Hubert Humphrey, the Democratic presidential nominee, and his Republican opponent, Richard Nixon, rejected unilateral withdrawal but campaigned on the promise that they would seek a way to end the war by negotiation.

Nixon was not explicit about the method except to say that it would be a new approach; the Democratic *protest* platform spoke of withdrawals without specificity. The issue that split the Democratic party and produced riots at its presidential convention in August was over a plank urging the *mutual* withdrawal of both (American and North Vietnamese) military forces from South Vietnam. The size of the proposed American withdrawal, as envisaged by Senator Edward 'Ted' Kennedy and other dovish Democrats, was specified only as 'of a significant number'.[26]

From our first meeting, Nixon had insisted on an honorable outcome in Vietnam as a component of American world leadership. During the transition period after the election, we defined 'honorable' as giving the people of Indochina, who had fought for freedom, an opportunity to determine their own fate. By then, the domestic protest had moved to urging unilateral withdrawal; Nixon adamantly rejected this. In his view, the national interest required navigating between victory and retreat. Unconditional retreat, in Nixon's view, was the road to spiritual and geopolitical abdication; in other words, a severe impairment of American relevance to international order.

Once inaugurated, Nixon discovered practical reasons for rejecting unilateral withdrawal. The joint chiefs of staff estimated that it would take sixteen months to prepare for the removal of a half-million troops and their equipment. Even allowing that the chiefs' estimate was affected by their dislike of the idea altogether, the chaotic experience of removing 5,000 American troops from Afghanistan in 2021 demonstrates the potential disorder of unilateral withdrawal in war conditions. In Vietnam in 1969, American forces of over 150,000 faced at least 800,000 North Vietnamese – and a comparable number of South Vietnamese whose conduct, if they felt betrayed, might range from hostility to panic.

Therefore Nixon, as he had said during the campaign, resolved to implement a diplomacy via linkage with the Soviet Union. He pursued this strategy even in the face of a North Vietnamese offensive that began within three weeks of Nixon's inauguration – before he had made any major military move – leading to more than 6,000 American fatalities during the first six months of his presidency.[27]

Nixon sought by a combination of diplomacy and pressure to induce Moscow to cut off its support for Hanoi. My staff produced an exploratory diplomatic plan whereby we would submit the concessions we were prepared to make to the North Vietnamese, possibly via Moscow. Concurrently, they also developed options for military escalation (essentially consisting of a blockade and the resumption of bombing) under the code name 'Duck Hook'.* If our offer were rejected by

---

* I have no recollection or documentation of why or by whom this code name was chosen.

Moscow, Nixon would seek to impose it by military force. (As it happened, the military portions would be largely implemented three years later, in May 1972, in response to Hanoi's all-out 'Easter' offensive.)

Cyrus Vance, who had negotiated with North Vietnam for the Johnson administration, seemed receptive to the idea of being appointed special negotiator in the event that our proposal gained favor. With Nixon's approval, I put the concept (without details) to Anatoly Dobrynin, the Soviet ambassador to the United States. We never received an answer from Moscow, but in an August 1969 meeting – my first with the North Vietnamese – Deputy Foreign Minister Xuan Thuy volunteered his awareness of the proposal by rejecting it on the ground that Hanoi would never negotiate through a third party.

While the diplomatic track was being considered, Nixon put before the world a comprehensive strategic concept for Southeast Asia on July 25, 1969.[28] For the site of his address, he chose the unlikely location of the Western Pacific island of Guam during an afternoon stop on an around-the-world trip – shortly after greeting the American astronauts who had just returned from the moon.

In a seemingly extemporaneous statement at a press conference – in fact carefully prepared at the White House and refined en route – Nixon presented his Southeast Asia policy as a way of emphasizing American relationships with regional partners. Invoking the dangers posed by communist China, North Korea and North Vietnam, Nixon proceeded to argue that the United States 'must avoid the kind of policy that had made countries in Asia so dependent on us that we are dragged into conflicts such as the one we have in Vietnam'. The traveling press inevitably asked for more detail, which Nixon had come prepared to supply. He responded:

> I believe that the time has come when the United States, in our relations with *all of our Asian friends*, should be quite emphatic on two points: one, that we will keep our treaty commitments . . . but, two, that as far as the problems of internal security are concerned, as far as the problems of military defense, except for the threat of a major power involving nuclear weapons, that the United States is going to encourage and has the right to expect that this problem will be increasingly handled by, and the responsibility for it taken by, the Asian nations themselves.[29]

What came to be known as the 'Nixon Doctrine' contained three essential principles:

- The United States would keep all of its treaty commitments.
- It would provide a shield if a nuclear power threatened the freedom of a nation allied with us, or of a nation whose survival the United States considered vital to our security and the security of the region as a whole.
- In cases involving other types of aggression – that is, conventional aggression by non-nuclear powers – the US would furnish military and economic assistance when requested. But it would look to the nation directly threatened to assume the primary responsibility of providing the manpower for its defense.[30]

Under 'Vietnamization', as it came to be called, the US would by the third of these principles provide military equipment and training as well as continued air support to enable Saigon to hold on until it was strong enough to defend itself alone. The purpose of the Nixon doctrine was to demonstrate American resolve and evoke sufficient South Vietnamese capability to enable Hanoi to agree to a political outcome that would permit the people of South Vietnam to determine their own future.

Nixon pledged to keep American commitments to treaty allies, such as South Korea and Thailand, but also to defend other nations in Asia that were threatened by nuclear powers, implicitly China and the Soviet Union. Where he departed from his predecessors was in tying the level of American assistance to the threatened nations' assumption of responsibility for their own defense. An underlying purpose was to reassure countries that had based their survival on faith in America's role that negotiations to end the war in Vietnam would not mark a strategic retreat from Asia.*

Meanwhile, a formal negotiation with North Vietnam had been established at the very end of Johnson's presidency and continued during Nixon's. Under it, representatives of Hanoi, the US, the Saigon administration and the South Vietnamese National Liberation Front

---

* In June, just before Nixon's departure for his trip around the world, a withdrawal of 30,000 troops had been announced. This reduction was designed to prepare the ground for the Guam statement, but likely came too early in the strategy.

would meet for weekly sessions at the Hotel Majestic in Paris. Hanoi never regarded these talks as part of a diplomatic process, but rather as another stage in its psychological strategy to undermine American will and overthrow the 'illegitimate' South Vietnamese government.

In these negotiations, which had been announced with so much hope by President Johnson in the last days of the 1968 presidential campaign, Hanoi's objective was twofold: with respect to the government of South Vietnam, to delegitimize it by first refusing to deal with it at all, then insisting that the communist National Liberation Front be the South Vietnamese negotiating partner. After a compromise enabling both of the South Vietnamese claimants to legitimacy to join the formal negotiations, Hanoi refused to discuss any substantive issues at all. Its objective remained to procrastinate until exhaustion or domestic discord would force the United States to abandon its South Vietnamese ally. The official forum at the Hotel Majestic, where the North Vietnamese were led by Xuan Thuy, achieved the unusual feat that in four years of so-called negotiations it made no progress whatever, leaving behind only a succession of empty formal statements.

By the summer of 1969, Nixon had explored the Moscow channel to achieve what we considered an honorable outcome. But before adopting the option of increasing pressure he decided to make another effort to jumpstart negotiations. It had two parts, detaching me from an around-the-world trip to meet in Paris on August 4, 1969 with Xuan Thuy. This was a first clandestine meeting, which by the following April had become a secret channel between Le Duc Tho and me.

France was the only NATO country to maintain diplomatic relations with Hanoi, and the meeting had been arranged by Jean Sainteny, the French ambassador to Hanoi. Sainteny's wife had become a personal friend after spending three months at the international seminar I taught at Harvard's summer school. As a result, the first secret meeting between the Nixon White House and Vietnamese officials took place in Sainteny's elegant apartment on the rue de Rivoli. He introduced us to the Vietnamese with the injunction not to break any furniture.

A discussion followed that previewed the next three years of deadlock. Xuan Thuy delivered a discourse on the epic nature of the Vietnamese struggle for independence and Hanoi's determination to pursue it to the end. I would hear repetitions countless times over the coming years, concluding with a statement of Hanoi's preconditions. I, in turn, explained our willingness to negotiate on the basis of a political process in which all groups – including the communists – could participate.

Nixon had instructed me to use the occasion for a bold step: I was to convey that if we received no meaningful response to our proposal in either negotiating channel by November 1, we would have to consider other than diplomatic measures – implying military force. Xuan Thuy, who like all Vietnamese negotiators I encountered conducted himself with impeccable courtesy, responded by repeating Hanoi's precon-ditions: withdrawal of all American forces and overthrow of the Saigon government before any meaningful negotiations.

Since Nixon had no intention to discuss such terms, he decided to repeat the ultimatum to Soviet ambassador Dobrynin at the White House on October 20. Pulling a yellow legal pad from his desk in the Oval Office, Nixon handed it to the ambassador, saying, 'You'd better take some notes.'[31] Dobrynin asked clarifying questions and pleaded ignorance as to the substance. To underscore the deadline to Moscow and Hanoi, Nixon went so far as to schedule a speech on Vietnam for November 3, emph-asizing the deadline. It turned out to be one of his most eloquent.

Defying protests that had paralyzed Washington for weeks, Nixon appealed to the 'great silent majority' in America to stand fast for an honorable peace:

> Let historians not record that when America was the most powerful nation in the world, we passed on the other side of the road and allowed the last hopes for peace and freedom of millions of people to be suffo-cated by the forces of totalitarianism.
>
> And so tonight – to you, the great silent majority of my fellow Americans – I ask for your support.[32]

But now, for the only time in my association with Nixon, he stepped back from a course he had proclaimed. As we were approaching the November deadline without a Hanoi change in attitude or presidential decision of consequence, I wrote two memoranda on the principle that the security advisor owes the president an analysis of matters of con-sequential decisions.

The first memorandum inquired whether Vietnamization could in fact achieve our agreed objectives. The second memorandum a day later analyzed the incentives for a diplomatic solution in the existing strategy.[33] Nixon decided to stay his de facto course.

Avoiding the military escalation he had threatened and for which his staff was preparing, but also the unilateral withdrawal demanded by Hanoi and the domestic protestors, he essentially opted for the 'Vietnamization' process that he had outlined in his Guam press conference. In his November 3 speech, he would describe his strategy as a progressive withdrawal of US troops while negotiations continued – holding on until Saigon was strong enough for a political outcome that would permit the people of South Vietnam to determine their own fate. Vietnamization as developed by Secretary of Defense Melvin Laird – and announced by Nixon – involved a process of gradual withdrawal of American forces and their replacement by South Vietnamese troops. By the time of the speech, the withdrawal of some 100,000 US forces was already being implemented.

At the time, I was uneasy with Nixon's decision. Over the years, in reflecting on the alternatives, I have concluded that Nixon had chosen the wiser course. Had he followed his first instincts, he would have had a cabinet crisis, compounded by national paralysis from protest demonstrations in major cities. The opening to China was still only an idea; the first reply from Beijing had not yet been received.* The Soviet Union had not yet been faced down in the Middle East or over Berlin, and negotiations with it were still in an exploratory stage. Also, earlier in that crucial year, our European allies had displayed their distaste for war in Southeast Asia during Nixon's trip to Europe.

So, despite my initial reservations, I implemented Nixon's decision in the years to come with conviction. Both Nixon and I were convinced that the stability of the evolving international structure had to be buttressed by American strategic credibility – not squandered, especially when it came to China and Russia. The scorn of the elites notwithstanding, Nixon strove to deliver on his promises to America's 'silent majority', both to avoid a humiliating defeat in Vietnam *and* to cease sending their sons into inconclusive combat. Whether these objectives were compatible was at the heart of an ongoing national debate, prompting constraints imposed by an atmosphere of upheaval on campuses and in the streets as well as constant reflection in Nixon's entourage.

* See Chapter 3, pages 170–71.

As for Hanoi, it had not fought for decades against both France and America for the sake of a political process or a negotiated compromise, but to achieve a total political victory. To explore every avenue of negotiations, Nixon now resumed secret political talks with Hanoi. Hanoi would send its chief negotiator and Politburo member Le Duc Tho to Paris, where I would connect with him every three months or so. But these meetings were substantive only in comparison with the formal negotiations and, even then, not significantly. In each session, Le Duc Tho would read a statement listing alleged American transgressions against Vietnam. Hanoi's minimum and maximum terms remained identical: that the Saigon government be replaced by peace-loving personalities and all American troops be withdrawn as a prelude to negotiations. When we explored his definition of 'peace-loving', it turned out that no established South Vietnamese political figure met his criteria.

Nixon did not budge. Two years later, on January 25, 1972, to the amazement of the media, which had long accused him of neglecting the peace process, he published the record of my two years of secret negotiations with Le Duc Tho. In a speech that same evening, he put forward what was essentially a final offer, combining a ceasefire, South Vietnamese self-government and American withdrawal, the strategy quietly adopted since the November 3, 1969 speech.[34]

Hanoi's response was to launch, on March 30, 1972, its 'Easter Offensive' against South Vietnam, deploying all but one of its combat divisions, during which it took a provincial capital, Quang Tri, for the first time since Nixon's inauguration. It must have calculated that America would not risk a summit scheduled for Moscow in May amidst military escalation during an election year.

By this stage, however, we were closing in on our objectives with Vietnamization: by the end of 1971, all combat units had been withdrawn. By the end of 1972, there would be fewer than 25,000 American troops remaining in the country, down from more than a half-million on the day Nixon took office. South Vietnamese ground forces, with American air support, were now conducting the entire battle repelling Hanoi's latest offensive. American fatalities had fallen dramatically from 16,899 in 1968, to 2,414 in 1971, to 68 in 1973, when the US withdrew its remaining troops after the Paris Peace Accords.[35]

The timing of the Easter Offensive had heightened the stakes of any action Nixon might take in response. His state visit to China had been a historic first step in transforming the Cold War; the Moscow summit meetings in late May would be another landmark event. The consensus in Washington advocated military restraint. Just as predictably, Nixon rejected that approach.

During an NSC meeting at the White House on the morning of May 8, 1972, the president acknowledged that escalatory retaliation could jeopardize the Moscow summit and the months of preparatory work that had gone into it. But doing nothing or being driven out of Vietnam ensured that we would enter negotiations with Moscow with a record of national abdication.

Addressing the nation in this spirit, Nixon laid out the American position – in essence, a reiteration of the peace offer he had made in January: a ceasefire and withdrawal of US troops in return for Hanoi accepting a Saigon government assembled through an agreed-upon political process. Nixon explained:

> There are only two issues left for us in this war. First, in the face of a massive invasion do we stand by, jeopardize the lives of 60,000 Americans [including civilian staffs], and leave the South Vietnamese to a long night of terror? This will not happen. We shall do whatever is required to safeguard American lives and American honor. Second, in the face of complete intransigence at the conference table, do we join with our enemy to install a Communist government in South Vietnam? This, too, will not happen. We will not cross the line from generosity to treachery.[36]

Following the maxim he frequently enunciated – that one pays the same price for doing something halfheartedly as for doing it completely – Nixon now ordered the package of measures originally designed in 1969, including the mining of the North's harbors and bombing of its supply lines wherever they were located, thereby abrogating the bombing-halt agreement in effect since 1968.

Moscow opted to ignore the challenge, and the summit took place as scheduled. While the Soviets condemned the escalation as well as the blockade, they confined their critique to one dinner at Brezhnev's dacha, issuing no threats and ending with Foreign Minister Andrei Gromyko and me resuming the SALT discussions that same evening. Shortly after the summit, the titular Soviet head of state, Nikolai Podgorny, visited Hanoi. No retaliatory actions were taken; Moscow had concluded that it could not abandon its efforts to balance our China initiative.

In July, our South Vietnamese allies recaptured Quang Tri. Hanoi was becoming isolated; neither the Soviet Union nor China came to its aid, other than by public protest. That same month, negotiations with Le Duc Tho resumed. While his formal positions remained unchanged, his tone had become somewhat more conciliatory. He raised questions exploring the speed with which a final agreement might be negotiated, assuming we made a breakthrough. Then, during a meeting on October 8, he suddenly introduced a formal document that he described as an acceptance by Hanoi of Nixon's final offer of January, stating: 'This new proposal is exactly what President Nixon has himself proposed: ceasefire, end of the war, release of the prisoners, and troop withdrawal.'[37]

That was essentially accurate, though many traps would emerge in the negotiations. Still the acceptance of the Saigon government as a continuing structure did meet one of our principal objectives. When Tho finished, I asked for a recess. After he left the room, I turned to Winston Lord, my friend and special assistant, shook his hand, and said, 'We may have done it.'*

Having procrastinated for nearly three years, Le Duc Tho behaved very differently now that Hanoi was eager to conclude negotiations before the looming US presidential election, after which it feared it might have to deal with a president reelected by an overwhelming majority.

Nixon was aware that in his second term he was likely to face a hostile Congress even now in the process of cutting off funding for the war effort. For a short moment, strategic calculations on both sides became parallel; the conflict had finally reached what scholars of negotiated settlements call 'ripeness'. As a result, Le Duc Tho and I spent three days and nights drafting a final text (subject to approval by Nixon and Saigon). Peace was tantalizingly close, with Hanoi pressing us to conclude our work immediately.

---

* Winston had been convinced not to resign in protest against the US incursion in 1970 against Hanoi's bases in Cambodia by my argument that he should choose between carrying a protest placard in front of the White House and staying for the time we would finish this operation together.

But neither Nixon nor I would end the war by imposing it on a people who had fought at our side for twenty years. And Saigon, aware that its struggle for survival would not end with a peace agreement, insisted on prolonged negotiations over details – in the process proving that the capacity for endurance was not confined to the North. But Saigon's procrastination had in fact a deeper meaning: the fear of being left alone with a determined enemy for whom the word 'peace' had only a tactical significance.

The situation was now exactly the reverse of what it had been through nearly all of Nixon's first term. Hanoi, pressing us to conclude an agreement it had evaded for a decade and to commit us to what we had discussed, published the entire text of where the negotiations stood. At a press conference on October 26, 1972, I explained the status of the negotiations, emphasizing that we remained committed to the negotiated endgame, which I introduced (with Nixon's approval) by using the phrase, 'Peace is at hand.' I ended with a paragraph designed to reflect both our urgency and our limits:

> We will not be stampeded into an agreement until its provisions are right.
> We will not be deflected from an agreement when its provisions are right.
> And with this attitude and with some cooperation from the other side we
> believe that we can restore both peace and unity to America very soon.[38]

After Nixon's re-election on November 7, Le Duc Tho, now judging time to be on his side, returned to his pre-breakthrough stalling tactics. By early December, Nixon concluded that Hanoi was trying to prolong talks into his second term and ordered an air campaign against military targets by B-52 bombers. It was widely criticized in the media, by Congress and internationally. But, two weeks later, Hanoi returned to the negotiations and agreed to modifications requested by Saigon. The Paris Peace Accords were signed on January 27, 1973; they included the principal terms Nixon had put forward a year earlier.

Nine nations – as well as the governments of Saigon and Hanoi and the South Vietnamese communists – formally endorsed the Accords, marking the pinnacle of Nixon's Vietnam policy.[39] By March, however, and in flagrant violation of the agreement, Hanoi once again began using the Ho Chi Minh Trail to infiltrate massive amounts of military equipment into South Vietnam. In early April 1973, Nixon decided on resuming an air attack on Hanoi's supply lines.[40] It was planned for

early April, when all American prisoners would have returned from
North Vietnamese captivity.

But then, in the middle of April, White House counsel John Dean
began cooperating with federal prosecutors regarding allegations of his
office's participation in wiretaps and other activities under investigation. This rapidly evolved into the scandal now known as Watergate.
Under its impact, congressional reservations turned into wholesale pro-
scriptions of military action in Indochina.

The Vietnam agreement had always depended on the willingness and
ability to enforce its provisions. It was based on the assumptions that,
during the 1972 North Vietnamese offensive, Saigon had demonstrated
its ability to withstand North Vietnamese military capacities so long as
it received the supplies allowed under the treaty (namely, one-for-one
replacements); and that, in case of an all-out attack, American airpower
would be available.*

Amidst the Watergate investigation, an exhausted public would not
support additional conflict in Indochina. Congress cut off military aid
to Cambodia altogether, condemning it to governance by the murder-
ous Khmer Rouge; reduced economic and military assistance to South
Vietnam by 50 percent; and prohibited all military action 'in or over or
from off the shores of North Vietnam, South Vietnam, Laos or
Cambodia'.[41] In these circumstances, enforcement of the limitations of
the Vietnam agreement became impossible, and restraints on Hanoi
disappeared.

With the Paris Accords, Nixon had brought his country to an outcome that merged honor and geopolitics, even though it was later
overwhelmed by domestic disaster. In August 1974, he resigned from
the presidency. Eight months later, Saigon fell to an invasion by the
entire North Vietnamese armed forces, including all combat divisions.
Aside from the US, none of the nine international guarantors of the
agreement so much as protested.

The Vietnam War initiated an internal division of American society
that has torn it to this day. The conflict introduced a style of public
debate increasingly conducted less over substance than over political

* Comparable assumptions had governed, and sustained, the Korean Armistice Agreement
of 1953.

motives and identities. Anger has replaced dialogue as a way to carry out disputes, and disagreement has become a clash of cultures. In the process, Americans have stood in danger of forgetting that societies become great not by factional triumphs or the destruction of domestic adversaries, not by victories over each other, but by common purpose and reconciliation.

GREAT POWER DIPLOMACY AND ARMS CONTROL

Nixon's significance as a statesman derives from his fundamentally geostrategic approach. Following his early 1969 trip to Europe, he began a diplomatic offensive to weaken Moscow's control over its Eastern European satellites by drawing them individually into the orbit of American diplomacy.

By August of that same year, having proposed a meeting with Nicolae Ceaușescu, the autocratic leader of Romania, he became the first US president to visit a member of the Warsaw Pact. So eager was Ceaușescu for the symbolism of an American presidential presence that he postponed the Communist Party Congress previously scheduled for Nixon's proposed date and cancelled a visit by the Soviet leader Leonid Brezhnev, who had planned to attend the Congress. Placards welcoming Brezhnev to Romania were taken down or painted over.

Nixon was greeted by a rapturous public, partly stage-managed to advance Ceaușescu's own effort to achieve autonomy within the Soviet orbit, but also reflecting the Romanian people's yearning for national freedom. (As part of Nixon's entourage, I was the beneficiary of communist leadership luxuries: a large suite with an indoor swimming pool.) Nixon encouraged these positive emotions in his toast, in public comments and, above all, in his conversations with Ceaușescu. He also used Ceaușescu as a means to open a dialogue with China by telling him of his interest in such a project. We found out five months later that this had been transmitted to Beijing, which occasionally thereafter used Romania – sparingly – as an alternative channel to Washington.

Nixon's strategic goal was to increase the cost to the Soviets of maintaining their European empire to the point where their continuing to do so would necessitate the diversion of funds and attention from other key objectives. In the course of his presidency, Nixon would visit additional Eastern European countries seeking autonomy from Moscow, including Yugoslavia in 1970 and Poland in 1972. When Willy Brandt became West Germany's first Social Democratic chancellor, the White House acquiesced to the outlines of *Ostpolitik*, his initiative intended to normalize relations with East Germany, the Soviet satellites and ultimately the Soviet Union. Nixon went along with this deviation from Adenauer's policy during the early days of the Brandt chancellorship while committing Brandt to the processes of allied consultation. We sought to keep *Ostpolitik* compatible with NATO objectives and achieve leverage on Soviet designs. This strategy proved effective for both the United States and the Federal Republic.

At the end of his first month as president and just before his trip to Europe, Nixon invited Ambassador Anatoly Dobrynin to the Oval Office and conveyed his willingness to deal directly with Soviet leaders. A few days later, the president designated me as the principal channel for communications with the Soviet ambassador on sensitive issues.

This arrangement established a pattern for the remainder of Nixon's term in office. Direct contact with Moscow was established through what was labeled 'The Channel', a Kissinger–Dobrynin conduit that ran from Nixon to the Soviet leadership. One of the principal topics turned out to be the impact of the two countries' vast stores of nuclear weapons on world order – and how to prevent them from setting off a global catastrophe, either in preemption or in an escalating conflict between them.

As vice president during the Eisenhower administration, Nixon had reflected on the impact of nuclear technology on strategy – considering both how to react to nuclear threats and how such fearsome weapons might theoretically be employed. He inherited the doctrine of massive retaliation, which based nuclear deterrence on the capacity to inflict damage believed to be unacceptable to an opponent. Subsequently modified to 'mutual assured destruction', this concept sought to reduce a paralyzing dilemma to a sober calculation on both sides of the risks of escalation. In practice, however, this theory – as a calculation of 'acceptable' versus 'unacceptable' destruction – implied the reckoning of casualties that, in a matter of hours, might exceed the total of the two World Wars.

Nixon once expressed to a journalist that executive leadership in the nuclear age required, among other qualities, a willingness to suggest one's readiness to perform irrational acts on behalf of the national interest.[42] Although this statement was an instance of Nixon trying to impress an interlocutor rather than to convey an operational message, it nonetheless elicited intense criticism of his supposed recklessness. And yet in its essence it reflected a fundamental and enduring truth about the destructiveness in the hands of the nuclear powers.

As we have seen in earlier chapters, Charles de Gaulle and Konrad Adenauer were both wary of basing their security on weapons in the hands of allies that offered no credible way to resolve conflict without cataclysmic destruction. Three questions had arisen regarding the use of nuclear arms: was it possible to convince either an adversary or an ally of one's willingness to undertake a type of warfare likely to impair one's own civil order? Was it possible to introduce rational calculation into an ultimately irrational act? And was it possible to strike a balance between self-destruction and diplomacy?

These dilemmas, arising nearly eighty years ago at the dawn of the nuclear age, have yet to be resolved. Since Nagasaki, no nuclear weapon has been detonated operationally. Even when engaged in conflicts with non-nuclear countries, nuclear powers have elected to suffer the casualties of conventional war rather than resorting to nuclear weapons to speed success. The examples of the Soviet Union in Afghanistan – as well as the United States in Korea, Vietnam and Iraq – all testify to this.

Nixon understood that, by the time he took office, the American nuclear capacity was becoming controversial in the congressional appropriations procedure. He therefore appointed Melvin Laird as secretary of defense, who had served for a number of years as the chairman of the defense subcommittee of the House Appropriations Committee. Nixon was determined to prevent a situation in which an aggressor could mount a plausible strategic threat by developing a superior nuclear capacity. Laird helped shepherd through Congress

Nixon's commitment to missile defense and his goal of greater variety in the design and capacity of strategic weapons. Laird also added to the flexibility and invulnerability of American strategic forces by developing cruise missiles and mobile land-based weapons.

Second, Nixon took arms control seriously. The Test Ban Treaty, signed by Kennedy and Brezhnev in 1963, represented the first formal measure in nuclear arms control. Four days after President Kennedy was assassinated, President Johnson proposed a resumption of strategic arms negotiations with the Soviet Union.[43] The preliminary agenda-setting talks proved so inhibited by day-to-day controversies, however, that not until the summer of 1968 – just before Nixon was elected – did both parties agree on terms to allow negotiations to begin.[44] This planned summit was, however, abandoned following the Soviet invasion of Czechoslovakia in August 1968.

Thus, an early issue for Nixon became whether to proceed with arms-control negotiations with the Soviet Union at all. The decision became symbolic for the larger direction of his administration. Applying linkage, Nixon would formally agree to open Strategic Arms Limitation Talks (SALT) with the Soviets only after he had settled on a Vietnam strategy. US accession to arms-control negotiations, announced in October 1969, required the adaptation of existing administrative institutions. For the Pentagon, arms control was a novel subject: the department's emphasis had previously been on developing nuclear capabilities, not on restraining them. Arms-control negotiations involving high-ranking military personnel, who were themselves only now being introduced to the subject, required novel command structures.

Nixon's proposal, made early in his presidency, to build a twelve-site missile *defense* system covering the entire country had also challenged the prevailing intellectual consensus that strategic equilibrium would be achieved via mutual assured destruction exclusively. A defensive initiative, critics charged, would undermine deterrence by eroding mutual vulnerability. This critique, as well as concerns over the program's cost and efficacy, led many in Congress to oppose it and seek to reduce its budget.

On the other side of the Cold War, the Soviet Union harbored an elevated estimate of our emerging anti-ballistic-missile (ABM) capacities and feared that American defenses would erode the Soviets' offensive capability. If, as a result of missile defense, America had less to fear from a Soviet second strike, the Soviets reasoned, the US might be more likely to launch a surprise attack meant to disarm its adversary preemptively.

The beginning of the SALT negotiations devolved into a stalemate over procedure and sequence. The Soviets argued for negotiating constraints on defensive weapons first, and only then turning to address offensive weapons. Nixon insisted on retaining the defensive option to provide the necessary pressure for negotiating offensive limitations – and to provide protection for our civilian population.

The imminence of nuclear arms-limitation negotiations produced a new set of domestic debates. The liberal consensus favored first the rapid opening of SALT negotiations, then their acceleration as a way of easing tensions. But now, as arms control was becoming established on the international agenda, an emerging combination of liberals and conservatives started to criticize them on the grounds that arms control dealt only with symptoms and not the underlying causes: the authoritarian nature of the communist system and its human rights violations.

In addition, the characteristics of the opposing nuclear-weapons systems complicated any workable definition of equilibrium. Soviet strategic systems were large and inaccurate; American weapons were more mobile and more accurate. That equilibrium would be disturbed if America added throw weight to its accuracy, or the Soviets magnified their throw weight with accuracy.

After months of wrangling, Nixon intervened directly. Setting an initial goal of four defensive sites, on March 11, 1971, he dismissed the Soviet request for 'zero' and asked me to break the agenda deadlock on the relationship of defensive weapons to offensive weapons through private talks with Dobrynin.[45] He did not disclose these talks – in part to forestall Congress from decimating the missile defense system during the interval and causing us to lose its bargaining value.

Nixon's decision to inject himself sped up the negotiations. At the end of March 1971, I activated the Dobrynin channel, proposing on behalf of Nixon that both offensive and defensive limitations be negotiated simultaneously. The ensuing exchanges established a process – through negotiations conducted by Gerard Smith on the American side and Vladimir Semenov on the Russian side in Vienna[46] – that led to the

SALT I agreement concluded between Nixon and Brezhnev at the Moscow summit in May 1972.

Though central in the design of the negotiations, Nixon took less interest in the details. At the beginning of each negotiating cycle, my staff and I would draw up a summary of internal deliberations, including projections of potential developments. Nixon would make marginal comments largely confined to general issues of principle. During negotiations, I would send him each evening a summary of where we stood. He would on the whole reserve his views for moments when a breakthrough was imminent. While technical discussions of weapons balances were unlikely to draw his attention, he was always crystal-clear on his three principal objectives: to prevent an adversary from achieving a first-strike capability; to avoid an automatic process of escalation in case of conflict; and to demonstrate to the American public his commitment to ending, or at least alleviating, the arms race.

The Moscow summit resulted in the first comprehensive strategic arms-control accords of the nuclear period. The agreements confined ballistic missile defense to two sites (ABM treaty), limited the numbers of offensive strategic weapons to existing levels (SALT I) and established ways of addressing incidents at sea and nuclear accidents. As a byproduct of these talks, the US (together with France and the UK) took the lead in negotiations with the Soviet Union to generate a new agreement that would keep access to Berlin unchallenged until the fall of the Berlin Wall in 1989.

For the rest of his life, Nixon regarded arms control as an essential component of international order. And, in one form or another, substantive negotiations on the subject were conducted during every subsequent presidency until the Trump administration. The Ford administration, in 1975, completed the Helsinki Accords, whose negotiations had been started by Nixon, in which every European nation save Albania, together with the Soviet Union and America, agreed to common principles in security, economics and human rights. The Carter administration would conclude the second SALT agreement, never ratified by the Senate though observed in its essentials. The Reagan administration would reach the only arms-control agreement with the Soviet Union to eliminate an entire class of weapons – those of intermediate range. Finally, the George H. W. Bush administration negotiated the Strategic Arms Reduction Treaty (START I), which led Washington and Moscow to reduce their strategic nuclear arsenals by nearly 60 percent, from a combined 48,000 warheads in 1991 to around 20,000 in 2001.[47] What started as a novelty under Nixon became a commonplace after him.

EMIGRATION FROM THE SOVIET UNION

When Nixon came into office, Jewish emigration from the USSR stood at only a few hundred per year.[48] Nixon authorized me to put the issue to Dobrynin in practical, not ideological, terms. I told the Soviet ambassador that we were paying close attention to Soviet emigration practices; Soviet respect for our concerns would be reflected in our treatment of Soviet priorities. In other words, an improvement in conditions for Jewish emigration would further American cooperation.

Dobrynin never offered a formal answer, but he agreed to discussions of specific hardship cases. By 1972, the end of Nixon's first term, annual Jewish emigration from the Soviet Union had reached more than 30,000.[49] Nixon never claimed credit for this development in election campaigns or announced the increase in numbers; the Soviets never acknowledged it as an agreed-upon outcome.

American domestic politics undermined this tacit arrangement. Senator Henry 'Scoop' Jackson of Washington, a serious student of international affairs who as a Democrat had lent bipartisan bona fides to the Nixon administration's effort to sustain adequate defense spending, reframed the issue of Jewish emigration in ideological terms. Arguing that the promotion of emigration should become a formal part of American diplomacy, he put forward an amendment to the Trade Act of 1974 conditioning US trade relations with the Eastern bloc on Soviet performance with respect to emigration. Thereafter, emigration took a steady downturn, decreasing from around 35,000 in 1973 to fewer than 15,000 by 1975.[50]

Nixon's objectives regarding Jewish emigration paralleled those of his successors, but his methods were more broad-ranging and more subtle, subordinating ideological confrontations to ad hoc practical arrangements.

THE OPENING TO CHINA

In 1967, Nixon – then out of office – published a pathbreaking article in *Foreign Affairs* raising the possibility that China could not be left 'forever outside the family of nations'.[51] He framed the proposition in grand strategic terms, emphasizing the benefits to global peace if China could curtail its support for revolutionary insurgencies around the world and one day be brought into diplomatic relationship with the West. Nixon's essay did not, however, define any specific way to achieve an eventual diplomatic opening.

Two years later, when Nixon became president, the opening became practical. China was then in the throes of the Cultural Revolution. As part of a grand scheme of ideological purification, Mao Zedong had recalled Chinese ambassadors from every country except Egypt. (Though in a handful of countries, such as Poland, Chinese diplomats below the rank of ambassador remained.) The first approach came from Nixon himself. During his visit to Romania in June 1969, as we have seen, he conveyed his intention to engage the Chinese through Ceauşescu, who indicated that he would pass on the suggestion. No response was forthcoming, probably because the Chinese were fearful of Soviet penetration of a satellite country, even one as challengingly autonomous as Romania.[52]

During the 1954 Geneva Conference at the end of France's war to retain Vietnam, the Warsaw embassy had been designated as a contact point between Washington and Beijing. In fact, 162 ambassadorial meetings had been conducted. They ended with each side rejecting the precondition of the other: the US refusing to discuss the unconditional return of Taiwan to China; Beijing refusing to give an assurance of pursuing its objective only by peaceful means. Not even those pro forma meetings had taken place for several years. But in January 1970, we decided to activate the channel. I instructed Ambassador to Poland Walter Stoessel to approach a Chinese diplomat at the next social occasion they both attended with our offer of a dialogue. Assuming the instruction was a private initiative by me, Stoessel ignored it – a symbol of rivalries between the White House and the State Department. Recalled for consultation, Stoessel found himself in the Oval Office, where the president delivered his instructions personally. Thereupon Stoessel presented the offer at a Yugoslav social function, where a Chinese diplomat first ran away from him but, when finally cornered, received our proposal.

Two weeks later, the Chinese ambassador to Poland appeared unannounced at the American embassy with instructions to begin a dialogue. Four meetings took place. On the American side, progress ran up against the bureaucracy's formal system of clearances, first within the government and then with Congress, and Nixon at one point exclaimed, 'They're going to kill this baby before it's born.'

In any case, soon after the American incursion into Cambodia in May 1970, the Chinese broke off the Warsaw channel in protest. That October, however, Nixon repeated his interest in establishing direct contact to Yahya Khan, the Pakistani president, who had called on him at the White House in connection with a visit to the UN.

This time, Nixon received a reply directly from Chinese Premier Zhou Enlai, writing on Mao's behalf. On December 9, 1970, in four cryptic sentences, Zhou elevated Nixon's conversation with Yahya Khan to the status of a formal message, characterizing it as the first time the US had approached China on the presidential level, 'from a head through a head to a head'.[53]

Zhou indicated that China was prepared to negotiate with the United States about Taiwan's return to the motherland. We replied, cryptically, that if dialogue were to proceed, each side should be free to raise issues of its own concern. Ensuing messages were sent back and forth without letterhead or signature to minimize the risk of disclosure and of a reaction in Moscow and uncertainty in the rest of the world. In a return to historic diplomatic methods, the messages were delivered via messenger from Washington to the Pakistani capital of Islamabad, and thence by Pakistan to Beijing – with the Chinese replies following the same route in reverse.

The pace of this exchange was slowed by both sides' determination not to permit their counterpart to exploit their respective eagerness and to screen it to the maximum extent from the Kremlin. As a result, the dialogue between Nixon and Mao was conducted over a period of many weeks through my exchanges with Zhou, each time conveyed in a few sentences. A Soviet miscalculation helped speed the issue.

During the spring of 1971, our secret exchanges were bearing fruit, and a visit by me to Beijing had been agreed. We were negotiating with both adversaries simultaneously on summits. Nixon solved the tactical dilemma by instructions to extend offers to both, starting with the Soviets. Were both to be accepted, we would take them in the order of their reply.

I submitted our proposal for a summit to Dobrynin at Camp David in June 1971. The Soviets solved the problem for us by making acceptance dependent on our support in the negotiations with the Federal Republic of Germany, Britain and France over a new Berlin agreement. By contrast, during my secret visit to Beijing in July 1971, Zhou Enlai proposed a Nixon visit to China without any preconditions. Three days after my return from China, Nixon accepted the Beijing invitation. Within a month, Dobrynin offered an unconditional invitation to Moscow. As planned, we placed it three months after the one envisaged for Beijing.

The secret trip was arranged by scheduling a visit by me to Vietnam, Thailand, India and Pakistan. Once in Islamabad, time for the final lap was found by announcing an indisposition that would explain my ensuing two-day absence as a visit to a hill station for recovery. The entire process – from Nixon's conversation with Yahya Khan on October 25, 1970[54] to my arrival in Beijing on July 9, 1971 – took eight months. The actual trip, from the departure from Washington to the arrival in Beijing, took eight days. Only forty-eight hours were spent in Beijing.

How best to use that brief period? For the ambassadorial talks in Warsaw, the US government had a well-established agenda. Items on the list included Taiwan, financial claims and assets arising from the expropriation of American property, prisoners and navigation in the South China Sea. But Nixon and I concluded that these and comparable topics were likely to lead into technical byways or ideological logjams that might obstruct progress toward the objective of a continuing relationship. I was instructed to express a willingness to discuss Taiwan but specifically only in relation to the overall Chinese–American relationship with the end of the war in Vietnam.

As part of this emphasis on geopolitics, Nixon delivered a speech in Kansas City, Missouri on July 6, 1971 while I was in transit. Elaborating his view of world order based on equilibrium among the great powers and omitting any reference to Taiwan, he said:

> instead of just America being number one in the world from an economic
> standpoint, the preeminent world power, and instead of there being just

two super powers, when we think in economic terms and economic potentialities, there are ... five great economic super powers: the United States, Western Europe, the Soviet Union, Mainland China, and, of course, Japan.[55]

The only agreement reached during the secret visit was an invitation for Nixon to visit China. Both sides concentrated on outlining their overall approach as a basis for further discussion. I elaborated on the Nixon speech; Zhou introduced a conversation with a quote from Mao: 'There is turmoil under the heavens, but the situation is excellent.'

A more specific diplomatic dialogue opened during my second visit three months later in October 1971. The purpose was to prepare the summit and to draw up a communiqué for it. The four-month interval between my second visit and the Nixon summit reflected our conviction that a deadlock between Nixon and Mao should not be risked in a first face-to-face meeting, where conversation would be limited by the domestic requirements of each side and the media waiting outside.

I had brought with me a standard communiqué affirming our general intentions but lacking concreteness. Zhou returned the next morning with an explicit message from the chairman: having avoided high-level contact for so many years, our countries should not now pretend that we were approaching general harmony. Mao suggested that a full statement of our disagreements on specific issues be part of the communiqué together with some clearly stated agreements. In such a context, the communiqué would draw much more attention to the agreements rather than boilerplate declarations of goodwill. A shared statement regarding Taiwan's future was left to the principals at the upcoming summit, but, as a warning to the Soviet Union, Zhou and I settled on an agreement to jointly oppose hegemony in Asia.

Beijing's sudden engagement was no doubt shaped by the pressure being exerted by the more than forty Soviet armored divisions that were deployed along China's Manchurian and Xinjiang borders. High-level cooperation with China in establishing a global equilibrium would now be announced explicitly and transform the nature of the Cold War.

There was no precedent for the pre-summit draft that emerged; nor would there be any comparable successor to it. As had been decided, both sides expressed long lists of their disagreements, coupled with some statements of agreement. Each side made itself responsible for their own formulations. As neither of us asked for a veto over the other side, this approach gave us the opportunity to state the American views on Taiwan explicitly as part of a joint communiqué. The draft was then subject to the approval of Nixon and Mao.

At the summit, Mao proved to be available for only forty-five minutes, due – as we were later told by Chinese doctors – to a grave medical crisis the week before. But he had approved the October draft communiqué, which stated the full American position on Taiwan and other issues. In light of this, a statement that he then volunteered in his brief meeting with Nixon took on special significance: China did not want Taiwan right away, he explained, because the Taiwanese 'were a bunch of counter-revolutionaries ... We can do without them for the time being, and let it come after 100 years.'[56]

Removing urgency from the issue that had long thwarted negotiations between the two countries at the summit made possible a statement expressing what has remained the governing principle of US–China relations for the fifty years since: 'The United States acknowledges that all Chinese on either side of the Taiwan Strait maintain there is but one China and that Taiwan is a part of China. The United States Government does not challenge that position.'[57]

Following a formal proposal by Nixon at the summit, this language was added to what is now called the Shanghai Communiqué, which was issued at the end of his visit.

Neither Nixon nor I invented this language; instead, we drew it from a statement drafted during the Eisenhower administration in preparation for negotiations with Beijing that never happened. The statement had the virtue of accurately rendering the stated objectives of both Taipei and Beijing. Abandoning US support of a 'Two China' solution, the communiqué remained equivocal regarding *which* China would accomplish the postulated wishes of the Chinese people.

After a few days, Zhou accepted our formulation. Its ambiguity freed both sides to conduct a policy of strategic cooperation that would tip the international equilibrium away from the Soviet Union. The statement implied that Taiwan would be treated as autonomous for the foreseeable future. Both sides would affirm the One China principle, while the US would stop short of offering statements or actions implying a Two China outcome, and neither side would seek to impose its preference. The US insistence on a peaceful solution was explicitly stated in the American section of the communiqué. Two additional communi-qués agreed during the Carter and Reagan administrations expanded upon these understandings. Together, they have remained the basis of relations across the Taiwan Strait. Were either side to challenge them, the risks of military confrontation would mount significantly.

For twenty years following Nixon's visit, the United States and China conducted a broad-range collaborative policy to contain Soviet power. During this period, US–China cooperation even extended to the intel-ligence field, albeit to a limited extent. Demonstrating the degree of China's commitment during a subsequent visit in February 1973, Mao urged me to balance my time in China with time devoted to Japan, lest the Japanese feel neglected and become less dedicated to the common defense against the Soviet Union: 'Rather than Japan having closer rel-ations with the Soviet Union,' Mao said, 'we would rather that they would better their relations with you.'[58]

The following month, Singaporean Prime Minister Lee Kuan Yew used a lecture at Lehigh University in Pennsylvania as an occasion to reflect on the significance of the Nixon administration's diplomacy:

> We live in stirring times. Not for some time has the world witnessed such dramatic changes in the relationship of the great powers as in the last two years. We are witnessing the shifts in the balance of power as the weight-ing has changed. And the great powers are learning to live peacefully with each other ...
>
> The old fixed divisions of the cold war appeared fluid and nebulous. Washington had moved from confrontation to negotiations with both Peking and Moscow. For whatever their different reasons, both commun-ist powers wanted the war in Vietnam scaled down and America allowed to withdraw honorably ...
>
> China, for her part, shows greater cordiality towards capitalist Amer-ica and Japan than towards communist Russia ...
>
> Ideological divisions appear to be less relevant. For the time being, national interests seem the most reliable guide for the actions and policies of governments.[59]

Nixon could have wished for no better appraisal of his policy.

Mao died in 1976. Two years later, Deng Xiaoping returned from his second purge and instituted the reform policy he had initiated in 1974 after returning from his first purge. From that point until the advent of the Trump administration in 2017, America's China policy rested on the essentially nonpartisan principles established during this period.

Today, China has become a formidable economic and technological competitor to the United States. In the prevailing circumstances, the question is sometimes raised whether Nixon, were he alive today, would regret the opening to China. It is a challenge he anticipated. His July 1971 Kansas City speech betrays an acute awareness of China's potential to impact the international system:

> The very success of our policy of ending the isolation of Mainland China will mean an immense escalation of their economic challenge not only to us but to others in the world . . . 800 million Chinese, open to the world, with all the communication and the interchange of ideas that inevitably will occur as a result of that opening, will become an economic force in the world of enormous potential.[60]

British Prime Minister Palmerston famously said: 'We have no eternal allies, and we have no perpetual enemies. Our interests are eternal and perpetual, and those interests it is our duty to follow.' Building cooperation with China to counter the Soviet Union was an overriding American interest during the Cold War; today, any US policy toward China has to take place in the context of its vast economy – comparable to that of the United States – growing military power, and skill in diplomacy hewn in preserving thousands of years of distinctive culture.

The opening to China, then, like every strategic success, was not only a response to contemporary problems but also an 'admissions ticket' to future challenges. The most pronounced among them is this: as modern technology continues to compound the destructive capacity of nuclear war through the advent of a variety of high-tech weapons and radical improvements in artificial intelligence, China, Russia and the US have begun modernizing their military arsenals. With weapons developing the capability to seek their own targets and learn from experience, and cyberweapons that can obscure rapid determination of their origin, establishing a permanent dialogue side by side with technological development is imperative to ensure the stability of world order – and perhaps the survival of human civilization. (See further discussion in the Conclusion.)

THE MIDDLE EAST IN TURMOIL

A pair of issues, at once perennially linked and seemingly contradictory, confronted Nixon at the beginning of his presidency: how to maintain the West's position in the (mostly Arab) Middle East while also fulfilling America's commitment to the security of Israel. Like his predecessors, Nixon embraced both objectives, but he also began to pursue them from a new strategic perspective.

The last year of the Johnson administration defined the shape of the Middle East crisis that Nixon would inherit. The 1967 war between Israel and its Arab neighbors – Egypt, Syria and Jordan – ended with Israel occupying the Sinai Peninsula from Egypt; the Golan Heights from Syria; and the Palestinian West Bank from Jordan. These conquests transformed the bargaining position of the two sides. Israel would start a peace process – if it could be started at all – in possession of the tangible territorial prize, which it intended to use for intangible strategic aims: namely, recognition of its legitimacy and existence, as well as secure borders which implied adjustment of the 1949 armistice lines.

The UN sought to create an international framework for this process by means of Security Council Resolution 242. Adopted in 1967, it contained all of the sacramental words – 'peace', 'security', 'political independence' – but in a sequence that drained them of operational significance by enabling each side to apply its own definitions. It read:

The Security Council . . .

1. *Affirms* that the fulfilment of [UN] Charter principles requires the establishment of a just and lasting peace in the Middle East which should include the application of both the following principles:

(i) Withdrawal of Israel armed forces from territories occupied in the recent conflict;

(ii) Termination of all claims or states of belligerency and respect for and acknowledgment of the sovereignty, territorial integrity and political independence of every State in the area and their right to live in peace within secure and recognized boundaries free from threats or acts of force . . . [61]

The extent of the territories from which Israel was to withdraw was left ambiguous, as was the definition of a 'just and lasting peace', a condition that in a world of sovereign states has in any case proved difficult to sustain. As a consequence, each party interpreted the text against the background of its existing convictions.

In March 1969, Egypt's President Nasser attempted to accelerate the process by shelling the Israeli positions along the Suez Canal with heavy artillery. Israel responded with deep-penetration air raids against Egypt's interior. Nixon made a number of immediate decisions: he assigned negotiations on the Middle East to Secretary of State William Rogers but simultaneously left it to me to bring about a sequence in which the Middle East diplomacy would come to a head only after our diplomatic efforts vis-à-vis Vietnam, so as to avoid simultaneous domestic controversy over two such different issues.

Rogers' mediation efforts produced a UN-sponsored ceasefire agreement along the Suez Canal which established a 50-kilometer- (32-mile-) wide demilitarized zone on each side of the canal. This was proposed by Rogers on June 19, 1970 and announced by him on August 7. Nasser and the Soviets violated it immediately by moving fifty Soviet-provided batteries of advanced anti-aircraft missiles into the demilitarized zone along the west bank of the canal.*

Military conflict along the canal thus seemed imminent, and a subgroup of the National Security Council concluded that Israel would be the most likely initiator of it. Nixon rejected this appraisal. He did not favor Israeli initiation of a conflict so far from its borders; such an action, he argued, might trigger a confrontation with the Soviet Union or a wider conflict. A conflict along the Suez Canal involved American security interests; if necessary, American forces should be involved so as to produce maximum deterrence of the Soviet Union. He reserved the initiation of such action to himself and proscribed exploring it until he were to approve it. The issue then settled down for a few weeks until the center of gravity in the Middle East crisis shifted from the Suez Canal to the future of the Jordanian state.

During this period, Nixon's quest for a comprehensive approach focused on diminishing the crucial role that Soviet military assistance

---

* This enabled Egypt to assemble forces, creating the conditions for the October War three years later under the protection of the surface-to-air missiles (SAM).

had been playing in fostering radical Arab designs.[62] In the daily morning discussions in Nixon's private White House office, we reasoned that Egypt and Syria would modify their pressures once they recognized that the US was prepared to thwart Soviet assistance, which ranged from supplying MiG aircraft and heavy artillery to some 20,000 on-the-ground advisors of ground forces. As a complement to blocking that strategy and constricting anti-aircraft batteries, we planned to support serious negotiations for Middle East peace provided the Arab states would deal with Israel directly.

Enthusiastic about this approach, Nixon urged me to begin referring to it publicly; accordingly, I explained during a conversation with a journalist early in the Nixon administration: 'We are trying to expel the Soviet military presence, not so much the advisors, but the combat pilots and the combat personnel, before they become firmly established.'[63]

The first test of the strategy came in September 1970, when the Palestine Liberation Organization (PLO), an anti-Israel terrorist group formed in Cairo in 1964, hijacked four Western passenger planes and landed three of them in Jordan. (The fourth, which landed in Cairo, was blown up shortly after the passengers were released.)[64] With this action, which began the series of events which in the Arab world came to be called 'Black September', Palestinian terrorists stood on the verge of transforming sovereign Jordan into an operational base.

King Hussein, the doughty monarch who had handled decades of hostility from Arab neighbors as well as Israel's security concerns with diplomatic skill and courage, threw down the gauntlet. He closed the Palestinian refugee camps on Jordanian soil, which had become PLO bases, and evicted the residents mostly to Lebanon.

Amidst rising tensions, Syrian and Iraqi armies began to concentrate forces on their frontiers with Jordan. A number of Washington Special Action Group (WSAG) meetings on our side followed. (The WSAG was a flexible interagency group at the deputy secretary level which coordinated crisis management under the chairmanship of the security advisor.) We concluded that Hussein would not yield and that Israel would not tolerate a military attack on Jordan by its neighbors. When these views were brought to Nixon, he emphatically repeated his instructions from the Suez crisis: Jordan needed to be preserved, but Israeli action to that effect should not be undertaken without US approval, and US military action could not take place or be specifically threatened without his consent.

On September 18, a Syrian armored division crossed the Jordanian frontier and advanced on the town of Irbid. King Hussein resisted and asked for American support.

The crisis had evolved into a direct strategic challenge. Were Jordan to disintegrate and Arab armies to appear on Israel's eastern frontier, a war could result that could bring Soviet forces into the region to support Soviet advisors already with the Syrian and Iraqi armed forces. Israeli military opposition was therefore probable, and American support for it, at least diplomatically, was essential.

Crisis management sometimes produces incongruities. When, on a Sunday night,[65] I brought news of the Syrian invasion of Jordan to Nixon, he was bowling in the basement of the Eisenhower Executive Office Building (a very rare event). It was important to prevent the crisis in Jordan from escalating, but neither could we allow a Syrian occupation of strategic parts of Jordan, achieved with Soviet weapons and advisors, to become a fait accompli. When I put the issues to him, Nixon authorized initial steps to contain the crisis and reverse the Syrian adventure. In his presence – still in the bowling alley – I telephoned Yitzhak Rabin, then the Israeli ambassador to Washington, to inform him that we would not let the Syrian invasion stand. We would support a mobilization of Israeli forces to threaten the Syrian flank, but military *action* should wait on further discussions. I then called Secretary of State Rogers to inform him of the president's thinking. He replied that he was uneasy about military action but that he would ask Joe Sisco, the assistant secretary of state, to come to the Situation Room in the White House to help coordinate the diplomacy. Characteristically, Nixon was not prepared to manage a crisis in the White House in bowling clothes. He disappeared for a few minutes to change into a business suit to join Sisco and me in the Situation Room.

Conventional diplomacy would suggest appealing to both parties for restraint and setting up some kind of diplomatic conference to settle outstanding issues. But in the existing circumstances, such moves would likely have accelerated the crisis by giving the aggressor time to extend its conquests. A call for an international conference *before* a Syrian withdrawal would have rewarded both the hijacking and the invasion.

It would also have established a Syrian military presence deep in Jordanian territory. And rather than separating the Arab regimes from their Soviet backers, as our policy envisioned, such an action by the US would likely have reinforced their dependence on Moscow.

The larger the conference, the more difficult it is to achieve a consensus. The refusal to recognize Israel's right to exist had been embedded in Arab diplomacy since Israel's founding. While, for their part, most European countries supported Israel's legitimacy, they were opposed to its insistence on direct negotiations before a ceasefire. And even if all this were not the case, the pace of diplomacy would still have been inherently slower than the advance of Syrian armed forces with their Soviet advisors on the ground in Jordan.

Therefore, Nixon decided in the Situation Room that any appeals for restraint from other countries be diverted to the Syrian invaders and their Soviet sponsors in the first instance. We would insist on Syrian withdrawal from Jordan as a precondition to negotiations. Such a policy required some demonstration of US commitment. Nixon therefore raised the alert level for US forces in Europe by one notch. Sailors of the Sixth Fleet were recalled to their ships in the Mediterranean, and in the United States the 82nd Airborne Division was readied for potential action.[66] The alert – almost exclusively for conventional forces – was designed to warn the concerned parties, especially the Soviet Union and Syria, that US military action was being considered.

Having set the strategy, Nixon followed his usual practice of leaving its implementation to subordinates. He departed the Situation Room, leaving Sisco, General Alexander Haig (then my deputy) and me to take care of the details. A message to Israeli Prime Minister Golda Meir, on Nixon's behalf, stated that the United States would resist the intervention of outside powers – meaning the Soviet Union – and urged her not to go beyond the existing mobilization in order to give our strategy time to take hold. The message to King Hussein indicated that he could rely on our support to restore the status quo. Messages were also sent to NATO allies advising them of the readiness decisions and the reasoning behind them.

In the face of this demonstration of American refusal to tolerate Syrian military pressure backed by the Soviet Union, Moscow ended its part in the crisis. Seeking me out at a diplomatic reception at an embassy the next afternoon, September 21, Dobrynin's deputy took me aside to inform me that Soviet advisors had left Syrian forces as they crossed into Jordan. With Soviet backing substantially removed, the Syrian troops duly returned to their bases, and Hussein retook control of his country.

This strategy of managing the Jordan crisis reflected a pattern that would recur in Nixon's subsequent crisis management: a period of reflection, followed by a sudden move comprehensive enough to convince the adversary that further escalation posed unacceptable risk. In both respects, the experience of September 1970 would preview the even more consequential Middle East crisis in October 1973.

THE 1973 MIDDLE EAST WAR

Even as the Soviet Union began to explore coexistence with the United States, aid and arms flowed from Moscow to Arab client states, raising the prospect of another confrontation. Within the United States, significant shifts had also taken place. In November 1972 Nixon was reelected by the second-largest popular vote margin in American history. He intended to replace Rogers as secretary of state but had not yet made up his mind about a successor, which accounted in part for the slowed pace of Middle East diplomacy. But the basic reason was Nixon's determination to avoid a simultaneous domestic debate over Vietnam and the Middle East, and therefore to postpone Mideast diplomacy until after the election. In August 1973, Nixon decided to appoint me as secretary; I was confirmed on September 21.

Two weeks later, on October 6, a Middle East war was started when Egypt and Syria invaded Sinai and the Golan Heights. Concurrently, the Watergate crisis had accelerated rapidly after John Dean, the White House Counsel, reported White House irregularities (and his own role in them) to the attorney general.

In the Middle East, the balance of Arab incentives had shifted under the impact of the Jordan crisis and the death in September 1970 of Egypt's Gamal Abdel Nasser, who had been the driving force behind the Arab confrontation policy. He was succeeded by Anwar Sadat, who at first pursued his predecessor's strategy of relying on the Soviets to elicit

American pressure on Israel to withdraw from the Sinai. But then, in the summer of 1972, Sadat abruptly expelled the more than 20,000 Soviet military advisors who had been deployed to Egypt and ordered the seizure of their installations and heavy equipment.* In February 1973, he sent his security advisor, Hafiz Ismail, to the White House to explore America's attitude in a renewed negotiation.

Ismail's terms remained essentially the same as those that had previously produced deadlock with Israel: withdrawal by Israel to the 1967 frontiers as a precondition for recognition and direct talks. One new aspect of the message was an implication that Egypt might undertake these steps on a national basis separate from its Arab allies.

Nixon received Ismail in the Oval Office and told him that we would launch a peace effort after the Israeli elections in November, fulfilling an understanding Nixon had reached in 1972 with Golda Meir. I reiterated Nixon's assurance in a subsequent private meeting and sketched possible applications. For Sadat, this was too uncertain a prospect, as Israeli elections were (and are) generally followed by weeks – sometimes months – of negotiations to form a cabinet. Instead, on October 6 – Yom Kippur, the holiest day on the Jewish calendar, when most Israelis are in synagogues – Sadat dealt a shocking surprise to both Israel and the United States. Egyptian forces crossed the Suez Canal, and Syrian forces advanced into the Golan Heights. The sudden assault caught Israelis, Americans and the world unaware and unprepared.

At that very moment, Nixon was dealing with Watergate and its consequences. On October 6, the first day of the war, he was faced with the impending resignation of Vice President Spiro Agnew, who had been accused of corruption in his previous position as governor of Maryland. On October 20, in what the media referred to as the 'Saturday Night Massacre', Nixon dismissed Attorney General Elliot Richardson and Deputy Attorney General William Ruckelshaus, who had been unwilling to fire Special Prosecutor Archibald Cox. Acting Attorney General Robert Bork did so, leading to the opening of impeachment proceedings against Nixon in the House of Representatives.

Despite this succession of domestic political disasters, the United States assumed a central role in bringing about a ceasefire and launching

* For a fuller account of these events, see Chapter 4, pages 230–33.

a peace process in the Middle East that would last well into the coming decades. Nixon never lost sight of the central strategic objectives: to continue a creative diplomacy with Arab states, to maintain Israel's security, to weaken the Soviet Union's position and to emerge from the war with a sustainable American diplomacy working toward peace. That diplomacy's central feature had been foreshadowed in the Jordan crisis three years earlier: to avoid deadlock and multiplying tensions, we were determined to forestall an unwieldy conference of all parties and covering all issues. The alternative was a step-by-step approach that involved the parties genuinely prepared to move toward peace. The feasibility of this approach would be determined by the outcomes of the battles then raging.

The surprise attack had thrown the Israeli military establishment off stride. Likewise, the unpreparedness of our own intelligence services had been exposed in their early assessment suggesting it was *Israel*, not Egypt and Syria, that had launched the surprise attack, and that a rout of the Arab armies was imminent. In fact, Egyptian armed forces crossed the Suez Canal and established themselves in a belt 10 miles deep into the Sinai Peninsula, which they maintained in the face of massive Israeli counterattacks owing to the cover of Soviet surface-to-air missiles that neutralized the Israeli air force. The Syrian army, meanwhile, captured part of the Golan Heights; at one point, a Syrian breakthrough into Israel proper appeared possible.

But by the fourth day, October 9, Israeli reserves had been fully mobilized and its forces were on the move. In Washington early that morning, an Israeli victory was thought to be imminent.

In pursuit of our objectives, Nixon had released, from the second day of the war, high-tech military equipment to be transported by Israeli commercial airlift. The challenge became how to replace extensive Israeli tank and airplane losses. The Israeli military attaché General Mordechai Gur called on me on October 9 with an urgent request. Israeli losses had been unexpectedly large – so large, in fact, that the prime minister was prepared to fly to Washington to plead her case in person. I told him that such a visit would convey an impression of desperation. Above all, Nixon was dealing with the imminent resignation of Vice President Agnew. By the end of that day, Nixon authorized me to assure the Israeli ambassador that we would replace all Israeli losses after the war and that the Israelis should use their reserves while the resupply was being organized and conducted.

There ensued a technical and political near-deadlock. US airlift capability during peacetime is enhanced by the Pentagon's authority to requisition civilian aircraft. But civilian airlines were reluctant to operate in a combat zone, and a technical obstacle turned into a political one: to reach Israel from the United States, civilian aircraft needed to stop for refueling, and Portugal and Spain – the most suitable stops – refused to allow refueling stops due to concern over Arab reactions and Soviet pressure.

When such complications stretched into the seventh day of the war (October 12), Nixon made a characteristic decision: he ordered the use of military airlift planes, which needed no refueling, to deliver what was necessary. No mere tactical decision, this provided the Israelis with the means to reverse their early setbacks and represented a major escalation of US involvement in the war. During a White House meeting to discuss the crisis on the morning of October 12, Nixon rejected suggestions for a limited use of military aircraft, observing, 'We are going to be blamed as much for three planes as for three-hundred.' Ultimately, the president noted, our strategy would be judged by its political outcome, explaining, 'our role must be such that we can play a constructive role in diplomatic initiatives to get a real settlement'. I agreed, adding, 'If we can keep our posture, we will be in the best position that we have ever been to contribute to a settlement.'[67]

The dominant objective remained the redress of the balance of forces first on the battlefield and then as a prelude to diplomacy. Nixon affirmed this general principle during a phone call to me two days later:

> The thought is basically – the purpose of supplies is not simply to fuel the war, the purpose [is] to maintain the balance ... because only with the balance in that area, can there be an equitable settlement that doesn't do in one side or other ...[68]

THE DIPLOMACY OF CEASEFIRE

While the air supply was being debated in Washington, Israeli Ambassador Simcha Dinitz informed me of a new initiative proposed from Jerusalem. Golda Meir had received proposals from her defense minister, Moshe Dayan, and the chief of general staff, David Elazar, to ask for a ceasefire. They argued that the new Egyptian line along the Suez would be too difficult to overcome until Israel had found ways to defeat the Soviet anti-aircraft missiles. She was prepared to go along, but only after an ongoing Israeli counteroffensive on the Golan Heights had made progress toward threatening Damascus. I said I would see whether Britain would support a Security Council resolution to that effect and scheduled it for Saturday, October 13.

The end of battlefield operations was accelerated by the US airlift and aided by a miscalculation of Sadat. As the Israeli offensive on the Golan Heights headed toward Damascus, Syrian President Hafez al-Assad appealed to him for help. Based on his commitment to his Syrian ally, and overestimating Egypt's achievement in crossing the canal, Sadat rejected the ceasefire proposal being explored by Britain. Instead, he ordered an attack by two armored divisions into the Sinai with the objective of seizing the passes in the central highlands. But this offensive moved the Egyptian armored forces beyond the belt of surface-to-air missiles along the canal, thus exposing themselves to the full power of the Israeli air force. On Sunday, October 14, 250 Egyptian tanks were destroyed. This enabled Israeli armor to break the stalemate along the Suez Canal – which its own commanders had considered as frozen three days earlier – and cross the canal into Egypt on October 16.*

By Thursday, October 18, Sadat spoke of ceasefire, and Dobrynin was exploring ceasefire language in Washington. On Friday, October 19, the Soviets invited me to Moscow to complete the process with Brezhnev.

The Egyptian military situation was by now sufficiently difficult to dissuade the Soviets from exploiting our domestic travails. In

* For a fuller account, see Chapter 4, pages 233–9.

Moscow, a ceasefire proposal was completed with Nixon's approval on Sunday, October 21, and was approved by the UN Security Council on Monday, October 22.[69] The ceasefire, which was to take effect twelve hours after it was approved, also included provisions to begin negotiations between the parties toward a political settlement.

Despite having asked us to propose a ceasefire three days earlier, the Israeli leadership hesitated to accept it, seeking to exploit their breakthrough across the Suez Canal further. As a result, I returned to Washington from Moscow via Israel, during the course of which Israel accepted the ceasefire. Arriving in Washington on the same day that had started in Moscow, I discovered that the ceasefire had proved easier to proclaim than to enact. It broke down almost immediately. In ceasefire negotiations, the parties frequently seek ceasefire lines favorable to themselves. This particular breakdown, however, was not tactical but strategic. For the Israeli forces advancing toward the city of Suez were on the verge of trapping the Egyptian Third Army east of the canal.

In Moscow, such a development occurring a few days after having worked jointly on a ceasefire proposal appeared as a direct and deliberate challenge. By the evening of Wednesday, October 24, communications from Moscow grew increasingly threatening, culminating in an ominous message from Brezhnev around 9 p.m. After recounting the Soviet version of events since the previous weekend's negotiations, he proposed that Soviet and American military forces undertake a joint action to enforce the ceasefire. He warned:

> I will say it straight that if you find it impossible to act jointly with us in this matter, we should be faced with the necessity urgently to consider the question of taking appropriate steps unilaterally. We cannot allow arbitrariness on the part of Israel.[70]

We were faced with the single most dramatic and humanly challenging period of the Nixon presidency. Intelligence informed us that Soviet airborne divisions were being readied and that Soviet high-tech weapons were entering the Mediterranean by ship. I called a WSAG meeting of principals in the Situation Room. (I was then serving simultaneously as secretary of state and national security advisor.) The challenge was to reject joint military deployment with the Soviets in the Middle East directed against a major ally (which, in the circumstances, would dramatically alter the political balance) and to deter Moscow from unilateral military action.

Our meeting took place in an atmosphere of drama. Weeks of personal and international strain had driven Nixon to exhaustion, obliging the White House doctors to urge him to retire before the message from Brezhnev arrived. It therefore became necessary to make decisions in an unusual way. The NSC was convinced that the United States could not consider deploying forces as a buffer between Israel, an American ally, and Egypt, a country whose military operations were enabled by Soviet weaponry and which was being supplied via a Soviet airlift. But neither could the US tolerate Soviet combat forces in the region unilaterally enforcing Soviet strategic designs. Views were unanimous on these subjects.

The NSC reached the consensus we needed to reject the Brezhnev proposal. But that left unilateral Soviet measures to be deterred. The meeting then proceeded in the absence of the president, with General Haig (who had replaced Haldeman as chief of staff) acting as liaison to him while I handled the diplomatic contacts. I called Ambassador Dobrynin from the meeting to warn against unilateral Soviet action and informed him that a formal reply to Brezhnev's note was being prepared. Following procedures based on previous decisions and the experience of the Jordan crisis, the NSC recommended measures to forestall immediate Soviet actions including to raise the nuclear alert level to DEFCON 3, signifying a serious crisis short of preparing for nuclear war.

In a reply to Brezhnev's letter on behalf of the president, we rejected the proposal for joint US–Soviet deployment in Egypt but reiterated the American commitment to consultative diplomacy on the peace process. We held the letter for some hours to allow the impact of the alert to sink in and internal and allied consultations to take place. In the interval, I briefed NATO ambassadors and other allies, especially Israel.

Because of the frequent interactions among the parties involved, I remained in the Situation Room while General Haig left from time to time to liaise with the president. In this manner, with the NSC's unanimous conviction – never challenged afterward in leaks or memoirs – that time was of the essence in preventing an irreversible Soviet move, Nixon's strategic purposes were carried out.

At dawn, Nixon returned to the Oval Office and endorsed the details of the NSC recommendation. By noon, Brezhnev, in full retreat, replied to the president, altering his demand for joint military intervention with a counter-proposal for both nations to send a limited number of observers to report on the ceasefire. In a press conference, Nixon summed up what had taken place, emphasizing American opposition to the introduction of Soviet forces into the existing conflict as well as our willingness to play a major role in the quest for peace.

What had prompted Brezhnev's retreat? His decision was in keeping with a general pattern of Soviet conduct during the entire 1973 crisis, which was careful to support its Middle Eastern partners diplomatically and materially by an airlift but to avoid compromising détente by confronting the United States militarily. It may also have foreshadowed the weakening of purpose and more general economic and societal decline that would culminate eighteen years later in the fall of the Soviet empire.

THE MIDDLE EAST PEACE PROCESS

For any peace process in the region to have a chance of moving forward, the first task was to bridge the apparently irreconcilable preconditions of the warring parties. Israel insisted on diplomatic recognition as a precondition for ending hostilities; Egypt and Syria's prerequisite was for Israel to agree to return to the frontiers of 1967. Neither side accepted the precondition of the other, and each side rejected an interim agreement as a starting point.

These were not the only complications. If all parties to the ceasefire, including the Soviet Union, were to participate in a peace process, the most intransigent would hold a veto at the resulting conference – giving the Soviets or radical Arab states an opportunity to stymie the West in pursuit of their Cold War purposes. Nonetheless, we decided to legitimize the negotiations by means of a multilateral conference involving all parties. Were a deadlock to develop, however, we would transform the process into a step-by-step enterprise with those parties that were prepared to proceed.

A conference was set for Geneva for December 22, 1973, inviting all the parties to the ceasefire. Assad refused to attend. Sadat – unwilling to become subject to a Soviet veto – took the diplomatic lead in urging a step-by-step approach. Israel insisted on a parallel course of action based on a series of mutual concessions, a process later described by Prime Minister Yitzhak Rabin as trading 'a piece of land for a piece of peace'. There was no possibility at this stage of an overall agreement, and it was the only meeting. A step-by-step approach followed.

A number of Middle East agreements were reached, with American mediation, during Nixon's presidency. In January 1974, Egypt and Israel struck a disengagement agreement that created a buffer zone along the Suez Canal, separated the military forces and placed restrictions on their military movements and arsenals in each zone. In June 1974, an essentially military disengagement agreement was reached between Syria and Israel. Its technical and observable provisions were based on proscribing either side's deployment of heavy weapons within range of the other's front line. This limitation has proved sufficient to maintain essential mutual restraints between the two countries for the half-century since the disengagement agreement was negotiated – including during the Syrian civil war that began in 2011.

These agreements were made possible because all of the parties involved accepted the step-by-step approach and also because they came to trust America in the mediator's role. All parties had to make sacrifices in accepting this route: Egypt and Syria, to modify the demand for return of the territories they considered their own as an entrance price into negotiations; Israel, to give up ground in the Sinai and its forward positions in Syria in return for pledges of peace that would be, by definition, reversible.

In 1975, these agreements were augmented by another Egyptian–Israeli agreement in which Israeli forces would withdraw to Sinai's mountain passes in return for Cairo's offering political concessions that would open the Suez Canal and include Israeli transit of it. The agreement was to be supervised by a US radar post in the Sinai. By the end of 1976, Egypt and Israel were negotiating an end to their state of belligerence in return for a further Israeli withdrawal from the passes in the center of Sinai to a line running from Ras Mohammad to El Arish, which is 20 miles from the Egyptian–Israeli border.

The Kremlin's acquiescence in this process constituted a major geopolitical transformation in a strategically important region where the USSR had very recently appeared ascendant. It was also a vindication of linkage and of Nixon's approach to negotiations. During the crisis, the diplomacy of détente enabled a constant channel of communication with Moscow, serving to prevent unnecessary collisions. Even more importantly, this diplomatic approach gave the Soviets a stake in other issues that they were reluctant to jeopardize, including talks over the status of Berlin and what would become the 1975 Helsinki Accords.

In 1979, a formal peace agreement between Israel and Egypt was signed in a dramatic ceremony on the White House lawn by President Carter, Israeli Prime Minister Begin and President Sadat. The peace process, sketched in 1974 at breakfast meetings in Nixon's private office, had been fulfilled.*

BANGLADESH AND THE INTERLOCKING COLD WAR

In the second half of the twentieth century, the international system based on European equilibrium in the nineteenth century was once again transformed. In a development foreshadowed a century earlier by the rise of an industrializing Japan, traditional Asian civilizations such as India and China began to enter the international system as great powers in their own right. Rather than relying on a contest of alliances that in the nineteenth century had characterized the competition for European preeminence, these emerging powers displayed a capacity to challenge the global equilibrium autonomously. If the decolonization of Asia and Africa had, for the first time, extended the Westphalian state system across the globe, now the growth of Indian and Chinese power further diminished the relative strength of the old imperial powers. International order – heretofore defined by the relationships of Western powers – was becoming world order.

Nixon's decision to introduce China into the Westphalian system – by negotiating with it not as an adjunct to the Soviet-led bloc but as a counterweight to it and as a new player entitled to serious attention in its own right – opened the field to unprecedented strategic combinations. By exploiting the mounting hostility between the two principal

* For a fuller account, see Chapter 4, pages 261–7.

communist powers, this move turned the quest for world order into a truly multipolar enterprise.

In March 1971, this emergent reality asserted itself. At almost exactly the same moment that exchanges with Zhou Enlai were bringing China into the international system – though for the moment still secretly – what had begun as an essentially regional disturbance in South Asia between Pakistan and India quickly drew in the United States, China and Russia. The emerging problem in East Pakistan thereby represented an unprecedented development: a crisis involving three nuclear-armed great powers, all competing as sovereign equals.

The origins of the crisis were rooted more than two decades earlier in the partition of the Indian subcontinent amidst appalling bloodshed. Governed during the colonial period as a single vast unit, the British Raj in 1947 was split by decolonization into two sovereign states, India and Pakistan; the latter was itself divided into two entities, both of them under Pakistani sovereignty but separated from each other by 1,200 miles of Indian territory.

Of the two states, India was secular in confession and largely Hindu in its population though with a substantial and growing Muslim element. Pakistan was explicitly Muslim, but its halves, ethnically and linguistically diverse and geographically detached, included peoples for whom a common Islamic faith did not provide a shared sense of unity, let alone political cohesion.

This divided Pakistani state was ruled from Islamabad in West Pakistan, where the Punjabi plurality dominated the national army and other significant institutions of governance. Historically, the largely Bengali population of East Pakistan had been split into a variety of factions which the central government in Islamabad regularly played off against one another. But in January 1969, a mass protest broke out in East Pakistan that would lead to the declaration of a new independent state, Bangladesh, on March 26, 1971.

The beginning of the crisis did not immediately elicit a strategic reaction from any of the major international players, with the exception of India. In October 1970, President Yahya Khan of Pakistan called on Nixon in connection with a session of the UN General Assembly, the same occasion when he would undertake to pass along to Beijing the president's expressed interest in an opening to China. He told us he intended to hold an election in December, from which he expected East Pakistan to emerge divided among factions, allowing him to continue exploiting divisions among the Bengalis.

But the December 1970 elections produced the opposite of Yahya Khan's expectations. In East Pakistan, the Awami League, a political party dedicated to Bangladeshi autonomy, achieved an absolute majority. By the following March, order in East Pakistan had broken down, and its independence – or, as West Pakistan saw it, secession – had been proclaimed under the leadership of Sheikh Mujibur Rahman.

Seeking to restore control in East Pakistan through systemic violence, Yahya Khan now abolished the electoral system and declared martial law. The result was appalling bloodshed and a torrent of refugees fleeing from East Pakistan, mostly across India's borders. While Islamabad treated the whole issue as a domestic matter and rejected foreign interference, India saw the crisis as an opportunity to end its strategic encirclement. Claiming that the growing number of Bangladeshi refugees on its soil strained its finances, it began organizing them as anti-Pakistan guerrillas.

In the United States, news of the conflict's devastating human toll made an immediate impact as the struggle in distant South Asia merged with the existing domestic debate over the character of American power and the moral issues raised by Vietnam. The Nixon administration fell under passionate criticism because its response did not involve, as many desired, publicly condemning West Pakistan with great intensity. American discourse about the situation in East Pakistan continued to be dominated by human-rights advocates, some of whom took to the pages of the major newspapers to urge Nixon to adopt largely symbolic gestures.

Proposals ranged from supporting a UN fact-finding mission and Red Cross presence in East Pakistan to suspending all US military and economic aid to West Pakistan.[71] For US decision-makers at the time, however, the calculus was much more complex. West Pakistan was already amply armed, and tragically neither an arms embargo nor a suspension of aid would divert Pakistani leaders from turning their army on the people of East Pakistan. To be sure, such measures would communicate US disapproval of Pakistani outrages, but they would also diminish American leverage and threaten the nascent opening to China – for which Pakistan was our principal intermediary.

Paradoxically, critics equated the administration's reaction to this latest crisis with its conduct in Vietnam – but on diametrically opposite grounds: in East Pakistan, the fault was asserted to be the *absence* of US intervention in a faraway crisis, described as if America condoned the iniquity; in Vietnam, America was condemned for its continuing involvement.

Washington's reticence to become publicly involved in the crisis had little to do with insensitivity (though some internal discussions did not reflect moral elevation); the Nixon White House was focused on the opening to China, and the tragedy unfolding in East Pakistan coincided with and complicated our communications over the date and agenda of my impending secret trip to Beijing. Moreover, Pakistan was a US treaty ally through the SEATO (South East Asia Treaty Organization) agreement negotiated by Secretary of State John Foster Dulles in 1954.

No Nixon policy was ever as one-dimensional as was ascribed to us in the evolution of the Pakistan crisis, which was blamed on his dislike of India's prime minister, Indira Gandhi. To be sure, her vocal criticisms of US policy in the Cold War, and especially of the Vietnam War, had long been an irritant – but only that. In any case, the actual policy was far more complex. As soon as the crisis began in early March, the NSC staff concluded that the probable – and desirable – outcome was East Pakistan's autonomy and eventual independence. But we wanted to arrive at this goal without challenging Pakistan directly or wrecking our channel to China.

The White House approved massive food aid for the relief of East Pakistani refugees. We also conducted covert CIA discussions with representatives of the Awami League with an eye toward creating contacts for possible follow-on official negotiations. The State Department was similarly authorized to establish contacts between the Awami League and India; these efforts, however, were refused by India, whose goal was to encourage East Pakistan not merely to seek political autonomy but to secede. Altogether, the substance of American policy during the first phase (roughly from March through July 1971) was to prevent a regional crisis from becoming a global one and to sustain the possible transformation of the Cold War through the opening to China.

Both purposes were complicated by my secret visit to China. En route to Beijing in July 1971 via Saigon, Bangkok, New Delhi and

Islamabad – and especially while in the last two capitals – I was exposed to a range of views on the South Asia crisis. The Indian attitude – particularly that of Prime Minister Gandhi – focused less on the refugee issue than on establishing East Pakistan as an independent country. While in India, I outlined American support on the refugee issue, especially via the supply of food, and our efforts to encourage a dialogue with the Awami League. While thoughtful and polite, my Indian interlocutors were largely – and emphatically – dedicated to transforming what was then one-half of an avowed adversary on their eastern border into a new country that would be neutral, or even friendly, toward India. In my report to Nixon, I raised the possibility that India might act on its professed geopolitical views and resolve the crisis through a decisive military intervention in East Pakistan – an aggressive step that could invite a response from China, Pakistan's longtime ally.[72]

At my next stop, Islamabad, from where I would depart for China the following morning, I met with President Yahya Khan and Foreign Secretary Sultan Khan. My report to Nixon summarized my discussions on the issue of East Pakistan:

> I emphasized the importance of attempting to defuse this issue [of East Pakistan] over the next few months. One way to do this, I suggested, might be to try to separate as much as possible, at least in international eyes, the refugee issue from the issue of rebuilding the political structure of East Pakistan. If this were to be tried, it would seem important for Pakistan to put together a collection of major steps in one package designed to have important impact both on the refugees and on the world community and perhaps to internationalize the effort.[73]

Our recommendation was thus to combine the various reform measures we were urging into one package to help rebuild the political structure of East Pakistan. The practical effect would be autonomy.

The opening to China was announced in July 1971, with Nixon's trip to Beijing scheduled for the following February. By that summer, the Bangladesh crisis had entered its second phase. In East Pakistan, the systematic human rights abuses had been substantially curtailed.* Gandhi,

---

* In the last stages of Pakistan's rule, however, some of the earlier atrocities were repeated.

to counteract the potential realignment of the international system through an American opening to China, no longer tried to obscure her own design of fostering the secession of East Pakistan. She accelerated India's support for the guerrilla campaign in Bengal, and in August took another step toward a showdown by concluding a friendship and military assistance agreement with the Soviet Union.

This treaty marked the USSR's first initiative in a South Asian strategy that would involve substantially expanding military aid and diplomatic support to India.[74] It was a direct answer both to China and to American strategy, transforming the conflict in Bangladesh from a regional and humanitarian challenge into a crisis of global strategic dimensions, exactly as we had been keen to avoid. If Pakistan were to disintegrate under Soviet–Indian pressure so shortly after having facilitated our opening to China, not only would Nixon's upcoming summit in Beijing be imperiled, but the very premise of the China strategy, which was to balance the Soviet Union, would be shaken.

Nixon was under extraordinary domestic pressure to side with India, whose democracy was widely admired. The issue for the White House, however, had never been East Pakistan's domestic structure but the maintenance of an appropriate international equilibrium. I emphasized this point to Indian Ambassador Lakshmi Jha during a series of meetings over the summer of 1971. On August 9, I reported to Nixon the following conversation with Jha:

> The American interest was in a strong, self-reliant independent India . . .
> East Bengal would be gaining autonomy even without Indian intervention. We, in turn, had no interest in the subcontinent except to see a strong and developing India and an independent Pakistan. Indeed, there was a difference in our approach to India and in our approach to Pakistan. India was a potential world power; Pakistan would always be a regional power. For all these reasons, the problem would sort itself out if we separated the issue of relief from that of refugees and the issue of refugees from that of political accommodation. The Ambassador said that he had no difficulty separating relief from refugees, but he saw no way of separating refugees from political accommodation.[75]

On September 11, with tensions mounting, I repeated the US position to Ambassador Jha:

We had no interest in keeping East Bengal a part of Pakistan. We did have an interest in preventing the outbreak of a war and preventing that issue from turning into an international conflict. As for the rest, we would not take any active position one way or another.[76]

As the crisis mounted, it began to show certain parallels to the weeks before the outbreak of the First World War, with two coalitions of great powers confronting each other over a regional conflict that, at its beginning, did not affect them. From the American point of view, we held that it would be undesirable to humiliate Pakistan so soon after it had enabled our initiative to Beijing. It was also important to preserve the strategic design that underlay the visit to China by Nixon – namely, to ease Soviet pressure globally and rebalance the international order. Allowing the Soviet Union to make inroads into South Asia through its new alliance with India would undermine that second objective.

But our immediate, overriding goal was to prevent the outbreak of war on the subcontinent. In October 1971, Yahya Khan again paid a visit to Washington, during which Nixon raised the subject of autonomy for East Pakistan. Shaken by the military deployments all around Pakistan and by international disapproval, Yahya Khan promised autonomy for East Pakistan following the establishment of a Constituent Assembly planned for March 1972. We interpreted autonomy for East Pakistan as a prelude to the early emergence of an independent Bangladesh.

Following Yahya Khan there came a disastrous visit by Gandhi to Washington on November 3–6, 1971. The intractability of the issues was compounded by the two leaders' reserve toward each other. When Nixon informed Gandhi that Khan had agreed to replace martial law with civilian rule and autonomy in Bangladesh, she showed little interest. She was invested in an independent Bangladesh, not an autonomous region sponsored by the United States. A brilliant and hardboiled realist, she had come to the conclusion that the existing balance of forces would enable her to impose India's preferred strategic outcome.

On December 4, in the aftermath of these coldly formal White House meetings, India invaded East Pakistan, reshaping the conflict once again and ushering it into its third and final phase. Like Sadat two years later, Gandhi understood how the unilateral use of force could transform the terms of an eventual settlement. While East Pakistan had been drifting inexorably toward autonomy, which seemed likely to lead to independence under the impact of superior Indian forces, Nixon had confined public criticism to statements in the UN about India's disregard for internationally recognized borders. But when Gandhi decided to settle the territorial disputes along India's *western* border by measures against the Pakistani-occupied portion of Kashmir – the Himalayan province that had itself been partitioned in 1947, with India holding the larger and most historically significant part – Nixon became increasingly active. India, backed by Soviet military and diplomatic aid, had the capacity to dismember Pakistan province by province. And if Pakistan were on the verge of dissolution as a result of an Indian–Soviet alliance, China might become directly involved in the fighting, leading to a major war that would rend the global order. In any event, such a sequence of events would demonstrate a kind of American irrelevance in a strategically important region.

Nixon had been prepared to leave East Pakistan's domestic evolution to the internal leadership of Bangladesh, which sought independence. But he drew the line at Indian–Soviet collusion threatening West Pakistan's existence. Characteristically, he permitted no ambiguity about the American position. To convey that the United States had a commitment to strategic balance in South Asia, he ordered a task force of the Seventh Fleet, led by the aircraft carrier USS *Enterprise*, to move to the Bay of Bengal. He also authorized me to hint in a background briefing that success at the forthcoming Moscow summit would depend on the Soviet Union's conduct in the South Asian crisis, implying a readiness to suspend the summit in case of Soviet challenges. To bring matters to a head publicly, Nixon made a formal proposal to all parties for an immediate ceasefire.

A dramatic moment of decision had arrived – two months before the Beijing summit and five months before the Moscow one. The night of Friday, December 10, 1971, I met with Huang Hua, Beijing's first ambassador to the United Nations. During the meeting, which had been asked for by China, its ambassador warned that China could not remain quiescent if existing military trends continued. On Sunday morning, the tension heightened when he requested another meeting, which raised concerns that its purpose might be to inform us of some Chinese military move. The request arrived when Nixon and I were about to leave for a flight to the Azores to meet with French President Georges

Pompidou to discuss America's recent abandonment of the gold stand-ard. Nixon did not think he could cancel the meeting on such short notice without causing a financial panic and asked me to accompany him should the situation on the subcontinent intensify.

So Alexander Haig, then my deputy, represented America in the second meeting with Huang Hua. What to say if China announced military action? And if the Soviet Union responded? Nixon instructed Haig to use the formula that we had employed for Israel during Syria's 1970 invasion of Jordan: Haig was not to make specific comments but was authorized to say that America would not be *indifferent* to a Soviet military move.

In the event, the instructions did not need to be used. The Chinese message merely repeated the same warning from two days earlier, now softened by support for our ceasefire proposal. On Thursday, December 16, 1971, India proclaimed a ceasefire in the western theater, at least in part as a response to Nixon's appeal.[77]

The resolution of the conflict proved to be a turning point in the Cold War, though it was not recognized as such at the time nor widely today. India's offer of a ceasefire resulted in part from Nixon's willing-ness to use military signaling and high-level diplomacy to rebalance the strategic equation and thereby to defuse the crisis. His conduct risked planned summits with both Beijing and Moscow. Concurrently, it demonstrated willingness to use American power with resolve for geopolitical purposes – a lesson that was also not lost on traditional allies.

The Bangladesh crisis is often described in terms of the 1960s debates over America's moral duties in the world. It can also be seen as the first crisis over the shape of the first genuinely global order in world history. In both respects, moral and strategic, the relatively swift conclusion to the East Pakistan crisis – in less than a year – in a manner favorable to world order and humane values contrasts sharply with the Syrian civil war, which lasted more than a decade from 2011 – not to mention the ongoing civil conflicts in Libya, Yemen and Sudan.

In Bangladesh, the United States acted on the basis of a carefully con-sidered definition of the national interest. It focused on its principal strategic objectives, adjusting them to evolving circumstances and American capabilities. It took serious account of humanitarian consid-erations and adopted significant achievable measures on their behalf.

The Bangladesh crisis represented a major step in the transformation of the Cold War from a rigid bipolar structure into a more complex global equilibrium involving Asia as a growing element. Thanks to the combination of diplomacy, audacity and restraint exercised at appropriate moments, the odds of a global war over Bangladesh slipped from possible to inconceivable. Ultimately, each participant in the crisis gained enough – or, in Pakistan's case, lost too little – so that for decades afterward no major country has disturbed the arrangement.

Within two months, the summit with Mao proceeded as scheduled, resulting in the Shanghai Communiqué, in which both China and the US declared their opposition to an attempt by any power to attain hegemony in Asia. Bangladesh achieved its independence; the United States recognized Bangladesh's new status less than four months after the ceasefire.[78] Although the United States had strained its relations with both India and the Soviet Union, the Moscow summit took place in May 1972 on the schedule established before the South Asian crisis and led to outcomes shaping the future of the Cold War toward an eventually peaceful outcome. US relations with India began to improve within two years and have stayed on a positive trajectory since. During my visit to New Delhi in 1974, the two countries created the US–India Cooperation Commission, which became the institutional basis for a synchronization of interests that has continued to accelerate to the present day.[79]

NIXON AND THE AMERICAN CRISIS

Historical memory is often endowed with the appearance of inevitability; gone are the doubt, risk and contingent nature of events that accompany – and, on occasion, threaten to overwhelm – participants in the moment. Nixon's leadership consisted in the fortitude to overcome his own latent sense of doom and, amid the anguish of uncertainty, to merge complex geopolitical trends into a broad definition of national interest and to sustain it in the face of adversity. Nixon worked on the conviction that peace was the fragile and dangerously ephemeral consequence of diligent statesmanship within a world where tension and conflict were almost preordained. It was the statesman's duty to seek to resolve conflicts on the basis of an inspired vision of the future.

At Richard Nixon's funeral in 1994, I observed that he had 'advanced the vision of peace of his Quaker youth'. This is true in an obvious and immediate sense: he brought American troops home from Vietnam, helped end wars in the Middle East and South Asia and introduced incentives for restraint in the superpower competition with the Soviets through diplomatic initiatives rather than unilateral concessions. But his vision of peace was also made manifest in the way he reshaped world order by introducing multipolarity into the global system by the opening to China while advancing American interests and overall stability.

By adjusting America's role from faltering dominance to creative leadership, Nixon was, for a time, successful. But the collapse of his administration in August 1974 due to the Watergate tragedy, compounded by the fall of Saigon eight months later, prevented his approach to foreign policy from achieving the influence on American thought it deserved. As a result, the eventual triumph of the United States in the Cold War and the unraveling of the Soviet empire were widely perceived in ideological rather than geopolitical terms and understood as a vindication of America's confident verities about the world.

Those verities, in turn, have guided much of the US approach to the post-Cold War period. Among them is the belief that adversaries will collapse due to their own dynamics or can be crushed; that friction between countries is more often the result of either misunderstanding or malevolence rather than of differing interests or values that each side regards as valid; and that, with only a push by the United States, a rules-based world order will naturally develop as the expression of inexorable human progress.

Today, a half-century after the Nixon presidency, these impulses have led the United States to a situation that is strikingly similar to the one Nixon inherited in the late 1960s. Once again, it is a tale first of exuberant confidence generating overextension and then of overextension giving birth to debilitating self-doubt. Once again, in almost every region of the world, the United States confronts major interlocking challenges to both its strategies and its values. Universal peace, long anticipated, has not arrived. Instead, there is renewed potential for catastrophic confrontation.

And, once again, swings between reckless triumphalism and righteous abdication signal danger for America's position in the world.

A Nixonian flexibility, at once realistic and creative, is needed for American foreign policy. Despite many important differences between Nixon's time in office and today, three familiar principles from his statesmanship would continue to benefit the United States: the centrality of the national interest, the maintenance of the global equilibrium and the creation of sustained and intense discussions among major countries to construct a framework of legitimacy within which the balance of power can be defined and observed.

Certain qualities of Nixon's leadership would help to actualize these principles: an understanding of how different aspects of national power relate to one another; an awareness of minute shifts in the global equilibrium and the agility to counterbalance them; an imagination for tactical boldness; a facility for relating the management of regional disturbances to a global strategy; and the vision to apply America's historic values to its contemporary challenges.

Managing the global order requires an acute US sensitivity to evolving and often ambiguous events. It also demands an ability to identify strategic priorities. We must ask ourselves: which threats and opportunities require allies? And which are so central to American national interests and security that we will deal with them alone, if necessary? At what point does multilateral commitment compound strength, and when does it multiply vetoes? To achieve the goal of peace, confrontational forms of competition must leave room for a sense of shared legitimacy. Together, balanced power and agreed-upon legitimacies supply the soundest structure for peace.

Toward the end of his first term in office, Nixon addressed a joint session of Congress at which he presented the results in foreign policy that his administration had secured to that point, framing them as at once a national achievement and a worldwide mission:

> An unparalleled opportunity has been placed in America's hands. Never has there been a time when hope was more justified – or when complacency was more dangerous. We have made a good beginning. And because we have begun, history now lays upon us a special obligation to see it through.[80]

The essence of Nixon's diplomacy lay in his disciplined application of American power and national purpose after it had been on the verge of being consumed by domestic controversies. There existed, after the

1972 election, a possibility that the methods and thinking behind the administration's first-term diplomatic achievements might be translated into a lasting 'school' of American foreign policy – a recalibration not only of strategy but also of mindset. In this scenario, America's exceptionalism would be understood to owe as much to the deft and measured exercise of its inherent strength as to its determination to validate its founding principles.

But only two weeks after Nixon delivered this speech, there was a break-in at the Watergate.

4

Anwar Sadat:
The Strategy of Transcendence

THE SPECIAL QUALITY OF ANWAR SADAT

The six leaders discussed in this volume are akin in their commitment to securing a new purpose for their respective societies and in each case seeking to relate that purpose to a meaningful tradition. Even when their legacies have been controversial, five of them have been recognized by posterity and incorporated in the history of their countries.

It was different with Anwar Sadat, president of Egypt from 1970 to 1981. His triumphs were mainly conceptual in nature, and their implementation was truncated by his assassination; his regional heirs, scant in number, adopted only the practical rather than the visionary aspects of his efforts and did not display the single-minded courage with which he had infused them. As a result, his great achievement – peace with Israel – is remembered by few, and his deeper moral purpose is ignored by almost all, even though it formed the basis of the Israeli–Palestinian Oslo Accords, peace between Israel and Jordan and Israel's diplomatic normalization with the United Arab Emirates, Bahrain, Sudan and Morocco.

During a period of seemingly intractable regional conflict and diplomatic deadlock, Sadat's contribution was a bold vision of peace, unprecedented in its conception and daring in its execution. Unimpressive in his earlier life, a revolutionary in his formative years, seemingly only a secondary figure even after achieving high national office and not taken seriously upon his rise to the presidency, Sadat put forward a concept of peace, the promise of which remains to be fulfilled. No other contemporary figure in the Middle East has professed comparable aspirations or demonstrated the ability to realize them. His brief episode thus remains a stunning exclamation point in history.

As president of Egypt, Sadat did not fit the mold of his regional contemporaries: national leaders dedicated to uniting the Arab Middle East and North Africa under a single banner. Unlike his charismatic predecessor Gamal Abdel Nasser, his histrionic Libyan neighbor Muammar Qaddafi or the dour military realist Hafez al-Assad of Syria, Sadat, after exploring their approach to the international system, shifted dramatically to the methods of diplomacy practiced in the West. His strategy prioritized national sovereignty and alignment with the United States over the pan-Arab nationalism and nonalignment then sweeping the Arab and Islamic world. To his strategic imagination Sadat added extraordinary human qualities: fortitude, empathy, audacity and a gravitas, at once practical and mystical. His policies flowed organically from his personal reflections and his own interior transformations.

This chapter is an effort to trace those evolutions, to understand how he inoculated himself against the conventional wisdom of his time and thus transcended ideologies that, for decades, had contorted the Middle East and bled Egypt dry.

THE IMPACT OF HISTORY

Egypt's history endowed it with an exceptional sense of continuity and civilizational wholeness. For millennia, the Nile valley north of Aswan has remained the core of the country's territory. And in spite of twenty-three centuries of nominal foreign rule – first under the Ptolemys and then under Romans, Byzantines, a succession of caliphs, Mamluks, Ottomans and finally the British – Egypt has typically been able to wrest local control from its ostensible conquerors. Though never fully independent since the days of Alexander the Great, Egypt also never fully acquiesced as a colony; instead, it was a civilization practicing eternity in a pharaonic guise. Such a distinctive character would always proclaim more than merely provincial stature. In this sense, Sadat's primary mission, before and during his presidency, was an expression of the aspiration of Egyptian civilization to secure lasting independence.

Despite its continuity, Egypt has for centuries vacillated between two civilizational identities. One originated with the ancient Mediterranean kingdom, based in Egypt, of the Ptolemaic dynasty, which was oriented toward Greece and Rome. Within that framework Egypt held a prominent place during the Hellenistic period and the early Roman empire. Alexandria served as a central entrepot of the ancient world, and the fertile banks of the Nile produced much of the Mediterranean basin's grain.

The country's second, more recent identity – that of an Islamic state, oriented toward Mecca – was rejuvenated by eighteenth- and early nineteenth-century expansionists such as the Mamluk Ali Bey and the Ottoman military commander Muhammad Ali, who aimed at influencing and conquering Arabia and the Levant. In 1805, after Napoleon's brief appearance in Egypt, Muhammad Ali established himself as the first Khedive – essentially a viceroy under Ottoman suzerainty – and began a dynasty that would rule Egypt for the next 150 years; his descendants, too, would be known as Khedives. The modern Egyptian view thus came largely, though not entirely, through an Islamic lens.[1]

Throughout the long nineteenth century, the spirit of Egyptian independence became intertwined with Western ideals. Egypt experienced a profusion of liberal Arabic thought (*el nahda*, the Egyptian Renaissance), much of it inspired by translations from liberal and revolutionist French writings.[2] In the late 1870s, the Ottomans, administrators of the country since the sixteenth century, temporarily established a written constitution that endorsed popular political representation and experimented with parliamentary rule.

In this moment of inspiration, the identities of Egypt layered upon each other to produce an intellectual fusion exemplified by the great reformist philosophers Jamal al-Din al-Afghani and his student Muhammad Abduh, who articulated a reinvigorated Islam compatible with the principles of Western political structures.[3] But these visionaries proved the exceptions to the rule. The country would wait three-quarters of a century for another who could rise above the divisions in Egyptian thought.

The Egyptian Khedives, who by the second half of the nineteenth century had achieved de facto independence from weakening Ottoman rule, saddled the country with debt, leading in 1875 to the sale to Britain of Egypt's stake in the Suez Canal and the surrender of Egypt's rights of operation there. In this way, beginning in 1876, Paris and London asserted control over Egyptian finances. In 1882, Britain occupied Egypt and named itself Egypt's 'protector'.[4] Henceforth, Egyptian nationalism began to express itself against the same European powers whose writers had once inspired it. Nationalism, newly combined with a sense of Arab solidarity and fueled by a resentment of Britain's ongoing interference, characterized the mindset of much of Egypt in the first half of the twentieth century.

This was the milieu into which Anwar Sadat was born in December 1918.

EARLY LIFE

Anwar Sadat was one of thirteen children born to a father of partly Turkish heritage who worked as a government clerk for the army and a mother whose Sudanese father had been forcibly brought to Egypt and enslaved.[5] The family lived in Mit Abu al-Kum, a rural village in the Nile delta, until Anwar was six, at which time they moved to a Cairo suburb.

The period in Cairo was difficult: Sadat's father took another wife, relegating Sadat's mother and her children to second-class status within the family. There were many mouths to feed, and the family was sometimes too poor to buy bread.[6] This was a time to which Sadat would almost never refer publicly, preferring to recall a childhood in the idyllic countryside rather than in a crowded and very ordinary urban flat.[7] In public appearances later in life he would often introduce himself as a child of the Nile and a farmer.[8]

In his youth Sadat showed an instinctive patriotism that predated any political theorizing or ideology. As a child in Mit Abu al-Kum, he had idolized the anti-colonial icon Mahatma Gandhi, dressing in a white sheet and 'pretending he did not want to eat'.[9] He was aware of continuing British power because it determined the nature of his father's employment; for instance, after the British forced withdrawal of Egyptian troops from Sudan in 1924, his father came home.

Young Anwar occasionally stole apricots from the royal orchard for his snacks.[10] At eight years old, he joined street demonstrations for the removal of Egypt's pro-British ministers. As an adolescent, he despised the British constable who rode his motorcycle through Sadat's Cairo neighborhood.

The family strongly emphasized education: Anwar's paternal grandfather was literate (a rarity in Egyptian villages at that time), and his father was the first man in Mit Abu al-Kum to obtain an educational qualification.[11] Despite their constrained finances, the family managed to pay for Anwar and his older brother's schooling. Raised a devout Muslim, he learned in both the Qur'anic and Christian traditions as a student at two different middle-class schools. He read widely and voraciously.

Sadat became more conscious of the distinctiveness of his class difference when he gained admission to the Royal Military Academy in Cairo, which had only recently begun taking students from the lower and middle classes.[12] His acceptance had to be achieved through the laborious and humbling process of asking for references from distant acquaintances sufficiently elevated in the state hierarchy to have influence.

In young adulthood, his patriotic instincts began to develop into a political philosophy and a sense of self. On the wall of the Cairo flat had been a portrait of Kemal Ataturk; he read the Turkish hero's biography while at the military academy.[13] Afterward, he frequented bookstores to keep up his education.

Sadat spent his youth feeling inferior, both in his family and at school. The circumstances of his early years trained him in survival, whether by theft or by the small deceptions of conformity. These adaptive skills would hold him in good stead as a revolutionary and early in his presidency.

Although intelligent, and spiritually inclined from childhood, the young Sadat was far from fully formed, and he did not begin with the ideas he would only later develop. Still, he was open to new understandings and genuinely curious. His natural openness allowed him to grasp a wide range of possibilities. And he had the persistence to follow through on what new thoughts implied.

Sadat's adolescence and early adulthood unfolded against a backdrop of contradictory political trends. From 1882 to 1914, the Ottoman Empire retained Egypt as an autonomous province, though British de facto control had turned it into a 'veiled protectorate'.[14] In 1914, with the outbreak of the First World War, Britain declared Egypt a sultanate under British protection and encouraged the Arab revolt against the vestiges of Ottoman rule.[15] In 1922, after years of unrest over Britain's sidelining of the popular Wafd Party,* Egypt was grudgingly granted its long-promised formal independence, transforming it from a protectorate and sultanate to a kingdom. Sultan Fuad I, ninth of the Ali dynasty, became King Fuad I. This was, at first, only a nominal change; Britain still reserved for itself the operation of the Suez Canal, the prevention of foreign interference in Egypt and the 'protection' of Egyptian security, foreign affairs and international communications.[16]

Token independence did lead gradually to real gains in self-governance, as in the Anglo-Egyptian Treaty of 1936, which enhanced some of the powers of the Egyptian government and reduced British military presence in the country. But optimism over this progress was countered by growing popular frustration at the failure of the Wafd Party to deliver either full independence or the restoration of Egyptian control over Sudan, which remained under British rule.[17]

Public despair of reform and opposition to the British reached a crescendo in February 1942, when British troops and tanks surrounded the Abdeen Palace, forcing King Farouk, Fuad's successor, to approve a government selected by the British.[18] Egyptian nationalists later pointed to the humiliation of the king as a direct cause of the revolution in the following decade.[19]

The principles espoused by revolutionary groups in Egypt appealed to Sadat's earliest religious and political convictions. Believing in an Islamic Egypt,[20] he idolized Sheikh Hassan al-Banna, the founder of the Muslim Brotherhood, and met with him.[21] Al-Banna also held an uncompromising stance on achieving real independence. Thanks to his Sudanese heritage, Sadat came to regard the continuing British rule in Sudan as a personal affront. For him, the British were criminal interlopers and Winston Churchill a 'thief' and 'hated enemy' who had humiliated Egypt.[22]

In 1939, as a nineteen-year-old lieutenant fresh out of the academy, Sadat met another young officer named Gamal Abdel Nasser. Nasser had formed the Free Officers, an underground revolutionary

---

* The Wafd Party was Egypt's leading political party and the spearhead of the independence movement. It was unusual in its secularism, having embraced the slogan 'religion is for God and the nation is for all'.

group within the Egyptian military. Like the Muslim Brothers, the Free Officers planned to employ armed efforts to gain independence. Sadat eagerly accepted Nasser's invitation to join the movement.

Sadat's anti-British fervor led him down the road of revolutionary violence. In June 1940, with the collapse of France and Italy's growing appetite for expansion, North Africa found itself a battlefield of the Second World War. Sadat, fixated on expelling the British even as his country nominally fought alongside them, took inspiration from Aziz al-Masri, a prominent leader of the Arab Revolt against the Ottoman empire during the First World War. Al-Masri had partnered with the British to drive the Ottomans out of the Arabian Peninsula.[23]

Drawing on al-Masri's example – treating the enemy of one's enemy as one's friend – Sadat began corresponding with and supporting German forces operating in North Africa. Stationed alongside British soldiers, Sadat nursed thoughts of rebellion. In his memoirs he would recollect that 'at that time, in the summer of 1941 ... I actually laid down the first plan for a revolution'.[24]

Then, in the summer of 1942, he attempted to send messages to associates of General Erwin Rommel, who was leading the Nazi offensive from Libya into Egypt. In this he was not alone: in February 1942, crowds in Cairo had shouted support for Rommel and his troops.[25] But Sadat's messages were intercepted; he was arrested by the British and imprisoned.

CONTEMPLATIONS IN PRISON

For the next six years, during the war and after, Sadat was in and out of prison (1942–4 and 1946–8). He escaped more than once from his imprisonment, living for these interludes as a fugitive and remaining active in the Free Officers movement. In January 1946, he was indicted on charges of involvement in the assassination of the pro-British finance minister, Amin Osman. He awaited trial for twenty-seven months, often in solitary confinement, until his ultimate acquittal – though he would later admit that he had in fact been involved.

While he was enduring imprisonment and extended isolation, the other Free Officers continued their activities. They built the nascent movement into a well-funded, hierarchical organization. Most, while secretly plotting revolution, remained in the ordinary ranks of the Egyptian military. Awaiting them was a shock that would transform their aims: namely, the establishment of the state of Israel on May 14, 1948.

Upon issuance of the new state's declaration of independence, read out by David Ben-Gurion at a meeting in Tel Aviv, and the immediate recognition of Israel by US President Harry Truman, neighboring Arab states entered the civil war that had been consuming the Arabs and Jews of Mandate Palestine. Egypt, Transjordan, Syria and Iraq invaded, the start of an unsuccessful ten-month campaign that attempted to forestall the formation of an independent Israeli state. Twenty-five years of intermittent warfare would follow.

By October 1948, Egyptian forces were taking heavy losses; by January 1949, they had been pushed back and surrounded in the Gaza Strip; by February, they had signed an armistice – the first but not the last of the Arab combatants to do so.[26]

The defeat was an embarrassment for the Arab League for failing to coordinate its members' disparate national armies. Veterans of the 1948–9 war, including future Egyptian Presidents Naguib and Nasser, believed that the rout had resulted from Arab disunity. This catalyzed a new, pan-Arab project: a military union of Arab states charged with confronting Israel and combating Western influence. Perhaps because the establishment of Israel was perceived by many Egyptians as a further European imposition on the region, even greater Egyptian identification with Arab causes and fiercer resentment of the West followed.

When Sadat emerged from prison and was reunited with the Free Officers (now as a member of its leadership body, the Constituent Council), he remained in some ways separated from them. Many of the Free Officers had fought in the 1948 war. Sadat, meanwhile, had only had an indirect relation to the war, and his enthusiasm for Arab unity was similarly diluted.

Moreover, in prison he had undergone a profound transformation. Rather than languishing in his solitary confinement, he had developed what he later recalled as an 'inner strength'. Already formed by the slow rhythms of his rural childhood, he professed to have found still greater serenity in prison. But his was not a serenity that lent itself to stillness. It was, rather, 'a capacity . . . for change'.[27] In his memoirs, Sadat would reflect: 'My contemplation of life and human nature in that secluded place had taught me that he who cannot change the very fabric of his thought will never be able to change reality, and will never, therefore, make any progress.'[28]

When finally released in August 1948, Sadat was still committed to the revolutionary cause, but he was no longer an uncritical adherent of his compatriots' ideas. He had cultivated the confidence to question his earlier convictions.

EGYPT'S INDEPENDENCE

The disgrace of the Egyptian monarch, the strain of the Second World War and the shame of the 1948 defeat added to the Egyptian public's anti-British sentiment. In October 1951, the country's parliament unilaterally abrogated the Anglo-Egyptian Treaty of 1936, which, for all its apparent advantages to Egyptian sovereignty, had served as the basis for a continued British military presence around the Suez Canal. When the British refused to leave, the Egyptians blockaded the remaining troops at the canal.

The standoff deteriorated into active skirmishes. On January 25, 1952, British tanks demolished the Egyptian police station in Ismailia, killing forty-three men. Two days later, thousands of outraged Cairenes took to the streets. The ensuing riots sent much of downtown Cairo up in smoke; it became known as 'Black Saturday'.[29] In the following months, government by parliamentary majority became impossible; three successive governments were formed and then dissolved.

The Free Officers saw that the situation had reached its critical point: the people were ready, and the government hapless. Hoping to 'neutralize the British' by convincing Britain's American ally of a fait accompli, the Officers sent word to the US embassy that a major move was imminent.[30] On July 23, 1952, they carried out a successful coup against Farouk, who abdicated in favor of his infant son, King Fuad II.

It was Sadat who drafted the king's abdication statement and declared the Officers' triumph over the radio. His subdued announcement emphasized the internal reconstitution of Egypt's government and military, the expulsion of foreign influence and the establishment of diplomatic relations with other states on the basis of equality.[31]

A council of regents stepped in to manage the monarchy, as was customary with an infant king. But the real power now lay with the Revolutionary Command Council (RCC), of which General Naguib was the head. The RCC proclaimed a new constitutional charter, by which it would rule for a transitional period of three years. In the summer of 1953, the RCC abolished the monarchy, declared Egypt a republic, and appointed Naguib as president and prime minister. Nasser was named deputy prime minister.

A leadership competition soon sprang up between Nasser and Naguib. The latter enjoyed broad national support, but he was from an older generation; meanwhile, Nasser's charisma continued to fire the imagination of the Free Officers. In the spring of 1954, Nasser convinced key army officers, a major Naguib constituency, that their leader's commitment to pluralism and parliamentarism had brought Egypt one step away from anarchy.[32]

Having won the army, Nasser was free to pursue his ambitions. In October 1954, as he was speaking at a podium, eight bullets were fired toward him. All miraculously missed. Unhurt, Nasser finished his speech: 'Go ahead and shoot me,' he extemporized. 'You can't kill Nasser because all the Egyptian people will become Nassers.'[33]

Some maintain that the shooting was staged. Whether it was or not, it had a major effect. In November 1954, Nasser rode the ensuing wave of popularity to the presidency under the three-year transitional constitution and took over the leadership of the RCC, ousting Naguib in the process.[34]

The contest between Nasser and Naguib was also a battle over the future of democracy in Egypt.[35] In 1954, Naguib's wing of the RCC had drafted a constitution giving significant powers to the parliament. But that faction was overcome by Nasser's supporters, and in June 1956, Egypt's first republican constitution created a relatively unchecked executive – one manifestation of the military's unease with sharing power.[36] Simultaneously, Nasser was re-elected president.

With shrewd maneuvering and extraordinary panache, Nasser had sidelined his main competitor. The Council had early on won goodwill from ordinary Egyptians with a series of popular policies: investment in industrialization and education, land reform (which weakened the aristocracy) and removal of titles (mostly held by Turco-Circassian elites). Responding to violent provocations by the Muslim Brotherhood, the

Council had also outlawed political parties in the winter of 1953. In this way, Nasser and his political allies managed to replace revolution with autocratic authority.[37]

MOUTHPIECE OF THE REVOLUTION

Under President Nasser, Sadat was the force behind Egyptian state media, founding the daily *al-Gumhuriah* ('The Republic') in December 1953 and serving for several years as its managing editor and a well-known columnist.[38] Led by him, the paper continued to denounce imperialism,[39] and during this period Sadat also wrote three books on the Egyptian Revolution, including a volume in English, *Revolt on the Nile* (1957), with a foreword by Nasser.

From September 1954 to June 1956, Sadat served as a minister of state (without portfolio) in Nasser's cabinet and, even though he had no legal training, became a member of the RCC's Revolutionary Tribunal, a judicial body. At first focused on rooting out monarchists and British loyalists, the Tribunal eventually turned against the Muslim Brotherhood.[40]

Soon Sadat was taking on greater responsibilities. In 1957, after Nasser's consolidation of power and reintroduction of political parties within the People's Assembly (Egypt's parliament), Sadat became secretary-general of the National Union (Egypt's most powerful party) and a member of parliament.[41] In 1960, he became speaker of the Assembly. Despite his elevated positions, Sadat maintained a low profile.

Over the next decade, even as he ascended to the vice presidency in 1969, he would continue to avoid drawing attention to himself. Later, after he became president, a journalist would ask if his relatively minor stature had been the reason for his good relationship with Nasser. The journalist, Sadat remarks in his memoirs, must have concluded that he was either 'of absolutely no consequence' or else extremely 'cunning' to avoid the friction that usually accompanied extended collaboration with Nasser. Sadat replied:

> I was neither inconsequential during Nasser's lifetime nor shy or cunning at any point in mine. The matter is quite simple. Nasser and I became friends at the age of nineteen. Then came the revolution. He became

President of the Republic. I was glad, for the friend I trusted had become President, and that made me happy.[42]

Sadat was right to note that he was hardly inconsequential. Even as he avoided publicity, he played key roles in Nasser's programs, particularly in foreign policy, foreshadowing many of the efforts he would pursue as president.[43]

Nasser sought to delegitimize and imprison the Muslim Brothers because they posed a political threat, but he also wanted to maintain support among Egypt's majority Muslim population. To that end, in 1954, he formed the Islamic Congress, an organization to develop relations between the state and prominent imams.[44] He appointed Sadat as chairman.

Of deep faith himself and formerly having corresponded with leading Muslim Brothers, Sadat was uniquely equipped to serve as a bridge between Nasser's secular government and the Brotherhood as well as other Islamic leaders. Later in his career, he would again attempt to blend secularism and spirituality in Egyptian society – in both cases with only mixed results.

The Islamic Congress also served an important purpose abroad: to align Egypt with Saudi Arabia against the British-sponsored Baghdad Pact, an anti-Soviet defensive alliance (also encouraged by the United States).[45] Nasser saw the Pact as a Western ploy to co-opt the Arab world – and to build up Iraq as a counter to Egypt – and, in 1954, refused to join.[46] That same year, Sadat disrupted Jordan's plans to join the Pact by putting pressure on some of its ministers to ensure the deal's failure. One Western observer named him as 'one of the direct causes of the breakdown of the negotiations'.[47] Sadat managed a similar outcome in Lebanon by comparable methods.

By the end of the 1950s, Sadat had become at once an indispensable and a relatively inconspicuous part of the Egyptian government. He controlled key domestic constituencies and enjoyed collegial relationships with other legislators. He had proved himself an able diplomat, with a particular quality of empathy.[48] He was a professional public figure adhering to President Nasser's line.

Yet, within those constraints, he had already started to formulate an original vision of where his country might be led.

NASSER AND SADAT

Nasser held hypnotic sway over Egypt and the Arab world's popular imagination. During his period in office, he particularly excelled in the management of confrontations – first against Britain, then against Israel – but was less skillful in the practicalities of administration. As one Middle East specialist wrote in 1967, Nasser had a

> remarkable talent for knowing what he wants at a given moment, and how to change his stance and seek reconciliations with opponents when he is over-extended … But he clearly dislikes making definitive long-range bargains, perhaps partly because of his temperament but more essentially because the Egyptian revolution, like other Arab revolutions, is still groping for a clear sense of its purposes.[49]

Through the mid-1950s, Nasser continued in what Sadat regarded as the original vein of the revolution: the defense of Egypt's national pre-rogatives. In October 1954, he negotiated a new agreement with Britain to formally replace the annulled 1936 Anglo-Egyptian Treaty: British soldiers would withdraw within two years, ridding Egypt's soil of foreign troops for the first time since the occupation in 1882.[50] Early on, Nasser maintained open channels with both the United States and the Soviet Union. He became, by the time of the Bandung Conference in 1955, an icon of the Non-Aligned Movement.

Nasser knew that to defend Egypt's sovereignty, he would need to bolster its economic self-sufficiency. In that spirit he embarked on the Aswan High Dam, a signature project that, once completed, would control the flow of the Nile, reducing flooding, increasing arable land and producing hydropower. In December 1955, the United States, Britain and the World Bank agreed to finance the dam's construction.

It soon became clear, however, that Egypt would not be able to repay the loan. Private investment and development since the revolution had been slow. Nasser's needling of the West – anti-American propaganda; support for anti-Western forces in the Congo, Libya and Algeria; an arms deal with Czechoslovakia;[51] recognition of the People's Republic of China[52] – led the United States and Britain to believe he was already on the Soviet side. Washington canceled its funding for the Aswan Dam on July 19, 1956. The United Kingdom and the World Bank rescinded their pledges shortly thereafter.

To compound the challenge, the United States announced publicly Egypt's economic inadequacies as the reason for the cancellation. 'No one likes being refused a loan by a bank,' as the World Bank President Eugene Black commented, adding that 'people get [especially] upset when they read in the paper the next day that they were refused because their credit wasn't any good'.[53] To Nasser and Sadat, the issue went beyond creditworthiness. The Egyptian leaders saw Western powers using debt to humiliate and stunt Egypt – just as they had done seventy years earlier when they occupied the country.

Within days, Nasser retaliated. The Suez Canal Company, owned mostly by French and British shareholders, had operated the canal since the late nineteenth century. On July 26, 1956, Nasser announced the Company's nationalization and, in its stead, established the state-owned Suez Canal Authority. Egypt, not Egypt's colonizers, was to reap the benefit of the lucrative tolls in the canal, the fastest and most-traveled sea route from Europe to Asia. Those new revenues, Nasser claimed, would fund the Aswan High Dam.[54]

The nationalization of the canal was a challenge to the entire British position in the Middle East. In August 1956, British Prime Minister Anthony Eden wrote to President Eisenhower: 'The removal of Nasser, and the installation in Egypt of a regime less hostile to the West, must . . . rank high among our objectives.' Eden was convinced that Nasser was a new 'Mussolini', one whose ambitions put Britain's very existence 'at his mercy'.[55]

That October, after secret collusion, Britain, France and Israel invaded Egypt to retake the canal. American diplomatic intervention led to a UN General Assembly vote against Britain and France – America's formal allies. There was a run on the pound sterling, and the United States blocked the IMF from supporting the currency. Abandoned by Britain's chief ally, in failing health and humiliated, Eden discontinued the project and resigned in January 1957.

Salvation by America did not alter Nasser's hostility to the West. Rather, he seized the occasion to raise the stakes. With the end of the conflict, he proceeded to keep the canal closed for another five months, disrupting Europe's supplies from Asia and denting the British, French and other European economies.

The canal's closure was a challenge for the Israelis, too; they had taken direct military losses in the invasion and now faced a suspension of US aid, an interruption in oil supplies and the proscription of their ships from the canal.[56] Under pressure from Eisenhower and the threat of US sanctions, Israel withdrew from the Sinai – creating the impression, in some Egyptian minds, that Washington could dictate Israeli policies. At the same time, a series of punitive actions by Nasser's government at home brought about the wholesale expropriation and forced exodus of roughly three-quarters of Egypt's 60,000 Jews.[57]

Though the canal closure enhanced Nasser's celebrity and helped propel Egypt onto the international stage, it was something of a Pyrrhic victory. In the aftermath of the Suez crisis, France, Britain and the United States blocked Egyptian government assets held in their respective countries.[58] Damaged by the invasion, the canal required expensive repairs and in the meantime generated no revenue for its new Egyptian operators. Tourism fell, businesses departed – wounds made only more painful by Nasser's sequestration in November of the Anglo-Egyptian Oil Company, several banks and insurance companies, and other European-owned entities.[59] Foreign capital fled Egypt.

The Soviets seized the occasion to build a new international alignment solidifying Egypt's alienation from the West. Over the next eight years, Soviet Premier Nikita Khrushchev would pledge large loans on favorable terms: $325 million for the Aswan High Dam, followed by nearly $175 million for other industrial projects.[60] Soviet aid, military equipment and military advisors by the tens of thousands poured into Egypt.[61]

In the Arab world, Nasser's nationalization of the Suez Canal Company and defense against the European and Israeli military operations had made him a hero. He relished his leadership role and cultivated it with slogans of Arab solidarity. But once he was crowned leader of the Arabs, the Arabs wanted him to lead. For Egypt, reliant for food on foreign aid from the United States and for arms on the Soviet Union, shouldering others' burdens was an unwelcome and infeasible project.

When Syria approached Egypt with a request for union, however, Nasser could not refuse. To do so would have been to reveal the limits of his commitment to the Arab world. Thus was born the United Arab Republic (UAR), an ill-fated experiment in Arab unity that lasted just three years, from 1958 to 1961. Increasing pan-Arab aspirations led Nasser to involve Egypt in the Yemeni civil war, a draining, unproductive conflict later dubbed 'Egypt's Vietnam'. Egyptian forces would not be fully extracted from Yemen until 1971.

Having already overextended Egypt's foreign commitments, Nasser, in 1967, decided to challenge Israel. On the basis of Soviet information – which turned out to have been faked – that Israel was about to attack Syria, Nasser closed the Straits of Tiran and moved his army into the Sinai Peninsula, which since the Suez crisis had been in effect demilitarized. In the resulting war, the Israeli air force wiped out its Egyptian counterpart while Israeli troops occupied the West Bank, the Gaza Strip, the Golan Heights, East Jerusalem and the entire Sinai. The Six-Day War, waged in June 1967 on the Arab side by the joint forces of Egypt, Syria and Jordan – aided in certain theaters by Sudanese contingents and in others by Palestinian guerrillas – ended with Israel more than tripling its territory, placing its forces on the Suez Canal and leaving its Arab neighbors humiliated.

Nasser was so embarrassed by the defeat that he resigned the presidency on June 9. Called back to office by popular demonstrations, he tried to restore his prestige by launching a war of attrition against Israel. But rather than regaining Egypt's former glory, the war in Yemen, the Six-Day War and the War of Attrition (which lasted until 1970) had the cumulative effect of draining Egypt's resources and further increasing its dependence on the Soviet Union.

In 1967 and 1968, Egypt's economy contracted.[62] Domestic development lagged. Productivity remained low. A second Suez Canal closure, which would persist for eight years, robbed Egypt of the very revenues that had motivated the canal's nationalization. In addition, Nasser's industrialization program had converted arable land into manufacturing space, with the consequence that Egypt was now reliant on imported grain.

The Soviet Union, the funder of Nasser's grandest domestic projects, soon proved more mercenary than ally. Khrushchev's fall in 1964 had precipitated a new, hard-nosed approach under Leonid Brezhnev, Alexei Kosygin and Nikolai Podgorny. Already by 1966, economic aid was drying up[63] – as was Soviet cooperativeness. Soviet leaders began advocating Egyptian austerity policies; in May 1966, Kosygin denied a request from Cairo to postpone its debt repayment.[64] The Soviet Union would maintain its influence as an arms supplier and occasional financier but ceased to be Egypt's great-power benefactor.

In June 1967, the Egyptian leader broke off relations with the United States over its military aid to Israel. By 1970, the Soviets had stopped responding to Nasser's appeals for aid, loans and debt relief.[65] In pursuit of pan-Arabism, Nasser had brought about Egypt's isolation.

SADAT'S PERSPECTIVE

Even at its height, the friendship between Egypt and the Soviet Union had been formal to the point of coldness. Sadat witnessed firsthand Soviet disdain for what they considered Egyptian dependency. In June 1961, while serving as speaker of Egypt's National Assembly, he was hosted in Moscow by Soviet Premier Nikita Khrushchev. Over dinner, Khrushchev reportedly told Sadat: 'We can hardly have confidence in your Nasser when he is losing his grip on the country and not solving his country's problems.' Sadat left the dinner immediately and departed Moscow without a farewell to his hosts.[66]

For another nine years, as Sadat watched Nasser simultaneously rely on, and be put off by, the Soviets, he became convinced that alignment with them was disastrous. On September 28, 1970, three months after a final, ineffectual plea to Moscow for greater assistance, Nasser suffered a heart attack and died. In his memoirs, Sadat quotes Zhou Enlai, the premier of the People's Republic of China, telling him that the Russians had caused the collapse of Nasser's health. Sadat himself was sure that their abuse had hastened the end: 'It was undoubtedly one important reason why his morale deteriorated and so precipitated a terminal heart condition and diabetes. How and when a man dies is, of course, preordained by God – but Zhou was right.'[67]

Nasser had believed that Egypt lay at the overlap of three circles – the Arab, the Islamic and the African[68] – and perceived 'a shared destiny' with the Arab world as a whole.[69] He considered it his mission to liberate the Arab world from the yoke of colonialism. He regarded Arab unity as the essential first step – the defeat of 1948 by Israel having demonstrated the risks of Arab countries acting alone – and saw himself as their unifier and charismatic leader.

But if 1948 was Nasser's formative conflict, 1967 was Sadat's; to him, the Six-Day War had illustrated the danger of placing pan-Arab solidarity above the national interest. For his part, Sadat felt 'the pull of the Mediterranean' and desired Egypt's full 'initiation into the world system'.[70] A high degree of engagement in the Arab world was a tactical obligation but not a civilizational one. In Egypt's long history, Arab ties were one of many influences; proposals of pan-Arabism could therefore be judged on their immediate practical merits.

Nasser's death came just days after his attempt to paper over Arab divisions between Jordan's King Hussein and Yasir Arafat, the chairman of the Palestine Liberation Organization (PLO), which in September 1970 had hijacked four commercial airplanes and had attempted to overthrow Hussein, who in turn evicted the PLO.[71] Even without attributing Nasser's death to the strain of these efforts, Sadat could see that Nasser had cornered himself. Breaking relations with the United States after 1967 had made Egypt solely dependent on Soviet aid. In Sadat's evolving view, alignment with the Soviet Union had brought few rewards and the freezing of Egypt's position. But any future alignment with the United States would have to be compatible with Egypt's autonomy.

Even before Nasser's death, Sadat started to act on his instincts. As Nasser tilted toward the Soviets, Sadat approached the United States with statements based on straightforward calculations of the national interest. In 1959, he told the US ambassador to Egypt that the American and Egyptian positions in Africa ought to be viewed as compatible.[72] In 1962 and 1963, as Egypt waded into Yemen on the side of an army-led insurrection against the ruling imam, Sadat kept in contact with Washington, urging the United States not to intervene on the side of the royalists; his purpose was to avoid direct conflict between the United States and Egypt.[73] But by 1964, despite these efforts, relations between Egypt and the United States had become outright hostile, strained over the Congo, Yemen and US aid policy.[74] Nevertheless in 1966, Sadat became the highest-profile Egyptian since the revolution to visit the United States in an official capacity. This time, he hoped to persuade America to play the role of honest broker as Egypt was attempting to strike a deal with Saudi Arabia over Yemen.[75]

These were unemotional appeals founded on rational considerations of mutual interest. Had Sadat, as a top Egyptian official, signaled any kind of unusual friendliness, one of his American interlocutors would surely have noted it. Neither in his years as a government minister nor in his decade as the leader of the legislature was his attitude toward the United States deemed by American officials to be especially warm.

At that point in time, Sadat had not yet developed visionary views on peace. He likely grasped, by the autumn of 1970, the practical futility of perennial war with Israel: intermittent fighting was costly, and Egypt's treasury was already depleted. Air raids, threatening Cairo, stalled Egypt's economy.[76] The conflict – putting Egypt at odds with the West – was precluding Egypt from operating in the wider international system. As a minister to Nasser, he had gravitated toward frameworks governed more by state sovereignty than by imperial hegemony or regional solidarity. And he understood the possibilities of neutrality as Nasser had not. But he had not fitted these pieces together into a coherent, long-term view of Egypt's future course, or of himself as its helmsman.

Nor was there public evidence at the time of his potential to become a peacemaker. In fact, nearly all of his signals pointed the other way. Despite his contacts with the United States, he was its frequent and vehement critic – a tendency that persisted, at least in public, through the early years of his presidency. In his 1957 book *Revolt on the Nile* he asserted that Israel had come into existence because 'the State Department dreamed of forcing its authority on the Islamic world, from the Caucasus to the Indian Ocean.'[77] And in 1970, he categorically rejected the possibility of recognizing Israel: 'Never! Never! Never! This is something no one can decide ... Our people here will crush anyone who would decide this!'[78] He treated Israel as a spearhead of American imperialism: 'Israel has been the first line of defense of American interests and ... the Americans gave her the green light to the Gaza Aggression.'[79]

These voluble criticisms of the United States were enactments of his penchant for dramatic impact. Sadat believed that, 'In Egypt, personalities have always been more important than political programs'.[80] Early in his presidency, he summoned a top Soviet advisor for a dressing-down. In the uniform of the supreme commander of the Egyptian armed forces, he warned the advisor: 'I am Stalin, not Kalinin [then the token president of the Soviet Union]. If you don't carry out this order of mine, I'll treat you exactly as Stalin would have treated you.'[81] His manner of speaking was one of emphasis trending toward exuberance; he occasionally recounted confrontations and bold actions for which the underlying evidence was ambiguous. At times this made him appear more a rhetorician, operating on levels of drama and status, than a figure of political purposefulness.

In the first two years of his presidency, opposition to the United States seemed to remain a central component of Sadat's policy. Thus, he contrasted the supposed benefits of Egypt's partnership with the Soviet Union to the miserliness of the West, which had 'refuse[d] to supply us with one single pistol, even if we were to pay its price in foreign currency',[82] or which had pretended 'to assist us and then reneged, hoping thereby to shake the confidence of our people in itself, in its dreams, and its revolutionary leadership'.[83] In early 1971, he would refer to proposals put forward by Golda Meir, then Israel's prime minister, as 'a pipe dream, based on the victory complex'.[84] Well into his presidency, Sadat was considered by American policymakers as a less dramatic version of Nasser.

THE CORRECTIVE REVOLUTION

Charismatic leaders such as Gamal Abdel Nasser base their politics on casting a spell. Their inspirational rhetoric and demeanor are designed to smother the bleaker truths of everyday life. Stubborn realities come into focus only when the singular, blinding personality disappears.

Such was the atmosphere in October 1970, after Nasser's death. Sadat, as vice president, took over the presidency as a transitional leader in accordance with the Egyptian constitution and subject to confirmation by the parliament. His inauguration was overshadowed by Nasser's funeral, as millions poured into the streets to pay their respects. The procession was so overwhelmed that Sadat feared the crowds might prevent Nasser's proper burial by taking his body away with them.[85]

Though he had spent nearly two decades in the upper echelons of national politics, his refusal to thrust himself into the limelight meant that Sadat was still not well known to the Egyptian people and even less to the outside world.[86] During his progression up the political ladder,

Sadat had not been held in high regard in Washington. In December 1969, when he was named vice president, it was the common belief not only in the press but also in Washington and in our Cairo embassy that Sadat owed his promotion primarily to his being inconsequential and therefore in no position to threaten Nasser's leadership.[87]

In late September 1970, Nixon learned of Nasser's death and Sadat's automatic succession to the presidency while aboard an aircraft carrier, the USS *Saratoga*, in the Mediterranean.[88] The shared instinct of most of those present – as well as of available intelligence reports – was that Sadat would not last long as president. He seemed to embody continuity with Nasser's aggressively nationalist ideology and, to boot, looked like a man of little influence or substance.[89] One senior advisor gave him six weeks, the assessment being that his succession was just a 'convenient way of blocking selection of a stronger rival'.[90] Likewise, a CIA report from the time failed to include Sadat among 'the most important men around Nasser at the time of his death' and predicted that he was 'most unlikely to make a bid to take over permanently'.[91]

Sadat's personal qualities contributed to his relative obscurity. Though he sometimes put on a show of assertiveness, as in his put-down of the Soviet advisor or his railings against America, these performances were to make a point. In reality, he was preternaturally calm. This attribute had somewhat insulated him from the pressures of ambition and the frenzy of political life. Over his eighteen years in government, he had remained at a remove from the center of the maelstrom. He was one of the few members of the RCC initially not given a ministerial position. Sometimes this detachment was intentional: at least once, he had suspended his membership in the RCC because of his dislike of the posturing and infighting.[92]

The combination of his quietist personality and his friendship with Nasser had limited the usual incentives to develop a political base of his own – and he was never a natural politician. He spent more time in reflection, and in a way at prayer, than at the podium. His tendency toward solitude endowed him with insight and independent thought but also marked him as a loner.

Like the foreign observers, many Egyptian onlookers also believed that Sadat would be no more than a transitional leader. His colleagues on the

RCC, particularly the powerful cluster headed by Ali Sabri, Sharawi Gomaa, Sami Sharaf and General Mohamed Fawzi, perceived him as easy to control.[93] Sabri was a member of the Egyptian aristocracy and was considered a logical successor to Nasser by virtue of having served as his vice president, prime minister and intelligence chief. Gomaa had been Nasser's minister of internal affairs, Fawzi his defense minister, and Sharaf a close presidential aide – indeed, his consigliere. (At the start of his presidency, Sadat would retain these three, the last as a minister of state.)

To succeed formally, Sadat needed to be nominated for the presidency by the executive committee of the Arab Socialist Union (ASU), Egypt's only political party. That group, with the support of the influential Council of Ministers, agreed to give him the nod on October 7, 1970.[94] They acquiesced in part because they could not agree on who among themselves could play Nasser's role, and because they judged Sadat too weak to challenge them. To ensure their control, they attached five conditions to his nomination, including a pledge to rule in tandem with the leaders of the ASU and the National Assembly, among them prominently the allies of Sabri and Gomaa. In effect, this cohort had given itself veto power over presidential policy. Sadat agreed, was nominated and duly elected.

Despite the pitfalls of the late president's efforts toward Arab unity, the inadequate state of the military forces and the economic mismanagement that had withered both the private and public sector, Nasser remained a beloved icon of the Egyptian people. Those disappointed with the economic and political situation he left behind cast about for someone else to blame. It was on the new President Sadat that these burdens fell.

To succeed a charismatic leader is in the best of circumstances a forbidding task; while policy can be transmitted, charisma is intangible. Capturing the imagination of the people, who were still mourning Nasser, was unlikely. And without control over the workings of his government, Sadat knew he would be a puppet. He needed, above all, to establish himself.

Within six months of his election, he made a number of unilateral decisions that were at odds with the views of those seeking to exercise a veto over him. He abolished by decree the seizure and sequestration of private property, hinted at a peace gesture toward Israel and declared an agreement of federation with Syria and Libya.[95]

Shocked by the new president's venture outside the bounds of their agreement, and threatened by a dilution of their power in the National Assembly, Sabri and Gomaa began plotting a military coup.[96] Sadat discovered the plot and fired them. The conspirators then resigned as a group, hoping to instigate a constitutional crisis. But Sadat, aided by relationships in the Assembly he had accumulated since 1952 and during his years as speaker, worked overnight to find replacements for each of the vacant positions in his newly reconstituted government.

Instead of bending to his opponents' demands as expected, he swept them away in a single stroke, a move that would become known as the 'Corrective Revolution'. Within twenty-four hours, he had imprisoned most of the plotters; ninety-one would ultimately face trial. Such decisiveness had not been evident in Sadat's earlier career, but it would become the hallmark of his presidency. Each of his bold and unexpected moves was deliberately calculated to serve a larger strategic objective. As one senior diplomat put it at the time: 'They badly misjudged the man if they thought he was going to be pliant ... They forgot that he carried bombs in his pocket as a young revolutionary.'[97]

STRATEGIC PATIENCE

The Corrective Revolution consolidated Sadat's power and liberated him from his colleagues' control. But he was still tethered to Nasser's legacy and Egypt's realities, and constrained by two contradictory imperatives: to retain popular legitimacy he would need to retain Nasserism and his link to Nasser's image; to reverse Egypt's fortunes, he would need to jettison many elements of Nasser's program. He therefore decided to reaffirm the Nasserist program while gradually, and at first imperceptibly, turning it in a new direction. By pursuing what looked like the established course, he would cloak his real intentions.

In a speech to the National Assembly shortly after his nomination on October 7, Sadat announced that he would continue to 'pursue the path of Gamal Abdel Nasser whatever the case may be and from whatever position'. Reaffirming Nasser's foreign policy, especially toward Israel, he would seek to free Arab lands from Israeli occupation, increase Arab unity and 'safeguard, fully, the rights of the Palestinian people'.[98]

Though domestic policy would play a large part in restoring Egypt's historic role, Sadat was convinced that his ability to resurrect a truly independent Egypt would depend in the end on his foreign policy. But when he entered the presidency, he gave no hint of a seminal foreign policy shift. As Nasser's successor and heir, he could not risk a dramatic dissociation even if in the innermost parts of his mind he was considering it.

Sadat's first move was to sign a Treaty of Friendship with the Soviet Union in May 1971 – a political step beyond Nasser's technically economic move of accepting Soviet aid for the Aswan Dam in 1956. In September of the same year, he also nodded to Nasser's pan-Arab legacy in following through on the formalities of a federation with Libya and Syria. Throughout, he kept up Nasser's usual barrage of criticism toward Israel and America:

> The principal party is [not Israel, but Israel's] guardian, America. It conveys open defiance to us in everything: defiance to our existence, defiance to our dignity, our independence, our will, to every value we and the past generations fought to accomplish after the July 23rd Revolution.[99]

As with many of Sadat's moves, this last one had a dual purpose: it placated Soviet uneasiness over the dismissal and arrest of the pro-Soviet Ali Sabri at a time when Egypt still depended on the Soviets for military equipment. It also provided a means of testing whether the Soviet alliance could be exploited to induce the United States to pressure Israel for a Middle East settlement on the basis of Arab demands.

At their summit in Khartoum in 1967, the Arab leaders had sworn never to recognize Israel, never to make peace with Israel and never to negotiate with Israel. In his early years in office, Sadat's domestic position did not allow any deviation from the Khartoum rules. To that end, he now continued – and, if anything, made more explicit – the Nasserite attacks on Israel and the United States. In his speech to the National Assembly in 1972, he averred: 'Armed colonialism of the brand we witness in Israel dislodges a people from their land . . . the means it uses to dislodge them is genocide and destitution.' For its part, the United States, though 'powerful, mighty, and tyrannical', was nevertheless also 'impotent'.[100] Whatever his ambitions in his first year in office, Sadat limited himself to paths in foreign policy charted by his predecessor, such as dispatching UN diplomats to engage Israel indirectly in the negotiation of interim ceasefires along the Suez Canal.

Yet, while operating under this guise of continuity, Sadat also embarked on gradual 'de-Nasserization'. Cautiously, he accelerated Egypt's transition toward capitalism. He also led the formation of a new constitution that, while retaining the basic institutional structure of strong presidential command laid down in the 1952 revolution, added a greater emphasis on democratic rights and greater lenience to religious groups, especially the Muslim Brothers, many of whom he released from prison.

In foreign policy, from his intimate vantage point in Nasser's entourage and then his vice presidency, Sadat interpreted his predecessor's end as a lesson in the importance of appreciating limits. With the Suez closure, and given Egypt's involvements in the Arab world, Nasser had taken on tasks beyond his capacities and failed to see the value in incrementalism, including (or especially) in the pursuit of ideological objectives. These had incurred reputational, economic and military costs – and also costs to Nasser's own flexibility by tying him up in impractical commitments and ideological rigidities.

With these insights, Sadat initiated an early peace feeler to Israel too ambiguous for dramatic results. In February 1971 – only five months after ascending to the presidency – he offered to reopen the Suez Canal if Israel would withdraw from the canal's immediate surroundings.*[101] This arguably marked a retreat from Egypt's 'and the Arab world's demand of full Israeli withdrawal to the pre-1967 borders.

Israel interpreted this offer as a maneuver to compromise the Bar-Lev Line, its set of fortified embankments along the eastern edge of the Suez Canal. It also objected to Sadat's indirect method of negotiation, involving UN officials as intermediaries, generally through a mediator designated by the UN secretary general. To keep channels open with Israel, Sadat went along with temporary ceasefire agreements along the Suez Canal and, even when they broke down, refrained from ordering a resumption of hostilities.[102]

Little more than a year later, in July 1972, Sadat's gradualism was replaced by a dramatic move: the abrupt expulsion from Egypt of roughly 20,000 Soviet advisors, without warning to Moscow or prior consultation with any Western country, including the United States,

---

* Reopening had not yet occurred because, though it would have afforded Egypt badly needed cash, it required equipment Egypt lacked and represented a significant concession to Israel and Europe, both of which relied on the canal for cheap oil transit.

about either the move or its consequences.[103] Though the full implications of this change in strategy took a while to reveal themselves, it
would develop into a turning point in Middle East diplomacy.

In retrospect, it appears that Sadat had given himself two years to
determine whether Nasser's reliance on Moscow might produce tangible results. That is why, after the May 1971 signing of a Friendship
Treaty between the Soviet Union and Egypt, Brezhnev began to urge
Nixon to accelerate peace efforts in the Middle East.

The overture from Brezhnev came during the concluding phases of
the Vietnam War and before the 1972 summits in Beijing (February)
and Moscow (May), which would redraw the global diplomatic map.
With this in mind, the American response was what we also told the
Middle East parties: that we were prepared to discuss principles of an
eventual settlement, including at the Moscow summit. The start of a
formal process would be based on progress in those talks.

The strategy adopted at the beginning of the Nixon administration
had involved creating for Egypt incentives to turn to American diplomacy. The Moscow summit had ended with a joint statement of
principles including a shared commitment to maintain stability in the
Middle East, which omitted any call for an immediate resumption of
active negotiations. Coupled with the Soviet refusal to supply Sadat
with arms at a level he considered adequate, this seems to have cemented
Sadat's judgment that the Soviet partnership lacked utility.

Every leading statesman I have encountered – with the possible
exception of de Gaulle – would have implemented a new strategy
incrementally, in stages that permitted measures of retreat if it proved
ineffective. By contrast, Sadat made a radical departure that could be
sustained only by forward movement.

Tension between Egyptian and Soviet officials had been building for
years.[104] The spectacle of foreigners visiting indignities on Egyptians
had, since childhood, struck a deep personal chord in Sadat. When in
1972 the Soviet leader Leonid Brezhnev demanded an explanation for
the expulsion of Soviet advisors, Sadat wrote him: 'You look on us as
though we were a backward country, while our officers have had
education in your academies.'[105] In his memoirs, Sadat reflects: 'I wanted
to tell the Russians that the will of Egypt was entirely Egyptian; I wanted
to tell the whole world that we are always our own masters.'[106]

Egypt would continue to accept Soviet economic aid – and the Soviets, intent on maintaining a modicum of influence, persisted in providing it. But Sadat had achieved his purpose of demonstrating that Egypt was capable of autonomous action and not merely the vassal of a distant superpower.

With the expulsion of Soviet personnel from Egypt, Sadat had removed a principal obstacle to American participation in a peace process. With Soviet influence waning, the diplomatic route via America appeared to be a natural path forward.

But foreign policy is as influenced by intangibles as it is by objective circumstances. Sadat was still held in low regard in Washington. His initial public steps as president contradicted his private overtures, which were in any case too indirect and subtle to suggest a potential opening for transformative dialogue. My personal assessment had not improved materially from the time of his ascension to the presidency. In February 1973, as part of Sadat's early outreach, his national security advisor Hafiz Ismail visited Washington and invited me to Cairo – if our talks made progress. I scribbled a note to a colleague: 'Would it be impolite to ask what the second prize is?'

The outreach was unappealing on a number of levels. In light of Sadat's frequent anti-American statements in 1971 and 1972, Cairo did not appear a promising site for negotiation. Also, Hafiz Ismail's visit to Washington occurred barely a month after the Paris Agreement ending the Vietnam War. Around the same time, Nixon had promised Israeli Prime Minister Golda Meir that another negotiation with Israel on a range of issues so seemingly intractable would not occur until after the forthcoming Israeli elections, then scheduled for late October. Sadat's apparent aim was to enlist the United States in producing a new Middle East arrangement on existing Arab terms, which began with the unconditional Israeli withdrawal to the 1967 frontiers as a prelude to negotiations regarding recognition of Israel. The Soviets had failed to produce this result for Nasser, and a number of Arab leaders, who had not been able to achieve it by force, refused to seek it by dialogue.

The fundamental challenge presented by the prevailing Arab–Israeli peace process was that both sides demanded an irrevocable concession as a condition for entering negotiations at all. The Arab countries required that Israel agree to return to the pre-war 1967 frontiers; Israel insisted on direct negotiations, which its adversaries refused on the grounds that this would constitute recognition.

Despite these obstacles, Nixon did agree to an exploratory conversation with Hafiz Ismail. At the meeting, which took place on February 23, 1973, Ismail made explicit what Sadat's expulsion of the Soviets had implied: that Egypt was ready to normalize relations with the United States. Nixon affirmed his intention to explore that possibility in good faith, and ended by summarizing his understanding of the difficulties of the Middle East negotiation as 'the irresistible force meeting the immovable object'. He suggested that a settlement would have to satisfy both the demand for Egyptian sovereignty and the imperative of Israeli security. Given what he called the 'gulf between the parties', however, he felt it would be prudent to pursue a step-by-step approach, seeking interim and partial solutions, rather than attempt a comprehensive resolution (though without categorically foreclosing the latter as an option).[107]

As had become standard operating procedure, Nixon stressed that the actual negotiation should be conducted through the security advisor's office and that Ismail and I should start the exploratory phase immediately – and indeed our discussions began the following day. To permit extended conversations and to emphasize their informal, confidential character, they took place at a private home in a New York suburb.

In our talks, Hafiz Ismail repeated what he had already told Nixon: that Egypt was tired of the 'no war, no peace' situation and that Sadat was prepared to reestablish diplomatic relations with the United States. He urged the United States to participate actively in the peace process, deviating from established Arab terms only by implying a readiness to explore a separate peace on the basis of total Israeli withdrawal. Sticking to Nixon's suggested step-by-step approach, I outlined some details as to how it might work.

It was, I pointed out, a significant departure from the methods that had characterized Middle East diplomacy heretofore. The prevailing approach to Middle East peace was comprehensive, involving the resolution of all contested borders between Israel and its neighbors as well as the Palestinian Arabs. It also envisioned an encompassing peace conference including the major regional players, together with Palestinian representatives, with the United States and the Soviet Union participating as great-power facilitators as well as guarantors of the projected agreement.

A step-by-step approach, by contrast, would seek to disaggregate the Israel–Palestinian dispute from the possibility of regional progress on particular issues. Some of these issues were related to sovereignty (jurisdictional and administrative arrangements, normalization of relations and ultimately mutual recognition), while others were related to security (creating nonproliferation regimes, countering terrorist networks and ensuring the free flow of energy resources). Taking steps forward on such practical issues, rather than tying them to the ultimate resolution of an importantly psychological and historic problem, could create an organic momentum by enabling those regional players who had the greatest interest in the resolution of the individual issues to sustain the outcome.

The conversations with Ismail were inconclusive in terms of immediate decisions, in large part because at that time, the spring of 1973, a step-by-step approach was altogether precluded by inter-Arab agreements. Nevertheless I outlined to Ismail how steps might be taken – for example, by separating Egyptian and Israeli sovereignty criteria from accommodations on mutual security concerns. Ismail did not receive a program from us embracing his stated goals, but he did receive a detailed and accurate picture of our proposed alternative (which, in the end, Sadat would accept).

That was in February. In the fall – on October 6, to be precise – Sadat decided, before returning to diplomacy, to deliver a shock that altered every country's perceptions of him.

THE 1973 WAR

As early as July 1971, at a session of the Arab Socialist Union Congress, Sadat had declared that he would not 'accept this state of no war and no peace'.[108] He had identified the problem – stasis with Israel – but it is unlikely that, so early in his presidency, he had made any decision about how to solve it. Rather, he was still exploring various ways of improving his negotiating position.[109]

It was not until sometime in 1972 that he decided to alter his strategy, but, at that time, he could not move toward a step-by-step approach in the Arab world and retain minimal support from the Soviet Union without some dramatic act that established his own authenticity.

Sadat decided to go to war. He may have hoped to achieve his stated

objectives in one fell swoop. Much more likely, he was initiating hostilities in the expectation that it might legitimize alternative diplomatic
options. Jehan Sadat, his extraordinary wife, recalled that he described
the situation to her as requiring 'one more war in order to win and enter
into negotiations from a position of equality'.[110] The White House
discussions in 1973 with Ismail confirmed for Sadat the US willingness
to become involved – and also its limits. They convinced him that, failing total Egyptian victory, the step-by-step approach might provide a
fallback position.

For more than a year, Sadat prepared for the right constellation of
forces to 'achieve a real peace'.[111] That period was described in August
1972 by the Egyptian journalist Mohammed Heykal as 'a constant
hemorrhage for Egypt, a death without heroism that is on the point of
suffocating the country'.[112] Jehan Sadat remembered of the period:

> Egyptian soldiers and freedom fighters continued to be killed in the spor-
> adic fighting along the Suez Canal. The windows of all the houses and the
> headlights of all the cars in the Canal Zone continued to be painted dark
> blue to stop any lights from showing during air raids. In Cairo sandbags
> were still piled in front of buildings, while the windows on museums and
> stores were taped to minimize damage from bombs. The atmosphere was
> very depressing during this time that the historians were to call 'no war,
> no peace'. We all hated it and wanted it to end. Especially Anwar.[113]

Determined to wait until the situation had evolved, so that his war
would be 'the last war',[114] Sadat made careful preparations. In mid-
1972, after the expulsion of Soviet advisors, Sadat ordered military
plans to be drawn up. In October 1972, when he inquired into progress,
he discovered that his generals, perhaps disbelieving the prospects, had
failed even to begin the task. After firing the war minister, Sadat set
aside additional funds and purchased more weapons from the Soviets.[115] He also secretly elaborated a joint war plan with Syrian President
Hafez al-Assad.[116]

As he primed his own military, Sadat confounded Israel's. Through
the spring and summer of 1973, Sadat goaded the Israelis with threats
of action, then duped them into readying for assault. Twice, the Israel
defense forces mobilized at great expense; twice, they realized the alarms
had been false. On six separate occasions, Egypt performed apparently
routine military exercises resembling a real operation. On the day prior

to the actual invasion, Soviet planes in the process of evacuating the USSR's diplomats – a gesture which should have alerted the Israelis and the United States – were misinterpreted to be part of Soviet training.[117] After the 1973 war, Israel's then-defense minister, Moshe Dayan, replying to the question of why he had not mobilized in October, would answer that Sadat 'made me do it twice, at a cost of ten million dollars each time. So, when it was the third time around I thought he wasn't serious. But he tricked me!'[118]

By the fall of 1973, Sadat had spent nearly eighteen months shaping the international landscape for an impending war. Public flexibility on transit of the canal had burnished his international reputation. Expelling the Soviets had increased his diplomatic options and ensured that the advisors would neither prevent nor subvert his plans. Exploratory conversations with the White House implied that he entered the war with a working relationship with Washington. He must have calculated that the United States would help to limit the consequences of a military setback and might enter negotiations.

Based on considerations such as these, on October 6, 1973, Egypt and Syria launched a coordinated offensive against Israel. Sadat had already called on the Egyptian people, in January 1972, to prepare for 'confrontation' and to embrace an ethic of forbearance:

> We have ahead of us many hardships and difficulties. But with God's help we will bear its burdens and sacrifices. Our people will give, in the battle, the living example that they are a great people like their history, their long civilization and their humanity and ideals ... Our Lord! Make our faith the best and be with us until victory.[119]

On the first day of the war, Sadat communicated to me, then secretary of state, that his aims were limited and he intended efforts to facilitate negotiations for peace after hostilities had ended. On the war's second day, I replied: 'You're making war with Soviet arms. Keep in mind that you will have to make peace with American diplomacy.'[120]

Managing to achieve the kind of military success that had eluded Nasser, Egyptian forces laid down pontoon bridges across the Suez Canal and crossed the Bar-Lev line. They advanced up to 10 miles into the Sinai, retaking territory that had been captured by Israel in 1967. At the same time, Syrian forces penetrated Israeli positions in the Golan Heights. As the two Arab forces pressed onward, equipped largely with

Soviet arms,[121] Israel suffered significant casualties and losses of equipment.

The early Egyptian–Syrian success stunned the world, confronting all sides with unexpected situations. Paradoxically, however, once the war was fully under way, the UN Security Council, which had the responsibility for preserving peace, shrank from proposing a ceasefire. Of the Council's two most powerful members, the Soviet Union was opposed because it did not want to impede the perceived Arab advance, while the United States was reluctant lest it prevent an Israeli counter-strike. The other members were undecided out of a mixture of fear and uncertainty. In the event, the Security Council would not meet to vote on a ceasefire until the United States and the Soviet Union had agreed on a text on October 22, more than two weeks after the war's outbreak.

During these weeks, Nixon's domestic crisis came to a head. On the same day as the outbreak of the 1973 war, Vice President Spiro Agnew began the process of his resignation as the result of activities conducted while he was serving as governor of Maryland (1967–9). This was con-cluded on October 10, coinciding with another wave of Watergate hearings on the issue of which of Nixon's taped conversations should be released. Nixon's efforts to avoid releasing these tapes would culminate on October 20, two weeks into the Middle East war (and while I was in Moscow negotiating a ceasefire), when Nixon requested the resignation of and dismissed the attorney general and the special prosecutor, respect-ively. The resulting uproar led to the initiation of impeachment proceedings against Nixon.

Despite his domestic difficulties, Nixon maintained his control of foreign affairs. Early on during the war, he established two primary objectives: to end the hostilities as quickly as possible and, as I said pub-licly on his behalf, to do so 'in a manner that would enable us to make a major contribution to removing the conditions that [had] produced four wars between Arabs and Israelis in the [previous] 25 years'.[122]

On the ground, the situation was changing almost daily. By Tuesday, October 9 – the fourth day of the war and the day Spiro Agnew's formal resignation as vice president was dealt with by Nixon – the Israeli ambassador Simcha Dinitz and the military attaché General Mordechai Gur appeared in the Map Room of the White House residence to inform me that Israel had lost hundreds of tanks and many tens of airplanes in the initial battles along the Suez Canal. They requested immediate resupply and a visit to Washington by Prime Minister Meir to plead her case.

After concluding the Agnew resignation, Nixon agreed to respond to the immediate needs with some emergency support. He directed an immediate resupply of three airplanes a day and an evaluation of the feasibility of mobilizing our civilian air fleet. To enable Israel to use its backup weapons, Nixon promised to replace all losses after the war.

On Thursday, October 11, Dinitz reappeared at the White House with another dramatic message: the Israeli chief of staff, David Elazar, and Defense Minister Moshe Dayan had convinced the prime minister that further Israeli attacks along the Suez Canal were too costly in the face of the belt of surface-to-air missiles (SAM) on the canal's west bank to provide air cover for the territory 15–20 miles east of the canal. Israel was therefore prepared to accept a ceasefire and was asking us to arrange it.[123] To improve its bargaining position, Israel would open an offensive on the more vulnerable Syrian front, thereby giving an incentive for the Soviet Union to support a ceasefire request in the Security Council. Nixon agreed, and we approached Britain to introduce such a resolution.

The British government – represented by Sir Alec Douglas-Home as foreign secretary – undertook the initiative. But Sadat, when asked to assent on Saturday, October 13, amazed us by refusing unless Israel committed itself to return to the pre-June 1967 frontiers. Another approach to him via Australia met the same fate.

By Sunday, October 14, Sadat's motives for these refusals became apparent: he had decided to lunge more deeply into Sinai with two armored divisions. Whether impelled by overconfidence in his military capacity after the crossing of the canal, or by a desire to relieve the pressures on his ally Assad, or by a brief loss of his sense of proportion, venturing beyond the territory covered by the SAM belt resulted in a disastrous setback. Between the Israeli air force – now freed from the SAM belt's restraints – and counterattacks by Israeli tanks, some 250 of Egypt's tanks were wiped out. This in turn enabled Israeli tanks to push the Egyptian Third Army back toward the canal. Within two days of that battle, in heavy fighting, Israeli forces had made a canal crossing of their own and started to destroy the Soviet-built SAM sites on the canal's west bank. Meanwhile, armored Israeli forces, growing to over 10,000 strong, thrust to the rear of the Third Army, threatening its encirclement and even Cairo.

In these circumstances, General Saad Shazli, the Egyptian field commander, urged Sadat to transfer the Third Army from the canal's east bank to its west bank so as to protect Egypt's population. But this would have defeated Sadat's larger design. He responded sharply – 'You do not understand the logic of this war' – and ordered Shazli to stand fast. Egypt needed only 'four inches' of the Sinai, Sadat argued, in order to transform the diplomatic situation.[124]

On Thursday, October 18, with two Egyptian divisions withdrawing in the Sinai, Sadat suddenly called for a ceasefire. The tide of battle having turned against him, he needed a pause while he still retained a foothold in the Sinai.[125] Even as he appealed for the ceasefire, he claimed a psychological victory: 'The enemy lost his balance and remains unbalanced until this moment. The wounded nation has restored its honor, and the political map of the Middle East has been changed.' In the same speech, he urged the United States to join with Egypt in a project for peace.[126] However dire Sadat's military situation, his analysis of policy options remained on the mark.

The crisis spread into the global economy on October 17, when the Organization of the Petroleum Exporting Countries (OPEC) announced an oil embargo, aiming to oblige the US and its European allies to push Israel into a settlement. The price of a barrel of oil rose precipitously, eventually reaching 400 percent of its pre-crisis level.[127]

The next day, Ambassador Anatoly Dobrynin and I began to discuss ceasefire language for possible joint submission to the Security Council. On October 19, Brezhnev invited me to Moscow to complete the ceasefire negotiations, and two days later the US and the Soviet Union presented a joint draft to the Security Council that on October 22 was adopted unanimously.

The turn toward a cessation of hostilities was temporarily overwhelmed when the ceasefire broke down and Israel could not resist the temptation to cut the supply route to the Third Army by surrounding the city of Suez. A tense forty-eight hours followed. The Soviets protested these violations of the ceasefire we had negotiated in Moscow a few days earlier, demanded its joint reconstitution by American and Soviet action and threatened unilateral military action to reimpose it. Sadat could have used the Soviet pressure for his own purposes, but he never resorted to it. After a robust American rebuff, the Soviets substituted a proposal enabling them to participate with non-combat observers to supervise the ceasefire. The outcome was UN Resolution 340, which provided for a UN Emergency Force of international observers drawn from non-permanent members of the UN Security Council.*

Sadat used the opportunity for a symbolic gesture expressing his commitment to a new approach to the conflict. Since the 1948–9 armistice, no Egyptian and Israeli officials had negotiated face to face. To the surprise of all parties, Sadat now informed the Israelis that he was sending military officers to kilometer 80 on the Cairo–Suez road to discuss the details of Resolution 340 and to arrange a resupply for Egypt's trapped Third Army. (For various technical reasons, the actual negotiation was moved from kilometer 80 to kilometer 101.) This did not amount to a formal recognition of Israel, or a diplomatic one; rather, it was a symbol of Sadat's determination to launch Egypt on a new course.

MEIR AND SADAT

After the war, on November 1, 1973, Prime Minister Meir came to Washington. Of all the Israeli leaders with whom I dealt, none was more difficult – and there was none that moved me more.

She was an original. Her wrinkled face testified to the turmoil of a lifetime pioneering a new society in a strange and forbidding environment. Israel, eked out on a tiny bit of land – precarious, ostracized, threatened by implacably hostile neighbors – had salvaged survival from its history by only a narrow margin. Mrs Meir's wary eyes seemed ever on the lookout for unexpected challenges, especially from her impetuous American allies. She saw it as her mission to protect what had been invested with such fervent hope by a people who for 2,000 years had endured a precarious existence in the Diaspora. My own childhood in Hitler's Germany gave me an understanding of her endemic apprehensiveness.

I also recognized a certain justice in her present attitude toward us. As the victim of a military attack, her government now faced a situation in which demands for a peace process were multiplying from the American ally on which she depended but which never quite seemed to grasp her traumas.

* Details of the diplomacy of the crisis are in Chapter 3, pages 186–9.

She treated me, being Jewish, as a favorite nephew who, when he disagreed, deeply disappointed her. Our relationship was familiar enough that I came habitually to call her Golda and still think of her as such. My wife, Nancy, used to say that arguments between Golda and me at dinner in Golda's home in Israel constituted some of the most dramatic theatrical performances she had ever witnessed. Nancy did not mention how they usually ended: Golda and I would withdraw to the kitchen and work out a solution.

Meir arrived in Washington at the first opportunity after the cease-fire. She was, above all, unhappy that we had insisted on a resupply – albeit of non-military supplies – for the Egyptian Third Army. She was railing, in effect, not against specific policies but against the change in strategic realities: the demonstration of Israeli vulnerability and the apparent emergence of Egypt as an accepted American negotiating partner. Restraint was being urged on her to permit the country that had attacked hers to evolve in a more peaceful direction. This, to Meir, was not a self-evident proposition:

> *Meir*: We didn't start the war, yet . . .
>
> *Kissinger*: Madame Prime Minister, we are faced with a very tragic situation. You didn't start the war, but you face a need for wise decisions to protect the survival of Israel. This is what you face. This is my honest judgment as a friend.
>
> *Meir*: You're saying we have no choice.
>
> *Kissinger*: We face the international situation that I described to you.[128]

For a nation to pretend to total autonomy is a form of nostalgia; reality dictates that every nation – even the most powerful – adapt its conduct to the capabilities and purposes of its neighbors and rivals. That Meir ultimately acted accordingly is a tribute to her leadership.

On her visit to Washington, Prime Minister Meir pursued two outcomes simultaneously: a consensus with her indispensable ally and a consensus of her people, a majority of whom were still in shock from the change in their circumstances and many of whom remained adamantly belligerent. UN supervision of the resupply meant that it could be accomplished without the direct cooperation of the combatants. At a dinner at the Israeli embassy, she engaged in some semi-public criticisms of the US administration (perhaps made for the benefit of the Israeli assistants, ministers and advisors in attendance). Setting aside these chastisements, I called on her the next day at Blair House (the residence of state guests) at a private meeting confined to advisors where she signaled openness to resupply under six conditions I outlined, including the start of talks on disengagement.* The six points also provided for the exchange of prisoners of war at the very beginning of the process, a salient concern to Israel.

With Israeli elections imminent, Meir's cabinet at first refused to authorize her to accept these terms while she was in Washington. But by now we understood Israeli politics well enough to recognize that the prime minister would not have put forward such a program had she judged the draft unacceptable. Her cabinet would not overrule her when she was actually in the chair.

Sadat's vision of a new negotiation could not have prevailed without Meir's participation. By entering negotiations at all, she was accepting the possibility of relinquishing territory for the first time in Israeli history. By agreeing to non-military resupply of the Third Army, she forwent the possibility of Israel's achieving a decisive military victory. At the same time, she created the precondition for a breakthrough in negotiations. She overcame her instincts for the sake of a possible move toward peace. Neither Sadat nor Meir could have achieved this first step without the other.

THE MEETING AT THE TAHRA PALACE

On November 7, 1973, just four days after Meir's visit, I met Sadat for the first time. He had prepared the ground for American diplomacy by

---

* The six points were: A. Egypt and Israel agree to observe scrupulously the ceasefire called for by the UN Security Council. B. Both sides agree that discussions between them will begin immediately to settle the question of the return to the Oct. 22 positions in the framework of agreement on the disengagement and separation of forces under the auspices of the UN. C. The town of Suez will receive daily supplies of food, water and medicine. All wounded civilians in the town of Suez will be evacuated. D. There shall be no impediment to the movement of nonmilitary supplies to the East Bank. E. The Israeli checkpoints on the Cairo–Suez road will be replaced by UN checkpoints. At the Suez end of the road, Israeli officers can participate with the UN to supervise the nonmilitary nature of the cargo at the bank of the canal. F. As soon as the UN checkpoints are established on the Cairo–Suez road, there will be an exchange of all prisoners of war, including wounded. (Kissinger, *Years of Upheaval*, 641.)

sidelining Soviet military action in the crisis over the erosion of the ceasefire. Egypt's strategic objective in launching the war, we later discovered, was to transform the situation psychologically in order to make a sustainable peace. Sadat's openness to negotiation then transformed our view of him. He was no longer a radical in our eyes.

Heretofore Sadat's moves had been more symbolic than fundamental. Were we dealing with a genuinely new approach or a tactical variation on the established pattern? The Arab demand for Israel's immediate return to the pre-June 1967 frontiers remained on the table as a precondition for negotiation. Recognition of the legitimacy of the state of Israel had not even been hinted at. The meeting might lead either to step-by-step progress or to an impasse if Sadat insisted on an overall settlement.

Major issues needed to be resolved during our discussions. The most immediate was resupply of the Third Army, which was happening on an ad hoc basis. Second came the goal of negotiations on Middle East peace, called for in the ceasefire but never formally defined. Third was the future of Egyptian–American relations, technically still based on Nasser's breaking of diplomatic ties at the end of the 1967 war.

The encounter took place in the Tahra Palace, in a once fashionable suburb of Cairo now struggling to maintain appearances. I was hurried toward a veranda where a mob of journalists was assembled, accompanied by a significant number of Sadat staffers. There were no visible security precautions.

Amidst this chaos, a deep baritone uttered the words, 'Welcome, welcome.' Without any formal ceremony, Sadat had arrived. He was wearing a khaki military uniform with an overcoat slung over his shoulders. (November in Cairo can be quite cold.) Dispensing with any opening statement and pausing only for a brief round of pictures by photographers, he escorted me into a large room with French doors that overlooked an expansive lawn; on it, wicker chairs had been placed for our aides.

We sat on a sofa facing the gardens, both of us affecting nonchalance though well aware that the nature of Egyptian–American and probably Arab–American relations in the immediate future could depend on the outcome. Appearing extremely relaxed, Sadat filled his pipe, lit it and started the conversation by saying that he had been longing for a personal meeting: 'I have a plan for you. I have named it the Kissinger Plan.'

At this, he walked across the room to an easel on which situation maps had been placed. Standing in front of them, he referred to my prior talks with Hafiz Ismail. As noted earlier, I had answered Ismail's proposal for Israeli withdrawal from all of Sinai by suggesting interim arrangements, to permit adjustment to a peace process before making final decisions. Ismail had rejected our step-by-step proposal; Sadat now accepted it, naming it the Kissinger Plan. He suggested as an initial step an Israeli withdrawal across two-thirds of the Sinai to a line from El-Arish (a city about 20 miles from the Israeli frontier and 90 miles from the Suez Canal) to the Ras Mohammad National Park at the southern edge of the Sinai Peninsula.[129]

It was a stunning opening for a negotiation that we had expected to be protracted and difficult – not because his suggestion was so unprecedented (it was in fact unrealistic) but because he was articulating a willingness to explore provisional phases of disengagement. In no other such instance had I encountered an opposite number who conceded the field in his opening move. Every Arab leader with whom we had raised the idea of an interim settlement had rejected it. Sadat had accepted it before it could even be proposed.

But Sadat must have known that it would be impossible to convince Israel's leaders to withdraw such a distance, including the strategic passes in the center of the Sinai, at the end of a war started by Egypt. To avoid beginning the dialogue with Sadat in a deadlock, I invited him to explain the considerations that led him to where we found ourselves.

Sadat at first deliberately, and then with growing intensity, described his purposes. He was disillusioned with the Soviets; they had been unable or unwilling to work with the United States to bring about a Middle East peace compatible with Egypt's dignity. The language in the communiqué ending the Moscow summit of 1972 had removed any doubt about Soviet priorities: they would not risk tensions with America over Egypt. The decision to expel some 20,000 Soviet advisors had been taken as a first step toward restoring Egyptian dignity, and the war was its further expression. He had given no advance warning for the expulsion and had asked America for no reward afterward.

Sadat spoke in excellent English if in a somewhat stilted manner, precise and formal – perhaps because he had taught himself from newspapers, short stories and books while in British prisons during the war.[130] His exposition was delivered emphatically, with his eyes slightly narrowed, as if viewing some distant horizon. He had concluded, he said, that no progress could be made without long-term American goodwill. He would therefore seek reconciliation with America and a lasting peace for the Middle East. His quest was for a change in basic attitudes, not of lines on a map.

He had given me his Kissinger Plan. What, he asked, was mine?

The objective of the dialogue, I said, was a lasting peace. Its durability, however, would depend on the parties' gaining each other's confidence in stages, thereby accruing confidence in the process itself. A first move could not possibly achieve either peace or confidence. At the present moment, I continued, Sadat's Kissinger Plan was too ambitious. A more realistic withdrawal line for Israeli forces would fall well short of his proposal, somewhere to the west of the Mitla and Gidi passes. It would probably require several months to negotiate. We would do our best to achieve the disengagement process, with a view to continuing it, and base a peace process on it.

A conversation with Sadat was frequently interrupted by pauses for reflection. Now, after one of those pauses, he responded with just two words: 'And Israel?' I replied, similarly cryptically, by handing him the six points worked out with Prime Minister Meir.

Sadat looked at the paper for a few minutes and accepted it without any discussion. Nasser had been unwise, he summed up, to seek to harass America into cooperation. The Third Army was not the heart of the matter between Egypt and America. Sadat's own aim, by contrast, was relations of confidence with America and peace with Israel. To express this symbolically, he would announce after our meeting what we had not even proposed: an end to Egypt's diplomatic boycott of the United States, in place since 1967, through the establishment of an Egyptian interest section in Washington, headed by an ambassador. The ambassador would be named in December 1973. (This was the same procedure we had followed earlier that same year in establishing relations with China.) Full diplomatic relations would follow the conclusion of a disengagement agreement.

These remarks were put forward not in conditional form, nor as a demand for reciprocity, but rather as a description of a desirable course. Against what we later learned was the near-unanimous sentiment of his advisors, Sadat had decided to take his chances on the word of an American secretary of state that the United States would facilitate significant progress in Egyptian–Israeli territorial negotiations over a period of three months. Throughout, the Third Army would remain trapped. If anything were to go wrong, Sadat would be ruined and Egypt humiliated.

A seemingly minor step – non-military supplies for the Third Army after it had become beleaguered – created an opportunity for preliminary cooperation and became a symbol for progress towards peace. While I was still in Cairo, the six points worked out with Mrs Meir in Washington and now accepted by Sadat were put into treaty language by Assistant Secretary of State Joe Sisco and Egyptian Foreign Minister Ismail Fahmy.

By the end of the visit, Sadat had achieved the initial purpose of his daring gamble: he had broken the status quo in order to open the possibility of negotiation with Israel under American auspices. His ultimate purpose was to end the conflict with Israel that had sapped Egyptian energy and confidence since the June 1967 war. In his mind, the existence of Israel was not a threat to Egypt's being; *war* with Israel was. That threat could be reduced and ultimately eliminated through a new concept of security based on the process of peace with Egypt's adversary rather than its annihilation.

Even successful negotiations sometimes leave in the negotiators' memories uneasy traces of their compromises, which cast a shadow over future efforts. Sadat's view of this meeting is contained in his memoirs:

> Our first session of talks took three hours. The first hour made me feel I was dealing with an entirely new mentality, a new political method ... Anyone seeing us after that first hour in al-Tahirah Palace would have thought we had been friends for years. There was no difficulty in understanding one another and so we agreed on a six-point program for action, including a U.S. pledge of return to the October 22 cease-fire line within the framework of the forces' disengagement.[131]

Sadat's willingness to accept disengagement, together with the six points, was a rare occasion where one side in a negotiation unilaterally abandons its prerogative for haggling. His insight was that establishing trust and goodwill would be more important, in the end, than securing immediate concessions. Such mutual confidence would prove essential because the parties had traversed only the first step in the long journey they would chart.

FROM GENEVA TO DISENGAGEMENT

Following the Tahra Palace meeting, the obvious next move would have been to continue the step-by-step approach immediately. But this was precluded by Sadat's obligation to his ally Assad not to settle separately. Also, the United States, in the ceasefire talks in Moscow, had agreed to pursue an overall negotiation in concert with the Soviet Union. In consequence, a Middle East Peace Conference was assembled in Geneva in December 1973.

The conference was meant to provide a forum to legitimize follow-on negotiations. All the regional parties were invited to initial discussions at Geneva, as well as the United States and the Soviet Union as facilitators of the peace process. Egypt was under political pressure, verging on obligation, to participate: it had joined the Khartoum declaration in 1967, which had rejected separate Arab negotiations with Israel, as had Sadat's own pronouncements before and during the 1973 war. Sadat, recognizing Egypt's and his allies' momentum toward the Geneva conference, decided to unilaterally ensure its abandonment.

Weary of inter-Arab disputes and distrustful of the Soviets, Sadat rejected an overall approach, fearing that the multiplication of vetoes would thwart agreement and that Cold War rivalries would overwhelm Arab priorities. And indeed any prospects for agreement at Geneva quickly dissolved. Assad of Syria refused to attend. The participation of Jordan, which was governing the West Bank, became a matter of controversy. The Soviet Union was more concerned with the evolution of détente than with the regional negotiation (or else it tolerated a step-by-step approach because it was convinced that it would fail). Thus the Geneva Conference of the United States, the Soviet Union, Israel, Egypt and Jordan suspended itself to permit exploration of separate component issues, which in any case had been the design of both Sadat and the United States.

Everything depended now on whether Egypt and Israel could

transform exploratory discussions into something tangible. This required agreement on the extent of Israeli withdrawal, on the definition between the parties of zones of armaments limitations, on the ending of Arab boycotts and on ways to control and legitimize any agreements.

Israel's willingness to undertake its first withdrawal from occupied territory would determine the outcome. For that reason, Moshe Dayan became a key player. As close to a professional military person as the Israeli system of citizen-soldier permits, distinguished by the range and suppleness of his intellect, Dayan was seemingly made to guide the emerging peace process for Israel. But the opportunity found him melancholy. He had been surprised by the outbreak of the war, tricked by Sadat's feints, and he knew that he would pay a political price for having misjudged the mobilization. Both he and Meir would be out of office by June 1974.

Yet Dayan performed his task with dignity. He understood the profound significance of Israel's first territorial withdrawal from the 1967 borders. And he knew that, although his personal participation was coming to an end, he stood at the beginning of a process that was expected to develop its own momentum.

On January 4, 1974, in Washington to begin the negotiations, Dayan proposed a withdrawal line of some 12 to 20 miles from the Suez Canal – far less than Sadat had put forward in his 'Kissinger Plan'. But, according to Dayan, it was the maximum feasible concession: any farther east and Israel would lose control of the only north–south road in the Sinai west of the passes. Dayan had no interest in assuming a tougher line for bargaining purposes, and he wanted to avoid political maneuvering. In seven hours of discussion extending over two days, he laid out his proposal on an elaborate map of new dividing lines, including zones of limited armaments.[132]

The following week, I delivered Dayan's meticulous map to Sadat. Our meetings on the details of disengagement had been set for Aswan, a desert city 425 miles south of Cairo, where Sadat was spending the winter. At our first meeting on January 11, he put forward two startling propositions. He would accept the Israeli withdrawal lines if I would remain in the region to accelerate the outcome in a shuttle between Egypt and Israel. Sadat then gave himself (and the American team) a deadline. For the next weekend, January 18, he had scheduled a visit to his Arab brethren to discuss the oil embargo that OPEC had imposed on the

United States during the October War. If a disengagement agreement were concluded by then – and Sadat hoped it would be – he would urge an end to the embargo. Although he felt that some of the Israeli proposals involved compromises to sovereignty that could not be countenanced, those issues could be raised at a later stage of the negotiations.

The shuttle sped up negotiations in an unprecedented manner. Seven shuttles took place between January 11 and January 18;[133] during one of them (January 12–13), Dayan came up with a complicated outline of the substance of demilitarization within the disengagement zones.

On January 14, Sadat, for the only time in my acquaintance with him, changed the arrangement from a face-to-face meeting to a conference, with the American team (Ambassador Hermann Eilts and Joe Sisco) facing him and Foreign Minister Fahmy and Defense Minister Gamasy across the table – perhaps in an effort to share the responsibility for painful decisions.

That occasion turned into a dramatic confrontation between Sadat and his associates. The withdrawal line was reaffirmed without controversy, but Dayan's proposal for zones of limited armaments in territory vacated by Israeli forces evoked passionate opposition. Sadat had expressed to me previously his firm conviction that a foreign country, especially a foreign country at war with Egypt, must not be allowed to prescribe the deployment of Egyptian forces to defend Egypt on Egyptian soil. Fahmy and Gamasy now objected on similar grounds, and in particular to the proposed limit of thirty Egyptian tanks across the Suez Canal. Gamasy vehemently closed his argument with, 'No self-respecting Egyptian officer will sign an agreement containing such a provision.'

Sadat sat silently for a few moments. He emerged from this pensive state with an odd question to me: 'Can we form a working committee from both sides here?' (He meant everyone around the table except him and me.) When I agreed, he suggested that the group develop limitations for armaments, reserving the issue of tanks to himself and me. He then invited me to follow him into an adjoining room.

Once alone, he asked (referring to the limit on tanks across the Suez Canal): 'Does she [Prime Minister Meir] mean it?'

I replied: 'She is bargaining. But you have to decide how much time you want to spend on this issue.'

Sadat replied: 'Let us join the others,' without telling me his decision.

At the conference table, he settled the controversy: 'I have accepted 30 [as the limit for Egyptian tanks across the canal]. Dr. Kissinger will get me more, and you, Gamasy, will sign it.'

Sadat had avoided the looming deadlock. The working group agreed on limits for major categories of weapons. These were then passed to the kilometer 101 technical group, established at the end of the war for implementing negotiated language. Meir then raised the number of Egyptian tanks permitted on the east bank of the canal to over 100.

The shuttle procedure not only speeded decisions, it enabled Sadat to deepen and advance the dialogue. Meir, he said, would understand that the size of the tank force across the canal was largely of symbolic significance:

> If I want to attack, I will put 1,000 tanks across the Canal in one night. So as a sign of my commitment to peace, you can convey to [Meir] my assurance that I will put no tanks across the Canal. But I want the Prime Minister to understand that the entire future of the agreement depends on psychological factors. Israel must not offend the dignity of the Egyptian armed forces by overbearing demands. You can tell her from me that I have committed myself to this course.[134]

During the next shuttle (January 16), Sadat asked for a map of the proposed arms-limitation zones between Egyptian and Israeli forces in the Sinai. He summarily struck out its many sub-divisions. In their place, he drew one simple dividing line, splitting the zones into two parts: one Israeli, the other Egyptian. Limitations, he said, should be spelled out as distances from those lines to the canal, not in terms of national forces.

He also came up with an ingenious idea for avoiding debates about who had yielded to whom. Israel and Egypt, rather than describing the agreement as a series of obligations each to the other, should express them as mutual commitments to the president of the United States. In this manner, the agreement would be indirectly guaranteed by Washington. To stress the American role in the supervision, he proposed two UN technical inspection units using American technology and American personnel along the Suez Canal.* It took only two more shuttles to put the first disengagement agreement into final form.

---

* The agreement became more complex as it was elaborated into formal language. This was demonstrated by the manner in which Sadat and I described the breakthrough to the

After months of war and tactical maneuvers, Sadat had needed a mere week of dialogue to construct a moment when both parties dared to pronounce the word 'peace'. After approving the working group's final document for transmission to Israel, he added a message to Meir about his dedication to a genuine peace; it paralleled what he had said during the discussion on tank limits a few days earlier:

> You must take my word seriously. When I made my initiative in 1971, I meant it. When I threatened war, I meant it. When I talk of peace now, I mean it. We never had contact before. We now have the services of Dr Kissinger. Let us use him and talk to each other through him.[135]

It was still a step short of direct dialogue. The Israeli prime minister received me while bedridden with the flu. 'It is a good thing,' she said laconically. 'Why is he doing it?' A day later, she decided on a formal answer. I brought the final text of the agreement to Sadat, together with Meir's reply – his first official, direct contact with an Israeli head of government. Her private letter read in part:

> I am deeply conscious of the significance of a message received by the Prime Minister of Israel from the President of Egypt. It is indeed a source of great satisfaction to me and I sincerely hope that these contacts between

---

working group. Sadat asked me to speak for him:

'*Sadat*: Please, you're much cleverer.
Kissinger: But not as wise. The president and I had discussions not only of the technical provisions but also of the pros and cons of moving quickly against moving slowly at Geneva. The technical provisions might be better if done at Geneva, but we assessed the advantages of moving quickly.
Sadat: That is our assessment.
Kissinger: The Egyptian line defends Egypt; the Israeli line doesn't defend Israel. So for the Egyptians to move back their own defense line on Egyptian territory is politically unacceptable. I must say I find this a very persuasive argument. So I am prepared to go back to Israel with something I had never heard – to abandon all these distinctions between zones. The Israeli forces will move back to this line, and the Egyptian forces will move back to this line, and the Egyptian line is defined here – so there is no Egyptian withdrawal required. So we'll describe any limits not in terms of withdrawal but in terms of distance between the Egyptian line and the Canal and the Israeli line. The second point President Sadat said is that it is very difficult for Egypt to sign in a document limitations of forces on their own territory.
Sadat: Quite right.'
(Kissinger, *Years of Upheaval*, 826).

us through Dr Kissinger will continue, and prove to be an important turning point in our relations.

I, for my part, will do my best to establish trust and understanding between us.

Both our peoples need and deserve peace. It is my strongest conviction that peace is the goal toward which we must direct all our energies.

Let me reiterate what you said in your message: 'When I talk of permanent peace, between us, I mean it.' [136]

Sadat had just finished reading the letter and folding it when an assistant entered the room and whispered something in his ear. Sadat walked over to me and kissed me on both cheeks: 'They have just signed the disengagement agreement at kilometer 101. I am today taking off my military uniform – I never expect to wear it again except for ceremonial occasions.'

Sadat added that he would depart that same day for Arab capitals, where he would describe what had been negotiated. I told him that I would be leaving that evening for Damascus to continue the step-by-step process with Assad, Sadat's ally in the war and partner in the 1967 Arab agreement never to negotiate on peace with Israel. It was important for Sadat's position in the Arab world that some progress be made on behalf of Syria.

Sadat, while approving the diplomacy, had another idea: 'It would be good for you to spend a day in Luxor to experience the greatness of history – and,' he added with one of his pauses, 'its fragility.'

THE SYRIAN DIMENSION

Of the individuals profiled in this volume, Sadat was the one whose philosophical and moral vision constituted the greatest breakthrough for his time and context. Syrian President Hafez al-Assad, in contrast, adopted a purely practical approach. Ruthless and highly intelligent, he aspired to leadership in the Arab world while conscious of his inability to achieve it.

Syria, unlike Egypt, had a relatively short history of self-government. Centuries of conquest and division, of achievements alternating with catastrophes, had reduced Syria's magnitude and self-confidence necessary to act autonomously. Without Sadat's faith in his country's internal capacities, Assad sustained Syria through confrontations with its international environment by tenaciousness, willpower and cunning.

Damascus is at one and the same time the fount of modern Arab nationalism and a case study of its frustration at the hands of foreigners. Assad said to me on one occasion that before the First World War, Syria had been betrayed by Turkey, after it by Britain and France, and after the Second World War by America in backing the state of Israel. He thus had no incentive to form a cooperative relationship with the United States and made no effort to relate Syria to Western proposals for peace. He was outraged by Sadat's separate efforts, to the point of refusing to receive the Egyptian president in Damascus after the disengagement agreement, instead accepting Sadat's report of the first shuttle at the airport.

But Assad was willing to promote Syria's specific interests. In particular, he wanted to regain the territory along the road to Damascus that had been acquired by Israel in its final offensive of the October War, and to apply the military disengagement of the Sinai agreement to the Golan Heights, which had been occupied by Israel since 1967.

Our dialogue thus consisted of highly granular discussions of military arrangements. No elevated language spurred the process. It was a practical progression that from time to time had to be salvaged from breakdowns that Assad himself would generate. I once described Assad's negotiating tactic as moving toward the edge of a precipice and occasionally jumping off it, counting on the presence of a tree to arrest his fall and enable him to climb back up.

Using as a model the Sinai principles on the separation of forces, but without the accelerant of Sadat's moral vision, Assad put the Syrian shuttle through thirty-five days of mile-by-mile negotiations. Every Damascus meeting involved three stages, each chaired by Assad: an initial, extensive discussion with Assad alone, using only my interpreter; a session with Assad's military advisors; and a meeting with civilian ministers. (He excluded even his interpreter from the first meeting so that he could limit what his subordinates learned of my report from Jerusalem.) It was a convoluted style of decision-making, but it allowed Assad to disburse information as he saw fit. It also made for protracted meetings for whose length Israeli leaders could find no explanation and which kept them on edge.

On the night of the thirty-fourth day, Assad drove matters to a point at which a breakup seemed inevitable. We had already drafted the com-muniqué announcing the end of the negotiations – literally as I was heading for the door of our presumed final meeting – when Assad found a way to resume the negotiations. He then expended five hours negoti-ating over negotiations and finally kept us haggling into the evening.

In the end, the Syrians squeezed the last drop of blood out of the stone: the demarcation line was adjusted by a few hundred yards in an overall neutral direction. Ultimately, Israel would withdraw from terri-tories 10 miles south of Damascus and from the town of Quneitra. The opposing forces and their weapons would be separated by 30 miles, so that heavy weapons could not reach the frontline of the adversary.* Assurances of enforcement, as in the Egyptian agreement, were made in a letter by the parties to the US president.

Needless to say, the Syrian shuttle did not end with the same elevated feeling as its Egyptian counterpart. The agreement between Syria and Israel was a brutal bargain between adversaries that adjusted only their relative position. Assad chose to follow Sadat's practical solutions while rejecting his moral framework. But, although there was no mention of the nature of peace, Assad was willing to make specific agreements that made the initiation of war much more difficult. Those realistic prov-isions, unleavened by emotion, were both practical and observable.

In the event, the provisions of the so-called Golan Agreement endured – in part because, though Assad could have broken them, he never did. For all his pride and shrewdness, he finally accepted – in practice – an indirect and silent form of recognition of Israel. It had to have been a searing process for a radical to come to grips with such a possibility. His convictions of enmity with Israel were stronger than Sadat's, and so his journey was harder, his progress shorter. But, like

---

* The complexity of this goal is shown by this late-stage proposal from the United States:
'All of Quneitra would be under Syrian administration.

A line would be drawn 200 meters west of Quneitra measured from the line of buildings on the west side of the western road. This line would be marked by a physical barrier. The area to the west of this line would be demilitarized. The UN would assure com-pliance. Israeli civilians would be permitted to cultivate the fields in this area.

The Israeli military line would be at the Eastern base of the two key hills, but no weapons would be allowed on the crest of the hills that could fire on Quneitra in a straight line. This assurance would be contained in a letter from President Nixon to President Assad.

The line to the north and south of Quneitra would be straightened out so Quneitra would not be encircled by Israeli positions.' (Kissinger, Years of Upheaval, 1087.)

Meir from the other end of the telescope, he had caught a glimpse of the virtue of an end to conflict.

Assad could not have achieved either his external purposes or his internal change if it had not been for Sadat's initiative. But he did substantially contribute, albeit through the pursuit of more mundane objectives, to the step-by-step resolution of regional disputes. And, paradoxically, Assad's ability to wring a negotiation dry of its idealism made it politically possible for Sadat to continue on the path to realizing his vision.

ANOTHER STEP TOWARD PEACE: THE SINAI II AGREEMENT

After the Syrian disengagement agreement, Sadat expected a return to the peace process with Israel. The logical next step would have been an agreement on the West Bank of the Jordan River, occupied by Israel in the June 1967 war. But that path was precluded by internal Arab politics.[137] Although the West Bank had been under the de facto governance of Jordan, it was neither part of Jordan nor itself sovereign. And, on October 28, 1974, soon after the Syrian agreement, the Arab League designated the PLO as the sole legitimate representative of the Palestinians. This ensured that any attempt by Israel to disengage from the West Bank by negotiating with King Hussein of Jordan would have led to immediate civil conflict in the Arab world. And Israel was not prepared to deal with the PLO, sworn to its destruction.

The West Bank was thereby removed from the step-by-step diplomacy. Another Egypt–Israel negotiation, on a further Israeli withdrawal from the Sinai, appeared as the sole feasible course for progress.

That, however, had to wait until the impact of the resignation of Nixon, in August 1974, could be absorbed. Time had to be left for President Gerald Ford to be briefed internally and to assemble his own White House staff. In his first public statement he appointed me as his secretary of state, thus assuring continuity.

Actually, the most significant assurance of continuity lay in the new president's personality. Raised and educated in Michigan, Ford embodied the most sterling qualities of Middle America: patriotism, confidence in fellowship, trust in American purposes, extraordinary common sense. In agreement with the peace principles for the Middle

East that had evolved during his predecessor's tenure, he was above all committed to overcoming America's own internal divisions.

Israel, too, had experienced a change of leaders. Prime Minister Meir had survived the previous December's elections, but public criticism over alleged failures in the prelude to the 1973 war convinced her to step aside. Her successor was Yitzhak Rabin, the first *sabra* (native-born Israeli) to become the nation's prime minister. Rabin had been commander of the Israeli army in the 1967 war, and its victories had made him a national hero. Like Sadat, he was a soldier who had turned his aspirations to transcending war. In a poignant speech as prime minister, he said:

> As a former military man, I will ... forever remember the silence of the moment before: the hush when the hands of the clock seem to be spinning forward, when time is running out and in another hour, another minute, the inferno will erupt.
>
> In that moment of great tension just before the finger pulls the trigger, just before the fuse begins to burn – in the terrible quiet of the moment, there is still time to wonder, to wonder alone: Is it really imperative to act? Is there no other choice? No other way?[138]

Rabin was as different from Meir as could be imagined. She had come to Israel as a pioneer. To her, every square inch of Israeli territory had been won by blood and was therefore sacred; in this thinking, to trade land for peace was to trade the absolute for the quite possibly ephemeral. To Rabin, born in the country, the wonder of Israel's existence loomed less saliently than the necessities of its survival. Rabin's view, informed by millennia of Jewish history, was that Israel's historical precariousness could only be overcome by linking his people to their Arab neighbors. Highly intelligent and well-educated, Rabin viewed the negotiating process through an analytical lens. To him, the step-by-step approach was a preference he expressed as 'a piece of land for a piece of peace'.

Rabin's cerebral version of the step-by-step approach was still not fully expressed in early 1975, when he and Sadat began exploring tentative negotiations along the Sinai model via American mediation.* The

---

* It gained full expression in the 1993 Israeli–Palestinian Oslo Accords with their three phases of withdrawal from the West Bank and Gaza.

early stages were smooth: the two men were committed to the idea of
peace and agreed on a gradual, multi-stage approach. For the next step,
both gravitated toward another Israeli withdrawal – Sadat in order to
continue Egypt's separate journey toward peace, Rabin to acquaint his
fractious cabinet with the facts of international life.

In March 1975, Rabin sent a letter through me to Sadat. He expressed
in his own way convictions similar to those Meir had written in January
1974:

> It has always been my firm conviction that Egypt, by virtue of its cultural
> heritage, its strength, its size, and its influence, carries a leading voice with
> respect to the peace-making effort in our region. From what Dr Kissinger
> has conveyed to me, as well as from your public statements, I feel assured
> that you are determined to make strenuous efforts to achieve a settlement.
>
> I, on my part, am determined to make all efforts to promote peace
> between us, and it is in this spirit that I express the aspiration that we
> shall yet succeed in reaching an agreement that will do honor to our two
> peoples.[139]

When I delivered the letter, Sadat asked me who had thought it up. I
admitted that I had encouraged it. He next inquired: 'Did they write it?
This is even more important.' I answered truthfully that the letter had
been drafted by Rabin. The next day, Sadat asked to see me alone and
made the following oral reply:

> My attitude is that power will never again play a role in the relations of
> our two peoples. I will try to handle the Arab people if Rabin handles the
> Israeli people. My determination is to bring about the ultimate with-
> drawal to agreed lines by peaceful means only. If a Geneva conference is
> assembled after this agreement is signed, I will not touch this agreement
> or change anything between us at Geneva. Assure Rabin from my side I
> am not dreaming of solving this at Geneva. Whatever the problems, I will
> not use force. I would be ready to meet Rabin whenever the Israeli occu-
> pation of Egyptian territory is ended.[140]

The concept now on the table was another Israeli withdrawal, this
time beyond the passes in the central Sinai. In return, Rabin expected an
Egyptian declaration of non-beligerency. A problem then emerged with
the formula 'a piece of land for a piece of peace': namely, that peace was

not as divisible as land. Sadat was not prepared to declare a general end
of belligerency, but he was willing to agree to refrain from a list of
defined belligerent acts. The steps toward peace to be put forward by
Egypt for the Israeli withdrawal beyond the passes proved controversial
in Israel and needed to be more than emotive phraseology. Insofar as
words could accomplish it, no further reassurance against Israel's nightmares could be imagined than Sadat's communication with Rabin via
American mediation. But Jewish history had taught that assurances
alone did not insure against tragedy; the fragility of human designs
required legal or constitutional provisions to ensure their efficacy.

An agreement needed to be approved by the Israeli cabinet and parliament, where Rabin, like all of his predecessors, possessed only a tiny
majority – 65 out of 120.[141] Divisions within the cabinet – voiced especially by Defense Minister Shimon Peres (later Israel's preeminent dove,
but at that time a hardliner) – could similarly jeopardize any peace plan.

By March 1975, a draft treaty existed. But it still had vague elements
that needed to be made explicit, especially on the state of belligerency.
On March 18, in response to Rabin's objections, Sadat and Fahmy committed Egypt to a pledge not to use force even if the peace process were
to falter. Sadat also promised, both to Israel and in a letter to the American president, not to attack Israel provided Israel made the same pledge
in the same form to Egypt. And Sadat explicitly accepted that the passes in
the Sinai from which Israel would withdraw were to be controlled by
UN forces rather than handed over to Egypt.

Nevertheless, the Israeli cabinet was not yet ready to embrace what
before the 1973 war would have been considered fulfillment of their
desires. Yigal Alon, the foreign minister, had opposed negotiations with
Egypt altogether, preferring talks with Jordan over the West Bank. Defense
Minister Peres, a lifelong rival of Rabin, continued to advocate a hard
line, categorically rejecting the idea of relinquishing control of the Sinai
passes for anything short of an explicit commitment to non-belligerency.

Since Sadat felt that he could not formally pledge to end belligerency
without rupturing Egypt's ties to the Arab world, the Israeli negotiators
sought as a substitute a multiplying list of contingencies. By this route,
Sadat could grant the substance of 'peace' item by item while not using
the phrase.

In the event, these pieces of peace proved insufficient for the expected
piece of land. Foundering on these nuances, the negotiations broke up

at the end of March 1975. The shuttle was put on pause. It was, as
Rabin put it to me, 'a Greek tragedy'.[142]

President Ford had never been engaged in Mideast diplomacy but
was very familiar with the military elements from his service on the
House Armed Services Committee. He met with both Rabin and Sadat.
The meeting with Sadat seemed beset by the jinx of presidential meetings with Arab leaders in that domestic issues suddenly overwhelmed
the issues of Middle East order. The first time Sadat met Nixon, Watergate was at its height, and Nixon resigned six weeks later. The weekend
of his introduction to Sadat, Ford felt obliged to dismiss his secretary of
defense, James Schlesinger, and CIA director, William Colby, to clear
the decks for the 1976 presidential campaign. A substantial amount of
time had to be devoted to presidential assurances to Sadat regarding the
constancy of Ford's administration.

Ford took the suspension of the shuttle hard. While making no secret
of his restlessness, which I shared, he had decided to give Rabin time to
conclude the internal Israeli debate. This was facilitated by Peres, who
had shifted to support the next step, provided the UN inspection system
was improved by its being placed near the center of the Sinai. Sadat
volunteered another incentive, proposing that warning stations in the
Sinai be manned by Americans, and instructing his foreign minister:
'This is an important proposal. Americans would be witnesses. It would
be a complete guarantee for the Israelis.'[143]

An agreement emerged on September 1, 1975. It did not produce the
elation of the first disengagement agreement, but it was substantively
more significant. Egypt and Israel were balancing military necessities
against political conditions. Both sides declared that, on defined issues,
force would not be used. Israel gave up the passes.* Egypt renounced the
use of force against Israel in a range of circumstances, even pledging not
to support Syria in another attack on Israel. These measures would
define Israel's and Egypt's entire perceptions of one another. Sadat and
Rabin were reaching for a comprehensive solution, not for the entire
region but in essence with each other.

Both sides' options were narrowed by their achievements: in Sadat's

---

* Defining the extent of the passes, initially controversial, was resolved by having UN
advisors and representatives of Israel and the US walk the length of them.

case by his increasing movement to the edge of what his people could understand or bear, and in Rabin's case by his own gradual movement toward a new definition of peace that was no longer a matter of pieces of land.

SADAT'S JOURNEY TO JERUSALEM

Both Israel and Egypt understood that little space was left for another interim agreement in the Sinai. But in late 1976, with an American election imminent, they began to explore another step, which would have been to draw a line from El-Arish to Ras Muhammad within 20 miles of Israel's border: indeed, to the same 'Kissinger line' that Sadat had proposed in our first meeting almost three years earlier. Had Ford won the election, the El-Arish–Ras Muhammad line, in return for an end of belligerency, would have been his first foreign policy move after inauguration.

Through the last year of the Ford administration and the first year of Jimmy Carter's, Sadat tried to keep the United States engaged in his vision of a wider peace. In August 1976, he told US Ambassador Hermann Eilts that he hoped a new American proposal would come soon – and if it did not, he would encourage the Israelis to 'put all cards on the table'.[144]

During the 1976 election campaign, the Carter team had committed itself to an overall agreement between Israel and all of its Arab neighbors, to be achieved at a conference of all the parties, with the future of Palestine as a key subject. President Carter's inauguration in January 1977 thus put an end to the step-by-step process as an American strategy.

On April 3, 1977, believing that 'the Americans hold more than 99 percent of the cards in the game', Sadat presented a plan for peace to the newly inaugurated President Carter.[145] In reiterating the need for a Palestinian state and for Israeli withdrawal to the 1967 borders, Sadat said he was also prepared formally to recognize Israel and would not object to US aid or guarantees to the prospective Palestinian state.[146]

Nothing could have been further from Sadat's mind – or the Israelis' – than a multilateral Middle East conference, let alone an attempt at a comprehensive settlement. For one thing, any such gathering would invite proposals for returning to the pre-state frontiers of 1947, which no political party in Israel accepted, at least where the West Bank was concerned: the 1947 partition plan called for a line on the West Bank within 10 miles of the road between Israel's two principal cities of Tel Aviv and Haifa and even closer to Ben-Gurion Airport, Israel's only international hub. For another, a multi-party conference would also resurrect the question of the PLO's presence – which Israel refused to consider – and the problematic issue of Soviet participation. Sadat continued to oppose a comprehensive conference because it would have reintroduced Soviet influence into the Middle East, given Syria a veto over Egypt's diplomacy and threatened his understanding of how peace might gradually be achieved.

But President Carter was unconvinced by Sadat's April proposal and disturbed by the Egyptian's resistance to the comprehensive approach. To overcome Sadat's objections, on October 21, 1977, Carter appealed directly to him to support the conference.[147] Afraid that the president might force him into a diplomacy in which hostile Soviets and suspicious Arab allies could block his efforts, Sadat leaped directly to ultimate goals. If a lasting rearrangement of the Egyptian–Israeli relationship was to be achieved, it would require another shock to the system. Sadat wrote later that Carter's advocacy for peace 'directed my thinking for the first time toward the initiative that I was to take'.[148]

By way of a response to Carter's letter, Sadat's address at the opening of the new Egyptian parliament on November 9, 1977, sounded familiar cues of 'going to the ends of the earth' for peace.[149] This time, however, he included a brief mention of a hypothetical visit to Israel: 'Israel will be surprised when it hears me say that I won't refuse to go to their own home, to the Knesset itself, to discuss peace with them.'[150]

Sadat buried the Knesset reference amidst positive mentions of Carter's proposed Geneva conference[151] – which he did not dare to reject. For the sake of Yasir Arafat, the PLO leader who was sitting in the audience, he insisted that the negotiating parties at such a conference include Palestinian representatives – a requirement he knew the Israelis would not accept. Though the seriousness of his commitment to peace was plain,[152] almost no one realized that he was actually floating the idea of a visit to Israel and had no intention of going to Geneva.

Israeli Prime Minister Menachem Begin, however, picked up on Sadat's signal. Begin had replaced Rabin as prime minister in May 1977.

Having emigrated from Poland in 1942, he had at first served as head of the Irgun, an underground paramilitary unit, and then three decades in political opposition. Begin was inflexible and legalistic in his view of negotiations. Yet he did not rule out a 'binding peace' with Egypt as long as it did not include the pre-1967 frontiers.[153] On November 15 – perhaps in good faith, or perhaps merely to place Sadat at a disadvantage in world opinion – Begin seized the initiative and formally invited the Egyptian president to Jerusalem.[154]

Just after dark on November 19, a Saturday – to respect the Sabbath – Sadat's plane landed in Israel to global astonishment. I had telephoned Sadat the day before to congratulate him on this latest daring peace initiative. I found him relaxed and at peace with himself. Which leading Israeli figure, he asked, did I think he would find most impressive? He himself thought it would probably be the dashing Ezer Weizman, Israel's former air force commander and now defense minister in Begin's government (and in his youth a member of the Irgun underground). I suggested Dayan as a possibility. We were both wrong. It turned out to be 'the old one' (Golda Meir); she was among the Israeli leaders in the reception line at the airport.[155]

The atmosphere upon Sadat's arrival was tense: the Israelis half-expected an ambush, while Sadat's security people feared for his safety. Radicals on either side might have used this dramatic moment to cut his effort short. But some events transcend ordinary calculations. The initial chill subsided as, to a fanfare of trumpets, wildly cheering Israelis welcomed the Egyptian president on a visit that nobody had previously dared to imagine.

The morning after his arrival, a Sunday, Sadat prayed at Al-Aqsa Mosque and then visited the Church of the Holy Sepulchre and Yad Vashem, the Israeli Holocaust memorial and museum. Thereafter, his first official act was to address the Knesset. His very presence in that body posed a radical challenge to the historic Arab stand. The speech itself, in traditional classical Arabic, discarded the established rhetoric of entrenched enmity. It rested the achievement of peace not in the tactics of decades of recrimination but in the souls of the adversaries:

Frankness makes it incumbent upon me to tell you the following:

First, I have not come here for a separate agreement between Egypt and Israel ... in the absence of a just solution of the Palestinian problem, never will there be that durable and just peace upon which the entire world insists. Second, I have not come to you to seek a partial peace, namely to terminate the state of belligerency at this stage and put off the entire problem to a subsequent stage ... Equally, I have not come to you for a third disengagement agreement in Sinai or in Golan or the West Bank. For this would mean that we are merely delaying the ignition of the fuse.

I have come to you so that together we shall build a durable peace based on justice to avoid the shedding of one single drop of blood by both sides. It is for this reason that I have proclaimed my readiness to go to the farthest corner of the earth.[156]

Settling for any half-measures, Sadat said, would mean that 'we are too weak to shoulder the burdens and responsibilities of a durable peace based upon justice'.[157] But he believed both parties were strong enough to make such a peace. In the emotional culmination of the speech, he asked: 'Why don't we stretch out our hands with faith and sincerity so that, together, we might destroy this barrier?'[158]

Sadat defined peace not so much as a finalized set of conditions as above all a fragile, vulnerable state, to be amended and defended with all possible tenacity against the rebirth of conflict. 'Peace,' Sadat proclaimed, 'is not a mere endorsement of written lines. Rather it is a rewriting of history ... Peace is a giant struggle against all and every ambition and whim.'[159]

Begin responded with an address that rose above his usual legalistic approach to overcome the inertia of conflict and embrace the full range of diplomatic options:

President Sadat knows, and he knew from us before he came to Jerusalem, that our position concerning permanent borders between us and our neighbors differs from his. However, I call upon the president of Egypt and upon all our neighbors: do not rule out negotiations on any subject whatsoever. I propose, in the name of the overwhelming majority of the parliament, that everything will be negotiable ... Everything is negotiable. No side shall say the contrary. No side shall present prior conditions. We will conduct the negotiations with respect.[160]

Sadat's journey to Jerusalem was that rare occasion in which the mere fact of an event constitutes an interruption of history and thereby transforms the range of the possible. It was his ultimate revolution, more consequential and truer to the spirit of his leadership than the coup of July 1952, the 'correction' of April 1971, the July 1972 expulsion of the Soviets or the war of October 1973 and its aftermath. The visit marked the fulfillment of Sadat's particular kind of nationalism, which expressed peace as a form of inner liberation.

THE TORTUOUS ROAD TO PEACE

The October War had cost Egypt more than 10,000 lives, including Sadat's youngest brother, a fighter pilot downed in a raid on an Israeli military airport. For Israel, the figures had been more than 2,600 killed and more than 7,000 wounded.[161] Meeting at an Egyptian military hospital during one of the shuttles, Sadat told me how much his country had suffered from war and that it did not need to produce more martyrs.[162]

The next four years would demonstrate that Sadat had set too high an initial hurdle for both sides. The first recriminations would come from the Arab world. Prior to the visit to Jerusalem, the last meeting between an Arab head of state and a Zionist or Israeli leader had been when Emir Faisal met with Chaim Weizmann in January 1919.[163] Since then, four wars had been fought on the very principles that Sadat proclaimed he was ready to abandon.

Aside from the immediate stakes, Arab leaders felt personally betrayed by Sadat's failure to consult them. On a practical level, they worried that his presence in Jerusalem would strengthen the Israelis' negotiating position.[164] Assad of Syria was outright contemptuous. When in 1975 I had asked him for his alternative, he replied, icily: 'You are abandoning Vietnam; you will abandon Taiwan. And we will be here when you grow tired of Israel.'[165]

Within Sadat's government, too, there was substantial opposition. On November 15, 1977, Foreign Minister Fahmy resigned in protest at the decision to visit Jerusalem.[166] Pressure on Israel from America increased. When, on November 19, Begin called Carter to confirm Sadat's arrival in Jerusalem, Carter told him: 'You must have observed Fahmy has resigned. There is the need for some tangible contribution for Sadat to take home. He has run high risks.'[167] Given this history, it is curious that in the aftermath of his visit, Sadat would sometimes be accused of going through Jerusalem to get to Washington. In fact, he sought to do just the reverse.

In July 1977, Libya under Muammar Qaddafi (for whom Sadat had only contempt) had provoked a brief war with Egypt over Sadat's insistence on his pursuit of peace with Israel and his rejection of Qaddafi's proposals of unity with Libya. He later described Sadat's actions as a 'betray[al] of the Arab nation'.[168] Syria and the PLO expressed similar outrage in a joint communiqué:

> [Sadat's visit], along with the Sadat–Begin plan, has no other aim but to impose a fait accompli on the Arab nation and thereby invalidate all genuine efforts to achieve a just peace based upon total withdrawal from all the occupied Arab territories.[169]

A formal 'Sadat-Begin plan' was at this point only a fantasy. Nevertheless, at a conference in Tripoli in December 1977, Syria, Algeria, Southern Yemen, Libya and the PLO described Sadat's actions as 'high treason'.[170] There they decided to apply punitive anti-Israel boycott laws to any Egyptian entities that traded with Israel.[171] Shortly thereafter, Egypt severed its relations with five Arab states and the PLO.

Sadat had hoped that the visit to Jerusalem would complement the exclusive relationship between Israel and America and jolt negotiations for peace into a new phase, to produce a more robust and permanent agreement.[172] He also anticipated that a divided Arab front would give Israel new opportunities for negotiating.[173] But, over the next year, Begin and Sadat achieved only faltering steps toward peace. In December 1977, Begin reciprocated the Jerusalem visit by traveling to the Egyptian city of Ismailia, but the only product of the summit there was an arrangement for meetings of the two sides' military and political experts, which quickly ran into the ground.

Begin, like Sadat, had started as a revolutionary. Unlike Sadat, he was the head of government in a country whose neighbors rejected its right to exist. He fought tenaciously on matters of symbol and language. In 1975, in response to the argument that Israel needed to give up territory in order to be recognized by its Arab neighbors, he shot back that the Israeli people 'don't need legitimacy ... We exist. Therefore, we are legitimate.'[174] Begin had an even deeper concern than recognition; more than his predecessors, he feared that Sadat would endanger the relationship with America that guaranteed Israel's existence.[175]

In March 1978, Sadat wrote to Begin in language recalling the formula Nixon had expressed to Hafiz Ismail in February 1973: 'security should not be at the expense of land or sovereignty.' That principle, Sadat wrote, had already been recognized by Egypt with respect to the existence of Israel, and he would do his part to convince the Arabs and the international community of it. But Israel would have to act according to the same principle: with respect to the Palestinian Arabs, it could not 'raise the issues in terms of land and sovereignty', and with respect to Egypt, it could not request the sacrifice of 'land and sovereignty' in exchange for peace. Sadat implied that security could be achieved as a stable equilibrium, an agreed-upon balance, sustained above all by overcoming established formulas and founded on a conception of justice that was rooted in the prospect of mutual benefit and the achievement of a shared vision of peace.

The two sides failed to come together even after renewed American participation in the spring of 1978. Sadat's frustration grew, as did his separation from his colleagues, who felt that his commitment to peace had become too overriding.

Exasperated, Sadat asked Carter to join the negotiating table. The president responded with invitations to both him and Begin for a meeting at Camp David in September 1978. At the outset of the talks, which lasted from September 5 to September 17, bilateral negotiations between the parties were still so fraught that Carter and Secretary of State Cyrus Vance had to mediate to get them started.

Sadat had problems even within his own delegation. As he said to one Foreign Ministry official:

> You people in the Foreign Ministry are under the impression that you understand politics. In reality, however, you understand absolutely nothing. Henceforth I shall not pay the least attention to either your words or your memos. I am a man whose actions are governed by a higher strategy which you are incapable of either perceiving or understanding.[176]

Not surprisingly, Fahmy's successor, Foreign Minister Kamel, also resigned, shortly before the conclusion of the Camp David Accords.[177] From the moment he set foot in Jerusalem, Sadat had committed himself irrevocably to an Egyptian–Israeli peace. Over twelve days of negotiations, he substantially modified elements of the standard Arab program.

Three months before the October War, in 1973, Sadat had rejected American views on the opening of the Suez Canal abruptly:

No partial solution, no separate solution with Egypt alone, no negotiations whatsoever . . . My initiative [for opening the Suez Canal] was not
designed at all as a partial or a step-by-step solution, and was not an end
in itself. What I said was: let me test your intentions regarding Israel's
retreat, so that I be convinced that she would indeed complete her
withdrawal . . . When the final date of evacuation is set, I would then clear
the canal. But today, no![178]

At Camp David five years later, Sadat agreed to a settlement that,
while leaving the fulfillment of its moral spirit to the future, contained
detailed steps to be taken immediately and others to be accomplished
further down the road. Despite lingering differences, it was built on the
trust gradually and mutually accumulated over the previous four years.
Both sides agreed to renounce the use of force, to normalize relations, to
sign a bilateral peace treaty and to allow the continued presence of UN
forces around the Suez Canal. Israel agreed to withdraw from the entirety of the Sinai.

The step-by-step approach had managed to attain nearly all that the
advocates of the comprehensive approach had set out to accomplish in
one major conference. At the same time, Egypt's national objectives had
been brought about by Sadat's strategy and, beyond that, the definition
of principles for regional peace and equilibrium; Israel reached the permanent binding agreement with one neighbor that it had sought with *all*
of them through the decades of its existence. Israel also agreed to explore
negotiations toward a peace treaty with Jordan, as well as separate
negotiations on the final status of the West Bank and Gaza; to allow a
self-governing Palestinian authority to form; and to include the Palestinians in negotiations on their own future, in a manner that satisfied
both Arab substantive and Israeli procedural requirements.

For the Camp David agreement, Sadat and Begin shared the Nobel
Peace Prize of 1978. In his acceptance speech on December 10, 1978,
Sadat reiterated his vision of peace: even this triumph, he said, was but
an interim 'end' in a much larger process aimed at 'security . . . liberty,
and dignity . . . for all the peoples of the region'. An ultimate and enduring peace – not yet achieved – would be 'indivisible' and 'comprehensive'.
The peace he desired would not just 'save man from death by destructive weapons' but also rid humanity of 'the evils of want and misery'.[179]
He concluded:

peace is a dynamic construction to which all should contribute, each adding a new brick. It goes far beyond a formal agreement or treaty, it
transcends a word here or there. That is why it requires politicians who
enjoy vision and imagination and who, beyond the present, look toward
the future.[180]

There was a six-month gap between the conclusion of the Camp
David Accords and the signing of the peace treaty. In the interim, negotiations continued, and Sadat took additional steps to reassure Israel:
accepting that Egypt would no longer claim a 'special role' in Gaza and
that it would not object to Israel's guarantee from the United States for
the loss of oil in the small Sinai oilfield.[181] Finally, on March 26, 1979,
after approval by the Israeli Knesset and the Egyptian People's Assembly, the peace treaty was signed on the White House lawn.

Two months later, Begin and Sadat met in El-Arish for the transfer of
that city from Israeli to Egyptian control. They looked on as Egyptian
and Israeli soldiers embraced each other and pledged themselves to
peace. As Begin remembered the scene in a letter to Sadat:

> we have learned to transform the Treaty into a living reality of peace,
> friendship, and cooperation. In stating this I cannot but make mention,
> with the deepest feeling, that meeting we witnessed together at El-Arish
> between the soldiers, the war invalids of Egypt and Israel who said to each
> other and to us: 'No more war.' What a unique, moving scene that was.[182]

THE UNRAVELING

Sadat's invocation of ancient partnership, 'the brotherhood of Ismail
and Isaac', failed to stir the imagination of those on both sides most
needed to fulfill it. Just after Egypt and Israel agreed to the Camp David
framework, and before they signed the bilateral treaty normalizing diplomatic relations, it became clear that Israel would resume building
settlements in the West Bank and Gaza as soon as the three-month suspension of construction expired.[183] Sadat wrote to Begin in late
November 1978, asking for a timetable for transferring authority 'to
the inhabitants of West Bank and Gaza'.[184] Begin responded with a list
of Egypt's failures to live up to its own commitments.

Begin interpreted the language of the peace treaty as not requiring the Israel Defense Forces to withdraw from the West Bank or Gaza and that the Palestinians had been granted the status not of a political entity but rather of an administrative council.[185] On July 30, 1980, the Knesset once again proclaimed Jerusalem to be Israel's capital. Sadat protested, proposing instead a unified administration but divided sovereignty over Jerusalem. Begin replied that the city was indivisible.[186] In a letter received by Begin on August 15, 1980, Sadat wrote that under such circumstances it would be impossible to resume negotiations.[187]

While Israel challenged particular provisions, the Arab world opposed the entire agenda of the Camp David Accords. Arab states saw the peace treaty as a violation of the 1950 Arab League agreement on joint defense and economic cooperation, which prohibited any member from entering into a separate peace with Israel.[188] Prominent Arab leaders repudiated the Camp David Accords for failing to settle the final status of the West Bank and Gaza and for not including the PLO in negotiations.[189] King Hussein of Jordan vehemently denounced the treaty and described himself as 'absolutely shattered' by Sadat's actions.[190] On March 31, 1979, the Arab League suspended Egypt from membership and resolved to move its headquarters from Cairo to Tunis. In December 1979, the UN General Assembly voted 102 to 37 to condemn the Accords and other 'partial settlements' on the grounds that they neglected Palestinian rights. Almost all of the Arab League members who had not already severed diplomatic relations with Egypt promptly did so.

External Arab opposition fueled existing hostility to Sadat within Egypt. After the 1973 war, he had gained the political legitimacy to shed Nasser's legacy by dint of crossing the Suez Canal. In the spring of 1974, he introduced his signature domestic legislation, the *infitah* or 'open door' policy that liberalized Egypt's economy. The *infitah* was intended to spur foreign aid and investment and bring about an economic boom.

Aid did arrive: from 1973 to 1975, Arab states gave Egypt more than $4 billion. And American economic assistance would also multiply, reaching $1 billion annually by 1977.[191] That figure, approaching quantitative parity with American aid to Israel, was greater than US aid to all of Latin America and the rest of Africa combined.[192] But, although Egypt's GDP growth rate accelerated, from 1.5 percent in 1974 to 7.4 percent in 1981,[193] the anticipated boom in investment and productivity never followed. Egypt failed to develop indigenous capital.[194] Short-term loans bore interest rates of up to 20 percent, and 90 percent of the funds used in public projects came from outside Egypt.[195] In January 1977, when Sadat tried to roll back subsidies on staple foods like bread, riots broke out across the country, with demonstrations of 30,000 people in Cairo alone.[196]

Sadat's economic policies also created a visible class of well-to-do foreigners. Militant Islamic groups, composed largely of members of the middle or lower-middle class, took to overt protest and opposition.[197] Some of his staunchest antagonists were Muslim Brothers whom Sadat had released from prison without realizing the degree to which many of them had become his enemies while incarcerated.[198]

The two most powerful Islamic militant groups at the time, Repentance and Holy Flight (*al-Takfir w'al-Hijra*) and the Islamic Liberation Organization (*Munazzamat al-Tahrir al-Islami*), both of which were dedicated to fighting Western influence and Zionism, also opposed Sadat's peace efforts,[199] interpreting his November 1977 Knesset speech, in which he described Israel as an 'established fact', as recognition of the Israeli state and thus a contravention of Islamist doctrine.[200] His proposal to build a church, mosque and synagogue on Mount Sinai, which had been made public in the summer of 1978,[201] was denounced as blasphemous. The fundamentalists were passionately opposed also to Sadat's legislative efforts promoting women's rights, dubbed 'Jehan's laws' after his young, half-English wife who advocated birth control and the liberalizing of divorce laws.

Opposition turned to violence. In July 1977, a fundamentalist group kidnapped and executed one of Sadat's former ministers.[202] In response, Sadat passed legislation ordering a death sentence for anyone belonging to a secret armed organization.[203] Jehan Sadat, then studying for a master's degree, became alarmed for her husband's safety. As she would recall in her memoirs,

> I wondered whether Anwar knew how deeply they were against him. My husband had advisers and intelligence reports, but I had more access to the people ... Anwar occasionally visited the universities, but I saw the fundamentalists with my own eyes every day. And unlike some advisers, I was not afraid to pass on an unfavorable report. 'Fundamentalism is growing, Anwar,' I cautioned him during the fall of '79. 'If you do not act

soon they may gain the political strength to overthrow everything you stand for.'[204]

Tensions in Egypt worsened after the formal conclusion of peace. In 1979, the Arab League declared the end of its economic aid as well as of private bank loans and oil exports to Egypt.[205] The Iranian Revolution pitted Sadat against the Islamists celebrating the rise of Ayatollah Khomeini. Sadat and the Shah had formed a personal friendship while the former was still vice president, and the latter had extended financial assistance after the 1973 war and oil supplies during a shortage in 1974.[206] He remained Sadat's supporter after the trip to Jerusalem.[207] In 1980, Sadat would welcome the exiled Shah to Egypt when his refuge in Panama was threatened by Iranian requests for his extradition.[208]

Sadat's domestic challenges were compounded by the disquiet among the 1952 revolutionaries who had since governed on the basis of the army's prestige and of Nasser's ability to evoke mass passions. Although Sadat undertook some political reforms – nominally replacing the single-party system with multi-party elections in 1976 and using referenda to circumvent the National Assembly – he had not fundamentally altered the constitution of the Free Officers' government, which enshrined authoritarian rule, and he had also maintained the dominance of the military elite. Sensing the growth in opposition, Sadat, out on a limb, followed his usual tactic of dealing with opponents by confronting them head on. He clamped down on free speech, dissolved student unions and banned vectors of religious extremism.[209]

In the process, Sadat shrank the group of those around him, finding himself in a classic dilemma. The deeper his conflict with the ideological majority, and the shallower his support, the more precarious his situation became. In September 1981, after a summer of Muslim–Coptic violence, Sadat carried out mass arrests, imprisoning more than 1,500 activists.[210] He even detained both the Coptic Pope and the Supreme Guide of the Muslim Brotherhood.[211]

The steady growth of religious extremism posed a central paradox for Sadat's domestic program. As one contemporary observer put it, 'the more liberal and democratic [Sadat] wants to be in order to carry out his dream, the more attentive and responsive he must become to popular demands to revert to the tradition of Islam'.[212] His pursuit of the dream of reconciliation turned into a choice for martyrdom.

ASSASSINATION

As a young boy, Sadat had admired the efforts of Egyptian patriots to fight for independence. He cherished one legend in particular: that of Zahran, a young Egyptian sentenced to hanging by the British. While others shuffled meekly to their fates, Zahran walked to the scaffold with his head held high, proclaiming in defiance: 'I am dying to free Egypt.' Sadat's daughter Camelia wrote that, all his life, her father had modeled his conduct on Zahran's example.[213]

On October 6, 1981, Egypt celebrated the eighth anniversary of the October War. Sadat was sitting on a reviewing stand at a military parade when suddenly one of the trucks slowed to a halt. A group of soldiers – fundamentalists within the Egyptian military, including an Islamic Jihad member who had escaped arrest in the earlier crackdown – started firing on Sadat. They killed the president and ten others.

Sadat had believed that Egypt's freedom would be achieved first through independence and then through historic reconciliation. His aim was to resurrect an ancient dialogue between Jews and Arabs, based on his understanding that their histories were meant to intertwine. It was precisely this belief in the compatibility and coexistence of societies founded on different religious faiths that his opponents found intolerable.

In the immediate aftermath of the attack, Prime Minister Begin praised Sadat's visit to Jerusalem and declared that he had been 'murdered by the enemies of peace', adding:

> His decision to come to Jerusalem and the reception accorded to him by the people, the Knesset, and the government of Israel will be remembered as one of the great events of our time. President Sadat did not pay attention to abuse and hostility, and went ahead with endeavors to abolish the state of war with Israel and to make peace with our nation. It was a difficult road.[214]

Sadat's funeral was held on October 10. President Reagan, having himself just survived an assassination attempt, could not attend. In his stead – and as a symbol of American respect – he sent Presidents Nixon, Ford and Carter, along with Secretary of State Alexander Haig, Secretary of Defense Caspar Weinberger and UN Ambassador Jeane Kirkpatrick. As a special courtesy, he attached me, then in private life, to the delegation.

The funeral was a strange affair: tightly managed by security forces, with a sense of shock still hanging in the air. The streets were quiet; there was none of the public outpouring of grief that had accompanied Nasser's funeral. The identity of the group responsible for his murder had not yet been clarified, but it was obvious that there had been high-level collusion, at least within the military.[215] This meant the prominent guests at the funeral procession – among them the three American presidents, Begin, Lee Kuan Yew, the Prince of Wales, former British Prime Minister James Callaghan, British Foreign Secretary Lord Carrington, French President François Mitterrand and former President Valéry Giscard d'Estaing, German Chancellor Helmut Schmidt and Foreign Minister Hans-Dietrich Genscher, and European Parliament President Simone Veil[216] – had to be protected as if potential targets.

Just two days earlier, insurgents had attempted to overrun a regional security headquarters to the south of Cairo. The Libyan government, rejoicing at President Sadat's death, was spreading false reports of more violence in Egypt. When several hundred mourners tried to merge into the procession, guards fired shots in the air to keep them out.

The hundred or so VIP guests had been assembled in a tent on the grounds of the parade route where Sadat was murdered. After a wait of well over an hour, we walked behind Sadat's coffin along the same route as the military parade four days earlier, passing the place of his assassination on our way to bury him.

The eeriness of the funeral echoed the unsettled prospects of the Middle East. Sadat's conduct had reflected his confidence that his counterparts might choose his path; his death symbolized the penalty they might have to pay. As radical regimes – exemplified by Qaddafi's reign of political violence, which sponsored terrorism from Scotland to Berlin – overwhelmed parts of the Arab world, those who stood for moderation were thrown into jeopardy. As I said on the night of his death: 'Sadat had taken from our shoulders the burdens of many difficult uncertainties'[217] – burdens that others would now have to assume.*

Sadat's epitaph contains a verse from the Qur'an: 'Do not consider those killed for the sake of Allah dead but alive and blessed by the

---

* To take one example, as the late professor and diplomat Charles Hill once wrote to me: 'With the killing of Sadat, Egypt dropped out of its role as state negotiator on behalf of the Palestinians with Israel'.

side of the Almighty.' Below that, it reads: 'Hero of war and peace. He lived for the sake of peace and was martyred for the sake of his principles.'[218]

On the occasion of a visit to Egypt in April 1983, I paid my respects at Sadat's tomb. I was the only mourner present.

EPILOGUE: THE UNREALIZED LEGACY

Anwar Sadat is best known for the peace treaty with Israel that he brought to Egypt. His ultimate design, however, was not a peace treaty, great though that achievement was, but a historic modification in Egypt's pattern of being and a new order in the Middle East as a contribution to the peace of the world.

From his youth, he recognized that Egypt, as a result of its history, was no more suited to being a subjugated province than it was to being the ideological leader of the Arab world. Its strength lay in its aspiration to an eternal identity.

Egypt's geographical location between the Arab world and the Mediterranean was both a potential asset and a liability. Sadat envisioned Egypt as a *peaceful* Islamic nation, strong enough to partner with its erstwhile enemy rather than either dominating it or being dominated by it. He understood that a just peace could be achieved only through an organic evolution and the recognition of mutual interests, not from imposition by outside powers. And the culmination of that process would be a universal acceptance of such principles.

Sadat's overall vision was too out of joint with that of his colleagues and contemporaries to be sustained. What survived him were the practical elements that he considered ephemeral.

The crucial contest in the modern Middle East is still with us: it is a competition between advocates of a religiously or ideologically pluralistic order – who treat their personal and communal convictions as compatible with a state-based system – and Sadat's repudiators, engaged in the articulation of a comprehensive theology or ideology across every domain of life. As imperial ambitions threaten to swallow states whole – and insurgencies divide them from within – Sadat's vision of international order among sovereign states, based on national interests defined in moral terms, could be a bulwark against calamity.

In an address delivered in May 1979 at Ben-Gurion University, where he was receiving an honorary degree, Sadat called for a revival of the spirit of relative tolerance of Islam's medieval Golden Age. He added:

> The challenge before us is not one of scoring a point here or there; rather, it is how to build a viable structure for peace for your generation and for the generations to come. Fanaticism and self-righteousness are no answer to the complex problems of today. The answer is tolerance, compassion, and magnanimity.
>
> We will be judged not by the hard positions we took but by the wounds we heal, the souls we saved, and the suffering we eliminated.[219]

One of Sadat's primary aims was to demonstrate Egypt's inherent independence. At a private dinner after our official relationship had ended, I remarked that the Americans he had worked with owed him a debt of gratitude for making us look better than we were. With some emphasis, Sadat replied that his work had not been done for the sake of his or anyone's reputation. He had embarked on his mission to restore the dignity and hope of the Egyptian people and set standards for peace in the world. As he said at the Egyptian–Israeli Peace Treaty signing ceremony in March 1979:

> let there be no more wars or bloodshed between Arabs and Israelis. Let there be no more suffering or denial of rights. Let there be no more despair or loss of faith. Let no mother lament the loss of her child. Let no young man waste his life on a conflict from which no one benefits. Let us work together until the day comes when they beat their swords into plowshares and their spears into pruning hooks. And God does call to the abode of peace. He does guide whom He pleases to His way.[220]

Yet Sadat did not merely 'express' his civilization; he modified and ennobled it. Much as he revered the epic past, his signal accomplishment was to transcend the pattern of Egypt's recent history. In the same way, as a prisoner, he had transcended confinement by opening himself to moral and philosophical change. As he reflected on those years in his memoirs:

> Inside Cell 54, as my material needs grew increasingly less, the ties which had bound me to the natural world began to be severed, one after another.

My soul, having jettisoned its earthly freight, was freed and took off like a
bird soaring into space, into the furthest regions of existence, into infinity . . .
My narrow self ceased to exist and the only recognizable entity was the
totality of existence, which aspired to a higher, transcendental reality.[221]

In this spirit, later in life, he bridged the gaps between Egyptian and
Israeli perceptions and the initial incommensurabilities of their negotiating positions. He understood that a zero-sum mindset would only
freeze in place a status quo as antithetical to the Egyptian national interest as it was to the cause of peace. He then had the extraordinary
courage to realize that revolution.

In this effort, he had important Israeli partners. Israel's geography
did not lend itself to heroic gestures. Yet the Israeli leaders who partnered with Sadat – Golda Meir, Yitzhak Rabin and Menachem
Begin – were moved by his vision of peace.[222] Rabin in particular articulated a notion of peace parallel to Sadat's. On the occasion of the
Jordanian Peace Agreement in 1994, he said to the American Congress:

In the Bible, our Book of Books, peace is mentioned, in its various idioms,
237 times. In the Bible, from which we draw our values and our strength,
in the Book of Jeremiah, we find a lamentation for Rachel the Matriarch.
It reads: 'Refrain your voice from weeping, and your eyes from tears: for
their work shall be rewarded, says the Lord.'

I will not refrain from weeping for those who are gone. But on this
summer day in Washington, far from home, we sense that our work will
be rewarded, as the prophet foretold.[223]

Both Rabin and Sadat were struck down by assassins hostile to the
changes that peace might bring.

Shortly after Sadat's assassination, I wrote that it was too early to
judge whether he had 'started an irreversible movement of history' or
had consigned himself to the fate of the ancient Pharaoh Akhenaten,
'who dreamed of monotheism amidst the panoply of Egyptian deities a
millennium before it was accepted among mankind'.[224] Forty years later,
the long-lived Egypt–Israel peace agreement, the parallel Israeli agreement with Jordan, even the Syrian disengagement agreement and most
recently the Abraham Accords – a series of diplomatic normalizations
between Israel and Arab nations signed in the summer and fall of

2020 – stand as Sadat's vindication. What is more, even where formal agreements have yet to be concluded, time has worn away some of the sands of illusion to expose the harder rock of Sadat's truth.

Early in our acquaintance, I sometimes wondered whether Sadat might have been playing a longer game than he was given time to finish. Once he had fulfilled his immediate purposes, might he have returned to earlier convictions, or reached for a different, even more sweeping perception?

The only version of Sadat that I can speak to with confidence is the one I knew. We spent hours together on the various negotiations described in this chapter and many evenings for the rest of his life in more abstract but equally edifying conversation as friends. The Sadat with whom I was familiar had moved from a strategic to a prophetic vision. The Egyptian people asked no more of him than the return to the pre-war borders. What he gave them, starting with his speech to the Knesset, was a vision of universal peace, which I believe was his definitive incarnation and the culmination of his convictions.

Our last conversation took place in August 1981 on a flight from Washington to New York after his first meeting with President Reagan. He had by then encountered four American presidents in seven years, each with a modified program. He was visibly tired. But suddenly he turned to me and spoke about a cherished symbolic project. 'Next March, the Sinai will come back to us,' he said. 'There will be a great celebration. You helped take the first step, and you should come celebrate with us.' Then there was one of his long and pensive pauses as empathy overtook exuberance. 'No, you shouldn't,' he continued:

> It will be very painful for the Israelis to give up this territory. It would hurt the Jewish people too much to see you in Cairo celebrating with us. You should come a month later. Then you and I can drive alone to Mount Sinai, where I intend to build a synagogue, a mosque, and a church. This will be a better commemoration.[225]

Sadat was assassinated at a parade to celebrate the watershed event which he had initiated and which had transformed the Middle East. He did not live to witness the return of the Sinai from Israel which he had brought about. The houses of worship on Mount Sinai that he envisioned are not yet being built. His vision of peace is still waiting for its incarnation.

But Sadat was both patient and serene. His perspective was that of ancient Egypt, which treated fulfillment as the unfurling of eternity.

5

Lee Kuan Yew: The Strategy of Excellence

A VISIT TO HARVARD

On November 13, 1968, Lee Kuan Yew, the forty-five-year-old prime minister of Singapore, arrived at Harvard University for what he described as a month-long 'sabbatical'.[1] Singapore had become independent only three years earlier, but Lee had been its prime minister since 1959, when the city gained autonomy in the twilight of British rule.

Lee told the *Harvard Crimson* – the student newspaper – that his aims were 'to get fresh ideas, to meet stimulating minds, to go back enriched with a fresh burst of enthusiasm for what I do', adding, in a touch of self-effacement, 'I intend to study all the things I've been doing ad hoc without the proper tutoring the past 10 years.'[2] *

He was soon invited to a meeting by the faculty of Harvard's Littauer Center (now the Kennedy School of Government), which comprised professors of government, economics and development. At the time, Americans knew little about Lee – or the tiny, newly established country he represented. The essence of the faculty's understanding was that our guest led a semi-socialist party and a post-colonial state. As such, when he sat down at the large oval table, he was warmly welcomed as a kindred spirit by my predominantly liberal colleagues assembled for the occasion.

Compact, and radiating energy, Lee wasted no time on small talk or

---

* As Lee wrote: 'I discovered early in office that there were few problems confronting me in government that other governments had not met and solved. So I made a practice of finding out who else had met the problem we faced, how they tackled it, and how successful they had been' (Lee Kuan Yew, *From Third World to First* (New York: HarperCollins, 2000), 687).

introductory remarks. Instead, he asked for the faculty's views on the war in Vietnam.[3] My colleagues, voicing passionate opposition to the conflict and to America's part in it, were divided primarily over whether President Lyndon B. Johnson was a 'war criminal' or merely a 'psychopath'. After a number of the professors had spoken, the dean of the Littauer faculty invited Lee to express his views, smiling in a way that clearly anticipated approbation.

With his first words, Lee went straight to the point: 'You make me sick.' Then, without making any attempt to ingratiate himself, he proceeded to explain that Singapore, as a small country in a tumultuous part of the world, depended for its survival on an America confident in its mission of providing global security and powerful enough to counter the communist guerrilla movements that were then seeking, with support from China, to undermine the young nations of Southeast Asia.

Neither a supplication for assistance nor an appeal to virtue, Lee's response was instead a dispassionate analysis of the geopolitical realities of his region. He described what he believed was Singapore's national interest: to achieve economic viability and security. He made clear that his country would do what it could in pursuit of both objectives, aware that America would make its own decisions about any assistance for its own reasons. He invited his interlocutors to join him less in a common ideology than in a joint exploration of the necessary.

To the astonished Harvard faculty, Lee articulated a worldview free of anti-American animus and post-imperial resentment. He neither blamed the United States for Singapore's challenges nor expected it to solve them. Rather, he sought American goodwill so that Singapore, lacking oil and other natural riches, could grow through the cultivation of what he said was its principal resource: the quality of its people, whose potential could develop only if they were not abandoned to communist insurgency, invasion by neighboring countries or Chinese hegemony. Earlier that year, British Prime Minister Harold Wilson had announced the withdrawal of all forces 'east of Suez', requiring the closure of the massive Royal Navy base that had been a pillar of Singapore's economy and security. Lee was therefore seeking an American hand to help counter the difficulties he saw looming. He framed this task less in terms of the prevailing moral categories of the Cold War than as an element in the construction of a regional order – in the sustaining of which America should develop its own national interest.

One of the essential qualities of a statesman is the ability to resist being swept along by the mood of the moment. Lee's performance in that long-ago Harvard seminar was instructive not only for the clarity of his analysis – of both America's and Singapore's positions in the world – but also for his courage in going against the grain. It was a quality which he would display many times in his career.

THE GIANT FROM LILLIPUT

Lee's achievements were distinct from those of the other leaders described in this volume. Each of them represented a major country with a culture formed over centuries, if not millennia. For such leaders, as they attempt to guide their society from a familiar past to an evolving future, success is measured by their ability to direct their society's historical experience and values so that its potential may be fulfilled.

The statesmanship practiced by Lee Kuan Yew developed from different origins. When he became leader of independent Singapore in August 1965, he took charge of a country that had never before existed – and hence, in effect, had no political past except as an imperial subject. Lee's achievements were to overcome his nation's experience, to establish a distinct conception of itself by conjuring up a dynamic future from a society composed of divergent ethnic groups and to transform a poverty-ridden city into a world-class economy. In the process, he grew into a world statesman and sought-after adviser to the great powers. Richard Nixon said he showed the 'ability to rise above the resentments of the moment and of the past and think about the nature of the new world to come'.[4] Margaret Thatcher called him 'one of the twentieth century's most accomplished practitioners of statecraft'.[5]

Lee accomplished all this in the face of seemingly crippling disadvantages. Singapore's territory was 'some 224 square miles at low tide', as he was wont to say – smaller than that of Chicago.[6] It lacked the most basic natural resources, including sufficient drinking water. Even the tropical rains – Singapore's main domestic source of drinking water at the time of independence – were an ambiguous gift, leaching the soil of nutrients and making productive agriculture impossible.[7] Singapore's population of 1.9 million was, by global standards, minuscule and rent by tension among three distinct ethnic groups: Chinese, Malay and

Indian. It was surrounded by much larger and more powerful states, particularly Malaysia and Indonesia, that envied its deep-water port and strategic location along maritime trading routes.

From this inauspicious genesis, Lee initiated an epic of leadership that transformed Singapore into one of the world's most successful countries. A malarial island off the southernmost tip of the Malay peninsula became – in the span of a single generation – Asia's wealthiest country on a per capita basis and the de facto commercial center of Southeast Asia. Today, by almost every measure of human well-being, it ranks globally in the highest percentile.

In contrast to countries whose persistence through the convulsions of history is taken for granted, Singapore would not survive unless it performed at the highest possible level – as Lee relentlessly warned his compatriots. As he put it in his memoirs, Singapore was 'not a natural country but man-made'.[8] Precisely because it had no past as a nation, there was no assurance it would have a future; its margin for error thus remained perpetually close to zero. 'I'm concerned that Singaporeans assume Singapore is a normal country,' he would say several times later in his life.[9] 'If we do not have a government and a people that differentiate themselves from the rest of the neighborhood . . . Singapore will cease to exist.'[10]

In Singapore's struggle to form itself and survive as a nation, domestic and foreign policy had to be closely intertwined. There were three requirements: economic growth to sustain the population, sufficient domestic cohesion to permit long-range policies, and a foreign policy nimble enough to survive among international behemoths such as Russia and China and covetous neighbors such as Malaysia and Indonesia.

Lee also had the historical awareness necessary for real leadership. 'City states do not have good survival records,' he observed in 1998.[11] 'The island of Singapore will not disappear, but the sovereign nation it has become, able to make its way and play its role in the world, could vanish.'[12] In his mind, Singapore's trajectory had to be a steep upward curve with no end in sight; otherwise, it would risk being engulfed by its hinterland or by the severity of its economic and social challenges. Lee taught a kind of global physics in which societies must constantly strive to avoid entropy. Leaders are tempted by pessimism, he observed to a private gathering of world leaders in May 1979, when Singapore was in the early stages of growth, but 'we have to fight our way out of it. You have to show a credible, plausible way that we can keep our head above water.'[13]

Parallel to Lee's dire warnings about the threat of extinction lay an equally vivid imagination of his country's potential. If every great achievement is a dream before it becomes a reality, Lee's dream was breathtaking in its audacity: he envisioned a state that would not simply survive but flourish through an insistence on excellence. In Lee's perception, excellence meant much more than individual performance: the quest for it needed to permeate the entire society. Whether in government service, business, medicine or education, mediocrity and corruption were not acceptable. There was no second chance in case of transgressions, very little tolerance for failure. In this manner, Singapore achieved a worldwide reputation for collectively outstanding performance. A sense of shared success, in Lee's view, could help to knit his society together despite the lack of a universally shared religion, ethnicity or culture.

Lee's ultimate gift to his multi-ethnic people was his unremitting faith that they were their own greatest resource, that they had the capacity to unlock possibilities in themselves that they had not known existed. He also devoted himself to encouraging a comparable confidence in his foreign friends and acquaintances. He was persuasive not only because he was a subtle observer of the regional politics of Southeast Asia but because his Chinese heritage, combined with his Cambridge University education, gave him exceptional insight into the dynamics of the interaction between East and West – one of the essential fulcrums of history.

Throughout his life, Lee insisted on describing his contributions as merely the unlocking of his society's existing capabilities. He knew that to succeed, his quest had to become the enduring pattern, not a personal tour de force. 'Anybody who thinks he's a statesman needs to see a psychiatrist,' he once said.[14]

In time, Singapore's success under Lee moved even China to study his approach and emulate his designs. In 1978, Deng Xiaoping came to the city-state expecting to see a backwater and to be cheered by throngs of ethnic Chinese. Deng had spent two days in Singapore on his way to Paris in 1920, and in the intervening years his information on the city had largely been provided by an obsequious entourage prone to paint the Singaporean leadership as the 'running dogs of American imperialism'.[15] Instead, the ethnic Chinese Deng met in Singapore were firm in their allegiance to their young nation. The gleaming skyscrapers and immaculate avenues Deng encountered provided him with both an impetus and a blueprint for China's own post-Mao reforms.

IMPERIAL YOUTH

Lee Kuan Yew was born in September 1923, scarcely more than a century after Sir Stamford Raffles, lieutenant-governor of the British colony in Sumatra, established a trading post on the small island near the Strait of Malacca known to locals as 'Singa Pura', meaning 'Lion City' in Sanskrit. Founded by Raffles in 1819, Singapore was technically ruled from Calcutta as part of 'further India', although the limited communications technology of the day allowed considerable leeway to locally based colonial administrators. Declared a free port by London – and enriched by natural-resource exports from the Malayan mainland – the new outpost grew swiftly, drawing traders and fortune-seekers from Southeast Asia and beyond. From 1867, Singapore was placed under the direct jurisdiction of the Colonial Office in London as a crown colony.[16]

Ethnic Chinese in particular flocked to Singapore and soon became its majority – some coming from the nearby Malay peninsula and Indonesian archipelago, others fleeing from turmoil and poverty in crisis-racked nineteenth-century China. Among the latter group was Lee's great-grandfather, who traveled to Singapore from the southern Chinese province of Guangdong in 1863. Malays, Indians, Arabs, Armenians and Jews likewise settled in the freewheeling entrepot, giving the city a polyglot character. By the 1920s, Malaya produced almost one-half of the world's rubber and one-third of its tin, exporting both via Singapore's port.[17]

By the time of Lee's birth, Singapore had also become a cornerstone of British military strategy in Asia. Britain had been an ally of Japan since 1902, going so far as to call in Japanese marines to help crush an Indian army mutiny in Singapore in 1915.[18] But by 1921, the Admiralty had become anxious about Japan's growing power and resolved to build a substantial naval base in Singapore, with the aim of turning it into 'the Gibraltar of the East'.[19] Despite the rise of Japan, the world of Lee's childhood was one in which the British Empire appeared both invincible and eternal. 'There was no question of any resentment,' he recalled decades later; 'the superior status of the British in government and society was simply a fact of life.'[20]

Lee's family prospered during the boom years of the 1920s. Influenced by a particularly Anglophilic grandfather, Lee's parents also took the unusual step of giving their sons English names in addition to their Chinese ones. Lee's was 'Harry'. From the age of six, he was educated in English-language schools.[21]

Despite these English influences, Lee's upbringing was traditionally Chinese. He was raised with his extended family – including seven cousins – in his maternal grandfather's house, where his parents shared a single room with their five children. From these childhood experiences and Confucian cultural influences, filial piety, frugality and a prizing of harmony and stability were early imprints on his mind.

His parents were not educated professionals and suffered when the Great Depression struck in 1929. Lee wrote in his memoirs that his father, a storekeeper for Shell Oil Company, would often 'come home in a foul mood after losing at blackjack ... and demand some of my mother's jewellery to pawn so that he could go back to try his luck again'.[22] She always refused, safeguarding the education of the children, who, in turn, adored her and felt a lifelong obligation to meet her high expectations.[23]

A clever but at times rebellious student, the twelve-year-old Lee graduated at the top of his primary-school class, thereby gaining admission to the Raffles Institution, alongside 150 of the best students of all ethnicities and classes in Singapore and Malaya who had been admitted exclusively on the basis of merit – including Miss Kwa Geok Choo, who was the only female student.[24] Then as now, the Raffles Institution was the most rigorous English-language secondary school in Singapore and the training ground of the city's future elite. It aimed at preparing the ablest colonial subjects for the entrance examinations to British universities. Later in life, upon meeting Commonwealth leaders from around the world, Lee invariably 'discovered that they also had gone through the same drill with the same textbooks and could quote the same passages from Shakespeare'.[25] They were all part of 'the easy old-boy network ... nurtured by the British colonial education system'.[26]

Cognizant of their son's academic promise, and regretting that they had not made more of their own careers, Lee's parents encouraged him to pursue medicine or law. He dutifully made plans to study law in London, being placed first in Singapore and Malaya in the senior Cambridge examinations.[27] But in 1940, with the outbreak of another world war in Europe, Lee decided it would be better to remain in Singapore and study at Raffles College (now the National University of Singapore), where he had been awarded a full scholarship.[28]

Lee excelled academically during his freshman year, competing with Miss Kwa for first place in various subjects. Returning to his dream to study law in England, he set his sights on attaining a Queen's scholarship, which would cover the costs of a university education in Britain. Since only two students in the Straits Settlements (Malacca, Penang and Singapore) were awarded a Queen's scholarship every year, Lee was perpetually anxious that Miss Kwa and a top student from another school would take the first two places, leaving him behind in Singapore.[29]

There were greater anxieties to come. In December 1941, the Japanese bombed the US Pacific Fleet at Pearl Harbor, Hawaii, and simultaneously attacked British Malaya, Hong Kong and Singapore. Two months later, in February 1942, the city was conquered by Japan in what Winston Churchill would call 'the worst disaster and largest capitulation in British history'. Lee, then eighteen years old, later described this as 'the first turning point of my life', contrasting the panicked departure of bourgeois British families with the stoic suffering of their colonial subjects and the 80,000 British, Australian and Indian soldiers who had been captured by the Japanese. For Lee and countless other Singaporeans, 'the aura of overwhelming superiority with which the British held us in thrall was broken, never to be restored'.[30]

A brutal occupation followed, as Singapore's trade-dependent economy was choked by war and its population demoralized by conditions of near-starvation. Japanese authorities renamed streets and public buildings, took down the bronze statue of Raffles from Empress Place and imposed their imperial calendar.[31] Lee himself narrowly avoided death after being arbitrarily rounded up by Japanese troops in a mass detention of Chinese men, most of whom were summarily executed – especially those with soft hands or spectacles, singled out as 'intellectuals' whose loyalties might lie with Britain. Tens of thousands were massacred.[32] Lee was spared, took a three-month Japanese language course and found work – first as a clerk at a Japanese company, then as an

English translator in the Japanese propaganda department, and finally as a black-market jewelry broker.[33] During the war years, Lee learned that 'the key to survival was improvisation' – a lesson that would shape his pragmatic, experimental approach to governing Singapore.[34]

With the war's end, Lee at last achieved a Queen's scholarship to study law at Cambridge, graduating with a first-class degree. Miss Kwa, whom Lee had begun courting during the war, followed the same path, and in December 1947 the two were quietly married in Stratford-upon-Avon.[35] 'Choo', as Lee called her, was an extraordinary woman, with an unusual combination of brilliance and sensitivity. She became the indispensable anchor of his life, not only in a day-to-day sense but above all as a pervasive emotional and intellectual support throughout his public activities. At Raffles College, she had majored in literature, reading from 'Jane Austen to JRR Tolkien, from Thucydides' *The Peloponnesian Wars* to Virgil's *Aeneid*', as Lee reflected later.[36] After their success at Cambridge, they returned to Singapore and co-founded a law firm, Lee & Lee.

Lee's views during his Cambridge years were firmly socialist and anti-colonialist, even anti-British. Some of this was personal: he was occasionally turned away from hotels in England because of the color of his skin,[37] but much more of it was to do with what he later called the 'ferment in the air'. The independence struggles of India, Burma and other colonies were leading Lee to ask: 'Why not Malaya, which then included Singapore?'[38] Convinced that 'the welfare state was the highest form of civilised society', Lee was an admirer of the postwar reforms of Prime Minister Clement Attlee's Labour government as well as Indian Prime Minister Jawaharlal Nehru's statist economic policies.[39]

Lee first entered the public eye while in Britain, campaigning on behalf of a Labour Party friend who was running for parliament. Standing on the back of a truck in the small town of Totnes in Devon, Lee delivered one of his first public speeches, trading on his identity as a British subject to advocate for Malaya's self-governance. His arguments foreshadowed his later style, more practical than ideological: independence would be most successful if achieved cooperatively and incrementally between the independence movement and the mother country. Lee closed his speech with an appeal to British reason and self-interest:

Even if you care nothing for fairness or social justice to the colonial peoples, then for the sake of your own self-interest, your own economic well-being, for the sake of the dollars you get out of Malaya and your other colonies, return a government that has the confidence of these peoples, who will then gladly cooperate with and be happy to grow up within the British Commonwealth and Empire.[40]

BUILDING A STATE

While Lee was studying in England, Singapore was suffering wrenching postwar disruptions. Well into the spring of 1947, food was rationed and tuberculosis rampant. The Malayan Communist Party and its trade union allies were organizing strikes that further damaged the economy.[41]

By the time of Lee's return to Singapore in August 1950, two major problems lingered: housing and corruption. Only one-third of Singaporeans had adequate housing, and construction was not keeping pace with demand. After stores closed for the day, it was common for employees to sleep on the floor.[42] Corruption, untamed under British rule, had been exacerbated by wartime conditions.[43] Inflation eroded the purchasing power of civil servants' salaries, creating greater temptations for graft.[44]

Lee had returned with the intention of practicing law but was quickly drawn into Singapore's politics. His gifts were immediately rewarded: in 1954, at the age of thirty-one, he founded the People's Action Party (PAP); within five years, galvanized by Lee's fearsome energy, it dominated the island's political landscape. Cyril Northcote Parkinson, the Raffles Professor of History at the University of Malaya in Singapore, described Lee's political positioning during these years as 'as far to the left as possible, short of Communism, and further to the left in words than action'.[45] With a strong social democratic message, the PAP emphasized the failure of colonial authorities to provide decent public services and clean, efficient government. PAP candidates campaigned without ties, in white short-sleeved shirts – intended at once as a no-nonsense accommodation to Singapore's tropical climate and a symbol of their commitment to honest governance.[46] * In May 1959, the city was granted self-government by London in all matters except foreign

---

* Their objective, according to the Singaporean sociologist Beng Huat Chua, was 'to equal if not better the asceticism and self-sacrificing attitude of the radical left'. (See Beng Huat

policy and defense. After the PAP secured a parliamentary majority in elections that month, Lee was appointed prime minister, a position he held until he stepped down in November 1990, more than three decades later.[47]

In the immediate aftermath of self-government, Singapore had three distinct constitutional arrangements within the space of a few years: as a British crown colony from 1959 to 1963, as part of a new confederation called Malaysia from 1963 to 1965, and as an independent sovereign state after 1965. It was during this period near the end of colonial rule that the foundations of the modern Singaporean state were laid. Lee assembled an impressive cabinet – including the economist Goh Keng Swee (appointed minister of finance) and the journalist S. Rajaratnam (appointed minister of culture) – who drew up plans to ameliorate the city's social conditions.*

The new Housing and Development Board (HDB) soon began constructing high-rise residential projects on a massive scale, with the goal of giving all Singaporeans access to affordable housing of essentially the same type; residents had the right to purchase their apartments from the HDB at established rates. Lee appointed a competent and dynamic businessman, Lim Kim San, to lead the board; at Lim's direction, it built more housing in three years than the British had in the preceding thirty-two.[48] In time, Singapore grew into a fully urban society of homeowners, providing every family with a stake in Singapore's future in the form of property.[49] As Lee pointed out in his memoirs, closely linking individual economic prosperity to the state's well-being also 'ensured political stability', which in turn reinforced economic growth.[50] At the same time, a system of racial and income quotas on Singapore's housing districts first put a limit on ethnic segregation and then progressively eliminated it. By living and working together, Singaporeans from disparate ethnicities and religions began to develop a national consciousness.

Lee moved just as quickly to eradicate corruption. Within a year of taking office, his government passed the Prevention of Corruption Act,

---

Chua, *Liberalism Disavowed: Communitarianism and State Capitalism in Singapore* (Ithaca, NY: Cornell University Press, 2017), 3.)

* Lee later wrote of Goh, Rajaratnam and two other trusted lieutenants: 'They were all older than I was and were never inhibited from telling me what they thought, especially when I was wrong. They helped me stay objective and balanced' (Lee, *From Third World to First*, 686).

which imposed severe penalties for corruption at every level of government and limited due process for suspected bribe-takers. Under Lee's leadership, corruption was swiftly and ruthlessly suppressed.[51] Lee also put all foreign investments under intense scrutiny, personally performing some of his administration's uncompromising due diligence. His rigorous enforcement of Singapore's laws buttressed its reputation as an honest, safe place to do business.

To achieve his objectives, Lee relied on penalizing civil servants for failure rather than encouraging them by raising their salaries; in fact, his government initially slashed them.[52] Only in 1984, when Singapore had become wealthier, did Lee adopt his signature policy of pegging civil servants' salaries at 80 percent of comparable private-sector rates.[53] As a result, government officials in Singapore became some of the best compensated in the world. Success against corruption remains the 'moral basis of [PAP] rule', as a prominent Singaporean academic has observed.[54]

Corruption in Singapore is understood not only as a moral failing of the individuals involved but also as a transgression against the ethical code of the community – which emphasizes meritocratic excellence, fair play and honorable conduct.[55] Singapore has regularly been ranked as one of the least corrupt countries in the world, fulfilling Lee's goals for his country.[56] * As Lee observed later: 'You want men with good character, good mind, strong convictions. Without that Singapore won't make it.'[57]

Reducing corruption made it possible to invest in government programs that ensured substantial improvement in Singaporeans' lives and provided a fair playing field based on equality of opportunity. Between 1960 and 1963, Singapore's educational expenditure rose nearly seventeen-fold, while the school population increased by 50 percent.[58] In the PAP's first nine years in power, Lee set aside nearly one-third of Singapore's budget for education – an astonishing proportion in relation to neighboring countries, or indeed any country in the world.[59]

---

* Transparency International, the Berlin-based non-profit, ranks Singapore as the third-least-corrupt country in the world for 2020 (a place it shares with Finland, Switzerland and Sweden. New Zealand and Denmark are tied for first). (See 'Corruption Perceptions Index' 2020, Transparency International website, https://www.transparency.org/en/cpi/2020/index/sgp.)

Emphasis on the quality of life turned into a defining aspect of Singapore's style. Beginning with a 1960 X-ray campaign against tuberculosis, Singapore made public health a major priority.[60] As George Shultz and Vidar Jorgensen have observed, 'The city-state spends only 5 percent of GDP on medical care but has considerably better health outcomes than the U.S., which spends 18 percent of GDP on health. Life expectancy in Singapore is 85.2 years, compared with 78.7 in the U.S.'[61] Within one generation, Singapore transformed itself from a disease-ridden slum into a first-world metropolis – all the while steadily shrinking the government's share of costs.[62]

To orchestrate this revolution in governance, Lee established a network of what he called 'parapolitical institutions' to serve as a transmission belt between the state and its citizens. Community centers, citizens' consultative committees, residents' committees and, later, town councils provided recreation, settled small grievances, offered such services as kindergartens and disseminated information about government policies.[63] The PAP played an important role in these institutions, blurring the boundaries between party, state and people.[64] For example, Lee established almost 400 kindergartens that were exclusively staffed by PAP members.[65]

Through a combination of public service and what Lee described as skilled political 'street fighting', the PAP steadily entrenched itself following the 1959 elections and then again around the 1963 elections.[66] By 1968, Lee had largely crushed his competitors; the opposition boycotted those elections, and the PAP won nearly 87 percent of the vote and all fifty-eight legislative seats. After that, the PAP maintained itself largely unchallenged. One source of its continuing strength was Singapore's first-past-the-post electoral system, a British legacy which makes no provisions for minority votes. Another was that Lee used the legal system to isolate his political opponents and curtail unfriendly media outlets.[67] He described his struggles with opposition figures as 'unarmed combat with no holds barred, in a contest where the winner took all'.[68]

Lee was passionately concerned about public order. When he first came to power, the counterculture and general relaxation of morals had not yet arisen in the West, but later Lee would reflect on this as freedom run amok. 'As a total system, I find parts of it totally unacceptable', he told Fareed Zakaria in 1994:

The expansion of the right of the individual to behave or misbehave as he pleases has come at the expense of orderly society. In the East the main object is to have a well-ordered society so that everybody can have maximum enjoyment of his freedoms. This freedom can only exist in an ordered state and not in a natural state of contention and anarchy.[69]

As Lee was building Singapore, he did not believe a city-state could stand on its own. His major effort was therefore to safeguard Singapore's impending independence from Britain by joining in federation with Malaya. Believing that 'geography, economics, and ties of kinship' created the basis for a natural unity between the two territories, Lee called a snap referendum on the merger for September 1962.[70] To rally the Singaporean populace, he made a series of thirty-six radio broadcasts in the course of a single month: twelve scripts, each recorded in three languages – Mandarin, Malay and English.[71] His oratorical talents produced an overwhelming endorsement of his plan in the popular vote. A year later, on September 16, 1963 – Lee's fortieth birthday – Singapore and Malaya combined in the Malaysian Federation.

The union was immediately challenged from within and without. Covetous of the augmented Malaysia's potential, dreaming of uniting the Malay peoples in a single country and enjoying the support of both Moscow and Beijing, Indonesian President Sukarno launched the *Konfrontasi* – an undeclared war involving jungle combat and terrorism that left hundreds dead on both sides. For Singapore, the most dramatic event of the conflict was the bombing on March 10, 1965 of MacDonald House – the first air-conditioned office building in Southeast Asia – by Indonesian marines, which killed three people and injured more than thirty.

Within Malaysia, many Malay politicians distrusted Lee, despite the PAP's efforts to reduce communal tensions in Singapore and promote Malay as the national language.[72] They feared that his dynamic personality and evident political gifts would outshine their own, leading to ethnic Chinese dominance of the new federation.

Malay leaders opposed to Lee stoked violent ethnic riots in Singapore, first in July and then again in September 1964, resulting in dozens killed and hundreds injured. The ostensible trigger for the riots was the demolition of Malay villages (*kampongs*) to make way for public housing, but there was clearly opportunism by ethnic chauvinists and communists at work as well.[73]

As a result, less than two years after they had been joined, Singapore and Malaysia separated again, ripped apart by intense partisanship and ethnic tensions. Singapore's independence came about in August 1965 not as a result of a homegrown liberation struggle but due to Malaysia's unceremonious decision to cut its tiny southern neighbor loose.

Expulsion left the island country entirely on its own, an outcome that Lee had neither expected nor sought. Announcing the failure of the merger brought him to the edge of tears. 'Every time we look back on this moment . . . it will be a moment of anguish,' he said at a press conference in which he uncharacteristically struggled to keep his composure, nearly overwhelmed by the enormous task now before him. In his memoirs, Lee wrote that Singapore had become 'a heart without a body' as a result of the separation. 'We were a Chinese island in a Malay sea,' he continued. 'How could we survive in such a hostile environment?'[74] It was the memory of this nadir which, for the rest of his life, gave Lee the sense that his country needed to overachieve because it was walking a perpetual tightrope between survival and catastrophe.

BUILDING A NATION

Writing in 1970, five years after Singapore's independence, the historian Arnold Toynbee predicted that the city-state in general had 'become too small a political unit to be practicable any longer', and that Singapore in particular was unlikely to last as a sovereign state.[75] Much as Lee respected Toynbee, he did not share the scholar's fatalism.[76] His response to Toynbee's challenge was to create a new nation out of the disparate peoples that the tides of history had deposited on the shores of Singapore.

Only what Lee deemed 'a tightly knit, rugged, and adaptable people'[77] – a people united by national feeling – could endure the manifold tests of independence and guard against his two daunting nightmares: internal disorder and foreign aggression. His challenge was not primarily a technocratic task. Sacrifices might be imposed by force, but they could be sustained only by a sense of common belonging and shared destiny.

'We didn't have the ingredients of a nation, the elementary factors,' Lee later reflected: 'a homogeneous population, common language, common culture and common destiny.'[78] To will the Singaporean nation into

being, he acted as if it already existed and reinforced it with public policy. At the end of the press conference on August 9, 1965, announcing
independence, Lee laid out an elevated mission for his people:

> There is nothing to be worried about . . . Many things will go on just as
> usual. But be firm, be calm.
>
> We are going to have a multi-racial nation in Singapore. We will set the
> example. This is not a Malay nation; this is not a Chinese nation; this is
> not an Indian nation. Everybody will have his place . . .
>
> And finally, let us, really Singaporeans – I cannot call myself a Malay-
> sian now – . . . unite, regardless of race, language, religion, culture.[79]

Lee's immediate concern was to build a military capable of deterring
further Indonesian aggression.[80] Separation from Malaysia had left
Singapore without a single loyal regiment of its own, and it had no leaders who knew how to build a military from scratch; the able Goh Keng
Swee, now minister of defense, had been only a corporal in the Singapore Volunteer Corps at the British surrender to the Japanese in 1942.[81]
(When Lee rode to the opening of the first Singaporean parliament in
December 1965, Malaysian troops had 'escorted' him from his office to
the session.)[82] Compounding the challenge, the island's Chinese majority did not have a tradition of soldiering – a profession that in
Singapore had been historically dominated by ethnic Malays – potentially
turning defense into a racial powder keg.

Immediately after independence, Lee appealed to President Gamal
Abdel Nasser of Egypt and Prime Minister Lal Bahadur Shastri of India
to send military trainers. Reluctant to antagonize Indonesia and Malaysia, both declined the request. In response, Lee made the audacious
decision to accept an offer of assistance from Israel, despite the back-
lash this risked among the significant Muslim population in Singapore
and the region. To head off that threat, Lee simply decided not to
announce the Israelis' presence. To anyone who asked, Singapore's new
military advisors would instead be described as 'Mexicans'.[83]

It proved to be an inspired combination, as Singapore's security
dilemmas roughly mirrored those of Israel. Both were resource-poor
countries without strategic depth, surrounded by bigger countries with
revanchist temptations. Lee adopted the Israeli practice of a small but
highly professional standing army, backed by a whole-of-society reserve

capable of rapid mobilization. All young male Singaporeans, regardless
of background, had to perform a period of military service and then
regularly conduct in-camp training as reservists. Lee saw 'political and
social benefits' in national service, as contributing to a feeling of national
unity and social equality across ethnic divides.[84]

In 1966, Indonesia extended diplomatic recognition to Singapore,
which had proven resilient against the *Konfrontasi*.[85] By 1971, Singapore
had built up seventeen national service battalions and an additional
fourteen reserve battalions. Despite enormous budget pressure, Lee
found funding for the rapid acquisition of air and naval forces required
for credible deterrence against Singapore's neighbors. He would go on to
emphasize the latest technology and rigorous training as 'force multipli-
ers' to compensate for the island's limited space and manpower. Within
a generation, Singapore's armed forces emerged as the most capable in
Southeast Asia – a source of national pride and unity as well as foreign
admiration, including by the United States Department of Defense.

Unlike many other post-colonial leaders, Lee did not seek to
strengthen his position by pitting the country's diverse communities
against each other. To the contrary, he relied on Singapore's ability to
foster a sense of national unity out of its conflicting ethnic groups.
Despite the intense inter-ethnic violence that preceded independence, he
defied the centrifugal forces intrinsic in Singapore's composition and
developed a cohesive national identity. As he put it in 1967:

> It is only when you offer a man – without distinctions based on ethnic,
> cultural, linguistic, and other differences – a chance of belonging to this
> great human community, that you offer him a peaceful way forward to
> progress and to a higher level of human life.[86]

Lee's approach was neither to repress Singapore's diversity nor to
discount it, but to channel and manage it. Any other course, he affirmed,
would make governance impossible.[87]

Lee's most innovative initiative was his language policy. How to govern a city-state where 75 percent of the population spoke various
Chinese dialects, 14 percent spoke Malay, and 8 percent spoke Tamil?
After the failure of the merger with Malaysia, Lee no longer favored
making Malay the national language. Making Mandarin the official
language, however, was 'out of the question', in Lee's view, as 'the 25 per
cent of the population who were not Chinese would revolt'.[88] English

had long been the working language of government, but few Singaporeans spoke it as their mother tongue, as Lee did.[89] * His solution was a
policy of bilingual education – requiring English-language schools to
teach Mandarin, Malay and Tamil while mandating English classes in
all other schools. Singapore's constitution enshrined four official languages: Malay, Mandarin, Tamil and English.[90] As Lee said in 1994:

> If I had tried to foist the English language on the people of Singapore I
> would have faced rebellion all around ... But I offered every parent a
> choice of English and their mother tongue, in whatever order they chose.
> By their free choice, plus the rewards of the marketplace over a period of
> 30 years, we have ended up with English first and the mother tongue
> second. We have switched one university already established in the Chin-
> ese language from Chinese into English. Had this change been forced in
> five or ten years instead of being done over 30 years – and by free choice –
> it would have been a disaster.[91]

Being an English-speaking country provided an economic benefit as
well. In the 1960s, Singapore stood out from rival developing economies
by its distinct Anglophilic orientation. Lee's decision to retain the statue
of Raffles preserved a non-sectarian figure from Singapore's past as a
unifying national symbol.[92] It also signaled to the world that Singapore
was open for business and not in the business of recriminations.[93]

'LET HISTORY JUDGE'

The rupture with Malaysia obliged Lee to reorient his initially socialist
approach toward pragmatic essentials. For Singapore to survive as a
state, its economy had to grow. For it to succeed as a nation, the fruits of
that growth had to be shared equitably among its people, regardless of

---

* Lee spoke Malay and English from childhood. He struggled to learn Mandarin beginning
in his teenage years, picked up again in his late twenties and was still working with a tutor
well into his eighties. To expand his political base, he began learning and making speeches
in Hokkien in his late thirties. (See Perry, *Singapore*, 192; Lee, *My Lifelong Challenge:
Singapore's Bilingual Journey*, 32-41; and Lee Kuan Yew, 'Clean, Clear Prose', speech to
senior civil servants at the Regional Language Centre, February 27, 1979, in *Lee Kuan Yew:
The Man and His Ideas*, 327.)

ethnic origin. And for it to persist as an international presence, it had to build influence among the major powers – especially the US and China.

'There are books to teach you how to build a house, how to repair engines, how to write a book', Lee would recall many years later:

> But I have not seen a book on how to build a nation out of a disparate collection of immigrants from China, British India, the Dutch East Indies, or how to make a living for its people when its former economic role as the entrepôt of the region is becoming defunct.[94]

Lee's experiences in the Second World War, in the contest for political power in Singapore and in the separation from Malaysia had given him convictions about the proper governance of states that no formal course of instruction could have offered. His travels and conversations with foreign leaders were consequential; by 1965, he had visited more than fifty countries and developed strong views about the reasons for their varying performance.[95] 'A nation is great not by its size alone,' he said in 1963. 'It is the will, the cohesion, the stamina, the discipline of its people and the quality of their leaders which ensures it an honorable place in history.'[96]

This is why Lee adopted 'Let history judge' as his operating maxim. He rejected communism because it meant dismantling existing institutions that were working. Similarly, his preference for market economics was derived from the observation that it produced higher growth rates.[97] When, at a dinner years later in my home, an American guest complimented him on including feminist principles in the development of Singapore, Lee disagreed. He had brought women into the labor force for practical reasons, he said. Singapore would not have been able to achieve its development goals without them. The same, he added, was true with respect to his immigration policy, which sought to convince talented foreigners to settle in Singapore. The purpose was not a theoretical notion of the benefits of multiculturalism but the requirements of Singapore's growth and its otherwise stubborn demographics.

Lee's thinking shows a strong utilitarian streak, as he demonstrated in his 1981 May Day address:

> Every rational government wants the maximum well-being and progress for the largest numbers of their citizens. To bring this about, the systems or methods, and the principles or ideologies on which their policies are

based, differ. Since the industrial revolution, two centuries ago, a kind of
Darwinism between systems of government is at work. It is sorting out
which ideological–religious–political–social–economic–military system
will prevail because of its efficacy in providing the maximum good to the
maximum numbers of a nation.[98]

BUILDING AN ECONOMY

One of the first major tests of Singapore's adaptability came in January
1968, when Britain, rattled by the devaluation of the pound and sapped
by conflicts in the Middle East, decided to abandon its military presence
east of Suez. In the House of Commons debate the previous year, Prime
Minister Harold Wilson had quoted Rudyard Kipling's 'Recessional' in
a vain attempt to defend the existence of the British base in Singapore;
now it read as a prophecy of Britain's imperial decline:

> Far-called, our navies melt away;
> On dune and headland sinks the fire:
> Lo, all our pomp of yesterday
> Is one with Nineveh and Tyre![99]

The closure of the naval base and departure of British troops, planned
for 1971, threatened to result in the loss of one-fifth of Singapore's gross
national product.[100]

Seeking outside advice, Lee turned to Dr Albert Winsemius, a Dutch
economist who had first visited Singapore in 1960 at Goh Keng Swee's
invitation as part of a UN Development Program mission.[101] Compared
with Western countries, Singapore was poor. But in the 1960s, its wages
were the highest in Asia.[102] Winsemius advised that, for Singapore to
industrialize, it needed to depress wages and make manufacturing more
efficient by embracing technology and training workers. He proposed
prioritizing textile manufacturing, followed by simple electronics and
ship repair, a stepping stone to shipbuilding. Lee and Goh (finance minister again from 1967 to 1970) followed his advice.[103] With the British
on their way out, Winsemius warned that Singapore could neither aspire
to total self-reliance nor depend on regional ties. Unable to count on a
common market with Malaysia, as it had from 1963 to 1965, it would
have to operate in a wider sphere.

Over the following years, Lee, Goh and Winsemius worked in tandem to recalibrate the Singaporean economy. While other leaders of newly independent countries rejected multinational corporations, Lee recruited them. Asked later whether such foreign investment constituted 'capitalist exploitation', Lee retorted unsentimentally: 'All we had was labor ... So why not, if they want to exploit our labor? They're welcome to it.'[104] To attract foreign investment, Singapore embarked on a project to raise the quality of its workforce while giving itself the appearance and the facilities of a first-class city. As Lee remarked to me in 1978: 'Others will not invest in a losing cause, it must look to be a winning cause.'[105]

Greening the city became a high priority: reducing air pollution, planting trees and designing infrastructure to incorporate natural light. Lee also saw to it that high-quality services were provided to visiting tourists and investors. The government mounted public-enlightenment campaigns promoting appropriate dress, comportment and hygiene. Singaporeans (or foreigners, for that matter) could be fined for jaywalking, neglecting to flush a toilet or littering. Lee even requested a weekly report on the cleanliness of the restrooms at Changi Airport – which, for many travelers, would provide a first impression of Singapore.[106]

The strategy worked. Decades afterward, Lee would recount that once he was able to convince Hewlett-Packard to set up a Singapore office, which opened in April 1970, other international businesses followed.[107]*

By 1971, Singapore's economy was growing at more than 8 percent per year.[108] By 1972, multinationals employed more than half of Singapore's labor force and accounted for 70 percent of its industrial production.[109] By 1973, Singapore had become the world's third-largest oil refining hub.[110] Within ten years of independence, foreign investment in manufacturing had risen from $157 million to more than $3.7 billion.[111]

In early 1968, the mood in the Singaporean parliament had been gloomy and fearful. No one believed that the island could survive the

* Hewlett-Packard was particularly impressed by Singapore's Economic Development Board's 'one-stop service' to assist relocating businesses. 'If you asked them about something, it would be on your desk the next day,' one executive reported (quoted in Edgar H. Schein, *Strategic Pragmatism: The Culture of Singapore's Economic Development Board* (Cambridge, MA: MIT Press, 1996), 20).

British military's departure. Lee later admitted that the years from 1965 to the scheduled withdrawal in 1971 were the most nerve-racking of his tenure.[112] Yet by the time the British departed, Singapore was able to absorb the economic shock; unemployment did not rise.[113] Against all expectation and conventional wisdom, Lee's determination to adapt to change launched Singapore on an astonishing trajectory.

To continue to attract investment, Singapore's productivity needed to keep climbing. To this end, Lee at first asked workers to accept temporarily reduced wages in the interest of long-term growth.[114] He gave urgent priority to education. And he frequently revised the nation's industrial and social targets upwards. As Lee said in his 1981 May Day message:

> The greatest achievement of the Singapore labour movement has been to transform revolutionary fervor during the period of anti-colonialism (i.e. antagonism towards expat employers) in the 1950s to productivity consciousness (cooperation with management, both Singaporean and expat) in the 1980s.[115]

Over three decades, Lee drove Singapore to ever higher levels of development: from subsistence to manufacturing, and from manufacturing to financial services, tourism and high-tech innovation.[116] By 1990, when Lee stepped down as prime minister, Singapore was in an enviable economic position. In 1992, looking back, he said to me that if I had asked him as late as 1975 – by which time he had already attracted substantial amounts of foreign investment to Singapore – he still would not have predicted the scope of his country's eventual success.

LEE AND AMERICA

Lee stunned my Harvard colleagues in 1968 with his defense of American involvement in Indochina. Had the political evolution of Southeast Asia attracted their attention earlier, they would have noticed that he had been propounding the same message for years. In fact, it was Lee's conviction of Washington's indispensable role for the future of Asia that had brought him to pay two important visits to America in as many years.

On Lee's first state visit to Washington in October 1967, President

Johnson introduced him at a White House dinner as 'a patriot, a brilliant political leader, and a statesman of the New Asia'.[117] Lee, with his habitual bluntness, took the opportunity of his high-level meetings to instruct his hosts about how the Vietnam drama had its antecedents in American decisions dating back over a decade and a half. To Vice President Hubert Humphrey, Lee likened the Vietnam crisis to a long bus ride: the United States had missed all of the stops at which it could have gotten off; the only option now was to stay on until the final destination.[118]

In the decades to come, Lee would be admired for his candor as much as for his intelligence by presidents and prime ministers around the world. The subtlety and precision of his analysis and the reliability of his conduct turned him into a counselor to many on whom he himself was dependent. How did the leader of a small and vulnerable city-state manage to exercise so significant an influence on so many leaders abroad? What was his perspective, and how was such a framework applied at moments of crisis?

In a sense, Lee Kuan Yew was on a permanent quest for world order. He understood that the global balance of power was a product not only of anonymous forces but of living political entities, each replete with individual histories and culture, and each obliged to make a judgment of its opportunities. The maintenance of equilibrium, on which Singapore's own flourishing as a trading nation depended, required not only the balancing of the major countries against each other but a degree of comprehension of their diverse identities and the perspectives that followed from them. For example, Lee observed in 1994:

> if you look at societies over the millennia you find certain basic patterns. American civilization from the Pilgrim Fathers on is one of optimism and the growth of orderly government. History in China is of dynasties which have risen and fallen, of the waxing and waning of societies. And through all that turbulence, the family, the extended family, the clan, has provided a kind of survival raft for the individual. Civilizations have collapsed, dynasties have been swept away by conquering hordes, but this life raft enables [Chinese] civilization to carry on and get to its next phase.[119]

Lee was respected by leaders of states far more powerful than his own to a unique degree because he furnished insights that enabled them to grasp their own essential challenges. Lee's reading of foreign affairs was, like his analysis of Singapore's domestic requirements, based on his perception of objective reality. Subjective preference did not enter into his assessments, which invariably cut to the heart of the matter. Some leaders seek to impress interlocutors by demonstrating their command of minute details; Lee, whose own factual knowledge was considerable, possessed a more precious quality: the capacity to distill a subject to its essence.

Just as the obstacles attending Singapore's birth had been defining experiences in Lee's political life, so, for the rest of his career, he placed special emphasis on the domestic evolution of other countries in evaluating their relevance to world order. Two countries were central to Lee's assessment of Singapore's survival and its place in the world: the United States and China. Lee defined the American relationship unpretentiously in a toast to President Richard Nixon at a White House dinner in April 1973:

> We are a very small country placed strategically at the southernmost tip of Asia, and when the elephants are on the rampage, if you are a mouse there and you don't know the habits of the elephants, it can be a very painful business.[120]

A May 1981 speech likewise captures his prescience and clarity with respect to the Soviet system:

> Thirty-six years after the end of World War II we know that in the contest of Western free-enterprise/free-market democracy versus communist command economy/controlled distribution, the communist system is losing. It cannot deliver the goods . . .
>
> Unless this contest ends in mutual destruction by nuclear weapons, the outcome will see the survival of that system which is superior in providing both more security and more economic/spiritual well-being to its members. If the West can prevent the Soviets from gaining easy spoils through their military superiority, the free-market system of personal initiatives and incentives will be clearly proved superior to the centrally planned/controlled market system.[121]

Ten years later, after the collapse of the Soviet Union, Lee's perspective would become the conventional wisdom; at the time, few perceived the imminence of Soviet decay.

In the American people, Lee discerned an unusual generosity and openness of spirit, reminiscent of elements in his own Confucian commitments. In the immediate postwar period, he observed, America did not abuse its nuclear monopoly:

> Any old and established nation would have ensured its supremacy for as long as it could. But America set out to put her defeated enemies on their feet to ward off an evil force, the Soviet Union, brought about technological change by transferring technology generously and freely to Europeans and to Japanese, and enabled them to become challengers within 30 years ... There was a certain greatness of spirit born out of the fear of Communism plus American idealism that brought that about.[122]

As his geopolitical attention shifted in the aftermath of the Deng reforms from the threat of Maoist subversion to the more complicated grand-strategic interplay among China, the Soviet Union and the United States – and later still to the management of China as a greatly empowered economic and political force – Lee's assessments shifted accordingly. But he never altered the theme of the indispensable role of America in the security and progress of the world and especially Southeast Asia.

It was not that Lee was sentimentally 'pro-American' – he was not sentimental at all. He could find a healthy amount to criticize in America's approach to politics and to geopolitics. He recorded his early views of Americans as 'mixed':

> I admired their can-do approach but shared the view of the British establishment of the time that the Americans were bright and brash, that they had enormous wealth but often misused it. It was not true that all it needed to fix a problem was to bring resources to bear on it ... They meant well but were heavy-handed and lacked a sense of history.[123]

With the Vietnam War, Lee refined his view: it became important not only to match support for American power with understanding and encouragement of American purposes; it was now imperative to enlist America in the defense of stability in Asia. Britain's exit from Asia had made America essential as a balancer of the complicated and violent forces inimical to the region's equilibrium. The Cambridge-educated Lee, who had once been told by British Foreign Secretary George Brown that he was 'the best bloody Englishman east of Suez',[124] adopted an attitude toward the United States that bore a resemblance to that of Churchill in establishing Britain's 'special relationship'. Lee made himself, so far as he could, part of the American decision-making process on matters of concern to Southeast Asia. Yet in his case, the relationship would be formed by an Asian leader of a tiny post-colonial city-state.

In Lee's view, the great American qualities of magnanimity and idealism were insufficient on their own; geopolitical insight was required as a supplement to enable America to fulfill its role. Sensitivity to the tension between national ideals and strategic realities was essential. Lee feared that America's tendency toward moralistic foreign policy might turn into neo-isolationism when faced with disappointment with the ways of the world. An overemphasis on democratic aspirations might hamper America's ability to empathize with less-developed countries which, by necessity, gave priority to economic progress over ideology.

Lee advanced these views in his characteristic style: a combination of history, culture and geography honed for relevance to contemporary concerns; an awareness of the interests of his interlocutor; and eloquent delivery stripped of small talk, extraneous matters or any hint of supplication. In 1994, he insisted that realism needed to be based on a clear moral distinction between good and evil:

> Certain basics about human nature do not change. Man needs a certain moral sense of right and wrong. There is such a thing called evil, and it is not the result of being a victim of society. You are just an evil man, prone to do evil things, and you have to be stopped from doing them.[125]

Lee presented his leadership to the world as operating within its cultural context and capable of relating regional developments to the wider world. Habitually analytic and prescriptive, he used the insights garnered from his network of contacts and extensive travels to answer questions and proffer advice. 'When I travel,' Lee wrote, 'I am watching how a society, an administration, is functioning. Why are they good?'[126]

After Lee stepped down from the premiership in 1990, reminding the United States of its responsibilities became a preoccupation. During the Cold War, Lee had been primarily concerned that America play a major role in maintaining the *global* equilibrium in the face of the Russian threat. After the collapse of the Soviet Union, his attention shifted to America's crucial importance in defining and maintaining the *Asian* equilibrium. Speaking at Harvard in 1992, at the very peak of American post-Cold War triumphalism, he warned that the geopolitical balance would be vastly impaired were the United States to turn inward, cash the post-Cold War 'peace dividend' and weaken in its global responsibilities:

> My generation of Asians, who have experienced the last war, its horrors and miseries, and who remember the U.S. role in the phoenix-like rise from the ashes of that war to the prosperity of Japan, the newly industri-alizing economies, and ASEAN [Association of Southeast Asian Nations], will feel a keen sense of regret that the world will become so vastly differ-ent because the U.S. becomes a less central player in the new balance.[127]

In 2002, he pointed out that global 'firefighting' was not the same as America understanding and using its considerable leverage to pro-duce lasting global stability.[128] Viewing foreign policy in terms of strategic design, he defined great-power balance as the key to inter-national order and, above all, to the security and prosperity of Singapore. 'We just want maximum space to be ourselves,' he said in 2011. 'And that is best achieved when big "trees" allow space for us, between them we have space. [When] you have one big tree covering us, we have no space.'[129]

Lee admired America and was made uneasy by its oscillations. He respected and feared China because of its single-minded pursuit of objec-tives. Out of historic proximity to China and necessary friendship with the United States, Lee distilled the security and future of Singapore.

LEE AND CHINA

Lee foresaw China's potential for hegemony in Asia. In 1973 – when China was considered economically backward – he was already saying: 'China will make the grade. It is only a matter of time.'[130] As late as 1979, however, he was still expecting China to remain comparatively weak for the medium term:

> The world imagines China as a giant. It's more like a flabby jellyfish. We have to see how something can be made of their resources [and] their two weaknesses: the Communist system, and the lack of training and know-how. Now, I fear they may not be sufficiently strong to play the role we want [for] them, balancing off the Russians. I do not fear a strong China; I fear the Chinese may be too weak. A balance is necessary if we are to be

free to choose our partners in progress. It will take them 15–20, 30–40 years.[131]

At the time, Lee's attitude toward China's rise was ambivalent, as Singapore had 'conflicting objectives': to make China strong enough to intimidate communist Vietnam (which Lee thought would provide 'relief'), but not so strong that it might aggress against Taiwan.[132] Yet even at that moment of relative weakness in China, Lee warned of the country's determination and the upheaval it could unleash: 'I don't know if the [Chinese] leadership can fully comprehend the nature of the transformation that is due them if they succeed. One thing is certain: they want to succeed.'[133] His prediction aligned closely with the way a great strategist of a previous era, Napoleon, is said to have viewed China: 'Let China sleep; for when she wakes, she will shake the world.'[134]

But when? By 1993, Lee's views had evolved. China's rise was no longer a far-off event; it had become the overriding challenge of the era. 'The size of China's displacement of the world balance is such that the world must find a new balance in 30 to 40 years,' he said. 'It's not possible to pretend that this is just another big player,' he added. 'This is the biggest player in the history of man.'[135] He elaborated on this view a few years later:

> Short of some major unforeseeable disaster which brings chaos or breaks up China once again into so many warlord fiefdoms, it is only a question of time before the Chinese people reorganize, reeducate, and train themselves to take full advantage of modern science and technology.[136]

Lee's approach to China, like his analysis of America, was unsentimental. If America's challenge, in Lee's view, lay in its fluctuations between insufficiently reflective idealism and habitual bouts of self-doubt, the problem posed by China was the resurgence of a traditional imperial pattern. The millennia during which China conceived of itself as the 'Middle Kingdom' – the central country in the world – and classified all other states as tributaries were bound to have left a legacy in Chinese thinking and to encourage a tendency toward hegemony. 'At this moment, I think the American outcome is best for us,' he told an interviewer in 2011:

> I don't see the Chinese as a benign power as the Americans. I mean, they say *bu cheng ba* (won't be a hegemon). If you are not ready to be a

hegemon, why do you keep on telling the world you are not going to be a hegemon?[137]

Determined to resist China's destabilizing policies during the Mao era, and afterward to ward off any impression that majority-Chinese Singapore should be viewed as naturally aligned with the motherland, Lee had long proclaimed that Singapore would be the last ASEAN country to establish diplomatic relations with Beijing. (Singapore had also relied on Taiwanese investments and knowhow to develop its industries, beginning with textiles and plastics.)[138] Following the opening to China by the West during the 1970s, Lee was true to his word. He defined Singapore as autonomous toward both neighbors and superpowers. In 1975, he ignored an invitation from Zhou Enlai to visit China – a decision which ensured that Lee and the ailing Zhou would never meet. Singapore officially recognized the PRC only in 1990.

In November 1978, however, Lee welcomed China's paramount leader, Deng Xiaoping, to Singapore. That event marked the beginning of the contemporary Singapore–China relationship. To symbolize the importance Lee attached to this visit, he arranged for an ashtray and spittoon to be placed in front of China's then-leader, who was an avid smoker, despite Singapore's laws against smoking (and Lee's strong allergy to smoke).

Deng's agenda on that trip was to build opposition to the Soviet Union and unified Vietnam among Southeast Asian countries; Lee was primarily concerned with easing domineering tendencies in Chinese policy toward Singapore. He explained to Deng that China's radio broadcasts aimed at radicalizing Southeast Asia's Chinese diaspora made it difficult to cooperate with Beijing. Lee asked that Deng halt the propaganda; within two years it was gradually stopped.[139] Years later, Lee identified Deng as one of the three world leaders he most admired (the other two being Charles de Gaulle and Winston Churchill). Deng, in Lee's view, 'was a great man because he changed China from a broken-backed state, which would have imploded like the Soviet Union, into what it is today, on the way to becoming the world's largest economy'.[140]

According to the distinguished Sinologist and Deng biographer Ezra Vogel, Deng was still undecided with respect to his economic policies when he visited Singapore, but the visit 'helped strengthen Deng's conviction of the need for fundamental reforms'.[141] The following month, he announced his Open Door policy, which created Special Economic Zones in coastal China to welcome foreign direct investment. As Vogel observed, 'Deng found orderly Singapore an appealing model for reform' and dispatched emissaries there 'to learn about city planning, public management, and controlling corruption'.[142]

During Deng's period of preeminence, Lee began to pay annual visits to China – even before full recognition – to examine its urban development and agricultural reform and establish contacts with its leading officials. Lee advised Zhao Ziyang, the Chinese premier and later general secretary of the Chinese Communist Party, that the openness required for economic growth did not have to come at the expense of 'Confucian values'. In a later reflection beginning with a riff on Deng Xiaoping's phrase 'crossing the river by feeling the stones', Zhao said that Lee had 'shortened this river crossing for us'.[143]

Lee's advice would be manifested in the creation of a Singaporean industrial park in Suzhou, an ancient Chinese city near Shanghai famous for its many beautiful traditional Chinese gardens. Opened in 1994, the park was designed to integrate Singaporean management practices with local labor, thereby accelerating industrialization and attracting foreign capital to China. Singapore's sovereign wealth funds, Temasek Holdings and GIC (formerly Government of Singapore Investment Corporation), became major investors in China.

In 1989, Lee joined most of the West in condemning the Chinese leadership's suppression of the student protests in Tiananmen Square. He decried the brutality of the methods and called their human cost unacceptable.[144] But he was also convinced that a political implosion in China would be a terrible risk for the world – posing a variety of dangers that the Soviet Union's own disintegration would soon illustrate. As Lee later put it, comparing the two cases:

> Deng was the only leader in China with the political standing and strength to reverse Mao's policies . . . A veteran of war and revolution, he saw the student demonstrators at Tiananmen as a danger that threatened to throw China back into turmoil and chaos, prostrate for another 100 years. He had lived through a revolution and recognized the early signs of one at Tiananmen. Gorbachev, unlike Deng, had only read about revolution, and did not recognize the danger signals of the Soviet Union's impending collapse.[145]

After Tiananmen, China's economic reforms appeared to be faltering, and they were revived only following Deng's 1992 'Southern Tour' – an epic and highly influential month-long trip through several southern cities in which the eighty-seven-year-old and nominally retired Deng persuasively restated the case for economic liberalization.

BETWEEN THE US AND CHINA

For the United States, Lee's message about China was sobering and, in its deepest sense, unwelcome: America would be obliged to share its preeminent position in the Western Pacific, and perhaps in the wider world, with a new superpower. 'It just has to live with a bigger China,' Lee said in 2011, and this would prove 'completely novel for the U.S., as no country has ever been big enough to challenge its position. China will be able to do so in 20 to 30 years.'[146]

Such an evolution would be painful for a society with America's own sense of exceptionalism, Lee warned. But American prosperity was itself due to exceptional factors: 'geopolitical good fortune, an abundance of resources and immigrant energy, a generous flow of capital and technology from Europe, and two wide oceans that kept conflicts of the world away from American shores'.[147] In the approaching world, as China became a formidable military power with cutting-edge technology, geography would provide no hedge for the United States.

Lee anticipated that the impending change would challenge the prevailing international equilibrium and make the position of intermediate states precarious. Julius Nyerere, the former prime minister of Tanzania, had warned Lee, 'When elephants fight, the grass gets trampled.' To which Lee, who as we have seen was himself fond of elephant analogies, had responded: 'When elephants make love, the grass gets trampled, too.'[148] * Singapore's aims of stability and growth would be best served by a cordial but cool relationship between the two superpowers, Lee believed. Yet in his own interactions with Washington and Beijing, Lee

---

* In 1973, Lee had said of détente between the US and the Soviet Union: 'It is only to be expected that the middle and small nations, whose interests may be affected, are concerned with the dangers of direct super-power diplomacy, that super-power differences being settled over their heads may well be at their expense' (Lee, 'Southeast Asian View of the New World Power Balance in the Making', 8).

acted less as a national advocate for Singapore than as a philosophical guide to the two awesome giants.

In his meetings with Chinese leaders, Lee tended to marshal arguments attuned to their historical traumas and delivered with an otherwise rare emotion. In 2009, he cautioned the rising generation of Chinese leaders who had not experienced the deprivations and cataclysms of their elders but felt a deep-seated resentment about their place in the world:

> This [older] generation has been through hell: Great Leap Forward, hunger, starvation, near collision with the Russians . . . the Cultural Revolution gone mad . . . I have no doubt that this generation wants a peaceful rise. But the grandchildren? They think that they have already arrived, and if they begin to flex their muscles, we will have a very different China . . . Grandchildren never listen to grandfathers.
>
> The other problem is a more crucial one: if you start off with the belief that the world has been unkind to you, the world has exploited you, the imperialists have devastated you, looted Beijing, done all this to you . . . this is no good . . . You are not going back to the old China, when you were the only power in the world as far as you knew . . . Now, you are just one of many powers, many of them more innovative, inventive, and resilient.[149]

As a counterpart to this advice, Lee counseled America not to 'treat China as an enemy from the outset', lest it 'develop a counterstrategy to demolish the U.S. in the Asia-Pacific'. He warned that, in fact, the Chinese could already envision such a scenario, but that an inevitable 'contest between the two countries for supremacy in the western Pacific . . . need not lead to conflict'.[150] Accordingly, Lee advised Washington to integrate Beijing into the international community and accept 'China as a big, powerful, rising state' with 'a seat in the boardroom'. Rather than presenting itself as an enemy in Chinese eyes, the United States should 'acknowledge [China] as a great power, applaud its return to its position of respect and restoration of its glorious past, and propose specific concrete ways to work together'.[151]

Lee considered that the Nixon administration had practiced this type of approach, describing President Nixon as 'a pragmatic strategist'. In the world ahead, America's posture should be to 'engage, not contain, China', but in a way that 'would also quietly set pieces into place for a fallback position should China not play according to the rules as a good global citizen'. In this way, should the countries of the region ever feel compelled 'to take sides, America's side of the chessboard should include Japan, Korea, ASEAN, India, Australia, New Zealand, and the Russian Federation'.[152]

I was present during presentations by Lee on both sides of the Pacific. His American interlocutors, while generally receptive to Lee's geopolitical analysis, tended to inquire after his views on immediate issues, such as the North Korean nuclear program or the performance of Asian economies. They were also imbued with an expectation that China in the end would achieve an approximation of American political principles and institutions. Lee's Chinese interlocutors, for their part, welcomed his arguments that China should be treated as a great power, and that differences, even in the long term, did not necessitate conflict. But beneath their smoothly polite manners, one also sensed a discomfort at being instructed by an overseas Chinese about principles of Chinese conduct.

Lee envisioned an apocalyptic scenario for war between the US and China. Weapons of mass destruction guaranteed devastation; beyond that, no meaningful war aims – including especially the characteristics of 'victory' – could be defined. So it is no accident that, toward the end of his life, Lee's appeals to China were persistently addressed to the generation that had never experienced the turmoil of his generation and that might be too reliant on its technology or power:

> It is vital that the younger generation of Chinese, who have only lived during a period of peace and growth in China and have no experience of China's tumultuous past, are made aware of the mistakes China made as a result of hubris and excesses in ideology. They have to be imbued with the right values and attitudes to meet the future with humility and responsibility.[153]

Lee never tired of reminding his interlocutors that globalization meant that every nation – including (perhaps especially) those that had created the system and written its rules – would have to learn to live in a competitive world.[154] Globalization had developed its ultimate form only in his lifetime with the collapse of the Soviet Union and the rise of China. In that world, great prosperity in close proximity to great want would generate flammable passions.[155] 'Regionalism is no longer the ultimate solution,' he said in 1979. 'Interdependence is the reality. It's one world.'[156] Global interconnection, he believed, could benefit everyone if handled wisely.

After all, as he said to me in 2002, Singapore's own engagement with the world was the main reason its development had outpaced China's.[157] In Lee's view, the end of the Cold War had produced two contradictory phenomena: globalization and potential strategic rivalry between the US and China with the risk of a catastrophic war. Where many detected only peril, Lee asserted the indispensability of mutual restraint. It was the essential obligation of both the US and China to invest both hope and action in the possibility of a successful outcome.

As few others, Lee foretold at an early stage the dilemmas that China's evolution would present for both China and the US. Inevitably the two nations would impinge on each other. Would this new relation lead to growing confrontation, or would it be possible to transform adversarial conduct into joint analysis of the requirements of peaceful coexistence?

For decades, Washington and Beijing proclaimed the latter goal. But today, in the third decade of the twenty-first century, both appear to have suspended efforts to give coexistence an operational expression and are turning instead toward sharpening rivalry. Will the world slide toward conflict as in the run-up to the First World War, when Europe inadvertently constructed a diplomatic doomsday machine that made each succeeding crisis progressively more difficult to solve until, finally, it blew up – destroying civilization as it was then perceived? Or will the two behemoths rediscover a definition of coexistence that is meaningful in terms of each side's conception of its greatness and of its core interests? The fate of the modern world depends on the answer.

Lee was one of the few leaders respected on both sides of the Pacific for both his insight and his achievements. Starting his career by developing a concept of order for a tiny speck of an island and its neighborhood, he spent his last years appealing for wisdom and restraint on the part of the countries capable of wreaking a global catastrophe. Though he would never have made such a claim for himself, the old realist had assumed a role as world conscience.

LEE'S LEGACY

After his long tenure, Lee resigned the office of prime minister in November 1990. In order to provide for a steady, managed transition, he gradually separated himself from day-to-day governance. With the titles first of senior minister and then minister mentor, he remained influential but progressively less visible through two prime ministerial successors.*

An assessment of Lee's legacy must begin with the extraordinary growth of Singapore's per capita gross domestic product from $517 in 1965 to $11,900 in 1990 and $60,000 at present (2020).[158] Annual GDP growth averaged 8 percent well into the 1990s.[159] It is one of the most remarkable economic success stories of modern times.

In the late 1960s, it was received wisdom that post-colonial leaders ought to shield their economies from international market forces and develop autonomous local industries through intensive state intervention. As an expression of their newfound liberation and out of nationalist and populist impulses, some even felt compelled to harass foreigners who had taken up residence on their soil during colonial days. The result, as Richard Nixon wrote, was that:

> We live in a time when leaders are often judged more by the stridency of their rhetoric and the coloration of their politics than by the success of their policies. Especially in the developing world, too many people have gone to bed at night with their ears full but their stomachs empty.[160]

Lee took Singapore in the opposite direction, attracting multinational corporations by embracing free trade and capitalism and insisting on the enforcement of business contracts. He prized its ethnic diversity as a special asset, working assiduously to prevent outside forces from intervening in domestic disputes – and thus also helping to preserve his country's independence. While most of his peers adopted a posture of non-alignment in the Cold War – which in practice often meant de facto acquiescence in Soviet designs – Lee staked his geopolitical future on the reliability of the US and its allies.

In charting a path for his new society, Lee attached decisive importance

---

* The second was his son, weakening somewhat the symbolic aspect of his retirement.

to the centrality of culture. He rejected the belief – held in the liberal democracies of the West as well as in the Soviet-led communist bloc – that political ideologies were paramount in defining the evolution of a society and that all societies would modernize in the same way. To the contrary, said Lee: 'The West believes the world must follow [its] historical development. [But] democracy and individual rights are alien to the rest of the world.'[161] The universality of liberal claims was as inconceivable to him as the notion that Americans would someday choose to follow Confucius.

But neither did Lee believe that such civilizational differences were insurmountable. Cultures should coexist and accommodate each other. Today, Singapore remains an authoritarian state, but authoritarianism per se was not Lee's goal – it was a means to an end. Nor was family autocracy. Goh Chok Tong (no relation of Goh Keng Swee) served as prime minister from November 1990 to August 2004. Lee's son Lee Hsieng Loong – whose competence no one questions – succeeded Goh and is now engaged in withdrawing from the premiership so that a successor can be determined in the next election cycle. They led Singapore further down the path on which Lee had set it.

Elections in Singapore are not democratic, but they are not without significance. While in democracies discontent expresses itself through the possibility of electoral change, in Singapore Lee and his successors have used voting as a performance evaluation to inform those in power of the efficacy of their actions, thereby giving them the opportunity to adjust their policies depending on their judgment of the public interest.

Was there an alternative? Might a different approach, more democratic and pluralist, have succeeded? Lee did not think so. He believed that at the beginning, as Singapore moved toward independence, it was in danger from the sectarian forces that tore apart many other postcolonial countries. As he saw it, democratic states with significant ethnic divisions run the risk of succumbing to identity politics, which tend to accentuate sectarianism.* A democratic system functions by enabling a majority (variously defined) to create a government through elections,

---

* The example of Sri Lanka was instructive to Lee: 'So if you believe what American liberals or British liberals used to say, then it ought to have flourished. But it didn't. One-man-one-vote led to the domination of the majority Sinhalese over the minority Tamils ...' (Lee, 'How Much is a Good Minister Worth?', speech before parliament, November 1, 1994, in *Lee Kuan Yew: The Man and His Ideas*, 338).

and then to create another government when political opinion shifts. But when political opinions – and divisions – are determined by immutable definitions of identity rather than by fluid policy differences, the prospects for any such outcome decline in proportion to the extent of the division; majorities tend to become permanent, and minorities seek to escape their subjugation through violence. In Lee's view, governance operated most effectively as a pragmatic unit of close associates untethered to ideology, prizing technical and administrative competence and ruthlessly pursuing excellence. The touchstone for him was a sense of public service:

> Politics demands that extra of a person, a commitment to people and ideals. You are not just doing a job. This is a vocation; not unlike the priesthood. You must feel for people, you must want to change society and make lives better.[162]

What, then, of tomorrow? The key issue for Singapore's future is whether continuing economic and technological progress will lead to a democratic and humanistic transition. Should the country's performance falter – causing voters to seek protection in ethnic identity – elections in the Singaporean system could run the risk of turning into authentications of one-party ethnic rule.

For idealists, the test of a structure is its relation to immutable criteria; for statesmen, it is adaptability to historical circumstance. By the latter standard, Lee Kuan Yew's legacy has thus far succeeded. But statesmen must also be judged by the evolution of their founding models. Scope for popular change will become an essential component of sustainability. Can a better balance be devised between popular democracy and modified elitism? This will be Singapore's ultimate challenge.

As in the mid-1960s, when Singapore first came into being, the world is today once again in a period of ideological uncertainty about how to build a successful society. Free-market democracy, which in the wake of the Soviet Union's collapse proclaimed itself the most viable arrangement, is simultaneously facing alternative external models and declining internal confidence. Other societal arrangements are asserting themselves as better at unlocking economic growth and instilling social harmony. Singapore's transformation under Lee's leadership bypassed such struggles. He avoided the rigid dogmas he decried as 'pet theories'. Rather, he devised what he insisted was Singaporean exceptionalism.[163]

Lee was a relentless improviser, not a theoretician of government. He adopted policies that he thought stood a chance of working and revised them if he saw that they did not. He experimented constantly, borrowing ideas from other countries and trying to learn from their mistakes. Nonetheless, he made sure that he was never mesmerized by the example of others; rather, Singapore had to ask itself constantly whether it was achieving goals imposed by its unique geography and enabled by its special demographic makeup. As he himself would put it, 'I was never prisoner of any theory. What guided me were reason and reality. The acid test I applied to every theory or science was, would it work?'[164] Perhaps Kwa Geok Choo had taught him the adage of Alexander Pope: 'For forms of government let fools contest; whatever is best administered is best.'[165]

Lee both founded a nation and laid down the pattern of a state. In the categories established in the Introduction, he was both a prophet and a statesman. He conceived the nation and then he strove to create incentives for his state to develop through exceptional performance in an evolving future. Lee succeeded in institutionalizing a creative process. Will it be adapted to evolving notions of human dignity?

The Spanish philosopher Ortega y Gasset asserted that man 'has no nature; what he has is ... history'.[166] In the absence of a national history, Lee Kuan Yew invented Singapore's nature from his vision of the future and wrote its history as he went along. In doing so, he demonstrated the cogency of his conviction that the ultimate test of a statesman lies in the application of judgment as he journeys 'along an unmarked road to an unknown destination'.[167]

LEE THE PERSON

'It was circumstances that created me,' Lee told an interviewer three years before his death.[168] In particular, he explained, it was his upbringing in a traditional Chinese family that explained his personality and made him 'an unconscious Confucianist':[169]

> The underlying philosophy is that for a society to work well, you must have the interests of the mass of the people, that society takes priority over the interests of the individual. This is the primary difference with the American principle, [which stresses] the primary rights of the individual.[170]

For Lee, the Confucian ideal was to be a *junzi*, or gentleman, 'loyal to his father and mother, faithful to his wife, [who] brings up his children well, [and] treats his friends properly', but who is most of all a 'good loyal citizen of his emperor'.[171]

Lee resolutely refused to engage in social chatter. He believed he was put into this world to accomplish progress for his society and, to the extent possible, for the world at large. He was disinclined to waste the time allotted to him. On his four visits to our weekend house in Connecticut, he would always bring his wife and generally one of his daughters. I would, by prior agreement, arrange meals with leaders and thinkers who were working on issues of concern to Lee, as well as some mutual personal friends. Lee used these occasions to inform himself on American affairs. Twice, at his request, I took him to local political events: one, a fundraiser for a congressional candidate; the other, a town-hall meeting. I introduced him, as he asked, simply as a friend from Singapore.

On the occasions when I visited Lee, he would invite leaders from neighboring countries as well as senior associates for a series of seminars. There would be a dinner and a discussion with him alone, the duration of which depended on the subjects that most moved either of us at the moment but was never brief. The meetings took place at the Istana, a stately government building in the center of Singapore. In my many trips to Singapore, Lee never invited me to his home; neither have I ever encountered or heard of any recipient of this gesture – an attitude similar to de Gaulle's at Colombey, to which Adenauer's visit was the single exception.

Our friendship also came to include another secretary of state, George Shultz, and Helmut Schmidt, who served as chancellor of Germany from 1974 to 1982.* We met as a group (sometimes only three of us when Shultz's or Schmidt's schedules interfered): first in Iran in 1978, and then in Singapore in 1979, in Bonn in 1980, and on the porch of Shultz's house in Palo Alto shortly after his appointment as secretary of state in 1982.[172] The four of us also attended a retreat in the redwood forests north of San Francisco: Schmidt, who incidentally shared Lee's disdain for small talk, as a guest of Shultz and Lee at my invitation. Though our views on specific policies were not always congruent, we

---

* See Chapter 1, pages 46–7.

shared a commitment: 'We always tell each other the absolute truth,' as Schmidt put it to a German journalist.[173] Conversations with Lee were a personal vote of confidence; they signaled an interlocutor's relevance to his otherwise monastically focused existence.

In May 2008, Choo, Lee's beloved wife and companion of sixty years, was felled by a stroke that left her a prisoner in her own body, unable to communicate. This ordeal lasted for more than two years. Every evening when he was in Singapore, Lee sat by her bedside reading to her aloud from books, and sometimes poems including Shakespeare's sonnets that he knew she cherished.[174] Despite the absence of any evidence, he had faith that she understood. 'She keeps awake for me,' he said to an interviewer.[175]

In the months that followed her death in October 2010, Lee took the unprecedented step of initiating several phone conversations with me in which he made reference to his grief – and specifically to the void left in his life by Choo's passing. I asked whether he ever discussed his solitude with his children. 'No,' replied Lee, 'as head of the family, it is my duty to support them, not lean on them.' After Choo's death, Lee's effervescence diminished. His intelligence remained, but his driven quality essentially disappeared. To the very end, he carried out what he considered his duties but, without his ultimate inspiration, joy had gone out of his life.

Though I considered Lee a friend for nearly half a century, he was restrained in expressing any personal ties. The closest he came was in the form of an unsolicited dedication that he inscribed in 2009 on a photograph of himself and Choo: 'Henry, Your friendship and support after our fortuitous meeting in Harvard, Nov. 1968, made a huge difference in my life. Harry.' In friendship as in politics, Lee let the significant speak for itself; verbal elaboration would only diminish its magnitude.

When Lee Kuan Yew died in March 2015, twenty-five years after stepping down as prime minister, dignitaries from all over the world converged on Singapore to offer their final respects. Many Asian heads of government attended, including the prime ministers of Japan, India, Vietnam and Indonesia, as well as the president of South Korea. China was represented by Vice President Li Yuanchao; the United States by former President Bill Clinton, former National Security Advisor Tom Donilon and myself. All of us had frequently encountered Lee on consequential questions in political life.

The most moving aspect of the obsequies was its demonstration of the bond that had grown between the people of Singapore and their nation's founder. For the three days of Lee's lying-in-state, hundreds of thousands defied drenching monsoons to stay in line and pay homage at his bier. Television news channels carried chyrons informing mourners of how long they would have to wait to pay their respects; it was never less than three hours. Out of an amalgam of races, religions, ethnicities and cultures, Lee Kuan Yew had forged a society that transcended his own life.

Lee meant his legacy to inspire, rather than inhibit, progress. That is why he requested that his home on Oxley Road be demolished after his death to avoid its becoming a memorial shrine.[176] His aim was for Singapore to develop the leaders and institutions relevant to the challenges ahead and to concentrate on its future rather than on worship of its past. 'All I can do', he told an interviewer, 'is to make sure that when I leave, the institutions are good, sound, clean, efficient, and there is a government in place that knows what it has got to do.'[177]

Regarding his own legacy, Lee was as always unsentimentally analytical. He allowed for regrets, including for some of his own actions as national leader. 'I am not saying that everything I did was right,' he told the *New York Times*, 'but everything I did was for an honorable purpose. I had to do some nasty things, locking fellows up without trial.'[178] Citing a Chinese proverb – a man cannot be judged until his coffin is closed – Lee said, 'Close the coffin, then decide.'[179]

Today, the name of Lee Kuan Yew is falling into obscurity in the West. Yet history is longer than contemporary biography, and the lessons of Lee's experience remain urgent.

World order today is being challenged simultaneously from two directions: the unraveling of entire regions where sectarian passions have overwhelmed traditional structures, and the intensifying antagonism of great powers with conflicting claims of legitimacy. The former threatens to create an expanding field of chaos; the latter, a cataclysmic bloodletting.

Lee's statesmanship is relevant to both of these circumstances. His life's work is a testament to the possibility of evoking progress and sustainable order out of the least promising of conditions. His conduct in Singapore and on the world stage alike is a tutorial in how to foster comprehension and coexistence amidst diverse perspectives and backgrounds.

Most significantly, Lee's statesmanship illustrates that the best determinants of a society's fate are neither its material wealth nor other conventional measures of power but rather the quality of its people and the vision of its leaders. As Lee said, 'if you are just realistic, you become pedestrian, plebeian, you will fail. Therefore you must be able to soar above the reality and say, "This is also possible."'[180]

6

MARGARET THATCHER: THE STRATEGY OF CONVICTION

A MOST UNLIKELY LEADER

Few leaders define the era in which they govern. Yet from 1979 to 1990, this was Margaret Thatcher's singular achievement. As prime minister of the United Kingdom, Thatcher labored to cast off the shackles that had limited her predecessors – particularly the nostalgia for lost imperial glories and the abiding regret of national decline. The Britain that emerged as a result of her leadership was, to the world, a newly confident nation, and to America, a valued partner in the late Cold War.

When she first took office, however, Thatcher's success was far from guaranteed; indeed, she was not expected to remain in power for long. Having wrested control of the Conservative Party from an exclusively male establishment that tolerated her under duress, she possessed only a meager share of political capital. Her previous record in government had been unremarkable; she had no great following in the country at large, and her experience in international relations was negligible. Not only was she Britain's first female prime minister, she was also at that time a rare Conservative leader drawn from the middle class. In nearly every way, she was a complete outsider.

Thatcher's greatest resource in these unpropitious circumstances was her unique approach to leadership. At the heart of her successes lay personal fortitude. As Ferdinand Mount, leader of the 10 Downing Street policy unit (1982–3), would succinctly put it in describing her reforms: 'What is remarkable is not their originality but their implementation. The political courage lay not in putting them into practice but *in creating the conditions* which made it possible to put them into practice.'[1]

Although I held no government position during Thatcher's tenure, it was my good fortune to witness her approach through the lens of a friendship that lasted nearly four decades.

THATCHER AND THE BRITISH SYSTEM

To appreciate Margaret Thatcher's ascent and years in office – as well as her fall – it helps to have an understanding first of the British political system. Americans tend to experience their presidential system as a succession of individual leaders. At least until the recent hardening of partisan differences in America, the electorate generally conceived of the political parties as embodied expressions of public preferences. Presidents won office by grasping those preferences, embracing them and projecting them into the future. British political parties, by contrast, are rigorously institutionalized; an electoral victory functions first to empower a party in parliament and, as a consequence of that, to install a new premier. As Thatcher put it in a 1968 speech to the Conservative Party's education wing: 'The essential characteristic of the British constitutional system is not that there is an alternative personality in the figure of the party leader but that there is an alternative policy and a whole alternative government ready to take office.'[2] That policy, moreover, is generally worked out in the party manifesto, which itself features as a major element in a UK election campaign.

The prime minister therefore sits within and, in some ways, below the political party to which he or she belongs. Unlike the American presidential system, in which legitimate decision-making power flows downward from the top, the British cabinet system elevates the importance of ministers, who represent the highest echelons of the party; authority moves in both directions between the prime minister and the cabinet. Ministers – though all appointed by the premier – are at once managers of the bureaucracy, the premier's supporters (actual or nominal) and sometimes aspiring leaders themselves. Within cabinet, the dissent of an influential clique, or the machinations of a single magnetic personality, can limit the premier's ability to pursue desired policy objectives. In extraordinary circumstances, a cabinet minister's resignation may even threaten the premier's hold on power.

While the prime minister's authority formally derives from the monarch, in practice it rests primarily on the maintenance of party discipline – that is, the leader's ability to sustain a parliamentary majority as well as the confidence of the party rank-and-file. Whereas the separation-of-powers system insulates the American executive from direct legislative pressure, in Britain the executive and legislative branches are largely fused together. In addition to being vulnerable during general elections, British premiers may be brought down by either a parliamentary vote of no confidence or a party mutiny. The former is rare; if a premier loses a no-confidence vote, a general election must be called, in which Members of Parliament (MPs) have to defend their own seats. Less rare is the party leadership contest. If MPs fear that their party leader is growing personally unpopular, putting them at risk of losing their seats in the next general election, they may attempt to elevate a new one.

When the party and the prime minister are in agreement and enjoy a solid majority, the system works smoothly. When prime ministers diverge from orthodoxy or appear weakened in parliament or public opinion, they must court both cabinet and party for continued support. Weak leadership can survive in the American system thanks to the executive's fixed four-year term; in the British system, however, retaining the executive position requires all of the leader's fortitude, conviction, mastery of substance and powers of persuasion. Since failure to convince colleagues to support one's policies can be catastrophic, a premier must also be nimble, lest a policy discarded foreshadow the end of one's political fortunes.

In November 1974, Margaret Thatcher challenged Edward Heath for leadership of the Conservative Party. Heath had lost the February 1974 general election and thereby his position as prime minister. Usually, following an electoral defeat, the outgoing prime minister also resigns as party leader; but Heath held firm, remaining as party leader even after a second consecutive electoral defeat in October 1974, because he expected the relationships he had cultivated over a decade of leadership to serve as a bulwark against a serious challenge. And so, when Thatcher stepped forward, the contest was expected to be a mere formality, which would end by reaffirming Heath's authority over the party. To the surprise of many, her challenge was successful.

Heath's electoral appeal was lackluster, and the Conservative right had sensed an opportunity to reorient the party. After two Conservative hopefuls, Keith Joseph and Edward du Cann, chose not to stand, the former endorsed Thatcher, his friend and intellectual ally. She thereby became the default selection of the right and the begrudging preference of the center. Besting Heath by eleven votes in the first ballot, she proceeded to outrun the centrist Willie Whitelaw by a wide margin in the second round, becoming the first female leader of a European major party.

Upon winning party leadership, Thatcher was asked by a journalist: 'What quality would you most like the Tory Party displaying [sic] under your leadership?' She responded: 'Win ... the winning quality.' The questioner pressed: 'What sort of philosophical quality?' 'You only win by being for things,' came Thatcher's spontaneous reply. 'For a free society with power well distributed amongst the citizens and not concentrated in the hands of the state,' she continued. 'And the power supported by a wide distribution of private property amongst citizens and subjects and not in the hands of the state.'[3] These were the fundamental beliefs which she would translate into policy as prime minister from 1979 to 1990 and for which she would become famous.

THE CHALLENGES AHEAD: BRITAIN IN THE 1970S

When Thatcher assumed office in May 1979, Britain's fortunes were at a low ebb. The country, as she put it in her memoirs, 'had had the stuffing knocked out of it'.[4] The challenges it faced, not least in economic performance, were very real, but no less real was a psychological handicap: the widespread belief that the country's best days were in the past.

In 1945, the United Kingdom had emerged from six years of total war victorious but exhausted and bankrupt. Its postwar foreign relations were marked by a series of disappointments. Wartime solidarity with the United States was replaced by watching with some unease as Washington proceeded to supplant Britain's global preeminence. Within weeks of the Allied victory, Britain suffered the indignity of having the generous US Lend-Lease program canceled, replaced by a loan on commercial terms that it could ill afford.

America's rising power and Britain's loss of status combined to produce new geopolitical realities. In his landmark 1946 speech in Fulton,

Missouri, Winston Churchill not only spoke of the 'Iron Curtain' descending across Europe but also proposed a 'special relationship' between the United Kingdom and the United States. Churchill hoped to cement a partnership that would secure Britain's influence in the world beyond what its raw power alone might allow – effectively *borrowing* US power through a close consultative relationship. While a shared Anglo-American assessment of the Soviet threat helped to place the transatlantic alliance on new foundations, in this postwar phase it was already painfully apparent that this was not a partnership between equals.

By 1956, the emerging balance of power, already disappointing for postwar Britain, was made both conspicuous and embarrassing. In July of that year, Egyptian President Gamal Abdel Nasser nationalized the Suez Canal. Three months later, during the Anglo-French invasion of Egypt to retake the canal, Britain came up against the might of the new American superpower – and folded. President Eisenhower had little patience for Britain's efforts to revive its imperial prerogatives, and even less for the invasion of a strategically important zone without prior consultation. The financial pressure he soon brought to bear put a swift end to the British–French venture and dealt a devastating blow to both nations' global aspirations. Chastened, Britain withdrew its forces and reduced its international role. The abiding lesson for many in the British governing class was never in the future to cross the Americans.

The burdens of decolonization abroad and a faltering economy at home further diminished Britain's standing. In 1967, Harold Wilson's Labour government was forced to devalue the pound sterling; a year later, his country beset by recurring financial crises, Wilson announced the withdrawal of all British forces east of Suez. A once-global actor had been forced to retreat to a regional stage. The final stanza of Philip Larkin's 'Homage to a Government' (1969) captures Britain's dour mood well:

> Next year we shall be living in a country
> That brought its soldiers home for lack of money.
> The statues will be standing in the same
> Tree-muffled squares, and look nearly the same.
> Our children will not know it's a different country.
> All we can hope to leave them now is money.[5]

As Britain's global influence receded, the continuing lure of the Atlanticist paradigm came up against the competing possibility of a closer relationship with continental Europe. The UK in those years exhibited a confusion over its broader identity that at times seemed to border on schizophrenia. Before the Suez debacle Prime Minister Anthony Eden had rejected British participation in what became the 1957 Treaty of Rome, which created the forerunner of today's European Union. The following year, however, Eden's successor Harold Macmillan, while seeking to maintain a close defense relationship with the United States, decided to set Britain on a pro-European course.[6] In 1963 and again in 1967, Britain belatedly tried to join the European Economic Community (EEC), only to find its efforts vetoed by French President Charles de Gaulle. Former Secretary of State Dean Acheson's assertion in 1962 that Great Britain had 'lost an empire but not yet found a role'[7] became famous – and wounded British pride – because it rang so true.

Edward Heath, who became prime minister in 1970, sought to turn the pro-European course first developed by Macmillan into the guiding principle of British foreign policy. Britain's entry into the EEC in 1973 proved to be Heath's crowning achievement. But it also placed a nettlesome burden on UK–US relations.

President Nixon had been delighted by Heath's victory at the polls, much preferring him to Harold Wilson, whose Labour Party the president identified with the US Democratic Party. In fact, the Labour Party under both Wilson and his successor, James Callaghan, unstintingly honored the 'special relationship', especially with respect to NATO and East–West relations, and also believed in the British independent nuclear deterrent. But Michael Stewart, the first Labour foreign secretary encountered by Nixon, had challenged him in the Oval Office over American intervention in Vietnam, and the sour impression lingered.[8]

In his years out of office, Nixon had become acquainted with Heath and expected their personally friendly relationship to continue once the Conservatives returned to power. As late as February 1973, Nixon was still speaking warmly of Heath as 'a friend in Europe . . . the only solid one we've got'.[9] Unfortunately, these sentiments did not prove reciprocal. As a result of de Gaulle's repeated vetoes of British membership in the European Community, Heath had drawn the lesson that the British prime minister had to be a 'good European'. Viewing a special relationship with the US as an obstacle to that goal, he strove to reduce the ties that had been nurtured for more than a generation – at least in their public manifestations. Only after Heath lost the February 1974 election did the incoming Labour government begin to restore the partnership. It thus remained to be seen whether the Conservatives, should they return to power, would revive the remoteness of Heath's later years or return to their historically Atlanticist roots.

British foreign-policy uncertainties of this period were compounded by the US domestic crisis – the Watergate scandal – which led to Nixon's resignation. In the aftermath, Congress imposed limits on executive authority, which in turn complicated efforts to carry out Allied Cold War strategy. Sensing opportunity, the Soviets embarked on renewed adventurism. In 1975, Moscow intervened militarily in Angola via Cuban proxies. The Soviets also flexed their muscles in South Yemen and Afghanistan without drawing an effective Western response.

In 1976, the Soviet Union began deploying SS-20 medium-range nuclear missiles to Warsaw Pact countries, establishing the greatest threat to NATO's defensive doctrine in a generation. NATO's equivalent weapons system – composed of medium-range land-based missiles – was then still under development; European member states would struggle to rally public support in favor of its eventual deployment. Europe therefore largely rested its defense doctrine on the viability of the American 'nuclear umbrella'. In other words, Soviet military planners had to assume that American policymakers would respond to a conventional military conflict in the European theater by drawing on the US long-range intercontinental arsenal. That an escalation of this nature would naturally invite Soviet nuclear retaliation, not only on Europe but also on the American homeland, placed a severe strain on the credibility of extended deterrence – as has been discussed in the chapters on Adenauer (page 43) and de Gaulle (pages 107–10).

By the late 1970s, moreover, Europeans had become increasingly attracted to the anti-nuclear movement, making it much more difficult for European leaders to base their security policies on nuclear deterrence. The most meaningful response was the deployment of US intermediate-range ballistic missiles on European soil, which was anathema to the nuclear disarmament movement.[10] The protesters favored seeking accommodation with the Soviets and, no doubt, an attendant drift toward neutrality in the East–West conflict.

*

The greatest challenge for Britain in the 1970s, however, was its moribund economy. Stifled by low productivity and onerous taxation, the British economy lagged behind its competitors for much of the 1970s. The high inflation of the period led to strife between employers and trade unions; as workers saw their earnings eaten up by higher prices, they pressed for wage increases, intensifying the inflationary cycle. The strains of this escalating conflict between the government and the National Union of Mineworkers led Heath to declare a three-day work-week starting on January 1, 1974. Television broadcasts were cut at 10:30 p.m.; commercial use of electricity was restricted to three days a week to conserve coal while the miners were on strike. By early March, a new Labour government had been elected. Prime Minister Harold Wilson immediately agreed to raise miners' wages by 35 percent.[11]

The economic crisis, however, was just beginning. In 1976, Britain suffered the indignity of having to approach the International Monetary Fund (IMF) for a $3.9 billion emergency loan (nearly $18 billion in 2020 dollars). Consumer prices, which had been rising at the stable pace of 2.5 percent as recently as 1967, increased by 24.2 percent in 1975 – a record in Britain's modern economic history. By the following year, Britain's economy appeared to have stabilized, but the reprieve was short-lived – creating a historic opening for the new leader of the Opposition, Margaret Thatcher.

By late 1978, inflation had returned with a vengeance. In November, Ford Motor Company's British operations gave striking workers a 17 percent raise – in contravention of the 5 percent cap on pay increases which the Labour government (now led by James Callaghan) had introduced. The government's strategy to fight inflation by imposing wage and price controls was thereby thrown into disarray.

The following January, temperatures averaged below freezing across Britain, making it the third-coldest winter of the twentieth century. Emboldened by Ford's 17 percent raise, truck drivers began a wildcat strike on January 3, 1979. Not only did they fail to show up for work, they also used their vehicles to block roads, ports and oil refineries. Fearful of shortages, customers emptied grocery store shelves in what became a self-fulfilling premonition of scarcity.

Conditions grew more severe as the strikes spread to the public sector: rail services ceased; buses idled. Leicester Square, the center of London's theater district, was transformed into a makeshift garbage dump. Emergency calls went unanswered, and, in more than one locality, the dead went unburied.[12]

This was the bitter harvest of a generation of British leadership which had embraced as its principal task the orderly management of decline. To get itself out of this sorry condition, the nation would soon turn to a very different kind of leader.

THE ASCENT FROM GRANTHAM

In 1948, Margaret Roberts, a recent graduate of Oxford with a degree in chemistry, applied for a research job at Imperial Chemical Industries (ICI). She was rejected. The internal assessment of her candidacy read: 'This woman is headstrong, obstinate, and dangerously self-opinionated.'[13] Three decades later, it was an inkling of these same qualities that persuaded the people of the United Kingdom to choose 'this woman' to tackle the challenges facing their nation.

Born in 1925 in the market town of Grantham, Margaret Roberts was brought up in a strict Methodist family that prized hard work, integrity and biblical teachings. Sundays were wholly devoted to church. Margaret and her older sister Muriel attended worship and Sunday school in the morning, often returning to church for another round of classes and prayer in the afternoon and early evening. Their father, Alfred Roberts, was a Methodist lay preacher. The Roberts home was modest, consisting of a few rooms above Alfred's grocery store and lacking hot water or an indoor bathroom.

Shortly before her eleventh birthday, Margaret enrolled as a scholarship student at the Kesteven and Grantham Girls' School, a selective grammar school, where she excelled academically. When she was granted a peerage later in life, she chose to style herself 'Baroness Thatcher of Kesteven', rather than 'of Grantham', as a tribute to the school that had shaped her. It was during these formative years – in April 1939, to be precise – that the Roberts family welcomed into their midst a seventeen-year-old Jewish girl from Vienna named Edith Mühlbauer, who had been Muriel's pen-pal. Shortly after the Nazi occupation of Austria, Edith's parents wrote to ask Alfred Roberts whether he could arrange a visa for her, and she ended up living with his family briefly before moving to more comfortable arrangements with another

Grantham household. Edith's parents were later able to flee Austria, eventually settling in Brazil. This and other early memories – such as Margaret's mother's weekly habit of baking loaves of bread to pass discreetly to needy families – reinforced the enduring pertinence in her upbringing of the biblical commandment to 'love thy neighbor as thyself'.[14]

After a strong academic performance in high school, Margaret Roberts gained admission to Oxford University, where she became president of the Oxford University Conservative Association. Following a brief stint as a research chemist, she passed the bar exam and became a barrister. Yet, even as she ventured far from her parents' home in Grantham, she always carried inside herself the values inculcated by her family and faith: discipline, thrift, sympathy and practical support.

In 1950s Britain, the political terrain was notably inhospitable to women. Through sheer persistence, determination and a healthy dose of charm, Mrs Thatcher (as she became following her 1951 marriage to Denis Thatcher, a businessman who was her lifelong support) secured the nomination for a safe Conservative seat and by 1959 had been elected to parliament for a north London constituency.

In 1960, at the age of thirty-four, she gave her first speech before the House of Commons. The purpose of the speech was twofold: first, to advocate for the legislation she was sponsoring and, second, to introduce herself to her colleagues and the country. The second goal she achieved briskly, omitting any introduction or preliminary embellishments. 'This is a maiden speech,' she said, 'but I know that the constituency of Finchley, which I have the honour to represent, would not wish me to do other than come straight to the point and address myself to the matter before the House.'[15]

Speaking without notes, she explained what she viewed as a serious constitutional problem. At the time, it was common for local elected officials to use procedural maneuvers to block members of the public from attending local government meetings. Then as now, local councils were responsible for overseeing schools, libraries, public housing and waste collection – the essential public services of everyday life. Without direct access, Thatcher noted, the public had to rely on the press alone for information, but the press, too, was barred from attendance. In her view, public access was a matter of first principles:

In England and Wales, local authorities spend £1,400 million a year and, in Scotland, just over £200 million a year. Those sums are not insignificant, even in terms of national budgets . . . the first purpose in admitting the Press is that we may know how those moneys are being spent. In the second place, I quote from the Report of the Franks Committee: 'Publicity is the greatest and most effective check against any arbitrary action.'[16]

The bill passed and remains in force across the United Kingdom. She would reprise the theme of fiscal stewardship throughout her career in public service.

Thus began Thatcher's climb up the parliamentary ladder; on each of its rungs, her competence and commitment left a clear mark. At the same time, she was carving out a position on the right of the political spectrum that was often at odds with the Conservative leadership's more moderate line. Although her self-description as a 'conviction politician' would come later, her uncommonly straightforward manner was already evident. As she said of the relationship between voters and politicians in 1968:

If the elector suspects the politician of making promises simply to get his vote, he despises him; but if the promises are not forthcoming, he may reject him. *I believe that parties and elections are about more than rival lists of miscellaneous promises – indeed, if they were not, democracy would scarcely be worth preserving* [emphasis in original].[17]

With the Conservative Party's return to power under Heath in 1970, Thatcher entered the cabinet for the first time as secretary of state for education and science. She immediately attracted controversy, in part for the sheer intensity of her pace. In an attempt to redirect funds for more promising educational investments elsewhere, she cut bloated budgets – including, notoriously, a free-milk program for primary-school children, for which she earned the sobriquet 'Milk Snatcher'. She also reversed Labour's attempt to mandate the closure of grammar schools and helped pass free-market legislation to make scientific research more competitive.

Heath's willingness to defer to the statist consensus, however, left Thatcher disillusioned. Convinced that the economic status quo was untenable, she turned to friends at the Institute of Economic Affairs, a free-market think tank, who introduced her to the contributions of Frédéric Bastiat, F. A. Hayek and Milton Friedman. Undertaking such a self-education in economics would have been an impressive intellectual feat for anyone – doubly so for an established politician in middle age. Meanwhile, with regard to foreign policy, Thatcher's instincts similarly ran counter to Heath's prioritization of Europe over a close relationship with the United States.* Having recognized their fundamental differences, she waited until Heath lost the October 1974 general election to challenge him for the party leadership.

Thatcher's decision to put herself forward, given the expectation that she would almost certainly lose, was a notable exhibition of courage and conviction. The Conservatives, long dominated by patrician men, surprised not only themselves but much of the Western world by electing her as their leader in February 1975. The party of Winston Churchill, Anthony Eden and Harold Macmillan was now led by a grocer's daughter.

Despite the novelty value of Thatcher's election, the widespread expectation was that her tenure would prove brief. As President Gerald Ford's national security advisor, I was hardly immune to this conventional wisdom. In May 1975, I highlighted the credentials of Winston Churchill's son-in-law, Christopher Soames, whom I felt was likely to become 'a big Conservative leader' in the future. My prognosis for the current leader was less positive: 'I don't think Margaret Thatcher will last.'[18]

While my judgment of her prospects was less than perspicacious, my evaluation of her character proved more enduring. I first met Thatcher in 1973, during her tenure as education secretary. The meeting came about at the urging of my future wife, Nancy Maginnes, who in connection with an educational study she was producing for New York Governor Nelson Rockefeller had consulted Thatcher. Impressed, Nancy suggested I seek a meeting of my own.

My request ran into considerable resistance from Heath, then at the height of his effort to distance Britain from the United States. Nevertheless, I managed to arrange a get-together through the auspices of a friend. I would see Thatcher again in late 1973 and in February 1975, days after she had outmaneuvered Heath and assumed party leadership.

From the first meeting, Thatcher's vitality and commitment fixed her

---

* Thatcher's pro-American views coexisted at this time with a more enthusiastic stance toward Europe than she would hold later in her career. For example, she supported Britain's remaining in the Common Market in the 1975 referendum.

notion of leadership firmly in my mind. Nearly every other politician of the era argued that to win elections, one had to capture the center ground. Thatcher demurred. That approach, she asserted, amounted to a subversion of democracy. The quest for the center was a recipe for vacuity; instead, different arguments had to clash, creating real choices for the voter.

Another event that helped shape our burgeoning relationship was Thatcher's visit to Washington in September 1977. President Jimmy Carter's attitude toward either large- or small-'c' conservatives recalled that of Nixon toward the Labour Party. Correspondingly, Carter's treatment of the visiting leader of the Conservative Party was correct but aloof. National Security Advisor Zbigniew Brzezinski advised Carter to 'plead a heavy schedule' and refuse to meet with Thatcher; Carter obliged.[19] As a result, she was treated with less attention than she had expected given her own warm feelings for the United States.

Nancy and I invited Thatcher to dinner one evening, together with leading Washington personalities from both parties, an informal occasion which set the tone for our future meetings. After becoming prime minister, Thatcher generally invited me for private discussions (by then I no longer held office) to exchange views on international topics – or simply to cross-check the prevailing views of her Foreign Office. If others were present, it was usually a close aide; cabinet officials were rarely invited to our meetings. From 1984 onward, a key figure in those meetings was Thatcher's foreign-policy advisor Charles Powell, one of the public servants to whom Britain owed its eminence.[20] Highly intelligent, self-effacing, and unostentatiously patriotic, Powell had been transferred from the Foreign Office after a distinguished diplomatic career that had taken him to Helsinki, Washington, Bonn and Brussels. He became a lifelong friend of Thatcher's, sustaining her through her difficult retirement.

Shortly after Thatcher became leader of the Conservative Party, she outlined her thinking at a meeting with me over a traditional English breakfast at Claridge's. Articulate and thoughtful, she made clear that her ambition was nothing less than to transform the country. She aimed to do so not by pursuing some vague middle ground, but by articulating a program that would make the middle ground see things as she did. Her rhetoric and policies would strike a genuine contrast to the staid conventional wisdom that, in her view, had doomed Britain to stagnation.

Then, after winning the next election, she would carry out fundamental reforms to overcome conventional wisdom, the doctrine of complacency, and the prevailing passivity with respect to the ravages of inflation, the power of the trade unions or the inefficiency of state-owned enterprises.

For Thatcher, there were no sacred cows, much less insurmountable obstacles. Every policy was up for scrutiny. It was not sufficient, she argued, for Conservatives to sand down the rough edges of socialism; they had to roll back the state before Britain's economy collapsed in catastrophic fashion. In the realm of foreign affairs, she was disarmingly honest about her inexperience, confessing that she had yet to formulate detailed ideas of her own. But she made clear that she believed passionately in the 'special relationship' with the United States.

By articulating her views as clearly and forcefully as possible, she aimed to shift the political center of gravity in her direction. And she had confidence that the British people would recognize the difference between sturdy principles and passing fads. As she put it in a 1983 interview: 'There would have been no great prophets, no great philosophers in life, no great things to follow, if those who propounded their views had gone out and said "Brothers, follow me, I believe in consensus."'[21]

Our meetings continued long after Thatcher left office and through the rest of her life. I describe our relationship in this way to make a point: unlike the president of the United States, the British prime minister does not have the ability to override the cabinet and still maintain his or her government. Thatcher was aware of these limits. To help her compensate, she would discreetly call on friends in Britain and around the world to discuss her vision and her options.

A FRAMEWORK FOR LEADERSHIP

Thatcher's foreign-policy views would, over time, come into tighter focus, in no small part thanks to her extraordinarily diligent habits of study – including reading and annotating briefing papers late into the night – and her practice of convening weekend seminars on long-term trends with university professors and other intellectuals. Some of her strategic convictions, such as the inviolable sovereignty of the nation-state, were apparent from our earliest meetings. An implacable advocate of self-determination, Thatcher believed in the right of citizens to choose their own form of government and in the responsibility of states to exercise sovereignty on their own behalf.

For Thatcher, British sovereignty was inextricably tied to the country's unique history, geographical integrity and fiercely guarded independence. Although she rarely spoke in abstract terms, in practice she subscribed to the broader notion, dating back to the Peace of Westphalia of 1648, that the sovereignty of individual nations was instrumental to stability between them. She believed in each country's right to uphold its own law-based governance and to act according to its interests without illegitimate interference. 'Although I am a strong believer in international law,' she remarked in her memoirs, 'I did not like unnecessary resort to the UN, because it suggested that sovereign states lacked the moral authority to act on their own behalf.'[22]

The logic of these convictions led Thatcher to an unqualified belief in a strong national defense. To her, credible deterrence was the only real guarantee of peace and of the preservation of Westphalian sovereignty. In practice, this meant that Western military capabilities would have to be restored before productive negotiations with the Soviet Union could be held.

Thatcher was also motivated by a staunch anti-communist conviction – fueled, in part, by her belief that Soviet expansionism posed an existential threat to the West. She did not hesitate to express her belief that communism's subjugation of the individual was intrinsically immoral. Actively promoting liberal democracy throughout her career as inherently morally superior, she emerged as a champion of freedom.

Thatcher's idealism was bounded by important limits – specifically, the existence of a nuclear-armed Soviet Union. Britain now had far fewer capacities to act unilaterally in the world than it did before the Second World War; national sovereignty could only be defended by closely partnering with America. Churchill's notion of a special relationship with the United States included a substantial element of realism: Britain could magnify its influence by gearing its policies closely to those of the United States. Such a relationship did not specify a formal structure, but it did include patterns of conduct. The US and the UK developed close intelligence cooperation during the Second World War and continued it during the Cold War, when they invited Australia, Canada and New Zealand into what became the Five Eyes intelligence alliance. Privately, both US and UK leaders would engage in intense consultation before major decisions; publicly, they would pay tribute to historical amity. British diplomats became exceptionally skillful at making themselves part of the American decision-making process – even inducing guilt in American policymakers if they disregarded British precepts.

No British prime minister had a deeper commitment to this transatlantic orientation than Margaret Thatcher. As leader of the Opposition, she had made it her mission to rebuild the relationship with the United States following the disappointments of the Heath years. She believed in the indispensability of US leadership for the wellbeing of both Britain and the world. As she once told me, 'Anything which weakened the United States weakened the free world.'[23] Beyond this practical judgment, she was a genuine admirer of the United States. She believed that the United States and the United Kingdom, inheritors of many shared values and much common history, needed to engage in a joint project to reinvigorate the Western Alliance. Under her leadership, Britain became less a beneficiary and more a partner in that joint enterprise.

While Thatcher's leadership was governed by principles, she never allowed her decisions to be overwhelmed by abstractions. Her strength lay in her indomitable willpower, made effectual by ample reserves of charm. Part of her genius as a leader inhered in the ability to adapt to the dictates of reality without relinquishing her larger vision. In her determination to effect change, she accepted results that in themselves were only stages in a lengthier process. As Charles Powell has observed, 'Like a sensible naval officer, she knew when to make smoke and retire to avoid tactical defeats, but always maintained the ultimate objective and battled on to achieve it.'[24] To her mind, acting imperfectly was always preferable to doing nothing.

THE ECONOMIC REFORMER

Outside Britain, Thatcher is remembered as a commanding presence on the international scene, but Britons elected her primarily as a domestic reformer. Her victory was not foreordained: in the autumn of 1978, the dramatic events that would lead to the Labour government's demise were unforeseeable. Thanks to her self-education in economics, however, Thatcher was intellectually prepared to exploit political opportunities when they presented themselves. She understood the sources of Britain's woes and would go on to propose compelling solutions that would win support in the May 1979 general election.

Measured against the exacting standards of Hayekian theory, Thatcher's economic program was perhaps slow and half-complete. Viewed within the context of electoral politics, however, her approach was decisive, unusually amenable to experimentation and ultimately history-making. Determined to whip inflation, Thatcher's new government raised interest rates to the recession-inducing level of 17 percent – to date, an all-time high.

And the recession came. In 1980, gross domestic product contracted by 2 percent. Hundreds of thousands of jobless workers were thrown on the dole. Yet as public sentiment and thinking within the Conservative Party – and even within her cabinet – grew increasingly skeptical of her reforms, Thatcher maintained her steely resolve. Initially, she was not as consistent in private as in her public appearances, but gradually her political resolve began to win out. She backed the reform proposals of her chancellor of the exchequer, Geoffrey Howe, frustrating consensus politicians such as the employment minister, Jim Prior. Despite intense public pressure to change course, she told the annual Conservative Party conference in October 1980: 'The lady's not for turning.' Echoing Hayek's thinking on the subject – but infusing it with a sharper cast, equal parts moral and patriotic – Thatcher saw inflation as a threat to the national interest: 'Inflation destroys nations and societies as surely as invading armies do,' she told the Conservatives. 'Inflation is the parent of unemployment. It is the unseen robber of those who have saved.'[25]

Thatcher did not reverse her monetary policy even when the preliminary results were unpopular. Her perseverance was all the more remarkable given that, unlike in the United States, where interest rates are set by an independent central bank, in Thatcher's Britain responsibility for setting interest rates was ultimately vested in the Treasury (until 1997), therefore resting directly with the prime minister.*

By 1982, the British economy had returned to growth. But unemployment continued to increase well into 1984, the year Thatcher

* The Bank of England gained control over monetary policy in 1997 – meaning it could set interest rates and employ quantitative easing autonomously – and became formally independent in 1998, under Prime Minister Tony Blair.

faced another domestic crisis that demanded all the political skill, foresight and sangfroid she could muster.

In March 1984, Arthur Scargill, head of the National Union of Mine-workers (NUM), declared a strike against the National Coal Board, the statutory corporation tasked with managing Britain's state-run mines. Under Thatcher, the Board had closed down the least productive coal-pits. Although Scargill never called an endorsing vote of his union members, the strike would continue for a year. In its course, more than a thousand police officers were injured during violent confrontations with the striking miners' 'flying pickets', mobile protests designed to prevent non-striking miners from entering their workplaces.

While public sympathy for the miners was widespread, so was public disapproval of both the violence resulting from the strike and Scargill's failure to call a vote before initiating it. Determined not to become trapped as Heath had been a decade earlier, Thatcher had initiated a policy of stockpiling coal that enabled her to hold her ground. As a result, Britain's electrical grid would not experience the blackouts endured during previous miners' strikes. As months passed, miners began to trickle back to work.

At one point during the strike, I had breakfast with former Prime Minister Harold Macmillan, a traditional Conservative and scion of a family-owned publishing house. Macmillan approved of Thatcher's courage during the miners' strike, he told me, adding that she had no other choice. Yet 'I could never have brought myself to do it,' he acknowledged, explaining that he, as a young officer in the First World War, remembered sending the miners' 'fathers and grand-fathers over the top' in the trenches of France.[26] He would not have had the heart to conduct the battle of human endurance Thatcher was now waging.

In March 1985, after 26 million days of labor lost, the strike ended. In Samuel Taylor Coleridge's *Statesman's Manual*, a 'lay sermon' for those who make politics their vocation, the Romantic poet observes that 'It is no uncommon foible with those who are honored with the acquaintance of the great, to attribute national events to particular persons ... rather than to the true proximate cause, the predominant state of public opinion'.[27] Yet, in Thatcher's case more often than not she was prepared to challenge public opinion in order to shape events and, in the end, bring public sentiment along with her.

Thatcher's reforms changed Britain irrevocably. During her premiership, the Conservatives ended foreign-exchange controls, eliminated fixed trading commissions and opened Britain's stock market to foreign traders in what became known as the 'Big Bang' – which, by the end of the 1980s, turned Britain into an international financial center. Conservative policies also restrained public expenditure, though they did not succeed in reducing it outright. Taxes on income and investment came down; the consumption tax went up. British Telecom, British Airways, British Steel and British Gas were all privatized. The number of Britons owning equities nearly quadrupled.[28]

Thatcher was equally determined to apply the logic of privatization to public housing. She established a 'right to buy' program which enabled more than a million council-house tenants to become homeowners on favorable terms. By translating her slogans of 'property-owning democracy' into operational policies, she helped working-class people build wealth. More than a handful of the new homeowners became Conservative voters, illustrating her maxim that good policy can build new political constituencies. When critics accused her of preaching Victorian values, Thatcher turned the charge against them:

> Winston [Churchill] put it best. You want a ladder, upwards, anyone, no matter what their background, can climb, but [also] a fundamental safety net below which no one can fall. That's the British character . . .
>
> Compassion doesn't depend upon whether you get up and make a speech in the marketplace about what governments should do. It depends upon how you're prepared to conduct your own life, and how much you're prepared to give of what you have to others.[29]

Thatcher lived by the principles she avowed. A full-throated champion of free markets, she was also proud that her government had improved the quality of social services. This was especially vivid in her approach to the National Health Service (NHS), the crown jewel of Prime Minister Clement Attlee's postwar Labour reforms. Despite her strong preference for market-based solutions, Thatcher never seriously considered privatizing the NHS. Instead, as she cut expenditure elsewhere, she *increased* NHS funding. This was made possible, she did not hesitate to note, by the wealth created by unshackling private enterprise:

> The National Health Service is safe with us ... this performance in the
> social services could never have been achieved without an efficient and
> competitive industry to create the wealth we need. Efficiency is not the
> enemy, but the ally, of compassion.[30]

Thatcher had assumed high office after years of apparent national
decline. Inflation had been at 18 percent in 1980 but had been cut to 8
percent by 1990, when she left office. From 1993 to 2020, it has largely
remained close to 2 percent. Likewise, unemployment had been reduced
from its high of nearly 12 percent in 1984 to 7 percent by 1990, while
over the same period incomes had more than doubled, from $7,805 per
capita to $19,095 (figures are in 2020 dollars). In 1983, nearly 100,000
workers left Britain, but by 1990 more than 200,000 were arriving annually.[31] The number of working days lost to labor disputes plummeted
from 29.5 million in 1979 to 1.9 million in 1990.[32] Not only was Britain
working again, but the economic turnaround engineered by Thatcher and
her capable lieutenants had restored Britain's standing in the world.

The success of Thatcher's economic reforms gave her a strong political hand, generating more resources and flexibility to achieve foreign
policy goals and increase defense spending. As the economy improved,
she led the Conservative Party to three consecutive electoral victories.
On the other hand, Thatcher never succeeded in winning a broad consensus in favor of her economic reforms, even after they began to show
results. She was admired by many, loved by some, but resented by much
of the working class and left-leaning intellectuals for the exertions of
the reform period. In 1988, the perception of Thatcher as cold-hearted
was revived by her embrace of the 'community charge' (a flat tax
imposed to fund local government), which sparked widespread protests
and contributed to her eventual political downfall.

By contrast, Thatcher achieved a lasting impact on the economic
views of the median voter and political elites. When Tony Blair's 'New
Labour' government was elected in 1997 – seven years after Thatcher's
departure from office – I wrote her a letter of congratulations for laying
the groundwork for this major turn away from the left:

> I never thought I'd congratulate you on a Labour victory in the British
> elections, but I cannot imagine anything that would confirm your revolu-
> tion more than Blair's program. It seems to me well to the right of the
> Conservative government that preceded yours.[33]

While Thatcher continued to be pained by the circumstances under which she was forced from office, on this occasion she managed good cheer. 'I think your analysis is the correct one,' she replied, 'but to make one's political opponent electable and then elected was not quite the strategy I had in mind!'[34]

Two weeks after Blair took office – and much to the consternation of his left flank – he invited Thatcher to tea at 10 Downing Street.[35] Ostensibly, the meeting's purpose was to seek her advice regarding an upcoming European summit, but there was clearly also an element of personal admiration.[36] Likewise, ten years later, Blair's successor Gordon Brown made a point of extending a similar invitation within his first three months as prime minister. On that occasion, Thatcher was seen leaving the prime minister's residence with a clutch of flowers in her hands.[37] It was proof that she had met the objective she had laid out in the baleful 1970s: creating a new center.

IN DEFENSE OF SOVEREIGNTY: THE FALKLANDS CONFLICT

Thatcher considered it her duty to defend British interests in the world, whether near or distant, and to protect Britain's capacity to maintain the Atlantic Alliance. She was eloquent in expressing the British point of view on these subjects, relentless in pursuing opportunities for British business abroad, and unyielding in her defense of British subjects. In April 1982, her willingness to act on these beliefs was put to the test when Argentina invaded the Falkland Islands, a British territory since 1833. For sovereignty – that is, the ultimate authority within a defined territory – to retain its meaning, she had to act. As she later wrote, the Argentine attack involved a 'crisis of Britain's honour'.[38]

But within the UN, whose founding documents had enshrined the Westphalian sovereign equality of states, Thatcher's defense of sovereignty was nonetheless contested. For many new members of the UN, who had achieved their independence by opposition to colonialism, Argentina's takeover of the Falklands appeared to be merely a long-overdue episode of decolonization. Thus, even many members of the Westphalian system were unlikely to support Thatcher's view of what was at issue in some lightly inhabited islands in the South Atlantic.

Furthermore, despite Ronald Reagan's high regard for Thatcher and the long-standing relationship with Britain, the American administration was ambivalent, and support among NATO was tepid too. By contrast, French President François Mitterrand saw the cogency of Thatcher's argument, assuring her: 'You should realize that others share your opposition to this kind of aggression.'[39]

Thatcher's conduct during the Falklands crisis was depicted by critics as unyielding, deaf to any effort toward compromise and bloody minded in its determination to enact her will. In fact, Thatcher's conduct during this conflict was built on her resolve to stand firm on principle, but it also reflected a shrewd understanding of when objective reality required a measure of diplomatic flexibility – especially in relations with Washington.

The Falkland Islands lie some 300 miles off the Argentine mainland. Their strategic importance lay in their proximity to Cape Horn, the southern tip of the American continent and, along with the Strait of Magellan, a historic passageway between the Atlantic and the Pacific. In the eighteenth century, control over the islands was a subject of dispute among France, Britain and Spain; the colony changed hands frequently, depending on the outcome of various European wars. During the early 1830s, the islands were governed from Buenos Aires, the capital of newly independent Argentina. Britain occupied them in January 1833, retaining continuous possession thereafter. By the early 1980s, therefore, the Falkland Islanders had been subjects of the British Crown according to international law for nearly 150 years, even as Argentina continued to assert its claim to sovereignty.

General Leopoldo Galtieri, who in December 1981 became president of Argentina by military coup amid economic chaos and substantial violence verging on civil war, resolved to increase his public support by summarily vindicating the country's longstanding claim to the Falklands. On April 2, 1982, Argentina invaded and quickly subdued the lightly defended islands.

News of the invasion shocked the British government. 'I could not believe it,' Thatcher later wrote, insisting, 'These were our people, our islands.'[40] But her instinct to act was met with little succor from her advisors. The Foreign Office saw no diplomatic route, and Defense Secretary John Nott advised that military action to retake the islands, some 7,000 miles away, was impossible.

An ultimate function of leadership is to inspire associates beyond what they deem possible. Bringing to bear her distinctive inner confidence, Thatcher pushed her government onward. 'You'll have to take them back,' she told Nott. When he insisted it could not be done, she simply repeated, 'You'll have to.'[41]

Thatcher's refusal to take no for an answer was vindicated when First Sea Lord Sir Henry Leach found a way forward. He advised her to assemble a naval task force capable of doing the job, albeit at substantial risk. Thatcher duly instructed him to undertake the necessary preparations. While this decision in no way bound her to a military solution, it preserved the possibility of one while Thatcher exhausted the diplomatic options that had been put forward by skeptical cabinet members and her American allies.

Having established a strategy, Thatcher wasted no time in implementing it. She publicly laid down her principles and made a solemn vow to defend them. An emergency debate was convened in the House of Commons the day after the invasion, a Saturday. Thatcher explained her thinking in clear terms: 'For the first time for many years, British sovereign territory has been invaded by a foreign power ... I must tell the House that the Falkland Islands and their dependencies remain British territory.' In short, this was not a colonial issue, but a challenge to Britain's national self-respect and sovereignty. Defiantly, she concluded: 'No aggression and no invasion can alter that simple fact. It is the Government's objective to see that the islands are freed from occupation and are returned to British administration at the earliest possible moment.'[42]

Thatcher had unequivocally conveyed her resolve by cutting off the possibility of her own retreat.

Thatcher hoped that the reaction from Britain's most powerful and important ally, the United States, would be positive. Washington's position, however, proved rather more conflicted.

Bolstered by the 1980 election of President Ronald Reagan, the Anglo-American relationship was in good standing by early 1982. Reagan and Thatcher first met in 1975, shortly after she became party leader and while he was preparing to campaign in the 1976 Republican presidential primaries. The meeting proved a great success. The two aspiring leaders, products of comparable ideological trajectories, found themselves in agreement on many policy issues. They also connected on a personal level: 'Please know you have an enthusiastic supporter out here in the "colonies",' Reagan wrote to her shortly afterward.[43]

Transatlantic ties grew stronger once Reagan was in office. In February 1981, Thatcher became the first European ally to visit Reagan's Washington, attending a glittering state dinner at the White House; and, in an unusual diplomatic honor, Thatcher proceeded to host a return dinner for Reagan at the British embassy the following evening. Recalling that night in his diary, Reagan noted that it was 'truly a warm & beautiful occasion', adding, 'I believe a real friendship exists between the P.M., her family & us – certainly we feel that way & I'm sure they do.'[44] Early in his term, Reagan proved supportive of Thatcher's economic reforms, and the two stood together in adopting a more assertive approach to East–West relations.

Yet for all the rejuvenated warmth between Washington and London, the US also maintained important ties with Argentina. Under Reagan, relations with the Argentine junta were upgraded, and Buenos Aires joined Washington in overt – and later covert – efforts to aid the anti-communist opposition forces (Contras) against the Soviet-backed Sandinista regime in Nicaragua. Some US leaders feared that any show of support for Britain in the Falklands conflict would compromise this joint venture with Argentina and weaken America's standing with the underdeveloped Third World. This picture was further complicated by CIA warnings that if the Galtieri government suffered a military defeat, it was likely to be replaced by 'a highly nationalistic military regime which would establish military ties with the USSR'.[45]

Facing these conflicting pressures, the US administration pursued a divided and sometimes contradictory course. Under the direction of Caspar Weinberger – a committed conservative – the Pentagon provided Britain with a broad supply of badly needed military materiel from the beginning of the conflict. Much of this assistance took place covertly, not least because the State Department, led by Secretary of State Alexander Haig, opposed public US support for Britain. Seeking to avoid a rupture with Argentina, Haig undertook a mediation effort. Though his sympathies lay with the British, Reagan acquiesced to Haig's shuttle diplomacy between London and Buenos Aires.

When Haig briefed me about his plans, I privately voiced serious doubts despite my own history of conducting shuttle diplomacy in the

Middle East. Then, the shuttles had been between capitals that were only a few hundred miles apart; in the South Atlantic crisis, the capitals were separated by nearly 7,000 miles. In the Middle East, not only could decisions be made overnight, enabling adjustment amid contingencies, but the principals on both sides were committed to making progress. By contrast, both Thatcher and the junta had taken fixed positions in the Falklands crisis, precluding compromise. In all likelihood, Thatcher agreed to the mediation largely to satisfy American wishes and to give her fleet time to reach the waters off the Falklands. Whenever the mediation threatened to impair her view of British sovereignty, she would doubtless have rejected it.

Thatcher expected the United States to take Britain's side without question. Haig's efforts, therefore, came as an unwelcome shock. Though she remained convinced of the virtue of her position that British sovereignty must be restored to the Falklands, she was now obliged to consider compromise measures. She agreed to listen to American proposals for a mediated outcome and not publicly insist that the solution had to be of a military nature. But, even as such diplomatic initiatives were pursued, the April 5 dispatch of the British naval task force ensured that pressure on Argentina would build. Acutely conscious of American public opinion – not to mention the need to maintain broad support and the appearance of flexibility at home – Thatcher entertained various options along the lines of turning the Falklands into a UN trusteeship.

At the end of April, shuttle diplomacy collapsed due to Argentine intransigence. As the likelihood of military conflict grew, pressure to find a negotiated solution intensified. On a visit to London in early May, I experienced the limits of Thatcher's diplomatic flexibility.

Months before the Falklands crisis, I had been invited by Foreign Secretary Lord Carrington to deliver a speech marking the 200th anniversary of the founding of the British Foreign Office. By the set date, however, Carrington was no longer in office. The perceived failure of the Foreign Office to foresee or prevent the Falklands invasion had aroused great ire on the Conservative backbenches. Reflecting a long-standing but by no means universally observed tradition, Carrington had chosen to accept responsibility for the government's failures by resigning, thereby shielding the prime minister and the cabinet as a whole. Carrington, the quintessence of honor, was not personally at fault. Under his conception of duty, resignation was the only appropriate course of action.*

In fact, in the year leading up to the crisis, Carrington had resolutely opposed the British decision that, as it turned out, had invited Argentine aggression: the planned withdrawal of the ice-breaking vessel HMS *Endurance* from the Falklands theater, which had been proposed by Defense Secretary Nott as a cost-cutting measure that would save around $2.5 million a year. Carrington argued that Argentina would interpret this decision 'as a stage in a deliberate British policy of reducing support for the Falkland Islands'.[46] In a debate in the House of Commons over HMS *Endurance* on February 9, 1982, Thatcher unwisely expressed support for Nott's view rather than Carrington's. But the price of gutting deterrence in the South Atlantic proved steep, as the cost of the Falklands War ran to more than $7 billion in all. As historian Andrew Roberts writes of the decision: 'Rarely has the truth been more starkly displayed that relatively high defense spending represents good value for money, because combat is always far more expensive than deterrence.'[47]

With Carrington out, the Foreign Office bicentennial proceeded under the stewardship of Francis Pym, the new foreign secretary. Having left office five years earlier, I was visiting in a private capacity, but official courtesies were nevertheless extended – a lunch with Pym and senior officials, followed by an afternoon tea with Thatcher.

Over lunch, the discussion focused on the putative compromises that had emerged from the Haig shuttle. There was neither consensus on details, nor a hint of any alternative course save some form of compromise. Over tea at 10 Downing Street, I asked Thatcher which of the new approaches she favored. 'I will have no compromise!' she thundered, 'How can you, my old friend? How can you say these things?' She was so irate I did not have the heart to explain that the idea was not mine but her chief diplomat's.

Her position, Thatcher explained, was a matter of principle and of strategy. Hence her disappointment that her closest ally had offered mediation in response to an unprovoked attack on British territory. In my speech that evening, titled 'Reflections on a Partnership', I endorsed

---

* Months later, I asked him why he had never told even his friends of the tense state of affairs. He replied: 'There is no point in accepting responsibility if afterwards you whisper to your friends that you are not really responsible.'

Thatcher's position on the Falklands crisis. The United States would be unwise to abandon a close ally, as it had over Suez in 1956:

> The strategic position or self-confidence of a close ally on a matter it considers of vital concern must not be undermined. It is a principle of no little contemporary relevance. In this sense the Falklands crisis in the end will strengthen Western cohesion.[48]

Still, as was occasionally the case with Thatcher, ideas she had resisted at the outset would later reach a point of apparent acceptance. This was no less true with respect to her position on the Falklands. She allowed her negotiating position to evolve inch by inch, even as Argentina foolishly showed little sign of responding in kind. By the time of what was described as the final British offer, transmitted via UN Secretary-General Javier Pérez de Cuéllar on May 17,[49] Thatcher had agreed to allow UN administration of the islands in exchange for Argentine withdrawal; Falkland sovereignty itself would be a matter for future negotiation. These concessions, made largely to maintain American support, had carried her a considerable distance from her initial insistence on restoring the status quo ante.

Was her 'final' proposal based on cold, rational analysis? Or was there a Machiavellian element in Thatcher's stance? Having witnessed Argentine intransigence throughout the negotiations, she may have concluded that chances were slim that Galtieri would accept her offer. The offer may also have been a fallback if the fleet by then approaching the Falklands were to suffer unacceptable losses. With such an uncertain outcome, and in pursuit of the high ground bestowed by a UN-brokered solution, she assumed considerable risk.

Had Buenos Aires accepted her proposal, she would have faced a Herculean struggle to persuade the House of Commons to accept such a settlement or to convince the UN to give up its administration to Britain after the dispute was resolved. Had this come to pass, I believe she would have drawn the negotiations onto a ground that would have enabled the British task force to achieve her initial objective of restoring British sovereignty. Fortunately for her, however, the gamble paid off: on May 18, the Argentines rejected the British offer point-blank. Three days later, British forces launched their assault.

Once the fighting began, British victory was by no means assured. With extraordinarily long supply lines, and finite in-theater resources, the British task force was quite vulnerable. Moreover, Argentina had acquired a number of Exocet missiles from France, which exacted a punishing toll on the British ships. Had either of the aircraft carriers HMS *Hermes* or HMS *Invincible* fallen prey, the British position would have become precarious.

Thatcher was only too aware of these dangers and the potential human toll. While projecting a public image of unremitting toughness, in private she felt each loss keenly. Her authorized biographer records that following news of one Argentine attack, Denis Thatcher found his wife sitting at the edge of their bed, weeping: 'Oh no, oh no! Another ship! All my young men!'[50] By war's end, she had sent 255 handwritten letters to the families of Britain's fallen servicemen.[51]

Thatcher's modus operandi as a wartime leader was to establish parameters and then leave the flag officers to manage the campaign as they saw fit, while providing steadfast political support. One such parameter was the 200-nautical-mile exclusion zone surrounding the Falklands, declared on April 30 by the British government. Within it, any Argentine vessel could be attacked without prior warning. This rule was soon put to the test, and a decision was required: On May 1, the Argentine cruiser *General Belgrano* was sighted skirting the edge of the exclusion zone. The following day, Thatcher ordered the sinking of the *Belgrano* despite the fact that it had since sailed some 40 miles outside the zone.[52] More than 300 Argentine sailors were killed. While her decision attracted much controversy, the *Belgrano*'s position had represented a latent threat to the British task force approaching the Falklands.

By the end of May 21, the first day of land combat, 5,000 British troops had landed on the islands. From that point onward, Thatcher's position hardened regardless of the increasing international pressure for a ceasefire. With British blood now spilled on land as well as at sea, she reverted to her basic position and refused to countenance anything short of full restoration of sovereignty.

This stance was unwelcome in Washington, where the administration was under growing pressure from Latin American allies to end the fighting. For a moment, the demands of British sovereignty seemed to have overstepped the bounds of US national interests. On May 31, with British forces advancing on the islands' capital of Port Stanley, President Reagan was persuaded to call Thatcher and appeal for magnanimity. She stood her ground: 'I'm not handing over the islands now,' she told

Reagan. 'I didn't lose some of my finest ships and some of my finest lives to leave quietly under a ceasefire without the Argentines withdrawing.'[53] As the rhetorical barrage continued, Reagan chose not to contest the substance of the argument. The US made no further effort to slow the British advance. In another indication of the underlying strength of the US–UK relationship, it was later revealed by former US Secretary of the Navy John Lehman that Reagan had even agreed that, in the event of the loss of a carrier of the Royal Navy, the US would lend the USS *Iwo Jima*, an amphibious assault ship (or helicopter carrier), which could accommodate Britain's vertical-takeoff Sea Harrier fighters. 'Give Maggie everything she needs to get on with it,' Reagan told Secretary of Defense Caspar Weinberger.[54]

After heavy fighting, the Argentine occupying forces surrendered on June 14. Britain's victory was complete and held an incalculable symbolic value. Taken in tandem with the decisive economic reforms Thatcher had instituted at home, the Falklands victory effectively transformed Britain's standing on the world stage. As she herself put it:

> We have ceased to be a nation in retreat. We have instead a new-found confidence – born in the economic battles at home and tested and found true 8,000 miles away ... we rejoice that Britain has rekindled that spirit which has fired her for generations past and which today has begun to burn as brightly as before.[55]

In the United States, the reaction was more ambivalent. Reagan's acquiescence to Thatcher's policy damaged relations with Argentina, which abruptly ended its cooperation with Washington. But for other countries, the broader picture was more favorable. By demonstrating credibility on the battlefield, Thatcher had also strengthened the West's hand in the Cold War. Her policy made a crucial distinction between colonial issues and strategic challenges and clearly placed the Falklands in the latter category.

NEGOTIATIONS OVER HONG KONG

Shortly after the Falklands war, Thatcher was obliged to confront a challenge arising out of Britain's explicitly colonial past: the future of Hong Kong.

Although the island of Hong Kong proper had been established as British territory since 1842, the New Territories surrounding it were governed by Britain only as part of a ninety-nine-year lease from China – which was due to expire in 1997. Rejecting Britain's historical claims regarding these arrangements, Beijing insisted that *both* territories revert to Chinese control by 1997 – two years before the Chinese Communist Party (CCP) would celebrate the fiftieth anniversary of its victory over the nationalist forces of Chiang Kai-shek.

China viewed British governance in Hong Kong and the New Territories as a historical aberration. The British position relied on three agreements: the Treaty of Nanjing (1842), by which China ceded Hong Kong island in perpetuity; the Convention of Kowloon (1860), by which China similarly ceded a neighboring peninsula; and the Convention for the Extension of Hong Kong Territory (1898), by which the New Territories were leased for ninety-nine years. As such, Thatcher believed that Britain's claims were well founded according to international law. From China's perspective, however, these treaties had been signed under duress, rendering Britain's claims no more legitimate than if London had taken the islands by force.

I was familiar with Chinese thinking on the matter, having heard it expressed in conversations with Zhou Enlai, China's chief diplomat and titular head of government under Mao Zedong from 1949 to 1975, and more extensively in speaking with Deng Xiaoping, China's paramount leader from 1978 to 1989. During these discussions, which dealt mainly with US–China relations, Hong Kong was broached only tangentially. Deng explained that China would be patient in negotiations but would not compromise on the issue of sovereignty, which it identified with the inviolability of Chinese territory. It might, however, agree to a degree of autonomy for Hong Kong if doing so would facilitate reunification with Taiwan.

By 1982, with the 1997 deadline for the New Territories lease on the horizon, China publicly communicated its intention to expand negotiations so as to include the island of Hong Kong itself. Thatcher, flush with success in the Falklands, had adopted an entrenched position against any surrender of British sovereignty – especially regarding Hong Kong proper.

Thatcher was also resolutely opposed to relegating British citizens to rule by the Communist Party. Given her belief that any communist system – Chinese, Soviet or other – subverted individual freedom, she felt that Beijing could not be relied upon to uphold the rights of Hong Kong citizens. On one occasion, she complained to me of the great cruelty of which Deng Xiaoping was capable;[56] during another meeting in Hong Kong (held on a private plane to avoid eavesdropping), she left me with no doubt regarding her negative view of the Chinese leadership as a whole.

But Thatcher's political choices were limited. Unlike the Falklands, there was no possibility of a military solution; against the People's Liberation Army, Hong Kong was indefensible. A solution would have to be found through negotiation; lurking in the background, however, was the fact that, should the two parties reach a stalemate, China had the power to settle the question unilaterally.

Thatcher's tactic was to hold flexibility in reserve. In early conversations, she avoided discussing sovereignty, instead seeking a Chinese pledge that Britain would continue to administer Hong Kong. This arrangement, she argued, was the only way to retain the confidence of international business, which was vital to Hong Kong's prosperity at the time and would continue to be essential after 1997.

In September 1982, Thatcher carried these sentiments with her to Beijing. But in strained meetings with Deng and Prime Minister (and later General Secretary of the Communist Party) Zhao Ziyang, she received a lesson in Chinese realities. Both publicly and privately, she was informed not only that the issue of sovereignty was non-negotiable, but also that continued British administration was out of the question. Beijing would permit Hong Kong's capitalist system to endure, but only under Chinese auspices. As one British official later noted, for the Chinese, 'If it came to the crunch, sovereignty took priority over prosperity.'[57]

There were few straws here at which Thatcher might grasp. Leaving her meeting with Deng, she stumbled down the steps of the Great Hall of the People. Chinese superstition held this to be a bad omen. Within ten days, the Hong Kong stock market had fallen by around 25 percent.

Thatcher's initial response was to dig in deeper, as I witnessed during a working dinner at 10 Downing Street that November. The meeting's purpose was to seek my views on how the British 'might best play our hand in our negotiations with the Chinese on the future of Hong Kong'.[58]

As I recall it, however, the substance of the discussion was rather different. Although British officials must have previously informed Thatcher of their view that sovereignty over Hong Kong would have to be ceded, she certainly did not show an awareness of it. Initially, she rejected the cession of sovereignty out of hand, adamantly asserting that she would never give up Hong Kong. Her every instinct militated against surrendering the island, with its unique British-Chinese way of life. Her first modification of that position was that Britain would negotiate only over the New Territories, where, in contrast to its freehold over Hong Kong, Britain maintained only a leasehold whose deadline was approaching.

Our dinner companions on this occasion included Foreign Secretary Pym, Foreign Office Permanent Under-Secretary Sir Antony Acland and Governor of Hong Kong Sir Edward Youde. The diplomats took on Thatcher's arguments. I admired their studied persistence as wave after wave of prime ministerial vehemence broke across the dinner table. Neither the Foreign Office contingent nor Youde flinched. While I did not participate in the internal British debate, I did reply to Thatcher's question regarding possible autonomy. Reflecting my discussions with Deng, I noted that China might have an interest in preserving some autonomy for Hong Kong, in order to establish the credibility of the One Country, Two Systems principle for the future of Taiwan. But Deng would not, in my opinion, yield on the principle of sovereignty. Much of the evening had gone by before, gradually, a few glimpses of prime-ministerial retreat could be made out. By the end of the meal, Thatcher had very reluctantly conceded that the whole package would be up for discussion, that is to say, that the future of Hong Kong island and Kowloon could be negotiated together with that of the New Territories.

I recall this dinner as a distillation of Thatcher's evolution during the Hong Kong negotiations. As with the Falklands crisis, she sought to avoid concessions of any kind, yet ultimately agreed to explore them. This time, the difference was that her concessions were not just tactical maneuvers against a ham-fisted enemy, and in Hong Kong no British fleet could save the day.

In March 1983, Thatcher made her decision. She wrote privately to Zhao that she was prepared to recommend to the British parliament that sovereignty over the entirety of Hong Kong revert to China – if an agreement could be reached between Britain and China on future administrative arrangements to ensure Hong Kong's prosperity and stability. This correspondence cleared the way for formal talks that would require successive, hard-fought concessions, including British acceptance of the Chinese condition that the British administrative link to Hong Kong be entirely severed in 1997.

In her memoirs, Thatcher recalled a conversation with Deng Xiaoping that reveals the tense nature of their negotiations:

> He said that the Chinese could walk in and take Hong Kong back later today if they wanted to. I retorted that they could indeed do so; I could not stop them. But this would bring about Hong Kong's collapse. The world would then see what followed a change from British to Chinese rule . . . For the first time, he seemed taken aback.[59]

In December 1984, Thatcher and Zhao signed the Sino-British Declaration under the terms of which the transfer of sovereignty would occur on June 30, 1997. The treaty dealt not only with the fixed conditions of sovereignty but, uniquely, with a fifty-year process through which the territory would transform itself from a British possession into a theoretically autonomous component of the Chinese state. With the completion of the handover, the agreement stipulated, China's sovereignty over Hong Kong would coexist with the contingent and subjective condition of 'autonomy' for a fifty-year period. Yet in any clash between the two, Chinese sovereignty was bound to prevail. The functional success of the fifty-year Hong Kong agreement thus depended on the perception that all parties were pursuing its terms.

But the perceptions of the two parties differed even as the agreement was drafted, and their differences only congealed with the passage of time. Whether at the end of the fifty-year autonomy period the ultimate transition would be smooth depended on whether Chinese evolution to that point was reconcilable with the British legacy. China for its part was unlikely to accept the final return of Hong Kong with political institutions that it considered vestiges of colonialism.

The interim preservation of Hong Kong's institutions ensured some level of democratic participation for its residents and restored confidence in its financial center, the foundation of the territory's wealth. Although the agreement was certainly not what Thatcher wanted, she had judged the situation reasonably. A harder line would have risked consigning the British to irrelevance; a more accommodating approach would likely have undermined all Hong Kong's hope for autonomy.

For the British negotiators, Thatcher's reputation for intransigence was a considerable asset. Experienced negotiators cannot but welcome to their side an apparently unreasonable third party with whom any deal must pass muster. Thatcher played this role skillfully, allowing her negotiators to reassure their Chinese counterparts of their own desire to agree on particular points while citing their terror of running afoul of a formidable prime minister – whose convictions on the subject were well known.

Thatcher's method – public intransigence to strengthen the hand of her negotiators, paired with private dialogue to ensure the two sides' common interest in a prosperous Hong Kong – maintained a measure of British influence over a tenuous situation. Her stance also showed that, even in disputes where Britain held the far weaker hand, there was a point beyond which it could not be pushed. In the final years of British administration, after she had left office, she returned to Hong Kong often and strongly supported Chris Patten, the last British governor of Hong Kong, in his efforts to embed more representative institutions and processes in the colony before it was handed over.

Diplomatic agreements are often completed with assurances of their longevity. The evolution of Hong Kong's autonomy did not fulfill British expectations. Thatcher and her chief negotiators were deeply committed to preserving British-type institutions and concepts of legal process, and they pursued them with skill and Thatcherian determination. They achieved a definition of autonomy that lasted for twenty-two of its stipulated fifty years. The arrangement on autonomy ended because the Chinese domestic evolution diverged increasingly from the expectations that had predominated when the concept of One Country, Two Systems was formulated by Deng. And in any handover of colonial territory, the recipient country is more focused on its own trajectory than on a legacy from the colonizers.

In this conflict between sovereignty and autonomy, the latter has been severely curtailed. The uncertainties that now loom over Hong Kong's future recall Thatcher's warning to Deng: where freedom is threatened, can economic dynamism long endure? Other questions inexorably follow. When agreements are prematurely abrogated, can strategic trust remain? Will the evolution of Hong Kong further strain tensions between China and the Western democracies? Or will a way be found by which Hong Kong can have a place in a dialogue over world order and political coexistence?

CONFRONTING A LEGACY OF VIOLENCE: NORTHERN IRELAND

No affair of state touched Margaret Thatcher more directly than the conflict in Northern Ireland, the six counties that remained part of the United Kingdom after Ireland was partitioned in 1921. Paradoxically, however, no major issue during her premiership provoked as much self-doubt.

Thatcher refused to submit to the intimidation tactics of the Irish Republican Army (IRA), frustrating its demand that Northern Ireland be absorbed into the Republic of Ireland (which consisted of the twenty-six southern counties). Through summit diplomacy, she mended relations between Britain and the Republic of Ireland to a great degree. In 1985, she secured the landmark Anglo-Irish Agreement, aimed at working toward an end to the 'Troubles': the violent, decades-long conflict between Northern Ireland's mainly Protestant Unionists and the mainly Catholic Nationalists.

Thatcher's actions were even more striking considering that, only weeks before she became prime minister in May 1979, Airey Neave, the man who would have been her secretary of state for Northern Ireland, was assassinated by an IRA splinter group. The murder of this close personal friend and hero of the Second World War reaffirmed Thatcher's basic instincts concerning how to approach Northern Ireland: reinforcing security while pressing the Irish Republic to combat terrorism. She understood that terrorists were following a strategic logic. Reflecting on the situation later, she defined her understanding of their approach as 'the calculated use of violence – and the threat of it – to achieve political ends', specifying: 'In the case of the IRA those ends are the coercion of the majority of the people of Northern Ireland, who have demonstrated their wish to remain within the United Kingdom, into an all-Ireland state.'[60]

In Northern Ireland as elsewhere, terrorism was the method of the weak. The IRA's supporters were a minority of a minority, seeking by use of spectacular violence to provoke the British government into either granting concessions or lashing out in a brutal overreaction that would drive the Catholic minority in Northern Ireland further into the Nationalist camp. Neave's killing failed to shake Thatcher, whose sympathies remained firmly with Northern Ireland's Protestant and Unionist majority – a view reinforced by her lingering grudge against the Republic of Ireland for its neutrality during the Second World War.[61]

On August 27, 1979, the IRA subjected the new prime minister to two additional tests, first by killing eighteen British soldiers in an ambush outside the Northern Irish town of Warrenpoint, and then by assassinating Lord Mountbatten, the Queen's cousin and former chief of the defence staff. The victims of the latter attack included not only Mountbatten, but also his fourteen-year-old grandson, his fifteen-year-old boatman and the Dowager Lady Brabourne. Though she mourned the dead, Thatcher refused to be provoked. Instead, she authorized her government to continue its regular meetings with the Irish government in pursuit of a peaceful outcome.

A year later, the IRA would throw another wrench into these ongoing negotiations. On October 27, 1980, IRA inmates in Northern Ireland's Maze prison launched a hunger strike. Protests of one form or another had been ongoing since 1976, when the Labour government had stripped these prisoners of the 'special-category status' that Heath had granted them two years earlier. Perhaps the prisoners now hoped that Thatcher would follow the example of her Conservative predecessor, but she immediately grasped what was at stake: acceding to the inmates' demand to be treated as 'political prisoners' would legitimate their cause and complicate effective control of the prison.[62]

When the UK's foreign-intelligence service (MI6) quietly reactivated its secret link with the IRA in early December 1980, it learned that some IRA leaders favored an end to the strike. This information was passed to Thatcher. While she was not willing to speak with the IRA directly, she said that if the hunger strike ended, she was prepared to extend 'humanitarian' concessions – such as the freedom to associate on weekends and wear 'civilian-type clothing' during the workday – to *all* prisoners in Northern Ireland, whether IRA or not.[63] On December 18, the prisoners called off their strike, and Thatcher's government duly announced the new measures. No prisoners had died as a result of the strike, and Thatcher's reputation for steadiness under pressure emerged enhanced.

But the calm was not to last. On March 1, 1981, Bobby Sands, the twenty-six-year-old leader of the Maze's IRA prisoners, announced another hunger strike, reiterating their demand that IRA inmates be treated as political prisoners. Thatcher was unimpressed. 'There is no such thing as political murder, political bombing, or political violence,' Thatcher said in a speech in Belfast on March 5, insisting, 'There is only criminal murder, criminal bombing and criminal violence. We will not compromise on this. There will be no political status.'[64] The battle lines were drawn.

Then, in a stroke of extraordinary luck for the IRA, a parliamentary seat opened up in a heavily Nationalist constituency in Northern Ireland. Sands declared his candidacy and, from his prison cell, became the first candidate affiliated with the Nationalist party Sinn Féin to win a seat in the UK Parliament since 1955. When the second hunger strike culminated in his death on May 5, riots broke out across Northern Ireland, and pressure mounted on Thatcher's government. Tens of thousands attended Sands' funeral in Belfast.

The hunger strike by other prisoners continued throughout the summer. Despite additional pressure from the Catholic Church and US House Speaker Tip O'Neill, Thatcher maintained her position, which enjoyed broad support from the British public. Pressed about Sands' fate during question time in the House of Commons, she replied, acidly: 'Mr Sands was a convicted criminal. He chose to take his own life. It was a choice that his organization did not allow to many of its victims.'[65] In total, ten prisoners died before those remaining gave up on October 3. With great steeliness, Thatcher had sacrificed compassion to duty.

Ireland, a non-permanent member of the UN Security Council from 1981 to 1982, had damaged relations with the United Kingdom by stridently criticizing the Falklands War at the UN. Nevertheless, Thatcher authorized the senior civil service to pursue confidence-building negotiations. Ireland's Dermot Nally and Britain's Robert Armstrong, the cabinet secretaries of their respective countries, led the steering committee of the Anglo-Irish Intergovernmental Council, which had been set up by Thatcher and her Irish counterpart in 1981. Nally and Armstrong's doggedness and dedication helped carry the relationship through its rough patches. Little was achieved at first, but after the June 1983 elections widened the Conservative majority in parliament, Thatcher and the Irish taoiseach (prime minister), Garret FitzGerald, communicated regularly, allowing them to overcome challenges such as the escape of thirty-eight prisoners from the Maze in September and the IRA's bombing of Harrods central London department store in December, which killed six people, including three police officers, and injured ninety others.

When another IRA-planted bomb ripped through Brighton's Grand Hotel in the early morning hours of October 12, 1984, Thatcher was awake in her suite, having just finished editing her address for the next day's Conservative Party conference. Unhurt but caked in dust, she changed into a navy suit and by 4 a.m. was speaking to the cameras. 'The conference will go on, as usual,' she informed the nation.[66] Her presence at the lectern the following afternoon was proof of the attack's failure:

> It was an attempt not only to disrupt and terminate our conference; it was
> an attempt to cripple Her Majesty's democratically-elected government.
> That is the scale of the outrage in which we have all shared, and the fact
> that we are gathered here now – shocked, but composed and determined –
> is a sign not only that this attack has failed but that all attempts to destroy
> democracy by terrorism will fail.[67]

Proceeding to thank the first responders who had raced to the scene, Thatcher expressed her sympathy for those who were suffering and then, in typically no-nonsense style, announced that her speech would cover 'business as usual': 'one or two matters of foreign affairs', as well as two economic topics 'selected for special consideration – unemployment and the miners' strike'.[68] Immediately after her address, she visited the bombing victims who had been hospitalized.

'Today we were unlucky,' the IRA said in its statement claiming responsibility for the attack, 'but remember, we have only to be lucky once. You will have to be lucky always.'[69] Five people were killed in the attack, including one MP, and thirty were injured, some very seriously. Had the bombers possessed more accurate intelligence about her location, the prime minister would likely have been among them.

Thatcher refused to permit the IRA's attempt on her life to jeopardize negotiations with the Republic of Ireland. After a brief pause, the summits resumed. By July 25, 1985, the British cabinet had approved a draft of the Anglo-Irish Agreement. The basic formula was for Britain to permit a formal consultative role for Ireland in the affairs of Northern Ireland in exchange for Dublin's agreement to temper its ambition to reclaim the province (which had been codified in Articles 2 and 3 of the 1937 Irish Constitution).

In signing the agreement, FitzGerald and Thatcher were acknowledging reality. Ireland formally agreed that 'any change in the status of Northern Ireland would only come about with the consent of a majority of the people of Northern Ireland', noting that at present this same majority favored remaining in the United Kingdom.[70] Britain agreed that, due to the province's significant Catholic minority, the Irish Republic would be given an opportunity to exert a significant influence in Northern Ireland. The agreement's importance lay in its directing Ireland's influence into legitimate channels – such as the new Intergovernmental Conference – without undermining British sovereignty.

The House of Commons approved the agreement by a vote of 473 to 47 – demonstrating British support as overwhelming as the Northern Irish Unionists' rejection of it. Thatcher and FitzGerald officially signed the document at Hillsborough Castle in Northern Ireland on November 15, 1985. Over the following months, the Protestant-majority counties of Ulster erupted in demonstrations, reserving the choicest venom for Thatcher.* Northern Irish Unionists in the British parliament collectively resigned their seats in protest. Meanwhile, Dublin's supporters in Washington cheered the British concession of a formal consultative role for the Republic of Ireland in Northern Irish affairs. It was not for nothing that Thatcher later confided to FitzGerald: 'You've got the glory, and I've got the problems.'[71]

Although the agreement permanently lifted Anglo-Irish relations into a friendlier stratum, it failed to curtail the IRA's violence, which intensified during the late 1980s and continued unabated into the early 1990s. Reflecting on Ireland in her memoirs, Thatcher characterized her approach as 'disappointing'. 'Our concessions alienated the Unionists without gaining the level of security cooperation we had a right to expect,' she wrote in 1993, concluding, 'In the light of this experience it is surely time to consider an alternative approach.'[72]

---

* Ian Paisley, leader of Democratic Ulster Unionists, publicly compared her to 'a Jezebel who sought to destroy Israel in a day' and prayed out loud: 'O God, in wrath take vengeance upon this wicked, treacherous, lying woman!' Even Enoch Powell, who had greatly admired Thatcher's stance on the Falklands, and whose good opinion mattered to her, asked her if she understood 'that the penalty for treachery is to fall into public contempt'. (See Moore, *Margaret Thatcher: At Her Zenith*, 333–8.)

Peace was not finally achieved in the province until the Good Friday Agreement of 1998. This successor accord to Thatcher's Anglo-Irish Agreement was much more ambitious, yet it stoked less Unionist rancor, with three of the four important Unionist parties agreeing to it.* The agreement established a devolved legislature and power-sharing executive in Northern Ireland, guaranteeing that both Nationalists and Unionists would be represented in the regional government. And, in accordance with its side of the agreement, the Republic of Ireland removed the territorial claim to Northern Ireland from its constitution.

Thatcher's Irish legacy is rife with ironies. She never developed her own distinct vision for Northern Ireland, allowing the negotiations to be led by Robert Armstrong, the cabinet secretary, to whom she delegated the task, yet the Anglo-Irish Agreement was a major diplomatic achievement. The agreement would not have been possible had she not kept Unionist leaders in the dark about the substance of the negotiations – which, had they known, would likely have led to a Protestant workers' strike and paralyzed the province.[73]

In the end, the peace she sought came by way of direct talks among Northern Ireland's factions – negotiations for which Thatcher's labors had helped establish the necessary conditions. Thus, the regret she later expressed over the policy her government carried out across the Irish Sea seems unwarranted. Her vision approached the limits of the possible in a region so deeply divided along religious lines and so indelibly stamped by a bitter legacy of violence. Despite seemingly insurmountable challenges, she laid the foundations for a generation of relative peace in Northern Ireland.

FUNDAMENTAL TRUTHS: THE 'SPECIAL RELATIONSHIP' AND THE COLD WAR

In Thatcher's time, East–West relations were debated largely in terms of absolutes. For realists, the Cold War would end by convincing Soviet

---

* The fourth Unionist party, Paisley's Democratic Unionists, formally opposed the Good Friday Agreement but continued to take part in elections and has been the most electorally successful party in Northern Ireland. Two Nationalist parties, including Sinn Féin, also signed the agreement.

leaders that their efforts to divide and defeat the NATO alliance were futile. Idealists, for their part, insisted that the issue was ideological; communism would be defeated when its philosophy was proven intellectually bankrupt and politically fruitless.

Thatcher had a major influence on the outcome of the Cold War by synthesizing the realists' and idealists' competing truths. She insisted on the overriding importance of national defense, an independent nuclear deterrent and allied cohesion – principles from which she never deviated – but her thought evolved to include a conviction that peace could best be preserved and Western values vindicated by exploring coexistence with the USSR. She was never tempted by prospects of appeasement; the child of a generation that had drawn lessons from Munich, she sought to combine strong defense with constructive negotiations. Further, she understood the importance of public diplomacy, receiving an enthusiastic popular welcome on official visits to Eastern bloc countries such as Hungary and Poland.

The management of East–West relations – the central foreign-policy challenge of Thatcher's age – required a broader approach than was needed with respect to the Falklands or Hong Kong, where her leadership was primarily aimed at protecting British concerns. In her early days as Conservative leader, her governing premise was that the Soviets posed a growing threat to the West. In early 1976, three years before she became prime minister, she castigated the Soviets in a manner that raised eyebrows. 'The Russians are bent on world dominance,' she insisted, 'and they are rapidly acquiring the means to become the most powerful imperial nation the world has seen.' Instead of seeking a relaxation of tensions, she argued, Moscow was engaged in a military build-up, expanding its influence around the globe in a manner that 'threatens our whole way of life'. She continued by warning that the Soviets' 'advance is not irreversible, providing that we take the necessary measures now'.[74]

In this rousing call to arms, Thatcher was laying out a personal manifesto for the Cold War. She included a searing judgment of Soviet leadership:

> The men in the Soviet politburo don't have to worry about the ebb and flow of public opinion. They put guns before butter, while we put just about everything before guns. They know that they are a superpower in

only one sense – the military sense. They are a failure in human and economic terms.[75]

Red Star, the newspaper of the Soviet Ministry of Defense, responded by calling Thatcher an 'Iron Lady'. The nickname, intended as an unflattering comparison with Bismarck, backfired; indeed, the history of propaganda offers few own goals as spectacular and long-lasting. Thatcher seized on the intended slur as a badge of honor, and the phrase became a defining sobriquet. Three years before she was elected prime minister, the Soviet Union had inadvertently elevated a previously obscure Opposition leader into a figure of global significance.

Thatcher's opposition to the Soviet Union derived not only from Britain's fear of Soviet aggression; it was more deeply rooted in a pronounced moral objection to state control and the negation of human dignity that were inherent in the communist system. In her youth, she had been profoundly affected by the imposition of the Iron Curtain. The formation of satellite states orbiting the Soviet sun had reinforced her view of East–West relations as a defining struggle between tyranny and liberty. The doctrine publicly outlined in 1968 by Soviet Communist Party leader Leonid Brezhnev asserted a Soviet right to defend embattled communist parties anywhere – and especially the totalitarian rulers of Eastern Europe – against their own people.[76] As Thatcher was wont to remind her audiences, Brezhnev had described his position with brutal honesty, maintaining that the 'total triumph of socialism all over the world is inevitable'.[77] Thatcher never hesitated to contrast this overweening ambition with the record of the West:

> We do not aim at domination, at hegemony, in any part of the world . . .
> Of course, we are ready to fight the battle of ideas with all the vigor at our
> command, but we do not try to impose our system on others.[78]

Thatcher understood that rhetoric alone would not end the Cold War or keep the West united. East–West relations would need to be reshaped – a task inconceivable without the support and leadership of the United States. This was perhaps chief among the many reasons for her fundamental commitment to reinvigorating transatlantic ties – the heart of her foreign policy.

In September 1975, shortly after she became party leader, Thatcher visited the United States. On American soil, she stressed the shared ideals – particularly the exercise of individual freedom – that under-pinned her vision of the relationship between the two countries. In a speech at Washington's National Press Club, she sought to shake off the pessimism that threatened to paralyze the free world, rallying spirits with a message based on both morality and efficacy:

> My real reason for believing in the future of Britain and America is because freedom under the law, the essence of our constitutions, is some-thing that both honors human dignity and at the same time provides the economic opportunity to bring greater prosperity to our people – a per-sonal prosperity based on individual choice. In short, it works incomparably better than other systems.[79]

The principal 'other' system to which she referred was, of course, communism. Her thinking about the Cold War thus combined an under-standing of the primacy of American power with a strong conviction that Britain, which had provided ballast to the occasionally fluctuating character of American foreign policy for more than forty years, could still play a vital international role.

Britain's international posture had long been defined by both a clear-eyed assessment of human nature in the raw and a high estimation of its own contributions to history.[80]

In the British political tradition, the concept of balance of power was treated as axiomatic. The British leaders of the nineteenth and early twentieth centuries – the high point of British influence – recognized the importance of maintaining alliances in at least part of the European continent, as well as bases in other parts of the world. They did not hesi-tate to intervene where they felt it was necessary to vindicate their multi-polar conception of international order.[81] This, together with Brit-ain's preponderant naval power, had engendered in its citizens a global perspective and in its politicians an ethos of permanent engagement abroad.[82] In contrast, the American perspective until the end of the Second World War had been to view foreign-policy achievements as dis-connected, practical 'solutions' without prescriptive value for the future. From this faith there developed an avoidance of permanent responsibili-ties and vacillation in external commitments.

On assuming office, Thatcher was determined to reassert the ear-lier theme of partnership, best exemplified by Anglo-American solidarity in the Second World War. She was prepared to support American diplomatic efforts in the Cold War, but she also insisted that the British government provide input on the direction of US policy. To this end, she supported President Carter's response to the Soviet invasion of Afghanistan in December 1979. But it was during the Reagan presidency that a true partnership developed and flourished.

Reagan's approach to the Soviets was the essence of simplicity: 'We win, they lose.'[83] Thatcher's view was more nuanced, but she nonetheless admired the assertiveness, energy and optimism Reagan brought to the struggle. Above all, she shared his commitment to democratic values. She encouraged him as best she could, while Reagan, for his part, understood the value of advice from a trusted and ideologically compatible outsider.

Communist doctrines continued to dominate Soviet policy, with the invasion of Afghanistan in December 1979 serving as a reminder of ongoing adventurism. Thatcher remained focused on the importance of a strong national defense and bolstering NATO's cohesion. She supported Reagan's efforts to strengthen the Alliance's credibility.

In 1982, Thatcher persuaded Reagan to supply Britain with the new Trident II submarine-launched ballistic missile on favorable financial terms, hoping to guarantee the future of Britain's independent nuclear deterrent. With the same convictions she helped guide NATO's response to the Soviet deployment of intermediate-range SS-20 missiles aimed at Europe and the consequent debate within the Alliance over accepting US Pershing and cruise missiles as a counterforce. By November 14, 1983, American intermediate-range cruise missiles were arriving in Britain; such weapons would also be sent to West Germany later that month. Thatcher's advocacy for an effective counterforce to the Soviet missile deployment had borne fruit.

Although the anti-nuclear movement had suffered a tactical defeat, it found an improbable sympathizer in Reagan; the president, who once described nuclear weapons as 'totally irrational, totally inhumane, [and] good for nothing but killing', harbored an unshakable distaste for them. His greatest obligation as president, he believed, was to bring about a world free of nuclear weapons. In March 1983, to the astonishment of the world, Reagan announced the Strategic Defense Initiative (SDI), a plan to develop a defensive shield of space-based weapons capable of intercepting and disabling incoming Soviet intercontinental ballistic missiles (ICBMs). In Reagan's words, SDI would help the world 'begin to achieve our ultimate goal of eliminating the threat posed by strategic nuclear missiles'.[84]

Thatcher harbored doubts about whether the SDI system was technologically feasible or could achieve the grand potential Reagan had assigned to it. She feared Reagan's plan was getting beyond a reasonable scope and directed her efforts to what she viewed as the more practical task of assuring Europe's defense. Further, she feared that even an imperfect SDI system might undermine the rationale for Britain's independent nuclear deterrent.

Navigating between Reagan's personal commitment and her own doubts, Thatcher opted, not for the first time, for constructive ambiguity. In public, she took pains to praise SDI – although she kept her focus firmly confined to the research component, which she supported as a matter of principle. She viewed the actual deployment of SDI, a more controversial matter, to be relegated to the distant future, and a subject for eventual negotiation within the Alliance and with the Soviet Union.

In candid exchanges with Reagan at Camp David in December 1984, she made clear her concerns. Although Reagan had no intention of retreating from his fundamental view, he offered one crucial concession. In a press statement at the conclusion of their meeting, Thatcher announced Reagan's concurrence that 'SDI-related testing and deployment would, in view of treaty obligations, have to be a matter for negotiation.'[85] The Pentagon bitterly opposed this promise, which went beyond anything to which the administration had previously agreed. But this measure not only offered a degree of reassurance to anxious NATO members, it also demonstrated the enduring closeness of the US–UK relationship. More than any other European leader, Thatcher saw it as her task to interpret between allies on both sides of the Atlantic. At the same time, she continued to back increased defense spending at home.

Thatcher's attitude toward SDI reflected the ambivalence of the European allies combined with special British circumstances. All NATO allies relied on the American nuclear guarantee while fearing a nuclear war that might devastate their territories. They were uneasy about any new weapons system that might limit American readiness to fulfill its guarantee or affect the nuclear equation. Thatcher's special concern derived from her commitment to protecting Britain's independent nuclear deterrent. The development of nuclear weapons in the United States had occurred with the cooperation of the British science community during the Second World War. Britain therefore had a moral claim to American assistance in its determination to develop nuclear weapons of its own or to acquire nuclear weapons from America. In September 1944, Roosevelt and Churchill had made a secret agreement at Hyde Park, New York, to continue cooperation on nuclear affairs after the war. After some turbulence in the relationship in the immediate postwar period, in 1958 the two countries concluded the US–UK Mutual Defense Agreement, which remains the gold standard for nuclear-weapons cooperation among states. The US agreed to supply nuclear weapons to the Royal Air Force until the British nuclear deterrent was of sufficient size, cooperate with Britain on nuclear submarine technology and allow transfers of enriched uranium and plutonium. The treaty remains in place.

The British commitment to a nuclear role was constant in every cabinet of both parties. It gave Britain a capacity to resist nuclear blackmail, as happened when the Soviet Union implied a nuclear threat during the Suez crisis in 1956. It also gave Britain the capacity to negotiate competently in arms-control discussions. On the American side, the attitude was not always uniformly shared, due to US concerns about nuclear proliferation. Nonetheless, a minority of us believed that a British nuclear capability was in the American long-term interest because it bolstered a partner on the other side of the Atlantic that had a historical record of shared objectives. It also increased Soviet difficulty in attempting to read, or anticipate, NATO's reaction in a potential crisis.

A PROBLEM IN GRENADA

Thatcher's desire for close Anglo-American relations did not override defending British interests even against Reagan, despite her high regard for him. A dramatic example came in October 1983 following the US invasion of the Caribbean island of Grenada. After a hardline Marxist faction seized power on the island, which was a member of the British Commonwealth, the Reagan administration sought to reverse the coup through military intervention. As early soundings suggested that the British would oppose such a course, the White House chose to exclude

Thatcher from its deliberations. She was told of American plans only hours before they were executed.

Grenada had shed its status as a British colony after choosing independence in February 1974. Because it remained within the Commonwealth, however, the Queen continued as its head of state, and the British government still felt a sense of responsibility for its sovereignty. A more searing objection was the humiliation Thatcher felt on discovering that her closest ally had acted against a Commonwealth nation without meaningful consultation. Worse, the invasion occurred mere days before US intermediate-range nuclear missiles were due to be deployed in Britain. If the US could not be trusted to consult Britain prior to the invasion of a small Caribbean island, how could it be relied upon to confer regarding the use of missiles on British soil?

Rejecting a charm-laden apology from Reagan, she made the disagreement public: 'We in the Western countries, the Western democracies, use our force to defend our way of life ... [not] to walk into other people's countries,' she told the BBC, pulling no punches as she explained, 'If you are pronouncing a new law that wherever Communism reigns ... there the United States shall enter, then we are going to have really terrible wars in the world.'[86] Thatcher's comments prompted a note from US national security advisor, Robert 'Bud' McFarlane, to the British cabinet secretary deploring her statement as 'unusually harsh' and stressing the administration's 'profound disappointment' at her stance.[87]

Meanwhile, events in Grenada moved apace. Within four days of the October 25 invasion, the Americans had deposed Grenada's ruling military junta; by December, the US had withdrawn from the island altogether. The pre-revolutionary constitution had been restored, and democratic elections were on the horizon.

Having reminded the US administration not to take Britain for granted, Thatcher chose not to allow the Grenada upset to linger. The deployment of intermediate-range missiles on British soil proceeded.

A STRATEGIC SHIFT: EAST–WEST ENGAGEMENT

In December 1983, four days before Christmas, Thatcher invited me to dinner at 10 Downing Street. Although we did not dwell on recent events in the Caribbean, I found her dispirited by the state of East–West relations. Moscow seemed 'rudderless', she said, observing that she could scarcely recall 'a situation where there was at once so much uncertainty and so little contact'.[88]

That September, the Soviets had shot down a South Korean civilian airliner (KAL Flight 007) that had inadvertently strayed into their airspace. Moscow's callous response to the tragedy heightened tensions and convinced the West that there was little to be gained from dialogue with Soviet General Secretary Yuri Andropov, whose health was known to be failing. In November, as US intermediate-range missiles began arriving on European soil, the Soviets had walked out of the Geneva arms-control negotiations. Soviet isolation had become as complete as Soviet intransigence.

Responding to Thatcher's disquiet that night at dinner, I asked whether she intended to urge a new East–West dialogue, and if so, how best to initiate it. As it turned out, her mind was already moving in that direction.

In the dying days of the Brezhnev era, when the Soviet gerontocracy was at its most rigid, Thatcher had consciously eschewed engagement. Only after her second electoral victory in June 1983 did she begin a formal reassessment of East–West relations and start to move toward it.

Over the weekend of September 8, Thatcher hosted a seminar of Soviet scholars at Chequers, the prime minister's official country residence. The meeting's stated purpose was ambitious: 'to consider the Government's strategy in international affairs with a view to establishing clear aims for the next few years'.[89] The Foreign Office initially attempted to staff the retreat with experienced hands from its own ranks, but Thatcher would have none of it. As she wrote in response to the proposed list of attendees, 'I want . . . some people who have really studied Russia – the Russian mind – and who have some experience of living there. More than half the people on the list know less than I do.'[90] In the end, eight Soviet specialists – all but one of them university professors – were invited. One attendee, Archie Brown, a lecturer on Soviet institutions at Oxford, suggested that Thatcher make contact with a promising leader in the younger echelon of Soviet leadership such as Mikhail Gorbachev, whom he described as 'the best-educated member of the Politburo and probably the most open-minded'.[91]

Thatcher was receptive to this proposal; the official record of the seminar noted: 'It was agreed that the aim should be to build up contacts slowly over the next few years.'[92]

When Thatcher visited Reagan in Washington later in September, she shared her thinking. While we should not 'deceive ourselves about the true Soviet character', she told the president; 'at the same time we must live on the same planet with the Soviets. Therefore the key question is what will be our future relations.' She favored establishing 'normal relations'. Reagan replied that he shared her views.[93]

Like Thatcher, Reagan had come into office determined to confront the Soviets. But unlike many of his supporters – and some of his staffers – his aversion to nuclear weapons made him favorably disposed to arms-control negotiations. As early as March 1981, shortly after surviving an assassination attempt, Reagan had written to Brezhnev from the hospital to suggest opening a dialogue.

George Shultz, who became secretary of state in July 1982, encouraged such a connection. The following February, at Shultz's urging, and in the face of vehement opposition from his national security advisor and secretary of defense, Reagan agreed to meet with Soviet Ambassador Anatoly Dobrynin. 'Some of the N.S.C. [National Security Council] staff are too hard-line & don't think any approach should be made to the Soviets,' Reagan wrote in his diary that April. 'I think I'm hard-line & will never appease,' Reagan continued, 'but I do want to try & let them see there is a better world if they'll show by deed they want to get along with the free world.'[94]

Thatcher, who fully agreed with this sentiment, sought to cultivate it within the Reagan administration. A more constructive relationship with the Soviet Union, however, required a willing partner in Moscow. Andropov's death in February 1984 propelled Konstantin Chernenko to the leadership, but the seventy-two-year-old apparatchik, who suffered from emphysema and a heart condition, gave Thatcher little reason to hope for an immediate improvement in relations.

Thatcher's crucial insight was to set aside Chernenko and his generation and look instead to the ranks of their likely successors. At her direction, the British Foreign Office developed a shortlist consisting of three younger members of the Politburo – Grigory Romanov, Viktor Grishin and Mikhail Gorbachev. Inviting Gorbachev, to whom she had already been alerted, made the most sense given his position as chairman of the Foreign Relations Committee of the Soviet legisla-ture.[95] With Chernenko still head of state, diplomatic protocol had to be observed. Thatcher arranged for Gorbachev to be invited to Britain as head of a visiting Soviet parliamentary delegation, a suitably innocuous overture that would allow her to meet him and take his measure.

Accepting, Gorbachev arrived in Britain with his wife, Raisa, in December 1984. Over lunch at Chequers, he and Thatcher entered into a robust argument over the relative benefits of capitalist versus com-munist systems. The record of their private conversation recounts that Thatcher 'did not wish to have the power to direct everyone where he or she should work and what he or she should receive'. Gorbachev replied that he 'understood the British system, but the Soviet system was superior'.[96] The discussion continued in this vein, with neither partici-pant giving ground. As their meeting drew to a close, no new initiatives or agreements had emerged. Notwithstanding the apparent impasse, however, this lunch would prove to be one of the most consequential meetings of Thatcher's premiership.

As she later wrote, Thatcher recognized that, while Gorbachev's remarks parroted familiar Marxist dogma, 'his personality could not have been more different from the wooden ventriloquism of the average Soviet apparatchik'. Later in the day, Thatcher 'came to understand that it was the style far more than the Marxist rhetoric which expressed the substance of the personality beneath'.[97] She sensed that Gorbachev was inherently more flexible than his predecessors. And, as usual, she did not hesitate to make her views known. 'I am cautiously optimistic,' she told the BBC the next day, adding, in a remark which became famous, 'I like Mr Gorbachev. We can do business together.'[98]

But at a Camp David visit with Reagan that December, she adopted a cautious tone. Yes, Gorbachev was charming and 'open to discussion and debate', White House records of the meeting recount, but Thatcher also mused, 'the more charming the adversary, the more dangerous'.[99] Yet this concern did not detract from her central conclusion. As Reagan later put it, 'She told me that she believed that there was a chance for a great opening. Of course, she was proven exactly right.'[100]

After Gorbachev became general secretary following Chernenko's death in March 1985, support grew for Thatcher's positive evaluation of the new Soviet leader – as did pressure on Reagan to participate in an early summit with him. Hardliners in the Reagan administration argued strongly against this course. Insisting that unremitting pressure would eventually cause the Soviet system to crash, they argued that through dialogue much Allied cohesion could be lost. Taking up the other side of the argument, Shultz sought to reinforce Reagan's instinctive desire to meet with the new Soviet leader.

My own view, as expressed to Thatcher, was that Reagan's efforts to build US strength and gain Soviet respect during his first term had put him in a strong negotiating position in his second.[101] By the early summer, Reagan had made up his mind, announcing plans for a summit with Gorbachev in Geneva that November. It proved to be a turning point. In the best tradition of the 'special relationship', Margaret Thatcher served as a trusted partner and counselor, providing the administration with independent and well-informed judgment. Reagan based much of his negotiating approach at Geneva on an unsolicited and unusually detailed letter from Thatcher dated September 12, 1985, in which she provided advice on how to engage with Gorbachev.[102] In effect mediating between Reagan and Gorbachev at this time, Thatcher was at the height of her international influence.

Thatcher's enthusiasm for dialogue with Gorbachev grew during the later 1980s as he embarked upon an extensive program of domestic reform. For the European left, Gorbachev's talk of reform and openness – glasnost and perestroika – sufficed to undercut the Thatcherite premise of a continuing Soviet threat. The anti-nuclear movement found new grist for the cause of complete disarmament. Such talk was anathema to Thatcher, who never tired of reiterating to her European colleagues the virtues of combining diplomatic flexibility with the need for a strong defense and awareness of a continuing Soviet threat.

Against this backdrop, a serious crisis in transatlantic relations erupted. In October 1986, Reagan and Gorbachev met in Reykjavik, Iceland, where they decided to pursue the American president's vision for a nuclear-free world. What had been billed as an informal meeting to prepare for a fully fledged summit in Washington evolved into exchanges of a magnitude rarely choreographed – much less improvised – on the international stage.

Gorbachev had come to Reykjavik prepared to agree to dramatic cuts in the Soviet nuclear arsenal, hoping to persuade Reagan not only to follow suit but also to abandon the Strategic Defense Initiative (SDI).

Behind closed doors, the two leaders discussed ever-greater cuts, reaching a crescendo with Reagan's suggestion that they agree to phase out nuclear weapons altogether. 'We can do that,' confirmed Gorbachev. 'We can eliminate them.'[103] The dialogue reached the point of preparing the draft of a memorandum of understanding to that effect.

The talks eventually foundered over the issue of SDI. Gorbachev insisted that SDI be confined to the laboratory for ten years. Reagan, convinced that SDI was needed as a hedge even in a non-nuclear world and that testing it in outer space was essential, refused. The American president ended the stalemate by abruptly walking out of the meeting, thereby scuttling the provisional agreement to abolish all nuclear weapons, which had already been drafted.

A decade or so later, I asked Anatoly Dobrynin, who was foreign-policy advisor to Gorbachev at the time of Reykjavik, why the Soviet negotiators had not accepted the main feature – freezing and then mutually and radically reducing the number of weapons; the issue of testing in outer space could have been relegated to a follow-up, technical conference in, say, Geneva. 'Because we had nobody in the room who knew much about nuclear deterrent strategy,' he replied, 'and because it never occurred to us that Reagan would walk out of the room.'*

Thatcher was profoundly unsettled. In urging Reagan to do business with Gorbachev, she had not thought it possible that such engagement might lead to a complete upending of existing US and British defense policy. Meeting with her two months after Reykjavik, I found her greatly disturbed by the course of events. The summit had been an 'earthquake' that would jeopardize 'all the good work done by the Reagan administration' to improve relations between the US and its European allies, she said. By attempting to undermine the longstanding NATO agreement over the role of nuclear weapons, Reagan had come close to delegitimizing a pillar of the transatlantic alliance.

Thatcher conceived her challenge now to help bring the president to a position on more solid ground. She was, she told me, 'determined to set aside Reykjavik'.[104] Her initial approach was to cocoon her message in the warmest of praise. Calling Reagan at the White House the day after the summit, she opened disingenuously by telling him he had

---

* The Soviets in the room included Gorbachev and Foreign Minister Eduard Shevardnadze; the Americans present were Reagan and George Shultz.

'done wonderfully at Reykjavik'. The summit, she judged, 'looked like a Soviet setup', and it was essential 'to put the blame for stalemate on Gorbachev'. Then she went on the offensive, warning Reagan that to advocate the elimination of nuclear weapons altogether would be 'tantamount to surrender, so we must be very, very careful'.

Her pleas left Reagan unmoved. When Thatcher reiterated her concern that if nuclear weapons were eliminated, 'the Soviets – with their conventional superiority – could just sweep across Europe', Reagan replied that he 'was sure we could develop a strategy to defeat the Soviets,' implying that he believed the task could be achieved by conventional military means.[105]

None of this was what Thatcher wanted to hear. She realized that on an issue as deeply imbedded in Reagan's mind as the abolition of nuclear weapons, he simply would not retreat – at least not directly. So she changed tactics. Her new vehicle of persuasion was a previously arranged visit to Camp David in November 1986, a month after Reykjavik. At the prompting of her longtime aide Charles Powell, she had decided to avoid asking Reagan to reject anything he had agreed to at Reykjavik. Instead, her goal was to 'pick out the elements of Reykjavik which we could accept and argue that they should receive priority', she told me at the time. 'By implication, everything else should be left aside, although not explicitly abandoned.'[106]

To her great relief, she found Reagan receptive. The two agreed that priority would be given to an Intermediate-Range Nuclear Forces (INF) agreement that would also include a 50 percent cut in strategic offensive weapons alongside a ban on chemical weapons. No mention was made of the more sweeping elements of the Reykjavik package, which now slipped out of the realm of active consideration.

This approach was not without costs. In supporting the INF agreement, Thatcher appeared to be offering her blessing to Reagan's ultimate aim of eliminating nuclear weapons from Europe altogether – far from her preferred outcome. Nonetheless, as she explained the decision to me, 'In order to preserve nuclear deterrence, to prevent the US from negotiating away its strategic nuclear weapons and ensure we would receive Trident [missiles], we accepted the lesser evil of a zero INF agreement.'[107]

Thatcher knew when to hold fast to a deeply held belief and when to accept a new reality – and, in her words, 'put the best face on it'.[108] The joint statement produced by the end of her Camp David visit also reaffirmed NATO's reliance on effective nuclear deterrence and Reagan's continuing support for Britain's Trident system. As far as public posture regarding nuclear deterrence was concerned, this statement represented, in effect, a rhetorical return to pre-Reykjavik norms. As I told Thatcher at the time, she was 'the only person outside the United States to whom the President listened'.[109] It remained important that she continue to offer him her advice – sympathetically, but by no means always agreeing.

Thatcher's arguments also benefited from the administration's weakening in the wake of the Iran-Contra scandal, as officials were exposed for having used the proceeds from unauthorized American weapon sales to Iran to fund the Contra insurgency against the Marxist-Leninist Sandinista regime in Nicaragua. As Reagan's friend and staunch supporter, Thatcher saw that her role was to help him find a way forward. She also did the West a great service by reaffirming the fundamentals of NATO's defensive doctrine. But the Reykjavik episode, in addition to illustrating the intimacy of Anglo-American relations, also revealed their limits. On issues where the imbalance of forces between the allies was a major factor – and presidential convictions especially strong – the ties of emotion and history could fray, and America might insist on pursuing its preferences unilaterally.

DEFENDING KUWAITI SOVEREIGNTY: THE GULF CRISIS

Under Thatcher's leadership, the British voice was heard not only on matters pertaining to NATO and the Cold War, but also on disputes around the globe. When Saddam Hussein's Iraq invaded and occupied the neighboring country of Kuwait in August 1990, it was not immediately obvious that Britain would have a special role to play. Britain's operational capability had declined markedly since an analogous episode in 1961, when Abd al-Karim Qasim, the army brigadier who had risen to power after overthrowing the Iraqi monarchy, appeared to threaten newly independent Kuwait's territorial integrity. At that time, the UK had successfully deployed troops and ships to deter Qasim, fulfilling its agreement to guarantee its former colony's defense.

In Thatcher's mind, Saddam Hussein was a reckless dictator in the mold of General Galtieri; as with the Argentine leader, appeasing Hussein would only embolden him. Should his aggression go unchallenged, the integrity of the international system would be severely strained. She took a dim view of historical episodes in which Britain had elected to appease aggressors. Reflecting on the 1938 Munich Agreement that helped precipitate the Second World War, she commented: 'British foreign policy is at its worst when it is giving away other people's territory, as in the Sudetenland and Czechoslovakia.'[110] From the beginning of the conflict in Kuwait – as on the Falklands – Thatcher determined that the only honorable course was to restore the status quo ante; the moral clarity she brought to bear ultimately had a significant impact on the American administration's decision-making during the crisis.

President George H. W. Bush's first reaction to the crisis was cautious. Speaking to the press from the White House the morning of August 2, Bush appeared guarded, stating that he was 'not contemplating' dispatching troops to the region, but then again, that he 'would not discuss any military options even if we'd agreed upon them'.[111] Immediately following Bush's remarks, the National Security Council convened to discuss the matter. Opinions drifted toward accepting the invasion as a fait accompli.[112]

It was serendipitous that, well before the crisis broke, Thatcher had accepted an invitation to appear alongside President Bush at a conference in Aspen, Colorado, on the afternoon of August 2. The time they spent together in Aspen would prove enormously consequential – for the Middle East, the US–UK relationship and the principles of world order. Thatcher's relationship with Bush was not as warm as the one she had developed with Reagan, but Bush understood its value. Charles Powell, who accompanied Thatcher to Aspen, noted that the two leaders were 'in very close agreement' on Kuwait, although Thatcher appeared to be more impressed than Bush with the urgency of marshalling a military response.[113]

At a joint press conference with Thatcher that afternoon, Bush spoke first. His brow furrowed, voice measured and hands buried deep in his suit pockets, the American president exuded caution. He recounted that he had been on the phone with Middle Eastern leaders, expressed his 'concern' over Iraqi aggression and called for a 'peaceful solution'.[114] After thanking Bush for welcoming her to Colorado, Thatcher lost no

time in getting to the 'main question', just as she had in her maiden
speech to Parliament thirty years earlier:

> Iraq has violated and taken over the territory of a country which is a full
> member of the United Nations. That is totally unacceptable. And if it
> were allowed to endure, then there would be many other small countries
> that could never feel safe.[115]

Although Thatcher chose these words carefully, it was not so much
the substance of her remarks as her method of delivering them that
made an immediate impression. She spoke in staccato bursts, with
great emphasis and total conviction. She was simply in her element as
a leader.

By the time Bush returned to the White House on August 5, his view
had hardened significantly: 'I view very seriously our determination to
reverse this aggression,' he said, declaring, 'This will not stand.'[116]
Speaking with Charles Powell a week later, I attributed much of the
president's shift in tone to Thatcher's presence: 'The White House party
had gone out to Aspen leaning toward the view that there was nothing
much to be done, but had returned braced and determined.'[117]

With the benefit of hindsight, I believe Bush was evolving toward
a more muscular response before he arrived in Aspen, but his discussions there with Thatcher strongly reinforced his instincts. Later that
month, she offered Bush similar encouragement following the passage of a UN resolution that permitted the use of force to interdict oil
tankers seeking to breach the sanctions against Iraq. 'This was no
time to go wobbly,' she insisted. The firm tone that Thatcher helped
to set during the early days of the conflict was an important factor in
the eventual liberation of Kuwait.

While Thatcher was quick to defend Kuwaiti sovereignty, she was
reluctant to grant the United Nations a major role in the country's liberation. She did welcome UN Security Council Resolution 660, passed
the day after Kuwait was invaded, which condemned Iraqi aggression
and demanded an immediate withdrawal; however, she viewed the prospect of greater UN involvement with pronounced skepticism. When it
became clear that an Iraqi withdrawal would not be achieved through
purely diplomatic means, she resisted efforts to seek an additional Security Council resolution that would authorize the use of force. If any
military action was treated as requiring a Security Council mandate, she

argued, a precedent would be set that would undermine the right of self-defense inherent in the principle of national sovereignty.

As a practical matter, she also wanted to preserve maximum freedom of action over the manner of Kuwait's liberation. On this point, she initially had President Bush's support: 'She does not want to go back to the UN on use of force; nor do I,' Bush wrote in his diary in early September.[118]

In the end, however, her intentions fell victim to the domestic situation in the United States. Bush understood the resistance in Congress and among the public to taking military action without UN backing. Thatcher did not face equivalent constraints in the United Kingdom and so, in private, she proceeded to argue intensely against an additional UN resolution. But the internal needs of US politics prevailed. In early November 1990, she conceded the argument. For entirely unrelated reasons, however, she would be forced from office mere weeks later.

THE LIMITS TO LEADERSHIP: GERMANY AND THE FUTURE OF EUROPE

Great statesmen operate at the outer limits of what is commonly thought possible; rather than parroting whatever orthodoxy defines the times, they probe its boundaries. Throughout her career, Thatcher had challenged the dictates of conventional wisdom, providing leadership that shifted the terms of debate.

On occasion, however, her belief in her ability to achieve the seemingly impossible turned out to be misplaced. Following the fall of the Berlin Wall on November 9, 1989, Thatcher deviated from the prudence and flexibility that generally served her well. Instead of leading the West toward a policy of German unification and anchoring a united Germany within NATO, she found herself increasingly at odds with her Atlantic peers.

For Thatcher, the fall of the Berlin Wall was indeed cause for celebration. Similarly, the subsequent collapse of communist regimes throughout Eastern Europe represented a culmination of the dismantling of the Soviet satellite orbit, what she had been working to achieve throughout her time in office. But she was left deeply troubled by the logical corollary to the Iron Curtain's demise: namely, that East and West Germany, artificially divided since the Second World War, should now unify.

Thatcher's concerns about German reunification had a legitimate basis. In 1871, the last time the newly unified Germany had entered the international system, Benjamin Disraeli had deemed it 'a greater political event' than the French Revolution.[119] The British statesman was proven prescient by a series of crises that erupted following Bismarck's 1890 retirement, culminating in the outbreak of the First World War in August 1914. A united Germany would once again inevitably alter the balance of power in Europe, and Thatcher was not alone in believing that the implications of such a change required careful consideration.

Seared by her experiences as a child of the Second World War, Thatcher doubted that the assertive and expansionist conduct of Germany had come to an end with Hitler's defeat. She distrusted what she perceived as an immutable German national character; in her pessimistic moments, she feared that not all the demons of Germany's past had been exorcized. 'To understand a man,' Napoleon is said to have observed, 'look at the world when he was twenty.' Thatcher had turned twenty in 1945.

She was not shy about giving expression to these skeptical sentiments. At a dinner we both attended in Toronto on the sidelines of the June 1988 G-7 summit,[120] I quoted Bismarck in a toast to her, suggesting that the best a statesman could do was to grasp the hem of God's cloak and walk with Him a few steps. Thatcher, who had only been half-listening, asked whose cloak I had proposed latching onto. When the host explained that I was quoting Bismarck, she asked, 'Bismarck, the German?' To the host's response in the affirmative, she replied: 'Time to go home.'

As momentum built for prompt unification, Thatcher remained resolutely opposed. While other leaders hesitated to air their doubts, she assumed a contrarian posture. Rather than contemplating unification, she argued that attention should focus on establishing genuine democracy in East Germany, insisting that two democratic German states could continue to exist side by side indefinitely. And attempting to underscore her concern that a united Germany might once again aspire to dominate Europe, she added another argument: German unification could derail Mikhail Gorbachev's historic experiment in reform – emboldening hardline factions in Moscow, which might oust him from office.

These arguments found little favor even among Thatcher's allies. The Bush administration considered reunification the natural outgrowth of Western victory in the Cold War. Just days before the Berlin Wall fell, Bush left no doubt as to his position: 'I don't share the concern that some European countries have about a reunified Germany,' he told the *New York Times*, 'because I think Germany's commitment to and recognition of the importance of the alliance is unshakable.'[121]

European leaders such as French President François Mitterrand, who had initially shared her hesitation, began to tiptoe toward accepting reunification while still seeking to shape the conditions under which it would take place. When I met with Thatcher in London on January 10, I urged just such a course. She proved unpersuadable. The record of our meeting illustrates her fixed position: 'The Prime Minister said that one should not regard anything in international relations as inevitable. Her starting point was to establish what would serve British interests and then try to make it happen.'[122]

These were laudable sentiments, but in January 1990 they were no substitute for a policy firmly tethered to the emerging reality in Europe. Her leadership, which was so often marked by creative agility and a firm grasp of realities, now displayed elements of rigidity. Without the pragmatic impulse that had served her so well in earlier crises, Thatcher was left with a policy that amounted to little more than ineffectual opposition. Her proposal to leave behind some Soviet forces to stabilize East Germany after reunification was a nonstarter.[123] The Germans, with US backing and French acquiescence, moved ahead. Thatcher was left sidelined and diminished.

German unification was further enmeshed in the broader project of European integration. The prevailing view on the continent was that a united Germany would be best managed by binding it closely to the European Community. Chancellor Helmut Kohl espoused this view and was prepared to bring German sacrifices to the enterprise; his foreign minister, Hans-Dietrich Genscher, echoed the novelist Thomas Mann's appeal to 'create not a German Europe but a European Germany'.[124]

Thatcher fundamentally disagreed with this strategy. Germany's large population and economic potential would guarantee it a substantial if not dominant weight in any integrated European structure. She understood that de facto German power could not be neutered by legalistic or institutional means. Yet she felt strongly that folding Germany into Europe would entrench German power rather than contain it. In the end, she was proven partly right, as Germany's economic progress has allowed it greater influence within the EU than any other member state. But on the fundamental question of German character and politics, she was wrong; Germany was transformed by Adenauer and his legacy and has remained an integral member of the Western Alliance since unification in October 1990.

EUROPE, THE ENDLESS DIFFICULTY

It was not simply German reunification, but the entire agenda of European integration, that was at odds with Thatcher's worldview. As a defender of parliamentary sovereignty, she regarded the transfer of powers from nation-states to European supranational institutions staffed by unelected bureaucrats as an abrogation of democratic and sovereign rights.

Thatcher's strategy had been to encourage economic liberalization in Europe without advancing political integration. Attempting to maintain this balance became her ultimate foreign-policy dilemma. In 1984, after years of painstaking negotiations, she had won a major political victory over Brussels, granting Britain an annual 'rebate' that reduced Britain's contribution to the European budget by two-thirds. In 1986, she had embraced the Single European Act in pursuit of a single market (indeed it had been principally drafted by the British). She failed, however, to foresee that the Act would be used to extend 'Qualified Majority Voting' in European Councils, thus accelerating the shift of power away from national capitals. As she later acknowledged in her memoirs:

> it is now possible to see the period of my second term as Prime Minister as that in which the European Community subtly but surely shifted its direction away from being a Community of open trade, light regulation, and freely cooperating sovereign nation-states toward statism and centralism.[125]

The stage had been set for a conflict – both between London and Brussels and within the Conservative Party – that would last for more than a generation.

How to manage Britain's relationship with Europe is a perennial question and, for the leader of the Conservative Party, a perilous one. From Margaret Thatcher in November 1990 to Theresa May in July 2019, four Conservative premierships foundered on the shoals of the European relationship.[126]

The first sign of Thatcher's struggle to manage her party's divides over Europe came with the resignation of Defence Minister Michael Heseltine in January 1986. The controversy was nominally about Westland, Britain's sole remaining helicopter manufacturer, but essentially about Heseltine's ambition to replace Thatcher as prime minister. The American company Sikorsky had expressed interest in becoming a minority shareholder in Westland, hoping to turn around the unprofitable British manufacturer by infusing it with capital – an option that appealed to Thatcher's free-market as well as her Atlanticist convictions.

But Heseltine favored a statist and European solution. Under the Heseltine plan, the struggling British company would join a consortium with British, French, German and Italian defense companies. A fracas ensued in which Downing Street sought to discredit Heseltine – touching off a brief period of turbulence that appeared to threaten Thatcher's grip on the Conservative Party. In the end, Heseltine resigned and Sikorsky bailed out Westland.

Charismatic, wealthy and fiercely ambitious, Heseltine positioned himself as a pro-European successor to Thatcher. His unsubtle insurgency would smolder on the backbenches for years before suddenly bursting into a conflagration in November 1990.

By then, plenty of tinder had accumulated. Conservative political giants rose and fell in relation to their stances on Europe. The United Kingdom had joined the European Economic Community (EEC) under Heath in 1973. But in 1979 Britain declined to enter the nascent European Rate Mechanism (ERM), a loose precursor to the euro currency that would require participating countries to keep their foreign exchange rates within a certain range of the value of the European Currency Unit (ECU) – which was itself determined by weighting member countries' currencies according to the size of their economies.

The knock-down, drag-out fights over the EEC, the ERM and the ECU had divided the British cabinet and steadily undermined Thatcher's leadership. She rejected the possibility of Britain's joining the ERM in 1985, but by early 1987 Chancellor of the Exchequer Nigel Lawson had found a workaround: without Thatcher's approval, he made sure that the pound sterling would 'shadow' the West German Deutschmark at a specified rate. By November 1987, however, Thatcher became aware of the tacit agreement and canceled the policy by early 1988.[127]

Amid this context of increasingly ambitious schemes for European integration, as well as an incurably divided Conservative Party, Thatcher accepted an invitation to deliver an address on the continent's future at the College of Europe in Bruges, Belgium. Aware that her audience of aspiring Eurocrats was not a natural constituency for her Euroskeptic message, she leavened the speech's opening with a joke. 'If you believe some of the things said and written about my views on Europe,' she said, flashing a broad smile, 'it must seem rather like inviting Genghis Khan to speak on the virtues of peaceful coexistence!'[128] Like Genghis Khan, however, Thatcher had come to conquer. The joke would be the extent of her gentility.

Rather than offering an encomium to the idea of Europe, Thatcher set out to prescribe its limits. In this way, the 'Bruges Speech' can be read as a declaration of independence from her cabinet critics. In Thatcher's view, the European Community was supposed to pursue five 'guiding principles': rely on 'willing and active cooperation among independent sovereign states'; 'tackle present problems in a *practical* way'; 'encourage enterprise'; 'not be protectionist'; and 'maintain a sure defence through NATO'.[129]

By 'practical', Thatcher meant a streamlined, politically accountable, pro-market European bureaucracy that would regulate with a light touch and focus on immediate problems rather than grand schemes. In line with this, her vision of Europe was based on retaining distinct nation-states:

> To try to suppress nationhood and concentrate power at the center would be highly damaging and would jeopardize the objectives we seek to achieve. Europe will be stronger precisely because it has France as France, Spain as Spain, Britain as Britain, each with its own customs, traditions and identity. It would be folly to try to fit them into some sort of identikit European personality.[130]

It was a passage Charles de Gaulle would have endorsed word for word.

Thatcher's skepticism of centralization, so prominent in the Bruges speech, had grown out of her study of Hayek before she became prime minister. By the time she spoke in Bruges, she had the experience of implementing reforms in Britain such as privatizing industry and public housing – initiatives that succeeded in large part because they returned the state's power to private enterprise. In her view, the European project's promoters were ignoring the major economic lessons of the age. She took direct aim at them in her speech, observing:

> Indeed, it is ironic that just when those countries such as the Soviet Union, which have tried to run everything from the center, are learning that success depends on dispersing power and decisions away from the center, there are some in the Community who seem to want to move in the opposite direction. We have not successfully rolled back the frontiers of the state in Britain, only to see them re-imposed at a European level with a European super-state exercising a new dominance from Brussels.[131]

This statement was crafted to shock, and it achieved its desired effect. It represented a direct rebuff to a speech given three months prior by European Commission President Jacques Delors, in which the French socialist had suggested that, within ten years, national legislatures would delegate as much as 80 percent of their economic decision-making to the European Parliament.[132] Thatcher could hardly have been more incensed.

The Bruges speech also offered a sage yet less frequently recalled meditation on the meaning of European civilization and Britain's place in it. It touched on two of her great convictions – her sympathy for those struggling for freedom in Eastern Europe and her deep admiration for the United States. The European Community was 'one manifestation of European identity', she observed, but not 'the only one'. Moving from detached analysis to passionate exhortation, she continued:

> We must never forget that east of the Iron Curtain, people who once enjoyed a full share of European culture, freedom, and identity have been cut off from their roots. We shall always look on Warsaw, Prague, and Budapest as great European cities. Nor should we forget that European values have helped to make the United States of America into the valiant defender of freedom which she has become.[133]

Thatcher's words were prophetic. Warsaw, Prague, Budapest and East Berlin were soon welcomed back to Europe, and the continent's prosperity, then and now, has depended on the security supplied by the United States, itself a great extension of European civilization.

This is why Thatcher's Bruges speech would eventually win a place in the British oratorical canon: not only for its pivotal place in her own biography but for its prescience and clear articulation of the enduring tensions between British identity and European integration.

THE FALL

The immediate effect of the Bruges speech, however, was to drive Thatcher and her cabinet colleagues further apart. This was a matter of no small moment, suggesting a hardening of differences on economic policy no less ominous than similar episodes over foreign and defense policy. As noted earlier, the British system elevates members of the cabinet to the highest echelons of their party, meaning that authority moves in both directions between the prime minister and the cabinet. An element of personal goodwill between the two is therefore crucial to the operation of effective government.

In June 1989, hours before Thatcher was to speak at a European Community summit in Madrid, Chancellor of the Exchequer Nigel Lawson and Foreign Secretary Geoffrey Howe paid her a Sunday-morning visit at Number 10. Here was a spectacle rare in British government: the two most powerful ministers in Thatcher's government threatening to resign if the prime minister refused to propose a deadline for formally joining the ERM, thus giving up her country's independent monetary policy. Thatcher carefully recorded their demands – and expressed willingness to amend her stance on the subject – but refused to accede to a public deadline.

Shortly after returning from Madrid, she demoted Howe to leader of the House of Commons while softening the blow by giving him the nebulous title of deputy prime minister. Thatcher was more merciful to Lawson, allowing him to remain in his post. However, he soon resigned over exchange-rate policy, as well as her refusal to dismiss her chief economic advisor Alan Walters, whose public views Lawson claimed were undermining his authority.

By October 1990, however, Thatcher had been forced by the newly minted chancellor of the exchequer, John Major, to acquiesce in Britain's joining the ERM. In an October 30 speech to the House of Commons, she defended this move while 'totally and utterly' rejecting economic and monetary union, which she saw as 'the back door to a federal Europe'. Furious at her cabinet and bent on forestalling additional challenges to her policies, she appeared to take her rhetorical cues from God's words of caution to Job: 'Hitherto shalt thou come, but no farther.' Setting up Jacques Delors as her foil, Thatcher recounted that 'he wanted the European Parliament to be the democratic body of the Community, he wanted the Commission to be the Executive, and he wanted the Council of Ministers to be the Senate.' Her response was straightforward: 'No, no, no!'[134]

'No, no, no,' quietly but emphatically uttered, would become another immortal Thatcher phrase – but not before it helped to topple her government, which was already bleeding support due to her espousal of the unpopular 'community charge' (a local government poll tax).

Two days later, Geoffrey Howe resigned his cabinet post over 'matters of substance as well as of style', as he would explain in a November 13 address to the House of Commons. Thatcher's policy on economic and monetary union, he argued in his resignation speech, 'increasingly risks leading herself and others astray'. Howe's oration was a masterpiece, peppered with backhanded compliments. After saluting Thatcher's 'courage and leadership' before a spellbound House, he then aimed squarely at her approach by invoking Harold Macmillan's belief that Britain

> had to place and keep ourselves within the EC. He saw it as essential then, as it is today, not to cut ourselves off from the realities of power; not to retreat into a ghetto of sentimentality about our past and so diminish our own control over our own destiny in the future.[135]

Growing more heated, Howe characterized Thatcher's rhetoric on Europe as 'tragic' and 'disturbing'. Then he modulated to a more-in-sorrow-than-in-anger tone:

> The tragedy is – and it is for me personally, for my party, for our whole people and for my right honorable Friend herself, a very real tragedy – that the Prime Minister's perceived attitude toward Europe is running increasingly serious risks for the future of our nation. It risks minimizing our influence and maximizing our chances of being once again shut out. We have paid heavily in the past for late starts and squandered opportunities in Europe. We dare not let that happen again. If we detach ourselves

completely, as a party or a nation, from the middle ground of Europe, the effects will be incalculable and very hard ever to correct.[136]

Howe's conclusion made clear that he saw no constructive future for the nation under Thatcher's leadership. Alluding to a 'conflict' between his loyalty to his friend the prime minister and allegiance to 'what I perceive to be the true interests of the nation', he concluded that it was no longer possible to continue serving in government. Claiming to have 'wrestled' at length with this decision, Howe urged others in the party to 'consider their own responses' and follow his lead in doing what is 'right for my party and my country'.[137] This appeal for 'others' in the Conservative Party to reconsider their loyalty to Thatcher's government implicitly blessed her overthrow. Michael Heseltine declared his leadership challenge the following morning.

The timing was highly inconvenient for Thatcher. She was due to visit Northern Ireland on November 16 and then travel to Paris for a three-day conference (scheduled for November 19–21) of the Commission on Security and Cooperation in Europe (CSCE), a period which now would be the final days of the new Conservative Party leadership campaign. Despite the challenge, Thatcher opted to honor her travel commitments.

Observing this (to an outsider) surprising leadership contest from afar, I was taken aback by Thatcher's decision. Perhaps overstepping previous bounds – which had always confined my judgments to foreign policy – I called Charles Powell, by now a close friend, and asked why she seemed to be absenting herself from the field at the height of battle. It was true that the conference represented a post-Cold War moment of great promise: Bush and Gorbachev were set to meet with their European counterparts and chart the future of the continent. But, for Thatcher, surely a more prudent course would be to stay in Britain and argue her case with wavering supporters.

My suggestion did not find favor: Thatcher believed her duty lay on the world stage. Eschewing the conference to conduct a Conservative Party dispute would, in her mind, have signaled a dangerous lack of confidence. Suffused as it was with character, her decision proved disastrous.

Thatcher left the management of her campaign to what may only be described as a posse of half-dedicated inadequates. On the evening of November 20, aides brought her news at the British embassy in Paris of the vote on the first ballot: 'Not quite as good as we had hoped and not quite good enough.'[138] She had won 204 votes to Heseltine's 152, with 16 abstentions. Under arcane Conservative Party rules, however, she had come up short of the supermajority required; had two of Heseltine's supporters backed her instead, she would have won. A second ballot would now be required. Putting on a brave face before the cameras, she told reporters that she would indeed contest this ballot.

The adverse events that built over the following forty-eight hours have an air of Shakespearean tragedy. Stores of goodwill that had accumulated in her cabinet over the years were running low; the same conviction, fighting spirit and charm that previously had won her allies were now coupled with a stubbornness that cost her friends and supporters. As Heseltine basked in media attention, some of Thatcher's loyalists began to quiver and defect. The cabinet murmured about drafting a 'stop Heseltine' candidate – either John Major or Foreign Secretary Douglas Hurd.

All night and into the next day, Thatcher witnessed fortune's tide receding. She interviewed cabinet members one by one, who all told her that, though of course he personally supported her, regrettably she could not prevail in another vote. By midnight on November 21, having run aground, she decided to resign. At 9 a.m. the following morning, she formally announced the decision to her cabinet. As I said to Powell at the time, her resignation felt 'worse than a death in the family'.[139]

To most American observers, Thatcher's fall was mystifying. The magnitude of her achievements on the world stage and the substantial confidence she enjoyed in America made it difficult to understand why her fellow Conservatives would oust her. President Bush was crestfallen when he heard the news during a trip to Saudi Arabia, where he was visiting coalition troops who were massing to repel Iraqi forces from Kuwait. General Norman Schwarzkopf spoke for many friends of Britain when he demanded of his British counterpart: 'What sort of a country have you got there when they sack the Prime Minister halfway through a war?'[140]

Equally remarkable to observers was the public grace Thatcher mustered despite her private grief. In the morning, she had announced her intention to resign; that same afternoon, she was obliged to face down a vote of no confidence in parliament. Labour had called the vote to take advantage of the disarray in Conservative ranks. What Thatcher

delivered that afternoon was, in the words of the Liberal Democrat
leader Paddy Ashdown, a 'bravura performance'. Mounting a rousing
defense of her government's policies – and, by extension, her own
leadership – she asked, 'When the windy rhetoric [of Labour] has blown
away, what are their real reasons for bringing this motion before the
House?' Her answer was unyielding:

> It cannot be a complaint about Britain's standing in the world. That is
> deservedly high, not least because of our contribution to ending the cold
> war and to the spread of democracy through [E]astern Europe and the
> Soviet Union – achievements that were celebrated at the historic meeting
> in Paris from which I returned yesterday.
>
>   It cannot be the nation's finances. We are repaying debts, including the
> debts run up by the Labour party . . .
>
>   The real issue to be decided . . . is how best to build on the achieve-
> ments of the 1980s, how to carry Conservative policies forward through
> the 1990s and how to add to three general election victories a fourth,
> which we shall surely win.[141]

In this, too, Thatcher was entirely prescient. John Major would best
Heseltine in the forthcoming leadership contest and win a fourth consecutive victory for the Conservatives in the 1992 general election.

The following week, Thatcher faced questions from parliament for
the last time. What strikes one most when revisiting this session is the
praise that was offered for her by politicians outside the Conservative
Party. For instance, the Northern Irish Unionist politician James Moly-
neaux took the opportunity to reflect somewhat penitently on their
earlier brawl over the Anglo-Irish Agreement:

> Does the Prime Minister recall an important debate in November 1985,
> when relations between us were a little strained? Does she recall my
> addressing her thus: 'Millions of our fellow British citizens throughout
> this nation feel that the Prime Minister has a lasting contribution to make
> to the destiny of the nation'? Is the Prime Minister now aware that the
> vast majority of those people wish that contribution to continue?[142]

Forgoing the opportunity to score on an adversary, Thatcher
graciously replied: 'The right honorable gentleman is very generous
indeed.'

The following day, November 28, 1990, Margaret and Denis Thatcher left 10 Downing Street. Her final statement as prime minister was, characteristically, to thank the staff who maintained the residence.

EPILOGUE

The revival of Britain brought about by Thatcher was at once an economic and spiritual undertaking. When she became prime minister, national decline was not merely a matter of a sputtering economy. Decline was a collective, self-reinforcing and ultimately debilitating belief. Its hallmarks were high inflation, slow growth and crippling labor strife. The political center of 1970s Britain simply was not working.

Rejecting that exhausted consensus, Thatcher conjured up a positive vision for the future as leader of the Opposition. And later, once she became prime minister, she proceeded to take her society where it had never been before. This required both courage and character: courage, in departing so dramatically from the received wisdom of the time, and character, in staying the course consistently as her tough medicine drew sharp complaint from the patient.

Again and again, Thatcher displayed calm nerves and unyielding commitment to her convictions – even when conditions were ambiguous, downside risks loomed large and public support appeared to be waning. Her strategy of tightening the money supply to curb inflation at the beginning of her time in office saw no U-turn. She prosecuted a vigorous response to aggression in the Falklands. And she assured Britain's power supply during the miners' strike, sustaining her policies even when public opinion threatened to turn against them.

To be sure, tenacity alone is rarely sufficient for success. To sustain her strategy to renew Britain, Thatcher had to rally supporters within the Conservative Party – particularly for domestic reform, which is inherently more polarizing than mobilization against an external foe. Her rhetoric had an impact on her supporters that recalls Isaiah Berlin's description of Churchill's words rousing the nation during the Second World War:

> So hypnotic was the force of his words, so strong his faith, that by the
> sheer intensity of his eloquence he bound his spell upon them until it

seemed to them that he was indeed speaking what was in their hearts and minds. Doubtless it was there; but largely dormant until he had awoken it in them.[143]

Likewise, in Thatcher's time, dismay at Britain's dysfunction was already in the air; her achievement was to channel it for the cause of domestic reform. Her rhetoric mobilized enough support from her wing of the Conservative Party to sustain her ambitious agenda, realigning the political center for decades. She balanced a strong government presence in society with individual freedom in the economy – not, perhaps, the program that a majority of her contemporary Conservatives were advocating but certainly ideals the party had followed in earlier periods of its history.[144] In the process, she assembled new coalitions of voters who had not traditionally voted Conservative, enabling her to win three elections in a row and laying the basis for a fourth victory shortly after her retirement. She had seen the future – and made it work.

Not that she was lacking for enemies; even Conservatives sometimes accused Thatcher of betraying her party's basic principles. She was, of course, an outsider: both as a woman who had trained as a scientist, and as one coming from a middle-class background, her father a grocer. Yet her actions, though assuredly disruptive, spoke of a total commitment to her party. Rather than betraying its principles, she was working steadfastly to restore them.

Thatcher's ideals echoed those of the greatest Conservative leaders since Disraeli: preservation of the United Kingdom, international engagement on the basis of democratic principles and domestic governance founded on individual self-sufficiency – supplemented by acknowledgement of Britain's postwar consensus on the need for a stable health service and welfare state.

In international affairs, although she initially saw little value in diplomatic outreach to the Soviet Union, she changed course when she came across Mikhail Gorbachev and judged the time right to make progress. With an eye firmly on the longer term, she engaged with Gorbachev on substantial issues, believing that opening such a dialogue would ultimately strengthen the position of the democratic West.

Thatcher also saw no conflict between her free-market principles and the obligation of environmental stewardship. A great champion of the Montreal Protocol, the rare international treaty that has been both universally praised and highly effective, Thatcher deserves her share of credit for the remarkable healing of the ozone layer in recent decades. Toward the end of her premiership, she became one of the first world leaders to speak out vigorously on the dangers of climate change. Addressing the Royal Society in 1988, she acknowledged that for all the benefits of the industrial revolution, it was also true that mankind had 'unwittingly begun a massive experiment with the system of this planet itself'.[145] Though it was left to younger generations to solve this vast and increasingly salient problem, Thatcher at least had sought to point the way.

Thatcher's foreign policy was a crucial testament to the importance of the British–American partnership within the Atlantic Alliance. The reinvigoration of the 'special relationship' secured her influence on the global stage. There was nothing about Great Britain's natural resources, economic performance or military prowess that would have qualified it for superpower status in the 1980s. Yet through her forceful personality, her skillful support when it mattered and her essential relationship with President Reagan, Thatcher acted as if Britain were on a par with the United States. And for the most part, the Reagan administration happily suspended disbelief.

Some leaders adjust to their retirement from politics with relative ease and elegance. They may even grow in stature, successfully writing a new, compelling chapter in their life's story. Lady Thatcher, as she soon became, was not one of those leaders. She lived for her vision and, once out of office, struggled to find anything as meaningful as the challenges she had encountered during her years at 10 Downing Street.

I continued to call on her on every trip to London, even in the years after illness had clouded her mind. Despite her fearsome reputation, largely acquired from her conduct in principled debates, with me she had always been the soul of personal kindness. To our very last visit, I found her unfailingly gracious, considerate and dignified.

On those final occasions, as I sat across from a treasured friend of more than three decades, I saw a leader who had faced down life's trials with courage and grace. Although she had been reduced to a mere observer in politics, to millions of her fellow countrymen and -women – and countless admirers abroad – she would always be a great and historic figure: an economic reformer of lasting significance, a premier ennobled by her resolve and daring when British sovereignty was threatened, the Iron Lady of the Western world. All who dealt with her recognized her outer toughness; all could sense the inner strength that carried her through the tribulations of leadership. In her presence, few could escape her personal charm and warmth.

To her critics, Thatcher's fortitude at times cloaked her human qualities. But her exceptional steeliness coexisted with the overlooked attribute that lies at the heart of her leadership: love of country. Exceptionally strong conviction and competitive drive were surely part of Margaret Thatcher's success in winning power; discipline and calculation helped her to retain it. But only love of her country and her people can explain how she wielded power and all that she achieved with it. That Queen Elizabeth II made the decision personally to attend her funeral – an honor extended to no previous prime minister except Winston Churchill – testifies to Lady Thatcher's historic impact.

The very last hymn to be sung at her funeral service in St Paul's Cathedral on April 17, 2013 captures her outlook:

> I vow to thee, my country, all earthly things above,
> Entire and whole and perfect, the service of my love:
> The love that asks no question, the love that stands the test,
> That lays upon the altar the dearest and the best.[146]

Conclusion:
The Evolution of Leadership

FROM ARISTOCRACY TO MERITOCRACY

These pages have traced the reciprocal impact of six leaders on historical circumstance, and of historical circumstance on the role of each. Konrad Adenauer, Charles de Gaulle, Richard Nixon, Anwar Sadat, Lee Kuan Yew and Margaret Thatcher: each transformed his or her society, and all contributed to the emergence of a new world order.

The six leaders were profoundly affected by the dramatic half-century when Europe, which for 400 years had shaped the unfolding of history while dominating an increasing portion of the globe, proceeded to consume much of its own substance in two world wars that were in effect a European civil war. They then helped shape its aftermath, in which economies had to be reorganized, domestic structures redefined and international relations reordered. The six also faced the challenges of the Cold War and the disruptions brought by decolonization and globalization – all of which continue to reverberate today.

The period in which these leaders had grown up was transformative in a cultural sense: both the political and social structures of the West were irrevocably changing from a hereditary and aristocratic model of leadership to a middle-class and meritocratic one. As they came of age, the lingering residue of aristocracy was combining with the emerging paradigm of merit, at once broadening the base of societal creativity and expanding its scope.

Today, meritocratic principles and institutions are so familiar that they dominate our language and thinking. Take the word 'nepotism', which implies favoring one's relatives and friends, especially in appointment to posts of responsibility. In the pre-meritocratic world, nepotism was omnipresent – indeed, the customary way of life – yet the practice

carried no implications of unfair advantage: to the contrary, blood relations were a source of legitimacy.

As originally conceived by the philosophers of ancient Greece, aristocracy meant 'rule by the best'. Such rule, emphatically *not* hereditary,
was morally justified by taking an aspect of human life assumed to be
given – the natural inequality of endowments – and harnessing it for the
public good. Plato's 'myth of the metals' portrayed an aristocratic political order based on what is now called 'social mobility'. In his telling,
youths (including girls) with souls of 'gold', even if born to parents of
'brass' or 'silver', could rise according to their natural talents.[1]

As a social system that shaped the history of Europe over the centuries, however, aristocracy took on an entirely different meaning: a
hereditary nobility which endowed its leaders with power and status.
The defects of aristocracy in the hereditary sense – such as the risk of
slipping into corruption or inefficiency – are easily recalled today. Less
well remembered are its virtues.

For one, aristocrats did not understand themselves to have acquired
their status through individual efforts. Position was inherent, not
earned. As such, although there existed wastrels and incompetents, the
creative aspect of aristocracy was bound up with the ethic of *noblesse
oblige*, as in the phrase 'to whom much is given much is expected'. Since
aristocrats did not achieve their station, the best of them felt an obligation to engage in public service or social improvement.

In the realm of international relations, leaders from different nations
belonged to this social class and shared a sensibility transcending
national boundaries. Hence, they generally agreed on what constituted
a legitimate international order. This did not prevent conflicts, but it did
help limit the severity of them and facilitate their resolution. The concepts of sovereignty, equilibrium, the legal equality of states and the
balance of power – which were the hallmarks of the Westphalian
system – developed in a world of aristocratic practices.

The banes of aristocratic foreign policy were overconfidence in intuition and a self-regard that invited stagnation. Still, in negotiations
where position was felt to be a birthright, mutual respect among competitors and even adversaries was expected (though not always
guaranteed), and flexibility was uninhibited by a prior commitment to
perpetual success, however short-term the issue. Policies could be judged

in terms of a shared conception of the future rather than of a compulsion to avoid even temporary setbacks.

As a result, an aristocracy at its best could maintain a sense of excellence that was antithetical to the demagogic temptations sometimes afflicting popular democracy. To the extent that an aristocracy lived up to its values of restraint and disinterested public service, its leaders would tend to reject the arbitrariness of personal rule, governing through status and moral suasion instead.

Over the nineteenth and early twentieth centuries, the assumptions underpinning hereditary aristocracy were steadily stripped away by the waning of religious belief, the unleashing by the French Revolution of movements toward greater political equality and shifts in wealth and status from the burgeoning market economy. Then, suddenly and unexpectedly, the First World War revealed the incongruity between waning aristocratic political values on the one hand and emerging technological realities on the other. Even as the former had stressed the imperative of restraint and peaceful evolution, the latter magnified the destructiveness of war. The system broke down in 1914 when rising national passions swept aside the previous safeguards, allowing technology to supply the means for a constantly escalating level of conflict, which over more than four years of attritional war undermined existing institutions.

Winston Churchill observed in *The Gathering Storm* (1948) that the First World War had been a conflict 'not of governments, but of peoples', in which the lifeblood of Europe was 'poured out in wrath and slaughter'.[2] By war's end, Churchill could write:

> Gone were the days of the Treaties of Utrecht and Vienna, when aristocratic statesmen and diplomats, victor and vanquished alike, met in polite and courtly disputation, and, free from the clatter and babel of democracy, could reshape systems upon the fundamentals of which they were all agreed. The peoples, transported by their sufferings and by the mass teachings with which they had been inspired, stood around in scores of millions to demand that retribution should be exacted to the full.[3]

Because Europe's leaders had failed to forestall the oncoming catastrophe, or to contain it once it erupted, the First World War eroded trust in the political elite – leaving behind a weakened leadership that in key countries would be overturned by totalitarian rulers. At the same time, the 1918 peace settlement proved at once insufficiently congruent with widely held values to induce a commitment to the new order and strategically unsound in failing sufficiently to weaken the defeated parties to eliminate their capacity for revenge. This had many consequences; the most momentous was the Second World War.

In both world wars, the all-out mobilization of peoples, commanding their energies and exploiting their mutual antipathies, represented the earliest and bleakest consequence of middle-class ascendancy. Yet after the turmoil of the Second Thirty Years' War (1914–45) had passed, this social transformation would reveal itself to be compatible with international stability and statesmanship. A world of self-confident nation-states, with the middle class wielding the major share of political and cultural power, proved capable of producing leaders who conducted responsible and creative politics.

Two related social forces, meritocracy and democratization, enabled and institutionalized the rise of middle-class leaders. One of the French Revolution's rallying cries had been 'careers open to talents'. From the middle of the nineteenth century, the adoption of meritocratic principles and institutions in the West – such as entrance examinations, selective secondary schools and universities, and recruitment and promotion policies based on professional standards – created new opportunities for talented individuals from middle-class backgrounds to enter politics. Simultaneously, the expansion of the franchise shifted both the social and the political center of gravity toward the middle class as well.

None of the six leaders studied in this volume came from an upper-class background. Konrad Adenauer's father had been a non-commissioned officer in the Prussian army and then a clerk; his son climbed through the standard levels of education in the German Empire. Charles de Gaulle's grandparents had been both well educated and prosperous, but his father was a schoolteacher; the son became the first in his family to serve at high levels of government. Richard Nixon was the product of a lower-middle-class upbringing in southern California. Anwar Sadat, the son of a clerk, struggled to obtain a reference in support of his application to the Egyptian military academy. Lee Kuan Yew, born to downwardly mobile Chinese Singaporean parents, relied on scholarships in Singapore and Britain to pursue his education. Margaret Thatcher was a grammar-school graduate and the daughter of a grocer – the second of a middle-class background (after Edward Heath) and the first woman to become leader of Britain's Conservative Party. None of them had a starting point that suggested later eminence.

Their humble backgrounds allowed them to defy the conventional political categories of 'insider' and 'outsider'. Both Sadat and de Gaulle were military officers who came to power through a crisis in their countries; Nixon and Adenauer were experienced and well-known politicians who nonetheless spent years in the political wilderness. Of the six, Thatcher and Lee entered office in the most orthodox manner – through party politics in a parliamentary system – but constantly questioned prevailing orthodoxy. Much like their aristocratic predecessors in the nineteenth century, but unlike many of their twentieth-century contemporaries, they were not primarily concerned with short-term, tactical advantage. Instead, their origins and experiences far from power lent them perspective, allowing them to articulate the national interest and transcend the conventional wisdom of their day.

The increasingly meritocratic institutions that had allowed them to harness their talents from an early age had arisen under aristocracy's shadow – and often as a consequence of war. Germany's General Staff and efficient, non-nepotistic bureaucracy had their antecedents in Prussian reforms adopted after the shock of battlefield defeats in the Napoleonic Wars. De Gaulle attended Saint-Cyr, the military academy founded by Napoleon in 1802 to develop a professional officer corps. Another such *grande école*, the selective and elite Institut d'études politiques ('Sciences Po'), was founded after the Franco-Prussian War (1870–71) had revealed inadequacies of French political and administrative leadership – deficiencies which were to be remedied by cultivating the talents of the next generation.

The industrial revolution also played its part in the growing emphasis on education, as the economic historian David Landes argues: 'all the old advantages – resources, wealth, power – were devalued, and the mind established over matter. Henceforth the future lay open to all those with the character, the hands, and the brains.'[4] With success increasingly ascribed to intelligence and effort rather than birthright, education became the quintessential road to advancement.

Thanks to these changes, the six leaders were able to attend rigorous secondary schools (most of them selective, and all of them public-spirited if not government-administered). Competition for high marks in examinations and scholarships was an important aspect of life.

Beginning in high school, and continuing in some cases into college, they were taught a wide range of subjects, including especially the humanities, as if in preparation for the challenges of leadership, for which a sense of history and the ability to deal with tragedy are indispensable. Above all, they received an education which would help them to understand the world, the psychology of others and themselves.

The meritocratic revolution affected nearly every aspect of life, valorizing achievement and the aspiration to careers transcending one's family origins.[5] The ideal of excellence was preserved from the earlier aristocratic age and, if anything, given a new and stronger, more individualistic, emphasis. As Thatcher observed in 1975, 'opportunity means nothing unless it includes the right to be unequal and the freedom to be different'.[6] Universities and careers were progressively (though still imperfectly) opened up to women, ethnic and racial minorities, and those from non-elite backgrounds. Societies benefited from the resulting intellectual diversity and openness to different leadership styles.

These factors enabled the leaders described in this volume to combine aristocratic qualities with meritocratic ambitions. The synthesis enshrined public service as a worthy endeavor, which encouraged aspirations to leadership. Both the school system and the broader society in which they were raised put a premium on academic performance, but both, above all, placed a strong emphasis on character. Correspondingly, the six leaders were brought up with priorities beyond their grades and test scores; these, while important, were not treated as an end in themselves. Hence Lee's recurring references to the *junzi*, or Confucian gentleman, and de Gaulle's striving to become 'a man of character'. Education was not merely a credential to be obtained in one's youth and set aside: it was an unending effort with both intellectual and moral dimensions.

The particular middle-class values in which the six leaders were steeped from childhood included personal discipline, self-improvement, charity, patriotism and self-belief. Faith in their societies, encompassing gratitude for the past and confidence in the future, was taken for granted. Equality before the law was becoming an entrenched expectation.

Unlike their aristocratic forebears, these leaders had a deeply rooted sense of national identity, which inspired their conviction that the loftiest ambition was to serve their fellow citizens through leadership of the state. They did not style themselves 'citizens of the world'. Lee may have received his university education in Britain, and Nixon may have prided

himself on the extent of his travels before becoming president, but neither adopted a cosmopolitan identity. To them, the privilege of citizenship
implied a responsibility to exemplify the particular virtues of their own
nations. Serving their people and embodying the greatest traditions of
their society was a high honor. The positive effects of this value system,
as manifested in the American context, were well described by the historian and social critic Christopher Lasch:

> Whatever its faults, middle-class nationalism provided a common ground,
> common standards, a common frame of reference without which society
> dissolves into nothing more than contending factions, as the Founding
> Fathers of America understood so well – a war of all against all.[7]

Another factor common to each of the leaders (except Lee) was a
devout religious upbringing – Catholic for Adenauer and de Gaulle,
Quaker for Nixon, Sunni Muslim for Sadat and Methodist for Thatcher.
For all the differences among these faiths, they uniformly served certain
secular purposes: training in self-control, reflecting on faults and orient-
ing toward the future.* These religious habits helped to instill
self-mastery and a preference for taking the long view – two essential
attributes of statesmanship which these leaders exemplified.

HARD TRUTHS

What were the commonalities in the meritocratic leadership of these six
figures? What lessons can be drawn from their experiences?

All were known for their directness and were often tellers of hard
truths. They did not entrust the fate of their countries to poll-tested,
focus-grouped rhetoric. 'Who do you think lost the war?' Adenauer
uncompromisingly asked his fellow members of parliament who were
complaining about the terms imposed by the Allies in their postwar

---

* As Alexis de Tocqueville observed, the devout are accustomed 'to consider for a long succession of years an unmoving object toward which they constantly advance, and they learn
by insensible progressions to repress a thousand little passing desires . . . This explains why
religious people have often accomplished such lasting things. In occupying themselves with
the other world they encountered the great secret of succeeding in this one.' See Alexis de
Tocqueville, *Democracy in America*, trans. Harvey C. Mansfield and Delba Winthrop
(Chicago: The University of Chicago Press, 2000), 522.

occupation of Germany. Nixon, who pioneered the use of modern marketing techniques in politics, still prided himself on speaking without notes based on his mastery of world affairs in a direct and plainspoken way. Skillful in maintaining political ambiguity, Sadat and de Gaulle nonetheless spoke with exceptional clarity and vividness when seeking to move their people toward ultimate purposes – as did Thatcher.

These leaders all had a penetrating sense of reality and a powerful vision. Mediocre leaders are unable to distinguish the significant from the ordinary; they tend to be overwhelmed by the inexorable aspect of history. Great leaders intuit the timeless requirements of statecraft and distinguish, among the many elements of reality, those which contribute to an elevated future and need to be promoted from others which must be managed and, in the extreme case, perhaps only endured. Thus both Sadat and Nixon, inheriting painful wars from their predecessors, sought to overcome entrenched international rivalries and initiate creative diplomacy. Thatcher and Adenauer found that a strong alliance with America would be most advantageous for their countries; Lee and de Gaulle chose a lesser degree of alignment, which was appropriate for adjustment to changing circumstances.

All six could be bold. They acted decisively on matters of overriding national importance even when conditions – domestic or international – appeared decidedly unfavorable. Thatcher dispatched a Royal Navy Task Force to recover the Falkland Islands from Argentina even as many experts doubted the expedition's feasibility and Britain itself remained mired in a devastating economic crisis. Nixon undertook a diplomatic opening to China and arms-control negotiations with the Soviet Union before withdrawal from Vietnam had been completed and against much conventional wisdom. De Gaulle's refrain, as his biographer Julian Jackson has observed, was 'I have always acted as if . . . ' – that is, as if France were larger, more unified and more confident than it really was.[8]

Each understood the importance of solitude.[9] Sadat enhanced his reflective habits in prison, as did Adenauer at a monastery during his internal exile. Thatcher made some of her most consequential decisions while reviewing her papers alone in the early hours of the morning. De Gaulle's home in the remote village of Colombey-les-Deux-Églises became an intrinsic part of his life. Nixon often separated himself physically from the White House, withdrawing to the Eisenhower Executive Office Building, Camp David or San Clemente. Away from the lights and cameras and daily impositions of command, these leaders benefitted from stillness and reflection – especially before major decisions.

A striking commonality among the six leaders – and a paradox – was their divisiveness. They wanted their peoples to follow along the path they led, but they did not strive for, or expect, consensus; controversy was the inevitable by-product of the transformations they sought. An example from de Gaulle's presidency is illustrative. During the January 1960 riots in Algeria known as the 'week of the barricades', I was in Paris meeting with members of the French defense establishment. Referring to de Gaulle's handling of the situation, one officer said to me: 'Whenever he appears, he divides the country.' Yet in the end it was de Gaulle who would overcome the Algerian crisis and return his country to a shared view of national purpose, just as he had brought the French nation back from the humiliation of capitulation in the Second World War.

Similarly, a leader does not undertake fundamental economic reforms as Thatcher did, or seek peace with historic adversaries as Sadat, or build a successful multiethnic society from the ground up as Lee, without offending entrenched interests and alienating important constituencies. Adenauer's acceptance of the restrictions accompanying Germany's postwar occupation invited vituperation from his political critics. De Gaulle survived – and provoked – countless confrontations, but his last great public act was to deescalate the protests by students and labor unions that had brought France to the brink of revolution in May 1968. Sadat was martyred not only for bringing peace between his people and Israel's but, above all, because of his justifying it by principles some considered heretical. Both during their years in government and afterwards, not everyone admired these six leaders or subscribed to their policies. In each case, they faced resistance – often carried out for honorable motives and sometimes by distinguished opposing figures. Such is the price of making history.

THE FALTERING MERITOCRACY

At least in the West, there are signs that the conditions which helped to produce the six leaders profiled in this book face their own evolutionary decay. The civic patriotism that once lent prestige to public service appears to have been outflanked by an identity-based factionalism and a competing cosmopolitanism. In America, a growing number of college graduates aspire to become globe-trotting corporate executives or professional activists; significantly fewer envision a role as regional- or national-level leaders in politics or the civil service. Something is amiss when the relationship between the leadership class and much of the public is defined by mutual hostility and suspicion.

The West's secondary schools and universities remain very good at educating activists and technicians; they have wandered from their mission of forming citizens – among them, potential statesmen. Both activists and technicians play important roles in society, drawing attention to its faults and the various means by which they might be corrected, but the broad and rigorous humanistic education that shaped prior generations of leaders has fallen out of fashion. The technician's education tends to be pre-professional and quantitative; the activist's, hyper-specialized and politicized. Neither offers much history or philosophy – the traditional wellsprings of the statesman's imagination.

Excellent test scores and sterling résumés lead today's elite 'to believe it has earned its power, and possesses it by right rather than by privilege', according to the political theorist Yuval Levin, a perceptive observer of today's faltering meritocracy.* We are substituting a 'cold and sterile notion of intellect for a warm and spirited understanding of character as a measure of worth'.[10] The most profound problem, in his view, is located in the realm of elite conduct:

> Americans have grown skeptical of our elite's claims to legitimacy not so much because it is too hard to enter the upper tier of American life (even if it is) as because those in that tier seem to be permitted to do whatever they want . . . The problem, in other words, is not necessarily the standards for entry, but the lack of standard *upon* entry. Precisely because our elite does not think of itself as an aristocracy, it does not believe itself to need standards or restraints.[11]

---

* The virtues and drawbacks of meritocracy as it is currently manifested have recently been the subject of widespread debate. Michael Sandel's *The Tyranny of Merit* and Daniel Markovits's *The Meritocracy Trap* argue that meritocracy – either inherently or as it has evolved – is dehumanizing and exclusive. Adrian Wooldridge's *The Aristocracy of Talent* counters that meritocracy remains an admirable, indeed transformative, way of organizing societies, but has become sclerotic and needs to be reinvigorated. James Hankins's *Virtue Politics* and the essays of Ross Douthat and Helen Andrews all emphasize the importance of character, values and codes of behavior in shaping the performance of elites.

Whereas nineteenth-century aristocrats understood much would be expected of them and the meritocrats of the twentieth century pursued values of service, today's elites speak less of obligation than of self-expression or their own advancement. What is more, they are being formed within a technological environment that challenges the very qualities of character and intellect that historically have served to bind leaders to their people.

DEEP LITERACY AND VISUAL CULTURE

The contemporary world is in the midst of a transformation in human consciousness so pervasive as to be nearly unnoticeable. This change – driven by new technologies which mediate our experience of the world and our acquisition of information – has developed largely without understanding of its long-term effects, including its implications for leadership. Under these conditions, reading a complex book carefully, and engaging with it critically, has become as counter-cultural an act as was memorizing an epic poem in the earlier print-based age.

While the Internet and its attendant innovations are unquestionably technical marvels, close attention must be paid to the balance between the constructive and corrosive habits of mind encouraged by new technology.[12] Just as the earlier transition from oral to written culture at once yielded the benefits of literacy and diminished the arts of spoken poetry and storytelling, the contemporary shift from print to visual culture brings both losses and gains.

What risks being lost in an age dominated by the image? The quality goes by many names – erudition, learnedness, serious and independent thinking – but the best term for it is 'deep literacy', defined by the essayist Adam Garfinkle as '[engaging with] an extended piece of writing in such a way as to anticipate an author's direction and meaning'.[13] Ubiquitous and penetrating, yet invisible, deep literacy was the 'background radiation' of the period in which the six leaders profiled in this book came of age.

To the politically concerned, deep literacy supplies the quality Max Weber called 'proportion', or 'the ability to allow realities to impinge on you while maintaining an inner calm and composure'.[14] Intense reading can help leaders cultivate the mental distance from external stimuli and personalities that sustains a sense of proportion. When combined with reflection and the training of memory, it also provides a storehouse of detailed and granular knowledge from which leaders can reason analogically. More profoundly, books offer a reality that is reasonable, sequential and orderly – a reality that can be mastered, or at least managed, by reflection and planning.[15] And, perhaps most importantly for leadership, reading creates a 'skein of intergenerational conversation', encouraging learning with a sense of perspective.[16] Finally, reading is a source of inspiration.* Books record the deeds of leaders who once dared greatly, as well as those who dared too much, as a warning.

Well before the end of the twentieth century, however, print had lost its former dominance. This resulted in, among other things, 'a different kind of person getting elected as leader, one who can present himself and his programs in a polished way', as Lee Kuan Yew observed in 2000, adding:

> Satellite television has allowed me to follow the American presidential campaign. I am amazed at the way media professionals can give a candidate a new image and transform him, at least superficially, into a different personality. Winning an election becomes in large measure, a contest in packaging and advertising.[17]

Just as the benefits of the printed era were inextricable from its costs, so it is with the visual age. With screens in every home, entertainment is omnipresent and boredom a rarity. More substantively, injustice visualized is more visceral than injustice described; television played a crucial role in the American civil rights movement. Yet the costs of television are substantial, privileging emotional display over self-command, changing the kinds of people and arguments that are taken seriously in public life.

---

* Charles Hill, the veteran American diplomat and advisor to secretaries of state, wrote an entire book on the significance of literature for statecraft: 'Literature's freedom to explore endless or exquisite details, portray the thoughts of imaginary characters, and dramatize large themes through intricate plots brings it closest to the reality of "how the world really works." This dimension of fiction is indispensable to the strategist who cannot, by the nature of the craft, know all of the facts, considerations, and potential consequences of a situation at the time a decision must be made, ready or not.' See Charles Hill, *Grand Strategies: Literature, Statecraft, and World Order* (New Haven: Yale University Press, 2010), 6.

The shift from print to visual culture continues with the contemporary entrenchment of the Internet and social media, which bring with them four biases that make it more difficult for leaders to develop their capabilities than in the age of print. These are: immediacy, intensity, polarity and conformity.

Although the Internet makes news and data more immediately accessible than ever, this surfeit of information has hardly made us individually more knowledgeable – let alone wiser. As the 'cost' of accessing information becomes negligible, as with the Internet, the incentives to remember it seem to weaken. While forgetting any one fact may not matter, the systematic failure to internalize information brings about a change in perception and a weakening of analytical ability. Facts are rarely self-explanatory; their significance and interpretation depend on context and relevance. For information to be transmuted into something approaching wisdom, it must be placed within a broader context of history and experience.

As a general rule, images 'speak' at a more emotional register of intensity than do words. Television and social media rely on images that inflame the passions, threatening to overwhelm leadership with a combination of personal and mass emotion. Social media in particular have encouraged users to become image-conscious spin doctors. All this engenders a more populist politics that celebrates utterances perceived to be authentic over the polished soundbites of the television era, not to mention the more analytical output of print.

The architects of the Internet thought of their invention as an ingenious means of connecting the world; in reality, it has also yielded a new way to divide humanity into warring tribes. Polarity and conformity rely upon and reinforce each other; one is shunted into a group, and then the group polices one's thinking. Small wonder that on many contemporary social-media platforms, users are divided into 'followers' and 'influencers'; there are no 'leaders'.

What are the consequences for leadership? In our present circumstances, Lee's gloomy assessment of visual media's effects is relevant: 'From such a process, I doubt if a Churchill, a Roosevelt or a de Gaulle can emerge.'[18] It is not that changes in communications technology have made inspired leadership and deep thinking about world order impossible, but that in an age dominated by television and the Internet, thoughtful leaders must struggle against the tide.

UNDERLYING VALUES

Today, merit tends to be understood narrowly as intellect compounded by effort. But Thomas Jefferson's earlier conception of a 'natural aristocracy' rested on a different and perhaps more sustainable basis: the merging of 'virtue and talents'.[19] For a political elite to render meaningful public service, both education and character are essential.

As we have seen, leaders with world-historical impact have benefited from a rigorous and humanistic education. Such an education begins in a formal setting and continues for a lifetime through reading and discussion with others. That initial step is rarely taken today – few universities offer an education in statecraft either explicitly or implicitly – and the lifelong effort is made more difficult as changes in technology erode deep literacy. Thus, for meritocracy to be reinvigorated, humanistic education would need to regain its significance, embracing such subjects as philosophy, politics, human geography, modern languages, history, economic thought, literature and even, perhaps, classical antiquity, the study of which was long the nursery of statesmen.

And since character is essential, a deeper conception of meritocratic leadership would also embrace the definition of virtue provided by the political scientist James Q. Wilson: 'habits of moderate action; more specifically, acting with due restraint on one's impulses, due regard for the rights of others, and reasonable concern for distant consequences'.[20] From youth to old age, the sheer centrality of *character* – that most indispensable of qualities – is an unending challenge, to leaders no less than to students of leadership. Good character does not assure worldly success, or triumph in statecraft, but it does provide firm grounding in victory and consolation in failure.

These six leaders will be remembered for the qualities that became associated with them and that defined their impact: Adenauer for his integrity and persistence, de Gaulle for his determination and historical vision, Nixon for his comprehension of the interlocking international situation and his strength in decision, Sadat for the spiritual elevation with which he forged peace, Lee for his imagination in the founding of a new multiethnic society, Thatcher for her principled leadership and tenacity. All showed extraordinary courage. No single person could ever possess all these virtues at any one time; the six leaders combined them in different proportions. Their leadership became as identified with their attributes as with their achievements.

LEADERSHIP AND WORLD ORDER

Since the end of what these pages have described as the Second Thirty Years' War (1914–45), instantaneous communication and the technological revolution have combined to give a new significance and urgency to two crucial questions confronting leaders: what is imperative for national security? And what is required for peaceful international coexistence?

These questions have been answered in different ways across history. Though a plethora of empires has existed, aspirations to world order were confined by geography as well as technology to specific regions; this was true even of the Roman and Chinese empires, which encompassed a vast range of societies and cultures within themselves. These were regional orders presenting themselves as world orders.

Starting in the sixteenth century, an explosion in technology, medicine and economic and political organization expanded the capacity of the West to project its power and systems of governance around the world.[21] From the middle of the seventeenth century, the Westphalian system based on respect for sovereignty and international law developed within Europe. That system, which became embedded worldwide after the end of colonialism, allowed the rise of states which – shedding Western dominance – insisted on their part in defining, and sometimes challenging, the rules of the established world order.

In his essay *Perpetual Peace*, the philosopher Immanuel Kant wrote three centuries ago that mankind was destined for universal peace either by way of human insight or by conflicts of a magnitude and destructiveness that would leave no alternative. The prospects stated were too absolute; the problem of international order has not appeared as an either/or proposition. For all of recent memory, mankind has lived with a balance between relative security and legitimacy established by its leaders and interpreted by them.

At no previous period in history have the consequences of getting this balance wrong been more fraught or catastrophic. The contemporary age introduced a level of destructiveness which has enabled mankind to destroy civilization itself. This is reflected in the period's established grand strategies famously abbreviated and conceptualized in the phrase 'mutual assured destruction' (MAD). These were advanced in pursuit not so much of traditional victory as of war's prevention, and ostensibly designed less for conflict – understood to be potentially suicidal – than for deterrence. Not long after Hiroshima and Nagasaki, the fielding of nuclear weapons became incalculable, the stakes disconnected from the consequences.

For more than seven decades, while advanced weapons have grown in power, complexity and accuracy, no country has persuaded itself actually to use them – even in conflict with non-nuclear countries. As previously described, both the Soviet Union and the United States accepted defeat at the hands of non-nuclear countries without resorting to their own deadliest weapons. These dilemmas of nuclear strategy have never disappeared; they have instead mutated as more states have developed advanced weapons and as the essentially bipolar Cold War distribution of destructive capacities has been replaced by a more complicated and potentially less stable kaleidoscope of high-tech options.

Cyber weapons and AI applications (such as autonomous weapons systems) exacerbate the existing range of dangers. Unlike nuclear weapons, cyber weapons and artificial intelligence are ubiquitous, relatively inexpensive to develop, and tempting to use. Cyber weapons combine the capacity for massive impact with the possibility of obscuring the attribution of attacks. Artificial intelligence is able to overcome even the need for human operators, instead allowing weapons to launch themselves based on their own calculations and their ability to choose targets with near-absolute discrimination. Because the threshold for their use is so low, and their destructive capacity so great, resorting to such weapons – or even their formal threat – may turn a crisis into a war or transform a limited war into a nuclear one through unintended or uncontrollable escalation. The impact of revolutionary technology makes the full application of these weapons cataclysmic while rendering their limited use difficult to the point of unmanageability. No diplomacy has yet been invented for threatening their use explicitly without the risk of preemption in reply. Arms control explorations seem to have been dwarfed by these enormities.

It has been a paradox of the age of high technology that actual military operations have been confined to conventional weapons or tactical deployment of small-scale high-tech weapons, from drone strikes to cyberattacks. At the same time, advanced weapons are expected to be contained by mutual assured destruction. This pattern is too precarious for the long-term future.

History remains a relentless taskmaster as the technological revolution has been accompanied by a political transformation. At this writing, the world is witnessing the return of great-power rivalry, magnified by the spread and advancement of astonishing technologies. When in the early 1970s China embarked upon its re-entry into the international system, its human and economic potential was vast, but its technology and actual power were comparatively limited. China's rising economic and strategic capacities have meanwhile obliged the United States to contend for the first time in its history with a geopolitical competitor whose resources are potentially comparable to its own – a task as unfamiliar to Washington as to Beijing, which historically has treated foreign nations as tributaries to Chinese power and culture.

Each side thinks of itself as exceptional, but differently. The United States acts on the premise that its values are universally applicable and will ultimately be adopted everywhere. China expects that its civilizational uniqueness and impressive economic performance will inspire other societies to show deference to its priorities. Both the United States' missionary impulse and China's sense of cultural eminence imply a kind of subordination of one to the other. By the nature of their economies and high technology, each nation is impinging – partly by momentum, importantly by design – on what the other has heretofore considered its core interests.

China in the twenty-first century seems embarked on an international role to which it thinks itself entitled by its achievements over millennia. The United States is acting to project power, purpose and diplomacy around the world to maintain a global equilibrium rooted in its postwar experience, responding to tangible and conceptional challenges to that order. For the leaders of each side, these requirements of security seem self-evident. And they are supported by public opinion. Yet security is only part of the equation. The key issue for the future of the world is whether the two behemoths can learn to combine inevitable strategic rivalry with a concept and practice of coexistence.

As for Russia, it conspicuously lacks China's market power, demographic heft and diversified industrial base. Spanning eleven time zones and enjoying few natural defensive demarcations, Russia has acted according to its own geographical and historical imperatives. Russian foreign policy transforms a mystical patriotism into imperial entitlement, with an abiding perception of insecurity essentially derived from the country's longstanding vulnerability to invasion across the East European plain. For centuries, its authoritarian leaders have tried to insulate Russia's vast territory with a security belt imposed around its diffuse border; today the same priority manifests itself once again in the attack on Ukraine.

The impact of these societies on each other has been shaped by their strategic assessments, which grow out of their histories. The Ukrainian conflict illustrates this. After the disintegration of the Soviet satellite states in Eastern Europe and their emergence as independent nations, the entire territory from the established security line in the center of Europe to the national border of Russia became open for a new strategic design. Stability depended on whether the emerging dispensation could calm historic European fears of Russian domination as well as account for traditional Russian concern over offensives from the West.

The strategic geography of Ukraine epitomizes these concerns. If Ukraine were to join NATO, the security line between Russia and Europe would be placed within 300 miles of Moscow – in effect eliminating the historic buffer which saved Russia when France and Germany sought to occupy it in successive centuries. If the security border were to be established on the western side of Ukraine, Russian forces would be within striking distance of Budapest and Warsaw. The February 2022 invasion of Ukraine, in flagrant violation of international law, is thus largely an outgrowth of a failed strategic dialogue or else of an inadequately undertaken one. The experience of two nuclear entities confronting each other militarily – even while not having recourse to their ultimate weapons – underlines the urgency of the fundamental problem.

The triangular relationship between America, China and Russia will eventually resume – though Russia will be weakened by the demonstration of its military limits in Ukraine, the widespread rejection of its conduct, and the scope and impact of the sanctions against it. But it will retain nuclear and cyber capabilities for doomsday scenarios.

In US–China relations, the conundrum is whether two different concepts of national greatness can learn to coexist peacefully side by side and how. With Russia, the challenge is whether that country can reconcile its view of itself with the self-determination and security of the countries in what it has long defined as its near abroad (mostly in Central Asia and Eastern Europe), and to do so as part of an international system rather than by means of domination.

It now seems possible that a liberal and universal rules-based order, however worthy in its conception, will be replaced in practice for an indeterminate period of time by an at least partially decoupled world. Such a division encourages a quest at its fringes for spheres of influence. If so, how will countries that do not agree on rules of global conduct be able to operate within an agreed design of equilibrium? Will the quest for dominance overwhelm the analysis of coexistence?

In a world of increasingly formidable technology that can either uplift or dismantle human civilization, there is no final resolution, not to speak of a military one, to great-power competition. An unrestrained technological race, justified by the ideologization of foreign policy in which each side is convinced of the malevolent intent of the other, risks creating a cataclysmic cycle of mutual suspicion like that which started the First World War, but with incomparably greater consequences.

All sides are thus now obliged to reexamine their first principles of international behavior and relate them to the possibilities of coexistence. For the leaders of high-tech societies in particular, there is a moral and strategic imperative to carry out, both within their own and with potential adversarial countries, a permanent discussion of the implications of technology and of how its military applications might be restrained. The subject is too important to neglect until crises arise. As with the arms-control dialogues that helped contribute to restraint during the nuclear age, high-level explorations of the consequences of emerging technologies could cultivate reflection and promote habits of reciprocal strategic self-control.

An irony of the contemporary world is that one of its glories – the revolutionary explosion of technology – has emerged so quickly, and with such optimism, that it has outrun thought of its perils, and inadequate systematic efforts have been made to understand its capacities. Technologists develop astonishing devices, but they have had little occasion to explore and assess their comparative implications within a frame of history. Political leaders too often lack an adequate grasp of the strategic and philosophical implications of the machines and algorithms at their disposal. At the same time, the technological revolution is impinging on human consciousness and perceptions of the nature of reality. The last great comparable transformation, the Enlightenment, replaced the age of faith with repeatable experiments and logical deductions. It is now being supplanted by reliance on algorithms, which work in the opposite direction, offering outcomes in search of an explanation. Exploring these new frontiers will require a committed effort from leaders to narrow, and ideally to close, existing gaps between the worlds of technology, politics, history and philosophy.

In the first chapter of these pages, the test of leadership was described as the capacity for analysis, strategy, courage and character. The challenges facing the leaders described here were as comparably complex as the contemporary ones, if less far-ranging. The criterion by which to judge the leader in history remains unchanged: to transcend circumstance by vision and dedication.

It is not necessary for the leaders of the contemporary great powers to develop a detailed vision of how to resolve the dilemmas described here immediately. They must, however, be clear on what has to be avoided and cannot be tolerated. Wise leaders must preempt their challenges before they manifest themselves as crises.

Lacking a moral and strategic vision, the present age is unmoored. The vastness of our future as yet defies comprehension. The increasingly acute and disorienting steepness of the crests, the depths of the troughs, the dangers of the shoals – all these demand navigators with the creativity and fortitude to guide societies to as yet unknown, but more hopeful, destinations.

THE FUTURE OF LEADERSHIP

The two questions Konrad Adenauer put to me during our final meeting in 1967, three months before his death, have gained new relevance: are any leaders still able to conduct a genuine long-range policy? Is true leadership still possible today?

After exploring the lives of six consequential twentieth-century figures and the conditions that enabled their achievements, the student of leadership naturally wonders whether parallel performances can be replicated. Are leaders coming forth with the character, intellect and hardiness required to meet the challenges facing world order?

The question has been asked before, and leaders have emerged who rose to the occasion. When Adenauer posed his questions, Sadat, Lee and Thatcher were largely unknown. Likewise, few who witnessed the fall of France in 1940 could imagine its renewal under de Gaulle in a career spanning three decades. When Nixon opened the dialogue with China, few contemporaries had an inkling of its possible consequences.

Machiavelli, in his *Discourses on Livy*, ascribes the slackening of leadership to social lassitude induced by long periods of tranquility. When societies are blessed with peaceful times and indulge the slow corruption of standards, the people may follow 'either a man who is judged to be good by common self-deception or someone put forward by men who are more likely to desire special favors than the common good'.[23] But later, under the impact of 'adverse times' – ever the teacher of realities – 'this deception is revealed, and out of necessity the people turn to those who in tranquil times were almost forgotten'.[24]

The grave conditions described here must, in the end, provide the impetus for societies to insist on meaningful leadership. In the late nineteenth century, Friedrich Engels predicted that the 'government of persons' would be replaced by the 'administration of things'.[25] But greatness in history resides in the refusal to abdicate to vast impersonal forces; its defining elements are – and must continue to be – created by human beings. Max Weber has described the essential qualities needed for transformative leadership:

> The only man who has a 'vocation' for politics is one who is certain that his spirit will not be broken if the world, when looked at from his point of view, proves too stupid or base to accept what he wishes to offer it, and who, when faced with all that obduracy, can still say 'Nevertheless!' despite everything.[26]

The six leaders discussed here developed parallel qualities despite the profound differences among their societies: a capacity to understand the situation in which their societies found themselves, an ability to devise a strategy to manage the present and shape the future, a skill in moving their societies toward elevated purposes, and a readiness to rectify shortcomings. Faith in the future was to them indispensable. It remains so. No society can remain great if it loses faith in itself or if it systematically impugns its self-perception. This imposes above all the willingness to enlarge the sphere of concern from the self to the society at large and to evoke the generosity of public spirit which inspires sacrifice and service.

Great leadership results from the collision of the intangible and the malleable, from that which is given and that which is exerted. Scope remains for individual effort – to deepen historical understanding, hone strategy and improve character. The Stoic philosopher Epictetus wrote long ago, 'We cannot choose our external circumstances, but we can always choose how we respond to them.'[27] It is the role of leaders to help guide that choice and inspire their people in its execution.

List of Illustrations

Notes

INTRODUCTION

1. Winston S. Churchill, *The Gathering Storm* (Winston S. Churchill, *The Second World War Book 1*) (Boston: Houghton Mifflin, 1948), 284.

2. Quoted in Andrew Roberts, *Leadership in War* (New York: Viking, 2019), 221.

3. Oswald Spengler, *The Decline of the West*, trans. Charles Francis Atkinson (Oxford: Oxford University Press, 1932), 383.

4. Charles de Gaulle, *The Edge of the Sword*, trans. Gerard Hopkins (New York: Criterion Books, 1960), 20–21. The full passage is: 'There is a close analogy between what takes place in the mind of the military commander when planning an action, and what happens to the artist at the moment of conception. The latter does not renounce the use of his intelligence. He draws from it lessons, methods, and knowledge. But his power of creation can operate only if he possesses, in addition, a certain instinctive faculty which we call inspiration, for that alone can give the direct contact with nature from which the vital spark must leap. We can say of the military art what Bacon said of the other arts: "They are the product of man added to nature."'

5. Quoted in Karl Joachim Weintraub, 1984 Ryerson Lecture, 'With a Long Sense of Time . . . ', *University of Chicago Magazine* 96, no. 5 (June 2004), https://magazine.uchicago.edu/0406/features/weintraub.shtml. For Huizinga, see: Johan Huizinga, *Het Aesthetishche Bestanddeel van Geschiedkundige Voorstellingen* (Haarlem: H. D. Tjeenk Willink & Zoon, 1905), 31–2.

6. Isaiah Berlin, 'The Sense of Reality', in *The Sense of Reality: Studies in Ideas and Their History*, ed. Henry Hardy (Princeton: Princeton University Press, 2019), 29–30.

7. Thomas Mann, *The Magic Mountain* (trans. 1927), quoted in Charles Hill, *Grand Strategies: Literature, Statecraft, and World Order* (New Haven: Yale University Press, 2010), 211.

8. Norman Angell, *The Great Illusion: A Study of the Relation of Military Power to National Advantage* (New York: G. P. Putnam's Sons, 1910), 186,

accessed via Project Gutenberg at https://www.gutenberg.org/files/38535/38535-h/38535-h.htm.

9. Ibid., 314.

10. Nadège Mougel, 'World War I Casualties', trans. Julie Gratz, 2011, Centre Européen Robert Schuman, http://www.centre-robert-schuman.org/userfiles/files/REPERES%20%E2%80%93%20module%201-1-1%20-%20 explanatory%20notes20%E2%80%93%20World%20War%20I%20cas ualties%20%E2%80%93%20EN.pdf.

11. François Héran, 'Lost Generations: the Demographic Impact of the Great War,' *Population & Societies* 2014/4 (No 510), 1–4.

12. W. H. Auden, 'September 1, 1939', https://poets.org/poem/september-1-1939.

13. National World War II Museum – New Orleans, 'Research Starters: Worldwide Deaths in World War II', https://www.nationalww2museum.org/students-teachers/student-resources/research-starters/research-starters-worldwide-deaths-world-war.

14. Roberts, *Leadership in War*, xii.

15. This typology originated in a 1966 essay for *Daedalus,* some phrases of which reappear here. See Henry A. Kissinger, 'Domestic Structure and Foreign Policy', *Daedalus* 95, no. 2 (spring 1966), 503–29.

16. Thucydides, *The Peloponnesian War*, I, 138. Emphases added.

17. Fernand Braudel, quoted in Oswyn Murray, 'Introduction', in Fernand Braudel, *The Mediterranean in the Ancient World* (London: Penguin, 2001).

1. KONRAD ADENAUER

1. Eugene Davidson, *The Death and Life of Germany* (Columbia: University of Missouri Press, 1999), 85. Richard Dominic Wiggers, 'The United States and the Refusal to Feed German Civilians after World War II', in Béla Várdy and T. Hunt Tooley, eds., *Ethnic Cleansing in Twentieth-Century Europe* (New York: Columbia University Press, 2003), 286.

2. Konrad Adenauer, *Memoirs 1945–53*, trans. Beate Ruhm von Oppen (Chicago: Henry Regnery Company, 1965), 56.

3. Charles Williams, *Adenauer: The Father of the New Germany* (New York: Wiley, 2000), 1–13, 16–17.

4. Ibid., 29.

5. Ibid., 220–23.

6. Ibid., 222–4.

7. Ibid., 237.

8. Ibid., 238, 232–5.

9. Ibid., 250.

10. Joseph Shattan, *Architects of Victory: Six Heroes of the Cold War* (Washington, DC: The Heritage Foundation, 1999), 95.

11. Williams, *Adenauer*, 284–90.

12. Ibid., 304–6.

13. Ibid., 314. See also Jeffrey Herf, *Divided Memory: The Nazi Past in the Two Germanys* (Cambridge, MA: Harvard University Press, 1997), 213.

14. Williams, *Adenauer*, 312–13.

15. The Zonal Committee (*Zonenausschuß*) of the CDU in the British Zone, 'Aufruf!', January 3, 1946, Konrad Adenauer Foundation, https://www. konrad-adenauer.de/download_file/view_inline/831.

16. Henry A. Kissinger, Memorandum for the President, 'Subject: Visit of Chancellor Adenauer – Some Psychological Factors', April 6, 1961, 2, https:// www.jfklibrary.org/asset-viewer/archives/JFKPOF/117a/ JFKPOF-117a-008.

17. *Volkszählungsergebnisse von 1816 bis 1970*, Beiträge zur Statistik des Rhein-Sieg-Kreises, (Siegburg: Archivbibliothek, 1980), Band 17 [*Population Outcomes from 1816 to 1970*, Postings for Statistics of the Rhein-Sieg-Kreises, vol. 17].

18. Williams, *Adenauer*, 326–30.

19. 'Text of Occupation Statute Promulgated on 12th May 1949 by the Military Governors and Commanders in Chief of the Western Zones', *Official Gazette of the Allied High Commission for Germany*. 23.09.1949, no. 1 (Bonn-Petersberg: Allied High Commission for Germany), 13–15.

20. Williams, *Adenauer*, 332–3. See also Amos Yoder, 'The Ruhr Authority and the German Problem', *The Review of Politics* 17, no. 3, (July 1955), 352.

21. 'Speech by Konrad Adenauer, Chancellor of the Federal Republic, at a Reception Given by the Allied High Commissioners (September 21, 1949)', in *United States Department of State, Germany 1947–1949: The Story in Documents* (Washington, DC: US Government Printing Office, 1950), 321, reprinted in Beata Ruhm von Oppen, ed., *Documents on Germany under Occupation, 1945–1954* (London and New York: Oxford University Press, 1955), 417–19; as cited here: http://germanhistorydocs.ghi-dc.org/docpage. cfm?docpage_id=3194.

22. Dean Acheson, *Present at the Creation: My Years in the State Department* (New York: Norton, 1969), 341.

23. George C. Marshall, 'Harvard Commencement Speech', June 5, 1947. https://www.marshallfoundation.org/marshall/the-marshall-plan/marshall-plan-speech/.

24. Adenauer, *Memoirs 1945–53*, 147. The speech was given on March 23, 1949, in Berne.

25. Thomas Hörber, *The Foundations of Europe: European Integration Ideas in France, Germany and Britain in the 1950s* (Heidelberg: VS Verlag für Sozialwissenschaften, 2006) 141.

26. Ronald J. Granieri, *The Ambivalent Alliance* (New York: Berghahn Books, 2004), 34, citing Herbert Blankenhorn, *Verständnis und Verständigung:*

Blätter eines politischen Tagebuchs (Frankfurt: Propyläen Verlag, 1980), entry for November 15, 1949, 40.

27. Quoted in Hans-Peter Schwarz, *Konrad Adenauer*, vol. 1, trans. Louise Willmot (New York: Berghahn Books, 1995), 450.

28. Letter from Konrad Adenauer to Robert Schuman, July 26, 1949, Centre virtuel de la connaissance sur l'Europe, University of Luxembourg (hereafter CVCE), https://www.cvce.eu/obj/letter_from_konrad_adenauer_to_robert_schuman_26_july_1949-en-a03f485c-0eeb-4401-8c54-8816008a7579.html.

29. Ernst Friedlaender, 'Interview des Bundeskanzlers mit dem Korrespondenten der Wochenzeitung', *Die Zeit*, November 3, 1949, https://www.cvce.eu/content/publication/1999/1/1/63e25bb4-c980-432c-af1c-53c79b77b410/publishable_en.pdf.

30. *New York Times*, December 5, 1949.

31. 'Deutscher Bundestag – 18. Sitzung. Bonn, den 24. und 25. November 1949', Konrad Adenauer Stiftung, https://www.konrad-adenauer.de/seite/24-november-1949/.

32. Adenauer, *Memoirs 1945–53*, 256.

33. Robert Schuman, Declaration of May 9, 1950. Foundation Robert Schuman, *European Issue*, No. 204, May 10, 2011, https://www.robert-schuman.eu/en/doc/questions-d-europe/qe-204-en.pdf.

34. Adenauer, *Memoirs 1945–53*, 260.

35. 'Entrevue du 23 mai 1950, entre M. Jean Monnet et le Chancelleur Adenauer', CVCE, 5, https://www.cvce.eu/obj/compte_rendu_de_l_entrevue_entre_jean_monnet_et_konrad_adenauer_23_mai_1950-fr-24853ee7-e477-4537-b462-c622fadee66a.html.

36. Konrad Adenauer, letter to Robert Schuman, May 23, 1950, Bonn, CVCE, https://www.cvce.eu/de/obj/brief_von_konrad_adenauer_an_robert_schuman_23_mai_1950-de-7644877d-6004-4ca6-8ec6-93e4d35b971d.html.

37. Konrad Adenauer, 'Where Do We Stand Now?', speech to students at the University of Bonn, February 1951, Konrad Adenauer Foundation, https://www.konrad-adenauer.de/seite/10-februar-1951-1/.

38. 'Ratification of the ECSC Treaty', in *From the Schuman Plan to the Paris Treaty (1950–1952)*, CVCE, https://www.cvce.eu/en/recherche/unit-content/-/unit/5cc6b004-33b7-4e44-b6db-f5f9e6c01023/3f50ad11-f340-48a4-8435-fbe54e28ed9a.

39. Ibid.

40. Michael Moran, 'Modern Military Force Structures', *Council on Foreign Relations*, October 26, 2006, https://www.cfr.org/backgrounder/modern-military-force-structures#:~:text=Division.,on%20the%20national%20army%20involved.

41. Adenauer, *Memoirs 1945–53*, 193.

42. 'Aide Defends Adenauer's Stand', *New York Times,* November 25, 1950.

43. Granieri, *The Ambivalent Alliance*, 56.

44. Arnulf Baring, *Außenpolitik in Adenauers Kanzlerdemokratie* (Berlin: R. Oldenbourg, 1969), 161–4.

45. Ibid.

46. The Soviet Ministry for Foreign Affairs to the Embassy of the United States, Moscow, May 24 1952, *Foreign Relations of the United States, 1952–1954*, vol. 7: part 1, document 102, https://history.state.gov/historicaldocuments/frus1952-54v07p1/d102.

47. Quoted in Granieri, *The Ambivalent Alliance*, 79.

48. Gordon Alexander Craig, *From Bismarck to Adenauer: Aspects of German Statecraft* (Baltimore: The Johns Hopkins Press, 1958), 110, citing *Der Spiegel*, October 6, 1954, 5.

49. Thomas A. Schwartz, 'Eisenhower and the Germans', in Gunter Bischof and Stephen E. Ambrose, eds., *Eisenhower: A Centenary Assessment* (Baton Rouge: LSU Press, 1995), 215.

50. Adenauer, *Memoirs 1945–53*, 456.

51. Leo J. Daugherty, 'Tip of the Spear: The Formation and Expansion of the Bundeswehr, 1949–1963', *Journal of Slavic Military Studies* 24, no. 1 (winter 2011).

52. Williams, *Adenauer*, 392–409.

53. Ibid., 410–23.

54. Jeffrey Herf, *Divided Memory: The Nazi Past in the Two Germanys* (Cambridge, MA: Harvard University Press, 1997, 282, quoting Konrad Adenauer, 'Regierungserklärung zur jüdischen Frage und zur Wiedergutmachung', in *Der deutsch-israelische Dialog: Dokumentation eines erregenden Kapitels deutscher Außenpolitik, Teil 1, Politik*, vol. 1 (Munich: K. G. Sauer, 1987), 46–7.

55. Ibid., 1:47.

56. Herf, *Divided Memory*, 288.

57. Ibid., 288, quoting Michael W. Krekel, *Wiedergutmachung: Das Luxemburger Abkommen vom 10. September 1952* (Bad Honnef-Rhöndorf: SBAH, 1996), 40.

58. Williams, *Adenauer*, 534.

59. 'Adenauer Fêted by Eshkol; Wants Jews to Recognize Bonn's Good Will', *Jewish Telegraphic Agency*, May 5, 1966, https://www.jta.org/archive/adenauer-feted-by-eshkol-wants-jews-to-recognize-bonns-good-will.

60. Ibid.

61. James Feron, 'Adenauer Begins 8-Day Visit to Israel', *New York Times*, May 3, 1966.

62. 'Adenauer Fêted by Eshkol'.

63. Williams, *Adenauer*, 442.

64. Felix von Eckardt, *Ein unordentliches Leben* (Düsseldorf: Econ-Verlag, 1967), 466.

65. Keith Kyle, *Suez* (New York: St Martin's Press, 1991), 467.

66. Department of State Historical Office, *Documents on Germany, 1944–1961* (Washington, DC, United States Government Printing Office, 1961), 585.

67. Kissinger, 'Visit of Chancellor Adenauer', 4. This was in preparation for Kennedy's first meeting with Adenauer, which took place on April 12.

68. Henry A. Kissinger, 'Remarks at the American Council on Germany John J. McCloy Awards Dinner', June 26, 2002, Yale University Library Digital Repository, Henry A. Kissinger papers, part II, series III: Post-Government Career, box 742, folder 10.

69. Niall Ferguson, *Kissinger 1923–1968: The Idealist* (New York: Penguin Press, 2015), 490–91, 906.

70. Ibid.

71. Walter C. Dowling, telegram from the Embassy in Germany to the Department of State, Bonn, February 17, 1962, 2 p.m. *Foreign Relations of the United States, 1961–1963*, vol. XIV: *Berlin Crisis, 1961–1962*, https://history.state.gov/historicaldocuments/frus1961-63v14/d298.

72. Ibid.

73. Neil MacGregor, *Germany: Memories of a Nation* (New York: Knopf, 2015), ch. 1, 'Where Is Germany?'.

74. For the definitive history of *Ostpolitik*, see Timothy Garton Ash, *In Europe's Name: Germany and the Divided Continent* (New York: Vintage, 1994).

75. Williams, *Adenauer*, 503–19.

76. Konrad Adenauer, speech on the possibilities of European Unification, Brussels, September 25, 1956, CVCE, https://www.cvce.eu/content/publication/2006/10/25/ea27a4e3-4883-4d38-8dbc-5e3949b1145d/publishable_en.pdf.

77. Barbara Marshall, *Willy Brandt: A Political Biography* (London: Macmillan, 1997), 71–3.

78. Helmut Schmidt, *Men and Powers: A Political Retrospective*, trans. Ruth Hein (New York: Random House, 1989), 4.

79. Marion Gräfin Dönhoff, *Foe into Friend: The Makers of the New Germany from Konrad Adenauer to Helmut Schmidt*, trans. Gabriele Annan (New York: St. Martin's Press, 1982), 159.

80. Helmut Schmidt died in 2015. I delivered one of the eulogies at a formal state service in Hamburg. The main speaker that day was Chancellor Angela Merkel, the leader of the Christian Democratic Union and head of a CDU–SPD coalition – a combination that illustrated how internal divisions in Germany had been overcome since the Adenauer period. I summed up Schmidt's contribution as follows: 'Helmut [Schmidt] lived in an age of transition: between Germany's past as an occupied and divided country and its future as the strongest European nation; between its concern with security and the need to participate in building a global economic world order ...'

See Henry A. Kissinger, 'Eulogy for Helmut Schmidt', November 23, 2015. https://www.henryakissinger.com/speeches/eulogy-for-helmut-schmidt/.

81. Blaine Harden, 'Hungarian Moves Presaged Honecker Ouster', *Washington Post*, October 19, 1989, https://www.washingtonpost.com/archive/poli tics/1989/10/19/hungarian-move-presaged-honecker-ouster/4c7ff7bd-code-4e82-86ab-6d1766abec3c/.

82. Jeffrey A. Engel, *When the World Seemed New: George H. W. Bush and the End of the Cold War* (New York: Mariner Books, 2017), 371–5.

83. Angela Merkel, 'Speech at the Konrad Adenauer Foundation on the 50th anniversary of Konrad Adenauer's Death', April 25, 2017, https://www.kas. de/de/veranstaltungen/detail/-/content/-wir-waehlen-die-freiheit-1.

84. 'Der Abschied', *UFA-Wochenschau*, Das Bundesarchiv-Inhalt. 'Ich habe den Wunsch . . . getan habe', https://www.filmothek.bundesarchiv.de/video/ 584751?q=bundeswehr&xm=AND&xf%5B0%5D=_fulltext&xo%5B0 %5D=CONTAINS&xv%5B0%5D=&set_lang=de.

2. CHARLES DE GAULLE

1. Address delivered by General de Gaulle at Orly Airport, on the arrival of Mr Richard Nixon, President of the United States, February 28, 1969.

2. In 1967, the French ambassador had invited me for a presidential audience but, in typical Gaullist style, had left the decision to me: 'If you find yourself in France, the president will be prepared to receive you.' This was shortly after the withdrawal of French troops from NATO command. Not wanting to offend the President Johnson administration, I had evaded the invitation – to my lasting regret.

3. See Charles de Gaulle, *Complete War Memoirs* (New York: Simon and Schuster, 1964), 80.

4. Ibid., 84.

5. Roger Hermiston, 'No Longer Two Nations but One', *The Lion and Unicorn* blog, June 4, 2016, https://thelionandunicorn.wordpress.com/2016/ 06/04/no-longer-two-nations-but-one/.

6. See de Gaulle, *Complete War Memoirs*, 74–80; and Hermiston, 'No Longer Two Nations but One'.

7. Hermiston, 'No Longer Two Nations but One'.

8. Julian Jackson, *De Gaulle* (Cambridge: Harvard Belknap Press, 2018), 128–33. De Gaulle gave several follow-up broadcasts in the following days.

9. From de Gaulle's reply to Pétain from London. See ibid., 134.

10. Ibid. The source on which Jackson is drawing is René Cassin, *Les Hommes partis de rien: Le reveil de la France abattue (1940–1941)* (Paris: Plon, 1975), 76.

11. Bernard Ledwidge, *De Gaulle* (New York: St Martin's Press, 1982), 76. Quoted in Jackson, *De Gaulle*, 135.

12. Quoted in Jackson, *De Gaulle*, 41.

13. Quoted in ibid., 17.

14. *Vers l'Armée de Métier*, 1934; the first English translation was published in 1940 as *The Army of the Future*.

15. Charles de Gaulle, proclamation dated July 1940, in *Discours et Messages*, vol. 1 (Paris: Librairie Plon, 1970), 19: Also quoted in Christopher S. Thompson, 'Prologue to Conflict: De Gaulle and the United States, From First Impressions Through 1940', in Robert O. Paxton and Nicholas Wahl, eds., *De Gaulle and the United States: A Centennial Reappraisal* (Oxford: Berg, 1994), 19. This sentiment happened to be entirely consistent with Churchill's conviction, expressed in the 'We shall fight on the beaches' speech of June 4, 1940, that 'in God's good time, the New World, with all its power and might,' would bring about 'the rescue and the liberation of the old'.

16. Henry Kissinger, 'The Illusionist: Why We Misread de Gaulle,' *Harper's Magazine*, March 1965.

17. Charles de Gaulle, '1939, Notes sur les idées militaires de Paul Reynaud', *Lettres, Notes et Carnets, 1905–1941* (Paris: Éditions Robert Laffont, 2010), 886.

18. Quoted in Jackson, *De Gaulle*, 44.

19. Walter Benjamin, *The Arcades Project* (New York: Belknap Press, 2002).

20. Paul Kennedy, *The Rise and Fall of the Great Powers* (New York: Random House, 1987), 99, 199.

21. Ibid.

22. Ulrich Pfister and Georg Fertig, 'The Population History of Germany: Research Strategy and Preliminary Results', working paper (Rostock: Max-Planck-Institut für demografische Forschung, 2010), 5.

23. Rondo E. Cameron, 'Economic Growth and Stagnation in France, 1815–1914', *The Journal of Modern History* 30, no. 1 (March 1958), 1.

24. Nadège Mougel, 'World War I Casualties', Robert Schuman Centre Report (2011).

25. De Gaulle, *Vers l'armée de métier*, 1934. De Gaulle was a lieutenant colonel at the time of publication.

26. Kissinger, 'The Illusionist', 70; also see 'Address by President Charles de Gaulle on French, African and Algerian Realities Broadcast over French Radio and Television on June 14, 1960', in *Major Addresses, Statements and Press Conferences of General Charles de Gaulle: May 19, 1958–January 31, 1964* (New York: French Embassy, 1964), 79, https://bit.ly/3rEDU8w.

27. The Molotov–Ribbentrop Pact.

28. Charles de Gaulle, *Memoirs of Hope: Renewal and Endeavor* (New York: Simon and Schuster, 1971), 3.

29. Ibid., 4.

30. Dorothy Shipley White, *Seeds of Discord* (Syracuse: Syracuse University Press, 1964), 87.

31. Jackson, *de Gaulle*, 138.

32. Charles de Gaulle, radio broadcast, August 27, 1940, https://enseignants. lumni.fr/fiche-media/00000003432/le-general-de-gaulle-salue-le-ralliement-du-tchad-a-la-france-libre-audio.html#infos.

33. Jackson notes that 'De Gaulle hinted later on one or two occasions that he had contemplated suicide' (*De Gaulle*, 149).

34. The full oath is: 'Jurez de ne déposer les armes que lorsque nos couleurs, nos belles couleurs, flotteront sur la cathédrale de Strasbourg.'

35. Quoted in Jackson, *De Gaulle*, 170.

36. De Gaulle, *Complete War Memoirs*, 192.

37. Ibid., 206.

38. Ibid., 195.

39. Ibid., 206.

40. Jackson, *De Gaulle*, 183.

41. Ibid., 254.

42. Charles de Gaulle, 'Télégramme au vice-amiral Muselier, à Saint-Pierre-et-Miquelon', December 24, 1941, in *Lettres, Notes et Carnets*, 1360.

43. See Jean Lacouture, *De Gaulle, the Rebel 1890–1944* (New York: Norton, 1990), 317.

44. Benjamin Welles, *Sumner Welles* (New York: St Martin's Press, 1997), 288.

45. Jackson, *De Gaulle*, 209.

46. Charles de Gaulle, speech delivered on June 18, 1942, at the Albert Hall in London, on the second anniversary of the formation of the Free French, in *Discours et Messages*, vol. 1 (Paris: Librairie Plon, 1970), 207–15.

47. Jackson, *De Gaulle*, 210–11.

48. The Conferences at Washington, 1941–1942, and Casablanca 1943. *Foreign Relations of the United States*, February 4, 1943.

49. See de Gaulle, *Complete War Memoirs*, 410.

50. Jackson, *De Gaulle*, 215.

51. Ibid., 277.

52. Quoted in ibid., 266.

53. Jackson, *De Gaulle*, 269–73. See also Lacouture, *De Gaulle, the Rebel*, 446–50.

54. See Jackson, *De Gaulle*, 276.

55. De Gaulle, *Complete War Memoirs*, 429.

56. Jackson, *De Gaulle*, 341.

57. Ibid., 315, quoting Henry L. Stimson and McGeorge Bundy, *On Active Service in Peace and War* (New York: Harper & Brothers, 1947), 549 (June 14, 1944).

58. De Gaulle's speech at Bayeux, June 14, 1944.

59. Jackson, *De Gaulle*, 317.

60. De Gaulle, *Complete War Memoirs*, 648.

61. Jackson, *De Gaulle*, 326.

62. Quoted in ibid., 327.

63. Ibid., 326.

64. Ibid., 331. For more on the dissolution of the Resistance, see Jean Lacouture, *De Gaulle, the Ruler 1945–1970* (New York: Norton, 1992), 25.

65. Jackson, *De Gaulle*, 336.

66. Ibid., 350.

67. See Jean Laloy, 'À Moscou: entre Staline et de Gaulle, décembre 1944', *Revue des études slaves* 54, fascicule 1–2 (1982), 152. See Jackson, *De Gaulle*, 350.

68. De Gaulle, *Memoirs of Hope*, 3.

69. Edmund Burke, *Reflections on the Revolution in France* (1790), in *The Works of the Right Honorable Edmund Burke* (1899), vol. 3, 359.

70. De Gaulle, *Complete War Memoirs*, 771.

71. Ibid., 771–2.

72. Ibid., 776.

73. Ibid., 778.

74. *Plutarch's Lives*, trans. John Dryden (New York: Penguin, 2001), vol. 1, 'Life of Solon', 118.

75. De Gaulle, *Memoirs of Hope*, 6.

76. Quoted in Jackson, *De Gaulle*, 381.

77. Quoted in ibid.

78. De Gaulle, *Complete War Memoirs*, 993.

79. Ibid., 977.

80. Jackson, *De Gaulle*, 499.

81. Ibid., 418.

82. De Gaulle, *Complete War Memoirs*, 996–7.

83. Quoted in Charles G. Cogan, *Charles de Gaulle: A Brief Biography with Documents* (Boston: Bedford Books, 1996), 183.

84. Ibid., 185.

85. Ibid., 186–7.

86. Ibid.

87. Ibid., 187.

88. Quoted in ibid., 185.

89. JFK Library, President's Office File, 'Memorandum of Conversation, President's Visit to Paris, May 31–June 2, 1961', Memorandum of Conversation at Elysée Palace between Kennedy and de Gaulle, May 31, 1961, https://www.jfklibrary.org/asset-viewer/archives/JFKPOF/116a/JFKPOF-116a-004.

90. Henry Kissinger, *Diplomacy* (New York: Touchstone, 1994), 541–3.

91. 'Proclamation of Algerian National Liberation Front (FLN), November 1, 1954', https://middleeast.library.cornell.edu/content/proclamation-algerian-national-liberation-front-fln-november-1-1954.

92. Quoted in Alistair Horne, *A Savage War of Peace: Algeria 1954–1962* (New York: Penguin, 1978), 99.

93. Central Intelligence Agency, 'Validity Study of NIE 71.2-56: Outlook for Algeria published 5 September 1956', CDG.P.CIA.1957.08.16.

94. Quoted in Jackson, *De Gaulle*, 447.

95. Quoted in 'Eyes on Allies: De Gaulle the Key', *New York Times*, May 20, 1962.

96. *Major Addresses* 6.

97. Jackson, *De Gaulle*, 463.

98. De Gaulle, *Memoirs of Hope*, 26.

99. Horne, *Savage War of Peace*, 301.

100. See ibid., L6333.

101. De Gaulle, *Memoirs of Hope*, 54.

102. Ibid.

103. Memorandum for the President from Henry Kissinger, May 16, 1969, 'Africa after de Gaulle', Richard Nixon Library, box 447 [218].

104. People's Republic of China Foreign Ministry Archive, 'Main Points of Chairman Mao's Conversation with Premier Abbas on September 30, 1960', trans. David Cowhig, October 4, 1960, Wilson Center History and Public Policy Program Digital Archive, http://digitalarchive.wilsoncenter.org/document/117904.

105. JFK Library, 'Staff Memoranda: Kissinger, Henry, February 1962: 13–28', https://www.jfklibrary.org/asset-viewer/archives/JFKNSF/320/JFKNSF-320-025.

106. Jackson, *De Gaulle,* 501.

107. Ibid., 518.

108. Ibid., 519.

109. 'Address Given by Charles de Gaulle (29 January 1960)', Centre virtuel de la connaissance sur l'Europe, University of Luxembourg, https://www.cvce.eu/en/obj/address_given_by_charles_de_gaulle_29_january_1960-en-095d41dd-fda2-49c6-aa91-772ebffa7b26.html.

110. 'Speech Denouncing the Algiers Putsch: April 23, 1961', in Cogan, *Charles de Gaulle*, 196.

111. '"Pieds-noirs": ceux qui ont choisi de rester', *La Dépêche*, March 10, 2012.

112. 'After 40 Years of Suffering and Silence, Algeria's "Harkis" Demand a Hearing', *Irish Times*, August 31, 2001.

113. Quoted in Cogan, *Charles de Gaulle*, 119.

114. Jackson, *De Gaulle*, 585.

115. De Gaulle, *Memoirs of Hope*, 176.

116. Address by President de Gaulle on May 31, 1960, in *Major Addresses*, 75, 78.
117. Eighth Press Conference Held by General de Gaulle as President of the French Republic [in Paris at the Elysée Palace on July 29, 1963], in ibid., 234.
118. *Major Addresses*, 159.
119. Quoted in Kissinger, *Diplomacy*, 606.
120. Ibid.
121. Ibid., 605.
122. Quoted in ibid., 575.
123. For the US policy, see McGeorge Bundy, 'NSAM 294 U.S. Nuclear and Strategic Delivery System Assistance to France', April 20, 1964, National Security Action Memorandums, NSF, box 3, LBJ Presidential Library, https://www.discoverlbj.org/item/nsf-nsam294.
124. See Wilfrid Kohl, *French Nuclear Diplomacy* (Princeton: Princeton University Press, 2016), 79.
125. This body should have the responsibility of taking joint decisions on all political matters affecting world security, and of drawing up, and if necessary putting into action, strategic plans, especially those involving the use of nuclear weapons. It should also be responsible for the organization of the defense, where appropriate, of individual operational regions, such as the Arctic, the Atlantic, the Pacific and the Indian Ocean. See Kissinger, *Diplomacy*, 611.
126. Henry Kissinger and Françoise Winock, 'L'Alliance atlantique et l'Europe', *Esprit*, n.s. 359, no. 4 (April 1967), 611.
127. Mark Howell, 'Looking Back: De Gaulle tells American Forces to Leave France', https://www.mildenhall.af.mil/News/Article-Display/Article/272283/looking-back-de-gaulle-tells-american-forces-to-leave-france/. August 1958 saw the first deployment of US nuclear weapons to (mainland) French soil, but they had been previously deployed to French Morocco. Robert Norris, William Arkin and William Burr, 'Where They Were', *The Bulletin of the Atomic Scientists*, November/December 1999, 29.
128. *Major Addresses*, 226.
129. Henry Kissinger, 'Military Policy and Defense of the "Grey Areas"', *Foreign Affairs* 33, no. 3 (1955), 416–28, doi:10.2307/20031108.
130. 'No Cities' speech by Secretary of Defense McNamara, July 9, 1962, https://robertmcnamara.org/wp-content/uploads/2017/04/mcnamara-1967-22no-cities22-speech-p.pdf.
131. Quoted in Kissinger, *Diplomacy*, 615.
132. Ibid.
133. De Gaulle, *Complete War Memoirs*, 81.
134. Ibid.
135. Ibid.
136. Julia Lovell, *Maoism: A Global History* (New York: Knopf, 2019), 273.

137. Jackson, *De Gaulle*, 721.

138. Ibid., 737.

139. Quoted in 'World: A Glimpse of Glory, a Shiver of Grandeur', *Time*, November 23, 1970.

140. Charles de Gaulle, *The Edge of the Sword*, trans. Gerard Hopkins (Westport, Conn.: Greenwood, 1960), 65–6. Quoted in Cogan, *Charles de Gaulle*, 218.

141. Quoted in Jackson, *De Gaulle*, 41.

142. De Gaulle, *Complete War Memoirs*, 997–8.

143. 'Sans Anne, peut-être n'aurais-je jamais fait ce que j'ai fait. Elle m'a donné le cœur et l'inspiration.' Pierrick Geais, 'Récit: La véritable histoire d'Anne de Gaulle, la fille handicapée du Général', *Vanity Fair* (France), March 3, 2020.

3. RICHARD NIXON

1. David Shambaugh, *China Goes Global: The Partial Power* (New York: Oxford University Press, 2013), 39.

2. Dale Van Atta, *With Honor: Melvin Laird in War, Peace, and Politics* (Madison: University of Wisconsin, 2008), 271–3.

3. 'Memorandum from President Nixon to his Assistant for National Security Affairs', *Foreign Relations of the United States*, vol. 17: *China, 1969–1972*, no. 147, State Department: Office of the Historian, https://history.state.gov/historicaldocuments/frus1969-76v17/d147.

4. Goodpaster was not national security advisor but helped to develop the procedures of the NSC. See C. Richard Nelson, *The Life and Work of General Andrew J. Goodpaster: Best Practices in National Security Affairs* (Lanham, MD: Rowman & Littlefield, 2016).

5. 'History of the National Security Council, 1947–1997', The White House Archives, https://georgewbush-whitehouse.archives.gov/nsc/history.html#nixon. David Rothkopf, *Running the World: The Inside Story of the National Security Council and the Architects of American Power* (New York: PublicAffairs, 2006), 84–5. As of 2017, the NSC staff has been statutorily limited to 200. See 'The National Security Council: Background and Issues for Congress', the Congressional Research Service, June 3, 2021, 8, https://crsreports.congress.gov/product/pdf/R/R44828.

6. Richard Nixon, *RN: The Memoirs of Richard Nixon* (New York: Grosset & Dunlap, 1978), 390.

7. Richard Nixon, 'Remarks to Midwestern News Media Executives Attending a Briefing on Domestic Policy in Kansas City, Missouri', July 6, 1971, https://www.presidency.ucsb.edu/documents/remarks-midwestern-news-media-executives-attending-briefing-domestic-policy-kansas-city.

8. Ibid.

9. *Time*, January 3, 1972.

10. Henry Kissinger, *Diplomacy* (New York: Simon and Schuster, 1994), 38–40.

11. Woodrow Wilson, 'Address of the President of the United States to the Senate', January 22, 1917, https://www.digitalhistory.uh.edu/disp_textbook.cfm?smtID=3&psid=3898.

12. Kissinger, *Diplomacy*, 709.

13. 'Text of President Nixon's Address at the 25th-Anniversary Session of the U.N.', *New York Times*, October 24, 1970.

14. Ibid.

15. Henry Kissinger, *White House Years* (Boston: Little, Brown, 1979), 135–6.

16. Richard Nixon to Melvin Laird, February 4, 1969. *Foreign Relations of the United States, 1969–1976*, vol. 1: *Foundations of Foreign Policy, 1969–1972*, State Department: Office of the Historian, https://history.state.gov/historicaldocuments/frus1969-76vo1/d10.

17. Richard Nixon, 'Remarks to the North Atlantic Council in Brussels', February 24, 1969, https://www.presidency.ucsb.edu/documents/remarks-the-north-atlantic-council-brussels.

18. Jeffrey Garten, *Three Days at Camp David: How a Secret Meeting in 1971 Transformed the Global Economy* (New York: HarperCollins, 2021), 4.

19. Ibid., 9–10.

20. Ibid., 77.

21. Ibid., 255.

22. Ibid., 250. Prominent German newspapers ran articles stating that 'there is almost a declaration of American trade war' and that 'Nixon's program . . . documents a relapse of the world's strongest economic power into nationalism and protectionism'.

23. Ibid., 308.

24. Richard H. Immerman, '"Dealing with a Government of Madmen": Eisenhower, Kennedy, and Ngo Dinh Diem', in David L. Henderson, ed., *The Columbia History of the Vietnam War* (New York: Columbia University Press, 2011), 131.

25. Harrison Salisbury, *Behind the Lines – Hanoi* (New York: Harper & Row, 1967), 137.

26. John W. Finney, 'Plank on Vietnam Devised by Doves', *New York Times*, August 24, 1968.

27. Defense Casualty Analysis System (DCAS) Extract Files, created, *c.*2001–4/29/2008, documenting the period 6/28/1950–5/28/2006, https://aad.archives.gov/aad/fielded-search.jsp?dt=2513&cat=GP21&tf=F&bc=,sl.

28. Richard Nixon, 'Informal Remarks in Guam with Newsmen', July 25, 1969, UC Santa Barbara American Presidency Project, https://www.presidency.ucsb.edu/documents/informal-remarks-guam-with-newsmen.

29. Ibid. Emphasis added.

30. Richard Nixon, 'Address to the Nation on the War in Vietnam', November 3, 1969, UC Santa Barbara American Presidency Project. https://www.pres idency.ucsb.edu/documents/address-the-nation-the-war-vietnam.

31. 'Memorandum of Conversation', Washington, October 20, 1969, 3:30 p.m. *Foreign Relations of the United States, 1969–1976*, vol. 12: *Soviet Union, January 1969–October 1970*, no. 93, State Department: Office of the Historian, https://history.state.gov/historicaldocuments/frus1969-76v12/d93.

32. Nixon, 'Address to the Nation on the War in Vietnam'.

33. The full text of the memorandum can be found in *White House Years*, 1480–82, together with a follow-up on p. 1482, with the following passage: 'Given the history of over-optimistic reports on Vietnam the past few years, it would be practically impossible to convince the American people that the other side is hurting and therefore, with patience, *time could be on our side*. First of all we are not sure about our relative position – we have misread indicators many times before. Secondly, even if we conclude that the allied military position is sound, we don't know how to translate this into political terms – and the political prospects in South Vietnam are much shakier. Thirdly, the Administration faces an extremely skeptical and cynical American audience – the President is rightly reluctant to appear optimistic and assume his own credibility gap. Finally, to a large and vocal portion of the dissenters in this country, the strength of the allied position is irrelevant – they want an end to the war at any price.' See Kissinger, *White House Years*, 1482, and 'Memorandum from the President's Assistant for National Security Affairs (Kissinger) to President Nixon', Washington, September 11, 1969, *Foreign Relations of the United States, 1969–1976*, vol. 6: *Vietnam, January 1969–July 1970*, no. 119, State Department: Office of the Historian, https://history.state.gov/historical-documents/frus1969-76v06/d119.

34. 'Address to the Nation', January 25, 1972, *The American Presidency Project*, UC Santa Barbara, https://www.presidency.ucsb.edu/documents/ address-the-nation-making-public-plan-for-peace-vietnam.

35. 'Vietnam War U.S. Military Fatal Casualty Statistics', National Archives, https://www.archives.gov/research/military/vietnam-war/casualty-statistics#toc--dcas-vietnam-conflict-extract-file-record-counts-by-incident-or-death-date-year-as-of-april-29-2008--2.

36. Richard Nixon, 'Address to the Nation on the Situation in Southeast Asia', May 8, 1972.

37. Quoted in Kissinger, *White House Years*, 1345.

38. 'Transcript of Kissinger's News Conference on the Status of the Cease-Fire Talks', *New York Times*, October 27, 1972.

39. 'Act of the International Conference on Viet-Nam', *The American Journal of International Law* 67, no. 3 (1973), 620–22, https://doi.org/ 10.2307/2199198. See also Henry Kissinger, *Years of Renewal* (New York:

Simon & Schuster, 1999), 485: 'There were twelve participants: United States, France, China, United Kingdom, Canada, Soviet Union, Hungary, Poland, Indonesia, Democratic Republic of Vietnam (DRV, i.e., North Vietnam), Republic of Vietnam (GVN, i.e., South Vietnam), and Provisional Revolutionary Government of the Republic of South Vietnam (PRG, i.e., the South Vietnamese Communists).'

40. Cf. Henry A. Kissinger, *Years of Upheaval* (Boston: Little, Brown, 1982), 316–27.

41. 'Vietnam – Supplemental Military Assistance (2)', Gerald R. Ford Presidential Library, box 43, John Marsh Files, 28 and 20–21, https://www.fordlibrarymuseum.gov/library/document/0067/12000897.pdf: 'The bill ... prohibits further military assistance or sales (including deliveries) to Cambodia after June 30, 1975'. 'For military assistance in FY 1974, the U.S. provided about $823 million (plus $235 million from prior year authorizations), about ⅓ of the previous year's funding and about half the level of $1.6 billion requested by the administration ... For economic assistance in FY 1974, the U.S. provided $333 million (including a supplemental of $49 million) or about ⅓ less than the level of $475 million requested by the Administration.' H. J. Res. 636 (93rd): 'Joint resolution making continuing appropriations for the fiscal year 1974, and for other purposes', July 1, 1973, https://www.govtrack.us/congress/bills/93/hjres636/text.

42. Jeffrey P. Kimball, *The Vietnam War Files: Uncovering the Secret History of Nixon-Era Strategy* (Lawrence, KS: University Press of Kansas, 2004), 57–9.

43. Hal Brands, 'Progress Unseen: U.S. Arms Control Policy and the Origins of Détente, 1963–1968', *Diplomatic History* 30, no. 2 (April 2006), 273.

44. A modest agreement had been reached on April 20, 1964 to jointly reduce the number of US and Soviet nuclear reactors and the quantity of fissionable materials, but this was not a major achievement, as it was not enshrined in a treaty and did not feature any limitations on nuclear weapons. See Brands, 'Progress Unseen', 257–8; 'Summary' of *Foreign Relations of the United States, 1964–1968*, vol. 11: *Arms Control and Disarmament*, State Department: Office of the Historian, https://history.state.gov/historicaldoc uments/frus1964-68v11/summary.

45. Kissinger, *White House Years*, 813.

46. 'Editorial Note', *Foreign Relations of the United States, 1969–1976*, vol. 13: *Soviet Union, October 1970–October 1971*, State Department: Office of the Historian, https://history.state.gov/historicaldocuments/frus1969-76v13/d234.

47. Hans M. Kristensen and Matt Korda, 'Status of World Nuclear Forces', Federation of American Scientists, last updated May 2021, https://fas.org/issues/nuclear-weapons/status-world-nuclear-forces/.

48. Sana Krasikov, 'Declassified KGB Study Illuminates Early Years of Soviet Jewish Emigration', *The Forward*, December 12, 2007.

49. Mark Tolts, 'A Half Century of Jewish Emigration from the Former Soviet Union: Demographic Aspects', paper presented at the Project for Russian and Eurasian Jewry, Davis Center for Russian and Eurasian Studies, Harvard University, on November 20, 2019.

50. Ibid.

51. Richard Nixon, 'Asia after Viet Nam', *Foreign Affairs* 46, no. 1 (October 1967), 121, https://cdn.nixonlibrary.org/01/wp-content/uploads/2017/01/11113807/Asia-After-Viet-Nam.pdf.

52. Kissinger, *White House Years*, 181.

53. '99. Memorandum from the President's Assistant for National Security Affairs (Kissinger) to President Nixon', *Foreign Relations of the United States, 1969–1976*, vol. 17: *China, 1969–1972*, State Department: Office of the Historian, https://history.state.gov/historicaldocuments/frus1969-76v17/d99.

54. 'Memorandum of Conversation', October 25, 1970, *Foreign Relations of the United States, 1969–1976*, vol. E-7: *Documents on South Asia, 1969–1972*, State Department: Office of the Historian, https://history.state.gov/historicaldocuments/frus1969-76ve07/d90.

55. Richard Nixon, 'Remarks to Midwestern News Media Executives', July 6 1971, *The American Presidency Project*, UC Santa Barbara, https://www.presidency.ucsb.edu/documents/remarks-midwestern-news-media-executives-attending-briefing-domestic-policy-kansas-city.

56. Quoted in Kissinger, *White House Years*, 1062.

57. 'Joint Statement Following Discussions with Leaders of the People's Republic of China', February 27, 1972, *Foreign Relations of the United States, 1969–1972*, vol. 17: *China, 1969–1972*, State Department: Office of the Historian, https://history.state.gov/historicaldocuments/frus1969-76v17/d203.

58. 'Memorandum of Conversation', February 17–18, 1973, *Foreign Relations of the United States, 1969–1976*, vol. 18: *China, 1973–1976*, State Department: Office of the Historian, https://history.state.gov/historicaldocuments/frus1969-76v18/d12.

59. Lee Kuan Yew, 'Southeast Asian View of the New World Power Balance in the Making', Jacob Blaustein Lecture no. 1, March 30, 1973, 1–3.

60. Richard Nixon, 'Remarks to Midwestern News Media Executives', July 6, 1971

61. United Nations Security Resolution 242, November 22, 1967, https://unispal.un.org/unispal.nsf/0/7d35e1f729df491c85256ee700686136.

62. Martin Indyk, *Master of the Game: Henry Kissinger and the Art of Middle East Diplomacy* (New York: Knopf, 2021), 162–3.

63. Kissinger, *White House Years*, 579–80.

64. See ibid., 601.

65. Indyk, *Master of the Game*, 66–8.

66. See Kissinger, *White House Years*, 605.

67. 'Memorandum of Conversation', October 10, 1973. Washington, 9:05–10:36 a.m., *Foreign Relations of the United States, 1969–1976*, vol. 25: *Arab–Israeli Crisis and War, 1973*, no. 143, State Department: Office of the Historian, https://history.state.gov/historicaldocuments/frus1969-76v25/d143.

68. 'Transcript of Telephone Conversation Between President Nixon and Secretary of State Kissinger', October 14, 1973, *Foreign Relations of the United States, 1969–1976*, vol. 25: *Arab–Israeli Crisis and War, 1973*, no. 180, State Department: Office of the Historian, https://history.state.gov/historicaldocuments/frus1969-76v25/d180.

69. UN Security Council Resolution 338, October 22, 1973, https://undocs.org/S/RES/338(1973).

70. National Archives, Nixon Presidential Materials, NSC Files, Kissinger Office Files, box 69, Country Files – Europe – USSR, Dobrynin / Kissinger, vol. 20, https://history.state.gov/historicaldocuments/frus1969-76v15/d146.

71. See Eqbal Ahmad et al., 'Letters to the Editor: Home Rule for Bengal', *New York Times*, April 10, 1971; Chester Bowles, 'Pakistan's Made-in-U.S.A. Arms', *New York Times*, April 18, 1971; and Benjamin Welles, 'Senate Unit Asks Pakistan Arms Cutoff', *New York Times*, May 7, 1971.

72. Margaret MacMillan, *Nixon and Mao: The Week That Changed the World* (New York: Random House, 2007), 222-7.

73. 'Memorandum from the President's Assistant for National Security Affairs (Kissinger) to the President's Deputy Assistant for National Security Affairs (Haig)', July 9, 1971, *Foreign Relations of the United States 1969–1976*, vol. 11: *South Asia Crisis, 1971*, no. 97, 242, State Department: Office of the Historian, https://history.state.gov/historicaldocuments/frus1969-76v11/d97.

74. Syed Adnan Ali Shah, 'Russo-India Military Technical Cooperation', https://web.archive.org/web/20070314041501/http://www.issi.org.pk/journal/2001_files/no_4/article/4a.htm.

75. 'Memorandum of Conversation, Washington, August 9, 1971, 1:15–2:30 p.m.', *Foreign Relations of the United States, 1969–1976*, vol. 11: *South Asia Crisis, 1971*, no. 117, 316–17, https://history.state.gov/historicaldocuments/frus1969-76v11/d117.

76. 'Memorandum of Conversation, Washington, September 11, 1971, 9:30–10:10 a.m.', *Foreign Relations of the United States, 1969–1976*, vol. 11: *South Asia Crisis, 1971*, no. 146, 408, https://history.state.gov/historicaldocuments/frus1969-76v11/d146.

77. UN Security Council Resolution 307, December 21, 1971, https://digitallibrary.un.org/record/90799?ln=en.

78. Benjamin Welles, 'Bangladesh Gets U.S. Recognition, Promise of Help', *New York Times*, April 4, 1972.

79. 'Agreement on Joint Commission on Economic, Commercial, Scientific, Technological, Educational and Cultural Cooperation', October 28, 1974, https://www.mea.gov.in/bilateral-documents.htm?dtl/6134/Agreement+on +Joint+Commission+on+Economic+Commercial+Scientific+Technological +Educational+and+Cultural+Cooperation.

80. 'Transcript of President Nixon's Address to Congress on Meetings in Moscow', *New York Times*, June 2, 1972.

4. ANWAR SADAT

1. Eugene Rogan, *The Arabs: A History* (New York: Basic Books, 2009), 65–71, 82.

2. See generally Albert Hourani, *Arabic Thought in the Liberal Age: 1798–1939* (Cambridge: Cambridge University Press, 1983); Rogan, *The Arabs: A History*, 88–9.

3. See John McHugo, *Syria: A History of the Last Hundred Years* (New York: The New Press, 2015), 39–40; Tarek Osman, *Islamism* (New Haven: Yale University Press, 2016), 50–52; Majid Fakhry, *A History of Islamic Philosophy* (New York: Columbia University Press, 2004), 349.

4. Rogan, *The Arabs: A History*, 124-31.

5. Lawrence Wright, *Thirteen Days in September* (New York: Vintage Books, 2015), 13–4.

6. Edward R. F. Sheehan, 'The Real Sadat and the Demythologized Nasser', *New York Times*, July 18, 1971.

7. Mohamed Heikal, *Autumn of Fury: The Assassination of Sadat* (New York: Random House, 1983), Chapter 2, 'Roots', 7–11.

8. Anwar Sadat, interviewed by James Reston, *New York Times*, December 28, 1970.

9. Sheehan, 'The Real Sadat'.

10. Ibid.

11. Anwar Sadat, *In Search of Identity* (New York: Harper & Row, 1977), 4.

12. Eric Pace, Anwar el-Sadat obituary, *New York Times*, October 7, 1981.

13. Mark L. McConkie and R. Wayne Boss, 'Personal Stories and the Process of Change: The Case of Anwar Sadat', *Public Administration Quarterly* 19, no. 4 (winter 1996), 493–511.

14. See, e.g., Sir Alfred Milner, *England in Egypt* (London: Edward Arnold, 1902).

15. Rogan, *The Arabs: A History*, 151, 164.

16. Ibid., 169.

17. Ibid., 196.

18. Ibid., 208–10.

19. Steven A. Cook, *The Struggle for Egypt* (New York: Oxford University Press, 2012), 30–31.

20. Ibid., 117.

21. In 1952, Sadat recalled al-Banna as 'an upright and honorable man, who I believe disapproved of the excesses committed by the Brothers' (Anwar Sadat, *Revolt on the Nile* (New York: The John Day Company, 1952)). See also Richard Paul Mitchell, *The Society of the Muslim Brothers* (New York: Oxford University Press, 1969, reprinted 1993), 24.

22. Jehan Sadat, *A Woman of Egypt* (New York: Simon and Schuster, 1987), 92–3.

23. Sadat, *In Search of Identity*, 18–19, 24–6.

24. Ibid., 27.

25. Raphael Israeli, *Man of Defiance: A Political Biography of Anwar Sadat* (Totowa: Barnes and Noble Books, 1985), 16–25.

26. Rogan, *The Arabs: A History*, 267–8.

27. Sadat, *In Search of Identity*, 303.

28. Ibid., 303.

29. 'Egypt Tense after Cairo's Mob Riots', Australian Associated Press, January 28, 1952.

30. Sadat, *In Search of Identity*, 108.

31. Sadat's declaration of independence, as quoted in Cook, *Struggle for Egypt*, 11–12.

32. Selma Botman, 'Egyptian Communists and the Free Officers', *Middle Eastern Studies* 22 (1986), 362–4.

33. Central Intelligence Agency, 'Memorandum for the Director: Subject: Thoughts on the Succession in Egypt', September 29, 1970, 1, https://www.cia.gov/readingroom/document/cia-rdp79r00904a001500020003-3. Several Muslim Brothers were executed for their alleged involvement. Steven A. Cook, 'Echoes of Nasser', *Foreign Policy*, July 17, 2013, https://foreignpolicy.com/2013/07/17/echoes-of-nasser/.

34. Cook, *Struggle for Egypt*, 60–61.

35. See Don Peretz, 'Democracy and the Revolution in Egypt', *Middle East Journal* 13, no. 1 (1959), 27.

36. The New Egyptian Constitution, *Middle East Journal* 10, no. 3 (1956), 304; see also Mona El-Ghobashy, 'Unsettling the Authorities: Constitutional Reform in Egypt', Middle East Research and Information Project (MERIP) (2003), https://merip.org/2003/03/unsettling-the-authorities/ .

37. See Anthony F. Lang, Jr, 'From Revolutions to Constitutions: The Case of Egypt', *International Affairs* 89, no. 2 (2013), 353–4.

38. Robert L. Tignor, *Anwar al-Sadat: Transforming the Middle East* (New York: Oxford University Press, 2015), 45–51.

39. Jon B. Alterman, 'Introduction', in *Sadat and His Legacy* (Washington, DC: Washington Institute, 1998), x, https://www.washingtoninstitute.org/media/3591.

40. Steven A. Cook, 'Hero of the Crossing?: Anwar Sadat Reconsidered', *Council on Foreign Relations*, October 7, 2013, https://www.cfr.org/blog/hero-crossing-anwar-sadat-reconsidered.

41. Peretz, 'Democracy and the Revolution in Egypt', 32.

42. Sadat, *In Search of Identity*, 75.

43. See generally Joseph Finklestone, *Anwar Sadat: Visionary Who Dared* (London: Frank Cass, 1996), 38–61; Tignor, *Transforming the Middle East*, 38–59.

44. Nicholas Breyfogle, 'The Many Faces of Islamic Fundamentalism: A Profile of Egypt', *Origins* (1993), 15, https://origins.osu.edu/sites/origins.osu.edu/files/origins-archive/Volume1Issue2Article3.pdf.

45. Jacob M. Landau, *Pan-Islam: History and Politics* (London: Routledge, 2015), 279; Martin Kramer, 'Anwar Sadat's Visit to Jerusalem, 1955', in Meir Litvak and Bruce Maddy-Weizman, eds., *Nationalism, Identity and Politics: Israel and the Middle East* (Tel Aviv: The Moshe Dayan Center for Middle Eastern and African Studies, 2014), 29–41, https://scholar.harvard.edu/files/martinkramer/files/sadat_jerusalem_1955.pdf.

46. See Tawfig Y. Hasou, *The Struggle for the Arab World* (London: Routledge, 1985), 75–84; Arthur Goldschmidt, Jr, *A Concise History of the Middle East* (New York: Routledge, 1979) 73. Nasser personally believed that the Baghdad Pact represented British and American attempts to control and influence the Middle East. See 'Excerpts from Interview with President Gamal Abdel Nasser of the U.A.R.', *New York Times*, February 15, 1970.

47. Kramer, 'Anwar Sadat's Visit to Jerusalem, 1955', note 12 (quoting Heath Mason, first secretary, dispatch of December 31, 1955, Foreign Office: Reference 371, Document 121476; https://discovery.nationalarchives.gov.uk/details/r/C2878966).

48. In 1958, in preparation for a visit to Iran, Sadat memorized a Persian proverb. He recited it for the Shah at the end of their meeting; the two went on to become lifelong friends. Camelia Anwar Sadat, 'Anwar Sadat and His Vision', in *Sadat and His Legacy* (Washington, DC: Washington Institute for Near East Policy, 1998) 5, https://www.washingtoninstitute.org/media/3591.

49. Malcolm Kerr, '"Coming to Terms with Nasser": Attempts and Failures', *International Affairs* 43, no. 1 (1967), 66.

50. Rogan, *The Arabs: A History*, 287.

51. This was an outcome of a meeting between Nasser and Zhou Enlai at the 1955 Bandung Conference; Zhou had offered to mediate between Nasser and the Soviets and Czechs. Finklestone, *Anwar Sadat: Visionary Who Dared*, excerpts on Sadat's opinions and advice under Nasser, 38–44, 46–47, 49, 53, 55–61.

52. Cook, *Struggle for Egypt*, 67.

53. William J. Burns, *Economic Aid and American Policy Toward Egypt: 1955–1981* (Albany: State University of New York Press, 1985), 106, quoting Eugene Black, John Foster Dulles Oral History Collection, Princeton University, 15, https://findingaids.princeton.edu/catalog/MC017_c0024.

54. Cook, *Struggle for Egypt*, 68.

55. Message from Prime Minister Eden to President Eisenhower, August 5, 1956, *Foreign Relations of the United States, 1955–1957*, vol. XVI: *Suez Crisis, July 26–December 31, 1956*, no. 64, State Department: Office of the Historian, https://history.state.gov/historicaldocuments/frus1955-57v16/d163.

56. United Nations Department of Economic and Social Affairs, *Economic Developments in the Middle East: Supplement to World Economic Survey, 1956* (1957), 106–7, https://www.un.org/en/development/desa/policy/wess/wess_archive/searchable_archive/1956_WESS_MiddleEast.pdf.

57. Michael Laskier, 'Egyptian Jewry Under the Nasser Regime, 1956–70', *Middle Eastern Studies* 31, no. 3 (1995), 573–619.

58. Ibid., 103–4.

59. Ibid., 106–7.

60. Karen Holbik and Edward Drachman, 'Egypt as Recipient of Soviet Aid, 1955–1970', *Journal of Institutional and Theoretical Economics* (January 1971), 154 ('growing dependence'); John Waterbury, *The Egypt of Nasser and Sadat* (Princeton: Princeton University Press, 1983), 86, 397.

61. 'Aswan High Dam Is Dedicated by Sadat and Podgorny', *New York Times*, January 16, 1971; Holbik and Drachman, 'Egypt as Recipient of Soviet Aid', 143–4.

62. Holbik and Drachman, 'Egypt as Recipient of Soviet Aid', 139–40; World Bank, 'GDP Growth (Annual %) – Egypt, Arab Rep.', https://data.worldbank.org/indicator/NY.GDP.MKTP.KD.ZG?end=1989&locations=EG&start=1961.

63. Waterbury, *The Egypt of Nasser and Sadat*, 298.

64. Ibid., 97.

65. Sadat, *In Search of Identity*, 128; Tignor, *Transforming the Middle East*, 64.

66. Dana Adams Schmidt, 'Cairo Rules Out a Pro-U.S. Stand', *New York Times*, June 7, 1961.

67. Sadat, *In Search of Identity*, 128.

68. Peter Mansfield, 'Nasser and Nasserism', *International Journal* 28, no. 4 (autumn 1973), 674.

69. Fouad Ajami, 'The Struggle for Egypt's Soul', *Foreign Policy*, June 15, 1979, https://foreignpolicy.com/1979/06/15/the-struggle-for-egypts-soul/.

70. Ibid.

71. Cook, *Struggle for Egypt*, 110.

72. 'Telegram from the Embassy in the United Arab Republic to the Department of State, Cairo, December 17, 1959', *Foreign Relations of the United States*,

vol. XIII: *Arab–Israeli Dispute*, no. 252, State Department: Office of the Historian, https://history.state.gov/historicaldocuments/frus1958-60v13/d252.

73. 'Telegram from the Department of State to Secretary of State Rusk in New York, Washington, September 27, 1962', *Foreign Relations of the United States*, vol. XVIII: *Near East, 1962–1963*, no. 59, State Department: Office of the Historian, https://history.state.gov/historicaldocuments/frus1961-63v18/d59; 'Telegram from the Embassy in the United Arab Republic to the Department of State, Cairo, October 10, 1962', ibid., no. 77, https://history.state.gov/historicaldocuments/frus1961-63v18/d77; 'Telegram from the Embassy in Saudi Arabia to the Department of State, Jidda, November 30, 1963', ibid., no. 372.

74. Waterbury, *The Egypt of Nasser and Sadat*, 320.

75. See 'Memorandum of conversation, Washington, February 23, 1966, 11.30 a.m.', *Foreign Relations of the United States*, vol. XVIII: *Arab–Israeli Dispute, 1964–1967*, no. 274, State Department: Office of the Historian, https://history.state.gov/historicaldocuments/frus1964-68v18/d274 (note: Sadat met with President Johnson); 'Memorandum of conversation, Washington, February 25, 1966, 5.05 p.m.', *Foreign Relations of the United States, Near East Region*, vol. XXI, no. 391, State Department: Office of the Historian, https://history.state.gov/historicaldocuments/frus1964-68v21/d391; 'Telegram from the Embassy in the United Arab Republic to the Department of State, Cairo, May 28, 1966', *Foreign Relations of the United States, 1964–1968*, vol. XVIII: *Arab–Israeli Dispute, 1964–1967*, no. 296, State Department: Office of the Historian https://history.state.gov/historicaldocuments/frus1964-68v18/d296.

76. Jehan Sadat, *A Woman of Egypt*, 282.

77. Sadat, *Revolt on the Nile*, (1952) 103.

78. Sadat, interviewed by James Reston, *New York Times*, December 28, 1970.

79. Raphael Israeli, *The Public Diary of President Sadat*, vol. 1: *The Road to War (October 1970–October 1973)* (Leiden: E. J. Brill, 1978), 19, quoting 'January 8, 1971 – Address to the Faculty of Universities and Higher Institutions of Learning'.

80. Sadat, *Revolt on the Nile*, 1952 27.

81. Thomas W. Lippmann, 'A Man for All Roles', *Washington Post*, December 26, 1977; James Piscatori, 'The West in Arab Foreign Policy', in Robert O'Neill and R. J. Vincent, eds., *The West and the Third World* (New York: St. Martin's Press, 1990), 141.

82. Israeli, *The Public Diary of President Sadat*, vol. 1, 11, quoting 'October 19, 1970 – Sadat's first public speech as president – address to military officers in the Suez Canal front'.

83. Ibid., 28–30, quoting 'January 15, 1971 – speech marking the completion of the Aswan Dam – delivered in the presence of Soviet President Podgorny, who was attending the ceremony'.

84. Ibid., 32–3, quoting 'February 16, 1971 interview with *Newsweek* Magazine – published February 22, 1971 in English'.

85. Finklestone, *Anwar Sadat: Visionary Who Dared*, 61.

86. The following material draws on, and in some cases repeats phrases from, *Years of Upheaval* and *Years of Renewal*.

87. 'Nasser rotated the vice presidency among non-threatening candidates, and so Sadat . . . unexpectedly became interim President of Egypt' (Kiki M. Santing, *Imagining the Perfect Society in Muslim Brotherhood Journals* (Berlin: de Gruyter, 2020), 119); 'Before becoming President, Sadat was reportedly nicknamed "Colonel Yes Yes"' (Robert Springborg, *Family Power and Politics in Egypt* (Philadelphia: University of Pennsylvania Press, 1982, republished 2016), 187); Edward R. Kantowicz, *Coming Apart, Coming Together* (Grand Rapids: William B. Eerdmans, 2000), 371; David Reynolds, *One World Divisible* (New York: Norton, 2001), 370.

88. 'A Gesture by U.S.: President Terms Loss Tragic – He Joins Fleet Off Italy', *New York Times*, September 29, 1970.

89. Central Intelligence Agency, 'Thoughts on the Succession in Egypt'.

90. Memorandum from Harold H. Saunders to Henry Kissinger, 'Subject: The UAR Presidency', October 8, 1970, 1. https://www.cia.gov/readingroom/document/loc-hak-292-3-14-9.

91. Central Intelligence Agency, 'Thoughts on the Succession in Egypt'.

92. Sadat, *In Search of Identity*, 125.

93. Cook, *Struggle for Egypt*, 114.

94. Raymond H. Anderson, 'Sadat Is Chosen by Egypt's Party to Be President', *New York Times*, October 6, 1970.

95. Raymond H. Anderson, 'Showdown in Egypt: How Sadat Prevailed', *New York Times*, May 23, 1971. As Sadat had predicted, the federation would never come into practical effect.

96. Cook, *Struggle for Egypt*, 122.

97. Anderson, 'Showdown'.

98. Cook, *Struggle for Egypt*, 117.

99. Sadat, address to the Nation, January 13, 1972. https://sadat.umd.edu/resources/presidential-speeches

100. Anwar Sadat, speech to the Second Session of the Egyptian People's Assembly, October 15, 1972, 1–3, https://sadat.umd.edu/resources/presidential-speeches.

101. See Sadat Peace Initiative of 1971, January 17, 1971, http://sadat.umd.edu/archives/speeches/AADD%20Peace%20Announcement%202.4.71.pdf.

102. John L. Hess, 'Deadline Comes and Cairo Waits', *New York Times*, August 16, 1971.

103. Martin Indyk, *Master of the Game: Henry Kissinger and the Art of Middle East Diplomacy* (New York: Alfred A Knopf, 2021), 91.

104. Edward R. F. Sheehan, 'Why Sadat Packed Off the Russians', *New York Times*, August 6, 1972.

105. Thomas W. Lippman, *Hero of the Crossing: How Anwar Sadat and the 1973 War Changed the World* (Sterling: Potomac Books, 2016), 62, quoting Sadat, *In Search of Identity*, Appendix I. Sadat, letter to Brezhnev, August 1972, 321.

106. Sadat, *In Search of Identity*, 231.

107. Full text: 'As the President sees it, the big issue is between Egyptian sovereignty and Israeli security. The two sides, he felt, were very far apart and their positions were very hard. The President did not think that it was possible to solve the entire Middle East problem all at once and perhaps not at all. He expressed his understanding of Mr Ismail's point about interim solutions turning into final solutions. The President gave his word that his goal was a permanent settlement, but he reiterated that he did not think it was possible, in view of the gulf between the parties, to reach such a settlement all at once. It may, therefore, be necessary to consider interim steps along the way. He said that perhaps the Egyptians would reject such an approach, but he urged Mr Ismail to discuss it with Dr Kissinger and he stressed that we were committed to a long-range solution to the problem. No possibility should be overlooked in our search for a way to move toward our goal. The President said he hoped that this would be only the first, and not the last, meeting. This should be the beginning of a dialogue, and if nothing concrete emerged, he hoped Mr Ismail would not report back to Sadat that the effort had failed. Once again, the President pointed out the sensitivity of the private channel negotiations – they must be kept quiet and private if they were to succeed.'

108. The President's Daily Brief, July 24, 1971, 3, https://www.cia.gov/readingroom/document/0005992769.

109. Jehan Sadat, *A Woman of Egypt*, 282–3.

110. Interview in *Yedioth Aharonoth*, June 11, 1987.

111. David Tal, 'Who Needed the October 1973 War?', *Middle Eastern Studies* 52, no. 5 (2016), 748, quoting Jehan Sadat, interview in *Yedioth Aharonoth*, November 6, 1987.

112. Sheehan, 'Why Sadat Packed Off the Russians'.

113. Jehan Sadat, *A Woman of Egypt*, 282.

114. Anthony Lewis, 'Sadat Suggests Return of West Bank, Gaza as Peace Step', *New York Times*, May 11, 1978.

115. David Hirst and Irene Beeson, *Sadat* (London: Faber and Faber, 1981), 144; Israeli, *Man of Defiance*, 79.

116. Moshe Shemesh, 'The Origins of Sadat's Strategic Volte-face: Marking 30 Years since Sadat's Historic Visit to Israel, November 1977', *Israel Studies* 13, no. 2 (summer 2008), 45.

117. See Elizabeth Monroe and Anthony Farrar-Hockley, *The Arab-Israeli War, October 1973: Background and Events* (London: International Institute for

Strategic Studies, 1975), 17; Henry Kissinger, *Years of Upheaval* (Boston: Little, Brown, 1982), 465.

118. Sadat, *In Search of Identity*, 241–2.

119. Ibid.

120. 'Remarks by the Honorable Henry Kissinger', May 4, 2000, Anwar Sadat Chair for Peace and Development, University of Maryland, https://sadat. umd.edu/events/remarks-honorable-henry-kissinger.

121. William B. Quandt, 'Soviet Policy in the October 1973 War', Rand Corporation (1976), vi, https://www.rand.org/content/dam/rand/pubs/reports/2006/ R1864.pdf.

122. 'Transcript of Kissinger's News Conference on the Crisis in the Middle East', *New York Times*, October 26, 1973.

123. Indyk, *Master of the Game*, 138.

124. Sadat, *In Search of Identity*, 244.

125. Cook, *Struggle for Egypt*, 131, citing Saad el Shazly, *The Crossing of the Suez* (San Francisco: American Mideast Research, 1980), 106.

126. 'I should like to say before you and before the world that we want the policy of détente to succeed and be fostered . . . I should like to tell [President Nixon] that our aims in waging this war are well known and need no further clarification; and if he would like to know our peace demands then I will submit to him our peace project.' See 'Excerpts of a Speech Calling for an Arab-Israeli Peace Conference', October 16, 1973, 91, https://sadat. umd.edu/resources/presidential-speeches.

127. US Department of State, Office of the Historian, 'OPEC Oil Embargo 1973–1974', https://history.state.gov/milestones/1969-1976/oil-embargo.

128. Memorandum of conversation, Saturday, November 3, 1973, 10:45 p.m.– 1:10 a.m., The Blair House, Washington, https://nsarchive2.gwu.edu/ NSAEBB/NSAEBB98/octwar-93b.pdf.

129. Ibid., 1031–38.

130. Sadat, *In Search of Identity*, 43.

131. Ibid, 291–2.

132. 'Memorandum from the President's assistant for national security affairs [Kissinger] to President Nixon, Washington, January 6, 1974', https://his tory.state.gov/historicaldocuments/frus1969-76v26/d1#fn:1.5.4.4.8.9.12.4.

133. I began the shuttle in Egypt (January 11–12); then Israel (January 12–13); then Egypt (January 13–14); then Israel (January 14–15); then Egypt (January 16); then Israel (January 16–17); then finally Egypt (January 18). See Department of State, Office of the Historian, 'Travels of the Secretary, Henry A. Kissinger', https://history.state.gov/departmenthistory/travels/sec retary/kissinger-henry-a.

134. Kissinger, *Years of Upheaval*, 824.

135. Ibid., 836.

136. Ibid., 844.

137. The scholar and diplomat Martin Indyk suggests that there was a chance to obtain such an agreement prior to that October summit. See *Master of the Game*, 413–44.

138. Yitzhak Rabin, *The Rabin Memoirs* (Berkeley: University of California Press, 1979), 421–2.

139. Letter from Yitzhak Rabin to Anwar Sadat, March 12, 1975, https://catalog.archives.gov.il/wp-content/uploads/2020/02/12-3-1975-מכתב-מרבי-לסאדאת-HZ-5973_13.pdf.

140. Reconstructed from handwritten notes.

141. 'The Seventeenth Government', *The Knesset History*, https://knesset.gov.il/history/eng/eng_hist8_s.htm.

142. 'Memorandum of conversation, Kissinger, Peres, Allon and Rabin, March 22, 1975, 6:35–8:14 p.m., Prime Minister's Office, Jerusalem', Gerald R. Ford Presidential Library and Museum, https://www.fordlibrarymuseum.gov/library/document/0331/1553967.pdf.

143. Henry Kissinger, *Years of Renewal* (New York: Simon and Schuster, 1990), 437.

144. Ibid., 1054.

145. Interview given by President Anwar El Sadat to the Irani newspaper *Etlaat*, June 13, 1976, 722.

146. Sadat, *In Search of Identity*, 297–8.

147. Letter from Carter to Sadat, October 21, 1977, https://sadat.umd.edu/sites/sadat.umd.edu/files/Letter%20from%20President%20Jimmy%20Carter%20to%20Egyptian%20President%20Anwar%20Sadat1.pdf.

148. Sadat, *In Search of Identity*, 302.

149. Eric Pace, Anwar el-Sadat obituary, *New York Times*, October 7, 1981.

150. 'Excerpts from the speech of H. E. President Mohamed Anwar el-Sadat to the People's Assembly, November 9, 1977', https://sadat.umd.edu/resources/presidential-speeches.

151. 'Since "we are on verge of going to Geneva" there was no need for [Arab] summit to determine new strategy', 'Telegram from the Embassy in Egypt to the Department of State, Cairo, November 10, 1977, Subj: Arab–Israeli Aspects of Sadat Nov 9 Speech', https://history.state.gov/historicaldocuments/frus1977-80v08/d145.

152. 'Telegram from the Embassy in Egypt to the Department of State, Cairo, November 10, 1977', https://history.state.gov/historicaldocuments/frus1977-80v08/d145.

153. He had Dayan, his foreign minister, convey to Sadat's advisor Tuhami, in a secret meeting in Morocco before Sadat's speech, that he would be prepared to make a full withdrawal from Sinai.

154. 'Prime Minister Begin's Letter of Invitation to President Sadat', November 15, 1977, in *Israel's Foreign Policy – Historical Documents*, volumes 4–5: *1977–1979*, https://www.mfa.gov.il/MFA/ForeignPolicy/MFADocuments/

Yearbook3/Pages/69%20Prime%20Minister%20Begin-s%20letter%20 of%20invitation%20to.aspx.

155. William E. Farrell, 'Sadat Arrives to Warm Welcome in Israel, Says He Has Specific Proposals for Peace', *New York Times*, November 20, 1977.

156. Anwar Sadat, 'Egypt–Israel Relations: Address by Egyptian President Anwar Sadat to the Knesset', November 20, 1977, https://www.jewishvirtuallibrary. org/address-by-egyptian-president-anwar-sadat-to-the-knesset.

157. Ibid.

158. Ibid.

159. Ibid.

160. *Peace in the Making: The Menachem Begin-Anwar El-Sadat Personal Correspondence*, edited by Harry Hurwitz and Yisrael Medad (Jerusalem: Gefen Publishing House, 2011), 'Begin Addresses the Knesset After Sadat', November 20, 1977, 35.

161. Abraham Rabinovich, *The Yom Kippur War: The Epic Encounter That Transformed the Middle East* (New York: Schocken Books, 2004), 497–8.

162. Henry Kissinger, 'Sadat: A Man with a Passion for Peace', *TIME*, October 19, 1981, http://content.time.com/time/subscriber/article/0,33009,924947, 00.html.

163. Sabri Jiryis, 'The Arab World at the Crossroads: An Analysis of the Arab Opposition to the Sadat Initiative', *Journal of Palestine Studies* 7, no. 2 (winter 1978), 26.

164. Ibid., 30–40.

165. Kissinger, *Years of Renewal*, 456.

166. Fahmy believed that 'Sadat had singlehandedly given away all that the Egyptian army had won with great effort and sacrifice without consulting anyone' (Tignor, *Transforming the Middle East*, 144, quoting Fahmy).

167. US Department of State, Office of the Historian, 'Memorandum of Telephone Conversation (Carter and Begin), November 17, 1977', https:// history.state.gov/historicaldocuments/frus1977-80v08/d147.

168. Joseph T. Stanik, *El Dorado Canyon: Reagan's Undeclared War with Qaddafi* (Annapolis: Naval Institute Press, 2003), 64.

169. Jiryis, 'The Arab World at the Crossroads', 29–30, citing General People's Congress statement as printed in *al-Safir*, November 19 and November 24, 1977.

170. Marvin Howe, 'Hard-Line Arab Bloc Is Formed at Tripoli', *New York Times*, December 6, 1977.

171. Jiryis, 'The Arab World at the Crossroads', 30–35.

172. Kissinger, *Years of Renewal*, 1057.

173. Ibid., 354.

174. James Feron, 'Menachem Begin, Guerrilla Leader Who Became Peacemaker', *New York Times*, March 9, 1992.

175. Kissinger, 'A Man with a Passion for Peace'.

176. Sadat, as quoted in Finklestone, *Anwar Sadat: Visionary Who Dared*, 249.

177. Thomas Lippmann, 'Sadat Installs New Government to Lead a Peaceful Egypt', *Washington Post*, October 6, 1978.

178. Israeli, *The Public Diary of President Sadat*, 354–5, 'May 1, 1973 – May Day speech at a mass rally at the Mahalla-al-Kubra stadium'.

179. Anwar Sadat, Nobel Lecture, December 10, 1978, https://www.nobelprize.org/prizes/peace/1978/al-sadat/lecture/.

180. Ibid.

181. Finklestone, *Anwar Sadat: Visionary Who Dared*, 251; Wright, *Thirteen Days in September*, 354.

182. Begin to Sadat, November 18, 1979, Israel Ministry of Foreign Affairs, vol. 6: 1979–1980, https://www.mfa.gov.il/MFA/ForeignPolicy/MFADocuments/Yearbook4/Pages/53%20Letter%20from%20Prime%20Minister%20Begin%20to%20President%20S.aspx.

183. Hedrick Smith, 'After Camp David Summit, A Valley of Hard Bargaining', *New York Times*, November 6, 1978.

184. *Peace in the Making*, 95–7, letter from Sadat to Begin, November 30, 1978.

185. Ibid., 85–6, 105.

186. Ibid., 209, letter from Sadat to Begin, received August 15, 1980; 224, letter from Begin to Sadat, August 18, 1980.

187. Ibid., 216.

188. M. Cherif Bassiouni, 'An Analysis of Egyptian Peace Policy Toward Israel: From Resolution 242 (1967) to the 1979 Peace Treaty', 12 Case W. Res. J. Int'l L. 3 (1980), https://scholarlycommons.law.case.edu/jil/vol12/iss1/2.

189. Judith Miller, 'Hussein, in Egyptian Parliament, Condemns Camp David Accords', *New York Times*, December 3, 1984.

190. Smith, 'After Camp David Summit'.

191. Jason Brownlee, 'Peace Before Freedom: Diplomacy and Repression in Sadat's Egypt', *Political Science Quarterly* 126, no. 4 (winter 2011–12), 649.

192. Burns, *Economic Aid and American Policy Toward Egypt*, 192.

193. World Bank, 'GDP growth (annual %) – Egypt, Arab Rep.' https://data.worldbank.org/indicator/NY.GDP.MKTP.KD.ZG?end=1989&locations=EG&start=1961. YES

194. Henry F. Jackson, 'Sadat's Perils', *Foreign Policy* 42 (spring 1981), 59–69.

195. Marvin G. Weinbaum, 'Egypt's *Infitah* and the Politics of US Economic Assistance', *Middle Eastern Studies* 21, no. 2 (April 1985), 206; interview given by President Anwar El Sadat to the Irani newspaper *Etlaat*, June 13, 1976.

196. Tignor, *Transforming the Middle East*, 140; Brownlee, 'Peace Before Freedom', 651.

197. Saad Eddin Ibrahim, 'Anatomy of Egypt's Militant Islamic Groups: Methodological Note and Preliminary Findings', *International Journal of Middle East Studies* 12, no. 4 (December 1980), 439.

198. Saad Eddin Ibrahim in 'Discussion', in *Sadat and His Legacy* (Washington, DC: Washington Institute, 1998), 103, https://www.washingtoninstitute.org/media/3591.

199. Ibrahim, 'Anatomy', 445.

200. Jiryis, 'The Arab World at the Crossroads', 35-6.

201. 'Middle East: War of Words, Hope for Peace,' *TIME*, August 7, 1978, http://content.time.com/time/subscriber/article/0,33009,948219,00.html.

202. Jackson, 'Sadat's Perils', 64.

203. Ibrahim, speaking in 'Discussion: Sadat's Strategy and Legacy', 102.

204. Jehan Sadat, *A Woman of Egypt*, 415.

205. Jackson, 'Sadat's Perils', 65; Don Schanche and *LA Times*, 'Arab Sanctions Leave Egypt Unshaken', *Washington Post*, April 2, 1979.

206. 'After the burning of el-Aqsa Mosque by a deranged tourist in 1969, Nasser had sent Anwar as Egypt's representative to discuss with other Muslim leaders what steps to take to protect the holy places under Israeli occupation. My husband had found the Shah's suggestions on the matter weak and, in Arabic, told the leaders so. The Shah had responded angrily. The quarrel was defused when Anwar, realizing that his remarks had sounded more inflammatory when translated into French so that the Shah could understand them, had addressed the Summit members in Persian. The Shah, who was known never to laugh and only rarely to smile, on this occasion had risen to his feet with a smile to applaud Anwar. The seeds of a lifelong friendship had been sown. "There can be no love except after enmity," Anwar was fond of telling the Shah, quoting one of our Arabic proverbs' (Jehan Sadat, *A Woman of Egypt*, 340-42).

207. Jehan Sadat recalled: '"I will go to Saudi Arabia to ask King Khalid and the Saudi princes why they are delaying their support for you," the Shah told my husband. "They must recognize that you are working for the whole area, for a comprehensive and just peace and for the return of Arab rights." The Shah's trip to Jedda would prove to be futile, but Anwar would never forget the lengths his friend, unasked, had gone to for him' (ibid., 384-6).

208. Ibid., 424-5.

209. Richard L. Homan, 'Opposition Parties Disbanding to Protest Sadat Crackdown', *Washington Post*, June 6, 1978. Brownlee, 'Peace Before Freedom', 661, Jackson, 'Sadat's Perils', 64.

210. William E. Farrell, 'Sadat, with Anger and Sarcasm, Defends His Crackdown on Foes', *New York Times*, September 10, 1981.

211. Brownlee, 'Peace Before Freedom', 664.

212. Raphael Israeli, 'Sadat's Egypt and Teng's China: Revolution Versus Modernization', *Political Science Quarterly* 95, no. 3 (1980), 364.

213. Camelia Anwar Sadat, 'Anwar Sadat and His Vision', in Alterman, ed., *Sadat and His Legacy*.

214. *Peace in the Making*, 244–5.

215. Henry Kissinger on *ABC News Nightline*, October 6, 1981, https://www.youtube.com/watch?v=N1nCpbUKc4E.

216. Howell Raines, '3 Ex-Presidents in Delegation to Funeral but Reagan Is Not', *New York Times*, October 8, 1981; 'Officials from Around the World Attending Sadat's Funeral', *New York Times*, October 10, 1981.

217. Kissinger on *ABC News Nightline*, October 6, 1981.

218. David B. Ottaway, 'Body of Sadat is Laid to Rest in Tightly Controlled Funeral', *Washington Post*, October 11, 1981, https://www.washingtonpost.com/archive/politics/1981/10/11/body-of-sadat-is-laid-to-rest-in-tightly-controlled-funeral/c72f4903-7699-42a8-b0c7-77f063695e81/.

219. Anwar Sadat, 'Address at Ben-Gurion University', May 26, 1979, https://mfa.gov.il/MFA/ForeignPolicy/MFADocuments/Yearbook4/Pages/15%20Statements%20by%20Presidents%20Navon%20and%20Sadat-%20and%20P.aspx.

220. https://www.presidency.ucsb.edu/documents/remarks-president-carter-president-anwar-al-sadat-egypt-and-prime-minister-menahem-begin.

221. Sadat, *In Search of Identity*, 79, 84–5.

222. Kissinger, *Years of Renewal*, 458.

223. Prime Minister Yitzhak Rabin, 'Address to the United States Congress, July 26, 1994', https://mfa.gov.il/MFA/MFA-Archive/Pages/ADDRESS%20BY%20PM%20RABIN%20TO%20THE%20US%20CONGRESS%20-%2026-Jul-94.aspx.

224. Kissinger, *Years of Upheaval*, 651.

225. 'Remarks by the Honorable Henry Kissinger', May 4, 2000, Anwar Sadat Chair for Peace and Development, University of Maryland, https://sadat.umd.edu/events/remarks-honorable-henry-kissinger.

5. LEE KUAN YEW

1. Lee Kuan Yew, 'Collins Family International Fellowship Lecture', delivered October 17, 2000 at the John F. Kennedy School of Government at Harvard University, https://www.nas.gov.sg/archivesonline/data/pdfdoc/2000101706.htm. Also see: Richard Longworth, 'Asian Leader Begins Brief Sabbatical', *The Harvard Crimson*, November 14, 1968, https://www.thecrimson.com/article/1968/11/14/asian-leader-begins-brief-sabbatical-plee/.

2. Longworth, 'Asian Leader Begins Brief Sabbatical'.

3. See Lee Kuan Yew, *From Third World to First* (New York: HarperCollins, 2000), 460–61.

4. Richard Nixon, *Leaders: Profiles and Reminiscences of Men Who Have Shaped the Modern World* (New York: Warner Books, 1982), 319.

5. Margaret Thatcher, *Statecraft: Strategies for a Changing World* (New York, HarperCollins, 2002), 117.

6. Lee, 'Collins Family International Fellowship Lecture'.

7. John Curtis Perry, *Singapore: Unlikely Power* (New York: Oxford University Press, 2017), 6.

8. Lee, *From Third World to First*, 3.

9. Han Fook Kwang et al., eds., *Lee Kwan Yew: Hard Truths to Keep Singapore Going* (Singapore: Straits Times Press, 2011), 19.

10. Ibid., 18.

11. Lee, *From Third World to First*, 690.

12. Ibid.

13. 'Aspen Meeting, May 6, 1979, 3.00 p.m., Singapore', Henry A. Kissinger papers, part III, box 169, folder 4, 12, Yale University Library, http://findit.library.yale.edu/catalog/digcoll:1193313.

14. Han et al., eds., *Hard Truths*, 390. Lee's interviewers were two young Singaporean journalists, Rachel Lin and Robin Chan.

15. Ezra Vogel, *Deng Xiaoping and the Transformation of China* (Cambridge, MA: Belknap Press, 2011), 290–91.

16. Perry, *Singapore*, 37.

17. Ibid., 124.

18. Ibid., 121.

19. Ibid., 124 for date. Fred Glueckstein, 'Churchill and the Fall of Singapore', *International Churchill Society*, November 10, 2015, https://winstonchurchill.org/publications/finest-hour/finest-hour-169/churchill-and-the-fall-of-singapore/.

20. Lee Kuan Yew, *The Singapore Story* (Singapore: Times Editions, 1998), 51.

21. Ibid., 35.

22. Ibid., 34. Lee opens his memoirs with the indelible image of his father dangling him over a balcony by the ears after one such loss.

23. Ibid.

24. Ibid., 35–8.

25. Ibid., 36.

26. Ibid., 43.

27. Ibid., 38.

28. Ibid.

29. Ibid., 39–40.

30. Lee, 'Collins Family International Fellowship Lecture'. Perry, *Singapore*, 146, records a similar sentiment of a Malay woman in Singapore upon the return of British forces after the war: 'We were certainly glad that the British had returned to liberate us from the Japanese, but we placed very little weight on their promise to protect us in the future . . . our gods had feet of clay.'

31. Perry, *Singapore*, 138.

32. Ibid., 140.

33. Ibid., 61–6.

34. Ibid., 66.

35. Ibid., 115.

36. Lee Kuan Yew, 'Eulogy by Minister Mentor Lee Kuan Yew at the Funeral Service of Mrs Lee Kuan Yew', Prime Minister's Office of Singapore, October 6, 2010.

37. Ibid., 113–14.

38. Lee, 'Collins Family International Fellowship Lecture', October 17, 2000.

39. Ibid.

40. Lee Kuan Yew, 'If I Were an Englishman' (speech on behalf of David Widdicombe, early February 1950), in *Lee Kuan Yew: The Man and His Ideas*, eds. Han Fook Hwang, Warren Fernandez and Sumiko Tan (Singapore: Times Editions, 1998), 255.

41. Constance Mary (C. M.) Turnbull, *A History of Modern Singapore* (Singapore: National University of Singapore Press, 2020), 371–2.

42. Ibid., 382.

43. An 1879 commission had decried rampant bribery in the police force. See Jon S. T. Quah, 'Combating Corruption in Singapore – What Can Be Learned?', *Journal of Contingencies and Crisis Management* 9, no. 1 (March 2001), 29–31.

44. Ibid., 30.

45. Cyril Northcote Parkinson, *A Law Unto Themselves: Twelve Portraits* (Boston: Houghton Mifflin, 1966), 173.

46. Perry, *Singapore*, 157.

47. Lee, *The Singapore Story*, 305–9, 319.

48. Turnbull, *Singapore*, 449–50.

49. Lee, *From Third World to First*, 96.

50. Ibid., 105.

51. Quah, 'Combating Corruption in Singapore'.

52. Turnbull, *Singapore*, 429.

53. Lee Kuan Yew, 'How Much Is a Good Minister Worth?', speech before parliament, November 1, 1994, in *Lee Kuan Yew: The Man and His Ideas*, 331.

54. Beng Huat Chua, *Liberalism Disavowed: Communitarianism and State Capitalism in Singapore* (Ithaca, NY: Cornell University Press, 2017), 3.

55. Muhammad Ali, 'Eradicating Corruption – The Singapore Experience', presented at the Seminar on International Experiences on Good Governance and Fighting Corruption, February 2000, 2.

56. Quah, 'Combating Corruption in Singapore', 29.

57. Lee, 'How Much Is a Good Minister Worth?', 338.

58. Turnbull, *Singapore*, 450.

59. Ibid., 495.

60. Ibid., 450.

61. George P. Shultz and Vidar Jorgensen, 'A Real Market in Medical Care? Singapore Shows the Way', *The Wall Street Journal*, June 15, 2020, https://www.wsj.com/articles/a-real-market-in-medical-care-singapore-shows-the-way-11592264057.

62. Lim Meng-Kim, 'Health Care Systems in Transition II. Singapore, Part 1. An Overview of Health Care Systems in Singapore,' *Journal of Public Health* 20, no. 1 (1988), 19.

63. Turnbull, *Singapore*, 510–11.

64. Ibid.

65. Turnbull, *Singapore*, 511.

66. Lee, *From Third World to First*, 112.

67. Perry, *Singapore*, 160, 250, 252.

68. Lee, *From Third World to First*, 112.

69. Fareed Zakaria, 'Culture Is Destiny: A Conversation with Lee Kuan Yew', *Foreign Affairs* 73, no. 2 (March/April 1994), 111.

70. Lee, *The Singapore Story*, 16, 401–2.

71. Ibid., 394–6.

72. Perry, *Singapore*, 157.

73. Ibid., 164.

74. Lee, *The Singapore Story*, 23.

75. Arnold Toynbee, *Cities on the Move* (New York: Oxford University Press, 1970), 55.

76. Perry, *Singapore*, 197.

77. Lee, *From Third World to First*, 7.

78. Seth Mydans, 'Days of Reflection for the Man Who Defined Singapore', *New York Times*, September 11, 2010.

79. Lee Kuan Yew, 'Transcript of a Press Conference on August 9, 1965', National Archives of Singapore, 32–3, https://www.nas.gov.sg/archiveson line/speeches/record-details/740acc3c-115d-11e3-83d5-0050568939ad.

80. Lee, *From Third World to First*, 6.

81. Ibid., 14.

82. Ibid., 11.

83. Ibid., 15.

84. Ibid., 19.

85. Ibid., 228.

86. Transcript of speech by the prime minister at a meeting of the Consultation on Youth and Leadership Training, sponsored by the East Asia Christian Conference held at the Queen Street Methodist Church on April 10, 1967.

87. 'Aspen Meeting, January 30, 1980, 3.30 p.m., Germany', Henry A. Kissinger papers, part III, box 169, folder 11, 10–11, Yale University Library, http://findit.library.yale.edu/catalog/digcoll:1193221.

88. Lee Kuan Yew, *My Lifelong Challenge: Singapore's Bilingual Journey* (Singapore: Straits Times Press, 2012).

89. Ibid., 53.

90. Constitution of the Republic of Singapore, Article 153A.

91. Zakaria, 'Culture Is Destiny', 120.

92. Perry, *Singapore*, 166. Lee even had a polymarble copy of the statue made and placed in a prominent location on the Singapore waterfront.

93. See Lee, *From Third World to First*, 50.

94. Ibid., 3.

95. Lee Kuan Yew, 'Make Sure Every Button Works', speech to senior civil servants at Victoria Theater, September 20, 1965, in *Lee Kuan Yew: The Man and His Ideas*.

96. Lee Kuan Yew, speech at Malaysia Solidarity Day mass rally and march-past on the Padang, August 31, 1963, 4, https://www.nas.gov.sg/archivesonline/speeches/record-details/740957c6-115d-11e3-83d5-0050568939ad.

97. 'Aspen Meeting, January 17, 1978', Henry A. Kissinger papers, part III, box 168, folder 31, 12–13, Yale University Library, http://findit.library.yale.edu/catalog/digcoll:1193335.

98. Lee Kuan Yew, 'Prime Minister's May Day Message, 1981', May 1, 1981, https://www.nas.gov.sg/archivesonline/speeches/record-details/73b03d18-115d-11e3-83d5-0050568939ad.

99. Perry, *Singapore*, 152; and Rudyard Kipling, 'Recessional', The Poetry Foundation, https://www.poetryfoundation.org/poems/46780/recessional.

100. 'British Withdrawal from Singapore,' *Singapore Infopedia*, Singapore National Library Board, http://eresources.nlb.gov.sg/infopedia/articles/SIP_1001_2009-02-10.html.

101. Perry, *Singapore*, 165.

102. Ibid., 157.

103. Ibid., 167. Lee traveled to Malta, Britain and Japan to study shipyards.

104. Quoted in *Lee Kuan Yew: The Man and His Ideas*, 109.

105. 'Aspen Meeting, January 18, 1978', Henry A. Kissinger papers, part III, box 168, folder 32, 2, Yale University Library, http://findit.library.yale.edu/catalog/digcoll:1193198.

106. Perry, *Singapore*, 196.

107. Memcon, Cabinet Conference Room, the Istana, Singapore, January 18, 2003, 3.40 p.m.

108. 'World Economic Survey, 1971', UN Department of Economic and Social Affairs (New York: UN, 1972), http://www.un.org/en/development/desa/policy/wess/wess_archive/1971wes.pdf.

109. Turnbull, *Singapore*, 491.

110. Ibid., 491.

111. *Lee Kuan Yew: The Man and His Ideas*, 111–12.

112. Lee, *From Third World to First*, 691.

113. Ibid., 63.

114. Lee Kuan Yew, 'Eve of National Day Broadcast 1987', August 8, 1987, https://www.nas.gov.sg/archivesonline/speeches/record-details/73fa03f6-115d-11e3-83d5-0050568939ad.

115. Lee, 'Prime Minister's May Day Message, 1981'.

116. Transcript of the prime minister, Mr Lee Kuan Yew's, discussion with five foreign correspondents, recorded at SBC on October 9, 1984, https://www.nas.gov.sg/archivesonline/speeches/record-details/7422b2ea-115d-11e3-83d5-0050568939ad.]

117. Lyndon Johnson, remarks of welcome at the White House to Prime Minister Lee of Singapore, October 17, 1967,https://www.presidency.ucsb.edu/documents/remarks-welcome-the-white-house-prime-minister-lee-singapore.

118. Hubert Humphrey, 'Memorandum from Vice President Humphrey to President Johnson: Meeting with Prime Minister Lee Kuan Yew of Singapore', October 18, 1967, Department of State, Office of the Historian.

119. Zakaria, 'Culture Is Destiny', 115.

120. Lee Kuan Yew, 'Exchange of Toasts between the President and Prime Minister Lee Kuan Yew of Singapore,' April 4, 1973, 7, https://www.nas.gov.sg/archivesonline/speeches/record-details/7337d52d-115d-11e3-83d5-0050568939ad.

121. Lee, 'Prime Minister's May Day Message, 1981'.

122. Zakaria, 'Culture Is Destiny', 124–5.

123. Lee, *From Third World to First*, 451.

124. 'Obituary: Lee Kuan Yew', *The Economist*, March 22, 2015, https://www.economist.com/obituary/2015/03/22/lee-kuan-yew

125. Zakaria, 'Culture Is Destiny', 112.

126. *Lee Kuan Yew: The Man and His Ideas*, 230, 233.

127. Lee Kuan Yew, 'East Asia in the New Era: The Prospects of Cooperation', speech given at the Harvard Fairbank Center Conference, New York, May 11, 1992. As cited in Graham Allison and Robert D. Blackwill, eds., *Lee Kuan Yew: The Grand Master's Insights on China, the United States, and the World* (Cambridge, MA: Belfer Center for Science and International Affairs/The MIT Press, 2012), 41.

128. 'Lee Kuan Yew, remarks to the U.S. Defense Policy Board, May 2, 2002', private files of Dr Henry Kissinger, 3.

129. Han et al., eds., *Hard Truths*, 313.

130. Lee Kuan Yew, 'Southeast Asian View of the New World Power Balance in the Making', Jacob Blaustein Lecture no. 1, March 30, 1973, 12, https://www.nas.gov.sg/archivesonline/speeches/record-details/73377f87-115d-11e3-83d5-0050568939ad

131. 'Aspen Meeting, May 7, 1979, Singapore', Henry A. Kissinger papers, part III, box 169, folder 5, 3, Yale University Library, http://findit.library.yale.edu/catalog/digcoll:1193268

132. Ibid., 6.

133. Ibid., 4.

134. Peter Hicks, '"Sleeping China" and Napoleon', Fondation Napoléon, https://www.napoleon.org/en/history-of-the-two-empires/articles/ava-gardner-china-and-napoleon/.

135. Nicholas D. Kristof, 'The Rise of China', *Foreign Affairs* 72, no. 5 (November/December 1993), 74.

136. Lee Kuan Yew, 'Asia and the World in the 21st Century', speech given at the 21st Century Forum, Beijing, September 4, 1996.

137. Han et al., eds., *Hard Truths*, 310.

138. Lee, 'Collins Family International Fellowship Lecture'.

139. Vogel, *Deng Xiaoping*, 292.

140. Han et al., eds., *Hard Truths*, 389.

141. Vogel, *Deng Xiaoping*, 291.

142. Ibid.

143. Quoted in Emrys Chew and Chong Guan Kwa, *Goh Heng Swee: A Legacy of Public Service* (Singapore: World Scientific Publishing Co., 2012), 17.

144. Lee, *From Third World to First*, 626.

145. Ibid., 627-8.

146. Summary of a conversation between Lee Kuan Yew and John Thornton at the FutureChina Global Forum, Singapore, July 11, 2001. As cited in Allison and Blackwill, eds., *Lee Kuan Yew*, 42.

147. Nathan Gardels, 'The East Asian Way – with Air Conditioning', *New Perspectives Quarterly* 26, no. 4 (fall 2009), 116.

148. Quoted in Henry A. Kissinger, *Years of Renewal* (New York: Simon and Schuster, 1999), 1057.

149. Question and answer session with Lee Kuan Yew at the Lee Kuan Yew School of Public Policy's fifth anniversary gala dinner, Singapore, September 2, 2009, as cited in Allison and Blackwill, eds., *Lee Kuan Yew*, 47-8.

150. Author interview, in Allison and Blackwill, eds., *Lee Kuan Yew*, 43.

151. Ibid., 45.

152. Lee Kuan Yew, 'America and Asia', speech given at the Architect of the New Century award ceremony, Washington, DC, November 11, 1996, as cited in Allison and Blackwill, eds., *Lee Kuan Yew*. 41.

153. Lee Kuan Yew, 'Shanghai's Role in China's Renaissance', speech given at the 2005 Shanghai Forum, Shanghai, May 17, 2005, as cited in Allison and Blackwill, eds., *Lee Kuan Yew*, 48.

154. 'Aspen Meeting, June 10, 1978, Iran', Henry A. Kissinger papers, part III, box 169, folder 2, 61–2, Yale University Library, http://findit.library.yale.edu/catalog/digcoll:1193349.

155. 'Aspen Meeting, May 6, 1979, Singapore', Henry A. Kissinger papers, part III, box 169, folder 3, 11, Yale University Library, http://findit.library.yale.edu/catalog/digcoll:1193222.

156. Ibid.

157. Lee, remarks to the US Defense Policy Board, May 2, 2002, 1.

158. World Bank Open Data, 'GDP per capita (current US$) – Singapore', https://data.worldbank.org/indicator/NY.GDP.PCAP.CD?locations=SG.

159. World Bank open data, 'GDP growth (annual %) – Singapore', https://data.worldbank.org/indicator/NY.GDP.MKTP.KD.ZG?locations=SG.

160. Nixon, *Leaders*, 310.

161. 'Aspen Meeting, June 9, 1978, Iran', Henry A. Kissinger papers, part III, box 169, folder 1, 33–4, Yale University Library, http://findit.library.yale.edu/catalog/digcoll:1193199.

162. Ibid., 336.

163. Lee, *From Third World to First*, 688.

164. Ibid., 687.

165. Alexander Pope, third epistle in *An Essay on Man* (1733–4).

166. José Ortega y Gasset, *History as a System, and Other Essays Toward a Philosophy of History*, trans. Helene Weyl (New York: W. W. Norton & Company, Inc., 1962), 217.

167. Lee, *From Third World to First*, 9.

168. Han et al., eds., *Hard Truths*, 388.

169. Tom Plate, *Conversations with Lee Kuan Yew* (Singapore: Marshall Cavendish Editions, 2015), 203.

170. Colin Campbell, 'Singapore Plans to Revive Study of Confucianism', *New York Times*, May 20, 1982.

171. Tom Plate, *Conversations with Lee Kuan Yew: Citizen Singapore: How to Build a Nation* (Singapore: Marshall Cavendish, 2010), 177.

172. There were meetings in Iran in 1978 (with Kissinger, Lee, and Shultz, but not Schmidt, at the first 'Aspen Roundtable'); in Singapore in 1979 (with Kissinger, Lee, and Shultz, but not Schmidt); in Germany in 1980 (with Kissinger, Lee, and Schmidt, but not Shultz); and in Tokyo in 1982 (with Kissinger, Lee, and Schmidt, but not Shultz). The first time all four met together was in summer 1982, in California. See Matthias Nass, 'Four Very Powerful Friends: Lee Kuan Yew, Helmut Schmidt, Henry Kissinger, George Shultz', *The Straits Times*, July 21, 2012, https://www.straitstimes.com/singapore/4-very-powerful-friends-lee-kuan-yew-helmut-schmidt-henry-kissinger-george-shultz.

173. Matthias Nass, 'Vier Freunde', *Die Zeit*, July 5, 2012, 4, https://www.zeit.de/2012/28/Vier-Freunde/seite-4.

174. Perry, *Singapore*, 237; and Seth Mydans, 'Days of Reflection for the Man Who Defined Singapore', *New York Times*, September 11, 2010. This despite Lee's 1968 proclamation: 'Poetry is a luxury we cannot afford.'

175. Seth Mydans, 'Days of Reflection for the Man Who Defined Singapore', *New York Times*, September 11, 2010.

176. Sadly, this is now the subject of a public feud within the Lee family.

177. Lee Kuan Yew, interview with Mark Jacobson, July 6, 2009, as cited in Allison and Blackwill, eds., *Lee Kuan Yew*, 149.

178. Mydans, 'Days of Reflection'.

179. Ibid.

180. Lee, 'How Much Is a Good Minister Worth?', 331.

6. MARGARET THATCHER

1. Ferdinand Mount, 'Thatcher's Decade', *The National Interest* 14 (winter 1988/9), 15. Emphasis added.

2. Margaret Thatcher, Conservative Political Centre Lecture, October 11, 1968, https://www.margaretthatcher.org/document/10163.

3. Margaret Thatcher, press conference after winning Conservative leadership, February 11, 1975, https://www.margaretthatcher.org/document/102487.

4. Margaret Thatcher, *The Downing Street Years* (London: HarperCollins, 1993), 5.

5. Philip Larkin, *Collected Poems* (New York: Farrar, Straus, and Giroux, 2003), 141.

6. See Peter Hennessy, *Having It So Good: Britain in the Fifties* (London: Penguin, 2007), Chapters 12 and 13.

7. Cited in Kathleen Burk, *Old World, New World: The Story of Britain and America* (London: Little Brown, 2007), 608.

8. Wilson too had refused to send troops to Vietnam, despite requests by Johnson.

9. Nixon tapes, February 3, 1973, 840-12, Richard M. Nixon Presidential Library, Yorba Linda, CA.

10. Odd Arne Westad, *The Cold War: A World History* (New York: Basic Books, 2017), 520–21.

11. BBC News, '1974: Miners' Strike Comes to an End', *On This Day*: March 6, 1974, http://news.bbc.co.uk/onthisday/hi/dates/stories/march/6/newsid_4207000/4207111.stm.

12. Christopher Kirkland, *The Political Economy of Britain in Crisis: Trade Unions and the Banking Sector* (London: Palgrave Macmillan, 2017), 76.

13. BBC News, 'In Quotes: Margaret Thatcher', April 8, 2013, https://www.bbc.com/news/uk-politics-10377842.

14. Leviticus 19:18, as cited by Jesus, Mark 12:31 and Matthew 22:39.

15. Margaret Thatcher, speech at the House of Commons, February 5, 1960, https://www.margaretthatcher.org/document/101055.

16. Ibid. The Franks Committee offered a report in 1957 that emphasized the need to practice openness, fairness and impartiality in British tribunals. The Committee was formed in response to the Crichel Down scandal and a general lack of system in governance; most of the Committee's particular recommendations were subsequently implemented in the 1958 Tribunals and Inquiries Act.

17. Thatcher, Conservative Political Centre Lecture, October 11, 1968.

18. Memorandum of conversation, 'May 9 1975, Ford, Kissinger', box 11, National Security Advisor, Ford Library, Ann Arbor, MI.

19. Charles Moore, *Margaret Thatcher: From Grantham to the Falklands* (New York: Knopf, 2013), 367.

20. Powell's brother Jonathan would perform a similar role for Tony Blair.

21. Thatcher, interview with Brian Walden for London Weekend Television, January 16, 1983, https://www.margaretthatcher.org/document/105087.

22. Thatcher, *The Downing Street Years*, 821.

23. See Charles Powell to Anthony C. Galsworthy, 'Prime Minister's Meeting with Dr Kissinger: Political Matters', December 3, 1986, National Archives of the UK, PREM 19/3586, 1, https://discovery.nationalarchives.gov.uk/details/r/C16481832.

24. Personal correspondence with Charles Powell, January 4, 2021.

25. Margaret Thatcher, speech to the Conservative Party Conference, October 10, 1980, https://www.margaretthatcher.org/document/104431.

26. Author's personal recollection.

27. Samuel Taylor Coleridge, *The Statesman's Manual* (London: Gale and Fenner, J. M. Richardson and Hatchard, 1816), 16.

28. Chris Edwards, 'Margaret Thatcher's Privatization Legacy', *Cato Journal* 37, no. 1 (2017), 95.

29. Thatcher, interview with Brian Walden for London Weekend Television, January 16, 1983.

30. Margaret Thatcher, speech to the Conservative Party Conference, October 12, 1984, https://www.margaretthatcher.org/document/105763.

31. World Bank Open Data.

32. UK Office for National Statistics, 'Labour Disputes in the UK: 2018', https://www.ons.gov.uk/employmentandlabourmarket/peopleinwork/workplacedisputesandworkingconditions/articles/labourdisputes/2018.

33. Henry Kissinger to Margaret Thatcher, May 6, 1997.

34. Margaret Thatcher to Henry Kissinger, May 20, 1997.

35. Rachel Borrill, 'Meeting between Thatcher and Blair "worries" left wing MPs', *Irish Times*, May 26, 1997, https://www.irishtimes.com/news/meeting-between-thatcher-and-blair-worries-left-wing-mps-1.75866.

36. Simon Jenkins, *Thatcher & Sons: A Revolution in Three Acts* (London: Penguin, 2006), 205.

37. Mark Tran, 'Thatcher Visits Brown for Tea at No. 10', *Guardian*, September 13, 2007.

38. Margaret Thatcher, 'Memoir of the Falklands War', https://bit.ly/3nFSvQO.

39. Quoted in Moore, *Margaret Thatcher: From Grantham to the Falklands*, 678.

40. Thatcher, *The Downing Street Years*, 179.

41. Quoted in Moore, *Margaret Thatcher: From Grantham to the Falklands*, 666.

42. Margaret Thatcher, April 3, 1982, Hansard: 21/633.

43. Ronald Reagan to Margaret Thatcher, April 30, 1975, THCR 6/4/1/7, Churchill College, Cambridge, available via the Margaret Thatcher Foundation, https://www.margaretthatcher.org/document/110357.

44. Ronald Reagan, *The Reagan Diaries*, ed. Douglas Brinkley (New York: HarperCollins, 2007), February 27, 1981, 5.

45. 'Monthly Warning Assessment: Latin America', April 30, 1982, CREST Program, CIA Archives, accessed at NARA, College Park, MD.

46. 'Franks Report' (Falkland Islands Review), presented to parliament in January 1983, paragraphs 114–18.

47. Andrew Roberts, *Leadership in War* (New York: Viking, 2019), 183.

48. Henry A. Kissinger, 'Reflections on a Partnership: British and American Attitudes to Postwar Foreign Policy', *Observations: Selected Speeches and Essays, 1982–1984* (New York: Little, Brown, 1985), 21.

49. Moore, *Margaret Thatcher: From Grantham to the Falklands*, 727.

50. Ibid., 735.

51. Roberts, *Leadership in War*, 193.

52. Ibid., 192.

53. Telephone conversation, Ronald Reagan and Margaret Thatcher, May 31, 1982, https://www.margaretthatcher.org/document/205626.

54. Sam LaGrone, 'Reagan Readied U.S. Warship for '82 Falklands War', *U.S. Naval Institute News*, June 27, 2012, https://news.usni.org/2012/06/27/reagan-readied-us-warship-82-falklands-war-0.

55. Margaret Thatcher, speech to Conservative rally at Cheltenham, July 3, 1982, https://www.margaretthatcher.org/document/104989.

56. John Coles to John 'J. E.' Holmes, November 15, 1982, National Archives of the UK, PREM 19/3586.

57. Roger Bone to John Coles, 'Points to Make', November 11, 1982, National Archives of the UK, PREM 19/1053, available via the Margaret Thatcher Foundation, https://www.margaretthatcher.org/document/138863.

58. Roger Bone to John Coles, 'Future of Hong Kong: Recent Developments and the Prime Minister's Dinner with Dr Kissinger on 12 November', November 11, 1982, National Archives of the UK, PREM 19/1053,

available via the Margaret Thatcher Foundation, https://www.marga
retthatcher.org/document/1388.

59. Thatcher, *The Downing Street Years*, 262.

60. Ibid., 383.

61. Personal correspondence with Charles Powell, January 4, 2021.

62. Moore, *Margaret Thatcher: From Grantham to the Falklands*, 597–601.

63. This is a controversial point, since Thatcher maintained that she never negotiated with terrorists, but she did tolerate MI6's link to the IRA and used it when she found it helpful. This account from ibid., 599–600.

64. Margaret Thatcher, speech in Belfast, March 5, 1981, https://www.marga
retthatcher.org/document/104589.

65. Margaret Thatcher, House of Commons PQs, May 5, 1981, https://www.margaretthatcher.org/document/104641.

66. Margaret Thatcher, TV interview for BBC, October 12, 1984, https://www.margaretthatcher.org/document/133947.

67. Thatcher, speech to the Conservative Party Conference, October 12, 1984, https://www.margaretthatcher.org/document/105763.

68. Ibid.

69. Quoted in Charles Moore, *Margaret Thatcher: At Her Zenith: In London, Washington, and Moscow* (New York: Vintage, 2015), 315.

70. Article 1 of the Anglo-Irish Agreement, https://cain.ulster.ac.uk/events/aia/aiadoc.htm#a.

71. Quoted in ibid., 336.

72. Thatcher, *The Downing Street Years*, 415.

73. See Moore, *Margaret Thatcher: At Her Zenith*, 333–8.

74. Margaret Thatcher, speech at Kensington Town Hall, January 19, 1976, https://www.margaretthatcher.org/document/102939.

75. Ibid.

76. Leonid Brezhnev, speech on November 13, 1968, https://loveman.sdsu.edu/docs/1968BrezhnevDoctrine.pdf.

77. 'Excerpts from Thatcher's Address', *New York Times*, February 21, 1985.

78. Margaret Thatcher, speech to Joint Houses of Congress, February 20, 1985, https://www.margaretthatcher.org/document/105968.

79. Margaret Thatcher, speech to the National Press Club, September 19, 1975, https://www.margaretthatcher.org/document/102770.

80. Henry A. Kissinger, 'The Special Relationship: "I Kept the British Better Informed than the State Department"', *Listener*, May 13, 1982.

81. Henry A. Kissinger, Keynote Address, Hong Kong Trade Fair, Hong Kong, 1983.

82. Henry A. Kissinger, 'We Live in an Age of Transition', *Daedalus* 124, no. 3, The Quest for World Order (Summer, 1995), 99–110.

83. Richard V. Allen, 'The Man Who Won the Cold War', *Hoover Digest* 2000 (1), https://www.hoover.org/research/man-who-won-cold-war.

84. Ronald Reagan, address to the nation on defense and national security, March 23, 1983, Public Papers of the Presidents, American Presidency Project, http://www.presidency.ucsb.edu/ws/index.php?pid=41093&st=&st1=.

85. Margaret Thatcher, press conference after Camp David talks, December 22, 1984, https://www.margaretthatcher.org/document/109392.

86. Geoffrey Smith, *Reagan and Thatcher* (London: Bodley Head, 1990), 131.

87. Robert McFarlane to Robert Armstrong, November 7, 1983, United Kingdom: Vol. V (11/1/83–6/30/84) [3 of 3], box 91331, Exec. Sec., NSC: Country File, Reagan Library, Simi Valley, CA.

88. This quote from the British record of our meeting. See John Coles to Brian Fall, December 21, 1983, National Archives of the UK, PREM 19/3586.

89. Quoted in Archie Brown, *The Human Factor: Gorbachev, Reagan, and Thatcher, and the End of the Cold War* (New York: Oxford University Press, 2020), 113.

90. Quoted in ibid., 114.

91. Quoted in Moore, *Margaret Thatcher: At Her Zenith*, 110.

92. Ibid.

93. Memorandum of conversation, Margaret Thatcher and Ronald Reagan, September 29, 1983, 'UK-1983-09/24/1983–10/10/1983', box 90424, Peter Sommer Files, Reagan Library, Simi Valley, CA.

94. Reagan, *Reagan Diaries*, April 6, 1983, 142.

95. Moore, *Margaret Thatcher: At Her Zenith*, 229.

96. Record of private lunchtime conversation with Mikhail Gorbachev, December 16, 1984, National Archives of the UK, PREM 19/1394, available via the Margaret Thatcher Foundation, https://www.margaretthatcher.org/document/134729.

97. Thatcher, *Downing Street Years*, 461.

98. Margaret Thatcher, TV interview for BBC, December 17, 1984, https://www.margaretthatcher.org/document/105592.

99. Memorandum of conversation, Margaret Thatcher and Ronald Reagan, December 22, 1984, Thatcher Visit – December 1984 [1], RAC box 15, NSC: EASD, Reagan Library, Simi Valley, CA.

100. *Newsweek*, December 3, 1990.

101. See Charles Powell to Len Appleyard, July 31, 1985, National Archives of the UK, PREM 19/3586.

102. Moore, *Margaret Thatcher: At Her Zenith*, 266–8.

103. Memorandum of conversation at Hofdi House, October 12, 1986 (3:25–4:30 p.m. and 5:30–6:50 p.m.), The Reykjavik File, National Security Archive, George Washington University, DC, https://nsarchive2.gwu.edu/NSAEBB/NSAEBB203/Document15.pdf.

104. This from the British record of our meeting. See Charles Powell to Anthony C. Galsworthy, December 3, 1986, 'Prime Minister's Meeting with Dr Kissinger: Arms Control', National Archives of the UK, PREM 19/3586.

105. Summary of telephone conversation with Prime Minister Thatcher, October 13, 1986, 'UK-1986-10/07/1986–10/19/1986', box 90901, Peter Sommer Files, Reagan Library, Simi Valley, CA.

106. See Powell to Galsworthy, December 3, 1986, 'Prime Minister's Meeting with Dr Kissinger: Arms Control'.

107. Charles Powell to Anthony C. Galsworthy, September 13, 1987, National Archives of the UK, PREM 19/3586.

108. Ibid.

109. See Powell to Galsworthy, 'Prime Minister's Meeting with Dr Kissinger: Political Matters'.

110. Cited in Charles Moore, *Margaret Thatcher: Herself Alone* (New York: Knopf, 2019), 599.

111. Quoted in Jon Meacham, *Destiny and Power: The American Odyssey of George Herbert Walker Bush* (New York: Random House, 2015), 424.

112. Ibid., 425.

113. Moore, *Margaret Thatcher: Herself Alone*, 602–3.

114. George H. W. Bush and Margaret Thatcher, joint press conference with President Bush (Iraqi invasion of Kuwait), August 2, 1990, https://www.margaretthatcher.org/document/108170.

115. Ibid.

116. George H. W. Bush, 'Remarks and an Exchange with Reporters on the Iraqi Invasion of Kuwait', August 5, 1990, Public Papers of the Presidents.

117. Charles Powell to Margaret Thatcher, August 12, 1990, National Archives of the UK, PREM 19/3075, cited in Moore, *Margaret Thatcher: Herself Alone*, 607.

118. Diary of George H. W. Bush, September 7, 1990, cited in George H. W. Bush, *All the Best* (New York: Scribner, 2013), 479.

119. Benjamin Disraeli, 'On the 'German Revolution', February 9, 1871, http://ghdi.ghi-dc.org/sub_document.cfm?document_id=1849.

120. Conrad Black, *A Matter of Principle*, Google Books version, 1966–7, https://bit.ly/3wk42YL.

121. *New York Times*, October 25, 1989.

122. Charles Powell to Stephen Wall, Prime minister's talk with Dr Kissinger, January 10, 1990, National Archives of the UK, PREM 19/3586.

123. Moore, *Margaret Thatcher: Herself Alone*, 512–22.

124. Quoted in Donald Edwin Nuechterlein, *America Recommitted: A Superpower Assesses Its Role in a Turbulent World* (Lexington: University Press of Kentucky, 2000), 187.

125. Thatcher, *The Downing Street Years*, 536.

126. Theresa May resigned after the failure of her withdrawal agreement, and David Cameron after campaigning for 'Remain' in the Brexit referendum. While internal rebellion did not force John Major to resign, his government

was severely damaged after the devaluation of the pound in 1992 and, for years thereafter, effectively kneecapped by the 'Maastricht rebels'.

127. Moore, *Margaret Thatcher: Herself Alone*, Chapter 4: 'The Shadow of Lawson', 94–111.

128. Margaret Thatcher, 'Speech to the College of Europe', September 20, 1988, https://www.margaretthatcher.org/document/107332.

129. Ibid.

130. Ibid.

131. Ibid.

132. Jacques Delors, speech to the European Parliament, July 6, 1988, https://www.margaretthatcher.org/document/113689.

133. Ibid.

134. Margaret Thatcher, remarks to the House of Commons on the Rome European Council, October 30, 1990, https://www.margaretthatcher.org/document/108234.

135. Geoffrey Howe, personal statement before the House of Commons, November 13, 1990, https://api.parliament.uk/historic-hansard/commons/1990/nov/13/personal-statement.

136. Ibid. Howe's assertions here almost anticipate the arguments of the 'Remain' camp during the 2016 Brexit referendum.

137. Ibid.

138. Moore, *Margaret Thatcher: Herself Alone*, 683.

139. 'Powell Record of Phone Conversation (Powell–Kissinger)', November 22, 1990, https://www.margaretthatcher.org/document/149456.

140. Quoted in Moore, *Margaret Thatcher: Herself Alone*, 716.

141. Margaret Thatcher, remarks on confidence in Her Majesty's Government, November 22, 1990, https://www.margaretthatcher.org/document/108256/.

142. Ibid.

143. Isaiah Berlin, 'Winston Churchill in 1940', in Henry Hardy and Roger Hausheer, eds., *The Proper Study of Mankind: An Anthology of Essays* (New York: Farrar, Straus and Giroux, 1998), 618.

144. Ivor Crewe and Donald Searing, 'Ideological Change in the British Conservative Party', *The American Political Science Review* 82, no. 2 (June 1988), esp. 362–8.

145. Margaret Thatcher, speech to the Royal Society, September 27, 1988, https://www.margaretthatcher.org/document/107346.

146. 'The Funeral Service of the Right Honorable Baroness Thatcher of Kesteven, St Paul's Cathedral, April 17, 2013', https://www.stpauls.co.uk/documents/News%20stories/BTOOS.pdf.

CONCLUSION

1. *The Republic of Plato*, trans. Allan Bloom (New York: Basic Books, 1991), 93–6.

2. Winston S. Churchill, *The Gathering Storm* (Boston: Houghton Mifflin, 1948), 4.

3. Ibid.

4. David Landes, *The Wealth and Poverty of Nations* (New York: Norton, 1998), 285.

5. See, generally, Adrian Wooldridge, *The Aristocracy of Talent: How Meritocracy Made the Modern World* (New York: Skyhorse Publishing, 2021).

6. Margaret Thatcher, 'Speech to the Institute of Socioeconomic Studies', September 15, 1975, https://www.margaretthatcher.org/document/102769.

7. Christopher Lasch, *The Revolt of the Elites and the Betrayal of Democracy* (New York: Norton, 1995), 48–9.

8. Julian Jackson, *De Gaulle* (Cambridge: Harvard Belknap Press, 2018), 772.

9. See William Deresiewicz, 'Solitude and Leadership', *The American Scholar*, March 1, 2010, https://theamericanscholar.org/solitude-and-leadership/.

10. Yuval Levin, 'Making Meritocrats Moral', *American Purpose*, December 7, 2021. See also Yuval Levin, *A Time to Build: From Family and Community to Congress and the Campus, How Recommitting to Our Institutions Can Revive the American Dream* (New York: Basic Books, 2020).

11. Ibid.

12. See, generally, Marshall McLuhan, *Understanding Media: The Extensions of Man* (New York: Signet Books, 1966).

13. Garfinkle credits the cognitive scientist Maryanne Wolf's concept of 'deep reading' and elaborates on it. See Adam Garfinkle, 'The Erosion of Deep Literacy', *National Affairs* no. 43 (spring 2020), https://nationalaffairs.com/publications/detail/the-erosion-of-deep-literacy.

14. Max Weber, 'Politics as a Vocation', in *The Vocation Lectures*, eds. David Owen and Tracy B. Strong, trans. Rodney Livingstone (Indianapolis: Hackett Publishing Company, 2004), , 77.

15. See Neil Postman, *Amusing Ourselves to Death: Public Discourse in the Age of Show Business* (New York: Penguin, 1985), 10. The retired Marine Corps general and former secretary of defense James Mattis has also elaborated on these points: 'If you haven't read hundreds of books, you are functionally illiterate, and you will be incompetent, because your personal experiences alone aren't broad enough to sustain you. Any commander who claims he is "too busy to read" is going to fill body bags with his troops.' James Mattis, *Call Sign Chaos* (New York: Random House, 2019), 42.

16. Garfinkle, 'The Erosion of Deep Literacy'.

17. Lee Kuan Yew, 'Collins Family International Fellowship Lecture', delivered October 17, 2000 at the John F. Kennedy School of Government at Harvard University, https://www.nas.gov.sg/archivesonline/data/pdfdoc/2000101706. htm.

18. Ibid.

19. Thomas Jefferson, letter to John Adams, October 28, 1813, in Adrienne Koch and William Peden, eds., *The Life and Selected Writings of Thomas Jefferson* (New York: Random House, 1944), 632–3.

20. James Q. Wilson, *On Character* (Washington, DC: The AEI Press, 1995), 22.

21. Niall Ferguson, *Civilization: The West and the Rest* (New York: Penguin, 2012).

22. 'Joint Soviet–United States Statement on the Summit Meeting in Geneva', November 21, 1985, Reagan Library and Museum website, https://www. reaganlibrary.gov/archives/speech/joint-soviet-united-states-statement -summit-meeting-geneva.

23. Niccolò Machiavelli, *Discourses on Livy*, trans. Julia Conaway Bondanella and Peter Bondanella (Oxford: Oxford University Press, 2009), 213.

24. Ibid.

25. Friedrich Engels, *Herr Eugen Dühring's Revolution in Science (Anti-Dühring)* (New York: International Publishers, 1966), 307.

26. Weber, 'Politics as a Vocation', 93–4.

27. Epictetus, *Enchiridion*, in *The Art of Living: The Classic Manual on Virtue, Happiness, and Effectiveness*, trans. Sharon Lebell (New York: Harper-Collins, 1995), 10.

Index